Computer
Hardware/Software
Architecture

Computer Hardware/Software Architecture

WING TOY

AT&T Bell Laboratories

BENJAMIN ZEE

AT&T Information Systems
(Formerly with AT&T Bell Laboratories)

PRENTICE-HALL, INC.
Englewood Cliffs, New Jersey 07632

Library of Congress Cataloging-in-Publication Data

Toy, Wing N. (date)
Computer hardware/software architecture.

Includes index.
1. Computer architecture. I. Zee, Benjamin.
II. Title.
QA76.9.A73T68 1986 004.2 85-24416
ISBN 0-13-163502-6

Editorial/production supervision and interior design: Nancy Milnamow
Cover design: Ben Santora
Manufacturing buyer: Gordon Osbourne

Printed in the United States of America

10 9 8 7 6 5 4 3 2

ISBN 0-13-163502-6 01

Prentice-Hall International (UK) Limited, *London*
Prentice-Hall of Australia Pty. Limited, *Sydney*
Prentice-Hall Canada Inc., *Toronto*
Prentice-Hall Hispanoamericana, S.A., *Mexico*
Prentice-Hall of India Private Limited, *New Delhi*
Prentice-Hall of Japan, Inc., *Tokyo*
Prentice-Hall of Southeast Asia Pte. Ltd., *Singapore*
Editora Prentice-Hall do Brasil, Ltda., *Rio de Janeiro*
Whitehall Books Limited, *Wellington, New Zealand*

To

Romayne, Liane, Arthur, and Sue-lin Toy

and

Shun-Ling, Kar-Ling, Phyllis, and Brian Zee

Contents

Preface

Numerous texts on computer architecture have been published, most of which are intended for computer engineers. They teach how to design ALUs, microprogram controllers, DMAs, and memory systems, and how these hardware components are organized within the computer and connected together. But the term *computer architecture* has evolved to take on a much broader meaning than just hardware organization. To us, computer architects are those who are responsible for designing a computer *system* whose principles of operation and specifications meet market requirements at the best possible cost performance. To produce a successful design, computer architects have to know how all the pieces of the *system* work and fit together. They must consider the available technology and its physical design implications. Computer architects need to understand various system hardware and software configurations, how they are interconnected, and how they interface with each other and the ''outside world.''

Computer architects must also ensure the maintainability, fault tolerance, and error recovery strategy of the system. They must consider the cost, limitations, benefits, and implementability of all the issues contributing to the design of the system. For example, architects must make sure their specifications can be implemented in the available time frame with the available personnel, and that their elegant solutions to complex problems are not prohibitively expensive. Furthermore, the architects must understand the interrelationships among the issues: how one design decision made for one issue affects the other issues. Developing sound computer architecture is unquestionably not a trivial task. The alternatives are many, the trade-offs subtle, and the interrelationships complex. The architects can seldom be certain that their choices are the right ones. They can only use their best judgment based on experience, analytical and simulation tools, and most important, an understanding of how the whole system will work together.

Computer Hardware/Software Architecture is a textbook that will help computer architects design systems in today's development environments. It serves as a text for a course intended for advanced undergraduates and graduate students, and can be used as a reference for computer architect professionals. Computer hardware designers and system software designers can gain better understandings of how their designs interface with those of their counterparts from this book.

To take full advantage of the material that *Computer Hardware/Software Architecture* presents, its readers should have had some exposure to programming languages, operating systems, and computer hardware organization. Many texts cover these areas separately. This book integrates the concepts of these separate areas. It explains, for example, how concepts in programming languages affect computer hardware design and organization, how operating system functions interact with the hardware, and how the system architecture influences system maintenance. The book's emphasis is not on how a processor works or what a process manager is supposed to do, but rather on how they *work together* to accomplish the *total* intended processing function.

In writing the text, we draw extensively from literature as well as from our own experiences as computer architects at AT&T Bell Laboratories in designing the 3B20D computer and earlier processors designed for high-availability electronic switching systems. The book proceeds from a discussion of the term *computer architecture*. Computer architecture includes both a hardware and a software component; the combination of the two components forms the total system. Chapter 1 reviews the basic logic elements that are fundamental in hardware design and progressively covers the major components: the control structure, the arithmetic and logic unit, memory organization, and the input/output structure. The effect of technology on architecture is summarized at the device, function, and system levels. Chapter 1 acknowledges the importance of VLSI technology to computer architects because of its effects not only on the cost but also on the reliability, performance, and increased functionalities of computer systems. This chapter covers these topics from the hardware viewpoint.

Chapters 2, 3, and 4 deal with the relationship between high-level languages and machine architecture. A high-level language is a powerful, expressive medium for programmers to describe and specify data objects and the algorithms for manipulating them. Their use plays an integral part in enhancing the quality and maintainability of software and the productivity of programmers. Chapter 2 discusses the major components of high-level languages: data objects, types, operators, flow control, exceptions, environment, and the major program units for grouping data objects: blocks, subprograms, and modules. These concepts have evolved through four generations of development. Chapter 2 states the relationships among various high-level languages in terms of the concepts they introduce and support. Chapter 3 covers the compilation process and the model of implementation. It begins with a discussion of the compilation step of translating a program in a high-level language to its semantic equivalent in a machine instruction set. Based on a model of implementation that represents the high-level-language concepts, the compiler generates the code that runs on the machine. The text concerns only the aspects of compilation that affect the architectural support of high-level languages. Chapter 4 discusses how a model of implementation is mapped onto a machine architecture. This mapping is supported by the instruction set and the hardware that executes it. The design of the instruction set is a key element in the design of a machine architecture to support high-level languages. It affects the complexity and efficiency of the hardware, firmware, and compiler designs.

Chapters 5, 6, and 7 cover the relationships between operating systems and machine architecture. Like high-level languages, operating systems are an essential part of modern programming methodologies. They manage hardware and software resources and create a friendly view of the computer system environment several levels of abstraction above that of the hardware of the machine. Chapter 5 identifies the basic operating system function: managing system resources. It gives a brief description of each of the four categories of resource management: memory, processor, device, and information. And Chapter 5 traces the historical development of operating systems from the 1950s to the present. Although operating systems are different because of their applications and hardware configurations, they have many common functions. They control software modules by protecting them from each other, synchronizing them, and providing communications among them. Chapter 6 discusses the basic functions of protection, synchronization, and communication in considerable detail. Its emphasis is on the architectural support for these fundamental operating system activities. Chapter 7 considers the compatibility and portability issues of the operating system in relation to previous machines of the same family, and discusses hardware support for various operating system functions. Examples of operating system directed architecture are also covered in Chapter 7.

Reliability requirements vary considerably from application to application. However, the major components of achieving high reliability are fault detection, fault recovery, fault diagnosis, and repair. Chapter 8 discusses these components and various techniques of implementing them. In addition, software faults and software techniques are included as an integrated system approach.

Finally, Chapter 9 describes the AT&T 3B20D processor. It covers many aspects of the architectural issues discussed in previous chapters. The 3B20D serves as a case study of a system that has fault-tolerant features built into an architecture for high-availability applications.

The field of computer architecture is vast, and the decisions architects make are many and intricate. This textbook does not catalog the "right" decisions for specific problems, nor can it because of the large (and growing) number of applications and implementation possibilities. Rather, the book presents a way of looking at the separate issues affecting a computer's architecture while constantly considering the total system. This *integrated* approach to computer architecture, we are convinced, must be done from the inception of a design to ensure the development of the best system at the least possible cost.

May you each acquire as much satisfaction as we have when you face the challenges of developing computer architectures—and overcome them.

ACKNOWLEDGMENTS

The authors are greatly indebted to Daniel E. Johns, who devoted himself wholeheartedly to the tedious process of reviewing and editing the manuscript. He spent considerable effort researching the material and ensuring the consistency of the text and references. His dedication throughout the last two years has shaped the material into its present readable form. We are also indebted to Deborah J. Fasbender for her support and direction in the preparation of this manuscript. The constructive criticisms made by the reviewers at AT&T Bell Laboratories have contributed substantially to our completely rewriting the first four chapters. The authors are very grateful to Liane C. Toy for her critical review, valuable suggestions in improving the manuscript, and assistance in providing some problem sets. We extend our appreciation to the mangement of AT&T Bell Laboratories, especially to L. E. Gallaher and J. J. Kulzer, for their support in writing this book. Finally, we want to thank our wives, Romayne and Phyllis, for their patience, understanding, and encouragement in making it all come true.

W. N. Toy
B. Zee

1

Overview of Computer Structure

1.1 INTRODUCTION

In recent years the field of computer architecture—once almost exclusively the study of hardware organization—has expanded to include software issues. Today's computer architects must consider the software component of the architecture as much as the hardware component in creating the most useful and cost-effective systems for the end users. Software issues are playing an increasingly important role in making the best use of the rapidly growing very large-scale integration (VLSI) and other technologies.

The architecture of the total system (the combination of the hardware and software components) may be viewed as a set of levels of interpreters or abstractions (Fig. 1.1) [1,2]. This, the functional view, implies that there are distinct types of architecture within the system. At the highest level (level 1), the system architecture determines which data processing functions the system includes and which belong to the external world (the end users). The communication between the system and the outside world is through two interfaces: languages and system application programs such as utilities, sorts, and information retrieval programs. The system architecture at level 1 defines both sets of interfaces.

Level 2 represents the various functions within the system's software architecture performed by high-level languages and operating systems. High-level languages have played an important role in reducing software complexity and development effort and in increasing programmer productivity and software reliability. These benefits have been obtained at the expense of increasing memory space and program execution time. Most general operating systems have sets of procedures that enable users to share computer hardware facilities efficiently; they also provide automatic control over the resources. Their services include memory management, process management, interrupt handling, file sys-

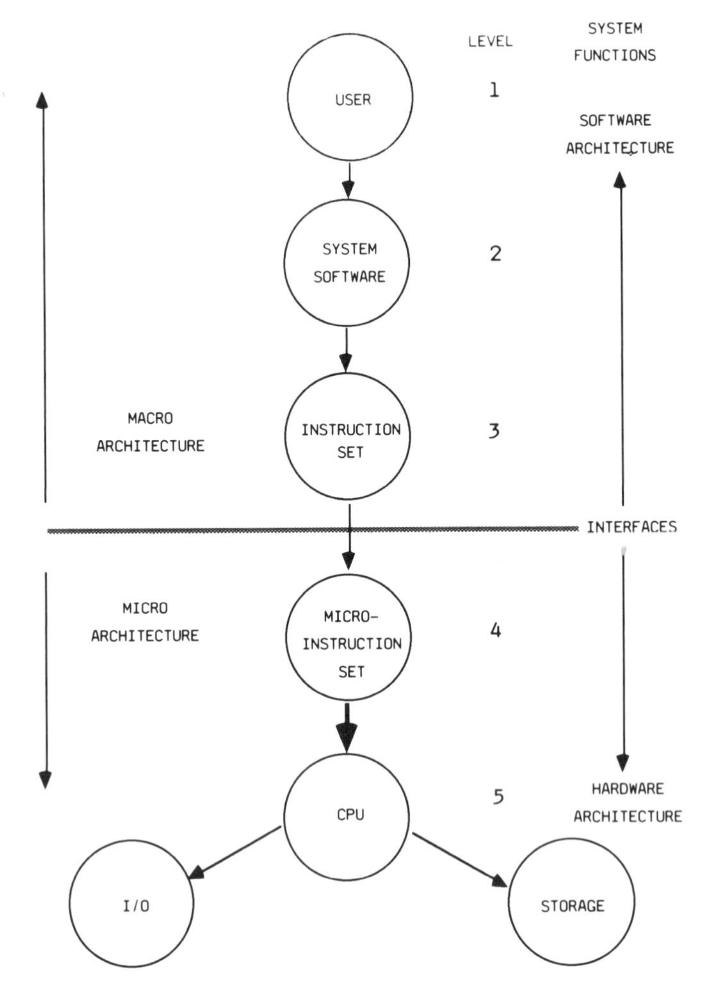

Figure 1.1 Levels of computer architecture.

tem management, and system maintenance. In these ways, operating systems free programmers from learning and specifying repeatedly machine details such as the physical characteristics and protocols of peripheral devices used for input/output operations.

The next level, level 3, is that of the instruction set. It is the lowet level accesssible to programmers. The instruction set is a collection of hardware features and characteristics of the bare machine that are visible to the software designers. These features include data operators, addressing modes, trap and interrupt sequences, and register organizations.

The architectures of levels 1, 2, and 3 form the software component of the computer architecture, or the *macroarchitecture*. Functional levels below the instruction set form the hardware component, or the *microarchitecture*. Considerable attention has been given to the placement of microcoded programs in the hardware/software dichotomy. Because microprograms are placed in read-only memory (ROM), they have been dubbed *firmware* (that is, they are software modules that are "firmly protected" from transient changes). In microprogram-controlled machines, the firmware is separated and considered level 4 of the hardware architecture.

Although the devices that implement the hardware architecture have improved dramatically because of technological advances, the structure of level 5 of the architecture today has the same components it had 40 years ago: the central processing unit, the storage unit (memory), the input/output unit, and the controls and interconnections among them. And digital logic, though now implemented by advanced chip technologies such as metal-oxide semiconductors and emitter-coupled logic devices, is still the basic building block of the hardware architecture.

This chapter provides an overview of the basic computer structure. Digital circuits are presented to provide the background in logic design necessary for understanding the issues presented in the remainder of the book. To supplement this background information, Chapter 1 reviews the major physical components of a computer and discusses VLSI technology and its impact on computer architecture.

1.2 DIGITAL LOGIC

1.2.1 Basic Logic Gates

The implementation of digital control logic requires three basic operators: OR, AND, and NOT. Used in combination, these three functions can perform any logical operation. Simple circuits, called *gates,* implement them. In most logic circuits, an input element such as a diode performs the logical operation. The transistor output stage that follows provides proper signal levels and adequate drive capability (fan-out).

Each input and output of most digital circuits is in one of two states, 0 or 1. Some logic gates have a third output state, the high-impedance state. The following discussion deals only with two-state logic gates. Two conventions are normally used to represent these logic values. The first convention, which uses the more positive voltage level to represent the 1 state, is called *positive logic*. The second convention, which uses the less positive potential to represent the 1 state, is called *negative logic*. The positive logic convention is more common and is used in this text. For transistor-transistor logic (TTL) series logic gates, the 0 state corresponds to near ground potential, and the 1 state corresponds to about 3 volts (V).

OR Gate. The OR circuit is arranged so that the output is in the 1 state when any one of its inputs is in the 1 state. The truth table and the logic symbol for the OR gate are shown in Fig. 1.2(a).

AND Gate. The AND circuit requires all its inputs to be in the 1 state to produce a 1 output, as the truth table in Fig. 1.2(b) shows. The logic symbols for the AND gate are also shown in the figure.

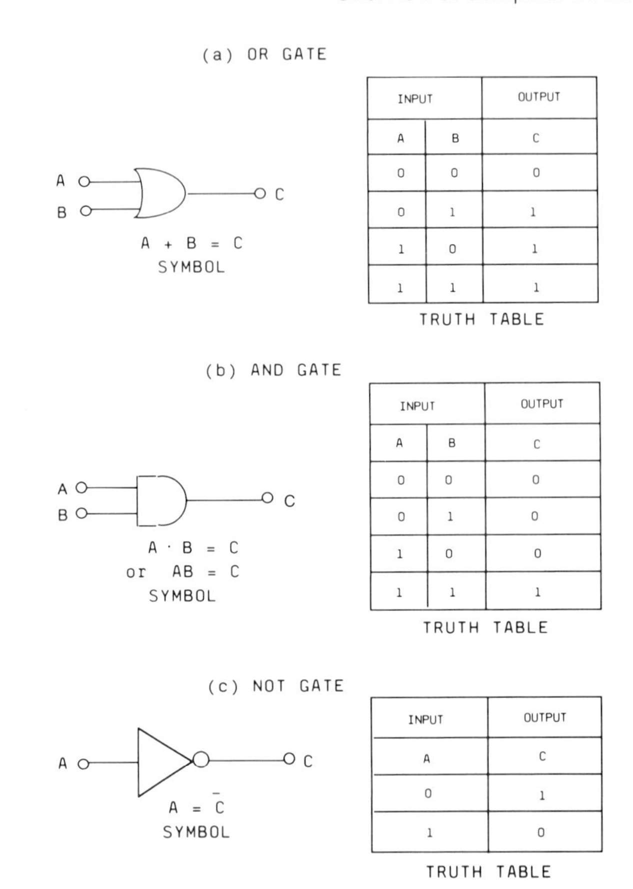

INPUT		OUTPUT
A	B	C
0	0	0
0	1	1
1	0	1
1	1	1

INPUT		OUTPUT
A	B	C
0	0	0
0	1	0
1	0	0
1	1	1

INPUT	OUTPUT
A	C
0	1
1	0

Figure 1.2 Basic logic gates.

NOT Gate. This curcuit is an inverter. Its single input and single output are complementary. The truth table and the logic symbol for the NOT circuit are shown in Fig. 1.2(c). The NOT function is one of the operations required to implement more complex logical functions such as NOR, NAND, and XOR.

NOR Gate. The combined OR and NOT function is called the *NOR gate*. The truth table and logic symbol are shown in Fig. 1.3(a). The gate symbol for NOR is the same as the symbol for OR except for the small bubble on the output side that denotes signal inversion.

A NOR gate configured with *two-rail logic* produces inverted and noninverted outputs; hence, the same gate implements OR and NOR. Two-rail outputs facilitate logic implementation because there is no need to go through two NOT states to generate the proper output, which would be necessary if there were only a single output.

NAND Gate. An AND circuit followed by a NOT circuit is called a *NAND gate*. Figure 1.3(b) shows the truth table and logic symbol for the NAND gate. The gate symbol

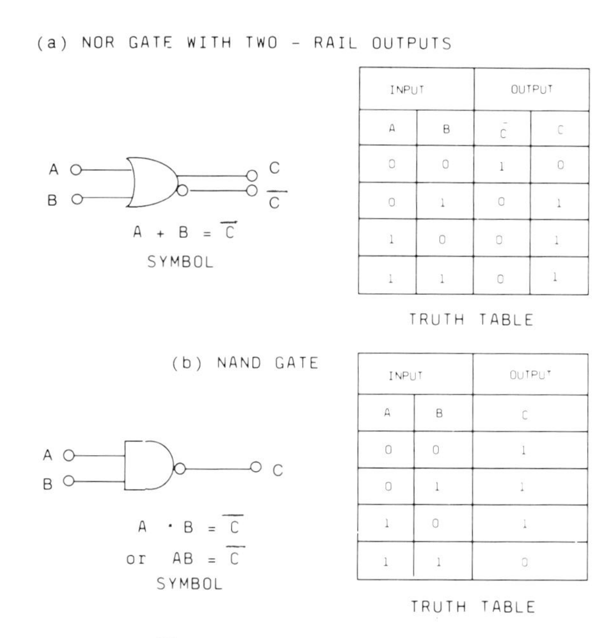

Figure 1.3 Other basic gates.

for NAND is the same as the symbol for AND except for the small bubble on the output side that denotes signal inversion.

1.2.2 Gate Representation

The basic gate representations for OR, AND, and NOT circuits are shown in Fig. 1.2. The shape of the symbols denotes the OR and AND functions. Although the NOT function is defined by the triangular symbol, the inversion of the input signal is indicated by a small bubble at the output. The single-input NOT function may be expressed by any of the three symbols shown in Fig. 1.4(a).

OR and AND gates, combined with possible signal inversions either at the input or the output, are shown in Fig. 1.4(b). The gates with the same inputs and outputs are equivalent. The duality of DeMorgan's theorem,

$$\overline{A + B + C} = \bar{A} \cdot \bar{B} \cdot \bar{C} \tag{1}$$

or

$$\overline{A \cdot B \cdot C} = \bar{A} + \bar{B} + \bar{C} \tag{2}$$

is a valuable aid in logic design, especially for implementing logic functions and expressions, because AND functions can be easily converted to OR functions, and vice versa.

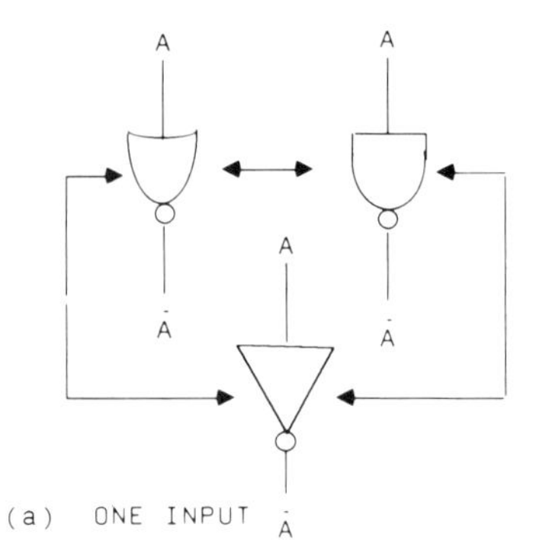

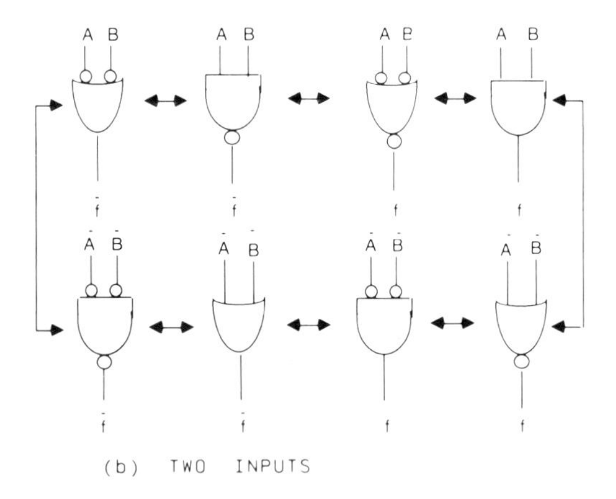

Figure 1.4 Gate representations.

For example,

$$f = \bar{A} \cdot B + A \cdot \bar{B} \tag{3}$$

$$\bar{A} \cdot B = \overline{(A + \bar{B})} \tag{4}$$

$$A \cdot \bar{B} = \overline{(\bar{A} + B)} \tag{5}$$

$$f = \overline{(A + \bar{B})} + \overline{(\bar{A} + B)} \tag{6}$$

By the use of DeMorgan's theorem, equation (6) may be expressed as

$$\bar{f} = \overline{\overline{(A + \bar{B})} + \overline{(\bar{A} + B)}} \tag{7}$$

which is a NOR gate realization. By rewriting, the original expression in equation (3) may be expressed as

$$\bar{f} = [\overline{\bar{A} \cdot B + A \cdot \bar{B}}] \tag{8}$$

$$\bar{f} = \overline{(\bar{A} \cdot B)} \cdot \overline{(A \cdot \bar{B})} \tag{9}$$

Forming the complement of $\bar{f}$,

$$f = (\bar{\bar{f}}) = \overline{\overline{(A \cdot \bar{B}) \cdot (\bar{A} \cdot B)}} \tag{10}$$

is a NAND gate realization.

1.2.3 XOR Gate

The exclusive-OR (XOR) function of two variables is given by the following logic expression:

$$f = \bar{A} \cdot B + A \cdot \bar{B}$$

Its implementation can be realized by various circuit arrangements formed from the standard logic gates previously described; one such circuit is shown in Fig. 1.5(a). Although the XOR gate is realized with a composite of several logic gates, a functional symbol has been adopted to denote it because of its wide usage in logic design [Fig. 1.5(b)]. According to the truth table [Fig. 1.5(c)], the XOR circuit gives a 1 output whenever its input signals are different ($A = 1$, $B = 0$; or $A = 0$, $B = 1$). The sum of two binary digits gives the same corresponding outputs as the XOR circuit when the carry is neglected. For this reason, the XOR circuit is sometimes called a *modulo-2 adder* or a *half-adder circuit*. A *full adder* may be built using a second XOR gate. The output of the first circuit and the carry-in from the preceding stage are used as the inputs to the second XOR gate. An XOR of three input variables is obtained by cascading two XOR circuits.

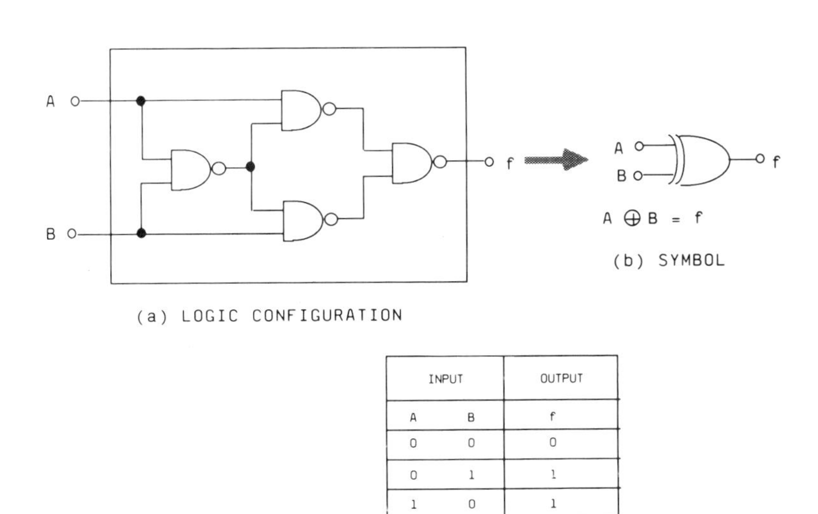

INPUT		OUTPUT
A	B	f
0	0	0
0	1	1
1	0	1
1	1	0

(c) TRUTH TABLE

Figure 1.5 XOR function of two-input variables.

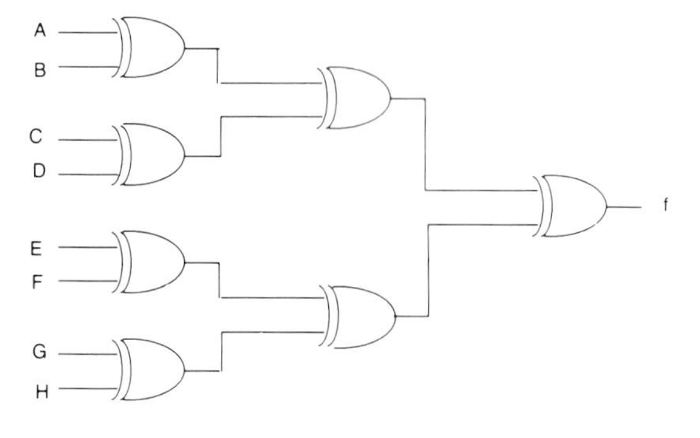

Figure 1.6 XOR *n*-input variables.

The parity check function uses XOR circuits in a tree-type structure since XORing *n* input variables gives a final output of 1 if an odd number of the input variables are 1s (Fig. 1.6).

Another commonly used logic function of two input variables is the exclusive-NOR circuit, which is the inverse or complement of the XOR function. The logic symbol is the same as the XOR symbol except that a small bubble is inserted at the output, indicating an inversion of the output signal. This circuit is also referred to as a *comparator,* since both inputs must be in the same state for the output to be a 1.

1.3 COMPONENTS OF A COMPUTER

Figure 1.7 shows the functional block diagram of a computer. The combination of the arithmetic and logic unit (ALU) and the control unit is commonly called the central processing unit (CPU), which is the core of the computer. The intermediate (temporary) stor-

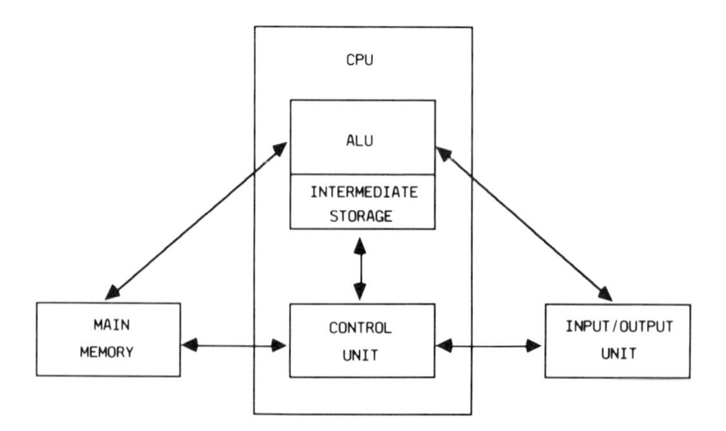

Figure 1.7 Components of a computer.

age unit is part of the ALU. The data and programs reside in the main memory unit. The machine shown in the figure consists of a CPU communicating with a main memory unit and an input/output (I/O) facility. This figure is the traditional computer block diagram. The three basic units are described below.

1. The *memory unit* stores instructions (programs) and operands (data). It may also function as a form of "scratch-pad" memory.
2. The *CPU* consists of one or more high-speed registers, the ALU, the control unit, and the circuitry necessary to perform bus control.
   (a) The *ALU* performs all the processing functions involving arithmetic and logic operations as well as the generation of partial results for a calculation; it includes high-speed registers for temporary storage.
   (b) The *control unit* coordinates the operation of all the units. A system clock that is closely synchronized to the memory cycle speed controls the overall operation. The control unit receives directives in a logical sequence from the memory unit. This logical sequence of instructions defines a program that will execute on the machine. The control unit, in conjunction with the ALU, provides for branching when decision points are encountered in the program sequence.
   (c) The *bus control circuitry* provides communication paths for addresses, data, and controls within the machine. In a time-multiplexed bus structure, this circuitry determines when information on a single bus will be treated as an address rather than data or control signals.
3. The *input/output unit* provides a means for the machine to communicate with its external environment. This unit links the machine with its operator and allows an orderly exchange of information to take place.

1.4 CONTROL STRUCTURE

The control section is the heart of the system; it interprets and executes stored instructions from main memory. The implementation of the instruction set, which is unique to each design, defines the control section of the machine. Three techniques are used to implement the control section in hardware: *conventional* or *random logic*, *programmable logic array (PLA)*, and *microprogram control*. Conventional logic is an outgrowth of the discrete-component era. Machines with conventional logic control sections minimize their number of logic gates to keep down the hardware cost. This produces an irregular structure; control signals are located throughout the machine in an apparently random manner. A large-scale integration (LSI) approach to conventional logic is the PLA. The logic structures of conventional logic and the PLAs are equivalent. Microprogram control, a highly successful development, places control sequences in random access memory (RAM) or read-only memory (ROM); the control sequences execute when the appropriate memory locations are accessed.

1.4.1 Control Functions

Control operations may be classified into four basic categories:

1. Instruction fetch
2. Instruction decode
3. Operand fetch
4. Instruction execute

These operations dictate the control signals required to implement the control functions defined by the instruction sets of computing machines. Although conventional logic, PLA, and microprogram controls all perform these operations, this discussion is directed toward conventional logic and PLA implementations. Microprogram control is covered in the following subsection.

The *instruction fetch* operation provides the control linkage between instructions and allows a continuous flow of instructions to be executed. Instructions are normally grouped into several types, for example, register to register (RR), register to storage (RS), and storage to register (SR). The *decode* function identifies the various classes of instructions that have common control sequences. This permits different instructions with identical operations to share the same hardware. For instructions requiring a memory reference (that is, RS or SR types), an *operand fetch* (commonly referred to as a *data fetch*) is required to obtain the prescribed data from memory. The number of operand fetches depends on the instruction set. To implement an instruction (*instruction execute*), various control signals need to coordinate activities occurring at different times. Each activity is an elementary operation and by itself may not accomplish the desired result. However, the orchestration of the various activities into a well-organized control sequence performs the operation specified by the instruction. The number of control signals for a given instruction depends on the complexity of the instruction and the internal structure of the machine. Since each instruction performs a unique function, the control sequences differ from instruction to instruction.

Figure 1.8 shows the relationships among the basic control functions. Figure 1.9 shows an implementation of the control structures, from the instruction fetch (1) through the decoding (2) to the instruction execution (5). The control functions implement not only the execution of instructions (5), but also perform the addressing operation (3) of sequencing (4) from instruction to instruction to form a *program sequence*. The address modification applies to both operand and instruction fetches. The many ways of altering an instruction sequence or performing a data fetch illustrate the strength and flexibility of stored programs. Figure 1.9 also illustrates the flow of data and instructions from the main memory. The address modification logic for programs and data normally shares the ALU hardware when indexing operations are performed under the control of the execution logic.

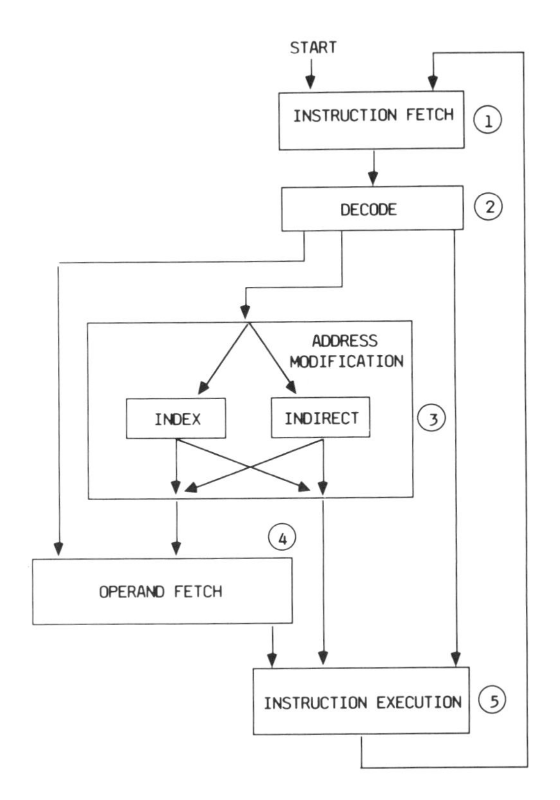

Figure 1.8 Basic control functions.

1.4.2 Microprogram Control

Microprogramming simplifies the design and maintenance of the control section by placing sequences of control signals in a RAM or ROM module called a *control store* or *control memory*. An elementary machine operation implemented in a control store is called a *control primitive* or a *microoperation*. The control primitives (signals) to be generated at a specific time are designated by the contents of the microinstruction currently being executed. A microinstruction is fetched from control storage in a manner that is directly analogous to the fetch of an instruction from main memory.

A sequence of macroinstructions (assembly language instructions) is called a *macroprogram* or *main program;* a sequence of microinstructions is called a *microprogram*. Figure 1.10 illustrates the basic structure of a microprogrammed machine. Using this arrangement, much of the complex control circuitry that has traditionally been implemented using conventional logic has been replaced by the regular structure of a random access memory that can easily be manufactured using very large-scale integration (VLSI) techniques. Microprogram control units are inherently more flexible than their conventional logic equivalents since the control sequences can be modified simply by

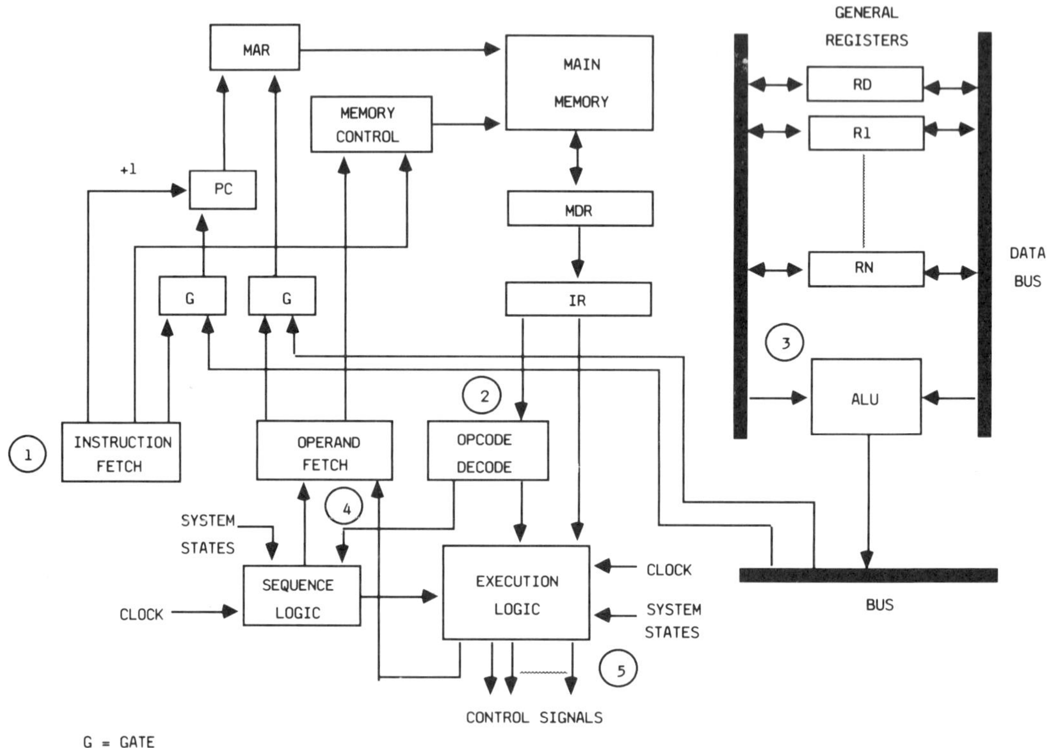

Figure 1.9 Simplified block diagram of instruction and data flow from main memory.

replacing the current control memory with another control memory containing a different microinstruction sequence. The speed of the microprogram control sequencer is slower than that of its hardwired, conventional logic equivalent since a memory access must be performed to fetch each microinstruction. However, the availability of high-speed, low-cost random access memories manufactured using VLSI techniques has greatly reduced this speed penalty and has made microprogram control an attractive procedure for implementing the control section of a computer.

Microprogram controls reduce the complexity and associated inflexibility of control units implemented using hardwired logic. They also help maintain the compatibility of operations between machines supplied by the same manufacturer. Such machines represent a *families of computers* that allow users to increase the capabilities of their systems by moving to more powerful machines in the same family. The expansion is done without rewriting any software or modifying any of the original system design assumptions.

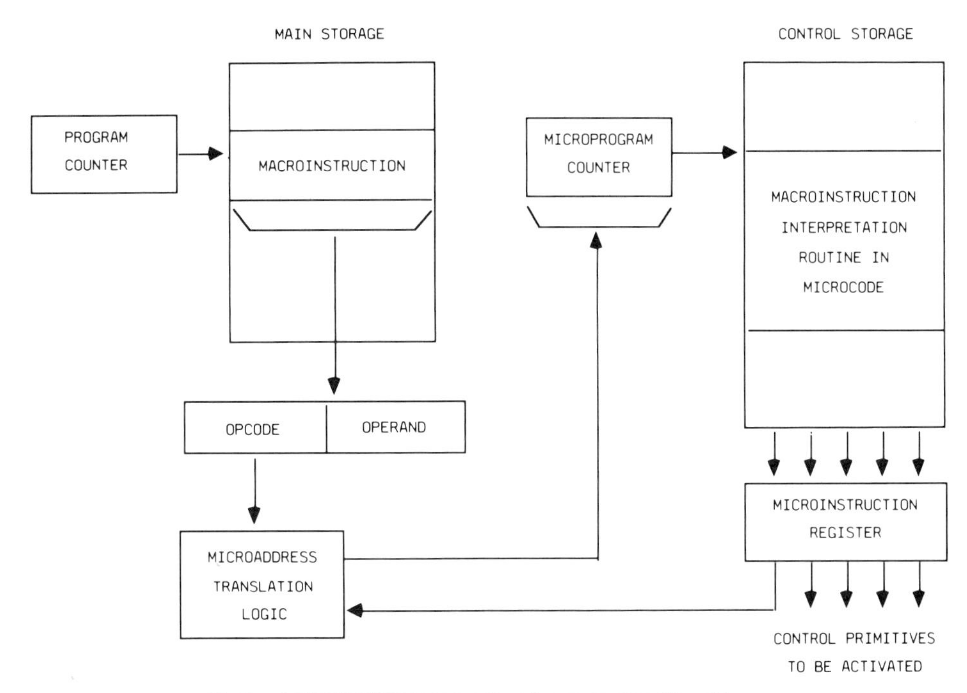

Figure 1.10 Basic structure of a microprogrammed machine.

1.4.3 Comparison of Conventional and Microprogram Controls [3]

Both the conventional implementation of the control section of a computer using random logic and a microprogram implementation perform the same functions: they generate the necessary microoperations or control primitives to execute each microinstruction, and they provide the sequencing logic that permits execution to step from one microinstruction to another. Although the purposes of implementing conventional control logic and microprogram control logic are the same, the methods of achieving those purposes differ radically. The conventional control section consists of four distinct functional parts: the operation code decoder, the timing and sequencing logic, the logic associated with the execution of the current macroinstruction, and the logic that combines the individual control primitives generated by all the macroinstructions. These four parts, and their microprogram equivalents, are shown in Fig. 1.11. Each macroinstruction is realized through the activation of a subset of the control primitives. Conventional control uses random logic to activate the appropriate control primitives in a prescribed sequence so that the host computer hardware interprets the current macroinstruction correctly. Microprogram control uses a sequence of microinstructions to specify the individual control primitives to be activated. Each microinstruction defines one or more control primi-

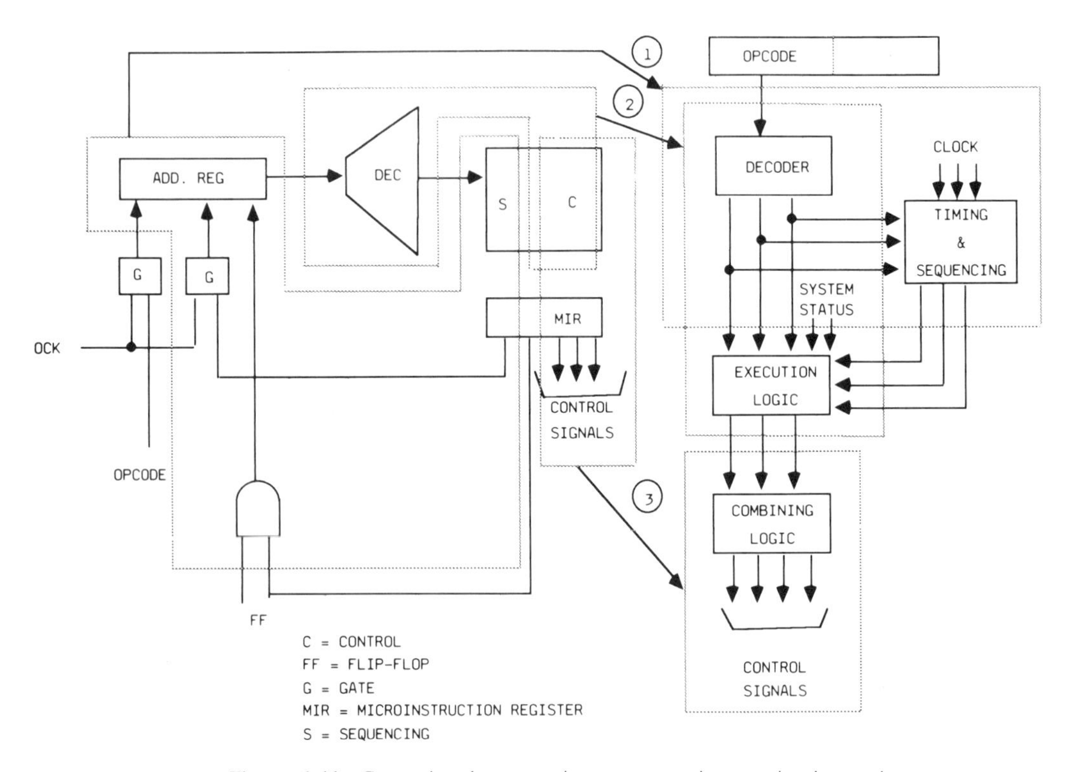

Figure 1.11 Comparison between microprogram and conventional controls.

tives that must be activated when the microinstruction is executed. A macroinstruction fetched from main memory is interpreted by a linked list of microinstructions fetched from control memory.

The sequencing logic (Box 1 in Fig. 1.11) in a conventional logic control arrangement is done by a device that generates the timing signals associated with each control primitive. The number of machine cycles allocated for interpreting each macroinstruction depends on the number of control primitives required by the macroinstruction and the *precise* sequence in which the control primitives should be activated. The *execution logic* (Box 2) found in the conventional control implementation is directly analogous to the execution of a sequence of microinstructions. The execution logic defines the time sequence in which the control primitives are activated. The outputs of the opcode decoder, in conjunction with the timing and sequencing logic, are intimately combined with the execution logic using a conventional logic implementation. This means that the sequencing between control primitives is not as autonomous as it is for an equivalent implementation using microprogram control.

The sequencing of control primitives in microprograms, handled by a hardwired sequencer in a conventional logic implementation, is administered by the addressing logic associated with the control memory. The opcode of the current macroinstruction points to a starting address in control memory corresponding to the first microinstruction in a microprogram. This microprogram interprets the macroinstruction by executing a sequence of microinstructions. Various techniques may be used to point to the location of the next microinstruction to be executed. However, the most straightforward approach is to store the address of the *next* microinstruction to be executed in a separate field of the *current* microinstruction. As each microinstruction executes, its successor is automatically fetched from control memory and placed in the microinstruction register (MIR) to be executed next.

The combinational logic (Box 3) found in the conventional control arrangement tends to be highly irregular in terms of its interconnections. Typically, the outputs that perform the same elementary control operations (control primitives) are logically ORed together so that one control signal is activated no matter which macroinstruction is being processed. This complex interconnection introduces irregularities in a control structure realized with conventional logic. On the other hand, microprogram control stores each control primitive as a part of the current microinstruction fetched from control memory. Even though the address of the next microinstruction may also be stored as a part of the current microinstruction, the sequencing information is separated from the control primitives, thus providing a regular pattern for the control logic implementation. The sequencing information and control primitives are not embedded together as they are in conventional implementations of the control section. Associations may be made as in Table 1.1.

A comparison of the hardware costs for each of the two methods used to implement control sections is shown in Fig. 1.12. The cost of microprogram control increases in steps because the control memory uses fixed-sized ROM modules [that is, modules consist of 1024, 2048, or 4096 (and so on) memory locations]. A disadvantage of this design approach is that if the control memory requires only a few locations, the minimum memory configuration still requires a full ROM module. It is therefore in the best interests of the designer to keep the step size or incremental cost as small as economically feasible. Another disadvantage of the microprogram control approach is that the control store address register, control store data register, and all the gating paths associated with the

TABLE 1.1 COMPARISON OF CONVENTIONAL LOGIC AND MICROPROGRAM CONTROLS

Conventional logic	Microprogram
Timing and sequencing logic, and macroinstruction opcode decoder	Addressing logic associated with the control memory
Execution logic section and decoder	Access circuitry and control section of the control memory (that is, the circuitry that selects the current microinstruction as a location in control store)
Combining logic section	Control and the microinstruction register (MIR) section of control memory (that is, the selection of the control primitives to be activated as specified by each microinstruction)

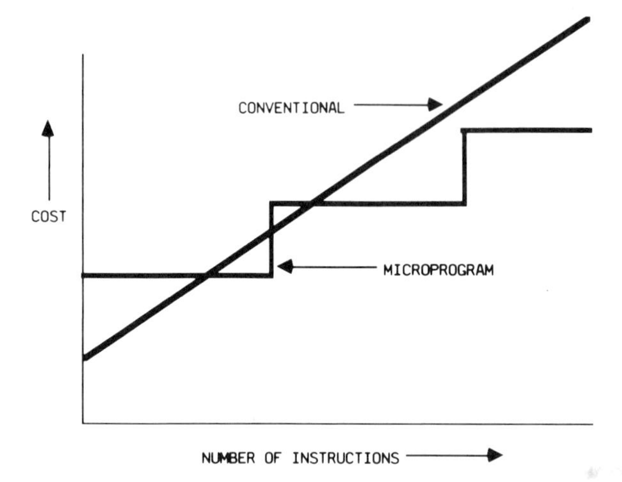

Figure 1.12 Cost comparison between conventional and microprogram control.

various control primitives must be implemented even if the control microprogram consists of a small number of microinstructions. Disadvantages such as these are referred to as *cost overhead*. The analogous cost overhead for conventionally implemented control circuitry is not as great. The cost of much of the control circuitry built from conventional logic grows linearly as the number of macroinstructions in the macroinstruction set of the processor increases.

The overhead circuitry associated with a microprogram implementation, however, is easier to design and incorporate into the overall logic of the processor than is the overhead circuitry for conventional logic implementations. The overhead circuitry of microprogram implementations is built from structurally well-defined logic elements such as the control store address register and the control store data register. The sequence of microinstructions that interprets the individual commands in the macroinstruction set need not be specified at the same time as the microprogram control section. Nor is it necessary for the designer of the microprogram control section concurrently to be involved in the development of the microprogram control sequences. In fact, another designer may develop the microprogram control sequences for the system after the early design has been completed. The microprogram sequences can be generated when the hardware design details are refined. Furthermore, the processor design can be continued before the details of the macroinstruction set are decided. The primary guideline logic designers must observe when designing the microprogram control is that control primitives must be included for interpreting any reasonable macroinstruction. For a control section designed using conventional logic design techniques, the macroinstruction set must be firmly established before beginning the design process. In general, the hardware designer must have also participated in the planning of the command elements in the macroinstruction set. In addition, because of the complexity and irregular nature of a control section implemented using conventional logic techniques, it is very difficult to partition the hardware design into distinct blocks that do not have an abundance of interconnecting leads between them and the rest of the system.

The differences between conventional logic and microprogram controls include ways of interpreting macroinstructions, the sequencing logic, and the cost overhead. But perhaps the most important difference between them is in the maintenance area. Maintaining conventional control structures is difficult compared to the ease with which maintenance concepts can be implemented in a microprogram control section. The regular structure of the control store and its sequencing logic allow fault detection logic to be integrated into the control hardware, where individual errors can be detected at the microprogram level. Since a microinstruction typically specifies one or more control signals, faults can be localized more accurately than in a conventional control implementation. The difficulty with introducing fault diagnosis techniques in a conventional control structure is that sequencing and timing information are embedded in the control logic in a random fashion. The logic of a conventional control structure is not systematic enough to lend itself to any reasonable error detection scheme. A unified scheme of checking the total conventional control implementation is quite difficult and in many cases may be impossible. In such cases, error checking can be done only at the macroinstruction level (that is, verifying that data has been correctly gated from one register to another and operated on properly by the ALU during the data transfer). A macroinstruction checking scheme, in many instances, is inadequate for realizing any effective fault diagnosis and fault correction philosophy. These disadvantages become more apparent as the processing power of a computer increases. At the microprocessor level, however, conventional logic control sections implemented using PLA techniques are used widely because of their low overhead and their efficiency.

1.5 ARITHMETIC AND LOGIC STRUCTURE

The ALU is the functional block within the CPU that performs the computing operations required to process data and solve scientific problems. The basic arithmetic and logical operations consist of binary addition, shift operation, rotation, and Boolean functions of two variables. Combinations of these operations either by means of microprogram sequences or subroutines can perform more complex arithmetic functions. For most applications, particularly control applications, the basic arithmetic and logical operations and combinations of them achieve satisfactory performance levels.

When higher performance is needed, the computing capabilities of the machine can be extended to include floating-point arithmetic. Floating-point arithmetic is used primarily for scientific calculations and signal processing. The early minicomputers did not offer hardware floating-point arithmetic units because they are expensive and needed by only a small percentage of machines. As a result, several companies manufacture floating-point processors (FPPs) as auxiliary, add-on units to meet the needs of those requiring high-speed floating-point calculations. An FPP is connected on the I/O bus and treated as an I/O device. The interface is well defined and the insertion of an FPP is relatively straightforward. In more recent minicomputers (such as the DEC VAX 11/780 and the DEC PDP 11/70), the FPP is an optional unit that fits integrally into the central processor. The cost of the FPP is comparable to the cost of the processor. Since the need for high-speed calculations concerns only a small segment of users, hardware FPPs will continue to be offered as optional units.

The concept of *co-processing* provides the hardware floating-point option at the microcomputer level. Co-processing is a technique of operating a specialized arithmetic processing unit (APU) concurrently with a general-purpose CPU. Both units examine the instruction stream from main memory. The CPU handles the standard instructions while the APU is in the standby state. When the system encounters a special numeric instruction, the CPU pauses and the APU assumes control and processes the numeric instruction. On completion of the numeric operation, both units return to examining the next instruction. The CPU and APU operate together in a manner that is transparent to the user's software. The floating-point operations are approximately 100 times faster than the equivalent software routing. Intel Corp. was the first company to pioneer the co-processing concept with their numeric processor, the 8087. The 8087 was developed to work with the Intel 8086, their 16-bit microprocessor. By using co-processing techniques, users incur the costs of specialized hardware only when they require it, and the chip set is optimized for specific applications. This appears to be the trend for implementing floating-point operations at the microcomputer level.

The techniques different ALUs have for performing arithmetic operations are covered extensively in many excellent textbooks. The following sections deal with only the basic logical operations and binary addition. Combinations of these basic operations accomplish the more complex numeric operations.

1.5.1 Common Logic Functions

In data processing, inputs are examined and modified logically to obtain desired results. The basic logic functions are AND, OR, and NOT. These functions can be implemented directly by using logic gates as the basic elements of the implementations as described in Section 1.2. Because they do not require much hardware, they are almost always included as an integral part of the data manipulation logic in the ALU. The basic logic functions are extremely useful in data manipulation for selecting, sorting, and reformatting information. For example, a 4-bit quantity n_1 in a 16-bit word is to be replaced by n_2 from another word [Fig. 1.13(a)]. Assume that word W_2 contains n_2 in the same bit location as n_1 and other bits are 0s. Also assume that a constant or mask M with four 0s in the corresponding position as n_1 and 1s in the other bit positions can be obtained either as part of the AND instruction or as data from an internal working register. Insertion of n_2 over n_1 is done first by ANDing M and W_1, as depicted in Fig. 1.13(b). This operation clears the specified 4 bits to 0s and leaves the others unchanged in W_1. The final result is obtained by ORing W_2 into W_1. Figure 1.13(b) and (c) shows functionally the two logical steps involved in inserting a 4-bit data field into a word without affecting the other bits. The hardware implementation, as indicated in the figure, uses AND gates to generate both the AND and the OR operation. By examining the truth table, the AND function is realized by setting the bits in W_1 to 0 if the corresponding bits in M are 0s. For any other input combinations, the

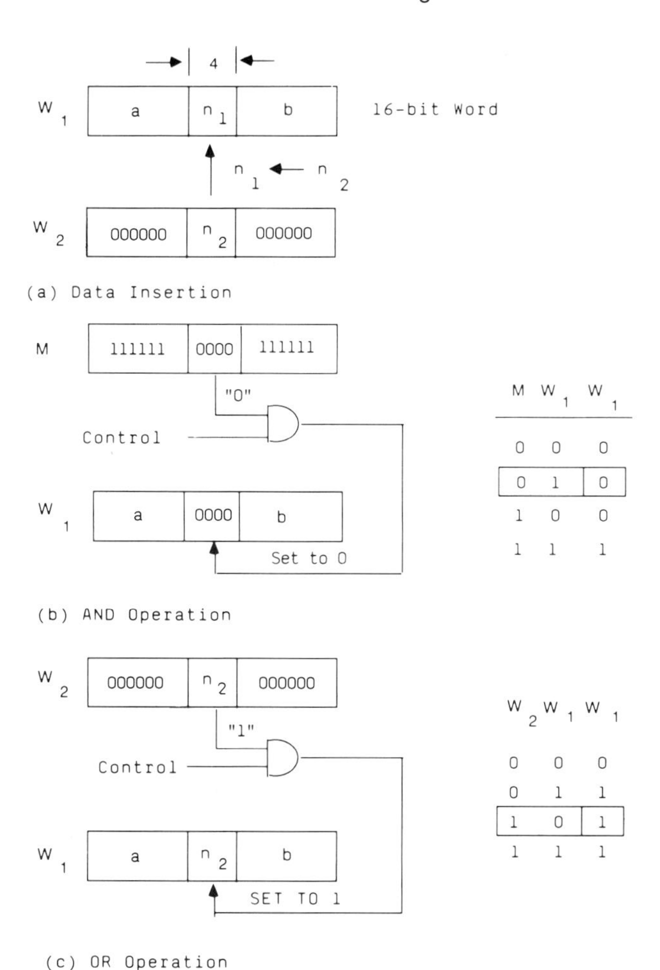

Figure 1.13 Data insertion by AND/OR operation.

values of W_1 are already in the correct state. Similarly, for the OR function, the 1 is examined instead of the 0. The bits in W_1 are set to 1s if the corresponding bits in W_2 are 1s.

Two other logic functions are frequently used: complementation and exclusive-OR (XOR). *Complementation* is a single operand operation. It is applied to every bit of a word and simply changes the bit states: 1s to 0s, and vice versa. Complementation is an important data manipulation function, particularly for converting binary numbers to negative representations in the one's- or two's-complement forms. The XOR function is commonly used for comparing two data words to determine whether they are alike bit by bit. If they are identical, the resultant outputs are all 0s. The all-0 condition is typically testable and allows a program to take an alternative action when a match occurs. Often, a search for a particular address or data is done for a block of memory words. XOR provides a powerful logical operation for control and data processing functions.

1.5.2 Boolean Functions of Two Variables

Although each logical function can be implemented individually, a more complete and more efficient arrangement is realized by taking into consideration the entire set of logical functions of two variables. AND, OR, NOT, and XOR are a subset of these functions. The Boolean function of two variables is expressed by

$$f_i = S_0 A_i' B_i' + S_1 A_i' B_i + S_2 A_i B_i' + S_3 A_i B_i$$

A_i and B_i are the input variables that combine logically to form the four minterms ($A_i'B_i'$, $A_i'B_i$, A_iB_i', and A_iB_i) bit by bit. The subscript i represents a unique bit i of A or B. The four function select controls (S_3, S_2, S_1, and S_0) specify the coefficients of the minterms to give the 16 possible Boolean functions (Table 1.2). As indicated in the table, the logical functions of AND, OR, NOT, and XOR are realized with $S_3S_2S_1S_0$ set equal to 1000, 1110, 0011/0101, and 0110, respectively. The implementation is straightforward and is shown in Fig. 1.14. Each of the four minterms is generated by an AND gate and the selected outputs (controlled) by $S_3S_2S_1S_0$) are logically combined to give the desired f_i output. The full Boolean functions of two variables by this technique of implementation require no more gates that those needed for the basic logical operations of AND, OR, NOT, and XOR.

In many of the data manipulations, the number of bits involved is not always the same as the number of bits in a word, particularly for the wider words of large machines. Four- or 8-bit quantities are frequently used to define items but they are packed and stored in memory as full words, so all the bits in a word are utilized. In processing these quantities, it is often necessary to focus and direct the operation only on specified bits. A combi-

TABLE 1.2 BOOLEAN FUNCTIONS OF TWO VARIABLES

Control, $S_3S_2S_1S_0$	Logic function, f
0000	0
0001	$A'B'$
0010	$A'B$
0011	$A'B' + A'B = A'$
0100	AB'
0101	$A'B' + AB' = B'$
0110	$A'B + AB' = A \oplus B$
0111	$A'B' + A'B + AB' = A' + B'$
1000	AB
1001	$A'B' + AB = (A \oplus B)'$
1010	$A'B + AB = B$
1011	$A'B' + A'B + AB = A' + B$
1100	$AB' + AB = A$
1101	$A'B + AB' + AB = A + B'$
1110	$A' B + AB' + AB = A + B$
1111	1

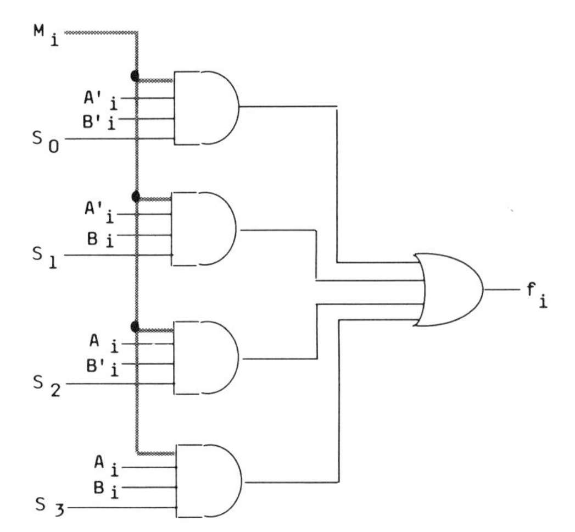

Figure 1.14 Boolean function of two variables.

nation of logical operations with an appropriate mask can effectively select and operate on a subset of bits within a word. Alternately, the mask (M_i) can be incorporated as part of the logical operation by enabling or disabling the logic function according to the mask bit M_i. The Boolean expression is then modified as follows:

$$f_i = M_i(S_0A_i'B_i' + S_1A_i'B_i + S_2A_iB_i' + S_3A_iB_i)$$

The heavy line in Fig. 1.14 represents the mask input M_i. The addition of the mask to the logic functions facilitates logical operations on selected bits. For example, a data word is packed with a 4-digit number. It is desirable to scan a block of these words and determine which words contain a unique digit (say, 9) in the rightmost digit position. In this example, shown in Fig. 1.15, the S control (0110) specifies the XOR operation between the corresponding bits of A and B with the mask M set up to enable only the rightmost 4 bits. The logical results of these 4 bits appear at the f output, while the high-order 12 bits are masked (0 output). When digit X in A matches with the corresponding digit (1001) in B, the f output is all 0s, indicating that the rightmost digit (X) in A has the value of 1001. This match condition can be determined by examining the f outputs for the all-0 state by another instruction. However, it can be done automatically by an additional hardware device called an all-zero detector as indicated in Fig. 1.15. Whenever any logical functions are performed and the resultant f outputs are 0s, a condition code is set. The program sequence needs only to test for the specified condition code instead of making the separate step of program testing the f outputs for the all-0 condition.

1.5.3 Arithmetic Shift and Rotate Functions

The shift and rotate operations used in arithmetic operations are for scaling binary quantities. These functions are necessary for implementing the more complex arithmetic calculations of multiplication, division, and floating-point operations. Shift left multiplies the quantity by 2^n, where n is the number of shifts in digit positions. Shift right divides the

(shift left = mult × 2^n)

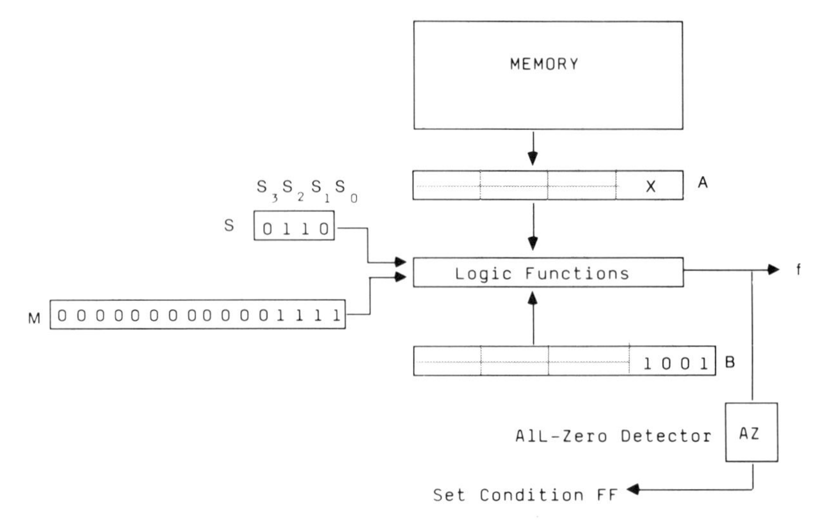

Figure 1.15 Example of logical operation.

quantity by 2^n. Figure 1.16 shows functionally the arithmetic shift and rotate operations. The standard algorithms of repeated addition and repeated subtraction implement multiplication and division. The link (L) bit stores the end bit shifted out for the purpose of testing and linking of two data words (Fig. 1.17). This permits double-word results in multiplication and division.

In arithmetic operations, shift and rotate are usually done on a bit-by-bit basis. This simplifies the implementation by using standard shift registers and allowing only one single-bit shift or rotate at a time. A variable number of shifts is obtained by repeating single shifts.

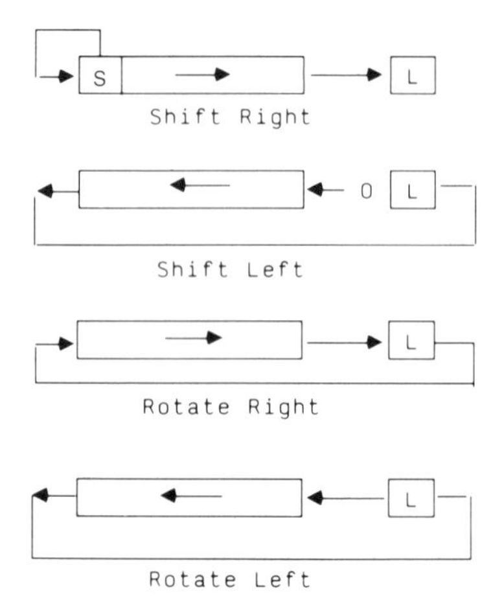

Figure 1.16 Arithmetic shift and rotate.

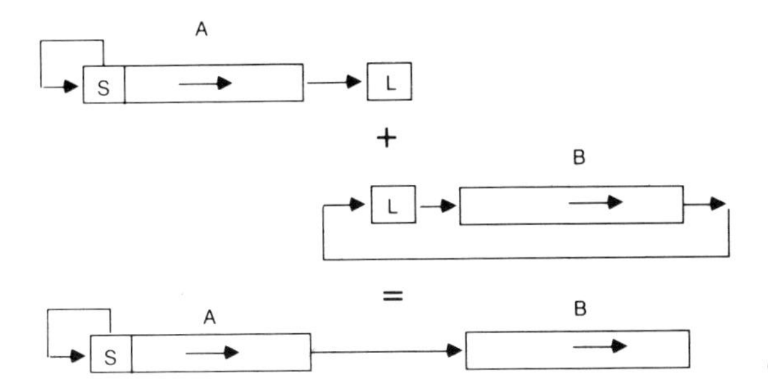

Figure 1.17 Double word shift by combination of shift and rotate.

1.5.4 *Logical Shift and Rotate Functions*

In addition to arithmetic operations, shift and rotate are extremely useful for editing. Editing includes packing and unpacking items of different bit lengths into and from words stored in memory, and inserting items into unused bits in a word or deleting items from a word. A considerable amount of juggling may be necessary to handle editing operations. Unlike the arithmetic type of function, it is not necessary to save the bit from the end position for testing or linking the data flow from one word to another to form a double-word shift. Figure 1.18 shows the logical shift and rotate function in which the link bit is not included in the operation. For control and logical types of data processing, a variable amount of bit rotation is often implemented to achieve more efficient data processing. Rather than repeating a single-bit rotation n times, a single instruction accomplishing the same result reduces the number of instructions required and also the execution time. One method of implementing variable bit rotation is the *barrel shifter* circuit, which is a network of gates that automatically rotates the bits as the data flows through the network.

Figure 1.19 shows one arrangement of a barrel shifter network using 4:1 multiplexers (Fig. 1.20) to rotate a 16-bit data word zero to 15 digit positions to the right. The rotation is done in two levels. The first level rotates the digit to the right by zero, one,

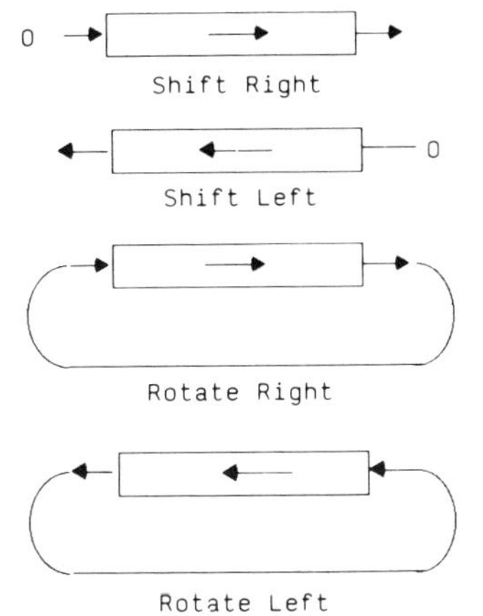

Figure 1.18 Logical shift and rotate.

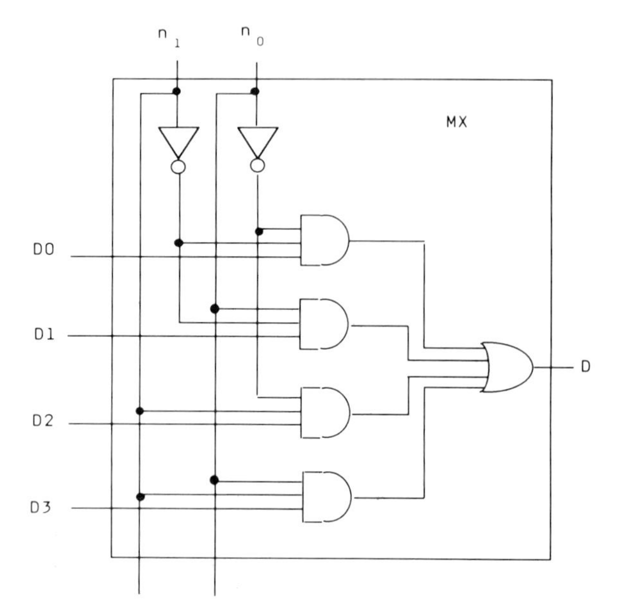

Figure 1.19 4:1 multiplier.

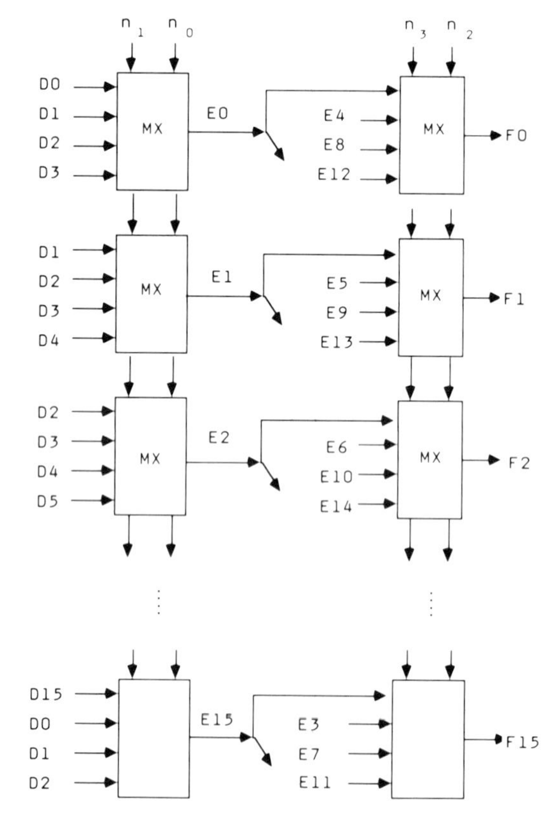

Figure 1.20 Two-stage barrel shifter network.

two, or three bit positions; the second level, by zero, four, eight, or twelve positions. There are 16 possible paths through which the data can flow in the two stages of multiplexers. If $n_3n_2n_1n_0$ specifies the amount of rotation, the low-order two bits n_1n_0 control the selection of the path in the first level; the high-order two bits n_3n_2 control the path of the second level. The end result is a right rotation by $n_3n_2n_1n_0$ having a value from zero to 15.

1.5.5 Binary Addition

1.5.5.1 Binary representation. A binary representation of a negative number may take either a sign and magnitude form or a complement form. The customary notation used in our daily decimal calculations is the sign and magnitude form. A separate symbol, (+) or (−), followed by the magnitude defines a signed number. The omission of a sign, the default condition, implies a positive number. Within a computer, the leftmost bit is usually defined as the sign bit and the remaining bits as the magnitude. A 0 is normally defined as positive (+) and a 1 as negative (−). Computations with this form of representation involve separate calculations of sign and magnitude. Multiplication and division are simplified with separate sign and magnitude calculations. However, the more frequent operations of addition and subtraction are more complex. For example, $(X - Y)$ requires the determination of the sign by comparing X and Y. If $Y > X$, the sign is negative and the magnitude is obtained by subtracting X from Y, $(Y - X)$. If $X > Y$, the sign is positive and the magnitude is $(X - Y)$. Although these decisions are easy to perform by human beings, computers require additional hardware and/or time to perform them.

Negative numbers can be represented in complement forms. There are two types: one's complement and two's complement. These forms require no sign computation and no subtraction. Positive and negative numbers are added by a single adder circuit. In the one's-complement representation, a negative number X is represented by $(2^{n+1} - 1 - X)$, with 2^n being the highest digit. The binary number $(2^{n+1} - 1)$ is an all-1s number (11...11) with the highest digit being 2^n. If $n = 7$ and $X = 01101011$, the calculation of $(2^{n+1} - 1) - X$ is

$$2^{n+1} - 1 = 11111111$$

$$X = 01101011$$

$$(2^{n+1} - 1) - X = 10010100$$

The result is the complement of X. Therefore, the conversion of a negative number to one's-complement form is straightforward. It is done simply by inverting the outputs of X.

The algebraic addition of one's representation requires the processing of *carry overflow* from the most significant bit. It is necessary to add 1 to the result when the overflow occurs. This correction is required to preserve the output in a consistent one's notation. For example, in adding X and $(-Y)$, the result could be positive or negative depending on whether X is larger or smaller than Y. In the one's representation, Y is converted to $(2^{n+1} - 1) - Y$. If $X > Y$, the addition of X and $(-Y)$ becomes

$$(2^{n+1} - 1) + (X - Y) \rightarrow (2^{n+1} - 1) + (X - Y) - 2^{n+1}$$

Since $(X - Y)$ is a positive quantity and $(2^{n+1} - 1)$ is the maximum binary value of $n + 1$ bits (bits 0 through n), the addition of these two quantities will generate a carry into the $(n + 1)$ digit position. This overflow is not retained and the net effect is the same as subtracting the value of 2^{n+1} from the result as indicated above. Simplifying the right-hand term, the result becomes

$$(2^{n+1} - 1) + (X - Y) \rightarrow (X - Y) - 1$$

To obtain the correct answer, a 1 must be added to the result. This is commonly referred to as an *end-around-carry*. If $Y > X$, then $(2^{n+1} - 1) + (X - Y)$ yields no overflow, and the result is a negative number in one's representation. Similarly, adding two negative numbers also yields an overflow. An end-around-carry gives the correct result in one's representation.

In the two's-complement representation, a negative number X is represented by $(2^{n+1} - X)$. This is simply the one's-complement notation plus one. The converson requires the extra step of adding one to the inverted output. The major advantage of two's-complement representation is that it requires no end-around-carry operation in an algebraic addition. The result is in the correct format without any further operation. Because of this, nearly all general-purpose computers use the two's-complement addition in the internal ALU structure.

Table 1.3 shows a 4-bit binary representation of +7 to −7 in the three forms discussed above. As indicated in the table, all positive numbers are the same in all three representations. Also, the highest or the most significant bit can be interpreted as the sign bit. Only the two's-complement representations of +0 and −0 are the same. This avoids the necessity of distinguishing between them.

TABLE 1.3 NUMBER REPRESENTATION IN VARIOUS FORMS

Number	Sign-magnitude	1's complement	2's complement
+7	0111	0111	0111
+6	0110	0110	0110
+5	0101	0101	0101
+4	0100	0100	0100
+3	0011	0011	0011
+2	0010	0010	0010
+1	0001	0001	0001
+0	0000	0000	0000
−0	1000	1111	0000
−1	1001	1110	1111
−2	1010	1101	1110
−3	1011	1100	1101
−4	1100	1011	1100
−5	1101	1010	1011
−6	1110	1001	1010
−7	1111	1000	1001
−8	—	—	1000

TABLE 1.4 TRUTH TABLE OF SUM AND CARRY OUTPUTS

Inputs			Outputs	
Carry-in, $C_i - 1$	Addend, a_i	Augend, b_i	Sum, S_i	Carry-out, C_i
0	0	0	0	0
0	0	1	1	0
0	1	0	1	0
0	1	1	0	1
1	0	0	1	0
1	0	1	0	1
1	1	0	0	1
1	1	1	1	1

1.5.5.2 Binary adder circuit. When two's complement represents negative numbers, the adder circuit handles all additions the same way. In binary addition, the logical expressions for the sum (S_i) and carry (C_i) are

$$S_i = a_i b_i c_{i-1} + a_i b_i' c_{i-1}' + a_i' b_i c_{i-1}' + a_i' b_i' c_{i-1}$$

$$C_i = a_i b_i + a_i c_{i-1} + b_i c_{i-1}$$

The truth table for the sum and carry equations is shown in Table 1.4. The implementation of the full-adder circuit according to the logical expression and truth table is shown in Fig. 1.21. The adders can be interconnected to form a multibit adder by cascading the carry

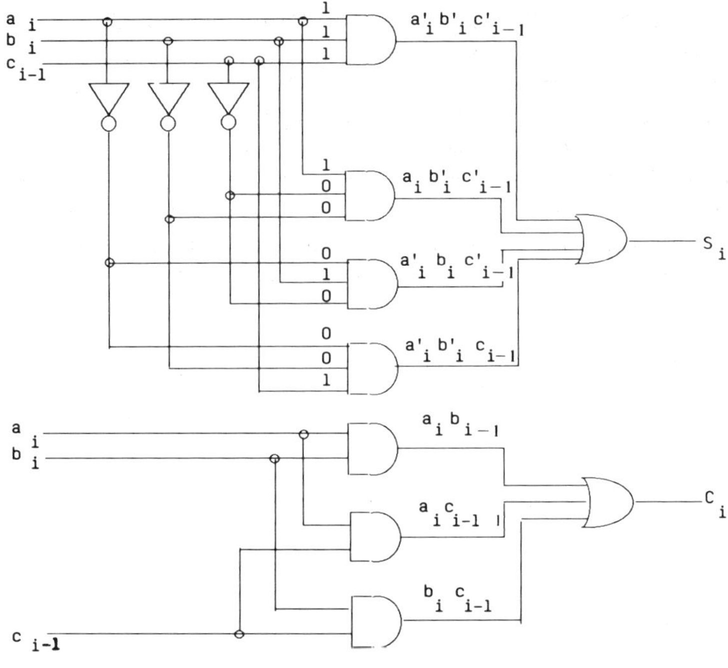

Figure 1.21 Binary adder.

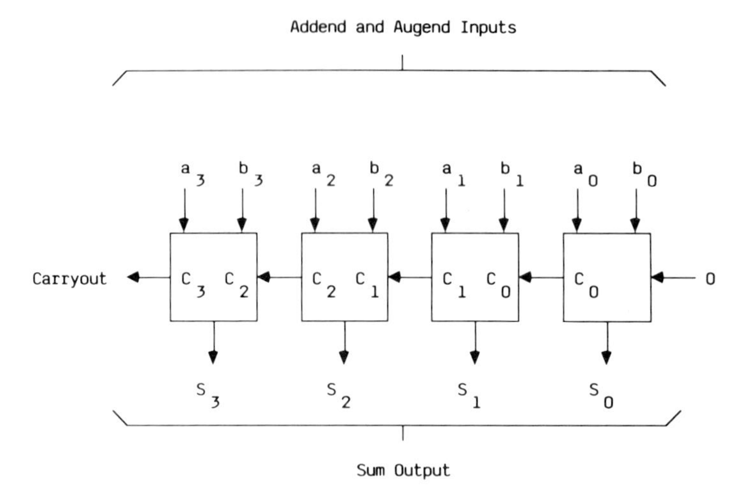

Figure 1.22 4-bit ripple carry adder.

outputs from one stage to the succeeding stage (Fig. 1.22). In this arrangement, the carry has a rippling effect and sufficient time must be allowed for it to propagate through each of the adder stages. Although the figure shows only 4 bits, the adder can be extended to any length. In high-performance applications, however, the settling time for large adders of this type may not be acceptable.

1.5.5.3 Look-ahead carry adders. The speed of adders is limited primarily to the carry circuit. There are several techniques for speeding up the process, such as completion recognition, carry bypass, and look-ahead carry. The look-ahead carry technique is commonly used in the current design of machines. The look-ahead carry structure is a parallel logic arrangement in which all carries are generated simultaneously and independently. Speed is obtained by generating the carry from the current stage before the carries from the previous counter stages have had sufficient time to ripple through to the current stage. The equations for the look-ahead carry are given in Table 1.5, where the generation $(G_i) = a_i b_i$ and the propagation $(P_i) = a_i \oplus b_i$. The implementation of a look-

TABLE 1.5 LOGIC EQUATIONS FOR THE GENERATION OF THE INDIVIDUAL LOOK-AHEAD CARRIES

$$C_0 = G_0 + P_0 C_{in}$$
$$C_1 = G_1 + P_1 G_0 + P_1 P_0 C_{in}$$
$$C_2 = G_2 + P_2 G_1 + P_2 P_1 G_0 + P_2 P_1 P_0 C_{in}$$
$$\vdots \quad \vdots \quad \vdots$$
$$C_i = G_i + P_i G_{i-1} + P_i P_{i-1} G_{i-2} + P_i P_{i-1} P_{i-2} G_{i-3} + \cdots + P_i P_{i-1} P_{i-2} \cdots P_1 P_0 C_{in}$$

ahead carry circuit using the previous logic equations is shown in the top portion of Fig. 1.23. As shown in the figure, each sum output is independently generated.

Large binary adders implemented with full look-ahead carry logic circuits become very expensive because of the fan-out and fan-in requirements of the circuits needed to implement the successive logic stages. A procedure for achieving a good compromise in cost is to incorporate a group look-ahead scheme in which an n-bit word is divided into m b-bit groups. The look-ahead carry concept can be applied to the groups as a whole, to bits within a group, or to both categories concurrently. The choice of implementation is dictated by the speed/cost trade-off requirements of the system design.

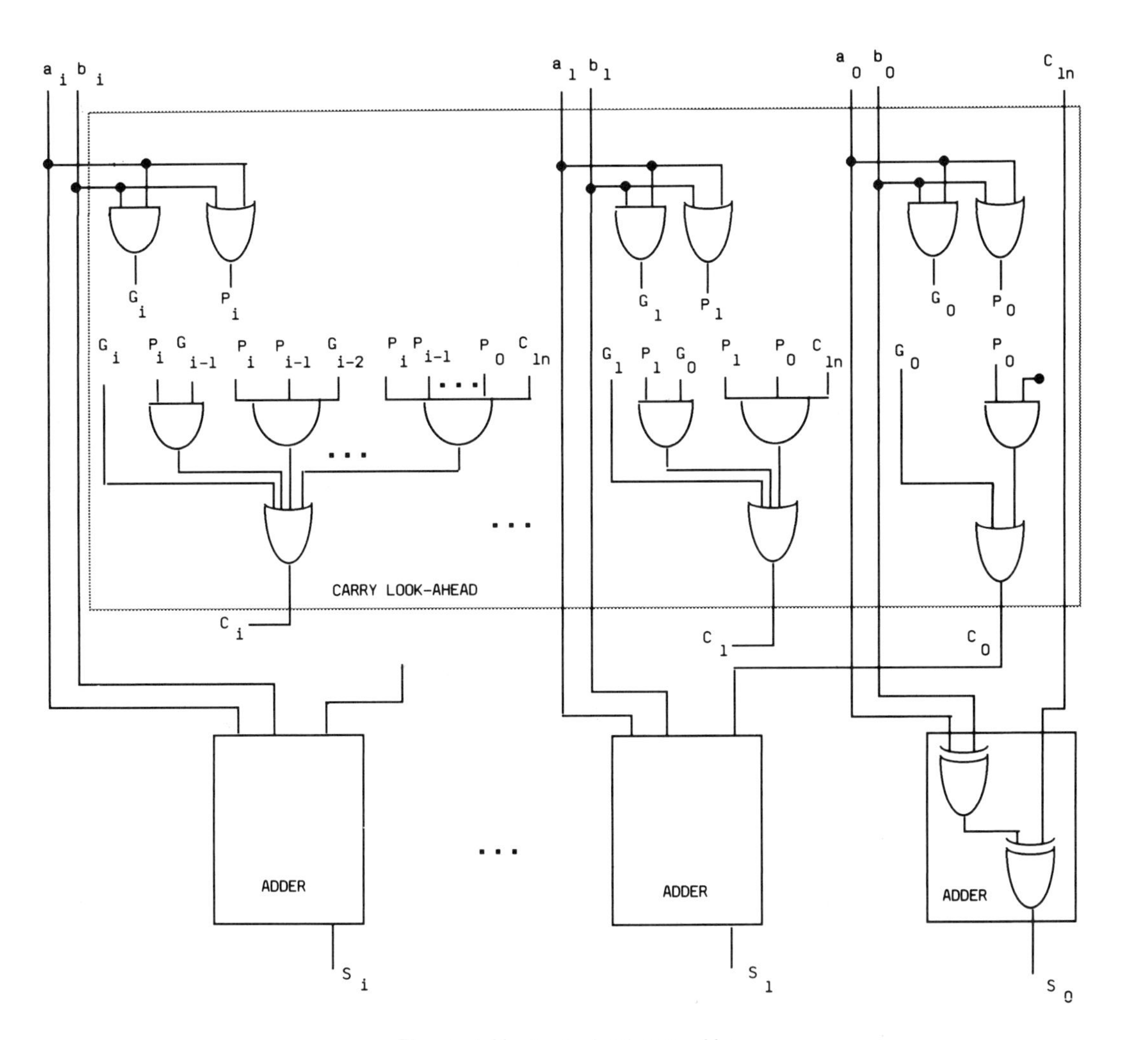

Figure 1.23 Look-ahead carry adder.

1.6 MEMORY ORGANIZATION

1.6.1 A Hierarchy of Storage Facilities

The CPU is composed of semiconductor logic gates with response times measured in nanoseconds. Main storage is made up of semiconductor memory modules with typical response times in excess of 100 nanoseconds. To match the processing capability of the CPU more closely with the response time of the available memory technology, a structured organization of storage facilities has evolved. This organization can be broken down into four categories. Each category may be distinguished by its speed of response, the technology employed to implement the devices found within the category, and the complexity of the control environment required by the associated devices. In essence, these categories form a hierarchy of storage facilities that may *all* exist on a particular computing system. Each category is distinguished by the response time of the memory device found within it. The four categories of memory facilities associated with a computing environment are these:

1. Very high-speed internal storage devices often contain the working register set and a cache-type memory structure. Specific functions performed by members of this memory group include the temporary storage of data and instructions and the imtermediate results of calculations.
2. The second category is represented by the main memory of the processor. The main memory stores the data and instructions of the currently executing program. Typically, such memories have cycle times ranging from 400 to 800 nanoseconds.
3. The category of on-line mass storage devices includes electromechanical devices such as magnetic tape units and magnetic disk storage. Mass storage devices are used for storing large files of programs and data that normally do not have to reside in main storage. Speed of access is less important than the capability of storing large amounts of data.
4. Off-line bulk storage devices typically store extremely large data files that are accessed very infrequently. The frequency of use is so low that manual intervention is required to load the storage media on the appropriate system device before the required data may be referenced by a program. Magnetic tape and cartridge disk packs fall into this category.

It is a characteristic of a device in this memory hierarchy that *its speed of response is inversely related to the complexity of its implementation*. In addition, *the capacity of the device varies inversely with the speed of its response*. For example, the working register set has the fastest response time of any memory element and it is implemented using straightforward logical gating circuits. In contrast, a magnetic tape unit can store millions of bits of data on a single reel of tape. But the tape must be retrieved from off-line storage and mounted on the tape drive, and the system must be alerted when the appropriate reel has been loaded. The magnetic tape system consists of a controller and one or more tape drives; each is usually housed in a separate enclosure, making the overall system highly complex.

1.6.2 Hardware Register Set

The early computers were organized around a small number of *special-purpose registers*. These included the instruction register (IR), the memory address register (MAR), and the program counter (PC). In addition to the IR, MAR, and PC, one or more other registers that could be associated with specific operations were provided, including *accumulators*, *index registers*, and *base registers*. The six types of hardware registers provided a faster, more efficient addressing environment than main memory since they had specific purposes. Soon it was seen that a set of general-purpose registers could perform the operations of the special-purpose registers. Hardware register sets evolved from being collections of special-purpose registers into groups of independent, directly addressable general-purpose registers called general-purpose register sets (GPRs).

The major significance of a hardware register set lies in the fast access time that the processor can achieve for operands when they are placed in it. This leads to a faster execution time for a program since the GPRs are not part of main storage. The use of GPRs to facilitate operand fetching provides a mode of memory referencing called *general register addressing*. The GPR set acts as a high-speed buffer memory between the CPU and main storage. Memory references are designed with such a structure so that the majority of operands will be found in the GPR set rather than in main storage.

1.6.3 Hardware Stack

One of the most powerful features of internal memory referencing has been the use of a *last-in, first-out (LIFO) buffer*, or *pushdown stack*. The device derives its name from the way it is loaded: items are added to the stack in sequential order and then retrieved from the stack in reverse order. A stack operation implicitly references the operand at the top of the stack (TOS). If the operation involves saving an operand, the item to be saved pushes down each of the other items in the stack one position from their former locations. Consequently, a stack-write operation is called a *push*. In a similar manner, if an item is removed from the stack, it appears as though each item in the entire stack has been moved up one position from its former location. A stack-read operation is referred to as a *pop*. Once an item has been "popped" from the stack, its stack location becomes available for future use. Items are always entered or withdrawn from the top of the stack. Because of this characteristic, a stack reference does not require a specific memory address to obtain an operand. Conceptually, all data enter and leave the logical stack from the same end. Information appears to move successively down one position on each push operation and up one position on each pop operation. Figure 1.24 illustrates the basic administration of a logical stack using push and pop operations.

Physically, however, it is not practical to implement a stack by moving the entire contents of the stack up or down each time a push or pop operation is performed. Instead,

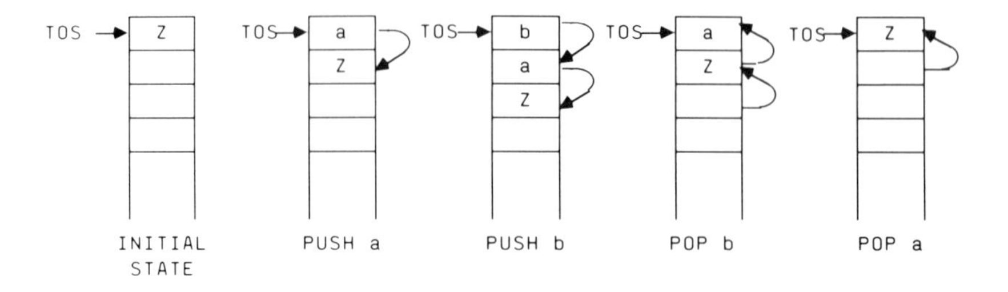

Figure 1.24 Basic stack push and pop operation.

the actual hardware stacks use an up-down counter as a pointer to the top of the stack. Using this method, the entire stack is never physically moved in memory. Rather, the top of the stack is moved up or down in memory as the stack pointer is incremented or decremented. Since the stack pointer always points to the top of the stack, the results of the last stack operation are immediately available to the program without an explicit memory reference.

Another characteristic of the stack is its ability to coordinate subroutines and interrupt service routines directly. Both the subroutine and the interrupt require the machine to save linkage information so that control can return to the point from which it was diverted when the interrupt processing completes. Typically, all the necessary linkage information is loaded onto the stack automatically when either the processor executes a subroutine call or recognizes an interrupt request.

1.6.4 Cache: Locality of Reference

Careful studies of programs executed on machines of various sizes have established the property of *locality of reference*. This is a characteristic of a program segment, spanning many instruction cycles, in which all references to memory for operands or instructions tend to cluster in localized areas of storage. The clustering of operands and instructions suggests that the highest speed of reference and access may only be necessary to a relatively small area of storage. The physical realization of this concept is the cache memory (Fig. 1.25). The cache-oriented machine uses hardware to examine the operand address and the address for the next instruction. If the hardware finds the addressed word in the cache (called a *hit*), execution proceeds very quickly since a typical cache cycle time is less than 200 nanoseconds. On the other hand, if the addressed word is not in the cache, the cache control logic must initiate a main memory read. The accessed data is loaded into the cache and a subsequent access to the cache results in a hit. Studies indicate that caches are effective in approximately 90 percent of memory reads for reasonably sized caches (for example, 8K bytes) and typical programs.

As shown in Fig. 1.25, the cache normally receives memory write requests from both the CPU and the direct memory access (DMA). The DMA must access the cache to

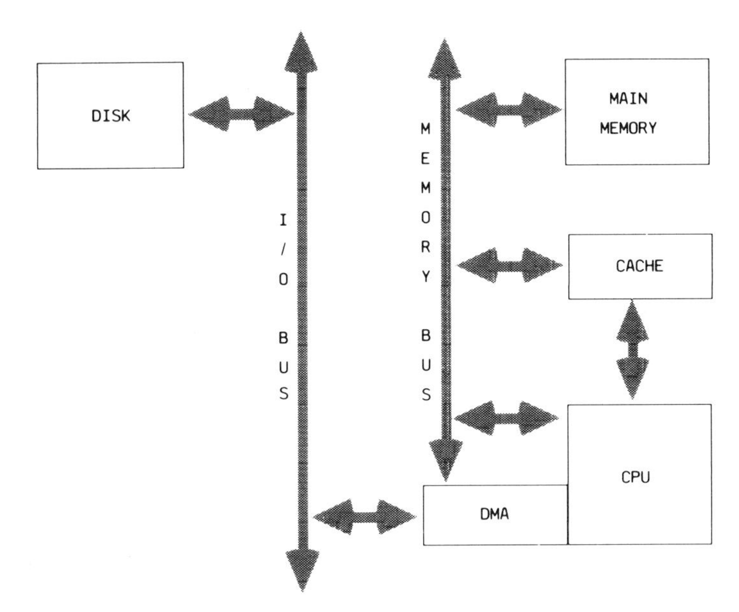

Figure 1.25 Use of a cache memory in a dual bus structure.

invalidate appropriate words on memory writes to ensure consistent data in both the main memory and the cache. Normally, the operation of the cache is completely transparent to the executing program. An example of cache implementation is given in Section 9.3.4.

1.7 INPUT/OUTPUT STRUCTURE

The input-output system provides the means for a CPU to interact with the external world, which is characterized by a peripheral device. Typically, the periphery is administered by a *device controller,* which interacts with the CPU in a well-defined manner. Information may be communicated between a device controller and the CPU in either parallel or serial form. *Parallel* I/O, which transfers all bits in a data word at the same time, has been the most common form of information transfer used in computer systems. But the advent of the microprocessor, with its emphasis on low-cost computing hardware, has stimulated the use of *serial* I/O. The emergence of computer networks has further encouraged the development of serial communications. A serial comunication mechanism provides a particularly straightforward technique for interfacing a peripheral device with the CPU. For instance, the RS-232C EIA data communications interface standard may be observed by both the CPU and the periphery [17], or a private serial communications convention may be used. In either case, the user simply inserts one end of a single coaxial cable into the appropriate mainframe serial I/O port and the other end into the corresponding connector slot of the peripheral device controller.

The I/O operations use the following three basic modes:

1. *Programmed data transfers,* including device polling, in which the CPU directs the entire I/O transaction by executing a sequence of I/O instructions.
2. *Interrupt-drive control,* in which the CPU interacts with its environment only when a hardware interrupt is directed to the CPU from its external system. The interrupt represents an immediate preemptive demand for service by an element in the system.
3. *Hardware-directed block transfers of data between an external device and main storage,* in which the transfers take place without the participation of the CPU. This technique is implemented via the DMA channel.

Communication between the processor and its peripheral system is administered under control of either software or hardware I/O controllers. Typically, hardware controllers function independently of the CPU and interface with specific external devices. The advantage of using independent hardware controllers is that the system can perform I/O operations concurrently with CPU processing. Essentially, useful work can be done in parallel with the normal execution of a program sequence. Consequently, such hardware controllers offer the possibility of achieving a higher data transfer rate than software controllers when operating on large blocks of data. Figure 1.26 shows the general steps required by software and hardware controllers for transferring data between the processor and the peripheral system.

Programmed I/O action can be initiated either internally or externally to service the peripheral devices. When the processor wants to communicate with an I/O device, it simply issues the commands for the action it deems appropriate. According to the program sequence, the commands can either return to the processor or wait if the device is busy. Once the program has control of the device, it initiates the desired I/O action. The communication from the processor to the device is straightforward. I/O communication problems arise when a peripheral device wants to communicate with the processor. The device can signal the processor to handle its request in one of two ways: program polling or external interrupt. In *program polling,* the program makes a periodic scan of all the peripheral devices and interrogates each one to determine whether it needs servicing. This procedure is time consuming and must be done frequently to avoid missing requests. For certain applications, such as low-performance or low-throughout systems, the polling technique is entirely satisfactory. Since no additional hardware is necessary, polling is economical; it does, however, sacrifice system time. Performance and throughput improve if the *external interrupt* technique is employed. Service is demanded from the processor when the peripheral device requests it. This technique also eliminates the need for the CPU to constantly poll each external device for service requests. The external interrupt technique is not as economical as program polling, however, because it requires additional hardware.

For high-performance applications, the serial nature of programmed I/O has often been inadequate to meet the high transfer rate of peripheral devices (for example, a fixed-head disk or a nine-track magnetic tape unit). An additional hardware facility has been devised to handle these devices without choking the system. Data can be transferred di-

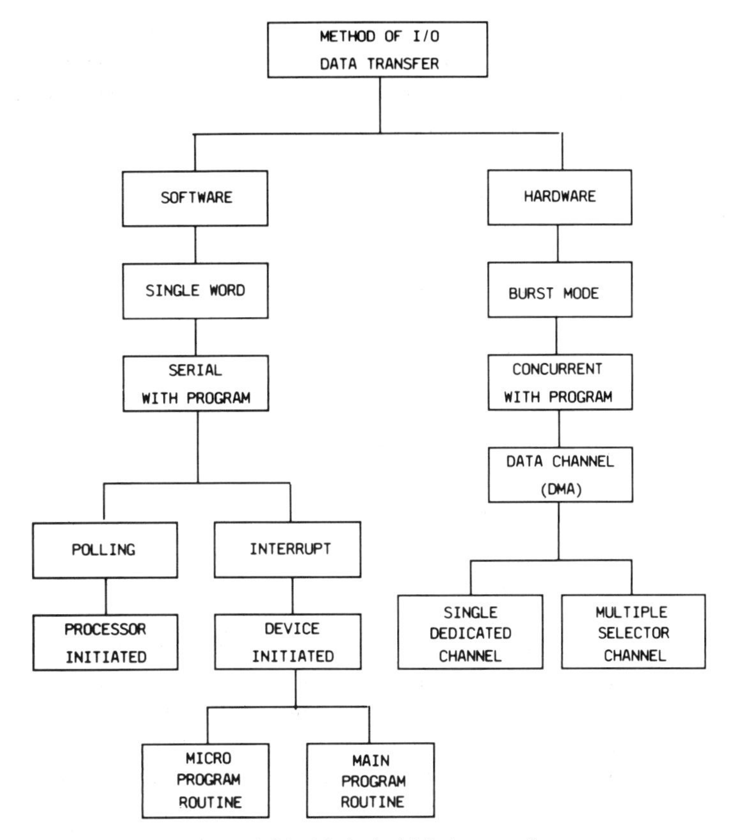

Figure 1.26 Method of I/O data transfer.

rectly into main storage from the external hardware (usually disks) by a DMA facility. High-speed data transfer is controlled entirely by the DMA hardware and is performed without program intervention once the block transfer process has been initiated. The operation involves time-sharing the main memory with the program sequence for the CPU on a cycle-stealing basis. Although the program sets up the initial conditions in the DMA channel, the data transfer is completely transparent to the main program sequence. At any given time, this concurrent operation allows a large block of data to be transferred at a maximum rate that corresponds to the cycle time of main storage. Note, however, that enhancing the data transfer speed and capacity by using a DMA facility means incurring additional hardware costs.

1.8 GENERAL CATEGORIES OF SOFTWARE

Software may be defined to include all the programs associated with a computer. Programs are made up of sequences of machine code that can be executed by the computer. Because of the many difficulties encountered in writing programs directly in machine code, programmers normally use some form of intermediate language to simplify the process. Programs written in an intermediate language must have their instruction sequences translated into the machine code of a particular computer. Such translators have been called *assemblers*, *compilers*, and *interpreters*.

There are three distinct software categories: system, application, and diagnostic. These categories are found in nearly all computing systems.

1. *System software* is oriented toward the efficient use of the computing system resources. Normally, this software is independent of any application. It is designed to administer functions that recur in the normal operation of the computing system such as file manipulation, operator interaction with the main console, and system generation procedures. System software provides a standard interface to the opening environment of the machine and permits the application programmer to concentrate on application code. System software may be subdivided as follows:
   (a) *Operating systems* or *monitors* administer I/O operations, schedule functions and tasks, and handle the details of coordinating application programs for execution on the system.
   (b) *Utility systems* include program composition software and program execution software. *Program composition software* lets the programmers use language processors, on-line text editors, library routines, and file administration capabilities to create and modify programs. *Program execution software* provides a real-time development environment for application-oriented and systems-oriented programs. In particular, program execution software includes packages such as device drivers, supervisory control programs, and on-line debugging modules that permit the programmer to debug code interactively in the actual environment in which it would normally execute.
   (c) *Language processors* such as FORTRAN, Pascal, Ada, C, and COBOL compilers provide the programmer with a graceful and precise way of generating application-oriented code. Programming is done in higher-level languages that use English-language-type statements and eliminate the need for the programmer to be concerned with the intimate details of machine operation. Higher-level languages make the computer largely transparent to the user.
2. *Application software* is developed by or for the user and relates directly to the requirements of the application. For commercially obtained machines, the users typically assume the responsibility for developing the application programs; the manufacturer supplies the system software. If the user obtains a *turnkey* system, the manufacturer supplies the system software and the application software. Examples of such software are turnkey business systems that perform specialized accounting functions.
3. *Diagnostic software* helps maintain and operate the CPU, the standard peripherals attached to the CPU, and the external devices interfaced to the CPU supplied by the application. Consequently, diagnostic software normally consists of vendor-supplied programs that test the manufacturer's equipment and user-supplied pro-

grams that test the application-related equipment. Diagnostic software has become increasingly significant as more and more emphasis has been placed on implementing highly reliable computing systems that may be easily diagnosed and maintained.

Software facilities of the small machine have been adopted from the larger computing structures. As new architectural features have made a small computer look like a large computer, the software techniques for the larger machine have been modified to run on the smaller machine. So the categories of software for the small computer are essentially the same as those of the large computer.

1.9 TECHNOLOGY IMPACT ON ARCHITECTURE

1.9.1 Hardware/Software Cost

Advances in computer technology offer opportunities for innovative hardware/software trade-offs that reduce system development costs and improve performance and software reliability. Software development is increasingly expensive. After being developed at a cost of $10 per line of code, it must be maintained. Developing a software system accounts for only 30 percent of the total software costs in a typical installation; maintenance accounts for the other 70 percent. Further, maintaining the software in an operational system requires from 50 to 80 percent of the total data processing budget. The increasing importance of software is readily apparent from Fig. 1.27 [4]. In the mid-1950s, about 80 percent of the system cost was attributed to the hardware and 20 percent to the software. This ratio will be reversed by 1987 because of rapidly decreasing hardware costs and the increasing rate of labor-intensive software costs.

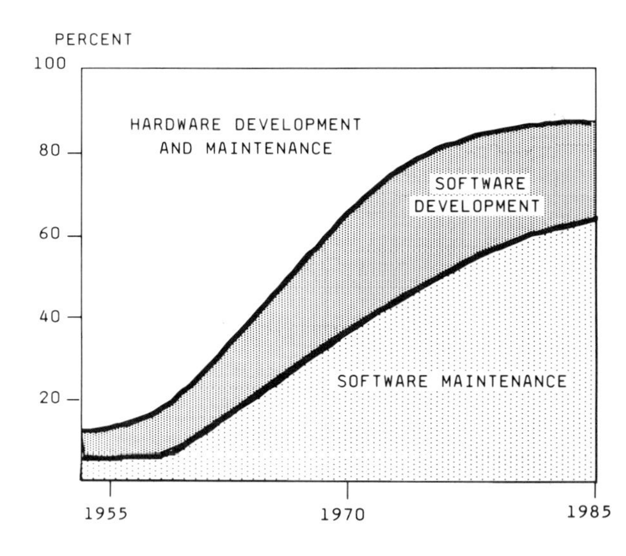

Figure 1.27 Hardware/software cost trends.

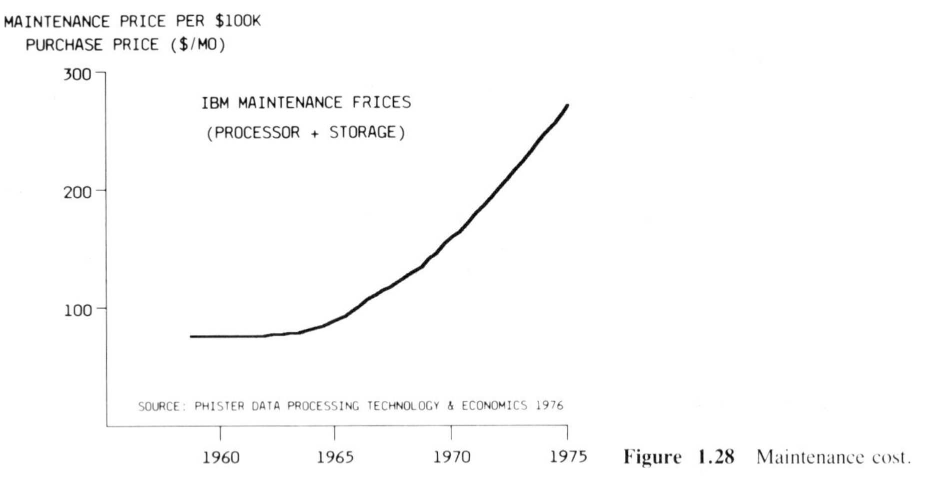

Figure 1.28 Maintenance cost.

Maintenance plays an important role in computer installations. Its cost is continually rising and reflects the highly labor-intensive effort. Figure 1.28 shows the maintenance price per $100,000 of purchase price for IBM processors and storage [5]. The monthly rate has increased by a factor of 3 from 1960 to 1975.

Advances in software engineering have not been as great as those in hardware. The price/performance ratio of hardware has improved greatly, but the improvement in programmer productivity has been slow (Table 1.6). This is reflected in the high cost of software development. To achieve the most cost-effective arrangement while ensuring adequate performance, architects are looking at hardware/software trade-offs in the designs of both of these components of computer systems.

1.9.2 Hardware/Software Trade-off Goals

A strong interest in hardware/software trade-offs is directed toward finding new hardware architectures that help alleviate the problem of low programming productivity. A considerable amount of recent work has been focused on the direct execution of higher-level languages, the replacement of data base management software with data base machines [7], communications processors for distributed data processing systems, and the implementation of parts of the operating system and procedural calls in microprograms. The flexibility of microprogramming offers other possible trade-offs. It is now both economically and technologically attractive to implement many software functions in microcode.

TABLE 1.6 DATA PROCESSING INDUSTRY GROWTH TRENDS

	1955	1965	1975	1985
Industry	1	20	80	320
Machine performance	1	10^2	10^4	10^6
Programmer productivity	1	2.4	5.6	13.3
System reliability	1	5	24	120

Source: Art Benjamin Associates; from [6].

Using hardware or microcode for functions that traditionally have been done by software can make systems faster and more reliable in the following ways [8]:

1. *Reducing software development costs*. Microcode supplies diverse instruction sets and represents data in various ways so that software compilers can scale variables and overlay memory efficiently, while the code remains portable.
2. *Simplifying software*. Using microcode for special instructions such as managing data bases reduces software development costs and also reduces the complexity of the software.
3. *Achieving better performance*. Hardware and firmware implementations of complex, but frequently used, functions such as floating-point arithmetic reduce the use of real time.
4. *Improving reliability*. With simpler programs and better performance, additional hardware checks may be added to detect errors and recover from them, increasing the tolerance of the system to faults.
5. *Securing system integrity*. Firmware and hardware improve memory protections by implementing them more simply and efficiently than their software counterparts.

In general, the trade-offs made between hardware, software, and firmware must be evaluated carefully to reduce costs. Both hardware and software architects must analyze these trade-offs before adding features to increase the size and complexity of their systems. They should also consider them when implementing ways of measuring performance and diagnosing the system.

1.9.3 Technological Advances

Semiconductor technology has progressed at an explosive rate. Innovations in processing techniques have led to higher-performance circuits and denser chip structures. This evolution has occurred in both metal-oxide semiconductor (MOS) and bipolar technologies. These technological advances have occurred to meet the needs of a variety of applications. For example, 256K dynamic RAMs, more powerful 32-bit microprocessors, and improved processor chip sets emerged from the semiconductor development state to commercial availability in just one decade.

Figure 1.29 summarizes the various semiconductor technologies and their circuit applications at the chip level. As indicated, the technologies are divided into two areas: MOS and bipolar. Although MOS technology had been around for many years, its potential was not realized until the early 1970s, when Intel Corp. introduced its Model 1103 1K RAM chip and its Model 4004 microprocessor chip. The early LSI chips were developed with P-channel MOS (PMOS) technology. Since then, great strides have been made with N-channel MOS (NMOS) and complementary MOS (CMOS). NMOS may be regarded as the second generation of MOS development. It is well suited for LSI RAMS and microprocessors.

Complementary MOS (CMOS) technology combines both P-channel and N-channel technology on the same substrate. Both transistors are connected in tandem in a "push-

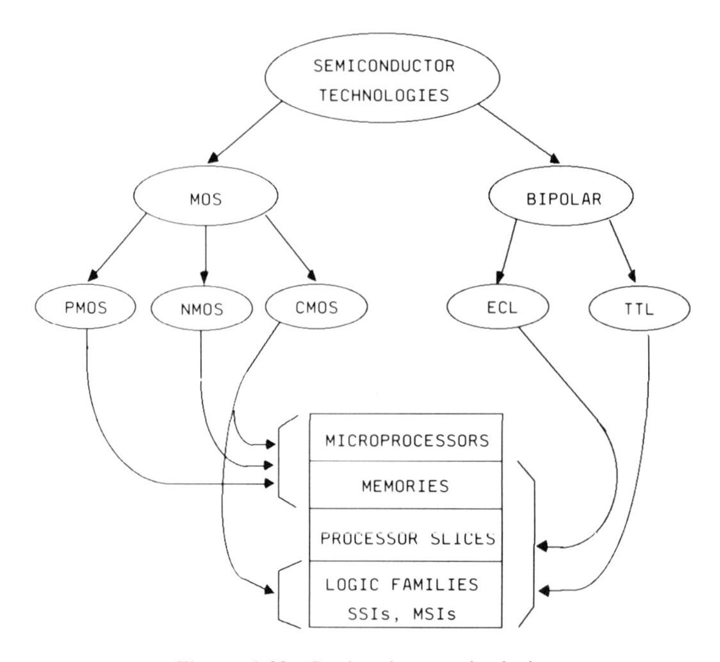

Figure 1.29 Semiconductor technologies.

pull'' arrangement. The N-channel transistor functions as the driver; the P-channel transistor functions as the load. Normally, only one transistor is on except during the switching interval. The great advantage of this structure is that it requires extremely low standby power. In addition, a single supply voltage with a wide range of voltages (3 to 15 volts) can be used without disturbing the circuit. CMOS circuits also have high noise immunity, with a guaranteed noise margin of approximately 1.5 volts. However, CMOS devices are more complex than either NMOS or PMOS devices, since both N-channel and P-channel transistors are required. They require more silicon real estate to accommodate what are basically two separate MOS transistors. As fabrication processing techniques continue making dramatic advances, though, the number of circuits that can be placed on a chip will not be limited by the silicon area as much as by the power dissipation. Because of their low power dissipation, CMOS devices may be regarded as the third generation of MOS development, and they are well suited for VLSI devices.

There are two major kinds of bipolar logic circuits: transistor-transistor logic (TTL) and emitter-coupled logic (ECL). The TTL family is the most widely used. A variety of TTL circuits have evolved to meet the needs of many different applications. The broad spectrum of available TTL circuits has allowed logic designers to optimize all portions of a system in the most cost-effective manner. The typical delay per gate is in the range of 3 to 15 nanoseconds. On the other hand, the fastest available integrated circuit logic is ECL. The speed is obtained by operating the transistors in the nonsaturated mode, resulting in a very fast switching speed, typically 1 nanosecond or less. However, this speed is realized at the expense of relatively high power dissipation. So far, ECL has been used almost exclusively in large computers.

Technological advances in the past decade have improved the cost-performance ratio significantly. They have made systems more reliable and have provided alternative technologies for the designers of computer architectures. Integrated-circuit technology has doubled the number of components per chip about once every 2 years during the 15 years between 1965 and 1980 (Fig. 1.30) [9]. This trend will continue well into the 1980s and therefore directly affects the design of processors, mass storage devices, terminals, peripherals, and system architectures. The 1980s will be the decade in which the next phase of integration in semiconductors, that of VLSI devices, becomes prevalent. In the near future, systems will use microchips with over 100,000 gates on them [10]. In 1981, Hewlett-Packard announced their 32-bit microprocessor chip containing 450,000 transistors; in late 1982, the chip was incorporated into their commercial products, the HP9000 computer systems.

1.9.4 Device-Level Impact

Each progression in the technology of logic and memory devices defines a new generation of computers. The first generation used vacuum tubes for the logic elements; the second generation used transistors. The third generation of integrated circuit (IC) devices was followed by large-scale integration (LSI). The fourth generation of VLSI devices is here now. In the past 30 years, the average switching speed of a logic circuit has increased 10^7 times, from 10 milliseconds for a relay to 1 nanosecond for a logic gate in an LSI or VLSI chip. No such rapid progress has been made in any other field, and these rapid developments have been the most important factor in the evolution of computers.

The complexity of an integrated circuit may be expressed by the number of active elements (transistors) it has. The 256K dynamic RAM device and the 32-bit

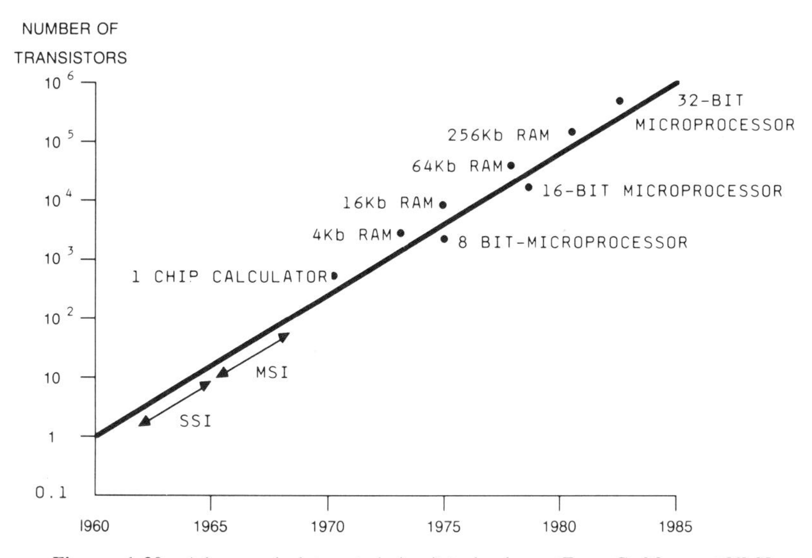

Figure 1.30 Advances in integrated circuit technology. (From G. Moore, "VLSI: Some Fundamental Challenges," *IEEE Spectrum*, April 1979.© IEEE.)

microprocessor represent the current state of the art. It is projected that new advances in electron beam lithography will bring the industry a 32-bit microcomputer chip with 1M byte of ROM by the late 1980s [11]. This means that by the end of this decade a single chip will have the same capacity as the CPU of an IBM 370/148 [5].

VLSI also means lower costs. For example, the storage capacity per chip has quadrupled every 2 years from 1972 to 1982 (1K in 1972, 4K in 1974, 16K in 1976, 64K in 1980, and 256K in 1982; see Figure 1.30), but the price per chip in the same time period increased only 20 to 30 percent [12]. Therefore, the price per bit has decreased remarkably. Further, the size of the chips has not increased significantly. One million gates per chip are being developed on the same size chip that in 1972 contained 1K gates. Improvements in microprocessor functions, cost, and speed have continued at a similar pace.

The statistics compiled by D. Queyssac in Table 1.7 reveal this: in just one year, the mean time between failures (MTBF) of a 3000-gate microprocessor chip increased from 877 years to 1901 years [11]. Compared with the failure rate of more traditional computers, this reliability is impressive. Also significant is that the reliability of IC chips does not vary appreciably with the number of components on them. Consequently, the reliability per gate or per function should increase tremendously with VLSI. As shown in Table 1.7, the reliability is increasing rapidly; in 1979, the failure rate was 6×10^{-8} failure/hour. With a million devices per chip (300,000 equivalent gates) and a failure rate of 6×10^{-8}, the failure rate per gate is 2×10^{-13}!

1.9.5 Function-Level Impact

Computer architects now have the problem of deciding how to use all those transistors and gates. Companies are creating products with larger memories at lower costs and better and faster processors. They are also increasing the complexity of the processors; the trend (4

TABLE 1.7 FAILURE RATES AND MEAN TIME BETWEEN FAILURE (MTBF) FOR MOTOROLA MC6800 MICROPROCESSOR

(Ceramic Package, 70°C Ambient Temperature)

Year	Failure rate (Percent 1000 hours)	MTBF [hours (years)]
1974	1.27	78,000 (9)
1975	0.5	200,000 (23)
1976	0.12	833,000 (95)
1977	0.08	1,700,000 (194)
1978	0.013	7,700,000 (877)
1979	0.006	16,666,666 (1901)

bits in 1972, 8 bits in 1974, 16 bits in 1978, and 32 bits in 1981) increases the power of microprocessors. However, it is unlikely that microprocessors will go beyond the 32-bit structure in the near future because of the inefficient use hardware makes of such large word sizes.

Microprocessors alone do not make up computer systems, so simply improving their cost and performance ratios will not necessarily make computers more versatile and understandable for their users. Architects must make computers that have more functions and are easier to use. They have two approaches for accomplishing this. Either they include program and data memory on the microprocessor chip, or they add functions directly to the chip (Fig. 1.31). Many of the dedicated control functions such as the TTY controller and the floppy disk controller have relatively short program control sequences and small memory needs. It is therefore logical to incorporate these functions into the on-chip memory. For example, the Intel 8051 is an 8-bit microcomputer with 4K bytes of program memory and 128 bytes of data memory [13]. Such a device allows the range of applications to increase as the amount of memory space on the chip increases. By including these types of program and data memories within the microprocessor chip, architects create single-chip microcomputers.

The second direction architects can take is the inclusion of functions and features on the chips. This enhances the performance capability of the microprocessor not only because it reduces the number of parts, but also because it increases the capabilities of microcomputers and allows them to compete with the minicomputer's spectrum of applications. For example, Intel is incorporating in their current generation of microprocessors (iAPX/286 and iAPX/432) on-chip memory management and protection, multilevel software protection, an integral operating system kernel, and other features that are currently available only in large and medium-sized minicomputers [13]. Migrating software functions into hardware will extend the capabilities of microprocessors and make them functionally equivalent to the largest current minicomputers.

At the mainframe level, the application of VLSI is more difficult. Several techniques are currently used: bit-slice processors, programmable logic arrays, gate arrays, and custom circuitry. Bit-slice processors contain the arithmetic and logic functions of the central processing unit. They operate on small "slices" of data (typically 4 bits). By cascading bit-slice processing chips, architects can build computers of various widths. For example, eight 4-bit slices give a 32-bit architecture. Available since 1975, the bit-slice processors are just starting to show up in large numbers of computers. DEC, for example, uses the AMD 2901 processor (4-bit slice) in its system.2020; UNIVAC's 1100/60 model uses the Motorola 10800 chip (4-bit slice). Fairfield Camera and Instrument Corporation

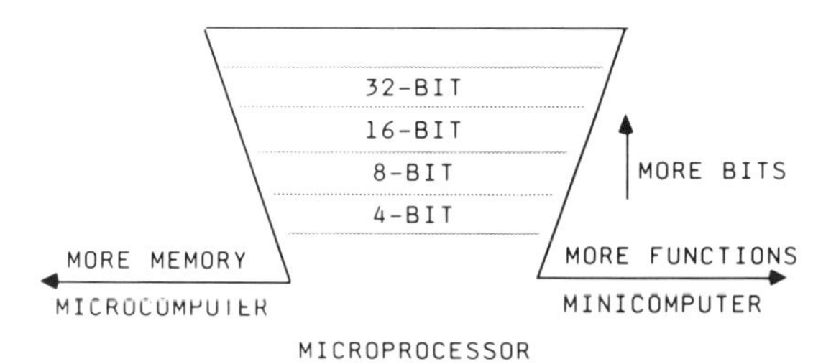

Figure 1.31 Microprocessor feature extensions.

has introduced a family of LSI ECL 8-bit slices (F100220) for use in mainframe computers [14].

Before VLSI achieves success in the marketplace, it must meet two basic challenges: interconnections and product uniqueness. Because the number of pins for a circuit has not increased rapidly with the increase in circuit components, it is necessary to develop an interconnection capability beyond the current technology. The standard 14- and 40-pin dual-in-line packages (DIPs) are no longer adequate. The CPU of the Intel iAPX/432, for instance, is packaged in 64-pin quad-in-line packages (QUIPs). Hundreds of pins will probably be needed for VLSI chips with customized logic. The other challenge VLSI designers face is that of developing unique products efficiently. The blocks on most VLSIs are specialized. This is a problem because it increases the number of different parts in a computer and reduces the quantities needed for each. Manufacturing computers becomes less efficient and more expensive. The challenges of developing cost-effective VLSI products are significant.

1.9.6 System-Level Impact

When improvements in basic technology become available, computers evolve in two directions. From each current model, two successors develop. The first successor holds performance constant; the second holds the cost constant. By holding performance constant, the improved technology is used to build lower-priced machines with new applications, thus increasing their volumes. This is the concept of the *minimal computer*. The minimal computer expands the market for computers and, as a result, continually attracts ideas for new applications. Each year the prices of the machines decline and new applications become economically feasible. The other direction in which computers evolve after a technological breakthrough holds the costs of the machine constant, increases their functionality, and improves their overall performance. The result of these evolutionary paths is shown in Fig. 1.32 [1]. Mainframe computers began their evolution around 1960; minicomputers, around 1965. The increase in the performance capability of minicomputers began to intersect the low end of the mainframe computers in the mid-1970s. The tremendous growth of the superminis was evident during this period. After their emergence in the early 1970s, microcomputers grew in popularity and will dominate the low end of the minicomputer market by 1985. The figure shows that the performance level of the small mainframes in 1970 was provided by the superminis in 1975, and microcomputers will probably meet this performance level by 1985.

1.9.7 Microarchitecture and Macroarchitecture

VLSI technology is drastically changing computer designs. The new integrated circuits affect the hardware structure more than the software structure. VLSI changes the configuration of the registers, the control circuitry, the arithmetic and logic units, the memories, and the interconnecting buses. The hardware structure of a computer, referred to as its *microarchitecture*, allows architects considerable freedom in implementing its

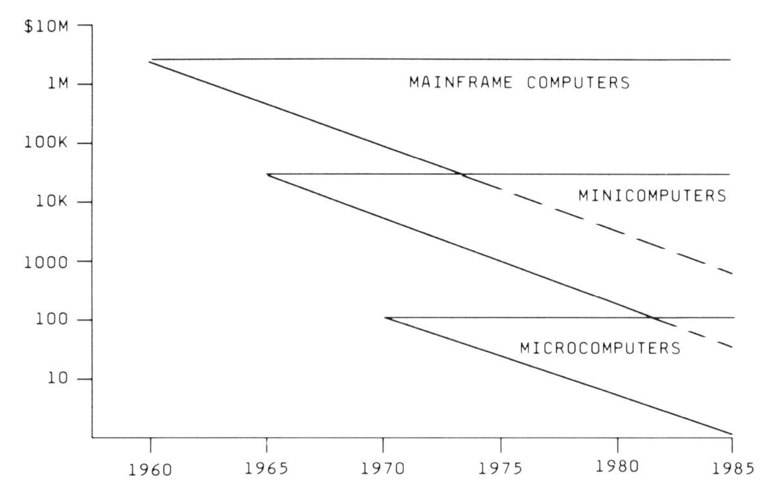

Figure 1.32 Computer evolution.

internal structures [15]. This freedom is extended by VLSI technology, which enables more sophisticated microprocessors and ALU units to be built.

Through all the changes in the microarchitecture, system designers have made concerted efforts to maintain a constant macroarchitecture. *Macroarchitecture* is the structure of the computer that is visible to the programmers. Programmers and other users are generally not aware of the buffers, ALUs, and buses that make up the microarchitecture. Instead, they see the intruction set, the types of data that may be manipulated (byte, half word, full word, fixed or floating point, etc.), and the principles of operation. Changes at the macroarchitecture level force a user to reprogram or change the jobs the computer performs. If all programs were written in higher-level languages, the amount of recoding to accommodate a change in the macroarchitecture would be relatively small. But much existing code is not written in high-level languages, so most computer designers and architects do not want to change the existing macroarchitectures. Another movement against changing existing macroarchitectures comes from those who advocate an industry-wide standard macroarchitecture. The U.S. Army recognized that in its own operations, the proliferation of computer types caused unnecessary expenses and complicated development and support activities. A recent survey showed that 92 Army systems used 57 different computers from 29 manufacturers [16]. This survey led directly to the proposal for a standard macroarchitecture for the family of military computers.

Because of the difficulty in introducing new macroarchitectures, computer architects use alternative techniques to achieve higher performance: these techniques do not require the users to rewrite existing code. One successful technique is building special-purpose processors and attaching them to existing machines. The attached processors preserve the existing user interface, but off-load certain functions and applications for more efficient execution. The off-loading is usually hidden from the user by the operating system. Potential tasks for off-loading onto attached processors are data base management systems, scientific processing systems, front-end communications, input/output channel control, and systems control and maintenance. Such special processors are considered the predecessors of larger, multiple-processor systems that include units dedicated to particular programming languages and data base management [17].

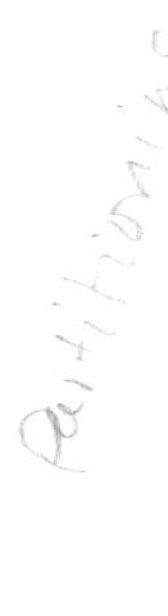

Architects have greater freedom for inventing new microarchitectures than macroarchitectures. One significant challenge they face is creating a microarchitecture structure that alleviates the partitioning problem (that is, the problem of using a VLSI chip only once in the system). To support the widely used S/370 macroarchitecture of the mainframes in its line, IBM designed two 4300 processors. They used gate arrays for the first time to implement a new microarchitecture. The number of plug-compatible machine (PCM) vendors available for the S/370 illustrates the scope of inventiveness possible in microarchitecture design.

1.9.8 Architecture Trends

Computer architecture trends have passed through several distinct stages (Fig. 1.33) [5]. During the early periods, macroarchitecture played an important role in computer design. Since software investment was not extensive, changing the software base was not costly. Consequently, there was considerable freedom in the design of the macroarchitecture of early computer systems. In the 1950s and early 1960s, architects designed the macroarchitecture of the CPU carefully to minimize hardware costs. By the mid-1960s, the price of the CPU had decreased substantially. Computer architects began recognizing the importance of software costs and development effort. IBM introduced the S/360 line of processors. These processors all had the same macroarchitecture, but each model had a different microarchitecture. IBM's goal for this design approach was achieving the proper balance between cost and performance. The development and accumulation of application software has made changing the macroarchitecture increasingly difficult.

During the late 1960s, another trend emerged: the characterization of memory architecture in terms of microprogramming, cache memory, and virtual memory. These new features of memory architecture take advantage of the rapid growth of semiconductor technology and integrated circuit technology and influence the design of the microarchitecture. An adjunct of this trend was the creation of mainframe and minicomputer families because of instruction set compatibility. Later, however, architects recognized that instruction set compatibility alone was not sufficient for compatible software. So the next architectural trend used deliberately planned software to achieve software compatibility [5].

Advances in microprocessors during the past years have shifted the emphasis from large central processors to distributed systems. Distributed systems represent the main trend for networks and in the organization of computer systems. Distributed systems offload specific functions from the main processor to improve program execution. Recent progress is creating efficient architectures for manipulating data bases. Although relational views of data are difficult to support within existing architectures, data bases are very regular and have inherent parallelism. The regularity and parallelism of the data

TREND	CPU ARCHITECTURE	SYSTEM ARCHITECTURE	DISTRIBUTED SYSTEMS ARCHITECTURE	SOFTWARE ARCHITECTURE
	-INSTRUCTION SET IMPROVEMENTS	-INSTRUCTION SET COMPATIBILITY	-SOFTWARE FAMILIES	-LANGUAGE PROCESSORS
	-MORE REGISTERS	-MICRO PROGRAMMING	-DATA BASES	-OS PROCESSORS
		-CACHE MEMORY	-COMMUNICATION NETWORK ARCHITECTURE	-DATA BASE PROCESSORS
		-VIRTUAL MEMORY	-INTELLIGENT SUB-SYSTEMS	
		-OPERATING SYSTEMS	-MULTI PROCESSORS	

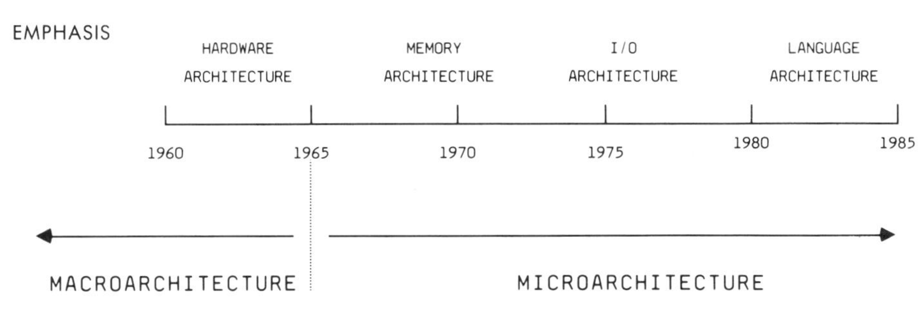

Figure 1.33 Architecture trends.

bases may be exploited by specialized architectures supporting the main processor. Similarly, intelligent peripherals and subsystems are economically attractive for expanding the capabilities of a computer system. The lack of balance between the speed and price of the CPU and the peripherals is increasing the emphasis architects are placing on I/O architecture.

In the future, architectural trends will emphasize software. Already evident is the increased sophistication of the microcoding for many of the system primitives for the operating system, interrupt handling, and language translation. Some of these functions will then migrate into the hardware. By the late 1980s, processors tailored for languages, operating systems, and data bases will probably be commercially available. Language architecture concepts for microprocessors are currently being explored by semiconductor manufacturers.

1.10 SUMMARY

Digital logic and the technologies used to implement it are the foundation of computer architecture. They affect the major hardware components of a computer system (the control unit, the ALU, memory devices, and I/O units) and the software that controls them. By reviewing the hardware components from an operational viewpoint and the three types of software (system, application, and diagnostic) from a functional viewpoint, the architect will be better to understand the trade-offs between hardware and software now available for reducing system development costs and improving performance and software reliability. These trade-offs, directed toward achieving the most efficient use of computing resources for specific applications, are the concerns of the subsequent chapters.

REFERENCES

[1] C. G. Bell, J. C. Mudge, and J. E. McNamara, *Computer Engineering: A DEC View of Hard ware Systems Design*, Digital Press, Bedford, Mass, 1978.

[2] G. J. Myers, *Advances in Computer Architecture*, Wiley, New York, 1978.

[3] G. D. Kraft and W. N. Toy, *Microprogrammed Control and Reliable Design of Small Computers*, Prentice-Hall, Englewood Cliffs, N.J., 1981.

[4] P. Wegner, ed., *Research Directions in Software Technology*, MIT Press, Cambridge, Mass., 1979.

[5] J. E. Juliussen and W. J. Watson, "Problems of the 80s: Computer System Organization," *Proc. Conf. Comput. 1980s*, Portland, Oreg. 1978, pp. 14–23.

[6] Electronics Staff, "Computer Technology Shifts Emphasis to Software: A Special Report," *Electronics*, May 8, 1980, pp. 142–150.

[7] R. I. Baum, D. K. Hsiao, and K. Kannan, "The Architecture of a Data Base Computer, Part 1: Concepts and Capabilities," *OSU-CISRC-TR-76-1*, Ohio State University, Columbus, Ohio, September 1976.

[8] R. Turn, "Hardware–Software Tradeoffs in Reliable Software Developent," *11th Annu. Asilomar Conf. Circuits Syst. Comput.*, 1978, pp 282–288.

[9] G. Moore, "VLSI: Some Fundamental Challenges," *IEEE Spectrum*, April 1979, pp. 30–35.

[10] R. N. Gossen, Jr., and G. H. Heilmeier, "100,000+ Gates on a Chip: Mastering the Minute," *IEEE Spectrum*, March 1979, pp 42–47.

[11] T. Kobayashi, "Very Large-Scale Integrated Circuits (VLSI) and the Future of the Computer," *Fujitsu Sci. Tech.*, December 1977, pp 1–19.

[12] R. Allan, "VLSI: Scoping Its Future," *IEEE Spectrum*, April 1979, pp. 30–37.

[13] "Microsystem 80 Advance Information," Intel Corp., Santa Clara, Calif., 1980.

[14] C. F. Wolfe, "Bit-Slice Processor Come to Main Frame Design," *Electronics*, February 28, 1980, pp. 118–123.

[15] B. R. Borgerson, "Computer Systems in the 80s," *Proc. Conf. Comput. 1980s*, Portland, Oreg., 1978, pp. 3–8.

[16] MIL-STD-1862, *Instruction Set Architecture for the Military Computer Family*, May 28, 1980.

[17] A. Durniak, "VLSI Shakes the Foundation of Computer Architecture," *Electronics*, May 24, 1979, pp. 111–133.

PROBLEMS

1.1 The exclusive-OR (XOR) function of two variables for function f is given by the following logic expression:

$$f = \bar{A} \cdot B + A \cdot \bar{B}$$

Its implementation can be realized with NAND gates as shown in Fig. 1.5(a). Implement function f with NOR gates.

1.2 The control section is the most complex portion of the system. Three techniques used to implement control sections are conventional or random logic, programmable logic arrays, and microprogramming. Compare the advantages and disadvantages of the three techniques.

1.3 The Boolean function of two variables is expressed by

$$f_i = S_0\bar{A}_i\bar{B}_i + S_1\bar{A}_iB_i + S_2A_i\bar{B}_i + S_3A_iB_i$$

Its implementation using AND and OR gates is shown in Fig. 1.14. Implement the Boolean function of two variables, f_i, using *only NAND* gates. Repeat the implementation using *only NOR* gates.

1.4 In the logical *shift* function as shown in Fig. 1.18, the shifted out bits are dropped and the incoming bits are filled with 0s. The logical shift operation is usually done on a bit-by-bit basis. This simplifies the implementation by using standard shift registers and allowing only one single-bit shift at a time. A variable number of shifts is obtained by repeating single shifts. In some applications, it is desirable from a performance viewpoint to implement in a single step the variable number (n) of shifts using a network of logic gates. This is shown in Fig. P1.4. The value n (4-bit number) ranges from 0 to 15. Design the network that implements the variable number n shifts directly.

1.5 Design a 16-bit ripple carry adder using the one's-complement form to represent negative numbers.

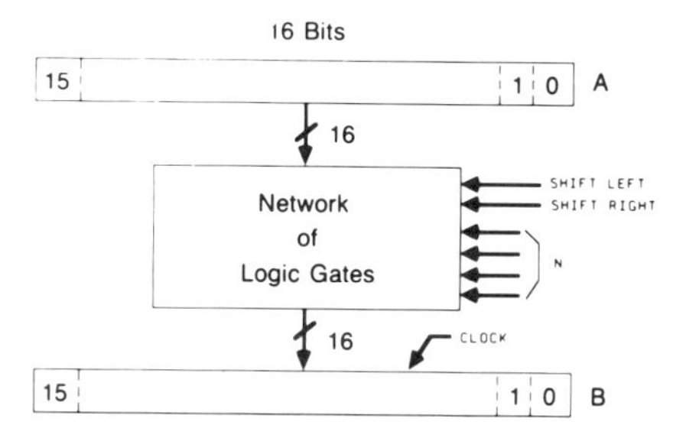

Figure P1.4 Logical shift logic network.

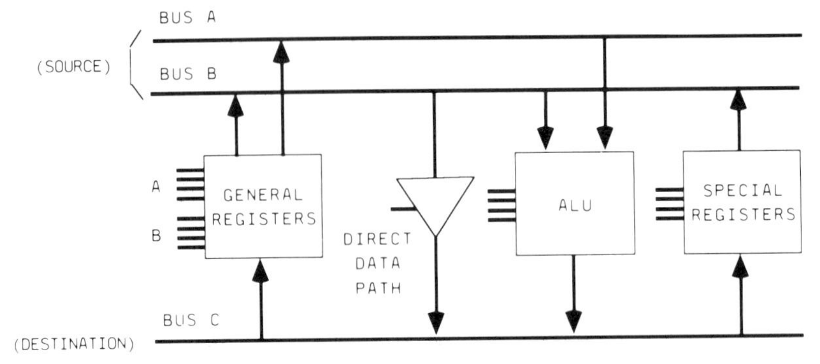

Figure P1.6 Three-bus arrangement.

1.6 Using a dual-port access RAM, implement a 16-bit general-purpose register structure as shown on the left side of Fig. P1.6. The RAM allows two operands specified by A and B to be made available simultaneously to the ALU. The results of the ALU operation can then be written into the word specified by B. Do not include the ALU or the special registers. Specify a microinstruction format that contains the necessary controls to effect a data move from one of the 16 GPRs specified by A to another GPR, specified by B.

1.7 The administration of a stack in terms of pushing and popping is handled by means of a register called the *stack pointer*, which always points to the top of the stack (TOS), as shown in Fig. P1.7. The control of the stack is determined by how the hardware is to interpret the contents of the TOS. This, in turn, determines when the stack pointer is to be incremented or decremented. Show the timing sequence of the control signals of the push and pop operations.

1.8 A cache system is a memory hierarchy used to improve the effective main memory speed. It accomplishes this by inserting a small high-speed buffer between a slower main memory system and the CPU. A cache may be classified as one of three types: *fully associative*, *direct mapping*, or *set associative*.

(a) A *fully associative cache* is organized so that any word in the main memory can be in any word in the high-speed buffer. Sketch a detailed block diagram for this structure.

(b) A *direct mapping cache* is organized so that if a given word in the main memory is in the high-speed buffer, it should be in a fixed word of the buffer. This location is determined by some low-order address bits of the memory word. Sketch a detailed block diagram for this implementation.

(c) A *set associative cache* is organized so that if any memory word is in the buffer, it will be confined to a fixed subset of buffer words. A fully associative cache and a direct mapping

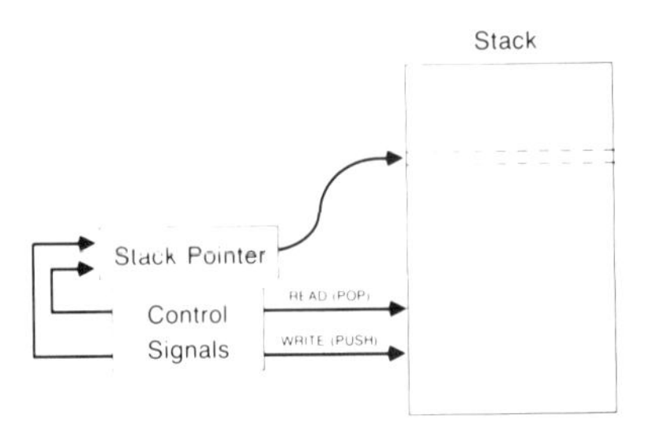

Figure P1.7 Stack control.

cache represent two extremes of a set associative cache. Sketch a detailed block diagram for this implementation.

(d) When the referenced word is in the high-speed buffer, the condition is said to be a *hit*. If the referenced word *is not* in the high-speed buffer, the condition is said to be a *miss*. One major problem in a fully or set associative cache is the replacement algorithm, which determines which member of the set (set associative) or which word in the buffer (fully associative) is to be replaced with the new word. Design three schemes implementing the replacement algorithm, and state the advantages and disadvantages of each scheme.

1.9 The basic elements in a DMA unit, in addition to the necessary control circuitry, are several key registers that coordinate the data transfer operation. These key registers address memory, count the number of words transferred, and receive or transmit data. Show in a functional block diagram the interrelationship between the processor and the DMA facility.

1.10 An interrupt is a hardware-generated signal supplied to the CPU indicating that an event external to the current executing program has occurred and requires immediate attention by the CPU. Before the execution of the interrupt program, all the information that is essential to characterize the state of the machine at the time of interruption must be preserved. Identify the information needs to be saved and explain why saving each of them is necessary.

1.11 CMOS technology is regarded as the technology of the future; it is well suited for VLSI devices. List the advantages and disadvantages of CMOS technology compared with NMOS technology.

1.12 As we extend the scale of integration to VLSI, what are some of the problems that must be overcome to produce cost-effective devices?

1.13 The VLSI impact on microprocessors has continually increased their processing power by increasing the word size (4-bit, 8-bit, 16-bit, and 32-bit). What do you think will evolve after 32-bit microprocessors? State the reasons for your projection.

1.14 The next step beyond VLSI is WSI (wafer-scale integration). What are some of the obstacles that must be overcome before WSI technology becomes commercially available?

1.15 Future architectural trends will emphasize software. State your reasons why this is or is not true?

2

Concepts of High-Level Languages

2.1 INTRODUCTION

Software development and maintenance costs make up the most significant portion of total computer system costs. By 1987, 80 percent of the system costs will be software related. Most of this figure will be for maintenance expenditures: one study indicates that 70 percent of the total costs of one life cycle of software occurs after the initial release [1]. As the range of computer applications grows and the size and complexity of software increases, the control of software expenses becomes increasingly important to the computer industry. Several techniques, including well-structured, well-documented designs and software management methodologies, have proved effective in minimizing software costs. The use of high-level languages ensures the effectiveness of these techniques.

A software management methodology divides the life cycle of software into distinct phases: definition, design, implementation, testing, and operation. In the definition phase, an *informal specification* documents the functional requirements of the system. A *formal specification* evolves from the less precise informal specification in the design phase. A formal specification is the basis for verifying that the finished system includes all the user's requirements. Some recent systems make the formal specification part of a data base for the integrated support of program development. After specifying the requirements, the system designers choose a programming methodology for implementing them.

Structured programming places restrictions on programming style but does not reduce programming power [2]. It emphasizes structure and simplicity instead of clever tricks and local efficiency. The *top-down design methodology* allows architects to specify intermodule interfaces and module functions before considering the implementation details of the modules [3]. The *Jackson methodology* allows the systematic development of programs whose structure fits the input and output requirements [4]. The implementation phase ends after the modules are coded. The system is then tested and made operational. During the operation phase, maintenance costs begin accruing for troubleshooting and enhancements.

High-level languages help reduce costs in all phases of software management methodologies. They allow programmers to concentrate on the algorithms of programs instead of the idiosyncracies of the machines on which the programs run. They provide a structured medium at a level far above the hardware for problem solving. They are easier to learn, easier to document, and easier to maintain than machine or assembly codes. Furthermore, high-level languages allow machine-independent code to be written, so software investment is less at the mercy of any one hardware vendor. Finally, the many types of high-level languages allow the system designers to choose the one most suitable for their applications.

The next three chapters discuss the relationships between high-level languages and machine architectures. Chapter 2 discusses the major concepts of high-level languages. The scope of the discussion is limited to procedural languages. Ada is used for illustrative purposes because it incorporates most of the important concepts of the earlier languages [5]. Chapter 2 also gives a historical perspective of the evolution of the high-level languages and the relationships among them in terms of the concepts they introduce and support. Chapter 3 examines the translation and implementation of the high-level language concepts introduced in Chapter 2. It separates the compile-time issues from the run-time issues. Chapter 3 begins with a discussion of compilation and ends with a discussion of the run-time implementations of high-level language concepts. The presentation concentrates on aspects of compilation that affect the architectural support of high-level languages. The chapter is not a text on the design and implementation of compilers, but a discussion of how the compilation process relates to the models of implementation of high-level languages and to high-level-language concepts. Chapter 4 discusses how a model of implementation is mapped onto a machine architecture. It presents different approaches to the architectural support for high-level languages and gives examples of high-level-language support in various machines. Chapter 4 also discusses trade-offs on instruction set design and their effects on high-level-language support.

2.2 PROGRAMMING LANGUAGE MECHANISMS

Programs implement mapping relations from sets of input objects to sets of output objects; programming languages precisely express these mapping relations and define their structures. They provide the mechanisms for inputting, outputting, manipulating, and grouping information, and for controlling the flow of the manipulations.

The most elemental form of programming language is the machine language. A computer machine instruction may be thought of as a primitive program. Each instruction involves fetching binary data words (input objects) from storage, examining and manipulating them (mapping relation), and possibly writing the result (output object) back into storage. A machine program comprises a set of these machine instructions.

The ones and zeros of machine languages soon proved inadequate for meeting the needs of the wide range of computer applications because they were hard to read, write, and maintain. Programmers needing a more useful and expressive medium began converting machine instructions into the symbolic forms of assembly languages. This was the first step in the evolution of high-level languages. Although assembly language programs are closely tied to the architecture of von Neumann machines, they allow programmers to deal with symbols instead of binary numbers [6]. In a von Neumann machine, one word at a time is sequentially fetched from linear memory. The word is interpreted as either an instruction or as input data. If the word is an instruction, it is executed. If the word is input data, it is used as the operand of an instruction. The output data is put back into memory.

Assembly language is sufficient for performing logical and manipulative operations (such as addition, subtraction, moves, compares, branches, and jumps) on meaningful objects (including integers, characters, and real numbers). But assembly language is too cumbersome for most applications. The instructions and data of an assembly language program are primitive actions and objects that directly reflect the capabilities of the hardware. For this reason, high level languages have been developed that contain *composites* of actions and objects, and they allow composites to be defined by programmers. Action *composites* include expressions, statements, procedures, functions, blocks, and tasks. *Object composites* include arrays, records, packages, files, lists, queues, stacks, strings, and matrices. Programmers use the action composites to develop algorithms and the object composites to structure information and form data bases. The algorithms, information, and data bases simulate the activities of real-life objects such as airline seats, stocks, chess pieces, and employees. The levels of increasing abstraction (composites) of actions and objects are shown connected by vertical arrows in Fig. 2.1. The horizontal arrows show the corresponding levels of abstraction for actions and objects.

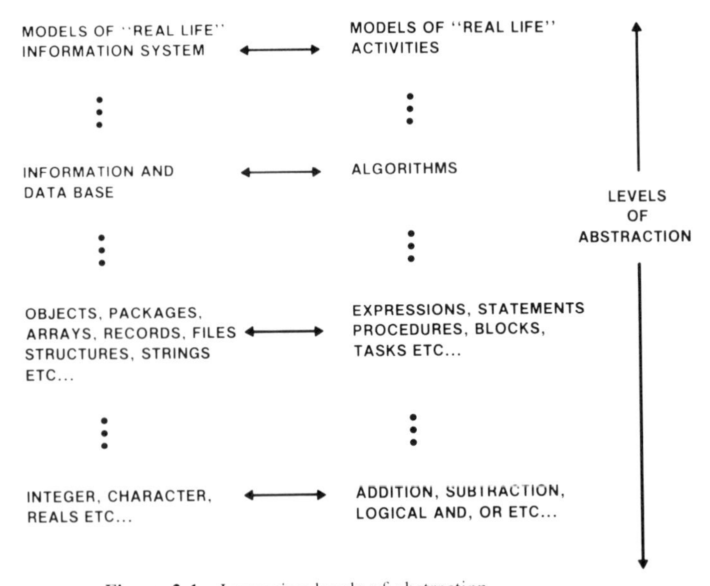

Figure 2.1 Increasing levels of abstraction.

2.3 DATA OBJECTS

High-level languages provide programmers with mechanisms that define and describe data objects as abstract models of real-life entities (for example, Mary, Veteran's Day, and John's profession). Mary is a person. More specifically, Mary is an *instance* of the person type of entity. Person is a *generic entity*, so Mary is an instance of the generic entity, person. High-level languages make clear the distinctions between instances and generic entities.

Programmers define generic entities in high-level languages by means of *type declarations*. A type declaration in Ada is of the form

type TYPENAME **is** ''attributes definition'';*

The type declaration names a generic entity TYPENAME, and defines its attributes. For example,

```
type PERSON is
   record
      HEIGHT : INTEGER ;
      WEIGHT : INTEGER ;
      SEX : (M,F) ;
   end record ;
```

where PERSON is the generic entity and HEIGHT, WEIGHT, and SEX are its attributes.

Programmers define instances of generic entities in high-level languages by means of *object declarations*. An object declaration in Ada is of the form

OBJECT_NAME : TYPENAME ;

For example,

MARY : PERSON ;

*This textbook uses Ada to exemplify the implementation of high-level-language concepts. Although it uses Ada syntax in the program examples, it is not an Ada tutorial. In the program examples, the text uses these documentation conventions:

Bold lowercase words are keywords (e.g., **type, or else**).

Uppercase words are names of entities, including type names, variable names, procedure names, labels, and other identifiers (e.g., TYPENAME, READ, INTEGER).

Quotation marks enclose descriptions of the information a programmer would need to supply.

Parentheses are Ada syntax; they enclose lists for enumeration types.

Brackets are not Ada syntax. They denote optional entries.

Other punctuation should be used as written. For example, := is an assignment operator and dashes set off comments. Abbreviated ellipses (. .) indicate ranges. Note that the authors use full ellipses (. . .) to indicate gaps in the programs to increase the clarity of specific examples.

Each data object in a high-level-language program has a name (MARY) and a type (PERSON).

2.4 TYPES

The *type* of a named data object specifies its attributes. The attributes include (1) the *structure* of the data object (the hierarchy of its components), and (2) the type of each of the *primitive components* of the structure. In the example above, the primitive components are HEIGHT, WEIGHT, and SEX. There is only one level of hierarchy. The type of HEIGHT and WEIGHT is INTEGER, and the type of SEX is male or female (M,F). A primitive component has no subcomponents (and hence, no structure); that is, it describes a *scalar object*. The type of a named scalar object specifies the set of values it may have and the set of operators to which it may be subjected. In Ada,

```
I : INTEGER ;
```

declares a scalar object named I to be of type INTEGER. The type INTEGER specifies the set of values I may assume (min_int, . . ., -3, -2, -1, 0, 1, 2, 3, . . ., max_int), where min_int and max_int, correspond, respectively, to the minimum value (largest negative value) and the maximum value of the integers in a machine representation. For example, a 16-bit word machine can represent the set (-32768, . . ., -3, -2, -1, 0, 1, 2, 3, . . ., 32767). The values of the set are called *literals*. The type INTEGER also specifies the set of applicable operators to which I may be subjected. In Ada, the set includes these: **, *, /, mod, rem, +, -, **unary** +, **unary** -, =, /=, <, <=, >, and >=. The operators are discussed in Section 2.5.

2.4.1 Built-In Types

A high-level language generally has certain *predefined* or *built-in* types. The language itself specifies the set of values and the set of operators applicable for objects of these types. More precisely, the set of values is specified by the language implementation. Built-in types commonly found in high-level languages are:

1. *Numeric* data types, including integers and reals
2. *Characters*
3. *Logical* data types, including Boolean and bit fields
4. *Access* types (pointers)

High-level-language designers choose the set of built-in types to include those commonly used by programmers. Built-in types eliminate the need for each programmer to define common types such as integer, Boolean, and character.

Built-in types in most high-level languages are scalar object types. Pascal's built-in types include INTEGER, REAL, BOOLEAN, and CHARACTER. Ada's built-in types include INTEGER, CHARACTER, FLOAT, and BOOLEAN. Programmers may use built-in types to define other scalar types, structured types, and access (also called reference) types.

2.4.2 Scalar Types

Scalar types are object types with a single primitive component. A scalar type defines the set of values and the set of operators for the component. The three kinds of scalar types are enumeration types, subtypes, and derived types.

2.4.2.1 Enumeration types. *Enumeration types* specify finite sets of ordered and discrete values. INTEGER, BOOLEAN, and CHARACTER types are built-in (or language-defined) enumeration types. Their implicit type definitions, for example, are:

```
type INTEGER is (-32768, . . ., -1, 0, 1, . . . , 32767);
type BOOLEAN is (FALSE, TRUE) ;
type CHARACTER is (''ASCII character set'') ;
```

so that -1 < 0, FALSE < TRUE, and A < B. The values listed in an enumeration type definition are ordered from left to right. In Ada, enumeration type definitions have the following form:

```
type EN_TYPENAME is (''list of values'') ;
```

Along with having built-in enumeration types, high-level languages such as Pascal and Ada allow programmers to define their own scalar types by enumerating (listing) the values the named objects of the type may assume.

For example, the statements

```
type MONTH is (JAN, FEB, MAR, APR, MAY, JUN, JUL, AUG, SEP,
               OCT, NOV, DEC) ;
```

and

```
THIS_MONTH : MONTH ;
```

define an enumeration type MONTH and declare an object named THIS_MONTH to be of the type MONTH.THIS_MONTH may assume any of the values listed in the type definition (JAN through DEC). The set of operators to which the named objects of a programmer-defined enumeration type may be subjected are the relational operators. For example, in Ada,

```
declare
type MONTH is (JAN, FEB, MAR, APR, MAY, JUN,
               JUL, AUG, SEP, OCT, NOV, DEC) ;
  NICE_MONTH, THIS_MONTH : MONTH ;
```

```
begin
  THIS_MONTH: = JUNE;                        --initialize THIS_MONTH
  NICE_MONTH : = MAY;                        --initialize NICE_MONTH
  if THIS_MONTH = NICE_MONTH then
            . . . ;
  else if THIS_MONTH > NICE_MONTH then
            . . . ;
  end if ;
end ;
```

The values listed in an enumeration type are assumed by the language to be ordered; in this example, JAN < FEB, FEB <MAR, and so on. Thus, the Boolean expression THIS_MONTH = NICE_MONTH has the value FALSE and the Boolean expression THIS_MONTH > NICE_MONTH has the value TRUE.

Since the values of enumeration types are ordered, they may be used to control iteration. For example, in Ada,

```
for I in 1 .. 5 loop
   .
   .
   .
end loop ;
```

specifies a loop that ends when I is greater than 5, and

```
for THIS_MONTH in JAN .. SEP loop
   .
   .
   .
end loop ;
```

specifies a loop that ends after processing JAN through SEP.

2.4.2.2 Subtypes. Programmers may define new types by constraining the range of assumable values in the set of a previously defined (built-in or programmer-defined) type. The previously defined type is considered the parent type, and the new type with range constraints is called a *subtype*. In Ada, a subtype definition is of the form

```
subtype SUBTYPENAME is PARENT_TYPENAME range . . .;
```

For example,

```
subtype DIGITS is INTEGER range 0 .. 9 ;
subtype SUMMER_MONTH is MONTH range JUN .. SEP ;
```

A named object of a subtype "inherits" the literals within the subtype's defined range and all the operators that are applicable to objects of its parent type. It can also be mixed with objects of its parent type in an expression. For example, with the type definition of the example above,

```
declare
subtype DIGITS is INTEGER range 0 .. 9 ;      --DIGITS is a subtype
  SON_AGE, DAUGHTER_AGE : DIGITS ;            --of INTEGER
  I, J : INTEGER ;
begin
          . . . ;
  I := SON_AGE - DAUGHTER_AGE ;               --object of subtype assigned
  J := SON_AGE + DAUGHTER_AGE ;               --to object of parent type
  SON_AGE := I + DAUGHTER_AGE ;               --object of subtype mixed
end;                                          --with object of parent type
                                              --in an expression
```

Thus, the only difference between a subtype and its parent type is the subtype's constraint on the range.

2.4.2.3 Derived types. Programmers may also define new types—other than subtypes—that inherit the set of values, literals, and operators from a previously defined type (parent type), and yet are considered by the language to be logically distinct from the parent type. That is, a named object of the new type cannot be mixed with the named objects of its parent type in an expression. These are called *derived types*. Derived types may also constrain the range of values in the set associated with its parent type. A derived type definition in Ada is of the form

```
type DER_TYPENAME is new PARENT_TYPENAME [range . . .] ;
```

where the range constraint is optional. For example,

```
type DOLLAR is new INTEGER ;
type POUND is new INTEGER ;
type SALARY is new DOLLAR range 1000 .. 2000 ;
```

DOLLAR, POUND, SALARY, and INTEGER are treated by Ada as different types and hence their objects cannot be mixed in an expression even though they share the same operations and the same literals. For example,

```
declare
  MARYS_ASSET : DOLLAR ;                      --types DOLLAR, POUND, and
  GEORGES_TRUST : POUND ;                     --SALARY previously declared
  JOHNS_EARN : SALARY ;
  I, J : INTEGER ;
begin
          . . . ;
  MARYS_ASSET := MARYS_ASSET + 5 ;
  GEORGES_TRUST := GEORGES_TRUST * 2 ;
```

```
        JOHNS_EARN := 1500 ;
        I := 200 ;
        JOHNS_EARN := JOHNS_EARN + I ;                          --illegal
        MARYS_ASSET := MARYS_ASSET + JOHNS_EARN ;               --illegal
        if MARYS_ASSET < GEORGES_TRUST then. . . ;              --illegal
      . . .;
   end if ;
end ;
```

The derived type mechanism allows programmers to define logically different scalar types that cannot be mixed in an expression but which share the same attributes (the set of values and the set of operators).

2.4.3 Structured Types

Objects of the scalar types are single-component, primitive objects. *Structured type* objects are made up of aggregates of components, in which the componenets obey well-defined structural relationships. A component of a structured type object may itself be a structured type object composed of its own components and structure, or it may be a scalar component. Ultimately, though, a structured type object is composed of scalar components. Each of the scalar components has a type defining its applicable set of values and set of operators.

A structured type definition not only defines the attributes (set of values and set of operators) of each of its scalar components, but also defines the structural (hierarchical) relationships among the components. The structural relationship is an attribute of the structured types. A structured type definition may be thought of as a *structural template* from which multiple instances of that structured type can be created. Each structured type object has a name and a type. Each component of a structured type object has a name, a type, and a relative position in the structure. A structured type object may be referenced as a unit, or its components may be referenced individually. High-level languages provide programmers with *constructors* to define structured types. The two commonly used constructors are the *array constructor* and the *record constructor*.

2.4.3.1 Array constructor. The array constructor allows programmers to define structured types in which the components of the structure have the same type and size. The components are selectable by an *index*. The index denotes the relative position of the component in an array object. Each component of an array object is named individually by specifying the name of the array object and the value of the index. A(10), for example, specifies the tenth indexed value in array object A; the generic format is ARRAY_NAME (''index value''). A type definition using the array constructor in Ada is of the form

type TYPENAME **is array** (''index definition'') **of** ''component type'' ;

The *index definition* specifies the number of indices (the dimensions of the array), the type of each index, and the range for each index (the bounds of each dimension). Indices may be any scalar type with ordered, discrete values. The most common index type found in high-level languages is the integer type. For example, an index definition of 1 .. 100, 5 .. 20 specifies two integer type indices. The range for the first index is 1 through 100; for the second index, it is 5 through 20. Some high-level languages such as Ada allow an index to be an enumeration type. For example, the index definition can be MONTH, where

```
type MONTH is (JAN, FEB, MAR, APR, MAY, JUN, JUL, AUG, SEP,
                                OCT, NOV, DEC);
```

The *component type* in an array type definition may be any previously defined type: built-in, programmer-defined, scalar, or structured. In this example

```
subtype GRADES is INTEGER range 0 .. 100 ;
type STUDENTS is (JOHNSON, JACKSON, WILLIAMS, SMITH, WHITE,
DOE, JONES) ;
type REPORT_CARD is array (1 .. 5) of GRADES ;
type CLASS is array (STUDENTS) of REPORT_CARD ;
```

CLASS is an array type, STUDENTS is the index type of the array, and REPORT_CARD is the component type. STUDENTS is an enumeration type and REPORT_CARD is an array type with five scalar components. The scalar components are of type GRADES, which is a subtype of INTEGER. With these type definitions, one can write, for example,

```
declare
  FRESHMAN : CLASS ;                              --array of arrays
begin
      FRESHMAN(JOHNSON) := (80, 75, 60, 90, 85) ;      --initialize first component
      FRESHMAN(JONES) := FRESHMAN(JOHNSON) ;  --of array FRESHMAN
        . . .;
  if FRESHMAN(JONES(3)) = 60 then
        . . .;
  end if ;
  if (FRESHMAN(JONES(1)) + FRESHMAN(JONES (2)))/2<
     FRESHMAN(JONES(3)) then
          . . .;
  end if ;
end ;
```

FRESHMAN is the name of an array object containing seven components. FRESHMAN(JOHNSON) is the name of the first component, which itself is an array of five scalar components. The second statement above initializes this component and assigns values to its five scalar components. FRESHMAN(JONES(1)) is the name of the first scalar component of the array FRESHMAN(JONES), which is the last component of the array FRESHMAN. The type of FRESHMAN(JONES(1)), FRESHMAN(JONES(2)), and FRESHMAN(JONES(3)) is GRADES, which is a subtype of INTEGERS and thus inherits the operators of the INTEGER type such as + and <.

Examples of commonly found arrays in scientific programming are vectors and matrices. In Ada, vector and matrix types are defined, for example, as follows:

```
type VECTOR is array (1 .. 10) of INTEGER ;
type MATRIX is array (1 .. 10, 1 .. 20) of INTEGER ;
```

Some high-level languages, including Ada, permit the bounds of array indices to be left unspecified in the type definition. For example,

```
subtype LE1000 is INTEGER range 1 .. 1000 ;
X, Y : LE1000 ;
type GEN_MATRIX is array (X, Y) of INTEGER;
```

where GEN_MATRIX defines a template from which matrices of different matrix types (sizes less than or equal to 1000 x 1000) can be instantiated by specifying the bounds of these matrices at object declaration time. For example,

```
A : GEN_MATRIX (1 .. 10, 1.. 10) ;
B : GEN_MATRIX (10 .. 100, 20 .. 500) ;
```

declares two matrix objects of different types, where A is of a matrix type having 10×10 elements and B is of a matrix type having 91×481 elements.

Whereas MATRIX, defined above, is a type from which multiple instances of objects can be declared, GEN_MATRIX, by leaving the bounds of indices unspecified, serves as a generic matrix type from which multiple instances of matrix types can be created, each with different dimensions. For each of these matrix types, multiple instances of objects can be declared. Hence, GEN_MATRIX is a *parameterized array type*. That is, different matrix types may be instantiated by assigning different values to the parameters X, Y associated with the GEN_MATRIX type definition.

2.4.3.2 Record constructor. Unlike the array constructor, in which the components of a structure must be the same type and size, the *record constructor* allows programmers to define structured types in which the components of the structure have different types and sizes. Each component is named by a *selector*. A type definition using the record constructor in Ada is of the form

```
type TYPENAME is
  record
    SELECTOR_NAME1 : TYPE1 ;
    SELECTOR_NAME2 : TYPE2 ;
          .
          .
          .
```

```
    SELECTOR_NAMEN : TYPEN ;
  end record;
```

where the component types (TYPE1, TYPE2, ..., TYPEN) have been defined previously. A record object is declared as

```
  RECORD_NAME : RECORD_TYPENAME ;
```

and its components are referenced by RECORD_NAME.SELECTOR_NAME.

For example,

```
declare
  type LNAME is (JOHNSON, SMITH, DOE, JACKSON);
  type EMPLOYEE is
     record
        FIRST_INITIAL : CHARACTER ;
        MIDDLE_INITIAL : CHARACTER ;
        LAST_NAME : LNAME ;
        DEPARTMENT : INTEGER ;
        YEARS_OF_SERVICE : INTEGER ;
     end record ;
  JACK, JOHN : EMPLOYEE;
begin
  JACK.DEPARTMENT := 5331 ;                    --initialize
                                                JACK.DEPARTMENT
  JOHN.DEPARTMENT := 5332 ;                    --initialize
                                                --JOHN.DEPARTMENT
     ...;
  if JOHN.DEPARTMENT = JACK. DEPARTMENT        --record object components
then
...;                                            --are compatible
end if ;
   ...;
JOHN.FIRST_INITIAL := "J" ;
JACK.FIRST_INITIAL := JOHN.FIRST_INITIAL;         -record object components
JACK := JOHN ;                                    --record objects are
                                                  --compatible
end ;
```

In this example, EMPLOYEE is a record type; its components are of different types—either built-in (CHARACTER, INTEGER) or previously defined (LNAME). JACK and JOHN are record objects of the same type, EMPLOYEE. Thus, they are compatible in the same expression. Furthermore, their corresponding components (JOHN.DEPARTMENT and JACK.DEPARTMENT) are compatible, and they can be mixed in an expression or an assignment statement.

Ada permits a record type to be *parameterized* much like it permits array types to be parameterized. A *parameterized record type* has one or more *variant* components, the size or type of which depends on the value of the parameter associated with the record type. A parameterized record type allows record types to be created that share many of the same attributes and structure but have one (or more) components that are different. For example, a "car" may be defined as a parameterized record type. All CAR record types share many of the same attributes, such as transmission, steering, and brakes. CAR record types may also be differentiated by a parameter (for example, CLASS) that may take on the values LUXURY, MEDIUM, and ECONOMY. CAR(LUXURY), CAR(MEDIUM), and CAR(ECONOMY) are different CAR record types, each with its own set of attributes. These attributes may be programmed as the variant components of a parameterized record type describing CAR. The parameter of a parameterized record type is called a *discriminant* because it "discriminates" among the variant components.

The parameterized record type may have a variant component of an array type that varies in size. It may also have variant components that vary in name and type. The next two sections give examples of the two kinds of parameterized record types: those with varying size and those with varying name and type.

2.4.3.3 Parameterized record type with varying size. A parameterized record type definition in Ada to denote varying size has the form

```
type TYPENAME (DISC : DISK_TYPE := "default value") is
  record
    NON_VAR_COMP : COMP_TYPE ;
    VAR_COMP : VAR_COMP_TYPE (1 .. DISC) ;
  end record;
```

where DISC is the discriminant variable of a previously defined discrete type DISC_TYPE. A parameterized record type may contain one or more nonvariant components NON_VAR_COMP as well as one or more variant components VAR_COMP. The variant component of type VAR_COMP_TYPE varies in size depending on the value assumed by DISC. The discriminant may be given a default value in the record type definition. The actual value assumed by the discriminant is specified in the object declaration. For example,

```
type MEMORY (NUMB_CELLS : INTEGER := 1000) is
  record
    SIZE : INTEGER ;
    MEM_ARRAY : array (1 .. NUMB_CELLS) of INTEGER ;
  end record ;
```

defines a parameterized record type MEMORY with a discriminant named NUMB_CELLS. These statements

```
CACHE : MEMORY ;
BUFFER : MEMORY(100) ;
MAIN_MEM : MEMORY(1000000) ;
DISK_CACHE : MEMORY(4000) ;
```

declare four objects of four different MEMORY types, each with a different size. The object CACHE assumes the default size (1000).

2.4.3.4 Variant record types. A parameterized record type with variant components that may differ in name and type depending on the value of a parameter (discriminant) is called a *variant record type*. A variant record type definition has the form

```
type TYPENAME (DISC : DISC_TYPE := "default value") is
  record
    COMP1 : TYPE1 ;
      :
    COMPN : TYPEN ;
    case DISC is
      when VALUE1 => 1VAR_COMP1 : 1TYPE1 ; --when DISC is
                                            --VALUE1, IVAR_
                                            --COMP1 to JVAR_
                                :
                     JVAR_COMP1 : JTYPE1 ;
      when VALUE2 => "variant component list 2" ; --COMP1 are chosen
                                                   --when DISC is
                                                   --VALUE2, variant
                                                   --comp list 2 is chosen
                                :
      when VALUEN => "variant component list N" ;
    end case ;
  end record ;
```

where COMP1 through COMPN are one or more nonvariant components of previously defined types, TYPE1 through TYPEN and 1VAR_COMP1 through JVAR_COMP1 are one or more variant components of previously defined types, 1TYPE1 to JTYPE1. Depending on the value (VALUE1, VALUE2, . . ., VALUEN) assumed by the discriminant object DISC, different variant record types with different variant components may be instantiated. For example,

```
type PWR is (POWER, MANUAL) ;
type TRAN is (STICK, AUTOMATIC) ;
type CAR_CLASS is (LUXURY, MEDIUM, ECONOMY) ;
type CAR (CLASS: CAR_CLASS :=MEDIUM) is
```

```
record
  TRANSMISSION : TRAN ;
  STEERING : PWR ;
  BRAKE : PWR ;
  case CLASS is
    when LUXURY  =>MERCEDES : BOOLEAN ;
    when MEDIUM  =>POPULARITY : INTEGER ;
    when ECONOMY  => SIZE : INTEGER ;
                     MPG : INTEGER ;
                     PRICE : INTEGER ;
  end case ;
end record ;
```

defines a variant record type where the value of the parameter CLASS determines the name and type of the variant components. Different objects of different types may be instantiated by assigning values to the discriminant in the object declaration. For example,

```
declare
  JOHNS_CAR : CAR(LUXURY) ;
  JOES_CAR : CAR(ECONOMY) ;
begin
  JOHNS_CAR.BRAKE := POWER ;
  JOHNS_CAR.MERCEDES := TRUE ;
  JOES_CAR.BRAKE := MANUAL ;
  JOES_CAR.PRICE := 6000 ;
end ;
```

declares objects JOHNS_CAR and JOES_CAR to be of types CAR(LUXURY) and CAR(ECONOMY). CAR(LUXURY) and CAR(ECONOMY) have four and six components, respectively, three of which are common in the two types. The statement

```
JOES_CAR.MERCEDES :=FALSE ;
```

is illegal since JOES_CAR is of type CAR(ECONOMY), which does not contain the component MERCEDES.

2.4.4 Access Types

High-level languages provide mechanisms for declaring objects that are *pointers* (that is, addresses) to other objects. Pointer objects are of the *access type*. An access type definition in Ada has the form

type TYPENAME **is access** ''type of object being pointed to'' ;

For example,

```
type BUFFER is array (1 .. 5) of INTEGER ;
type IPTR is access INTEGER ;
type BPTR is access BUFFER ;
```

defines IPTR and BPTR as access types. Objects of access types IPTR and BPTR point to objects of type INTEGER and BUFFER, respectively. They are declared by

```
A : IPTR ;
B : BPTR ;
```

These declarations create the pointer objects only and not the data objects pointed to. The respective data objects are created in Ada by means of a call to the storage allocator using the **new** command.

```
A := new INTEGER(25) ;
B := new BUFFER (10, 10, 10, 10, 10) ;
```

These statements create an integer object with its value initialized to 25 and a buffer object with its values initialized to five 10s. The addresses of these data objects are assigned to pointer objects A and B [Fig. 2.2(a)].

Pointer objects may be manipulated to assume different values, thus allowing them to point to different data objects of the same type or to keep track of the address of a data object that has relocated. Pointer objects assume the value **null** when they do not point to any object. When pointer objects are first declared, they are given the default initial value of **null.**

The data objects created by the **new** command do not have names. A and B in the example above are names for the pointer objects. The integer and buffer objects created can be accessed only through their respective pointers. In Ada, the **.all** operation (the *dereferencing* operation) accesses the object to which a pointer points. A**.all** and B**.all** reference the integer object and the buffer object. Unlike names specified with object declarations, A**.all** and B**.all** are not bound to the objects they reference for the lifetime of the objects. The values of A and B may be changed so that A**.all** and B**.all** become associated with different integer and buffer objects. Furthermore, more than one pointer object may point to the same object. Hence more than one name may be associated with an object. This is called *aliasing*. For example,

```
declare
  C : IPTR ;
  D : BPTR ;
begin
  C := A ;
  D := B ;
end ;
```

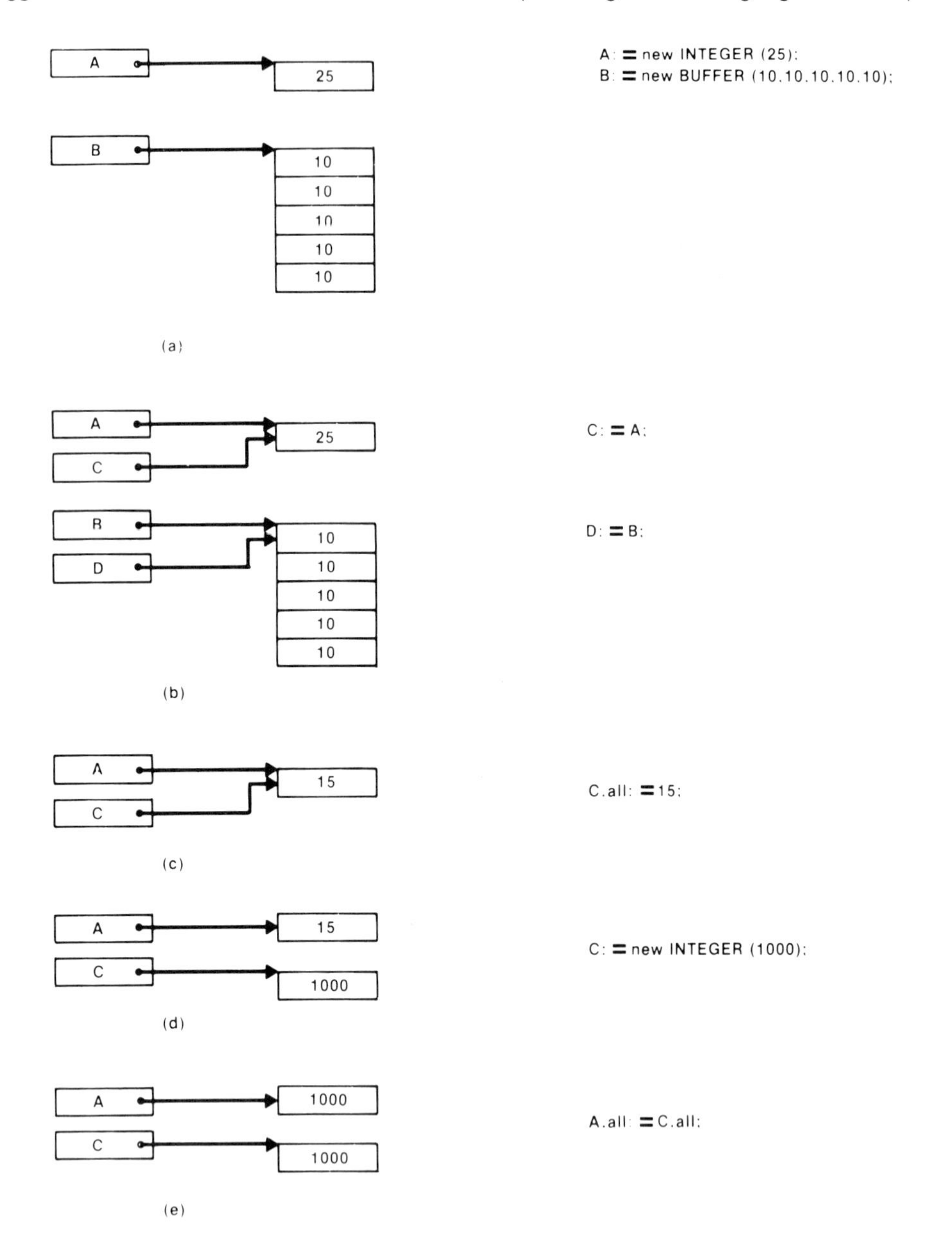

Figure 2.2 Pointer object: access type.

C and A point to the same integer object, while D and B point to the same buffer object [Fig. 2.2(b)]. Thus C.**all** and A.**all** are *aliases* for the integer object with value 25, while B.**all** and D.**all** are aliases for the buffer object with five 10s. With the assignment statement

C.**all** := 15 ;

A.**all** automatically also has the value 15, since A and C point to the same object [Fig. 2.2(c)]. Now when the statement

C := **new** INTEGER(1000) ;

is executed, C points to a new integer object initialized with the value 1000 [Fig.2.2(d)]. With

A.**all** = C.**all** ;

A and C still point to different integer objects, but the value of the object (1000) pointed to by C is assigned to the object pointed to by A [Fig. 2.2(e)].

2.4.5 Recursive Type Definitions

High-level-language mechanisms for recursive type definitions allow commonly used data structures such as *trees* and *linked lists* to be built. In both of these structures, the basic building block is a record object consisting of data components and pointer components. The pointer components in turn point to other record objects of the same type with data components and pointer components. Hence, the building blocks and their links are recursively defined. The recursive definition has the form

```
type BLD_BLOCK ;                            --incomplete type definition
type POINTER is access BLD_BLOCK ;          --BLD_BLOCK previously defined
type BLD_BLOCK is                           --complete type definition
  record
    DATA_COMP1 : TYPE1 ;                    --TYPE1 previously defined


    DATA_COMPN : TYPEN ;                    --TYPEN previously defined
    ACC_COMP1, ACC_COMP2.. ACC_COMPM : POINTER ;
                                            --POINTER previously defined
  end record ;
```

where the first declaration type BLD_BLOCK is an incomplete type declaration to start the recursion in the access and record type definitions. It allows the access type POINTER to be defined to point to a previously (although incompletely) defined type, BLD_BLOCK. The record type definition then completes the definition of BLD_BLOCK after the POINTER type is defined. The data components DATA_COMP1 through DATA_COMPN are of previously defined types (TYPE1 through TYPEN). The pointer components ACC_COMP1 through ACC_COMPM are of type POINTER; they point to BLD_BLOCK type objects. The basic building blocks for trees are called *nodes;* for linked lists, they are referred to as *elements*. For *binary trees* and *doubly linked lists* there are two pointer components in each node and element. Binary tree nodes have the *right* and *left branches*. For example,

```
type NODE ;
type BRANCH is access NODE ;
type NODE is
  record
    DATA : DATA_TYPE ;
    LEFT, RIGHT : BRANCH ;
  end record ;
```

An object of type NODE in which the components LEFT and RIGHT have the value **null** is a "leaf" of the tree. Doubly linked list has elements with pointer to the preceding and succeeding elements of the list. For example,

```
type ELEMENT ;
type POINTER is access ELEMENT ;
type ELEMENT is
  record
    DATA : DATA_TYPE ;
    PRECEDING, SUCCEEDING : POINTER ;
  end record ;
```

For a singly linked list, the access component points only to the succeeding element of the list.

2.4.6 Type Equivalence

High-level languages permit only objects of the same or equivalent types to be operated on in the same expression or to be assigned to each other. Different high-level languages define different criteria for types to be equivalent. In ALGOL 68, types are equivalent if they are structurally equivalent, that is, if they contain equivalent type definitions. Thus, two types of different names but equivalent type definitions are equivalent. On the other hand, Ada specifies that only objects with the same type name have equivalent types. For example,

```
declare
  type A is
    record
      AB : REAL ;
      AC : BOOLEAN ;
    end record ;
  type B is
    record
      AB : REAL ;
      AC : BOOLEAN ;
    end record ;
```

```
    OBJ1, OBJ2 : A ;
    OBJ3 : A ;
    OBJ4 : B ;
begin
    OBJ4 := OBJ3 ;              --legal in ALGOL 68; illegal in Ada
end ;
```

In Ada, only OBJ1, OBJ2, and OBJ3 have equivalent types. In ALGOL 68, all four objects have equivalent types. The assignment statement is thus legal in ALGOL 68, and illegal in Ada. ALGOL 68 specifies *structural equivalence* while Ada specifies *name equivalence*.

2.5 OPERATORS

Operators are the high-level-language mechanisms for manipulating data objects. High-level languages have *built-in operators*. Ada also allows programmers to define their own operators by means of *operator overloading*. The set of built-in operators varies from language to language. Almost all languages provide *numeric* operators, *logical* operators, and *relational* operators. Some also have *string* operators. The different categories of operators are distinguished by the type of data objects they can operate on, and the type of the resulting data object. The different categories of operators in Ada are shown in Table 2.1 and discussed below.

TABLE 2.1 TYPES OF OPERATORS IN ADA

Numeric	Logical	Relational	String	Membership
+	and	=	&	in
−	or	/=		not in
abs	xor	<		
*	and then	<=		
/	or else	>		
mod		>=		
rem				

2.5.1 Numeric

Numeric operators operate on numeric data objects of the INTEGER and FLOATING POINT types. The resulting data object has the same type as the operands (for example, adding two floating point operands gives a floating point result).* Numeric operators in-

*Earlier languages (e.g., FORTRAN) do not allow adding an integer to a floating-point operand. This restriction has been removed from some later languages (e.g., Pascal) in which adding an integer to a floating-point operand gives a floating-point result. Ada, on the other hand, requires an explicit type conversion to be stated by the programmer in adding an integer to a floating-point number. For example, if X is of type FLOAT, and I is of type INTEGER,

```
X := X + FLOAT(I) ;
```

is a legal statement. Different high-level languages have different conversion rules.

clude +, -, **abs** (absolute), *, /, **mod** (modulus), and **rem** (remainder). They carry the same semantics as their counterparts in mathematics. The symbols + and - are used to represent both the unary operators *identity* and *negation* as well as the binary operators *addition* and *subtraction*. The **mod** and the **rem** operators operate only on data objects of the INTEGER type.

2.5.2 Logical

Logical operators are sometimes referred to as *Boolean* operators since they operate on data objects of the BOOLEAN type and return results of the BOOLEAN type. Logical operators include **and, or,** and **xor.** Ada also provides two *short-circuit logical operators*. These are **and then** and **or else.** They give programmers control over execution optimization. The short-circuit logical operators **and then** and **or else,** unlike their counterparts **and** and **or,** evaluate the second operand of a Boolean expression only if the first operand cannot determine the result of the expression. Programmers can use these operators to define the precedence of the operands in a Boolean expression (that is, the first operand always takes precedence over the second operand in determining the result of the expression). The precedence provided by a short-circuit logical operator, in certain situations, creates different effects from those obtained by using the corresponding logical operator. For example, the expression

expression A **or** expression B

causes a program error if expression B causes a program error. On the other hand, the expression

expression A **or else** expression B

does not cause a program error if expression A is evaluated to the Boolean value TRUE.

2.5.3 Relational

Relational operators operate on data objects of types that define an *ordering* in the set of values assumable by the data object. Numeric types and enumerated types fall in this category. In an enumerated type, literals listed from left to right are assumed to be in increasing order. For example,

type BOY **is** (JOHN, JAMES, JERRY);

would result in the ordering JOHN<JAMES<JERRY. Relational operators include =, /=, <, <=, >, and >=. The operators = and /= test for equality and inequality; they can be used with data objects of any type. The result of a relational operation is of the BOOLEAN type.

2.5.4 String

Many high-level languages provide the **&** (concatenation) operator, which concatenates two strings together. In Ada, strings are implemented as a one-dimensional array of characters, and the **&** operator concatenates two arrays of characters. The **&** operator in Ada may be used with any two arrays with components of the same type. For example,

A := (1, 2, 3, 4, 5) ;
B :=(10, 20, 30, 40) ;
C := A **&** B ;

where A, B, and C are arrays of INTEGER elements. The result of the operation is

C = (1, 2, 3, 4, 5, 10, 20, 30, 40)

Other string operators supported by high-level languages include the *length* operator to produce the length of a string, and the *substring* operator to insert or extract substrings from strings.

2.5.5 Membership

Ada provides the membership operators **in** and **not in** to test whether the first operand is a value belonging to a range, type, or subtype as specified by the second operand. The result of the operation is of the BOOLEAN type. For example,

type BOY **is** (JOHN, JAMES, JERRY) ;

the expression

JOHN **not in** BOY

would evaluate to the Boolean value FALSE. The membership operator is used extensively in iteration. For example,

for I **in** 1 .. COUNT **loop**

where 1 .. COUNT defines the range that I may assume in the iteration. Thus, as long as the expression I **in** 1 .. COUNT evaluates to TRUE, the loop continues.

2.5.6 Others

High-level languages intended for system programming like PL/I and C also have bit string operators. Bit string operators include *bitwise and, bitwise or, bitwise xor, one's complement, right shift,* and *left shift*. C also provides the *increment* and *decrement* arithmetic operators.

2.5.7 Expressions and Operator Precedence

High-level languages, as in mathematics, use expressions that contain more than one operator and more than two operands to avoid the necessity of naming intermediate results. As in mathematics, high-level languages define the precedence of operators in evaluating an expression. Operators of the same precedence are evaluated from left to right, and parentheses are used to override predefined precedence. In high-level languages, the numeric operators and the concatenation operator have precedence over relational and membership operators, which, in turn, have precedence over logical operators. As in mathematics, the order of precedence among the numeric operators is exponentiation, multiplication, division, remainder, modulo, addition, and subtraction.

2.5.8 Operator Overloading

The symbols + and - are used to denote both the unary operations identity and negation as well as the binary operations addition and subtraction. The use of the same operator symbol to denote two semantically different operations is called *overloading* the operator. In Ada and other high-level languages, the symbols + and - are usually overloaded to denote both floating-point addition and integer addition. These forms of overloading are built into the languages and they reflect the usage of overloaded operators in mathematics.

Ada allows programmers to define their own overloaded operators. Ada's mechanism for the definition of derived types, as discussed in Section 2.4.2.3, specifies that derived types inherit the operators of the parent type. The inherited operators have special meanings since their use is restricted to the operands of the derived type. For example, in Ada,

```
declare
   type CARS is new INTEGER ;
   type TRUCKS is new INTEGER ;
      A, B : CAR ;
      C, D : TRUCK ;
      I : INTEGER ;
begin
   A := A + B ;        --add CAR to CAR
   C := C + D ;        --add TRUCK to TRUCK
   A := A + C ;        --illegal, cannot add CAR to TRUCK
   A := A + I ;        --illegal, cannot add CAR to INTEGER
   I := A + B ;        --illegal, cannot assign CAR to INTEGER
end ;
```

The first two statements are legal and the last 3 statements are illegal. The + operator carries different programmer-defined meanings in the first two statements depending on the type of its operands. In the first statement, the + operator adds two objects of type CARS; in the second statement, the + operator adds two objects of type TRUCKS.

Programmers may further overload operators in Ada by means of function definitions with names having the same symbol. For example, the function definitions,

```
function "+" (A, B : MATRIX) return MATRIX is
        .
        .
        .
end "+" ;
function "+" (A, B : RATIONAL) return RATIONAL is
        .
        .
        .
end "+" ;
```

further overload the + operator to signify the addition of objects of type MATRIX and objects of type RATIONAL. When the expression X + Y is encountered, the meaning of "+" is determined by the type of operands X and Y.

2.6 FLOW CONTROL

After data objects are operated on, the results are assigned to data objects through the *assignment* statements of a program. A program in its simplest form comprises declarations of data objects and their types, and a sequence of assignment statements. Implicit in the semantics of high-level languages is that the control of execution flows sequentially from one statement to the next. But the languages also provide programmers with decision-making mechanisms to explicitly control the flow of execution. They permit programmers to specify which statements are to be executed based on conditions encountered by the program during execution.

Flow control mechanisms commonly found in high-level languages include *selection, iteration, exit,* and *goto* statements. Some high-level languages also provide mechanisms for flow control to handle abnormal conditions encountered during program execution. These are the *exception definition* and *exception handling* mechanisms. Selection, iteration, exit, and goto statements are discussed in this section; exceptions and exception handling are discussed in Section 2.8.

2.6.1 Selection

Selection mechanisms allow programmers to select one set of statements for execution from multiple sets of statements. A condition guards each set of statements. The set of statements selected for execution is the set for which the guard condition is evaluated TRUE. One selection mechanism, the **if** statement, scans the guard conditions sequentially. It executes the set of statements having the first TRUE guard condition. The **if** statement hence provides programmers with the ability to establish precedence of conditions among multiple conditions that may evaluate to be true. Another selection mechanism, the **case** statement, permits only exactly one of the guard conditions to be evaluated TRUE. The statements guarded by that condition are then executed. The next two sections give examples of the **if** and **case** statements.

2.6.1.1 If statement.

The **if** statement in Ada has the form

```
if CONDITION_1 then
      "sequence of statements 1" ;
   [elsif CONDITION_2 then
      "sequence of statements 2" ;



   elsif CONDITION_N then
      "sequence of statements N" ; ]
[else
   "sequence of statements" ; ]
end if ;
```

where the **else** and **elsif** clauses are optional.

The conditions are Boolean expressions that may be true or false. The sequence of statements corresponding to the first true condition is executed. If none of the conditions evaluates TRUE, the sequence of statements corresponding to the **else** clause is executed. If the optional **else** clause is not specified, no statement is executed. For example,

```
if A < 5 then
      A := A + 1 ;
   elsif A < 10 then
      A := A - 1 ;
end if ;
```

If A has the value 4, it will become 5. If A has the value 6, it will become 5. Note that for the case A = 4, both conditions are satisfied, but only the first statement is executed. If A = 11, neither case is satisfied. No **else** clause is specified, so no statement is executed.

2.6.1.2 Case statement.

The **case** statement in Ada has the form

```
case EXPRESSION is
   when CHOICE1  => "sequence of statements 1" ;
   when CHOICE2  => "sequence of statements 2" ;
              .
              .
              .
   when CHOICEN  => "sequence of statements N" ;
   when others  => "sequence of statements" ;
end case ;
```

where the expression evaluates to a result of a discrete type. The choices (1 through N and **others**) comprise the total set of values defined by the discrete type. A choice (for example, **others**) may be a discrete range of values within the set of values. Since the expression can evaluate to one and only one value out of this set of values, only one choice is true. The sequence of statements corresponding to the true choice is executed. For example,

```
case A + B is
  when 0 => READ(X) ;
  when 1 => WRITE(X) ;
  when others => ERROR ;
end case ;
```

where A and B are of the INTEGER type, and **others** denotes all integer values other than 0 and 1 representable by the machine on which the program executes. As another example, the expression may simply be a variable of the enumeration type:

```
declare
  type DAY is (MON, TUE, WED, THURS, FRI, SAT, SUN) ;
  D : DAY ;
begin
  case D is
    when MON .. FRI => WORK ;
    when others => REST ;
  end case ;
end ;
```

Here also the choice MON .. FRI is a range of values within the set of type DAY.

2.6.2 Iteration

Iteration is a flow control mechanism that repeats a set of statements until a condition is satisfied. Iteration is also known as looping or repetition, and the set of statements repeatedly executed is known as a loop. The condition to be satisfied to exit the loop is called the exit condition. It may be a check to test whether a control variable is within a discrete range of values, as in the DO loop in FORTRAN and the **for** statement in other high-level languages. These mechanisms control repetition by counting. The control variable is incremented (or decremented) each time through the loop. The exit condition may also be a Boolean expression, as in the **while** and the **repeat . . . until** statements. The exit condition is evaluated at the beginning of the loop in the **while** statement and at the end of the loop in the **repeat . . . until** statement. Some languages, such as Ada, also provide a mechanism for defining an infinite loop, the **loop** statement, were no exit condition is present. The **for, while, repeat . . . until,** and **loop** statements are discussed in the following sections.

2.6.2.1 For statement. The **for** statement in Ada has the form

```
for CONTROL_VARIABLE in [reverse] ''discrete range'' loop
  ''sequence of statements'' ;
end loop ;
```

where the sequence of statements is executed once for every value the control variable assumes in the specified discrete range. The **reverse** keyword specifies whether the values in the discrete range are to be assumed in reverse order. For example,

```
for I in 1 .. 10 loop
    A(I) := I **2 ;
    WRITE (A(I)) ;
end loop ;
```

Within the loop body, the control variable I is treated as a constant having the value in the discrete range for that particular iteration. On the fifth iteration in the example above, I = 5 whenever it appears within the loop and its value cannot be modified. On the sixth iteration, I is assigned the constant 6, and so on. When the **for** loop is finished, I has the value 10.

2.6.2.2 While statement. The **while** statement in Ada has the form

```
while CONDITION loop
  ''sequence of statements'' ;
end loop ;
```

where the condition is a Boolean expression evaluated before each iteration of the loop is executed. For example,

```
while READ(X) /= END_OF_FILE loop
  A := READ(X) ;
  WRITE(X) ;
end loop ;
```

where the loop iterates until END_OF_FILE is read. The loop body is not executed at all if END_OF_FILE is read on the first try.

2.6.2.3 Repeat . . . until statement. The **repeat** . . . . **until** statement is defined in Pascal and has the form

```
repeat
  ''sequence of statements'' ;
until CONDITION
```

where the condition is a Boolean expression evaluated at the end of each loop iteration.

The loop is repeated until the condition is found true. The **repeat** . . . **until** statement causes the loop to be executed at least once. Ada does not provide the **repeat** . . . **until** statement.

2.6.2.4 Loop statement. In certain applications, some actions need to be repeated indefinitely. For example, an operating system needs to monitor and control resources continuously. These actions can be done by infinite loops. In Ada, an infinite loop can be expressed as

```
loop
   "sequence of statements" ;
end loop ;
```

For example,

```
loop
   INITIATE (PROCESS) ;
   SCHEDULE (PROCESS) ;
   TERMINATE (PROCESS) ;
end loop ;
```

where the three statements are repeated indefinitely.

2.6.3 Exit Statement

A loop may be exited by an **exit** statement, either conditionally or unconditionally. The **loop** and **exit** statements provide a generalized repetition mechanism because the exit condition may be placed anywhere within the loop. In Ada, it has the form

```
loop
   "sequence of statements preceding exit condition check" ;
   exit [when CONDITION] ;
   "sequence of statements following exit condition check" ;
end loop ;
```

where the condition to be evaluated is a Boolean expression and is optional. A **while** loop is equivalent to the combination of **loop** and **exit** statements if the sequence of statements in the loop preceding the **exit** statement is a null set. A **repeat** . . . . **until** loop is equivalent to the **loop** and **exit** statements if the sequence of statements in the loop following the exit statement is a null set. For example, the loop with the **exit** statement

```
loop
   exit when READ(X) = END_OF_FILE ;
   A := READ(X) ;
   WRITE(X) ;
end loop ;
```

is equivalent to the **while** loop example in Section 2.6.2.2.

An **exit** statement may also be used with the **for** and the **while** statements. It provides an exit condition that can be checked in addition to the exit condition specified by the **for** and the **while** statements. For example,

```
for I in 1 .. 10 loop
   A(I) := I ** 2 ;
   exit when A(I) > B(I);
end loop ;
```

where the loop may be exited by either condition depending on which condition is met first.

2.6.4 Goto Statement

In contrast to an **exit** statement, which restricts the transfer of the flow of execution on an exit to the statement immediately following the loop in which it is embedded, an unrestricted **goto** statement allows a program to transfer the flow of execution to anywhere in the program. A statement can be prefixed with a label, and a **goto** statement can transfer execution to the statement whose label it specifies. Much has been written about the potential harmfulness of **goto** statements because of the tendency to produce hard to understand "spaghetti" programs if they are overused. To prevent their overuse, Ada restricts **goto** statements from transferring control out of a subprogram unit (procedure, function) or out of a module (task, package). It also restricts **goto** statements from transferring control into other flow control statements (**if, case,** and **while**) and into a compound statement from outside the compound statement.

PL/I, on the other hand, allows labels to be declared as variables. Like any other variable, a label variable may be assigned values. A **goto** statement to a label variable causes control to be transferred to the label that is the current value of the label variable. For example,

```
DCL LB LABEL;
...
IF ...
THEN LB=LABEL1 ;
ELSE LB=LABEL2 ;
GO TO LB ;
...
LABEL1 : ...
...
LABEL2 : ...
```

Depending on how the IF statement sets the value of LB, flow control is transferred to either LABEL1 or LABEL2.

2.7 ENVIRONMENT

Programs are sets of type definitions, data object declarations, and statements operating on the data objects and controlling the flow of the operations. High-level languages provide mechanisms for grouping related data objects and the statements that manipulate them into program units (*environments*). Environments include *blocks, subprograms* (functions and procedures), and *modules* (packages and tasks). Data objects are said to be "visible" (that is, referenceable) within their environments. The environment in which an identifier is visible is called the *scope* of the identifier.

"Block-structured" languages (including ALGOL, PL/I, Pascal, and Ada) allow environments to be nested within other environments. One implication of nesting is that the environment in which an identifier is visible includes all the environments nested within it. In other words, the innermost environment may have statements that use identifiers that are declared not within it but in one of its enclosing environments. If the same identifier is used to denote different data objects (variables) in multiple environments, the data object declared in the innermost environment enclosing the statement in which the identifier appears is the data object referred. For example, in Fig. 2.3, environment D is nested within environment C, which is nested within B, which is nested within A. The data objects declared in D are x and t; in C they are x and y; in B, y and z; and in A, x and z. In the expression x + y + z in environment D, the identifier x refers to the data objects declared in D, not to the data objects declared in C and A. The identifier y refers to the data objects declared in C, and the identifier z refers to the data object declared in B. Thus, a reference of the identifier z in environment D is satisfied by an outward search of data object identifiers declared in D, then in C, until the identifier z is found in data object declaration statement in B.

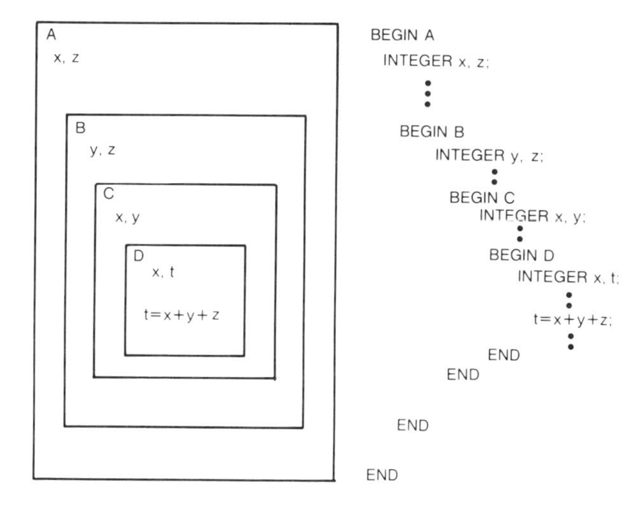

Figure 2.3 Scope of names in a nested block structure.

2.7.1 Blocks

A block is a grouping of an optional set of data object and other identifier declarations, and a sequence of statements. This grouping forms an environment. It is the simplest form of a program unit. In Ada, a block has the form

```
[declare
   ''data objects and other identifier declarations'' ;]
begin
   ''sequence of statements'' ;
end ;
```

The declared data objects are local; that is, they are visible only within the block. Data objects declared in an outer block that encloses an inner block are visible in the inner block. Data objects declared in the inner block, however, are not visible in the outer block. For example,

```
declare                                          --outer block
   QUARTERS, DIMES, NICKELS, PENNIES :
      INTEGER ;                                  --local variables of
   X : INTEGER ;                                 --outer block
begin
   READ (X : out INTEGER) ;
   declare                                       --inner block
      TEMP : INTEGER ;                           --local variable of
   begin                                         --inner block
      QUARTERS := X/25 ;
      TEMP := X rem 25 ;
      DIMES := TEMP/10 ;
      TEMP := TEMP rem 10 ;
      NICKELS := TEMP/5 ;
      PENNIES := TEMP rem 5 ;
   end ;                                         --end inner block
   WRITE (QUARTERS, DIMES, NICKELS, PENNIES) ;
end ;                                            --end outer block
```

In this example, the local variable in the inner block is TEMP. It is not visible in the outer block. The data objects declared in the outer block (QUARTERS, DIMES, NICKELS, PENNIES, and X) are visible in the inner block.

2.7.2 Subprograms

Whereas blocks are mechanisms for defining environments that must be placed in line and executed in sequence, subprograms and modules are mechanisms for defining environments where the transfer of the flow of execution between environments is not restricted to simple sequencing. Subprograms and modules are also separately compilable; blocks are not. In Ada, subprograms include procedures and functions, and modules include packages and tasks.

Subprograms, like blocks, are groupings of declarations of data objects and other identifiers, type definitions, and a sequence of statements. Unlike blocks, however, subprograms may be invoked from many places in a program without repeating the declarations and statements at each place they are invoked. A single invocation (call) statement causes execution control to transfer to the subprogram, wherever it is defined. For the invoker, subprogram invocation is an abstraction of the functionalities of the subprogram; that is, the invoker only needs to know the effects of a subprogram rather than the details of its implementation. High-level languages provide well-defined information passing mechanisms between the invoker (caller) and the invoked (called) units. As an invoked unit, a subprogram is a template for performing a specific function on a given set of parameters passed to it and possibly returning some result. Its manipulations are expressed in terms of *formal parameters*. Each invocation (or instantiation) of a subprogram requires that *actual parameters* be passed from the caller unit to the subprogram. The subprogram initializes its formal parameters with the information from the actual parameters. High-level languages use several different conventions to achieve this information exchange: call by value, call by result, call by value-result, call by reference, and call by name.

1. *Call by value:* The information passed is the *value* of the actual parameter in the caller unit at the point of the call. The value of the actual parameter passed is used to initialize the formal parameter. The formal parameter is a copy of the actual parameter. Updating the copy (the formal parameter) in the called unit does not affect the original (the actual parameter) in the caller unit.
2. *Call by result:* Whereas call by value is a mechanism for passing information from the caller unit to the called unit, call by result is a mechanism by which the called unit returns information to the caller unit. The *address* corresponding to the actual parameter's location at the point of call is passed to the called unit. At the point of return, the value of the formal parameter in the called unit is copied and stored at this address, thus updating the value of the actual parameter in the caller unit.
3. *Call by value-result:* Call by value and call by result are unidirectional information-passing mechanisms. In contrast, call by value-result is a bidirectional information exchange mechanism. The information passed is both the *value* and the *address* of the actual parameter in the caller unit. The formal parameter in the called unit is a copy of the actual parameter. The *value* passed initializes the formal parameter at the point of call. At the point of return, the *address* passed stores the value of the formal parameter. The actual parameter thus passes its value at the point of call, and receives a new value at the point of return.
4. *Call by reference:* In the call by reference convention, the information passed to the called unit is the address of the actual parameter in the caller unit at the point of call. The formal parameter shares this address with the actual parameter. Whenever the

formal parameter is updated in the course of the execution of the called routine, the actual parameter in the caller routine is updated. Call by reference is different from the call by value-result mechanism because the latter mechanism updates the actual parameter with the value of the formal parameter only at the point of return.

5. *Call by name:* The information passed to the called unit, as in call by reference, is the address (or name) of the actual parameter in the caller unit *at the point of call.* Unlike call by reference, however, the formal parameter is not bound to this address in the course of execution of the called unit. Rather, it is bound to the name of the actual parameter. If the name-address binding of the actual parameter changes in the course of the execution of the called unit, a statement in the called unit updating the formal parameter would update the contents of an address in the caller environment (the current address of the actual parameter) different from the address passed at the point of call (the address of the actual parameter at the point of call). In short, the formal parameter is bound to the actual parameter's name that may bind to different addresses in the course of execution of the called routine. For example, the name A(I) binds to different addresses depending on the value of I. If I and A(I) arc actual parameters passed to a called unit and the called unit changes the value of the actual parameter I from the value passed to it at the point of call (I_0) to the current value (I_1), the formal parameter in the called unit would be bound to the address of A(I_1) instead of A(I_0).

Ada uses the keywords **in, out,** and **in out** to distinguish three modes of parameter passing. **Out** and **in out** specify the call by result and the call by value-result, respectively. The **in** mode, however, is different from call by value or any of the mechanisms described above. Whereas call by value passes a value to initialize the formal parameter (which is treated as a local *variable*), the **in** mode in Ada passes a value to initialize the formal parameter (which is treated as a local *constant*). That is, a formal parameter with the **in** mode cannot appear on the left-hand side of an assignment statement.

High-level languages support two types of subprograms: functions and procedures (also called subroutines in FORTRAN). A function, like a mathematical function $f(x, y, \ldots)$, is a variable expressed in terms of some other variables $(x, y, \ldots)$. The variables $x, y, \ldots$ correspond to formal parameters in programming languages. Functions, being variables, appear in expressions as operands, for example, $f(x) + g(y)$. Each invocation of a function generates a new value for the function variable. A procedure, on the other hand, is invoked by a statement. It is invoked for its effect on the actual parameters and global variables. It performs a ''service'' for the caller unit. In Ada, functions return results and may have **in** parameters only; procedures may have **in, out,** and **in out** parameters.

2.7.2.1 Functions.

Functions in Ada have the form

function FUNC_NAME (''formal parameter list'') **return** ''function result type'' **is**
  ''declarations'' ;
begin
  ''sequence of statements'' ;

```
   return FUNCTION_RESULT ;
end FUNC_NAME ;
```

where the function result type is the type of the function variable. For example,

```
function CUBE (I : INTEGER) return INTEGER is
   RESULT : INTEGER ;
begin
   RESULT := I* I* I ;
   return RESULT ;
end CUBE ;
```

defines a variable CUBE(I) of type INTEGER, which is a function of another variable I of type INTEGER. It may be invoked, for example, as

```
X := CUBE(5) + CUBE(3) ;
```

or

```
I := 5 ;
J := 3 ;
X := CUBE(I) + CUBE(J) ;
```

Note that FUNC_NAME may be "+," "-," and so on, overloading the + and - operator symbols (see Section 2.5.8). In such cases, the function is not invoked as FUNC_NAME(ACTUAL PARAMETERS) but as an actual operator in an expression, for example A + B. When such an expression is encountered, the meaning of "+" is determined by the types of A and B. If the types match the types of the formal parameters of a function named "+", that function is invoked.

2.7.2.2 Procedures. Procedures in Ada have the form

```
procedure PROC_NAME ("formal parameter list") is
   "declarations" ;
begin
   "sequence of statements" ;
end PROC_NAME ;
```

For example,

```
procedure CUBE (I : in out INTEGER) is
begin
   I := I* I* I ;
end CUBE ;
```

In the caller unit, it may be invoked as

```
I := 5 ;
CUBE(I) ;
J := 3 ;
CUBE(J) ;
X := I + J ;
```

This sequence of statements affects X in the same manner as the sequence of statements in the example given previously for functions. However, the effect of these statements on the variables I and J illustrates the difference between functions and procedures. The procedure updates the variables I and J to their respective cubic powers. The variables I and J are unchanged by the function call. Alternatively, the procedure could be written

```
procedure CUBE (A : in INTEGER, B : out INTEGER) is
begin
  B := A* A* A ;
end CUBE ;
```

and the sequence of statements written

```
I := 5 ;
CUBE (I, I3) ;
J := 3 ;
CUBE (J, J3) ;
X := I3 + J3 ;
```

in which case I3 and J3 are the cubic powers of I and J; the variables I and J are unaffected by the procedure call.

2.7.2.3 Coroutines. Another type of subprogram unit supported by some high-level languages (for example, SIMULA 67) is *coroutines*. Whereas a procedure or function is a unit subordinate to the caller unit (that is, it performs a service or a function for the caller and then returns control to it), coroutines are units that maintain a symmetrical relationship with each other, passing control back and forth between them. A coroutine passes control to another coroutine when it calls that coroutine and receives control back when it is called. Control passes from one coroutine to another in an interleaved manner. Execution resumes in a coroutine at the point where it last made a call.

2.7.2.4 Recursive subprograms. Many high-level languages allow procedures and functions to call themselves; this is termed *recursion*. Recursion may be direct or indirect. In direct recursion, a unit calls itself directly. In indirect recursion, a unit calls itself through a unit that it has called.

An example of a recursive function is shown below.

```
function SUM (I : INTEGER) return INTEGER is
begin
  if I = 1 then
      return 1 ;
  else
    return I + SUM (I-1) ;
  end if ;
end SUM ;
```

This function calculates the sum $\sum_{n=1}^{I}$ by calling itself iteratively I-1 times. For example, if I = 5, SUM(5) calls SUM(4), which calls SUM(3), which calls SUM(2), which calls SUM(1). SUM(1) returns the value 1, which enables SUM(2) to be calculated and return, which then enables SUM(3) to be calculated and return, and so on.

2.7.3 Modules

Whereas blocks and subprograms group together related data objects and statements that manipulate the data objects into units, modules group together related data objects and subprograms into units. Blocks, subprograms, and modules, as discussed above, define nestable environments for specifying the visibility of identifiers. Any environment may be nested within other environments. For example, even though modules are composed of subprograms, a module may be nested within a subprogram. The subprogram may be embedded within another module, which in turn may be embedded in another subprogram, which may be embedded in a block, and so on.

The concept of modules allows programmers to divide (modularize) programs into units that interact with each other through well-defined interfaces. A module is an abstraction mechanism; another module that interacts with it needs to know only its interfaces (called the *module specification*) and not its implementations (called the *module body*).* Modules are abstracted from the details of implementations of other modules. Thus, as long as the interfaces and the effects of a module remain the same, the implementation of a module may be changed independently of the implementation of other modules.

There are two types of modules supported in Ada: *packages* and *tasks*. A package is a mechanism for data abstraction; a task is a mechanism for functional abstraction and concurrency.

*This level of abstraction is the same as that provided to the caller of subprograms who also needs to know only the subprogram interface given by a subprogram specification. A subprogram specification has the form

procedure (''formal parameter list'');

and

function (''formal parameter list'') **is return** (''return result type'');

2.7.3.1 Packages. As a mechanism for data abstraction, a package groups together a set of related data resources and the possible operations on the resources. These operations are visible to the modules that interact with the package. There are two common uses for packages: sharing data resources and creating new data types.

Shared Data Resources. The simplest use of packages is grouping together data declarations that may be shared by multiple program units. This mechanism is similar to the COMMON statement in FORTRAN where a set of data objects is declared to be common to multiple subprogram units.

A package to implement shared data resources has this form in Ada:

```
package PCK_Name is
   ''data declarations'' ;
end PCK_NAME ;
```

This is a package specification, the part visible to other modules. For example,

```
package DATA_RESOURCE is
   X, Y : INTEGER ;
   Z : FLOAT ;
end DATA_RESOURCE ;
```

Program units that share the data resources in this package may refer to the data objects DATA_RESOURCE.X, DATA_RESOURCE.Y, and DATA_RESOURCE.Z.

Abstract Data Type. A more powerful use of the package mechanism is allowing programmers to define their data object types. Programmers may define new types by defining subtypes and derived types of high-level-language built-in types, or by using language-provided array and record constructors to build new structured types. In all these cases, the new types *inherit* operators from their parent types, which are the built-in operators associated with the built-in types. Packages, on the other hand, provide a mechanism for programmers to completely define their own types, including the operators associated with them. Packages allow a type definition to be grouped together with subprogram specifications that define the possible operators on the type. The implementations of the subprograms are hidden from other modules, as are the implementations of built-in operators of built-in types. To other modules, such a package defines an abstract data type. Multiple data objects of this type may be declared. These data objects are subjected to operations defined by the abstract data type.

A package to define an abstract data type has the form, in Ada, of a package specification visible to other modules:

```
package ADT is
   ''type definition'' ;
   ''subprogram specifications'' ;          --defining possible ;
   end ADT ;                                --operations on the type
end ADT ;
```

and a package body not visible to other modules:

```
package body ADT is
  ''subprogram implementation'' ;
end ADT ;
```

For example, an abstract data type, COMPLEX, may be defined by

```
package COMPLEX_NUMBERS is
  type COMPLEX is
    record
      REAL : FLOAT ;
      IM : FLOAT ;
    end record ;
  function NEW_COMP(X, Y : FLOAT) return COMPLEX ;
  function ''='' (X, Y : COMPLEX) return BOOLEAN ;
  function ''+'' (X, Y : COMPLEX) return COMPLEX ;
end COMPLEX_NU_ MBERS ;
package body COMPLEX_NUMBERS is
  function NEW_COMP(X, Y : FLOAT) return COMPLEX is
    ''implementation of NEW_COMP'' ;
  end NEW_COMP ;
  function ''=''(X, Y : COMPLEX) return BOOLEAN is
    ''implementation of ''='' '' ;
  end ''='' ;
  function ''+''(X, Y : COMPLEX) return COMPLEX is
    ''implementation of ''+'' '' ;
  end ''+'' ;
end COMPLEX_NUMBERS ;
```

Data objects of the abstract data type COMPLEX have the allowable set of pairs of values determined by the machine implementation of FLOAT, and an allowable set of operations NEW_COMP, ''='', and ''+''. The user module is abstracted from the implementation of these operations. For example,

```
declare
  A : COMPLEX ;
  B : COMPLEX ;
  X, Y : FLOAT ;
begin
  X := 3.4 ;
  Y := 5.8 ;
  A := NEW_COMP(X, Y) ;
  B :=A + A ;
end ;
```

When the operators NEW_COMP and "+" are used, the corresponding functions in the package body are executed.

Information Hiding. Besides the package body being hidden from other modules, the type definition in a package specification may also be hidden from other modules. Hiding the type definition in a package specification prevents other modules from misusing the type by making illegal assignments and other illegal operations on the components of objects of the type. The user module only sees the type name and the operations associated with the type. The type definition is hidden by declaring it to be *private* in the package specification. It has the form

```
package IH is
  type PRV_TYPE_NAME is private ;
  "subprogram specifications" ;
private
  "PRV_TYPE_NAME definition" ;
end IH ;
```

For example,

```
package COMPLEX_NUMBERS is
  type COMPLEX is private ;
  function NEW_COMP (X, Y : FLOAT) return COMPLEX ;
  function "=" (X, Y : COMPLEX) return BOOLEAN ;
  function "+"(X, Y : COMPLEX) return COMPLEX ;
private
  type COMPLEX is
    record
      REAL : FLOAT ;
      IM : FLOAT ;
    end record ;
end COMPLEX_NUMBERS ;
```

defines an abstract data type, COMPLEX, where the type definition of COMPLEX is hidden.

General Packages. A single package combining the mechanisms of data resource grouping, abstract type definition, and information hiding has the general form

```
package PCK_NAME is
  "type definitions" ;
  "data declarations" ;
  "subprogram specifications" ;
private
  "private type definitions" ;
end PCK_NAME ;
```

```
package body PCK_NAME is
   ``subprogram implementations'' ;
end PCK_NAME ;
```

The subprogram implementations can be changed independently of the program modules that use the package as long as the subprogram specification and the effects of the subprogram remain the same.

2.7.3.2 Tasks. Certain high-level languages (for example, PL/I, concurrent Pascal, and Ada) allow related data objects and subprograms to be grouped together into modules that can be *active* at the same time. These *concurrent* modules are called *processes* or *tasks*. Whereas packages provide a mechanism for data abstraction, tasks provide a mechanism for functional abstraction and concurrency. Packages are passive entities; they are data resources and related subprograms that become active only when used. Tasks are active entities; they are asynchronous sets of activities that perform various functions. Once initiated, tasks remain active until they are terminated.

Concurrency. Concurrent modules (tasks) are active at the same time. On multiple processor systems, one task executes on one processor at the same time as other tasks are executing on other processors. Single processor systems simulate concurrency by making the tasks time-share the processor. A task executes for a while and is then suspended for a while letting other tasks execute on the processor. In both types of concurrent systems, each task is active until it is terminated. A task that is temporarily suspended is still active because it has not been terminated; it is simply waiting to run again. Tasks are an asynchronous set of activities. The order and rate at which they run with respect to each other does not determine the correctness of their execution. Only when they cooperate with each other or compete with each other for resources do they need to be synchronized. Synchronizations occur at well-defined sychronization points contained within the tasks. Once the synchronization point is passed, tasks can run asychronously again until their next meeting (synchronization point).

Tasks, like other structures in a program, are declared. In Ada, task declarations consist of a task specification

```
task TSK_NAME is
   ``type declarations'' ;
   ``entry specifications'' ;
end TSK_NAME ;
```

and a task body

```
task body TSK_NAME is
   ``declarations'' ;
begin
   ``sequence of statements'' ;
end TSK_NAME ;
```

Like a package specification, a task specification defines the interfaces, called *entries,* that are visible to other tasks. A task's entries are used by other tasks for synchronizing and communicating wth the task; they may be called by other tasks.

Entry and entry call have the same syntax as procedure and procedure call. As in a procedure call, communication between the calling task and the called task is by means of parameters. An entry call is a statement in the calling task. An entry specification is part of the task specification of the called task. An entry **accept** statement is part of the task body of the called task. An entry **accept** statement signifies that the called task is ready for its corresponding entry to be called. The statements associated wth an entry to be executed when called are part of the entry **accept** statement. The set of statements is called the entry body. For example,

```
  task body CALLING is                              --calling task
        .
        .
        .
    ENTRY1 (''actual parameters'') ;                --entry call statement
        .
        .
        .
  end CALLING ;
  task CALLED is                                    --called task's specification
      entry ENTRY1 (''formal parameters'') ;        --entry specification
        .
        .
        .
  end CALLED ;
  task body CALLED is                               --called task's body
        .
        .
        .
    accept ENTRY1 (''formal parameters'') do        --accept statement
      ''sequence of statements'' ;                  --entry body
 end ENTRY1;
   .
   .
end CALLED ;
```

Like a package body, a task body defines the implementation of the task and may be changed independently of other tasks as long as its task specification and the effect of the entry calls remain the same.

Tasks are initiated when the execution part of the program unit in which they are declared is entered. For example,

```
procedure MAIN is
   procedure A is
      task T1 is
         .
         .
         .
      end T1 ;
      task T2 is
         .
         .
         .
      end T2 ;
      task T3 is
         .
         .
         .
      end T3 ;
      task body T1 is
         .
         .
         .
      end T1 ;
      task body T2 is
         .
         .
         .
      end T2 ;
      task body T3 is
         .
         .
         .
      end T3 ;
         .
         .
         .
end A ;
begin
         .
         .
         .
   A ;
         .
         .
         .
end MAIN ;
```

When procedure A is called by the MAIN program and begins execution, tasks T1, T2, and T3 are initiated in parallel. They run concurrently until their termination. The flow of execution cannot leave procedure A until all three tasks have terminated.

The MAIN program is the parent task. It runs in parallel with the three "offspring" tasks it has initiated. Each offspring task can, in turn, initiate its own offspring tasks. A parent task cannot terminate until all its offspring tasks have terminated.

Synchronization and Communication. When tasks cooperate with one another, one task may not continue until it obtains some input from another task. When tasks compete with one another for resources, they must not use the same resources at the same time in an interfering manner. Cooperating and competing tasks must be synchronized at the points where they need to communicate their needs and inputs to one another. The many synchronization mechanisms designed and implemented are reviewed in Chapter 6 in the context of operating systems. In this chapter, only Ada's *rendezvous* mechanism, a synchronization mechanism that is part of a high-level-language definition, is discussed.

A rendezvous is a synchronization point. It is the point when two tasks "meet" possibly to exchange information. A rendezvous is achieved when one task makes or has made an *entry* call and another task *accepts* or has accepted an entry call. The calling task must wait when it makes an entry call if the called task has not yet accepted the entry call. On the other hand, the called task must wait before it accepts an entry call if the calling task is not yet ready to make the call. Both tasks must be ready for a rendezvous to occur.

When a rendezvous occurs, the calling task remains blocked until the sequence of statements (the entry body) associated with the accepted called entry is executed. Once the entry body is executed, both tasks can proceed independently (asynchronously) of each other until the next rendezvous. For example,

```
task body WORKER is
      .
      .
      .
   PAY (INCOME : out INTEGER) ;
      .
      .
      .
end WORKER ;
task TREASURER is
   entry PAY (SALARY : out INTEGER) ;
      .
      .
      .
end TREASURER ;
      .
      .
      .
```

```
task body TREASURER is
   accept PAY (SALARY : out INTEGER) do
   SALARY := (NET_INCOME)/NO_WORKERS ;
   end PAY ;
        .
        .
        .
end TREASURER ;
```

A rendezvous occurs when the WORKER unit executes or has executed the PAY statement and the TREASURER unit executes or has executed the **accept** statement. The entry body is the SALARY calculation statement. On a rendezvous, the WORKER unit is blocked while the SALARY is calculated. The WORKER unit continues only after the SALARY is calculated and the amount is communicated to the WORKER unit by means of the **out** parameter SALARY of the entry.

Delay. A task may suspend itself by executing a **delay** statement. A **delay** statement has the form

delay ''delay period specification'' ;

where the delay period specification is an expression calculating the time period that the task is to be suspended.

Terminate. A task may terminate itself by executing the **terminate** statement,

terminate ;

A task is allowed to terminate only if (1) all its offspring tasks have terminated or are waiting to be terminated, and (2) there are no calls pending for the task.

Select. Often it is not possible for a task to know the order in which its entries will be called by the various tasks it interacts with since the rate and order of execution of the tasks are nondeterministic. If a task places an **accept** statement for an entry that is not called for a long time in front of other **accept** statements whose entries have been called, the rendezvous for the other entries may be unnecessarily delayed. Since the rate and order of task execution are nondeterministic, the Ada tasking mechanism provides a nondeterministic selection of possible rendezvous. This is accomplished by the **select** statement, which has the form

```
select
  [when ''condition 1''] =>
     ''alternative 1'' ;
or [when ''condition 2''] =>
      ''alternative 2'' ;
        .
        .
        .
```

```
or [when ''condition N''] =>
     ''alternative N'' ;
[else
     [''else alternative''] ;
end select ;
```

where the **when** conditions are optional. If a **when** condition is absent, the corresponding alternative can always be selected. An alternative may be an **accept** statement, a **delay** statement followed by other statements, or a **terminate** statement. A **select** statement is executed by first determining the set of *open alternatives,* that is, all the alternatives with no **when** condition specified or with a **when** condition that is true. If there is no open alternative, the else alternative is executed. If there is neither an open alternative nor an else alternative specified, an exception is generated. This is the first level of selection of a **select** statement. The second level of selection is performed if there is more than one open alternative. Of the open alternatives, the ones with rendezvous immediately possible (that is, with waiting entry calls) are selected. Among these, one is randomly chosen to execute. If there are no open alternatives with pending rendezvous, the open alternative with the **delay** statement with the shortest delay period executes. If a rendezvous subsequently becomes possible for an open alternative during the delay period, that alternative executes. Otherwise, the statements following the **delay** statement execute. If there are no open alternatives with pending rendezvous or **delay** statements, an open **terminate** alternative may be selected, but only if it is allowed. Otherwise, the task suspends itself and waits for the first rendezvous possible for any of the open alternatives. For example,

```
task EXECUTIVE is
  type DEPT_PROB is (MANUF, R&D, SALES, NONE) ;
  type DAY is (MON, TUE, WED, THU, FRI) ;
  type FIGURES is array (1 .. 10) of INTEGER ;
  entry MANUF _(REPORT : in  FIGURES) ;
  entry R&D_(REPORT : in FIGURES) ;
  entry SALES_(REPORT : in  FIGURES) ;
  entry ASSISTANTS_(REPORT : in  FIGURES) ;
end EXECUTIVE ;
task body EXECUTIVE is
  PROBLEM : DEPT_PROB ;
  TODAY : DAY ;
begin
          .
          .
          .
  loop
    select
      when PROBLEM = MANUF =>
        accept MANUF_(REPORT : in FIGURES) do
```

```
                    .
                    .
                    .
          end ;
                    .
                    .
                    .
      or when PROBLEM = R&D =>
          accept R&D_(REPORT : in FIGURES) do
                    .
                    .
                    .
          end ;
                    .
                    .
                    .
  or when PROBLEM = SALES=>
  accept SALES_(REPORT : in FIGURES) do
                    .
                    .
                    .
          end ;
                    .
                    .
                    .
      or when TODAY = FRI =>
          accept ASSISTANTS_(REPORT : in FI GURES) do
                    .
                    .
                    .
          end ;
                    .
                    .
                    .
      or
        delay 10 ;
                .
                .
                .
      end select ;
    end loop ;
  end EXECUTIVE ;
```

The EXECUTIVE receives a REPORT from either MANUF, R&D, or SALES depending on which department has a PROBLEM. If TODAY is FRI, the EXECUTIVE may also choose to receive a REPORT from the ASSISTANTS instead. Thus, if a PROBLEM exists in SALES and TODAY is FRI, the EXECUTIVE nondeterministically selects a REPORT from either the ASSISTANTS or from SALES. If TODAY is not FRI and there is no PROBLEM, the EXECUTIVE waits for 10 seconds to see if any PROBLEM develops or the day changes to FRI. If a PROBLEM develops or the day changes to FRI during the 10-second delay, the EXECUTIVE will attend to the PROBLEM by receiving a REPORT from the department with the PROBLEM or from the ASSISTANTS. Otherwise, the EXECUTIVE does some of its own work (the statements following the delay statement) until it starts a new cycle (loop) to deal with a PROBLEM or FRI again. In this example, there is always an open alternative since the **delay** statement is not guarded by a **when** condition.

The selection mechanism of a **select** statement is more flexible than other high-level-language selection mechanisms. The **case** statement allows only one condition to be true. The **if** statement allows multiple conditions to be true but always selects the first true condition found by **if** or the first **elsif.** The **select** statement allows multiple conditions to be true and selects one nondeterministically among the ones with possible rendezvous.

In the example above, there may be multiple ''assistant'' tasks that may call the ASSISTANTS_ entry. If more than one ''assistant'' has called the entry, they are placed in a queue in a first-in, first-out ordering. When the EXECUTIVE executes the **select** statement and chooses the ASSISTANTS_ alternative, the first ''assistant'' in the queue has a rendezvous with the EXECUTIVE.

2.7.4 Generic Subprograms and Modules

Just as type definition is a high-level-language mechanism for specifying a generic entity of which multiple instances of objects may be created, certain high-level languages, such as Ada, provide mechanisms for defining *generic subprograms* and *generic modules* from which multiple instances of subprograms and modules may be instantiated. Generic subprograms and modules are declared in Ada with a generic specification and a generic body. A generic specification has the form

```
generic
   ''generic formal parameters''
''subprogram or module specification''
```

and a generic body has the same form as the body of an ordinary subprogram or module.

An ordinary subprogram is in itself a parameterized template of an execution unit from which multiple instances can be generated by substituting the *values* of actual parameters into the formal parameters of the subprogram. A generic subprogram is a parameterized template from which multiple ordinary subprogram templates can be generated by substituting the *type* of generic actual parameters into the generic formal parameters of the generic subprogram. For example, a generic subprogram can be defined to SWAP the values of two entities. The type of entity swapped is a generic formal parameter. Multiple swap subprogram templates can be generated by specifying the type of entity: a swap integer subprogram, a swap float subprogram, a swap array subprogram, and so on. Multiple instances of each of the swap subprogram templates can in turn be generated by calls to them with actual parameters. For example, the generic subprogram swap may be specified by

```
generic
  type ENTITY ;
procedure SWAP (A, B : in out ENTITY) ;
```

and SWAP subprogram templates may be instantiated by

```
procedure SWAP_INT is new SWAP (INTEGER) ;
procedure SWAP_FL is new SWAP (FLOAT) ;
procedure SWAP_ARRAY is new SWAP (ARRAY) ;
```

where INTEGER, FLOAT, and ARRAY are generic actual parameter types substituted for the generic formal parameter **type** ENTITY. Procedures SWAP_INT, SWAP_FL, and SWAP_ARRAY may then be called by substituting actual parameters:

```
SWAP_INT (I, J : in out INTEGER) ;
SWAP_FL (X, Y : in out FLOAT) ;
```

In these examples, I, J, and X, Y are actual parameters substituted for the formal parameters A, B.

Modules, unlike subprograms, are not in themselves parameterized units. They are instances of groupings of data and functional resources. Generic facilities allow modules to be parameterized. For example, a generic package defining a buffer may have parameters that specify the size of the buffer and the type of elements in the buffer:

```
generic
  SIZE : INTEGER ;
  type ELEMENT ;
package BUFFER is
  procedure ADD (IN : in ELEMENT) ;
  procedure REMOVE (OUT : out ELEMENT) ;
  OVERFLOW : exception ;
end BUFFER ;
```

This generic package specification is not an instance of a buffer but a parameterized template. It allows multiple buffer packages to be instantiated, each with a different value for the size or type of elements. For example, a buffer with 20 integer elements, a buffer with 10 floating-point elements, and a buffer with 50 vectors may be instantiated by

```
package BUFFER1 is new BUFFER (20, INTEGER) ;
package BUFFER2 is new BUFFER (10, FLOAT) ;
package BUFFER3 is new BUFFER (50, VECTOR) ;
```

where VECTOR is a previously defined array type.

Generic modules may also be specified without parameters. For example, the task EXECUTIVE in a previous example defines a set of activities and functions the EXECUTIVE performs when it is initiated. Multiple "executives," each performing exactly the same set of activities and functions may be instantiated. The generic EXECUTIVE may be declared by

```
generic
task EXECUTIVE is
      .
      .
      .
end EXECUTIVE ;
task body EXECUTIVE is
      .
      .
      .
end EXECUTIVE;
```

where the contents of the specification and body of the task are the same as in the previous example. Multiple EXECUTIVE tasks may be instantiated by

```
task EXEC1 is new EXECUTIVE ;
task EXEC2 is new EXECUTIVE ;
task EXEC3 is new EXECUTIVE ;
```

and be executed in parallel.

2.8 EXCEPTIONS

Some high-level languages permit programmers to distinguish between conditions and events that are part of the normal program execution and abnormal conditions and events that cause programs to terminate or require them to be handled specially. The abnormal conditions and events are called *exceptions*. Programmers declare them, *raise* them, and provide *exception handlers* to handle them when they are raised. An exception causes the flow of execution to be transferred from the statement where it is raised (detected) to the statement where the corresponding exception handler is defined. The exception handler may be located in the same program unit (environment) or in an enclosing program unit. In the latter case, control is transferred to the enclosing program unit.

An exception declaration in Ada has the form

```
EXCEPTION_NAME : exception ;
```

These statements, for example,

```
OUT_OF_BOUNDS, OSCILLATORY : exception ;
INF_LOOP : exception ;
```

declare three exceptions. An exception is raised by a **raise** statement of the form

```
raise EXCEPTION_NAME ;
```

Exceptions are handled by exception handlers of the form

```
when EXCEPTION_NAME =>
  ''sequence of statements'' ;
```

For example,

```
N := 0 ;
loop
  exit when READ(X) = END_OF_FILE ;
  A :=READ(X) ;
  WRITE(X) ;
  N := N + 1 ;
  if N > 10000 then
    raise INF_LOOP ;
  end if ;
end loop ;
      .
      .
      .
exception
  when INF_LOOP =>
    PUT (''INFINITE LOOP'') ;
```

This program is intended to exit normally from the loop on encountering the END_OF_FILE condition. If after iterating 10,000 times the END_OF_FILE is not found, an exception (INF_LOOP) is raised. Execution control transfers to the last statements, the exception handler, which prints the error message ''INFINITE LOOP''. In Ada, the **raise** statement has the same effect as a **goto** statement: it ''goes to'' the exception handler. After the exception handler is executed, the statement following it is executed. Execution flow does not return to the statement following the **raise** statement.

In Ada, the exception handlers are placed at the ends of blocks, subprograms, and modules. The general positions of exception handlers are as follows:

In blocks:

```
declare
   ... ;
begin
   ... ;
exception
   ''exception handler'' ;
end ;
```

In procedures:

```
procedures PROC_NAME(...) is
   ... ;
begin
   ... ;
exception
   ''exception handler'' ;
end ;
```

In functions:

```
function FUNC_NAME (...) return ... is
   ... ;
begin
   ... ;
   return ... ;
exception
   ''exception handler'' ;
end ;
```

In packages:

```
package body PCK_NAME is
   ... ;
begin
   ... ;
exception
   ''exception handler'' ;
end ;
```

And in tasks:

```
task body TSK_NAME is
   ... ;
begin
   ... ;
exception
   "exception handler" ;
end ;
```

This placement allows the subprogram, module, or block to be exited once an exception is handled. Execution flow does not return to the body of the subprogram or the module in which an exception is raised. It returns to the invoker of the subprogram or module. In the case of a task, the task that raised the exception terminates after the exception is handled.

Exception handlers handle exceptions locally; that is, they handle only the exceptions raised within the environment in which they are defined. In other words, exceptions may be propagated to their enclosing environments for handling. The block structure allows programmers to control whether exceptions should be handled locally or propagated. For example,

```
declare                                                   --outer block
  QUARTERS, DIMES, NICKELS, PENNIES : INTEGER ;           --local variables
  X : INTEGER ;                                           --of outer block
  GT_DOLLAR : exception ;
begin
  READ (X : out INTEGER) ;
  declare                                                 --inner block
    TEMP : INTEGER ;                                      --local variables of inner
                                                          --block
  begin
    if X >= 100 then
      raise GT_DOLLAR ;
    end if ;
    QUARTERS := X/25 ;                                    --outer block local variables
    TEMP := X rem 25 ;                                    --visible within inner block
    DIMES := TEMP/10 ;
    TEMP := TEMP rem 10 ;
    NICKELS := TEMP/5 ;
    PENNIES := TEMP rem 5 ;
  end ;
    WRITE (QUARTERS, DIMES, NICKELS, PENNIES) ;
exception
  when GT_DOLLAR =>
    PUT ("GREATER_THAN_DOLLAR_SUBMITTED") ;
end ;
```

In this example, the exception GT_DOLLAR is raised in the inner block. Because no exception handler is defined in the inner block to handle the exception locally, it is propagated to the outer block and handled by the exception handler defined there. The **raise** statement, when executed, has the effect of an unrestricted **goto** to the body of the exception handler, that is, the PUT statement.

Exceptions are propagated outward searching for the corresponding exception handler, much like the outward search of a data object identifier for its declaration. The search starts locally, goes to the immediately enclosing environment, and proceeds to the next enclosing environment until the corresponding exception handler is found, or until the search reaches the main program. If the exception reaches the main program without being handled, the program is terminated. Thus, in Ada, a raised exception has the effect of an unrestricted **goto** *(possibly across environments)* to its exception handler.

The PL/I exception signaling mechanism, on the other hand, has the effect of a procedure call. After the exception handler completes execution, the execution flow returns to the statement following the one in which the exception is raised (*signaled* in PL/I terminology). The PL/I exception declaration and exception handler definition are combined by means of the

ON condition on-unit ;

statement, where the on-unit is the exception handler comprising one or more PL/I statements. The on-unit is executed whenever the specified condition (exception) occurs *after* the ON statement executes. That is, the on-unit is not executed at the time the ON statement is executed, but when the specified condition subsequently arises. Conditions are explicitly raised by programmers using the SIGNAL statement, which has the form

SIGNAL condition ;

The ON statement is equivalent to a procedure definition while the SIGNAL statement is equivalent to a procedure call statement.

2.9 DEVELOPMENT OF HIGH-LEVEL LANGUAGES

The four generations of high-level languages have evolved from the machine-oriented languages of the earliest computers to abstract, modularized modern languages [7–9]. This section discusses the relationships of the languages to each other, and gives a historical perspective of how the concepts just discussed in this chapter evolved. The review covers only the major concepts of each generation's major languages and not the intricacies of each language.

2.9.1 First-Generation Languages

Before high-level languages existed, stored program computers were programmed using ones and zeros. John von Neumann outlined a one-address machine language for these machines in the 1945 "First Draft of a Report on the EDVAC"; the computers that evolved from von Neumann's developments are known as von Neumann machines [6]. In the 1950s, *assemblers* were developed to translate symbolic instruction codes into the ones and zeros of machine instruction codes. Even while assemblers were being developed, the idea of high-level languages was formulated. Despite skepticisim about their efficiency, a successful high-level language was developed between 1954 and 1958. This language is FORTRAN I; its name derives from its chief function, formula translation. FORTRAN I is a scientific computation language with simple data structures. It is oriented toward solving numerical algorithms.

FORTRAN I introduces the first high-level-language concepts of simple action composites such as statements and expressions, object composites such as arrays, and the COMMON and EQUIVALENCE definition mechanisms for data sharing and storage sharing. FORTRAN I also introduces control mechanisms (action composites) that allow iteration (DO loops), unconditional flow control transfer (GOTO statements), conditional flow control transfer (IF statements), and the use of labels. In FORTRAN I, typing is implicit depending on the variable's name; that is, the starting character of the name determines whether the variable is an integer or a real. FORTRAN I allows subroutines to be compiled independently. Although FORTRAN I is a higher level of abstraction from the machine than assembly language, its design approach is still *bottom-up;* that is, the hardware (the lowest level) dictates the language design. One of the major preoccupations of the FORTRAN I designers was creating the language so its compilers could generate efficient machine code. The bottom-up approach ensured successful and efficient compilations and thus proved the viability of high-level languages.

The success of FORTRAN I resulted partly from the restrictions it places on programs and data. For instance, FORTRAN I allows only *static storage allocation;* that is, the storage requirements for programs and data must be known at compilation and do not change during execution. Therefore, FORTRAN I does not permit dynamic data structures (variably sized data structures); nor does it allow recursion. This model of implementation produces efficient machine code since all the data structures are of known sizes.

FORTRAN I is not the only high-level language produced in the early period (1950–1958). Other languages include FLOWMATIC for data processing and IPL 5 for list processing. These first-generation languages introduce many other basic ideas of high-level languages. They are the direct predecessors of the more-well-known second-generation languages developed between 1957 and 1961: FORTRAN II [10], ALGOL 60 [11], COBOL [12], and LISP [13].

2.9.2 Second-Generation Languages

ALGOL 60, developed between 1957 and 1960, plays a major role in the development of high-level languages. It introduces many new language concepts that set the direction for the development of a large class of high-level languages. It was designed using a *top-down* design approach, unlike the bottom-up approach of FORTRAN I. A top-down approach emphasizes the needs of programming from the programmer's viewpoint. The careful design of ALGOL 60 represents the beginning of theoretical studies of the syntaxes and semantics of high-level languages. ALGOL 60 introduces the Backus-Naur Form (BNF) as a syntax specification language, or *metalanguage*.

The innovations of ALGOL 60 are many and varied. ALGOL 60 introduces the use of stacks during execution for allocating storage and directing program control. Run-time stacks permit dynamic storage allocation which, in turn, permits recursion. ALGOL 60 introduces the high-level-language concepts of nested block structures, scope rule for variables, explicit type declarations for variables, and call by value and call by name for passing procedure parameters. It also introduces the **if-then-else** statement as a selection mechanism, the **for** statement and the **while** concept for loop control, the **own** variables, and the **switch** concepts.

Own variables, unlike local variables, are variables whose values are preserved after the block in which they are declared is exited. Unlike global variables, however, **own** variables may only be accessed within the blocks in which they are declared. An ALGOL 60 **switch** statement is a flow control mechanism that allows transfer of control to any one of a number of statements, depending on the value of an integer. An ALGOL 60 **switch** statement may be thought of as a restricted **case** statement in which the test conditions are integers and the statements corresponding to the conditions are **goto** statements.

ALGOL 60 has three built-in data types (integer, real, and Boolean). It introduces the capability of treating labels as variables and of passing labels as paramcters of procedures. The designers of ALGOL 60 included in their definition of dynamic storage allocation concepts such as variably sized arrays and dynamically created variables. Except for the **own** variables and the **switch** concepts not retained in later languages because they were found to have limited usefulness, the concepts ALGOL 60 introduces appear in many modern languages.

COBOL was developed between 1959 and 1961 as a business-oriented programmng language; it is still in use today. A business language, the designers of COBOL realized, has to access and manipulate large volumes of data. So they divided COBOL programs into four divisions. The *data division* allows programmers to concentrate on the design of the data base; it specifies the files used by a program and the usage and formats of the data elements. The *procedure division* describes the processing to be done. The procedures are written using verbs to describe the required actions (such as, open, read, move, and calculate). COBOL's design uses a natural language style of programming, which makes reading the procedures of COBOL programs easy. The other divisions of a COBOL program are the *identification division,* which identifies the program that follows it, and the *environment division,* which describes the input and output devices to be used and localizes the machine dependencies of the programs. The four divisions of COBOL programs allow data to be treated as importantly as procedures. COBOL was designed with machine independence as a goal; equipped with a COBOL compiler, most machines are able to run COBOL programs after appropriate alterations are made to their environment divisions and possibly their data divisions.

LISP was also developed in the period between 1959 and 1961. LISP is a list-processing language that maps programs uniformly onto list structures. It is object oriented rather than value oriented; that is, it is designed for nonnumeric processing. It is an applicative language. Applicative languages are also known as functional languages because they are based on functions and demand a functional style of programming reminiscent of mathematics. LISP defines a few primitive operators and data types from which a programmer can build more complex structures. The two primitive data types are atoms and lists. The operators allow the selection of elements from a list, the construction of lists from their components, and testing for equality and atomicity. These are the essential operations for nonnumeric processing. Because of its list and nonnumeric processing capabilities, LISP is widely used for writing programs in artificial intelligence applications.

2.9.3 Third-Generation Languages

The 1960s and the 1970s saw the emergence of the third-generation languages: PL/I [14], ALGOL W [15], ALGOL 68 [16], Pascal [17], SIMULA 67 [18], APL [19], SNOBOL 4 [20], BASIC [21], and C [22]. PL/I (Programming Language One) was developed between 1964 and 1969 with the goal of synthesizing and combining the important concepts of FORTRAN, ALGOL 60, and COBOL. It was designed as a general-purpose computing language to satisfy the needs of scientists, commercial users, and system programmers. It takes from FORTRAN the ideas of separate compilation, subroutines, sharing common data, and the DO loop. It takes from COBOL data structures, input/output facilities, and report-generating facilities. From ALGOL 60, PL/I takes the concepts of block structures, arrays, and recursion. PL/I is a large language that provides many additional features to fulfill its design goal of being a general-purpose language. It introduces exception handling mechanisms and parallel processing. PL/I accepts various forms of input commands; its flexibility includes the ability to interpret words based on their context in a program. The language also allows a variety of storage allocation techniques: static, automatic, and controlled. PL/I also accommodates concurrency in the form of signals, multitasking, and exception handling. Although PL/I is a large and flexible language, it is difficult to learn and tends to compile slowly.

ALGOL 60 is the basis for several third-generation languages, including ALGOL W, ALGOL 68, SIMULA 67, and Pascal. ALGOL W, the immediate successor to ALGOL 60, was developed in the mid-1960s. It extends the number of built-in types of ALGOL 60 to include sequences (bits and strings), complex numbers, long real and long complex numbers (for extended precision), and the important access (or reference) type. ALGOL W eliminates the ALGOL 60 **own** variable concept, and does not allow the assignment of labels to variables and the passing of labels as parameters of procedures. It introduces the important concepts of call by result as an alternative procedure parameter-passing mechanism, the **case** statement, records as aggregates of heterogeneous components (although COBOL did introduce a form of record structure), and discriminants and unions (variant records). ALGOL W was designed as a strongly typed language; that is, no type checking needs to be done at run time.

ALGOL 68, like ALGOL 60, is a block-structured language; it was developed between 1963 and 1969. It further evolves the concepts of ALGOL 60, and includes the improvements of ALGOL W. It supports fully typed procedure parameters, references (pointers), structures (records), and a rich set of built-in types, including the union type. It introduces automatic mode conversion (coercion), and collateral (parallel) evaluation with synchronization by semaphores, where semaphores are a built-in type. ALGOL 68 also introduces the important principle of language extensibility. As an extensible language, ALGOL 68 provides mechanisms to programmers for defining their own data types and operators, and provides constructors for building data type composites or primitive data types. The constructors include reference, array, record, and variant record. ALGOL 68 supports **if-then-else, goto, loop,** and **case** statements for control mechanisms. It supports the treatment of procedures as objects with values and types. The type of a procedure is determined by the type of its parameters and the type of its result. Procedures may also be passed as parameters to other procedures.

Pascal was designed around 1970 with the goal of simplifying certain aspects of ALGOL 60 for programming ease and for enhancing program verifiability. It is based on ALGOL 60, stemming from investigations by N. Wirth into types of possible data structuring facilities. It has a rich set of built-in data types including range types and enumerated types. For defining new types, Pascal has several constructors including record, variant record, array, file, set, and pointer. Pascal allows the passing of procedures as parameters. It introduces the concept of parameterized type and excludes ALGOL 60 dynamic arrays.

SIMULA 67 is another language that is heavily influenced by ALGOL 60. A process-oriented language, SIMULA 67 was developed in 1967 to help build better computer models of events and data. To do this, SIMULA 67 introduces the idea of *class*. Class extends the block structures of ALGOL 60, which contain local procedures and data structures, to include global definitions that survive even after program control leaves a block structure. Assigning variables and procedures to classes allows them to be accessed from other parts of an executing program; this is a disadvantage only when programmers neglect to control intermodule communication sufficiently. The consideration of classed variables and procedures represents an early stage in the development of the principles of modular programming. SIMULA 67 also introduces the concept of coroutines.

Other third-generation languages developed in the 1960s include the following.

- APL, like LISP, is an applicative language. It was designed for mathematical applications, and was developed in the early 1960s and implemented as an interactive language in 1967. It is an interpreted rather than a compiled language. APL is a dynamically typed language, that is, the binding between variables and their types is dynamic. It treats arrays as a primitive type of the language and supports a set of operations on arrays without requiring language level iteration.
- SNOBOL 4 was developed between 1962 and 1967. It is a string manipulation language developed at AT&T Bell Laboratories with powerful pattern-matching operations to support strings and pattern data types. SNOBOL 4 is also a dynamically typed language.
- BASIC is another third-generation language. BASIC is a simple interactive language that is widely used as a first language for beginning programmers.
- The C language, also developed at AT&T Bell Laboratories, supports and encourages structured programming. C is efficient in its use of primitive machine instructions, making it ideal for writing low-level operating system functions.

2.9.4 Fourth-Generation Languages

Most of the fourth-generation languages, developed in the 1970s, evolved from Pascal. The major fourth-generation languages include CLU [23], ALPHARD [24], Euclid [25], Concurrent Pascal [26], Modula [27], and Ada. A distinctive feature of these languages is that they support modularity by means of abstraction. *Abstraction* involves hiding implementation details from the users by the compiler or by a language-supported encapsulation mechanism. Modularity permits the specification of well-defined interfaces among program modules. Most of the fourth-generation languages also support concurrency for parallel processing. They include facilities for defining concurrent modules, and they support the intermodule transfer of control among concurrent modules with well-defined synchronization mechanisms.

The languages CLU, ALPHARD, Concurrent Pascal, and Modula are modular languages designed with the goal of making programs easier to verify, modify, and understand. They incorporate structures that hide some information and allow only a subset of their attributes to be "exported" or made known to external programs. These structures are referred to as "clusters" in CLU, "forms" in ALPHARD, "monitors" in Concurrent Pascal, and "modules" in Euclid and Modula. In addition to modularity and abstraction, CLU has well-defined exception-handling mechanisms. Concurrent Pascal and Modula have well-defined concurrency mechanisms. The concept of class in Concurrent Pascal serves as a data abstraction mechanism and monitors serve as synchronization mechanisms. Concurrent Pascal also supports the notion of processes as language entities for implementing concurrency. Modula is a language for modular multiprogramming. It incorporates several notions: modules for defining abstract data types, processes for concurrent executable units, interface modules, and signals for synchronization. The design of these languages and their facilities strongly influenced the design of Ada.

Ada is a general-purpose language that supports modularity with packages and concurrent programming with tasks. Ada was developed by the U.S. Department of Defense in the late 1970s. It provides facilities that allow suitable structuring of programs including:

1. A set of program constructs and data types, procedures, and functions
2. Type declarations and operator declarations to allow the introduction of operators to act on the new types
3. Module facilities to allow the encapsulation of abstract data types
4. Separate compilation and linkage facilities
5. Ways of checking the validity of proofs of correctness

Ada is based on Pascal; for example, the mechanisms for type definition are similar to those of Pascal. Ada, however, avoids some unsafe features of Pascal in areas such as variant records. Like Euclid, it does not allow the discriminant of variant records to be assigned value independently so inconsistencies do not occur between the discriminant

WIDELY USED LANGUAGES	USE
FORTRAN (FORmula TRANslator)	SCIENTIFIC
ALGOL (ALGOrithmic Language)	GENERAL PURPOSE, SCIENTIFIC
LISP (LISt Processor)	LIST PROCESSING, ARTIFICIAL INTELLIGENCE
COBOL (COmmon Business-Oriented Language)	BUSINESS
PL/1 (Programming Language 1)	GENERAL PURPOSE
BASIC (Beginners All-purpose Symbolic Instruction Code)	EDUCATION
APL (A Programming Language)	MATH, MODELING
SIMULA 67	MODELING
PASCAL (Blaise PASCAL)	GENERAL PURPOSE
C	GENERAL PURPOSE, SYSTEM PROGRAMMING

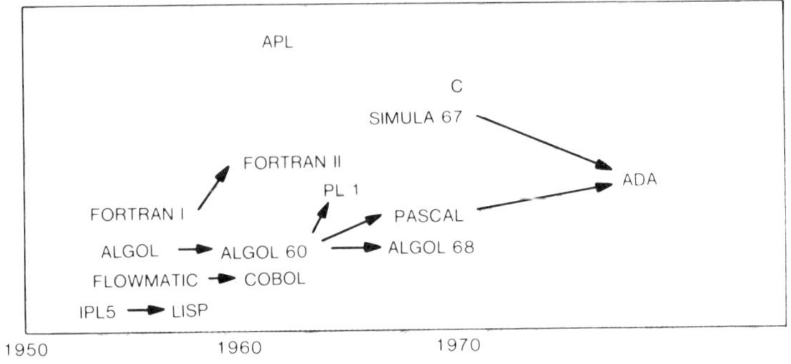

Figure 2.4

value and the variant component type and value of the variant record. Ada's exception-handling mechanisms are based on those of CLU.

The chronology of the development of some of the key languages is shown in Fig. 2.4.

2.9.5 Current State of Language Development

Concepts of modularity and information hiding developed in high-level languages are direct attempts to address the concerns about the reliability and verifiability of software. However, even with these improvements from the 1960s and 1970s, FORTRAN and COBOL are still the most common languages. They have become the de facto standards for programming in scientific and business environments. In comparison, PL/I, ALGOL 68, SIMULA, and others have enjoyed success mainly in the university and research environments.

Occasional efforts to standardize languages have been made. Recently, the Department of Defense nominated Ada as its standard. Ada is based on Pascal, and it retains most of the good features of Pascal. It remains to be seen, however, whether Ada will have the success in the 1980s and 1990s that FORTRAN and COBOL had in the 1960s and 1970s. Adopting a standard language such as Ada will minimize the possibility of software obsolescence as hardware technology changes.

The movement to adopt a standard language has been particularly strong at the microcomputer level. Many of the problems with mainframes are also problems with microcomputers, except with microcomputers they occur at an accelerated rate. Rapid technological changes cause software obsolescence, although this problem is minimized by the use of machine-independent, portable code. Currently, Pascal is the most popular language for microcomputers. Pascal has other advantages: it is available for mainframe computers, and its range of uses has been broadened considerably from its original role as a teaching tool. Current uses of Pascal range from real-time processing for NASA's Deep Space Network to general ledger systems on a minicomputer [28]. Machines built with microprocessors like the Motorola 68000 and the National NS16000 are designed with Pascal in mind [29]. More specifically, the Pascal Microengine from Western Digital Corporation and the MK-16 from Mikros Systems Corporation execute P-code, the immediate interpretive language generated by some Pascal compilers. Pascal will continue to be popular for many years. Advances in integrated circuit technology have vastly expanded microprocessor capabilities. Before the recent advances, minicomputers and microcomputers were slow and had little memory space. Assembly languages were therefore used to program them. But now, memory costs are decreasing and processing power is increasing. These changes minimize the primary disadvantage of high-level languages: their inefficiency in terms of the size and speed of the compiled machine code. The use of high-level languages is gaining momentum because of the cost benefits achieved by it: high-level languages simplify software development and make it easier to maintain. Even more significantly, software becomes more easily portable when written in a high-level language. Once developed, software may be used on newer, more efficient microcomputers as they appear on the market. With the rapid growth of integrated-circuit technology, algorithms coded in high-level languages will have a longer life expectancy than the hardware on which they are executed.

2.10 SUMMARY

The cost of software development and maintenance is an issue of great concern in the computing community. Research into software engineering has resulted in various methodologies to enhance the quality and maintainability of software and the productivity of programmers. The use of high-level languages plays an integral part in the application of these methodologies because the semantics of the languages determine the way programmers think.

High-level languages provide a medium for programmers to describe and specify data objects and the algorithms for manipulating them. An important high-level language concept is that of the data object type. A type defines the attributes (the set of applicable operations and the set of assumable values) of data objects. Each high-level language has a set of built-in types. They usually include *integer, real, character,* and *Boolean*. From these basic types, high-level languages provide mechanisms for programmers to define their own data types. Programmers may define a *subtype* or a *derived* type from a previously defined type. They may define an *enumerated type* by listing the literal values of the type. The subtypes, derived types, enumerated types, and the built-in types constitute the *scalar* types. Scalar types are data object types with single components. High-level languages also allow programmers to construct *aggregate* or *structured* data types. An aggregate or structured type is a data object type with more than a single component. Common constructors to build aggregate data types include the *array* constructor and the *record* constructor. The resulting array types have components of the same type; record types may have components of different types. Another mechanism to construct aggregate data structure types is with the use of the *access type*. Access type components in a record type provide the capability to define recursive types.

The built-in operators of high-level languages provide the mechanisms for manipulating the data objects. The built-in operators commonly include arithmetic, logical, and relational operators. High-level languages also allow programmers to define its operators and operations on data objects by means of *function* and *procedure* definitions. Modern high-level languages allow programmers to define an abstract data type completely specifying its set of operators with the set of values and structures.

High-level-language mechanisms for controlling the flow of operations include *selection, iteration,* and unconditional *goto*. Procedures and function calls also provide a form of flow control. In addition, procedures and functions define environments by grouping together a set of data objects and their operations. They define the *scope* of visibility of data object identifiers. High-level-language *blocks* are also mechanisms for defining the scope of identifiers.

Modern high-level languages provide ways of defining modules that have well-defined interfaces. This permits programs to be modularized. Modules include *packages* and *tasks*. Packages are modules for defining abstract data types; tasks are modules for concurrent processing. Associated with the task concept are mechanisms for synchronizing tasks. High-level languages also provide mechanisms for defining exceptions (abnormal events) within environments and modules and the handling of the defined exceptions.

High-level-language concepts evolved through four generations. The first generation, which includes FORTRAN I and IPL 5, provides the foundation for high-level languages. It is the first step away from assembly-level programming. The languages of the first generation developed the basic set of high-level semantics and syntaxes in the different application areas. The second generation, of which FORTRAN II, COBOL, and ALGOL 60 are the dominant members, introduced many important concepts such as recursion, dynamic data structures, blocks, and type definitions. FORTRAN and COBOL, although greatly enhanced since their inception, are still the standard languages for numerical and business programming. The high-level languages were becoming more general and flexible. The third generation, of which Pascal is an important member, refined the concepts of ALGOL 60, eliminating some of the less useful and difficult to implement concepts, while extending others such as user-defined type mechanisms. The fourth generation, of which Ada is a dominant member, is concerned with reliability, maintainability, and concurrency of high-level-language programs. The fourth-generation languages incorporate many of the concepts of ALGOL 60 and Pascal, while introducing modularization and concurrency mechanisms.

REFERENCES

[1] *Reference Manual for the Ada Programming Language,* Proposed Standard Document, Department of Defense, Washington, D.C., July 1980.

[2] R. Bernhard, "Computers: Emphasis on Software," *IEEE Spectrum,* Vol. 17, January 1980.

[3] W. P. Stevens et al., "Structured Design," in *Tutorial: Software Methodology,* C. V. Ramamoorthy and R. T. Yeh, eds., IEEE Catalog EH0 142-0.

[4] C. L. McGowan and J. K. Kelly, *Top-Down Structured Programming Techniques,* Petrocelli/Charter, New York, 1975.

[5] M. A. Jackson, "Information Systems: Modeling, Sequencing and Transformations," *Proc. 3rd Int. Conf. Software Eng.,* IEEE, 1978.

[6] H. H. Goldstine, *The Computer from Pascal to von Neumann,* Princeton University Press, Princeton, N.J., 1972.

[7] P. Wegner, "Programming Languages—The First 25 Years," *IEEE Trans. Comput.,* December 1976.

[8] P. Wegner, "Programming Languages," in *Research Directions in Software Technology,* P. Wegner, ed., MIT Press, Cambridge, Mass., 1979.

[9] E. Horowitz, *Programming Languages: A Grand Tour,* Computer Science Press, Rockville, Md., 1982.

[10] "FORTRAN vs Basic FORTRAN," *Commun. ACM,* October 1964.

[11] P. Naur, ed., "Report on the Algorithmic Language ALGOL 60," *Commun. ACM,* May 1960.

[12] *COBOL 1961: Revised Specifications for a Common Business Oriented Programming Language,* U.S. Government Printing Office, Washington, D.C., 1961.

[13] J. McCarthy et al., *LISP 1.5 Programmer's Manual,* MIT Press, Cambridge, Mass., 1965.

[14] *PL/I, Current IBM System 360 Reference Manual,* 2nd ed., Prentice-Hall, Englewood Cliffs, N.J., 1975.

[15] N. Wirth and C. A. R. Hoare, "A Contribution to the Development of ALGOL," *Commun. ACM,* Vol. 9, No. 6, June 1966.

[16] V. Wingaarden et al., "Report on the Algorithmic Language ALGOL 68," *Numer. Math.,* February 1969.

[17] N. Wirth, "The Programming Language Pascal," *Acta Inf.,* 1971.

[18] O. J. Dahl et al., "SIMULA 67 Common Base Language," *Publ. S-22,* Norwegian Computing Center, Oslo, October 1970.

[19] A. D. Falkoff and K. E. Iverson, "The APL Terminal System," in *Interactive Systems for Experimental Applied Mathematics,* M. Klerer and J. Reinfeld, eds., Academic Press, New York, 1968.

[20] R. Griswold et al., *The SNOBOL 4 Programming Language,* Prentice-Hall, Englewood Cliffs, N.J., 1971.

[21] J. G. Kemeny and T. E. Kurtz, *Basic Programming,* Wiley, New York, 1967.

[22] B. W. Kernighan and D. M. Ritchie, *The C Programming Language,* Prentice-Hall, Englewood Cliffs, N.J., 1975.

[23] B. H. Liskov et al., *CLU Reference Manual,* Laboratory for Computer Science, MIT, TR-225, October 1979.

[24] W. Wulf et al., "Abstraction and Verification in ALPHARD: Introduction to Language and Methodology," *Carnegie-Mellon Univ. Dept. Comp. Sci. Rep.,* June 1976.

[25] B. W. Lampon et al., "Report on the Programming Language Euclid," *SIGPLAN Notices, Vol. 12,* No. 2, February 1977.

[26] P. Brinch Hansen, "The Programming Language Concurrent Pascal," *IEEE Trans. Software Eng.* Vol. SE-1, No. 2, June 1975.

[27] N. Wirth, "Modula: A Language for Modular Multiprogramming," *ETH Institute for Informatics, Rep. TR18,* March 1976.

[28] M. Conrad, "Pascal Power," *Datamation,* July 1979.

[29] J. G. Poso, "Microprocessor and Microcomputers," *Electronics,* October 15, 1979.

PROBLEMS

2.1 What limits high-level-language designers from defining a large number of built-in types? What are the advantages and disadvantages of a large number of built-in types?

2.2 In what ways do Ada's mechanisms for defining subtypes and derived types allow programmers to enhance the reliability of their programs?

2.3 High-level languages are intended to facilitate a programmer's thought processes. Do the parameterized array type and the parameterized record type mechanisms achieve this purpose? If so, give examples of programming with and without these mechanisms and indicate how they might facilitate a programmer's thought processes.

2.4 In the following program excerpt

```
type IPTR is access INTEGER;
A, B, C, D, : IPTR;
A:= new INTEGER (1);
B:= new INTEGER (2);
C:= A;
D:= B;
C.all := B.all;
B:= new INTEGER (3);
```

what are the values of A.**all,** B.**all,** C.**all,** and D.**all** after the last statement is executed?

2.5 Compare the advantages and disadvantages of structural equivalence and name equivalence as notions of type compatibility. (*Hint:* Which enhances the readability of programs? Which is easier to implement?)

2.6 Rewrite the following iteration construct using the **loop** and **exit** statements only.

```
while READ (X) /= END_OF_FILE loop
    M:= READ(X);
    for I in 1..10 loop
        A(I):= I ** M;
        WRITE (A(I));
    end loop
end loop;
```

Compare the **loop** and **exit** solution with the above in terms of readability.

2.7 In the following program excerpt

```
procedure SWAP(X,Y);
    TEMP:INTEGER;
begin
    TEMP:= X;
    X:= Y;
    Y:= TEMP;
end SWAP;
for I in 1..3 loop
     A(I):= 1;
end loop;
I:= 2;
A(2):= 3;
SWAP(I,A(I));
```

what are the values of A(1), A(2), and A(3) after the SWAP procedure is invoked in the last statement of the excerpt if (a) call by value, (b) call by value-result, (c) call by reference, or (d) call by name is assumed?

2.8 In Problem 2.7, do the call by value-result and the call by reference assumptions produce the same results? If so, why? Suppose that the SWAP procedure in Problem 2.7 terminates abnormally. Do the call by value-result and the call by reference assumptions produce the same results? Why?

2.9 Top-down design is a proposed programming methodology for developing large programs. In this methodology, the design is decomposed into small programs called modules. All the module interfaces and behaviors are specified. The implementation of each module can then proceed independently. How does this methodology relate to the Ada's mechanisms for defining and programming modules?

2.10 In what ways are the built-in types of high-level languages abstractions like abstract data types?

2.11 What are some possible ways to program exceptions and exception handling in high-level languages that do not provide built-in exception and exception-handling mechanisms?

3

Compilation Process and Model of Implementation

3.1 INTRODUCTION

Compilation is the process of translating a high-level language into a language interpretable by the computer. The program that performs the translation is the compiler. Based on a *model of implementation* that represents high-level-language concepts, the compiler generates the code that runs on the machine. Some high-level-language concepts are handled completely by the compiler at compile time. Other concepts are run-time issues. The compile-time issues determine the complexity and efficiency of the compiler; they are transparent to the machine architecture. The run-time issues determine the complexity of the code generator of the compiler and the efficiency of the generated code running on a particular computer.

This chapter discusses the implementation of the high-level-language concepts reviewed in Chapter 2. After presenting an overview of the compilation process, it introduces the model of implementation and discusses the implementation of data objects, types, and flow control. It describes ways of implementing program units such as blocks, subprograms, packages, and tasks. This chapter also covers the implementation of exceptions, exception handling, and the allocation of storage for representing high-level-language concepts.

3.2 COMPILATION

A *compiler* is a program that translates programs written in a high-level language to their semantic equivalents in a machine instruction set. It filters out the aspects of the high-level language that are of no concern to the run-time environment, such as the syntax, the comments, the blanks, and the tabs. It also filters out certain errors in the semantics (such as type inconsistencies). A compiler is usually built in two sections: the front end and the back end. The front end performs lexical, syntactic, and semantic analyses and generates an intermediate representation of the high-level-language programs. The back end allocates storage, allocates and assigns registers, and generates code from the intermediate representation.

3.2.1 Lexical Analysis

The front end of a compiler is usually implemented in three phases: lexical analysis, syntactic analysis, and semantic analysis. The phases may execute as subroutines and coroutines or sequentially in multiple passes over the program to be compiled. For instance, the first phase, lexical analysis, may execute as a subroutine of the second phase, syntactic analysis. The *lexical analyzer* scans a program and recognizes basic symbols or *tokens* of the high-level language. The tokens consist of identifiers, literals, keywords, and operators; they are delineated by blanks, operators, special symbols, and punctuation marks. Each token may be represented (stored) by the compiler as an integer. This permits the later phases of a compiler to work with fixed-length integers rather than variable-length character strings. Each of the integers is an index into a table of all possible token syntactic types. Unique integers identify each operator and keyword. Identifiers and literals share a single integer; to distinguish among them, a second integer is used in their representation. The second integer of the pair is an index into a data structure (the symbol table) containing the rest of the information about the identifier or literal including the actual literal value and the spelling of the identifier. The *symbol table* contains the semantic information associated with each identifier or literal. In producing the tokens, the lexical analyzer also deletes the comments of a program and performs textual substitutions for macros.

3.2.2 Syntactic Analysis

Once a program (or a statement of a program) has been decomposed into a sequence of tokens, the tokens are passed through the *syntactic analyzer* or *parser*. The parser recognizes from the sequence of tokens the syntactic constructions (declarations, statements, control structures, and specifications) of the high-level language. When it recognizes a syntactic construction, the parser runs an *action routine* that converts the construction into a *parse tree* according to the rules of the language's *grammar*.* A parse tree is a graphical representation of the hierarchical syntactic structure of a program's syntactic constructions. The rules of the grammar specify the language's syntactic structure. For example, the syntactic construct

```
x := (a+b)*c + d;
```

*There are many types of parsers (e.g., operator precedence, recursive descent, LL, and LR) and many types of grammars (e.g., operator, operator precedence, LL, and LR). A discussion of these is beyond the scope of this book. They are aptly covered in references 1 and 2.

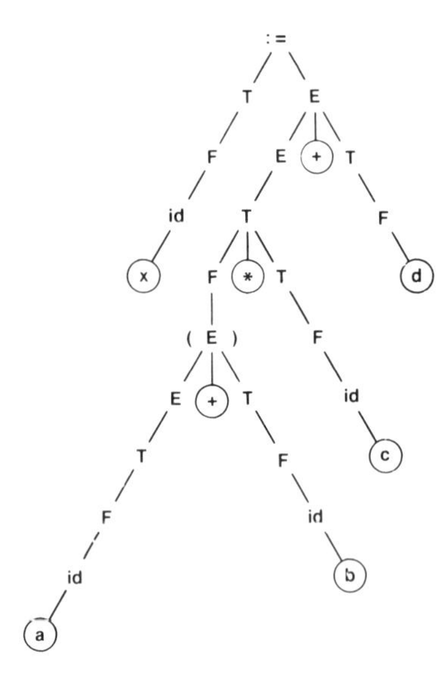

Figure 3.1 Parse tree for $x := (a + b)*c + d$.

may be parsed into the parse tree shown in Fig. 3.1 using this production rule grammar:

Rules of Grammar		Abbreviation
Expression	→ Expression + Term	E → E + T
Expression	→ Term	E → T
Term	→ Factor * Term	T → F * T
Factor	→ (Expression)	F → (E)
Term	→ Factor	T → F
Factor	→ Identifier	F → id

The parse tree in Fig. 3.1 is in fact a subtree of a larger tree that represents the source program itself. To build a parse tree, the parser needs only to examine the integer representation of the tokens. For identifiers and literals, it needs to know only the first integer of the integer pair. That is, the parser only needs to know the syntactic type of each token, not the semantic information associated with it.

The lexical analyzer usually runs as a subroutine of the parser, returning the integer representation of each token to the parser. The second integer in an integer pair denoting an identifier or literal token indexes into the symbol table. The symbol table contains the attribute information associated with all the identifiers and literals used in the source program. The identifiers and attributes include those listed in Table 3.1. These lists are not all-inclusive; nor must every identifier have all the attributes. When the parser recognizes a declaration, for example, it fills in the appropriate attribute information in the symbol table. Some high-level languages allow identifiers to be implicitly declared (for example, identifiers starting with the characters I through N in FORTRAN are implicitly declared as integers). Most languages also use the syntax to implicitly declare identifiers to be labels

TABLE 3.1 IDENTIFIERS AND ATTRIBUTES

Identifiers	Attributes
Data object names	Types
Type names	Structural templates or types and subtypes
Subtype names	Ranges of values
Parameter names	Initialized values
Block names	Bases
Program unit names	Scales
Operator names	Precisions
Loop names	Run-time addresses
Statement labels	Types of parameter correspondences (call by value, call by name, etc.)
	Types of program units (functions, packages, tasks, etc.)
	Block structures (lexical levels)

(an identifier followed by a colon followed by a statement is a label), and procedure specification syntax to implicitly declare procedure names and formal parameters. These implicitly declared identifiers and their attributes are entered by the parser into the symbol table.

As the lexical analyzer scans a program, it enters newly found identifiers and literals into the symbol table if they are not there already. Some languages, however, permit the same character string to denote tokens of different types. For example, the character string *IN* within a procedure may denote a procedure name, a label, or a keyword. For these languages, the lexical analyzer cannot determine the type of the token and its integer representation. The parser must use the syntactic context to determine the type of the token.

To facilitate the search of the symbol table for the entry containing information about an identifier or literal, the spelling of the identifier or literal may be hashed into a pointer to a symbol table entry. Since multiple spellings may hash to the same pointer, *chaining* can be used to link together all the symbol table entries containing identifiers or literals that hash to the same value. This scheme is illustrated in Fig. 3.2, where SPELLING(i + k), SPELLING(i + 2), and SPELLING(i) all hash to the same pointer.

To support block-structured languages in which the same identifier may appear in different blocks referring to different objects, the symbol table contains block structure information. There are various ways of representing block structure information in a symbol table. One method is to associate each identifier and literal with a unique number corresponding to the program unit that defines a scope for it. As the parser recognizes the syntactic constructions denoting the beginning and end of these environments, identifiers and literals declared within an environment (program unit) are paired with a unique number assigned to that program unit.

It is not necessary to represent block structure information in the symbol table this way. An alternative is to organize the symbol table as linked list. Environment nodes are created to denote blocks, subprograms, and modules defining the scopes of the identifiers. The environment nodes are linked together as shown in Fig. 3.3. The nesting of program units is described by the order of the linked list. Each environment node links to a list of symbol nodes denoting the identifiers and literals declared in that program unit.

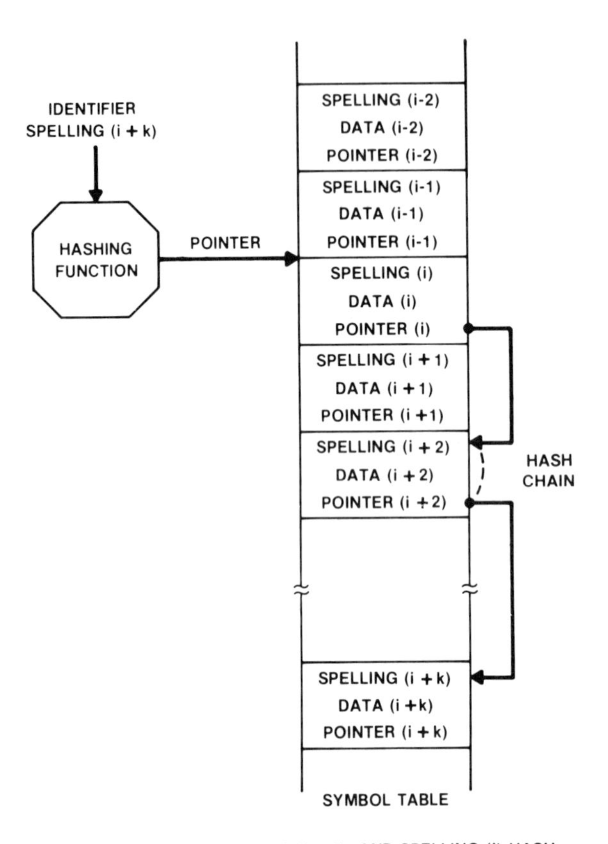

Figure 3.2 Hashed symbol table.

Symbol table entries contain attribute information that requires different amounts of storage for its representation. Identifiers denoting scalar types and variables have fixed requirements on the amount of storage needed for their representation. They may be completely specified in a symbol table entry. Identifiers denoting aggregate types and variables are usually represented by *indirection*. For example, the array type MATRIX

type MATRIX **is array**(1...N,1...M) **of** INTEGERS;

may be represented as shown in Fig. 3.4. The record type PERSON

```
type PERSON is
    record
        FIRST:CHARACTER;
        LAST:CHARACTER;
    end record;
```

may be represented as shown in Fig. 3.5.

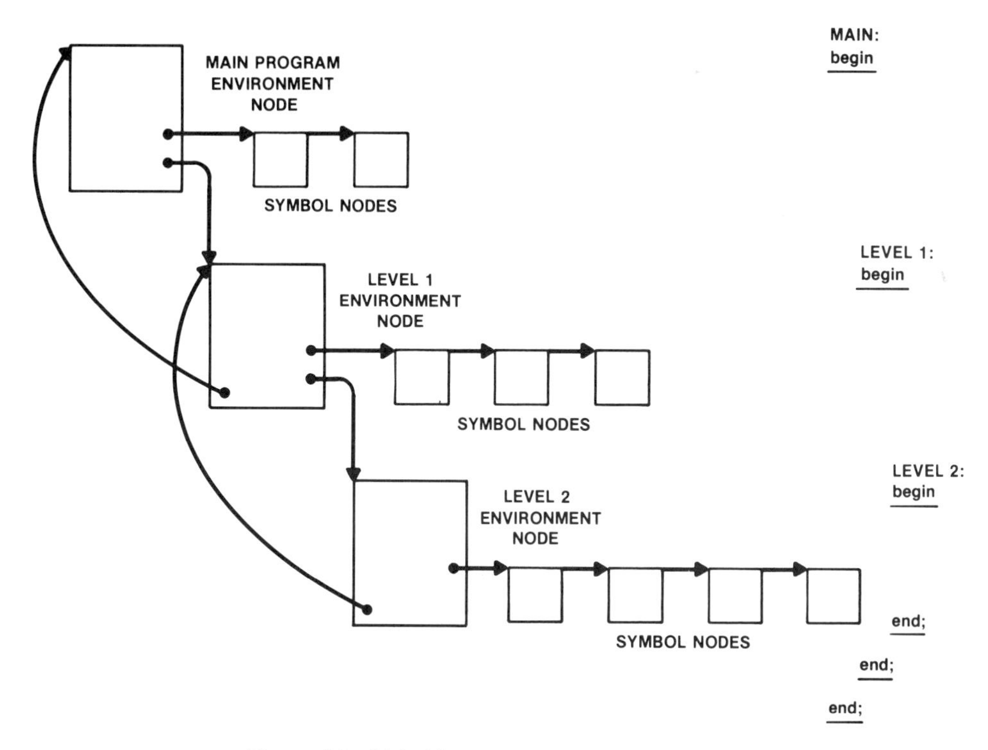

Figure 3.3 Linked list representation of block structure.

The parser, with the cooperation of the lexical analyzer, transforms the source program written in a high-level language into a parse tree and a symbol table. The symbol table describes the objects, their types, their values, their structures, their names, and the environments in which these objects are visible; the parse tree describes the manipulations of these objects and the flow control of the manipulations.

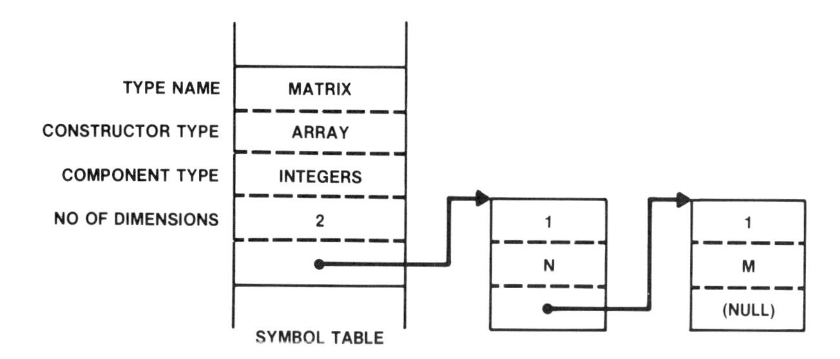

Figure 3.4 Symbol table representation of arrays.

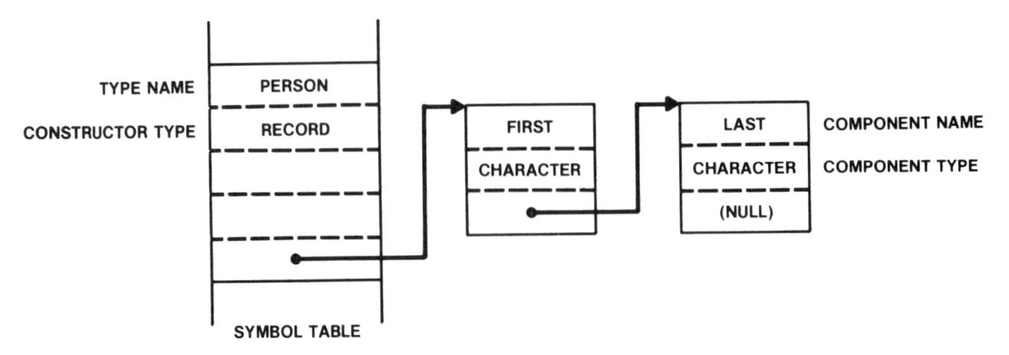

Figure 3.5 Symbol table representation of records.

A parse tree is an intermediate representation of the syntactical structure of the program. When a parse tree is produced, it usually contains redundant information. Such redundant information can be eliminated during syntactical analysis to produce an *abstract syntax tree*. An abstract syntax tree contains an operator for each node and an operand for each leaf. For example, the parse tree in Fig. 3.1 may be reduced to the abstract syntax tree in Fig. 3.6.

During syntactic analysis, the parser detects syntactic errors when constructs do not result in a legal action routine. Some high-level languages, like Ada, also have context-dependent syntax rules. Some examples of Ada's context-dependent syntax rules include these:

1. The literals in an enumeration type definition must be distinct.
2. A fixed-point type declaration must include a range constraint.
3. An **exit** statement is only allowed within a loop.
4. An **accept** statement is only allowed within a task body.
5. A **private** type declaration is only allowed as a declarative item of the visible part of a package.
6. All parameters of a function must have the mode **in**.

Adherence to these rules is checked after the abstract syntax tree is built and before semantic analysis.

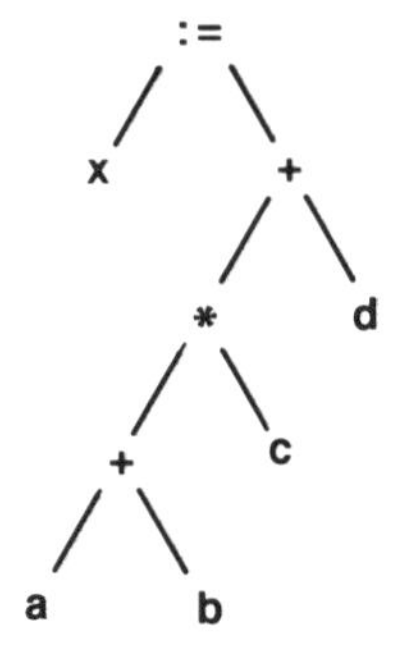

Figure 3.6 Abstract syntax tree for $x := (a + b) * c + d$.

3.2.3 Semantic Analysis

An abstract syntax tree does not contain any semantic information. Each node of the tree represents a syntactic type. *Semantic analysis* assigns semantic information to each identifier node of the tree. It associates each identifier node with an entry in the symbol table containing semantic information for that node. The resulting tree is interwoven with the symbol table.

Just as the syntactic analyzer checks the program's adherence to the syntactic rules of the language, the semantic analyzer checks the program's adherence to the *static semantic rules*. The static semantic rules are the nonsyntactic rules that may be checked at compile time (that is, they do not require run-time values). Examples of static semantic rules include these: the types of operands must be equivalent in an expression; **case** statements must be exhaustive; **goto** statements must not transfer control out of a subprogram body; and, the range of subtypes must be a subrange of the parent types.

Type checking is a large part of the semantic analyzer's activities. Semantic analysis associates each operand with its type, determines the type of every expression, and checks that the types of operands in an expression are consistent. It also clarifies the semantics of overloaded operators by determining the types of the operands, and inserts a conversion operator node into the abstract syntax tree to support the implicit and explicit conversions allowed by the high-level language. Semantic analysis also evaluates static expressions whenever necessary while performing semantic rule checks or processing declarations. As an example, semantic analysis transforms the abstract syntax tree of Fig.

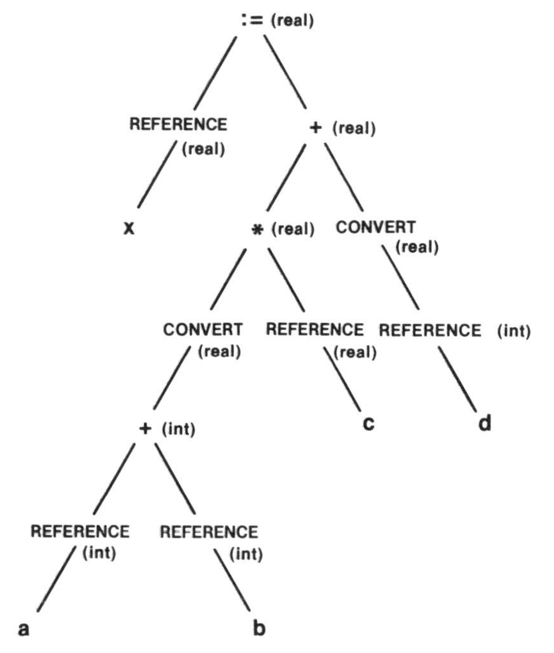

Figure 3.7 Decorated tree for $x := (a + b) * c + d$.

3.6 into the tree of Fig. 3.7, where x and c are reals, and a, b, and d are integers. This *decorated tree* (decorated with semantic information and conversion nodes) is an *intermediate representation* of the high-level program statement x:= (a+b)*c +d;

3.2.4 Compiler Back Ends

There are other forms of intermediate representation used by compilers, including *Polish notation, triples,* and *quadruples.** It is desirable for the intermediate representation of a high-level-language program to be independent of the high-level language as well as of the machine's architecture. That is, different compiler *front ends* (lexical, syntactic, and semantic analyzers) may be used to translate different high-level languages into the same intermediate representation. Similarly, different compiler *back ends* (*storage allocators, register allocators,* and *code generators*) may be used to translate the same intermediate representation into the machine code of different architectures. The careful design of the intermediate representation following a strategy of partitioning the compiler into distinct front and back ends minimizes the development effort when an existing compiler is modified to support a different high-level language and when an existing compiler is ported to another machine.

The intermediate representation should be the boundary between machine-independent and machine-dependent optimizations. A machine-independent optimization is performed on the intermediate representation as a part of the activities of the front end. Machine-independent optimizations include:

1. Elimination of common subexpressions (that is, subexpressions occurring more than once in the same statement should be computed only once).
2. Allocation of only a single copy of a constant.
3. Reordering expression evaluation to minimize the number of temporary variables required.
4. Elimination of all induction variables except one in a loop.
5. Generation of only a single copy of an argument list if two functions or subroutines have the same arguments.
6. Movement of computations involving nonvarying operands out of loops (code motion).
7. Use of the properties of Boolean expressions to minimize their computation. For example, a high-level-language statement with expression A logically ANDed with another expression B may be optimally compiled into intermediate code that com-

*For a discussion of these, see references 1 and 2.

putes the less complex expression of the two (for example, A) and tests it. If A is false, it bypasses (branches around) the computation for expression B.

Symbol table entries are representations of the declarations of data objects and their types; of program unit specifications, parameters, entries, and exceptions; and of statement labels and literals. Decorated trees are representations of the program manipulations and flow control. These are the *static representations* needed by the various phases of the compiler for translating a high-level-language program. Implementing a compiler back end requires determining the *run-time representation* of the data objects and their types; of program units, parameters, and exceptions; of statement labels and literals; and of data object manipulations and flow control. The run-time representation is sometimes referred to as the *model of implementation* of a high-level language.

Once the run-time representation and the machine address organization is known, the compiler may perform *storage allocation* for static data objects. Static data objects are data objects whose size and structure do not vary during program execution. Each static data object may be allocated storage and assigned an address relative to some origin.* Storage allocation routines also assign temporary locations for storing the intermediate results of the program. The run-time addresses are made part of the information associated with data objects in the symbol table. That is, for each data object, an address descriptor to keep track of its location at run time is stored in the symbol table. Storage allocation is a back-end activity.

Another activity of the back end is *register allocation and assignment*. Register allocation and assignment determines which program data objects should be stored in a register and assigns actual physical registers (register numbers) to selected data objects. Some compilers keep a count of the static references to a variable and allocate registers to variables with high counts. Compilers may also allocate registers to variables and loop indexes within a loop. Compilers may attempt to keep track of the run-time contents of the registers to check for optimization by eliminating redundant load and store operations to memory. Register allocation and assignment is sometimes performed as a part of code generation. The allocation and assignment algorithm must be congruent with the machine register set and the model of implementation.

Code generation is the process of transforming the intermediate representation into *object code, assembly code,* or code in some other language where a compiler or interpreter already exists. Object code may be *absolute* (that is, absolute addresses in the code are possible) or *relocatable* (no absolute addresses in the code are allowed). Relocatable object code may be separately compiled, linked together, and loaded with other relocatable object code for execution.

For each source code sequence, the code generator may produce many object code sequences to perform the same computation. The code generator must decide (1) which machine instructions to use, (2) which sequential order of instructions to generate, and (3)

*The absolute address cannot be assigned for local static data objects that are allocated storage on the run-time stack.

which variables to assign to registers. Different code sequences may require different numbers of instructions and different numbers of registers. For example, the high-level-language statement

A = B*C + D*E

may be parsed and reduced to the following tree:

The code generator executes a *tree walk* to produce one of these possible code sequences:*

Code Sequence 1

```
MOVW B,R1          --R1 contains B
MOVW, C,R2         --R2 contains C
MULW3 R1,R2,R3     --R3 contains B*C
MOVW D,R1          --R1 reused, contains D
MOVW E,R2          --R2 reused, contains E
MULW2 R1,R2        --R2 contains D*E
ADDW2 R2,R3        --R3 contains B*C+D*E
MOVW R3,A          --A contains B*C+D*E
```

Code Sequence 2

```
MULW3 B,C,R1       --R1 contains B*C
MULW3 D,E,R2       --R2 contains D*E
ADDW3 R1,R2,A      --A contains B*C+D*E
```

Code Sequence 3

```
MULW3 B,C,R1       --R1 contains B*C
MOVW R1,A          --A contains B*C
MULW3 D,E,R1       --R1 contains D*E
ADDW2 R1,A         --A contains D*E+B*C
```

Code sequences 2 and 3 are possible on machines with architectures that permit operations to be directly performed on store operands.

At each node of the tree, several alternative implementations may be available to the

*The assembly notation used in the example sequences are from the VAX 11/780 instructions set [3].

code generator. The alternatives are kept in *code templates*. Following is an example of a code template for the + operator:

<table>
<tr><td rowspan="2">oper1</td><td colspan="2">oper2</td></tr>
<tr><td>RN</td><td>OP2 (store variable)</td></tr>
<tr><td>RM</td><td>ADDW2 RN, RM
or
ADDW2 RM, RN
or
ADDW3 RM, RN, R</td><td>MOVW OP2, R
ADDW2 RM, R
or
ADDW2 OP2, RM
or
ADDW2 RM, OP2
or
ADDW3 OP2, RM, R</td></tr>
<tr><td>OP1
(store variable)</td><td>MOVW OP1,R
ADDW2 RN, R
or
ADDW2 OP1, RN
or
ADDW2 RN, OP1
or
ADDW3 OP1, RN, R</td><td>MOVW OP2, R
ADDW2 OP1, R
or
MOVW OP1, R
ADDW2 OP2, R
or
ADDW2 OP1, OP2
or
or
ADDW3 OP1, OP2, R</td></tr>
</table>

The alternatives specified in the code template for an operator node depend on the branches (operands) of the node. In this example, the operands oper1 and oper2 may be in registers (RM and RN) or in main store with addresses OP1 and OP2, respectively. The alternatives also depend on the resources available (that is, whether there are free registers) when the point of execution is reached. In this example, R is a free register. The alternatives also depend on the type of instructions (for example, ADDW2, MOVW, and ADDW3) and the addressing modes (such as register operand or store operand) available in the machine. Finally, the alternatives depend on where the compiler stores the results of the operation. On encountering an operator node, the compiler determines all these conditions and selects one of the alternatives from the code template.

The template becomes more complicated in real machines where there are more alternative addressing modes that can be used to access the store variable. Hence, even a simple subtree with an add operator node with two operands contains many alternatives. The code generator analyzes each alternative in the template according to predefined cost metrics. In the example above, the different code sequences use different instructions and a different number of registers. Each has a different execution time and code size. The code generator analyzes each alternative in terms of its contribution to the cost of a larger subtree. The cost depends on the hardware implementation of the target machine. The cost of an alternative using registers also depends on the number of free registers, the current contents of the registers, and the future possible uses of the registers. Registers, besides being faster, also support various addressing modes (such as indexing), which causes the cost analysis to be even more complex. Because it is unfeasible for the code generator to examine all the alternatives, code generators must follow some heuristics. Although there are algorithms for optimizing code generation, they are restricted to idealized machines [4].

3.2.4.1 Machine-dependent optimizations.

Code generation optimizations constitute a large part of machine-dependent optimizations. Knowing the machine's data types and formats, compiler designers can perform certain other machine-dependent code optimizations. These include:

1. Compile-time computations of operations whose operands are constants to save both space and execution time for the object code
2. Compile-time constant conversions
3. Compile-time evaluations of constant subscript expressions in array calculations

Machine-dependent optimizations are more difficult to implement in a compiler than machine-independent optimizations. Efficient register allocation and assignment and the efficient use of a machine's instruction set require extensive compiler code.

3.2.4.2 Peephole optimization.

Code generation attempts to optimize the code sequence for a subtree. The code sequence that is optimal for a subtree when juxtaposed with the code sequence for another subtree may result in a suboptimal sequence of instructions. Many compilers have another optimization phase after the code is generated for the whole program. This phase is called *peephole optimization*. Peephole optimization looks at a small sequence of instructions at a time. Some of the optimization include these:

1. Replacing a jump instruction to another jump instruction with a single instruction.
2. Removing redundant loads and stores
3. Removing unreachable code
4. Reversing the sense of tests in conditional jumps
5. Eliminating jumps over jumps
6. Eliminating algebraic identities (e.g., $x=x*1$)
7. Replacing an expensive operation with a cheaper one (e.g., x^2 *by* $x*x$)
8. Combining instructions by utilizing some of the machine's special instructions and addressing modes

Peephole optimizations are also part of machine-dependent optimizations.

3.3 MODEL OF IMPLEMENTATION

To generate code for a high-level language, the compiler must know the run-time representations of the concepts of the language. The collection of run-time structures to implement the concepts of a high-level language is called its *model of implementation*.

A model of implementation is important because it provides a cohesive framework for designing a high-level language. Without a model of implementation, the design of the language may include complexities that are extremely difficult for a compiler to handle. FORTRAN is based on a model of implementation in which subroutine and COMMON storage areas occupy fixed-size storage blocks. Each object in a storage block is characterized by an address relative to the beginning of the block. No storage allocation is dynamic during program execution. Because of its fixed storage allocation scheme, the model of implementation restricts the language from having arrays with dynamic bounds and recursive routines.

ALGOL 60 is based on a stack model of implementation. It handles arrays with dynamic bounds and recursive routines. However, it cannot handle pointer-valued variables or procedures that return procedures as their values. ALGOL 68 can be modeled with a run-time environment with two stacks and one heap. SIMULA 67 requires each created instance of a class to be modeled by a stack. PL/I has no clear model of implementation. It was designed entirely using a top-down approach; an underlying model of implementation was not considered during its development. In general, however, the design of a high-level language still depends on a model of implementation. Languages designed without models of implementation are difficult to support. The remainder of this chapter presents the run-time mechanisms used to represent and implement the high-level-language concepts discussed in Chapter 2.

The mechanisms discussed in the following sections are examples of the implementations of high-level-language concepts. Many alternative mechanisms exist. The efficiency of a particular model of implementation is highly machine dependent; models should be chosen based on the capabilities of the underlying hardware that executes them.

3.4 DATA OBJECTS

To implement high-level-language data objects, the compiler needs to determine their run-time representations, their storage allocation, their access mechanisms and the access mechanisms of their subcomponents, the run-time structures needed to implement their scopes, and the run-time representations of their attributes.

Compilers represent data objects at run time as a set of bits in memory locations. Compilers represent data object *names* as the addresses of the memory locations containing the set of bits. The bit pattern represents the value of the data object. The way the bit pattern is encoded depends on the type of the data object. Data objects of different types require different instructions to interpret their bit representations and require different layouts in linear memory space.

Each data object name has a *lifetime* and a *scope*. The lifetime of a name is the time the name is bound to memory locations. When the lifetimes of two names* overlap, the names must be bound to disjoint locations. Names bound to memory locations at any moment in time are not all usable (referenceable). The scope is that part of the program over which a name is usable. Lifetime is a dynamic property; scope is a static property.

*The exception is when the two names are aliases of the same data object.

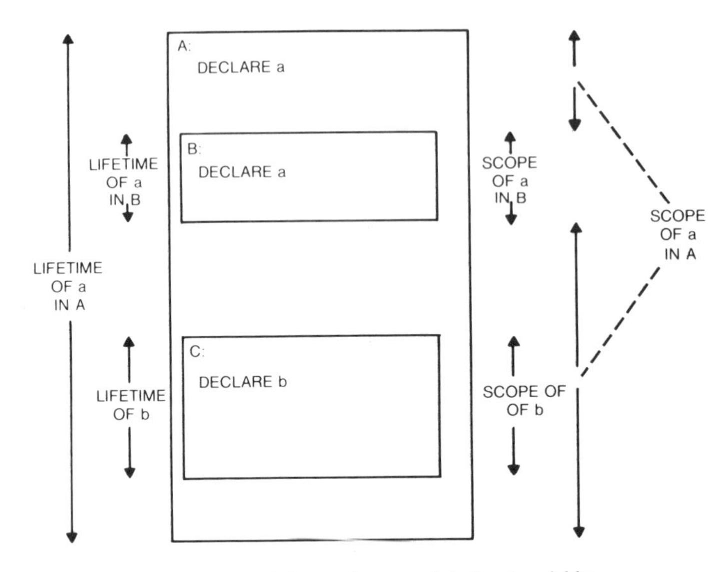

Figure 3.8 Lifetime and scope of declared variables.

For example, in Fig. 3.8, the lifetimes of the same name **a** in different procedures **A** and **B** overlap. They are bound at run time to distinct memory locations. In the different procedures, the same name **a** has different scopes. When name **a** in **A** is usable, name **a** in **B** is not, and vice versa, even though they coexist while procedure **B** is active. On the other hand, the lifetimes of the distinct names **a** in procedure **B** and **b** in procedure **C** do not overlap and may be bound to the same memory location during different times of program execution.

3.5 TYPES

High-level languages are *typed languages* in which the interpretation of a data object is determined by its declared type. A data object type specifies the structure of the data object as well as the set of values and set of operations to which each of its components may be subjected. Data object types determine the interpretation of generic operators in an expression. For example, in the expression A + B, the meaning of + is determined by the type(s) of A and B. Most machine languages, on the other hand, are *typeless languages* in which the interpretation of a data object is determined by the operator applied to it. For example, in the instructions

```
ADD M1, M2          --Integer add instruction
FADD M1, M2         --Floating-point add instruction
```

the interpretation of operands M1 and M2 (that is, the interpretation of the bit pattern in memory locations M1 and M2) depends on the opcodes ADD and FADD. The different opcodes interpret and manipulate the bits in different ways to carry out respectively the integer add and floating-point add operations.

The run-time model on a von Neumann machine of a high-level-language data object depends on the data object type. The type of data object specifies its attributes. The attributes are collected and placed in the symbol table by the compiler as it processes a declaration statement. The compiler uses the type declaration to determine the representation of an object and the amount of storage to be allocated.

Operations between objects with static attributes may be checked during compilation to ensure that they are meaningful; this is called *type checking*. To manipulate and access objects with static attributes, the compiler's code generator generates the appropriate instruction types and addressing modes based on the attributes.

Some languages, such as SNOBOL and APL, permit the *dynamic binding* (binding that occurs during program execution) of attributes to an object. Dynamic binding allows attributes to be changed while the program is running. To support dynamic binding, the compiler must generate code that examines the data type during program execution and, depending on the type, must call a routine to allocate storage dynamically and perform the correct machine operations. Languages like Ada permit variably sized arrays and variant records in which the attributes of an object may change dynamically. To accommodate dynamically changing attributes, the languages place the attributes in a template linked to the data object itself. The template becomes the run-time representation of the data object type.

3.5.1 Built-In Types

High-level-language built-in types include integer, real (fixed and float), Boolean, and character. As discussed in Chapter 2, these types are predefined by the high-level languages. High-level-language built-in types often correspond to built-in *instruction types* in computers. The instruction types commonly include integer instructions, floating-point instructions, packed decimal instructions, logical and test instructions (to operate on Boolean operands), and various conversion instructions (such as packed decimal to integer and floating point to integer). The instruction types determine how a set of bits are encoded, interpreted, and manipulated by the machine. The special ways bits are encoded determine the various *machine data types*.

Machine data types may have a variety of representations in different machines. The representations differ in size (number of bits) and in the way the bits are encoded. The representations are machine specific and so is the hardware that interprets them. An example of the sizes and ranges of machine data types in the VAX 11/780 is shown in Table 3.2.

Different computers use different encodings for characters. Many computers use the American Standard Code for Information Interchange (ASCII) while IBM uses the Extended Binary Coded Decimal Interchange Code (EBCDIC). Hardware can convert from the ASCII representation of the characters to the EBCDIC representation. Boolean data is encoded as zeroes and ones. Floating-point numbers are encoded as mantissa-exponent

TABLE 3.2 SIZE AND RANGE OF DATA ELEMENTS

Data Type	Size	Range (decimal)	
Integer		Signed	Unsigned
Byte	8 bits	−128 to 127	0 to 255
Word	16 bits	−32,768 to 32,767	0 to 65,535
Long word	32 bits	−2**31 to 2**31-1	0 to 2**32-1
Quad word	64 bits	−2**63 to 2**63-1	0 to 2**64-1
Floating point	32 bits	+/−2.9*10**-37 to 1.7*10**38, approximately seven decimal digits precision	
Double floating point	64 bits	Approximately 16 decimal digits precision	
Packed decimal	0 to 16 bytes (31 digits)	Numeric, two digits per byte, sign in low half of last byte	
Character string	0 to 65,535 bytes	One character per byte	
Variable-length bit field	0 to 32 bits	Dependent on interpretation	

Source: Reference 3.

TABLE 3.3 IEEE FLOATING-POINT STANDARD ENCODING[a]

Single-precision format:

s	e	f
0	1 … 8	9 … 31

Double-precision format:

s	e	f
0	1 … 11	12 … 63

[a]s, sign; e, exponent; f, fraction.

Source: Reference 5.

pairs. The Institute of Electrical and Electronic Engineers (IEEE) floating-point standard encoding is shown in Table 3.3.

The standardization of floating-point data type encoding and the associated interpretation and manipulation of the encoded bit pattern ensures that machines adhering to the standards produce identical numeric results in the presence of exceptional conditions such as overflow, underflow, and denormalization.

3.5.2 Scalar Types

Scalar types are object types with a single component. They include built-in types, enumeration types, subtypes, and derived types. Scalar data objects are usually represented by at most two 32-bit words. Some floating-point-number representations may require four words; packed decimal numbers, depending on the precision, require multiple words (as in the example in Table 3.2). The packed decimal numbers on the IBM S/360 require up to 31 digits plus a sign; they are represented by four words (16 bytes, with each half-byte representing a digit). Integers are usually represented by one 32-bit word, one half-word (16 bits), or one byte depending on their range. Eight-bit quantities (bytes) usually represent characters.

3.5.2.1 Enumeration types. A high-level-language enumeration type specifies a set of literals that objects of the type may assume as their values. The set of literals may be conveniently represented by the compiler as a set of integers at run time. For example, the enumeration type definition

type DAY **is** (SUN,MON,TUE,WED,THU,FRI,SAT);

may be represented by integers in the range of 1 through 7.

The data object declaration and assignment statements

```
TODAY:DAY;
TODAY:=WED;
```

at run time are implemented with TODAY as an integer with a value initialized to 4. For run-time input and output of enumeration type objects, the compiler must generate code to convert literal values to their corresponding integer values, and vice versa.

Using integers to represent enumeration literals is consistent with Ada's specification of ordering among enumeration literals, and with its use of enumeration literals as control variable values in an iteration. For example, WED<THU is consistent with the representations 4<5, and

```
for TODAY in MON .. WED loop
    .
    .
    .
end loop;
```

is consistent with the control variable assuming the values 2, 3, and 4 in the iteration.

3.5.2.2 Subtypes. Ada's subtypes are types with range constraints. For example,

subtype DIGITS **is** INTEGER **range** 0..9;

and

COUNT:DIGITS;

The machine representation of the data object (in this case, COUNT) is the same as the representation of the parent type (INTEGER). To support the concept of subtype, the compiler generates *range checking* code whenever a value is assigned to the data object COUNT. That is, it generates code to check that the value falls within the range 0 through 9 specified by COUNT's type DIGITS.

3.5.2.3 Derived types. Derived types in Ada inherit the set of values, and all the operators, from a previously defined parent type. Derived types share the same representation of the parent type. Derived types and their parent type, however, are nonequivalent and cannot be mixed in an expression or an assignment statement. The compiler performs checking at compile-time. That is, during semantic analysis the compiler checks the validity of expressions and assignment statements by checking the types of the operands for incompatibility between a derived type and other derived types and between a derived type and its parent type. A derived type may also constrain the range of values in the set of its parent type. In this case, the implementation of the derived type requires a combination of compile-time checking for type compatibility and the compiler-generated code for run-time range checking.

3.5.3 Structured Types

Data objects of structured types are commonly referred to as data structures. Data structures are aggregates of components in which the components obey well-defined structural relationships. In high-level languages, data structures and components of data structures are directly referred to by names such as A, A(30), and EMPLOYEE.DEPT. To implement these high-level references, compilers transform the names into memory location addresses. But before the compiler is written to perform these transformations, the compiler writers and computer architects must decide how to represent the structures in one-dimensional memory and the addressing modes needed to access them.

How data structures are represented in a one-dimensional memory has much to do with the way they are accessed. The representations should be compact and facilitate accesses.

3.5.3.1 Arrays. Chapter 2 defines arrays as data structures whose components have the same type and size. To take advantage of this property, the components of arrays are usually stored in consecutive memory locations. Representing arrays this way allows array components to be accessed by an index relative to the beginning of the array. The index is a measure of the distance along an array dimension and corresponds directly to the high-level-language index in an array component reference. For example, A(10) is a specific example of the array component reference format ARRAY_NAME(index). The high-level-language index 10 is used to locate the array component named A(10) in the machine representation. In other words, components of an array are found at integral points from a lower limit to an upper limit along each dimension. This representation allows the retrieval or modification of the values of random components in an array in a constant amount of time once the index is given. It allows the compiler to translate a name $A(i_1, i_2, \ldots, i_n)$ directly to the correct location in memory. In general, the address for A $(i_1, i_2, \ldots, i_n)$ in a row major order representation is

$$\alpha + s \sum_{j=1}^{n} (i_j - 1)\, a_j \text{ with } \begin{cases} a_j = \prod_{k=j+1}^{n} u_k \text{ where } 1 \le j \le n \\ a_n = 1 \end{cases}$$

where α is the address of the first component of the array, s is the number of memory bytes that each array component occupies, and u_k is the number of components in the kth dimension. The compiler determines the number of bytes, s, by examining the component type in the array type definition:

> **type** TYPENAME **is array** (''index definition'') **of** ''component type'';

The component type is a previously defined type (scalar or structured) having a known number of bytes, s. The compiler determines the number of components in the index dimension, u_k, from the index definition by subtracting the lower limit from the upper limit plus one in the range specified for the kth dimension. For example, in the array type definitions,

> **type** ARRAY_ELEMENTS **is array** (1 .. 4) **of** INTEGER;
> **type** ARRAY_EXAMPLE **is array** (1 .. 5, 5 .. 20, 2 .. 10) **of**
> ARRAY_ELEMENTS;

data objects with type ARRAY_ELEMENTS have sizes four times the size of INTEGER, or 16 bytes (assuming data with INTEGER type occupies four bytes). The number of components in the three dimensions in ARRAY_EXAMPLE are determined from the ranges given in the ARRAY_EXAMPLE type definition: $u_1 = 5$, $u_2 = 16$, and $u_3 = 9$.

In a row major order representation, the components are stored so that the subscript at the right moves the fastest, the subscript second from the right moves the second fastest, and so on. For a three-dimensional array A having a type with index definition 1...2, 1...2, 1...3 in which each component occupies four memory bytes, the representation in computer memory has the order A(1,1,1), A (1,1,2), A(1,1,3), A(1,2,1), A(1,2,2), A(1,2,3), A(2,1,1), A(2,1,2), A(2,1,3), A(2,2,1), A(2,2,2), and A(2,2,3). Applying the formula above to the high-level language reference A(2,1,2) and noting that $s = 4$ bytes, $i_1 = 2$, $i_2 = 1$, $i_3 = 2$, $u_1 = 2$, $u_2 = 2$, and $u_3 = 3$, the following address is obtained:

$$\begin{aligned} \text{address of } A(2,1,2) &= \text{address of } A(1,1,1) + \\ &\quad [(2\text{-}1)(2)(3) + (1\text{-}1)(3) + (1)(1)]*4 \text{ bytes} \\ &= \text{address of } A(1,1,1) + 28 \text{ bytes} \end{aligned}$$

This result may be verified by counting 28 bytes or seven components to the right of A(1,1,1), which is A(2,1,2).

The computation of addresses in a row order major representation using the equation above each time an array component is randomly accessed is time consuming, especially as the number of dimensions of an array increases. To alleviate this problem, the compiler may generate an *array descriptor block* (also known as a *dope vector*) for each array. For an array with N dimensions in which the number of components in the nth dimension is u_n, the array descriptor block is a linear array with $N + 1$ entries. The nth entry of the array descriptor block stores the product of $s(u_1)(u_2) \ldots (u_{n-1})$, where s is the size of each component of the array being described. Thus, the following dope vector describes an array having N dimensions, where the number of components in the nth dimension is u_n and where each array component is four bytes long:

$$\begin{aligned}
DV(1) &= 4\\
DV(2) &= (4)(u_1)\\
DV(3) &= (4)(u_1)(u_2)\\
&\ \ \vdots\\
DV(N) &= (4)(u_1)(u_2)\ \ldots\ (u_{N-1})\\
DV(N+1) &= \text{base address of array}
\end{aligned}$$

The last entry of the dope vector stores the pointer to the first component of the array.

The array descriptor block makes the computation of the address of an array component efficient. A high-level reference of an array component $A(m_1, m_2, \ldots, m_N)$ may now be translated to the following address by the equation

$$\text{Address of } A(m_1, m_2, \ldots, m_N)$$
$$= DV(N+1) + DV(1)*(m_1 - 1) + DV(2)*(m_2 - 1) + \ldots + DV(N)*(m_N - 1)$$

Once the compiler evaluates DV(1) through DV(N) and stores them, the products do not need to be calculated during run time for each array component access.

3.5.3.2 Records. A record is a data object whose components have different types and sizes. The component types are previously defined types and may themselves be records. Records are represented during run time by having their components placed next to each other within a block of memory. By examining the size of each component of the record and its position in the hierarchy of the record, the compiler generates the offset for each component relative to the beginning of the record. The compiler also generates the accessing function for the various components and determines the amount of storage occupied by each record.

Within each record, the offset of a component is the sum of the sizes of the preceding components. The size of each component depends on the type of the component. The components of a record, for example, may be records or arrays. The size of a component is the sum of the size of its subcomponents or itself if there is no subcomponent. If one of the components of the record is an array, the size of the component is the size of the array. In this case, a component of the array is a record subcomponent. The offset of a subcomponent with respect to the beginning of the record is the sum of its offset within its "parent" component and the offset of its parent component from the beginning of the record. By going down the hierarchy and determining the size and offset of each component and subcomponent, the address of any component or subcomponent can be determined. If any component or subcomponent of a record is another record, the offsets and sizes are calculated as above recursively. The transformation of a high-level-language reference RECORD_OBJ.COMP1 into a run-time address using the representation and offset calculation methods above are done by the compiler. For example,

```
type LNAME is (JOHNSON,SMITH,DOE,JACKSON);
type SALARY is
   record
      MONTHLY_PAY:INTEGER;
      LAST_RAISE:INTEGER;
```

```
    end record;
type EMPLOYEE is
    record
        FIRST_INITIAL:CHARACTER;
        MIDDLE_INITIAL:CHARACTER;
        LAST_NAME:LNAME;
        PAY:SALARY;
        DEPARTMENT:INTEGER;
        YEARS_OF_SERVICE:INTEGER;
    end record;
JOHN:EMPLOYEE;
```

The run-time representation of an enumerated type object is an integer. An integer may be represented as one byte, two bytes, or four bytes depending on its range. An enumeration type in most cases can be represented by an integer with one byte. With an enumeration type and a character being represented by one byte each, and an integer being represented by four bytes, the data object JOHN may be represented as in Fig. 3.9 (where, for simplicity, the word width of the machine is assumed to be one byte). The compiler transforms the reference JOHN.DEPARTMENT into an address equal to the record base address plus an offset. The offset is given by two bytes to represent the sizes of

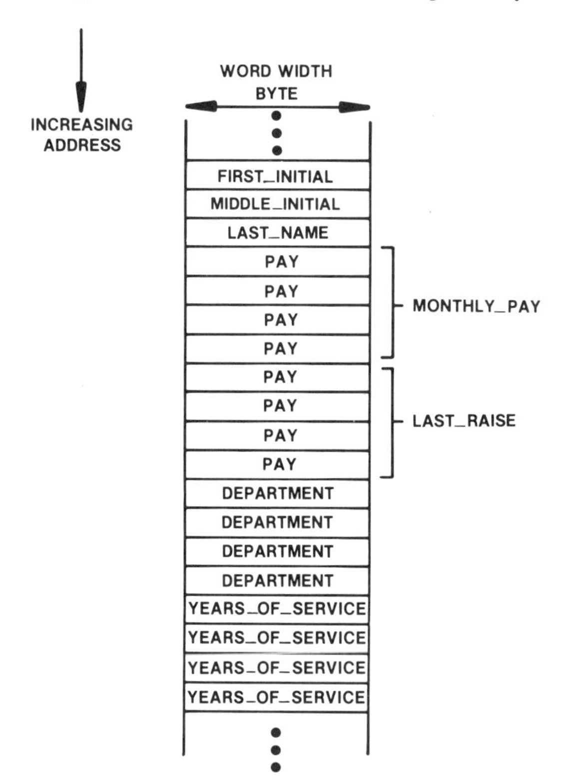

Figure 3.9 An example of representation of data objects of type employee.

FIRST_INITIAL and MIDDLE_INITIAL, plus one byte to represent LAST_NAME, plus eight bytes to represent PAY, for a total of 11 bytes. The compiler then generates code to access this address using an appropriate addressing mode supported by the instruction set of the machine.

3.5.3.3 Packing and padding data structure representations. A data structure is an aggregate of components. Memory is essentially an array of words. When a data structure is mapped into memory, each component of the data structure may not fit exactly into an integral number of memory words. In these cases, padding or packing is employed [6].

Rounding the number of words needed to represent a component up to the next whole number is called *padding*. For example, a data object of type EMPLOYEE (in the example of the preceding section) in a machine where the word size is four bytes and characters are one byte each may be represented as in the top of Fig. 3.10. The compiler usually generates padding automatically. The omission of padding requires partial word accesses, which are usually inefficient for machines without byte addressing capabilities and requires the addition of unnecessary code. Even for machines with byte operations, byte writes are usually less efficient than word writes. However, padding is an inefficient utilization of space when the size of the components is less than half the size of a memory

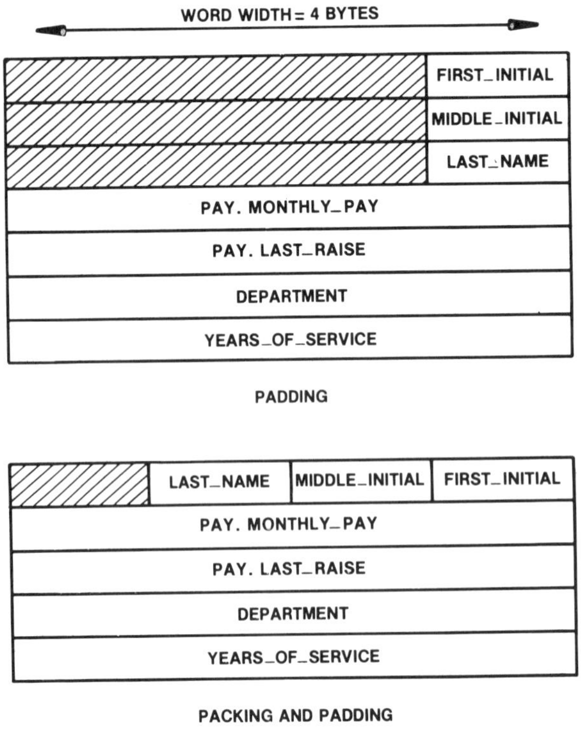

WORD WIDTH = 4 BYTES

FIRST_INITIAL
MIDDLE_INITIAL
LAST_NAME
PAY. MONTHLY_PAY
PAY. LAST_RAISE
DEPARTMENT
YEARS_OF_SERVICE

PADDING

LAST_NAME | MIDDLE_INITIAL | FIRST_INITIAL
PAY. MONTHLY_PAY
PAY. LAST_RAISE
DEPARTMENT
YEARS_OF_SERVICE

PACKING AND PADDING

Figure 3.10 Packing and padding of data objects of type employee.

word. By *packing* more than one component into a memory word, the compiler obtains better use of system memory as shown in the bottom of Fig. 3.10. It can be seen that the offset calculation must include the space occupied by padding. That is, once the compiler has packed and padded a data structure representation, it can determine the offset for each component. To access a component, an address must also specify the position of the component within a memory location. For high-level languages that support bit field types as components of records, accessing the bit fields requires a code sequence to extract the bit fields. Some computers, such as the VAX 11/780 and the AT&T 3B20D, have field instructions that allow a field within a memory word to be extracted in a single instruction. Packing is desirable if an aggregate is mostly used as a unit and the difficulty of accessing individual components is of secondary importance.

3.5.3.4 Constrained parameterized types. Certain high-level languages, like Ada, allow attributes of a data object to be specified in an object declaration rather than in a type definition. That is, in a type definition, a certain value is left unspecified, allowing it to be specified in an object declaration. The type definition is a generic type definition; the value to be specified in the object declaration is the value of a parameter (discriminant). Each parameter value determines a particular type instance to be created from the generic type definition. For example, in Ada,

```
type INDEX is range 1 .. 1000;
type ARRAY_GEN is array (INDEX) of INTEGER;
```

is a generic type definition of arrays with fewer than 1000 integers. INDEX is an enumeration type serving as the array parameter whose value is left unspecified. Multiple type instances may be created with object declarations:

```
A1:ARRAY_GEN(1 .. 10);
A2:ARRAY_GEN(1 .. 100);
A3:ARRAY_GEN(1 .. 500);
```

ARRAY-GEN(1 .. 10), ARRAY_GEN(1 .. 100), and ARRAY_GEN(1 .. 500) are distinct types with one different attribute, the size of the array. As another example, a parameterized record type definition

```
type MEMORY (NUMB_CELLS:INTEGER: = 1000) is
   record
      SIZE:INTEGER;
      MEM_ARRAY:array(1..NUMB_CELLS) of INTEGER;
   end record;
```

is a generic type definition with the discriminant NUMB_CELLS. Object declarations with type constraint such as

```
BUFFER:MEMORY (100);
DISK_CACHE:MEMORY (4000);
```

creates instances of MEMORY types with 100 and 4000 elements. The parameter values, once constrained in the object declaration, cannot change during run time.

Constrained parameterized types need no special run-time support. During compilation, the compiler merely has to complete filling the attributes into the symbol table as it compiles the object declaration statement.

3.5.3.5 Unconstrained parameterized types. Ada also allows unconstrained parameterized types. For unconstrained parameterized types, the parameter value is not only unspecified at type definition, but it is also unspecified during object declaration. An object declaration with constraint fixes the value of the parameter. An object declaration without constraint allows the parameter value to be changed at run time. A common parameter is the size of a data object type. An unconstrained parameterized type is thus a language mechanism for defining dynamic data structure types and for declaring variably sized data structures. For example, with the MEMORY type definition in the previous example, an object declaration

CACHE: MEMORY;

may have no constraint specified. The object CACHE is initialized to 1000 elements as specified by the type definition. Without constraint, the object CACHE may assume different sizes at run time. The contents of the data object CACHE, as well as its size, may be changed by an assignment statement, for example:

```
CACHE:MEMORY;                        --CACHE size initialized to 1000
BUFFER:MEMORY (100);
DISK_CACHE:MEMORY (4000);
    .
    .
    .
CACHE := BUFFER;                     --CACHE size becomes 100
    .
    .
    .
CACHE := DISK_CACHE;                 --CACHE size becomes 4000
```

For data objects whose attributes may change during run time, the run-time representation must include not only the data object itself, but the changeable attributes as well. These attributes may be placed in a *run-time descriptor* (sometimes referred to as a *type template*). Run-time descriptors contain all the information the machine needs to know about the object they describe. The contents of the descriptor may be changed at run time. The descriptor is linked to the run-time representation of the data object. The size of the descriptor does not change although the size of the data object may change. Hence, the descriptor is the fixed part of the representation and the data object itself is the dynamic part of the representation. A run-time representation of the data object CACHE and its descriptor are shown in Fig. 3.11. In this case, the run-time descriptor of the object CACHE is the array descriptor (dope vector). It contains the parameter value (NUMB_CELLS) and the pointer to the array object. When the object CACHE is refer-

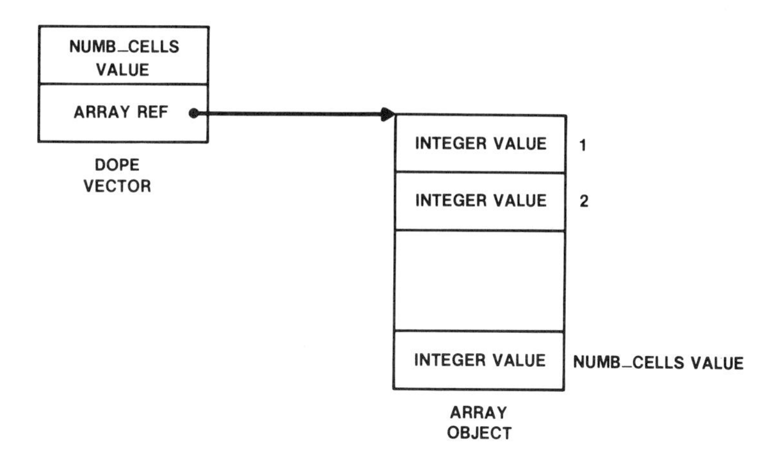

Figure 3.11 Run-time representation of cache.

enced at run time, code is required to determine the size of the object (NUMB_CELLS) in the descriptor. The object CACHE is always referenced through the descriptor.

An array descriptor is efficient for representing variable arrays whose dimensions change during run-time. The values of the entries of the array descriptor are changed to reflect the dynamic changes of the array dimension limits. This allows the compiled address of an array component to remain the same during execution even though dimensions of the array itself may change. Since the base address of the array is also part of the array descriptor, the array itself may be dynamically relocated by simply changing the value of the base address in the array descriptor without the compiler having to regenerate the addresses of the array components.

Ada and other high-level languages also allow variant records. In a variant record, the type as well as the size of the variant components may change at run time. For example,

```
type PWR is (POWER,MANUAL);
type TRAN is (STICK,AUTOMATIC);
type CAR_CLASS is (LUXURY,MEDIUM,ECONOMY);
type CAR (CLASS: CAR_CLASS:= MEDIUM) is
   record
       TRANSMISSION:TRAN;
       STEERING:PWR;
       BRAKE:PWR;
       case CLASS is
           when LUXURY   => MERCEDES:BOOLEAN;
           when MEDIUM   => POPULARITY:INTEGER;
           when ECONOMY  => SIZE:INTEGER;
                            MPG:INTEGER;
                            PRICE:INTEGER;
       end case;
   end record;
```

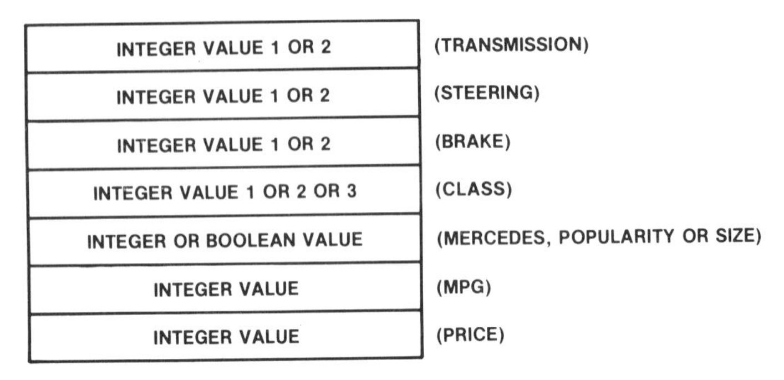

Figure 3.12 A run-time representation of JOHNS_CAR.

where car is a variant record type definition with discriminant CLASS. Since all the alternatives of a case construct in a variant record type are known, the maximum size of a variant record object can be determined at compile time. The compiler can assign enough storage to contain the record object when it has the largest variant component. In the example above, this is the case when CLASS is ECONOMY. A possible run-time representation of an object of type CAR (for example, Johns_CAR; CAR;) in a machine where the word width is one byte is shown in Fig. 3.12. If JOHNS_CAR.CLASS is LUXURY, the record object only needs five entries (bytes) for the representation. At compile time, however, seven entries are allocated for the representation so that when an assignment statement occurs (for example, JOHNS_CAR := (AUTOMATIC, POWER, POWER, ECONOMY, 40, 35, 4000);) during run time that assigns JOHNS_CAR.CLASS to be ECONOMY, there is enough storage allocated to contain the values of the record components. When a variant component is accessed (such as JOHNS_CAR.MPG), the compiler generates code that checks the current value of the variant record discriminant (JOHNS_CAR.CLASS) at run time and determines whether the reference is legal.

3.5.4 Other Ada Run-Time Determinable Attributes

Ada's types and objects have attributes that may be determined at run time; examples as discussed above include objects of parameterized types and variant record types. Also in Ada, the subrange of the subtypes of discrete types may be determined at run time as the

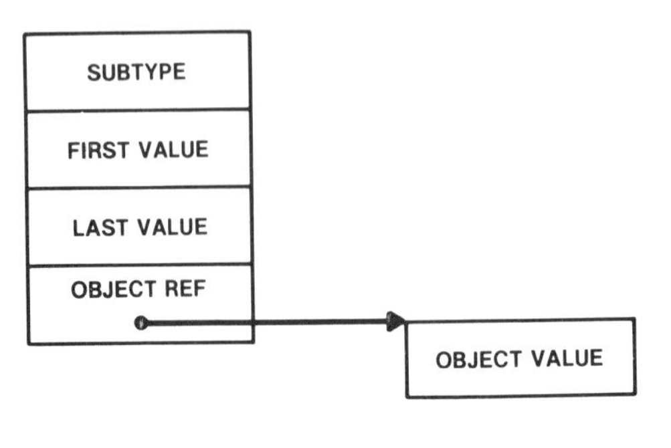

Figure 3.13 A run-time representation of object with subtypes having dynamic ranges.

result of evaluating an expression. An assignment of a value to an object with this subtype at run time must check whether the value falls within the subrange. For the run-time check to be performed, the minimum (FIRST) and maximum (LAST) values of the subrange must be stored in a template representing the attributes of the subtype. An object with this subtype may be represented as shown in Fig. 3.13.

3.5.5 Access Types

Data objects of the access type (pointers), like integers, are represented by a set of bits contained in a memory word. The bit pattern represents the value of the pointer variable. The pointer variable value is the address of a memory location where the data object pointed to by the pointer variable may be found.

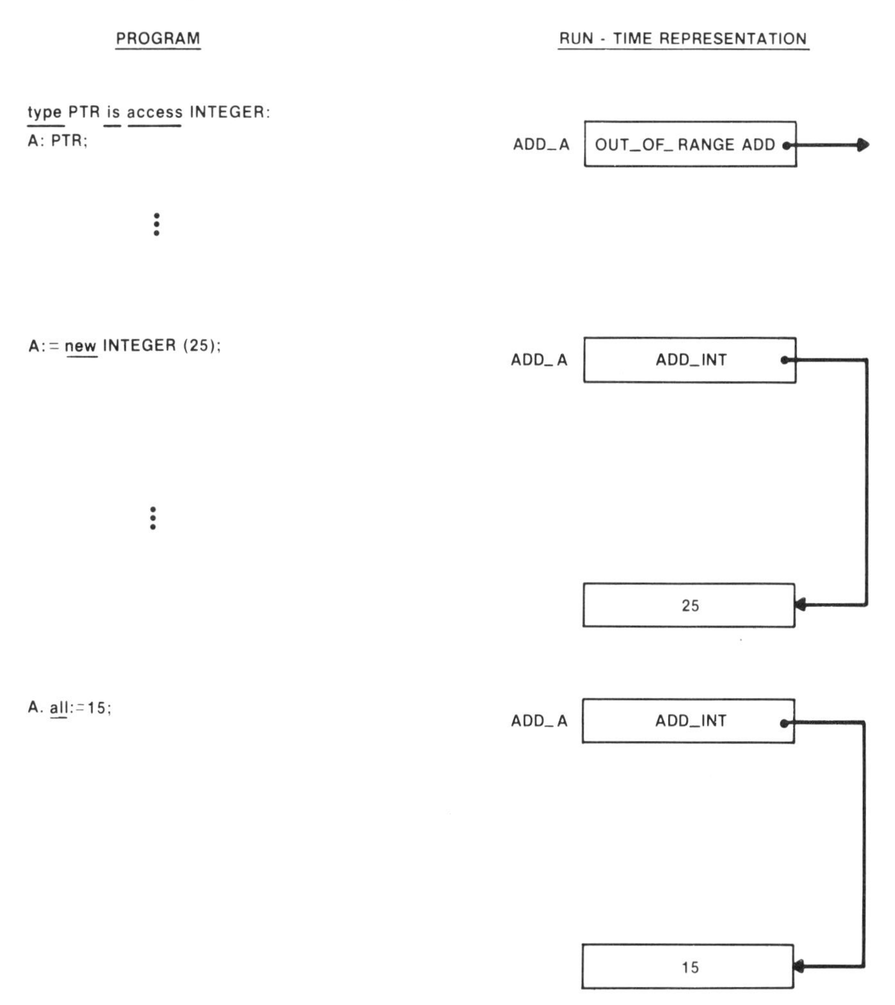

Figure 3.14 Run-time representation of pointers and their operations.

When the compiler encounters a pointer declaration,

```
type PTR is access INTEGER;
A:PTR;
```

the compiler assigns a run-time address (ADD_A in Fig. 3.14) of a memory location to represent the name A. The content of this location is the value of the variable named A. If A is uninitialized, it has the value **null.** The value **null** may be represented by an address value that causes an error when it is used to access data. For example, an out-of range address may be used to represent the value **null** (OUT_OF_RANGE ADD in Fig. 3.14). When A is initialized to point to a data object,

```
A:= new INTEGER(25);
```

the run-time code causes the storage allocator to obtain a storage location, places the value 25 into the location, and places the address (ADD_INT) of the location into the location (ADD_A) representing the variable A.

When the dereferencing operation is used,

```
A.all:= 15;
```

the run-time code accesses the memory location, ADD_A, and uses its contents (ADD_INT) as the address of the location to place the integer 15.

For many languages, when the statement

```
A:= new INTEGER(25);
```

is executed, the corresponding run-time code causes the storage allocator to obtain a storage location from a *heap*. A heap is a collection of memory locations where allocation and deallocation does not depend on a fixed algorithm (queues, for example, use a fixed first-in, first-out algorithm). Rather, the storage allocator depends on a free list or some other method to denote the locations in the heap that have not been allocated. Heap and heap storage management are discussed further in Section 3.10.2.

3.5.6 Common Data Structures

Array, record, and access constructors can be used to build other data structures, including matrices, character strings, stacks, queues, linked lists, and trees. Ways of representing these common data structures are discussed below.

Matrices are common data structures in mathematical computations. A natural representation of a matrix in storage is a two-dimensional array. The elements of an array can be found quickly and their addresses can be translated easily. Unfortunately, representing large matrices that are only sparsely populated with nonzero elements as two-dimensional arrays makes inefficient use of storage space. For example, storing a 100 by 100 matrix with only 100 nonzero elements (out of a possible 10,000) in a two-dimensional array uses only 1 percent of the storage allocated for it. A solution to this problem is setting up a new array that specifies where the nonzero elements are. To do this, each nonzero element is represented as a 3-tuple with the row index, column index, and value of the data element. The 3-tuples are stored in an $(n+1)$ by 3 two-dimensional array, where n equals the number of nonzero elements. The columns store the row number and the column number of the original matrix corresponding to the nonzero elements, and the values of the nonzero elements. The additional row, usually the first row, stores the number of rows, columns, and nonzero elements of the original sparse matrix. For example, the sparse matrix with seven rows, eight columns, and nine nonzero elements

i/j	1	2	3	4	5	6	7	8
1	0	0	0	0	0	1	0	0
2	0	0	0	0	-1	0	0	0
3	0	0	-2	0	0	0	0	-6
4	3	0	0	0	0	0	0	0
5	0	0	0	0	0	0	3	0
6	0	10	0	0	0	0	0	0
7	0	0	0	5	0	4	0	0

may be represented by the following two-dimensional array:

i/j	1	2	3
1	7	8	9
2	1	6	1
3	2	5	-1
4	3	3	-2
5	3	8	-6
6	4	1	3
7	5	7	3
8	6	2	10
9	7	4	5
10	7	6	4

The first row indicates the size of the original matrix (7 by 8) and the number of nonzero elements in it (9). The remaining rows designate the locations of the nonzero elements in the original sparse matrix. Algorithms may be written to transpose, add items to, erase items from, and manipulate in other ways this representation of the sparse matrix [7].

Character strings are usually represented as one-dimensional arrays of characters. They are represented as static arrays in Pascal. In Ada, the length may vary dynamically during run time. A data descriptor holding the information on the number of characters currently in the string must be used together with the string itself. Alternatively, as it is implemented in C, a character string with varying length may have an endmarker, represented by a noncharacter-coded byte, stored at the tail of the character string. Character strings which need not have a maximum length specified, as in ALGOL 68, must have their storage allocated from a heap.

A queue is a list of items in which items may be inserted only at one end and deleted or selected from the other end. A stack is a list in which insertion, deletion, and selection occur at one end, the top of the stack. Queues and stacks may be stored as one-dimensional arrays. A pointer denotes the top of a stack, and two pointers denote the head

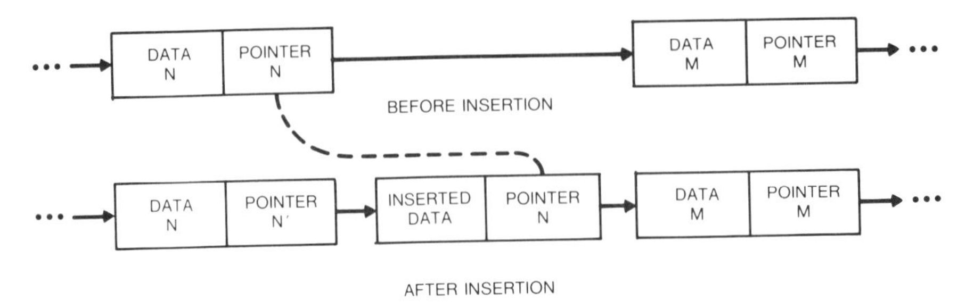

Figure 3.15 Insertion of data element into a singly-linked list.

and tail of a queue. If a queue is to be implemented in a restricted set of linear memory, it may be implemented as a *circular queue* with wraparound. This data structure is the software counterpart of a hardware circular buffer. Before an element is inserted into a circular queue, a check must be made to determine whether the end of the restricted set of linear memory is reached. If a pointer is updated past this point, it is reset to point to the beginning of the restricted set of linear memory. When inserting elements into the circular queue, the pointers must also be checked to ensure that the tail of the queue has not caught up with the head of the queue. If the queue is full, further insertion is prevented until elements are removed from the head of the queue.

For general ordered lists, an element may be inserted and deleted anywhere in the list, not just those at the ends. A sequential mapping of a general ordered list into storage makes inserting and deleting elements cumbersome. Inserting an element in the middle of a queue, for example, would cause all subsequent elements in the queue to be "bumped" one position. A solution to this problem is representing such lists as linked lists. In a linked list, each element has a link pointer to the next element. When each data element has a pointer, successive elements are not necessarily stored in adjacent locations in memory. To insert an element in the middle of a linked list, the pointer of the preceding element is adjusted to point to the new element, and the pointer of the new element is adjusted to point to the next element (Fig. 3.15).

Since the pointers in a linked list all point forward, scanning the list forward from element to element is easy. Singly linked lists are inadequate, however, for applications where a list needs to be scanned forward and backward. A doubly linked list is needed for such applications. In a doubly linked list, two pointers are associated with each data ele-

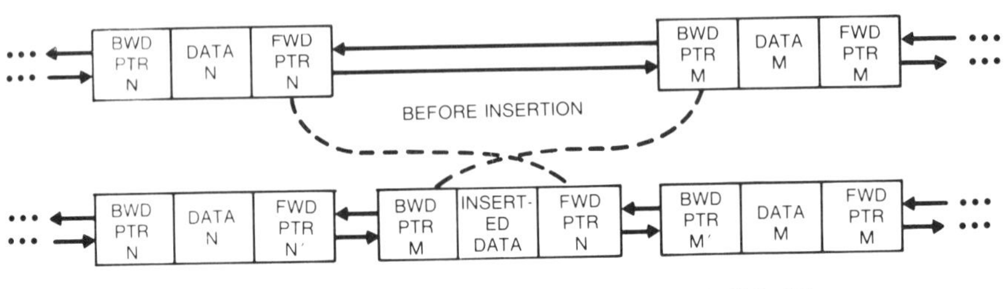

Figure 3.16 Insertion of data element into a doubly-linked list.

ment: one pointing forward to the next element and another pointing backward to the preceding element. When an element is inserted, the forward pointer of the preceding element and the backward pointer of the next element are updated to point to the inserted element (Fig. 3.16).

If a pointer takes as much memory space to store as the data element in the list, the storage overhead of the doubly linked list is 200 percent. Improved performance justifies this cost overhead, however, if insertions and deletions of arbitrary elements in the list are performed frequently.

Trees may be built using record constructors and access constructors. The nodes and the leaves of a tree may be linked by pointers. A record type for a tree may be recursively defined as discussed in Chapter 2. Special categories of trees include binary trees and B-trees; they are useful for applications in data base and operating systems. The representations of these trees and algorithms for traversal on them are beyond the scope of this book.*

3.5.7 Type Equivalence

High-level languages permit only operations and assignments among objects of equivalent types.† ALGOL 68 specifies structural equivalence of types; Ada specifies name equivalence of types. Type checking (that is, checking to ensure that the type equivalence rules are met in assignments and operations) is for the most part done by the compiler. During the semantic analysis, the compiler determines the type of every object and decides whether the types are used appropriately by the program. The compiler also determines the type of every expression.

For objects whose attributes may vary during run time, type checking must be done at run time when the objects are used in an operation or assignment. When such situations occur in the program, the compiler generates code to access the run-time descriptor containing information about an object type, and code to use the descriptor information for verifying the validity of the operation in terms of type equivalence. For example, the validity of the assignment of one variant record to another of the same type depends on whether, at the time of the assignment, their discriminants contain the same value.

3.6 OPERATORS

The built-in operators of high-level languages usually include numeric operators, logical operators, and relational operators. In many cases, these operators are mapped onto corresponding machine instructions. Numeric operations (+, -, *, /, **mod,** and **rem**) on integers and reals have corresponding machine instructions (such as ADD, SUB, MUL, DIV, MOD, REM, FADD, FSUB, FMUL, FDIV, where the last four are floating-point instructions). In some machines, there are no floating-point instructions; numeric operations on

*For a discussion, see reference 7.

†Some high-level languages allow operations of an integer with a floating-point number, where the integer is implicitly converted to a floating-point number before the operation.

real numbers are implemented by a sequence of machine instructions embedded in a subroutine. Complex numeric operators such as ** and **sqrt** (square root) are also implemented by subroutines in most machines.

Assignment operators (such as :=) are implemented by the MOV instruction. Logical operators (*and, or, XOR*) on Boolean type objects also have single corresponding machine instructions (AND, OR, XOR). Relational operators (=, /=, <, <=, >, and >=) are implemented by machine instruction sequences composed of compare (COMP) and conditional branch instructions (BE, BNE, BLT, BLE, BGT, BGE). For example, the statement

```
if A<=B then
    A := C;
end if;
```

may be compiled into the sequence*

```
        CMP A,B             --Compare A to B
        BLE L1              --Branch if <=
        B L2                --Unconditional branch
    L1:MOV C,A              --A<-C
    L2: . . .
```

or into

```
        CMP A,B             --Compare A to B
        BGT L1              --Branch if >
        MOV C,A             --A <- C
    L1:
```

where the second sequence has been optimized to eliminate a branch over another branch. String operators such as *concatenation* (**&**), *length,* and *substring* usually require a sequence of instructions that may be embedded in subroutines. High-level-language bit manipulation operators as those found in PL/I and C are directly mapped into the corresponding machine instructions. In fact, since C and PL/I are used for system programming, where the program controls the machine hardware, the bit manipulation operators are derived bottom-up from the machine instructions *bitwise and, bitwise or, bitwise exclusive or, one's complement, right shift,* and *left shift*. C also has the ++ and -- operators, which are also derived from the increment and decrement machine instructions, and have the same semantics.

Ada's membership operators **in** and **not in** may be implemented by COMP instructions that compare the operand with the upper and lower limits of the range, type, or subtype.

3.6.1 Expressions and Operator Precedence

While high-level languages permit expressions with a large number of operands and operators, assembly languages permit only two source operands and one operator in an instruction. Hence a multioperand expression in a high-level language is implemented by a

*The assembly notation in the example sequences are from the PDP 11/70 instruction set [8].

sequence of instructions; the result of each instruction is stored in a temporary location. Compilers generate temporary variables to hold these intermediate results. Compilers also observe the operator precedence rules of high-level languages in determining the order of the sequence of the instructions.

3.6.2 Operator Overloading

High-level languages are typed languages: each object includes its type information. Operators, on the other hand, are generic and have generic symbols; that is, they are overloaded. Three types of operator overloading are possible. First, in most languages, the symbol + is overloaded to denote both the addition of integers and the addition of reals. This is the case of built-in overloading. Second, Ada allows programmers to define derived types; a derived type permits an operator to operate only on objects of the particular derived type. The same operator symbol is overloaded and is used to denote operations on objects of the parent type. Finally, Ada allows programmers to define overloaded operators by means of function definitions. The examples given in Chapter 2 illustrate the overloading of the symbol "+" to denote addition of complex numbers and of matrices. The following example illustrates the overloading of the + operator.

```
C:= A + B;                   --A, B, and C are integers

ORCHARD:=                    --ORCHARDs are objects of derived types, with
  ORCHARD1+ORCHARD2;         --INTEGER as their parent type
X:= Y + Z;                   --X, Y, and Z are reals
COMP:= COMP1 + COMP2;        --COMPs are COMPLEX NUMBER types
```

Assembly languages are typeless languages; their operands do not carry any type information. The ways the bit encodings of the operands are interpreted and manipulated depend on the operators. Operators are not overloaded in assembly languages. Compilers examine the type of the operands in high-level languages, detect the legality of the operation between the operands in terms of type equivalence, and generate the appropriate machine instructions (such as ADD, FADD, etc.). In the case of an overloaded operator that is defined by a function, compilers determine the type of the operands and generate code to jump to the sequence of instructions that implements the function. In the examples above, the addition operator is implemented by ADD in the first and second cases, by FADD in the third case, and by a sequence of instructions in the fourth. The difference in the addition of ORCHARDs and the addition of its parent type INTEGERs is transparent in the run-time model. In this case, the overloading mechanism merely provides compile-time checks on type equivalence.

3.7 FLOW CONTROL

Implicit in the semantics of high-level languages is that the control of execution flows sequentially from one statement to the next. Similarly, implicit in the semantics of assembly languages is that the control of execution flows sequentially from one instruction to the next. Flow control is implemented in assembly programs by a variable called the *pro-*

gram counter. The program counter contains the address of the next instruction to be executed; that is, it specifies the point of flow in the program. By controlling the value of program counter, an assembly program implements flow control.

Sequential flow is implemented by automatically incrementing the program counter with the size of each instruction once it executes so that the program counter points to the next instruction. This eliminates the need for the compiled code to denote the location of the next instruction after every instruction.

Flow control mechanisms in high-level languages beyond simple sequencing include selection, iteration, and goto statements. To support these mechanisms, the compiler uses machine instructions denoting the program counter as an operand. These are the branch and conditional branch instructions; they are used with label operands. After the condition is met for the branch or conditional branch, the content of the label operand is loaded into the program counter, hence controlling the flow of the program. A **goto** statement in a high-level language may be implemented simply by a branch instruction in an assembly language.

3.7.1 Selection

The **if** statement and the **case** statement are the high-level-language selection mechanisms. They may be implemented using branch and conditional branch instructions and labels. For example, the **if** statement

```
if A > 5 then
   A:= A + 1;
elsif A< 10 then
   A:= A - 1;
end if;
```

may be compiled into the sequence*

```
      CMP A,5            --Compare A to 5
      BLE L1             --If A ≤ 5, check the next condition
      INC A              --Otherwise A:= A + 1
      BR L2              --Branch to L2
   L1 CMP A,10           --Compare A to 10
      BGE L2             --If A ≥ 10 go to L2
      SUB A,1            --Otherwise A:= A - 1
   L2 . . .
```

The **case** statement

```
case A+B is
   when 0 => READ(x);
   when 1 => WRITE(x);
   when others => ERROR;
end case;
```

*The assembly notation is from the PDP 11/70 instruction set.

may be compiled into

```
        MOV A,T             --T←A
        ADD B,T             --T←T + B= A + B
        BR L                --Branch to L
    L1: .                   --Code for READ(x)
        .
        .
        BR EC               --Branch to EC
    L2: .                   --Code for WRITE(x)
        .
        .
        BR EC               --Branch to EC
    DL: .                   --Code for ERROR
        .
        .
        BR EC               --Branch to EC
    L: CMP T,0              --Compare A + B to 0
        BEQ L1              --If A + B = 0, jump to L1
        CMP T,1             --Compare A + B to 1
        BEQ L2              --If A + B = 1, jump to L2
        BR DL               --If A + B ≠ 0, and A + B ≠ 1
                            --Jump to DL
    EC:                     --Exit of case statement
```

3.7.2 Iteration

Iteration is a flow control mechanism that repeats a set of statements until a specific condition is satisfied. In Ada, an infinite loop can be expressed as

```
loop
  .
  .
  .
end loop;
```

where the statements are repeated indefinitely. In assembly language, this loop may be implemented by a backward branch.

```
L1: .
    .
    .
    BR L1
```

High-level languages allow a loop to be exited at its beginning (**while** statement), its end (**repeat** . . . **until** statement), or anywhere within it (**exit** statements). These alternative mechanisms may all be implemented in assembly languages by a conditional branch instruction where the conditional branch instruction is placed respectively at the beginning, the end, or anywhere within the loop. For example,

```
while A < 100 loop
      A:= A + 1;
end loop;
```

may be compiled into

```
L1: CMP A,100          --Compare A to 100
    BGE L2             --Exit from loop if ≥100
    INC A              --A←A + 1
    BR L1              --Branch to L1
L2: .
    .
    .
```

whereas

```
repeat
    A := A + 1;
until A ≥ 100
```

may be compiled into

```
L1: INC A              --A←A + 1
    CMP A,100          --Compare A to 100
    BGE L2             --Exit from loop if A ≥ 100
    BR L1              --Branch to L1
L2: .
    .
    .
```

The **for** statement may be implemented similarly by calculating the control variable and testing it as the exit condition. The conditional branch instruction is placed before the instructions in the loop as in the **while** statement.

3.8 ENVIRONMENT

Blocks and *subprograms* are high-level-language mechanisms to describe the environments (*scopes*) in which data objects are visible. An environment may be represented at run time by a set of contiguous locations in storage called an *activation record*. An activation record contains the *context* of an environment, that is, all the data objects making up the environment. The run-time locations of these data objects may be represented by offsets relative to the base address pointing into the activation record.

Environments may be nested; within an environment, not only are the data objects of that environment visible, but the data objects of all the environments enclosing it are also visible (referenceable). The set of referenceable environments are represented by multiple activation records. At any point of execution, the compiled program needs to have available all the base addresses of the referenceable activation records. This set of activation record base addresses is called a *display*.

3.8.1 Blocks

Each nested environment assigned a lexical level corresponding to its level of nesting. The main program is assigned lexical level 0. All the environments that the main program immediately encloses are assigned lexical level 1; these in turn enclose environments at lexical level 2, and so on. An environment at lexical level n encloses an environment at lexical level $n+1$.

Even though the activation of environments is dynamic during execution, the lexical level of an environment and the position of the declared variables within it are static. High-level languages allow only one referenceable environment at each lexical level at any point of execution. A *display* is the set of base addresses of activation records corresponding to referenceable environments, one at each lexical level. When a program is executing in an environment at lexical level n, there are $n + 1$ entries in the display, one for each lexical level from 0 to $n - 1$, its enclosing environments. Each referenceable data object may be unambiguously specified by its lexical level and an offset. The lexical level is used as an index into the display to obtain the base address of the activation record representing the environment. The offset is used to index into the activation record to reference the data object. This addressing scheme is called *lexical-level addressing*.

In the example of Fig. 2.3, environment **D** is nested within environment **C,** which is nested within environment **B,** which is nested in environment **A.** The variables declared in **D** are **x** and **t;** in **C** they are **x** and **y**; in **B, y** and **z;** and in **A, x** and **z.** If, within an environment, the first declared variable is given the index of 0 and the second variable the index 1, the lexical level addresses of the variables in the example in Fig. 2.3 are shown in Fig. 3.17.

3.8.2 Subprograms

Subprograms in high-level languages are not only mechanisms for defining environments in which data objects are visible, but are also mechanisms for flow control. In a subprogram call or return, flow control transfers from one subprogram to another. In a subprogram call, the environment switches from that of the caller subprogram to that of the called subprogram; in a subprogram return, the environment switches from that of the called subprogram back to that of the caller subprogram.

Since a display describes the environment nesting *as seen by the current environment* (that is, it contains all the base addresses of all the *currently referenceable activation records*), each time flow control switches environments (by a procedure call or return, a

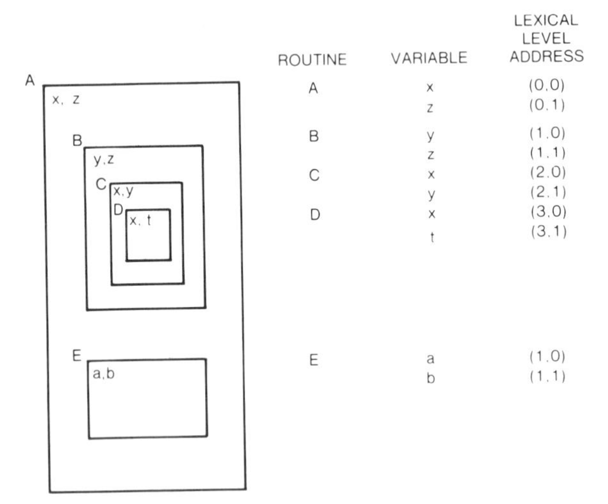

Figure 3.17 Lexical level addressing support of block structured languages.

function call or return, or by entering or exiting from a block), a new display is needed to denote the *set of referenceable activation records as seen by the new environment*. Languages like ALGOL and PL/I are not only block structured, they allow recursion. For example, if subprogram B in Fig. 2.3 calls itself, the display is changed so that it contains the base address of only the most recent activation record of B. That is, the display contains the most recent activation record at each lexical level.

Display entry 0 points to the most recent activation record of a lexical level 0 environment, display entry 1 points to the most recent activation record of an environment in lexical level 1, and so on. Figure 3.18 shows the display and the activation records of the program used in the example above (where the B subprogram has recursively called itself twice).

With a display, the first part of the lexical-level address couple serves as an index for selecting one of the display entries. The selected display entry points to an activation record. The second part of the address couple is an index into the activation record selecting one of the variables. In the example in Fig. 3.18, the address (1,0) references the variable y within the most recent activation record of the subprogram B.

In Fig. 3.17, the variables **a** and **b** in environment **E** have the same lexical-level addresses as the variables **y** and **z** in environment **B.** At any time during the execution, only one environment at each lexical level is referenceable. That is, if E is referenceable, B cannot be, and vice versa. In this case, the same address allocated at compilation to reference two distinct variables is not a problem since the displays are different at the different times that the variables **y** and **a** are referenceable. The same lexical-level address with different displays accesses different storage cells. The lexical-level addresses (1,0) and (1,1) access variables **y** and **z** or **a** and **b** depending on the contents of the display.

When flow control switches environments, the display changes. If flow control eventually returns to the same environment (on a procedure or function return, for instance), the display of that environment is restored. An environment switch must there-

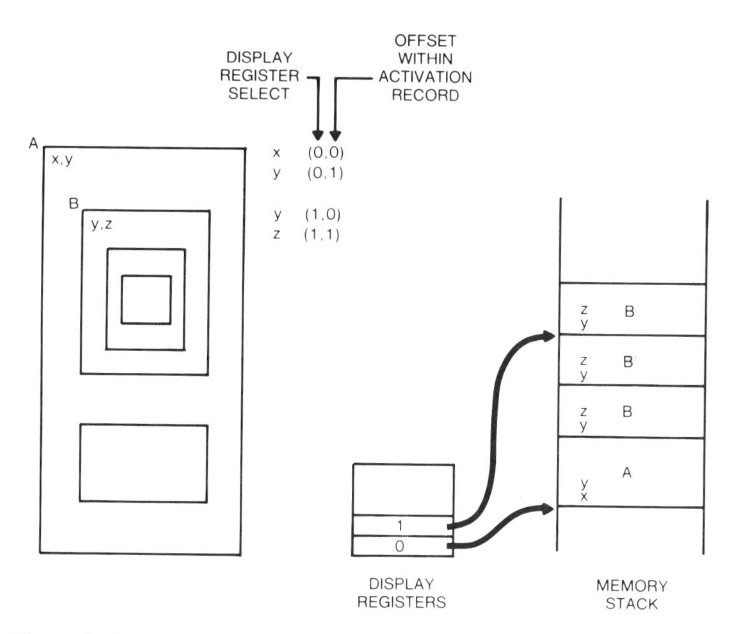

Figure 3.18 Use of display registers to support recursion in block structured languages.

fore preserve the display of the old environment; the display may be saved in the activation record of a subprogram or block as part of its context.

Because subprograms must run to completion before returning control to their caller, activation records representing subprograms are usually allocated on a stack. Each time a subprogram is called, its activation record is created and placed on top of the stack. When the subprogram returns, its activation record is removed from the top of the stack. When a subprogram calls another subprogram, the called activation record is placed on top of the caller activation record in the stack structure. The top activation record on the stack must be removed (that is, the called subprogram must run to completion and return) before the activation record below it may become active (that is, before control returns to the caller subprogram).

During a subprogram call or return, data may also be passed from one environment to another. The caller and the called subprogram each have access to different information required to complete the linkage. The caller subprogram has access to the data arguments it needs to pass to the called routine. It also has knowledge of its own state (the program counter and the temporary variables stored in the machine's general registers). The values of this information are available at the point of call. Before the environment is switched, the caller subprogram pushes the data parameters (arguments) onto the top of the stack and saves the contents of the program counter. It may also save the contents of the general registers. To minimize the number of general registers that need to be saved, the model of implementation may require that only the general registers that will be used by the called

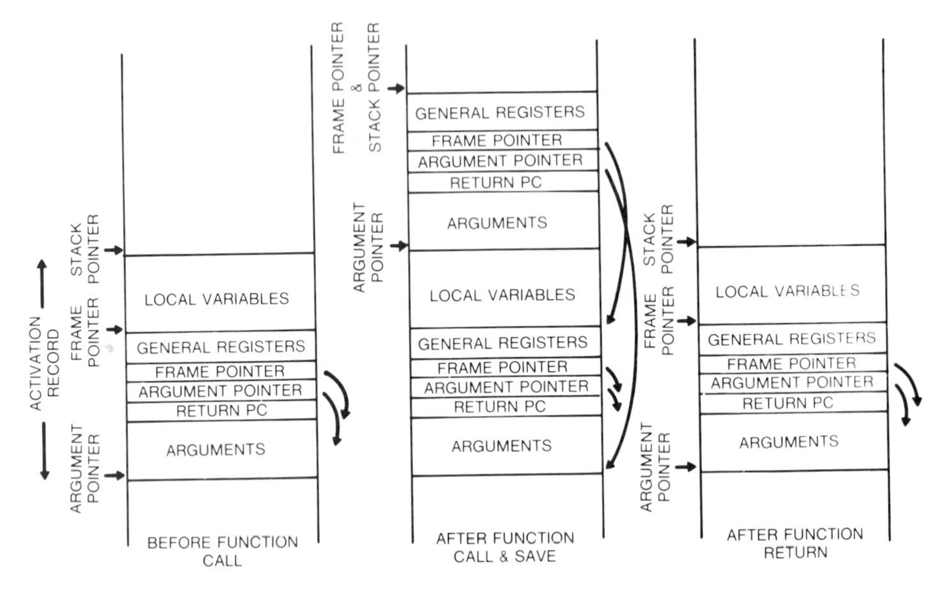

Figure 3.19 Function stack before and after function call, save, and return.

subprogram be saved. Since only the called subprogram has knowledge of which registers it needs, the called subprogram saves the contents of the selected general registers after the environment is switched. The called subprogram also has knowledge of its own lexical level and the amount of local storage it needs for its local variables. At the point of return, the general register values are restored, the activation record of the called routine is popped from the stack, the saved program counter is restored, and the values of the data to be returned are placed in the caller's activation record.

Many machine architectures use dedicated pointers to access activation records and the arguments and local variables stored in them. The pointers must be saved and restored during calls and returns. If the pointers are used frequently to reference a subprogram context while a subprogram is active, they are usually allocated hardware registers. Many machines have registers for a stack pointer, a frame pointer, and an argument pointer. The stack pointer points to the top of the stack. The frame pointer points to the current *stack frame;* a stack frame is a region of stack memory allocated on a subprogram call to store the activation record of the called subprogram. The argument pointer points to the base of the list of arguments passed to the executing subprogram. Thus, arguments may be accessed by means of an offset from the argument pointer. Local variables may be accessed from an offset from the frame pointer. The activation record for a C function call, and the pointers implemented in the 3B20D, are shown in Fig. 3.19.

The stack pointer, the frame pointer, and the argument pointer always point to the current (most recent) activation record on the stack. The location on the stack that is pointed to by the current frame pointer (offset by a fixed number of locations to store the general registers) contains the previous frame pointer that points to a location in the previous activation record. This location in turn contains the frame pointer that points to its predecessor activation record, and so on. The chain of frame pointers is shown in Fig. 3.19.

At the machine level, the support of the call and return statements in high-level-language programs may be provided by corresponding save, call, and return machine instructions. These "jumbo" instructions replace a series of primitive machine instructions. Microprograms implementing these instructions perform the needed operations of:

1. Saving the program counter of the caller subprogram in its activation record
2. Passing control to the called subprogram
3. Saving the state of the general registers
4. Saving the state of the various pointers (frame pointer and argument pointer)
5. Allocating the storage (a new stack frame) for activation record of the called subprogram
6. Deallocating the activation record and restoring the context of the previous activation record

In the implementation in Fig. 3.19, all the accessible variables are contained in a subprogram's activation record, and hence can be referenced as offsets to the frame pointer. The frame pointer pointing to the activation record has the same function as the display. In a language like C, the display needs to have only one value, since only the current activation record is accessible. In a language like Algol, the display may have several values to keep track of the multiple nested environments that are accessible.

An alternative to using displays and lexical-level addressing is to place a pointer in each activation record pointing to the activation record of the environment enclosing it. This chain of pointers links together all the referenceable activation records of the enclosing environments. Since the nesting relationship among environments is static, this chain of pointers is referred to as the static link. By descending the static link, a program has access to all the referenceable activation records at any point of execution.

As discussed above, the chain of frame pointers linked together caller environments and called environments. Since the relationship among caller environments and called environments is dynamic, the chain of frame pointers is referred to as the dynamic link. For example,

```
procedure A is
    procedure R is                  --procedure R
                                    --nested within A
        .
        .
        .
    end R;
begin
    .
    .
    .
```

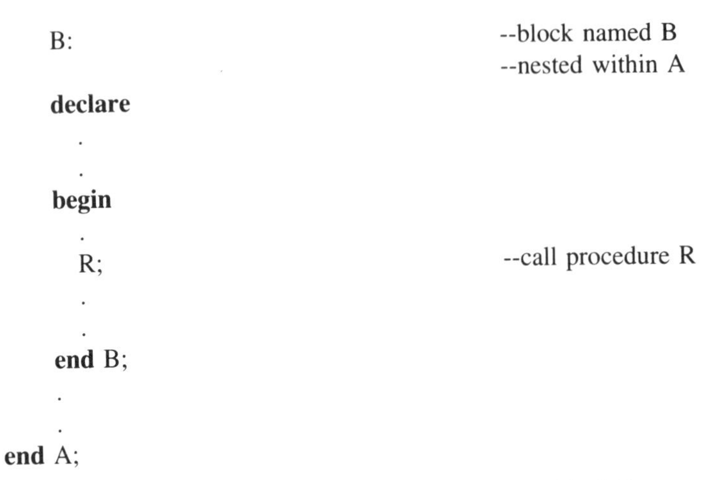

```
        B:                          --block named B
                                    --nested within A
        declare
          .
          .
        begin
          .
          R;                        --call procedure R
          .
          .
        end B;
        .
        .
    end A;
```

When the program executes procedure R, the data declared in block B is not visible since procedure R is not enclosed by block B. Thus, the static link is needed to point to the activation record that belongs to its immediately enclosing environment, in this case, procedure A. The dynamic and static links for this example are shown in Fig. 3.20.

3.8.2.1 Parameter passing. The type of protocol for parameter passing (call by value-result, call by reference, and call by name) determines the implementation required to pass parameters between two environments. Before an environment is switched, the caller subprogram pushes the data parameters onto the top of the stack.

- In call by value-result, the parameters pushed are copies of variables within the caller's activation record. They contain the values of these variables. When the called subprogram returns, the values of these variables are available as results for the caller subprogram.
- In call by reference, the parameters pushed by the caller subprogram are the addresses of variables (actual parameters) within the caller's activation record. A reference to a formal parameter is implemented as an indirect reference (through the

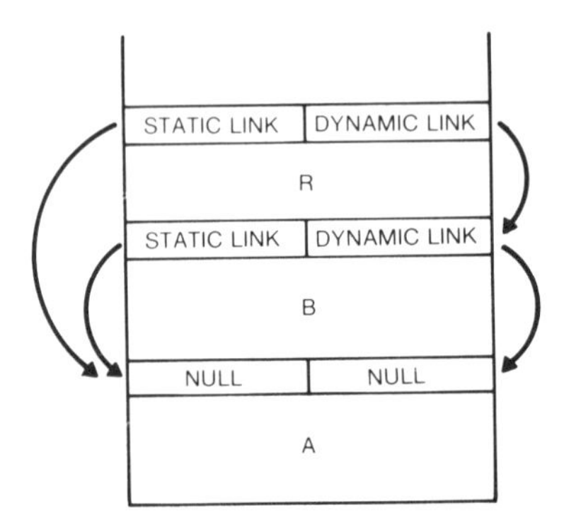

Figure 3.20 Static and dynamic links of block structured language support.

pointer passed) to the actual parameter. An update of the formal parameter results in updating the actual parameter within the caller's activation record.

- In call by name, the parameters pushed by the caller subprogram are also the addresses of variables (actual parameters) within the caller's activation record. However, these addresses may change during the called subprogram execution. Each time a formal parameter is referenced, a subprogram is called to determine the address of the corresponding actual parameter. A formal parameter may be bound to different actual parameters at different points of execution when it is referenced.

3.8.2.2 Coroutine call and return. Coroutines, unlike procedures and functions, do not restrict the relationship between caller and called routines to the last-called, first-returned structure that maps naturally to an implementation by the last-in, first-out structure of stacks. The activation records of coroutines may not be assigned on the same stack. Instead, they are allocated from a heap the first time a coroutine is activated, and returned to the heap when the coroutine runs to completion. While a coroutine is active, it may call subroutines. When a coroutine calls a subroutine, a stack is allocated from the heap storage assigned to the coroutine to store the activation records of the subroutines. Hence each coroutine may require a stack independently of other coroutines. A mechanism of transferring control from one coroutine to another may be implemented using a transfer primitive with a single argument, the pointer to the destination context (activation record). The transfer primitive suspends the current coroutine and begins the execution of the destination coroutine. The transfer primitive uses two global variables. The first variable holds the program counter of the caller routine at the point of transfer so processing control can return to the coroutine when it resumes execution. The second variable is a pointer to the arguments that are passed to the destination routine. The destination routine uses the second global variable to access the arguments. This model of support for transferring control from one routine to another is used in the architecture of the Mesa system [9].

3.8.3 Packages

Packages are program modules that implement data abstraction. A *package specification* groups together a set of related data resources with the subprograms of a package that may operate on the resources. The data resources and subprograms of a package that are visible to other program units are placed in the package specification. The *package body* includes the subprogram implementations, local variables, and other subprograms that are not visible to external program units. Ada specifies that data objects declared in a package specification or body exist between calls to subprograms declared in the package specification. The package data objects have the same lifetime as the innermost block or program unit in which the package is nested. For example, if a package has no enclosing block or program unit except the MAIN program, the data objects declared in the package exist for the duration of the program, including the period between calls to subprograms of the package. The data objects continue to exist after the statements of the package body have been executed.

Since the data objects declared in a package specification have the same lifetime as the block or program unit enclosing the package, a run-time model of implementation stores the data objects in the activation record (stack frame) of the enclosing block or program unit. The data objects declared in a package specification are not stored in the activation records or frames of the subprograms in the package body. The implementation of packages is further detailed in Chapter 6.

3.8.4 Concurrency, Tasks, and Synchronization

The development of the concept of concurrency was a result of the development of multiuser operating systems. Multiuser operating systems were developed because a program performing I/O functions under a single-user operating system uses the processing unit inefficiently. In a multiuser operating system environment, while one user program is waiting for an I/O operation to complete another user program can use the processing unit. As a result, the operating system treats a user program as a concurrent module (called a *process*) so that it can be *active* at the same time as other processes. A process is *active* once it is initiated, even while it waits for I/O completion. If there is more than one processing unit, the processes can run at the same time asynchronously.

PL/I introduced the concept of concurrency in high-level languages in the late 1960s. More recent languages such as Ada also make concurrency and synchronization mechanisms available. Ada calls its concurrent modules *tasks*. High-level language tasks and operating system processes are similar: they are concurrent modules that must be synchronized and must communicate with each other. However, an important difference exists between them. Processes belong to different users and must be protected from each other. Tasks are created by a single programmer and may not need protection. Hence, embedded in the concept of processes is a protection mechanism. Each process exists in its own address space and that address space is inaccessible to other processes. Tasks, on the other hand, share an address space. The concepts of processes, protection, synchronization, and communication are discussed further in Chapter 6. This chapter explains some of the implementation issues of tasks, specifically the task and synchronization mechanisms of Ada.

Tasks may run independently until they need to be synchronized with each other. Synchronizations occur at predetermined points called rendezvous. If a task reaches a rendezvous before another task—that is, it has called an entry that has not been accepted or it has accepted an entry that has not been called—it must wait. Such a task is said to be in a *wait state*. If a programmer initiates more tasks than there are available processing units, the active tasks not having a processing unit to run on are said to be in a *ready state*. Tasks in the ready state are placed in a ready queue. The tasks that are actually running on the processing units are in the *run state*. Whenever a task in the *run state* switches into the *wait state* because of an unfulfilled rendezvous, a processing unit becomes available. A task from the ready queue switches from the ready state to the run state and executes on the processing unit.

The run-time code that manages the active tasks in a processing unit is part of the *operating system kernel*. A task may contain subprograms and hence is represented by a run-time stack. In addition, a task's run-time representation includes a *task descriptor* to be used by the kernel in managing the task when it switches states. The task descriptor contains status information about the task and the state of the processing unit (the register contents) at the point when the task switches from run state to either the wait state or the ready state. This information is used to restore the processing unit registers when the task switches back to the run state.

A task may enclose other program modules, for example, another task. When a task initiates other tasks within its environment, the stacks of the initiated tasks must be linked to the stack of their parent task. Since the parent task may not resume until its offspring tasks have terminated, the stacks of the offspring tasks may be built on top of the stack of the parent task. Since there may be more than one offspring task to a parent task, the stack structure must be able to accommodate multiple stacks emanating from a single stack. This representation is termed a *cactus stack*. For example, the program

```
procedure MAIN is
    procedure INITIATE_TASKS is
        task A is
           .
           .
           .
        end A;
        task B is
           .
           .
           .
        end B;
        task body A is
           .
           .
           .
        end A;
        task body B is
           .
           .
           .
            task C is
               .
               .
               .
            end C;
            task D is
               .
               .
               .
            end D;
```

```
                        task body C is
                            .
                            .
                            .
                        end C;
                        task body D is
                            .
                            .
                            .
                        end D;
                        .
                        .
                        .
                    end B;
            begin
            end INITIATE_TASKS;
        begin
            .
            .
            .
            INITIATE_TASKS;
            .
            .
            .
        end MAIN;
```

specifies the task family shown in Fig. 3.21(a). The cactus stack representing the activation records of the tasks is shown in Fig. 3.21(b). The activation records of offspring tasks are each linked to the activation record of the procedure or block in their parent task. The linked activation records in the cactus stack form the access environment of a task in execution. Figures 3.22(a) and 3.22(b) show the access environments of tasks A and C from the task family of Fig. 3.21(a). The main task's access environment is its own stack. Task A, an offspring of the main task, has its own stack as well as the main stack in its access environment. Task C, an offspring of task B (which in turn is an offspring of the main task), has its own stack, task B's stack, and the main task's stack in its access environment.

3.8.4.1 Synchronization. A task may define a set of entries specifying synchronization points with other tasks. Each entry may be represented at run time by an *entry descriptor*. One field in the entry descriptor points to the task in which the entry is defined (the entry's owner task). A second field in the entry descriptor describes whether or not the entry has been accepted by its owner task. A third field in the entry descriptor points to a wait queue of tasks that have called the entry. Hence, in this model, a system implements multiple wait queues, one for each entry. Alternatively, a system may imple-

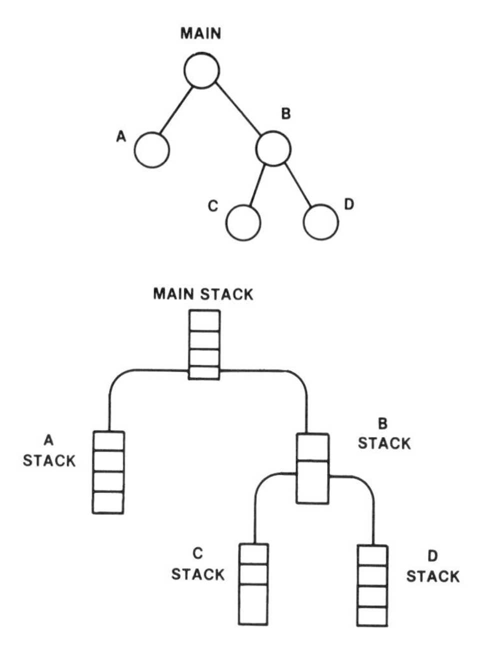

Figure 3.21 (a) A family of tasks; (b) cactus stack representation.

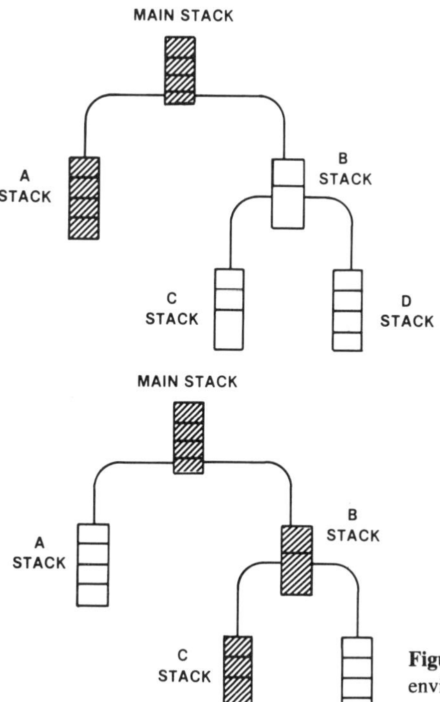

Figure 3.22 (a) Task A's access environment; (b) task C's access environment.

ment a single wait queue, where the tasks in the wait queue waiting for a particular entry are linked. A fourth field in the entry descriptor points to the entry body.

An entry call in Ada may be implemented by a kernel procedure that saves the processor state into the caller task's task descriptor. The kernel procedure then accesses the corresponding entry descriptor of the entry being called to determine whether the entry has been accepted by its owner task. If the entry has been accepted by its owner task, the kernel switches the state of the owner task from the wait state to the run state. The kernel then restores the processor state using the task descriptor of the owner task and determines the address for the entry body using the entry descriptor. Since the entry body in Ada must be executed as an indivisible unit, the kernel also inhibits interrupts, allows the entry body to be executed, and places the calling task into the ready queue by switching its state from the run state to the ready state. After the entry body is executed, the kernel reallows the interrupts. The owner task then continues to execute. If the entry has not been accepted by its owner task, the kernel switches the state of the calling task from the run state to the wait state and places it in the wait queue associated with the entry. The kernel then selects another task from the processor's ready queue to run.

An accept statement of an entry in Ada may be implemented by a kernel procedure that first saves the processor state in the owner task's task descriptor and accesses the corresponding entry descriptor. The kernel updates the entry descriptor field to indicate that the entry's owner task has accepted the entry. If the wait queue corresponding to the entry is not empty, the kernel allows the entry body to be executed, and changes the state of the tasks in the wait queue from the wait state to the ready state. It then restores the processor state and allows the owner task to continue execution. If the wait queue is empty, the kernel switches the state of the owner task from the run state to the wait state and updates the entry descriptor to point to the owner task descriptor.

Ada's **select** statement permits a nondeterministic selection of possible rendezvous. A **select** statement may be implemented by a kernel procedure that first saves the processing unit state in the owner task's task descriptor. It then checks the list of entries for the open alternatives. If none are found, the **else** alternative is executed. If there is no **else** alternative, the kernel raises an exception. If there are open alternatives, and among these there are no entries with wait queues, the kernel switches the state of the owner task from the run state to the wait state, and changes the entry descriptor field of all open entries to indicate that the owner task has accepted the entries. The kernel then selects another task from the processor's ready queue to run. If among the open alternatives there are entries with wait queues, the kernel arbitrarily selects an entry among these and switches the state of the tasks in the corresponding wait queue from the wait state to the ready state. The entry body then executes and the owner task may continue to run.

3.9 EXCEPTIONS

Exceptions are abnormal conditions or events that may occur during the execution of a program. They need to be handled specially. Some high-level languages, such as PL/I and Ada, permit programmers to declare exceptions, raise exceptions, and define handlers to manage exceptions when they occur. PL/I and Ada define different protocols for handling exceptions that determine their run-time models of implementation.

PL/I exceptions and handlers are declared by ON statements. Exceptions are raised by SIGNAL statements; they are handled by handlers declared within their environments (scopes). If no handler has been declared in its environment when an exception is raised, a default action (such as flagging a semantic error) is taken. After an exception is handled, it returns to the statement following the SIGNAL statement. For the run-time model, exceptions and handlers may be stored with the activation record since they are associated with an environment. When an ON statement is encountered during program execution, the compiled code stores the exception name and its handler (or pointer to the handler) in the activation record of the current environment. When the environment is exited, the activation record (including the exceptions and exception handlers) are popped off the stack. When a SIGNAL statement is encountered during program execution, the compiled code saves the program counter and initiates a search for the handler corresponding to the raised exception. The search starts with the most recent declared exceptions and exception handlers stored in the activation record. When the corresponding handler is not found in the current activation record, the default action is taken. Otherwise, when the handler is found, its code is executed. Upon completion, the saved program counter is restored and the program continues past the point where the exception was raised.

In Ada, the environment in which an exception is raised may not contain the corresponding exception handler. In that case, the exception propagates outward to its enclosing environment to search for the corresponding exception handler; the propagation continues until the handler is found. If the search reaches the main routine without encountering the handler, the program terminates. If the search finds the handler, the handler executes and the environment containing it is exited. Flow control returns to the point that activated the environment containing the exception handler. Flow control is not returned to the point where the exception was raised.

Ada's exception-handling mechanism may be implemented by the following run-time model. The activation record of each environment contains an exception handler entry. This entry may either contain zero or the address of the exception handler table in the environment of that routine. When an exception is raised, the compiled code examines the exception handler entry. If the entry contains zero, the activation record is popped. If the entry contains the handler table address, the table is searched for the desired handler. If it is not found, the activation record is popped. The activation record of its caller rises to the top of the stack. Its exception handler entry is in turn examined. If the entry contains zero or its exception handler table does not contain the desired handler, the activation record is popped. This process continues until the exception handler is found. The exception handler then executes. Any activation record popped during the search is lost. When the exception handler finishes execution, the activation record containing the handler is popped, and flow control returns to its caller. The caller's activation record would be at the top of the stack. If the search reaches all the way to thc base of the stack without finding the exception handler, a program error is implied and an operating system exception handler is called.

3.10 STORAGE ALLOCATION

So far, this chapter has described data elements and data structures of various types and how they may be represented in machine storage. It has also discussed how the data objects may be grouped into data areas to represent an environment of a program unit. Once the representation is determined, storage is allocated to contain the representation of data objects. Storage allocation may be done at compile time by the compiler or at run time by code generated by the compiler. The following discussion covers storage allocation for data elements and data structures as they appear in program modules for the various languages. Different high-level languages require different storage allocation methods. To exemplify the differences, this section discusses aspects of storage allocation for FORTRAN, ALGOL, PL/I, and Ada.

3.10.1 Static Storage Allocation

Static storage allocation is performed at compile time. Static allocation and the assignment of addresses are possible if the compiler is able to determine the address that each object will occupy during program execution. The compiler can make this determination only if the following conditions are met:

1. The size of all possible objects of the program are known at compile time, thus permitting only static data structures such as arrays with constant bounds.
2. Each object has only one occurrence at any given moment during the execution of the program, thus permitting only nonrecursive procedures.
3. Each object and its name are bound to a particular memory location throughout the execution of the program throughout all subprogram calls.

The compiler can determine the number, type, and size of the possible objects and generate the address of each object. In other words, the position of each object at run time can be determined during compilation, and storage for all data can be allocated before the program executes.

3.10.2 Dynamic Storage Allocation

Dynamic storage allocation is performed at run time by code generated by the compiler. In high-level languages in which new data objects are created at run time and dynamic data structures are permitted, storage allocation is dynamic. Because dynamic data structures can vary in size, the compiler is not able to assign a fixed amount of storage to them. Nor can it associate specific addresses with the components of the data structures. Instead, the compiler allocates a fixed amount of storage to hold the addresses of the dynamically allocated components instead of the components themselves. Dynamic storage allocation is also required to support recursion because it is not possible during compilation to determine how many times a procedure will call itself recursively during program execution. The number of times a procedure calls itself recursively determines the number of occurrences of data objects declared within the procedure. Dynamic storage allocation is also required to support concurrent processing. When a process is created, storage space is allocated to it. After a process terminates, algorithms are needed to recover the storage allocated to the terminated process.

Two types of dynamic storage allocation are stack allocation and heap allocation. Stack allocation handles recursion and procedure calls efficiently. It depends on a last-in, first-out order for the allocation and release of storage. That is, the last storage space allocated is the first storage space released. The compiler generates a sequence of instructions for each procedure entry and exit to allocate and deallocate a stack frame for the procedure's activation record.

Storage allocation for blocks may be treated the same way as storage allocation for procedures using the stack mechanism. On entry into a block, a stack frame is created that contains storage for all the variables within the block and its inner blocks. When an inner block is entered, a stack frame is allocated from the space in the stack frame allocated for the enclosing block. When a block is exited, its stack frame is popped off. Heap allocation is a more general dynamic allocation method. It does not depend on any specific order of allocation and release of storage. It is useful for implementing dynamic data structures and concurrent processes but requires more overhead than stack allocation.

Records and arrays stored in space allocated from a heap are referenced by pointers. These pointers in turn are kept in locations allocated on a stack. That is, if a procedure contains a record, the record object is kept in the heap; its pointer is kept in the procedure's stack frame. The pointers in the stack frame point to blocks of memory in the heap. Blocks pointed to by at least one pointer are called *used blocks;* they contain the data objects. Each data object usually has some descriptor space allocated with it for storing information used by the storage allocator. The descriptors contain, for example, the block length (size of the data objects) and pointers inside the data objects that reference other heap data objects. All the unused free blocks are linked together by pointers into a free block list. A used block becomes free when no more pointers point to it. If a count is kept of the pointers to a used block, the block is linked to the free block list when the use count is zero.

Instead of keeping use counts, *garbage collection* may be done. Garbage collection is the process by which each block is checked to see whether there is a path of pointers to that block. Garbage collection occurs periodically or when there is no more available free space. All blocks having pointers to them are marked (usually by a bit) as the whole heap is examined. The unmarked blocks are put into the free list.

One disadvantage of heap allocation is that storage is prone to fragmentation. Fragmentation of storage results when blocks in noncontiguous storage locations are freed. The free blocks that are linked by pointers individually may not be large enough to store a data structure, although collectively they are. In this case, several free blocks must be joined to make a large enough storage space. This is called *storage compaction*. Storage compaction is time consuming because the data blocks must be relocated and all the pointers to them updated. Storage compaction and garbage collection are discussed further in Chapter 6.

In a fixed storage space, the stack is often placed at one end and the heap is placed at

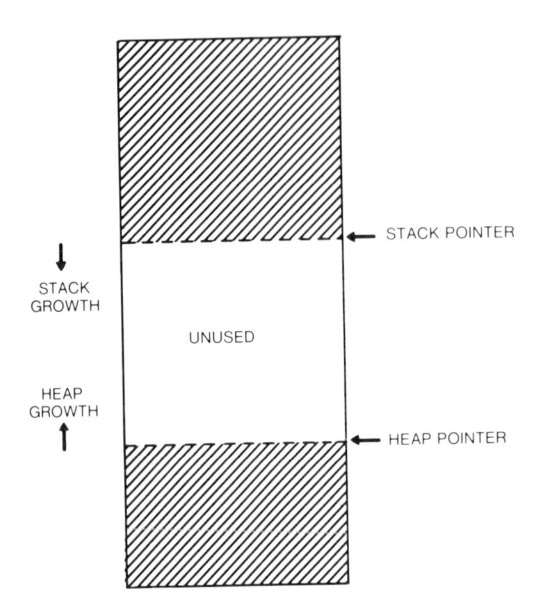

Figure 3.23 Storage allocation using heap and stack.

the other end (Fig. 3.23). They are allowed to grow toward each other until they meet. When they meet, the heap is collapsed and the process begins again. If the stack frames to store the activation records of the procedures that do the garbage collection and storage compaction algorithms are also placed on the same stack, space must be set aside for them. That is, garbage collection and storage compaction must have space to run before the stack and heap meet.

3.10.3 Storage Allocation in FORTRAN

FORTRAN permits neither dynamic data structures nor recursion. Thus *all* storage allocation is done statically during compilation. The FORTRAN compiler allocates a data area (block of storage) for each routine. In addition, FORTRAN allows additional data areas to be specified by the COMMON statement. Each COMMON statement specifies a set of names; the objects referred to by these names are stored in a "common" data area, which is not specific to any routine.

Static storage allocation results in the inefficient use of memory for data structures accessed only once in a small part of the program because the data structures must occupy the allocated space throughout the execution of the whole program. To alleviate this problem, FORTRAN allows programmers to overlay one data object on top of another (that is, to use the same storage) if their lifetimes do not overlap. FORTRAN does this by means of the EQUIVALENCE statement. For example, the statement

EQUIVALENCE (X[1,1],Y[1])

specifies that the starting location for array X is the same as the starting location for array Y. The same storage area is used for both the X and Y arrays. This feature takes advantage of the fact that the use of X is completed before the use of Y begins, or vice versa. The EQUIVALENCE statement is highly oriented to the pragmatics of machine storage space utilization.

3.10.4 Storage Allocation in ALGOL

ALGOL allocates storage dynamically for a variable on entry to the block in which the variable is declared. ALGOL supports dynamic arrays with bounds that may change during program execution; however, the bounds of a dynamic array are fixed at block entry. The bounds of an array are calculated before entering the block in which the array is declared. Once the block is entered, the array is allocated storage with the appropriate bounds. An ALGOL compiler stores the array in two parts on a stack. The first part (an array descriptor) contains the pointer to the array and the bounds of the array. The storage required to store the first part is fixed. The second part contains the array itself and may be of variable size. Both parts are allocated storage only when the block or procedure containing the array is entered. The allocated storage is freed upon exiting the block. Thus, with dynamic allocation, storage overlay by the programmer (such as that provided by the EQUIVALENCE statement) is not required. However, dynamic allocation needs to be performed every time the program executes; static allocation is done only once during compilation.

3.10.5 Storage Allocation in PL/I

In PL/I, the programmer specifies the storage allocation attributes of data objects. There are four types of allocated storage: static, automatic, controlled, and based. Static storage is permanent and assigned during compilation, as in FORTRAN. PL/I allows internal and external static storage. Internal static storage is local to a program. External static storage, like FORTRAN COMMON storage, may be referenced by the procedures of another program. Hence, external storage is allocated in a separate segment from the program segment. The loader usually loads both the program segments of a particular job and their external static segments. It checks whether two external static segments contain the same variables and ensures that no storage is duplicated. All references to the external static variables are made indirectly through a series of pointers located in the internal static area of the program. This is how it is done on machines like the IBM S/360. In the MULTICS system, the pointers to the external static area are not placed with the program segment, but in a separate segment called a linkage segment.

Automatic storage in PL/I is similar to the dynamic allocation method used in ALGOL. Storage is allocated automatically when a procedure or a block executes. For example, procedure X with an automatic variable A has storage allocated for A when procedure X is entered. When procedure X is exited, A's space is automatically released for use by other procedures. It is possible that different storage locations will be assigned to A each time procedure X is called. The use of automatic storage promotes efficient memory usage.

Controlled storage allows the programmer to have explicit control over storage allocation at execution time. Specific blocks of storage may be allocated and deallocated (freed) by the programmer by means of the ALLOCATE and FREE statements. Controlled storage may be internal or external. Internal controlled storage allows the programmer to allocate a work space within a program. External controlled storage may be referenced or freed by the procedures of another program. Controlled storage is not allocated at compile time or at the activation of the procedure in which it is declared. Instead, it is allocated at the execution of an ALLOCATE statement. Similarly, it is released only at the execution of a FREE statement.

Based storage is also controlled by the programmer; an ALLOCATE statement creates it and a FREE statement releases it. The difference between controlled and based storages is that controlled storage is allocated on a stack and based storage is allocated from a heap and referenced through a base pointer. The compiler translates the ALLOCATE and FREE statements by generating calls to procedures in the operating system. In response to an ALLOCATE statement, the operating system returns a pointer to an unused block with the specified length from a free storage pool. In response to a FREE statement, the operating system returns the deallocated block of storage indicated by a pointer back to the free storage pool. The pointer to an internal based storage block is placed in the internal static area. The pointer to an external based storage block is placed in the external static area so other procedures may reference it.

3.10.6 Storage Allocation in Ada

Storage allocation in Ada is in many ways similar to storage allocation in ALGOL since Ada is derived from ALGOL and its successors. Storage allocation in Ada uses stack allocation for holding activation records containing the variables and the parameters of procedures, functions, nested blocks, and package bodies. An activation record on the stack also contains run-time representations of types and subtypes (templates), exception-handling information, lexical scoping data, and procedure and function linkage information. When a procedure or function is called, when a nested block is entered, or when the sequence of instructions constituting the initialization of a package body is entered, a new stack frame is allocated and pushed onto the stack to hold the activation record.

Ada's variably sized arrays may be allocated storage on top of the stack or from a heap. A task is allocated storage from a heap. The allocated storage holds the stack containing the activation records of the procedures within the task. That is, when a task is initiated, a block of storage is allocated from a heap, and out of this storage stack frames are allocated when procedures of the task are entered.

3.11 SUMMARY

The compilation process is composed of an analysis stage followed by a synthesis stage. The analysis stage (lexical analysis, syntactical analysis, and semantic analysis) reads and recognizes language symbols, their syntactic constructs, and their semantic contents. It checks the validity of these symbols, constructs, and contents to ensure that they have not violated any of the high-level-language rules. It also filters out any of the high-level-language program constructs that have no bearing on the run-time implementation. The synthesis stage uses the results of the analysis stage (a decorated parse tree and a symbol table) to generate machine or assembly code based on a framework or model of implementation. It optimizes the generated code by judiciously using the resources (storage, registers, etc.) of the underlying machine.

The run-time model of implementation provides the cohesive framework from which the compiler generates the code. The model of data objects of different types determines how they are represented, how they are encoded, and how they are manipulated. The model for the data objects and their scopes determines whether they are accessible and how they are accessed at the point of execution. The model for the data objects and their lifetimes determines how storage is allocated and deallocated dynamically to hold the data objects. The model for program units that obey a last-activated, first-terminated relationship fits naturally on a stack implementation. For other program units (such as coroutines and tasks), a heap implementation is used. The model for concurrent program modules requires the cooperation of an operating system kernel to manage the concurrent units.

REFERENCES

[1] D. Gries, *Compiler Construction of Programming Languages,* Wiley, New York, 1971.

[2] A. V. Aho and J. D. Ullman, *Principles of Compiler Design,* Addison-Wesley. Reading, Mass., 1978.

[3] *VAX 11/780 Hardware Handbook,* Digital Equipment Corp., Maynard, Mass., 1978.

[4] A. V. Aho and S. C. Johnson, ''Optimal Code Generation for Expression Tree,'' *J. ACM,* Vol. 23, No. 3, 1976.

[5] Draft 8.0 of IEEE Task P754, ''A Proposed Standard for Binary Floating-Point Arithmetic,'' *Computer,* March 1981.

[6] M. Elson, *Concepts of Programming Languages,* Science Research Associates, Chicago, 1973.

[7] E. Horowitz and S. Sahni, *Fundamentals of Data Structures,* Computer Science Press, Rockville, Md., 1976.

[8] R. H. Eckhouse, Jr., and L. R. Morris, *Minicomputer Systems Organization: Programming and Applications (PDP-11),* Prentice-Hall, Englewood Cliffs, N.J., 1979.

[9] R. K. Johnson and J. D. Wick, ''An Overview of the Mesa Processor Architecture,'' *Symp. Archit. Support Program. Lang. Oper. Syst.* ACM, March 1982.

PROBLEMS

3.1 The phases of a compiler (lexical analysis, syntactic analysis, semantic analysis, storage allocation, code generation, and code optimization) may be executed in a single pass or in multiple passes. A *pass* is a module that reads the source program or output from a previous pass, makes the required analysis and manipulations, and generates an output file that may be read by a subsequent pass. The grouping of phases into passes and the number of passes are characteristics of the compiler. What are the advantages and disadvantages of single-pass compilers versus multiple-pass compilers? (*Hint*: Is a single-pass compiler more or less efficient than a multiple-pass compiler? Does a single-pass compiler require more or less memory space to perform a compilation than a multiple-pass compiler? Do all languages lend themselves to single-pass compilation? What are some of the language features that may not lend themselves to single-pass compilation?)

3.2 Register allocation and assignment is an important part of compilation because operations with register operands in most machines are much more efficient than operations with memory operands. The C language allows programmers to assign registers to specific variables. What are the advantages and disadvantages of this language feature?

3.3 FORTRAN was designed with the intent of being an easily compilable language where very efficient compiled code can be generated. What characteristics of FORTRAN and its model of implementation enhance the efficiency of the compiled code?

3.4 When the lifetimes of two names overlap and are bound to the same memory location, the names are said to be aliases of one another. Give examples of aliases possible in high-level languages.

3.5 List the compile-time and run-time checks needed to support Ada's types. Compare them with the checks needed to support FORTRAN.

3.6 If enumeration types are represented by integers and enumeration type literals assume integer values, what are some possible compile-time and run-time mechanisms to check that objects with different enumeration types (each represented by integers) are not mixed in an operation?

3.7 What is a possible mechanism to check that the indices of an array element reference are within the bounds of the array type definition? Is this check done at compile time or at run time?

3.8 Certain high-level language operators are supported directly by a machine instruction. Why shouldn't all high-level language operators have one-to-one mappings to machine instructions?

3.9 Compare the advantages and disadvantages of the static and dynamic link mechanism versus the display mechanism to support block-structured languages.

3.10 Consider the following nested structure:

```
procedure A is
    procedure B is
        procedure C is
        begin
            •
            •
        end C;
    begin
        •
        •
        •
        C;
    end B;
```

```
          procedure D is
          begin
             •
             •
             •
             B;
          end D;
begin
   •
   •
   •
   D;
end A;
```

Describe the creation and deletion of activation records on the stack as the procedure A is executed.

4

Instruction Set Design

4.1 INTRODUCTION

The compilation process maps high-level language concepts into run-time representations. The run-time representations constitute a model of implementation. The aspects of the architecture that must account for the model of implementation are the instruction set and the hardware that executes it. The code generator of a compiler uses the instruction set to produce instruction streams. The efficiency of an instruction set in supporting a high-level language corresponds to the efficiency of the instruction streams in implementing run-time representations of the high-level-language concepts. The design of an instruction set is optimally done in conjunction with the designs of the model of implementation and the code generator.

An instruction set defines the primitive operations implied by the semantics of high-level languages that, when supported by the firmware or hardware of a machine, increase the efficiency of program execution. An instruction set defines the operators, data types, and addressing modes to be recognized by the hardware and firmware of a machine. Architects and compiler designers faced with designing an instruction set must not only know *how* to support high-level-language constructs, they must judge *why* the constructs should be directly supported by the instruction set. That is, the architects and compiler designers must decide which high-level-language constructs should be supported by software (by sequences of compiler-generated instructions) and which should be supported by hardware or firmware by single, compiler-generated instructions. They must take into account cost and performance constraints when determining the complexity and size of the instruction set.

To be compiled, each high-level language requires a minimal set of instructions.

Each high-level-language construct is represented by a single instruction or by a sequence of instructions from the minimal set. The architect determines from measurements of the frequency of occurrence of a high-level-language construct whether the machine may be made more efficient by adding an instruction to the minimal instruction set to replace a sequence of instructions. Each instruction is incorporated into the machine as a primitive that is interpreted by microcode and executed by hardware.

This chapter discusses the many aspects of instruction set design. It examines the different considerations computer architects and compiler writers have in designing an instruction set, and presents the two philosophies of instruction set design: that of reduced instruction set computers (RISCs) and that of complex instruction set computers (CISCs). This chapter presents as examples the instruction sets of the PDP 11, VAX 11, S/360, and S/370. The addressing modes and ways of encoding instruction formats are also covered. The decisions and trade-offs encountered by the instruction set designer may be approached through the use of a design methodology and through the study of instruction mix. Finally, the chapter presents the set of heuristics for efficient instruction set design.

4.2 INSTRUCTION SET DESIGN FROM A COMPUTER ARCHITECT'S VIEWPOINT

Computer architects and compiler designers determine the primitives to include in a machine instruction set. After supporting the minimal set of instructions necessary for compilation, they expand the instruction set to accommodate additional primitives until the point of diminishing returns is reached. Computer architects design the hardware and firmware to match the instruction set. They must consider code density, processing and memory access speeds, and improvements in technology to ensure that the size of the instruction set is optimal for the overall efficiency and cost of the computer [1,2].

4.2.1 Code Density

One of the most often cited advantages of a large instruction set is code density, where single powerful instructions replace sequences of instructions. Dense code is advantageous because it requires less memory storage and fewer memory accesses to perform the same functions of less dense code. It also enhances cache and paging performance as the working set becomes smaller. The compaction of code by increasing the number of instructions in an instruction set eventually reaches a level where the extra bit required per instruction to encode a larger instruction set increases the amount of storage required for a program as much as instances in a program where a single instruction replacing multiple instructions reduces the amount of storage required. Long before such a level is reached, however, the cost of supporting new instructions needs to be justified using other metrics such as size of the microstore and difficulty of the design. These metrics are discussed in the next sections.

4.2.2 Speed of Memory versus Speed of Processing Unit

If a processing unit has to be idle while accessing memory for instructions, a denser representation of the code would enhance performance. If a processor is pipelined, however, the operations of the processing unit and the memory accesses can proceed in parallel. The level of pipelining has increased in processors since the late 1960s. The architect must then compare the speed of memory and the speed of the processing unit. If memory is slower than the processing unit, performance may be improved by reducing the load on the memory unit; that is, by giving it denser code. On the other hand, when the processing unit is the bottleneck, denser code does not improve performance significantly. The imbalance of memory and CPU speed was very large in the days of the IBM 701 when the processing unit was about 10 times faster than the core memory. With the prevalent use of cache memory to reduce memory access time, the architect must reevaluate the speed ratio and how it affects trade-offs in the instruction set design. With the advent of multiprocessor systems (systems with shared memory), memory access again becomes quite costly. In such architectures, denser code enhances performance.

4.2.3 Speed of Instruction versus Speed of Microinstruction

In a microcoded machine, an instruction is implemented by a sequence of microinstructions. A large instruction set includes instructions to perform activities that, without them, would be performed by sequences of simpler instructions. The execution of a single instruction (that is, a sequence of microinstructions) replaces the execution of a sequence of instructions. Thus the ratio of the speed of an instruction to the speed of a microinstruction is an important metric for evaluating instruction set design. The frequency of occurrence of a high-level language construct and the speed ratio of its implementation in a microinstruction sequence to its implementation in an instruction sequence determine the performance gain.

4.2.4 Size of Microstore

One of the disadvantages of a large instruction set is that it requires a large microstore. Since the size of microstores is allocated in powers of 2, the instruction set may sometimes be made more complex at no extra hardware cost by expanding the microprogram to fill the control memory completely. The extra space in the control memory, however, is often used for other purposes such as diagnostic and console functions, the support of multiple instruction sets, and system functions such as memory management and interrupt handling. The size of the microstore is a cost metric to consider when evaluating any performance gains of larger instruction sets.

4.2.5 VLSI Implementation

Just as a larger instruction set takes more microstore space in a microprogrammed implementation, it takes a larger control PLA in a VLSI implementation. Again, the valuable chip area may be put to better use by implementing functions with even a larger effect on performance than dense code. For example, if the chip area for implementing additional powerful instructions is used for on-chip address translation, a cache, or pipelining, the performance gain achieved may be larger.

4.2.6 Design Difficulty

The cost of an architecture relates directly to the complexity of its design. One may argue that a larger instruction set complicates microcode design. On the other hand, the microcode design simply replaces parts of the software design. For example, a string edit instruction or an integer-to-floating point conversion instruction implemented by microcode merely replaces software subroutines performing the same functions. Thus the architect must evaluate the relative difficulties of coding in software and microcoding. In general, microcoding is more difficult than coding in software.

4.2.7 Compatibility

The processors in a family of processors have compatible architectures based on the same instruction set. New members of the family must include all the instructions found in the other machines. To ensure that existing application software can run on the new member of the family, instructions are seldom removed from an architecture. To enhance performance, though, new instructions are usually added. As a result, the number and complexity of instructions of a series of computers of the same family tend to increase. Removing instructions from an instruction set is more difficult than adding instructions to one. Given this tendency, it is important to keep the initial instruction set design simple.

4.2.8 Technology

The life of a computer system may span many hardware implementations. The overall performance of the instruction set is thus much more important than the performance of a particular current implementation of it. Optimization of the instruction set based on the current technology should therefore be done carefully; that is, current technology should not be the primary factor designing an instruction set. A new technology may make new architectural support possible for the instruction set. The architect should weigh the trade-offs carefully because once an instruction is added to the instruction set of a family of computers, it is seldom removed.

4.3 INSTRUCTION SET DESIGN FROM A COMPILER WRITER'S VIEWPOINT

While a computer architect is concerned with matching the instruction set to the machine organization and technology for the best cost/performance trade-offs, a compiler writer matches the designs of the model of implementation to the design of the instruction set. A compiler writer is concerned with the correctness and simplicity of the compiler in translating high-level-language semantics to machine operations, data types, and addressing modes. A compiler writer's viewpoint of the principles for an instruction set design are reviewed below [3].

4.3.1 Regularity

Instruction sets are regular when similar operations are specified in the same way. A machine instruction set is regular, for example, if any addressing mode may specify an instruction operand. In other words, register, memory, source, and destination operands are all treated symmetrically by the instruction set.

Irregularity appears in an instruction set, for example, if the operations on words are not symmetric with the operations on bytes, and when condition codes are set differently for byte operations and full-word operations. Arithmetic shift instructions are another example of irregularity. On most machines, the arithmetic right shift is not a division by a power of 2, but the arithmetic left shift is a multiplication by a power of 2. Other examples of irregularities are (1) special provisions for handling immediate mode arithmetic with only a few constants (0, +1, and −1), (2) carries that do not propagate beyond the size of an address, (3) operations that are restricted to operate on a selected set of index registers, (4) general registers with special purposes so they are not treated uniformly (for example, multiplicands placed only in even registers), and (5) specifying that some operations be performed only between registers while others are performed only between a register and memory or any of many other variations.

From a compiler writer's viewpoint, every irregularity must be considered individually. The consideration of a special case manifests itself not only in code generation and optimization but in many phases of the compiler design. The selection process required to generate an optimized object program becomes much more complex if many special cases have to be treated.

4.3.2 One or All

To compile efficiently, a compiler should have to perform a minimal amount of analysis. To minimize the analysis, the instruction set should perform similar operations one way or all ways. Neither of these positions requires the compiler to analyze individual cases while generating code. Difficulties arise when there are several ways of performing the same operation and the compiler must decide the best way for each case. This is not a simple decision because each combination may create different side effects.

4.3.3 Orthogonality

Instruction sets that are *orthogonal* treat addressing modes, operations, and data types independently. In an orthogonal instruction set, the effect of an operation is independent of the addressing modes and data types used; the behavior of an addressing mode is independent of the operations and data types used; and the behavior of a data type is independent of the operations and addressing modes used. For example, the ADD operation in an orthogonal instruction set has identical effects regardless of the data types (bytes or words) it adds.

Two common violations of orthogonality, for example, are whether sign extension is performed on an operation result depends on its destination, and whether a long or a short form of a multiplication result is created depends on the address (even or odd) of the destination register. The compiler performs a separate analysis for each of these cases. The compiler writer's viewpoint is that instruction sets should be orthogonal: they should separate the definitions of data types, addressing modes, and operations and define each of these independently.

4.3.4 Composibility

Composibility is the characteristic of an instruction set that allows all operations to be available to all addressing modes and all data types. That is, a composible instruction set is a full cross-product among its orthogonal elements. Any addressing mode, for example, available for a particular operation and data type is available for all other operations and data types. But because of the large number of orthogonal elements, an unreasonable number of instructions are needed to implement a full cross-product. Therefore, only the reasonable cross-products are composed. In the VAX architecture, for example, there are six exclusive-OR instructions: two- and three-operand versions for bytes, words, and long words [2]. Although some of these are used infrequently, their presence simplifies code generation in the VAX compiler.

4.4 REDUCED INSTRUCTION SET AND COMPLEX INSTRUCTION SET

To protect the large investments in software, manufacturers build architecturally compatible computers. Each member of a computer family has software that can be ported easily from one computer to another. From the user's viewpoint, the machines are architecturally compatible. The concept of machine families began with IBM's S/360 series. The IBM S/360 computers all have the same instruction set.

The concept of portability makes the removal of instructions from an instruction set very difficult. On the other hand, instructions sometimes are added to improve performance and to support other high-level-language concepts. A machine with an instruction set that is a superset of the instruction set of another machine is said to be an upwardly compatible member of the same family. The design of an instruction set for a machine member in an existing family is restricted to the design of an upwardly compatible instruction set.

A design approach to architecture for high-level-language support belongs to the school of thought that argues for narrowing the semantic gap between high-level languages and the machine instruction set [4]. This school of thought contends that a large semantic gap between a high-level language and an instruction set complicates the compiler design, lessens the efficiency with which the high-level language is supported, and causes the compiled code to be large in size. An approach to instruction set design, they argue, is to raise the semantic level of the instructions to match the semantic constructs of high-level language. The IBM S/360 and the VAX 11 instruction sets are designed with this approach. These computers are classified as complex instruction set computers (CISCs) because their instruction sets support large sets of opcodes, addressing modes, and data types. They also support semantically high-level (more complex and powerful) instructions such as call, branch on index low or equal, and so on.

Narrowing the semantic gap by means of more complex instruction sets eventually reaches a point of diminishing returns. There are two reasons for this. First, instruction mix statistics have shown that only a few instructions are executed frequently. Introducing more complex and powerful instructions to replace sequences of more primitive instructions may not be justifiable in terms of cost and performance. Second, as the added instructions occur at high levels semantically (that is, as they replace long sequences of primitive instructions), the compiler must determine whether they can be matched to the many different instances of the same construct in high-level languages. By their nature, machine instructions are more restrictive than high-level-language constructs in their format (for example, in their specification and number of operands). The compiler must detect the instances of a high-level-language construct that exactly fit the architectured format. The instances that do not fit must be implemented by sequences of instructions. Code generation needs to find just the right instructions. Furthermore, as machine instructions become higher level semantically, possibilities arise that they may be usable with some, but not other, high-level languages because the seemingly same construct in different high-level languages may contain slight semantic differences (side effects and constraints).

In the past few years, an alternative school of thought for supporting high-level languages has emerged. This school argues for reduced instruction sets [1]. It claims that reduced instruction set computers (RISCs) can provide as good a high-level language support as complex instruction set computers (CISCs) [5]. Examples of RISCs include the IBM 801 [6] and the Berkeley RISC I project [7]. Because the PDP 11 minicomputer has a simple instruction set, it may also be classified as a RISC.

Some of the basic concepts of RISCs are illustrated by the IBM 801. The fundamental aim of the 801 architecture is to execute the instructions in the instruction set in a single machine cycle. Any instruction that cannot achieve this goal is not included in the instruction set unless it can justify its cost. Its addition must not slow down the execution of the other instructions of the machine. For example, if a complex instruction adds logic levels, lengthens the basic machine cycle, and hence slows the execution rate, it is rejected unless its performance improvement compensates for the cycle-time degradation and justifies its cost.

Vertical migration has been the driving force for CISCs. Vertical migration is the concept of moving software-implemented functions into firmware-implemented functions. It has great appeal because CPU-firmware executes out of a CPU-resident fast control store. Each microinstruction is designed to execute in a single cycle. A high-level function can be implemented much more efficiently by a sequence of microinstructions than by a sequence of assembly level instructions. However, the aim of RISCs like the 801 is to reduce and simplify the instruction set so that instructions at the assembly level can also be made to execute in a single machine cycle. If most of the instructions can be executed out of a CPU-resident fast store, the advantages of vertical migration are obtained by RISCs without the need of a complex instruction set. In other words, if RISCs can implement software as fast as CISCs can implement firmware, they achieve a great advantage because they eliminate an intermediate level of abstraction.

Even though RISC instructions can be implemented very efficiently, the question arises whether the instruction sets of RISCs, because of their primitiveness, require the compiler to generate more instructions than CISCs to perform the same functions. The 801 designers found that, for system code, the number of 801 instructions executed compares favorably with the number of IBM S/370 instructions executed. For scientific and commercial application code, they found that the number of 801 instructions required is only about 50 percent more than that required on the S/370.

A recent study of the performance of a pattern matching program in hand-coded assembly language and in C on the Berkeley RISC I and the VAX 11/750 and VAX 11/780 finds that the program in both languages executes* faster on the RISC I than on the VAX computers [8]. Further, the study concludes that whereas the hand-coded assembly version and the high-level-language version perform similarly on the RISC I, the hand-coded assembly version is much more efficient on the VAX. The study suggests that even though the VAX contains complex and powerful instructions, most of the instructions produced by the VAX compiler are simple instructions like those available on the RISC I. These instructions take longer on the VAX than on RISC I because the RISC I is optimized for simple instructions. The more complex instructions are only taken advantage of in hand-coded assembly programs.

Instruction sets in CISCs contain instructions designed specifically for the benefit of the assembly programmers (for example, the IBM S/370 edit and mark and translate and test instructions). The designs of the 801 instruction set and compiler has the goal that code generated by the compiler perform as well as code hand-generated by an assembly programmer. The achievement of this goal obviates the need for special instructions in the instruction set that are designed for the assembly programmer rather than for the compiler writer.

The approach to architecture for high-level-language support using the RISC philosophy is the best approach when starting a new family of machines where there are no compatibility and portability constraints. Its philosophy of simplicity is desirable in both the architectural and the compiler designs. The resulting design of the total system is more amenable to optimization to enhance performance and at the same time tends to cost less than CISC designs.

*The execution of the benchmark program on the RISC I was simulated.

4.5 EXAMPLE INSTRUCTION SETS

The instruction sets of the PDP 11 minicomputer, its successor the VAX 11, and the IBM mainframes S/360 and S/370 are examined in this section. These three instruction sets are selected as examples because they are extensively used and are well known. The PDP 11, although not truly a RISC, supports a simple instruction set. The VAX 11 and the IBM S/360 and S/370 supports a wide variety of special instructions and are examples of CISCs.

4.5.1 PDP 11 [9]

The PDP 11 supports a basic set of instructions. They may be divided into the following categories:

- General-purpose binary integer
- Logical and bit
- Unconditional and conditional branch
- Subroutine linkage
- Operating system
- Floating point

1. *General-purpose binary integer instructions* include move, clear, increment, decrement, compare, and negate. They also include fixed-point arithmetic instructions: add, subtract, arithmetic shift, and rotate. The arithmetic shift and rotate instructions implement multiplication and division in software. The PDP 11 family has an extended architecture and instruction set to enhance its basic architecture and instruction set. Fixed-point multiply and divide instructions are parts of the extended instruction set (EIS) for the PDP 11. *Double-* and *multiple-precision arithmetic* with the add carry and subtract carry instructions are also supported.
2. *Logical* and *bit operations* including bit clear, bit set, bit test, complement, and exclusive-OR. The logical AND and OR operations are implicit in the bit clear, bit set, and bit test instructions. The rotate right and rotate left instructions further allow sequential bit testing and manipulation. The bit and logical operations are useful for testing and setting bits within status and control words where information is stored on a bit basis. In a memory-mapped I/O system such as the PDP 11, the I/O control and status registers are treated in the same way as all the other operands stored in memory and thus may be tested and set using the logical and bit operations.
3. The PDP 11 includes a rich set of *unconditional* and *conditional branch instructions*. The conditional branch instructions examine condition codes set by operations treating the data either as signed or unsigned numbers.
4. For *subroutine* linkage, the PDP 11 provides the jump to subroutine (JSR) and return from subroutine (RTS) instructions.

5. The PDP 11 also has a set of *operating system* instructions useful for system programming, controlling exceptions and events, input/output, and multiprogramming. These include HALT, WAIT, return from interrupt (RTI), return from trap (RTT), input/output trap (IOT), RESET, emulator trap (EMT), TRAP, breakpoint trap (BPT), and no operation (NOP).
6. The floating instruction set (FIS) supports *floating-point* arithmetic: floating point add (FADD), subtract (FSUB), multiply (FMUL), and divide (FDIV) instructions. To further enhance floating-point performance, the later PDP 11 models offer the floating-point processor (FPP), and a set of single- and double-precision floating-point instructions. The floating-point processor is available as a hardware accelerator on the PDP 11/34, /45, /55, /60, and /70.

As can be seen from these instructions, the PDP 11 instruction set is simple and contains the basic instructions. But it does include some optimized instructions such as clear, increment, and decrement. The clear instruction is more efficient than a move of a zero operand. Increment and decrement are more efficient than adding and subtracting one. A true RISC architecture may not contain these instructions unless they are found to be used very frequently and the efficiency they introduce in the instances when they are used is greater than the efficiency that is possible with a simpler instruction set running on an efficient but simple architecture.

4.5.2 VAX 11 [10,11]

The VAX 11 supports many instructions with a rich set of addressing modes. The instruction set includes 243 instructions. In addition to the categories supported by the PDP 11, the VAX 11 supports these types of instructions:

- Packed decimal
- Conversion
- Character string
- Loop and case
- Field
- Address manipulation
- Index
- Queue
- Procedure and stack

1. *Integer instructions* include most of the standard move, compare, arithmetic, multiple-precision arithmetic, rotate, and shift instructions. The integer instructions in the VAX 11 are similar to the instructions in the PDP 11 instruction set.
2. *Logical* and *bit* instructions include bit clear, bit set, bit test, exclusive-OR, AND, and OR instructions. The logical and bit instructions in the VAX 11 are similar to the ones found in the PDP 11.

3. A rich set of *branch instructions* is included in the VAX 11. It is similar to the branch instruction set in the PDP 11. The set includes the unconditional branch and jump instructions; the branch on bit, bit set, and bit clear instructions; and the branch on condition code instructions. As in the PDP 11, the branch on condition code instructions include both signed branches and unsigned branches. The signed (unsigned) branch instructions branch on a condition code as a result of testing data treated as signed (unsigned) numbers.
4. *Subroutine instructions* include branch to subroutine with byte and word displacement from the program counter, jump to subroutine, and return from subroutine instructions.
5. *Operating system instructions* are used specifically by the operating system. They set and clear bits in the program status word and move bits from the program status word. Operating system instructions that change the mode of access* (kernel, executive, supervisor, and user), and return the program to the original mode of access are included in the VAX 11 instruction set. The VAX 11 also includes instructions to probe (PROBER, PROBEW) the previous access mode to validate arguments passed in interaccess mode calls.
6. *Floating-point instructions* include move, compare, test, add, subtract, multiply, and divide instructions on floating-point and multiprecision floating point numbers. In addition, they include the POLY instruction, which calculates the value of a polynomial using three operands, the order of the polynomial, the address of a table containing the coefficients of the polynomial, and the polynomial base variable.
7. *Packed decimal instructions* include move, compare, and conventional arithmetic instructions on packed decimal operands. An edit instruction to convert packed decimal strings to character strings is also available. An arithmetic shift and round instruction is used for decimal point scaling and rounding.
8. *Conversion instructions* make conversions between floating-point numbers and integers, and between packed decimal numbers and long word integers, leading decimal strings, and trailing embedded strings. Also, a special convert rounded instruction implements ALGOL rather than FORTRAN conventions for converting from floating-point numbers to integers.
9. *Character string instructions* include the move character string instruction, the compare character string instruction, the move character string with translation instruction, the move character string with translation until the specified escape character is encountered instruction, instructions to locate either the first occurrence or the nonoccurrence of a character string, instructions to locate the first matched substring, and instructions to locate either the first occurrence or the nonoccurrence of a character within a specified character set in a string.
10. *Loop and case instructions* support the FORTRAN DO loops and the FOR loops in other high-level languages. These instructions add one to or subtract one from an index; then they cause the program to branch to a specified loop location until the

*Access modes control the accessibility of memory pages. They provide protection, for example, for the kernel pages from being written when the program is executing in the user access mode.

index reaches a specified limit or zero. A somewhat more powerful instruction allows the increment to the index to be specified also.

The VAX 11 also includes a case instruction to support case statements in high-level languages. The case instruction takes selector operand and subtracts a base operand from it to produce an offset into a table of program-counter relative branch displacements. The selector operator is checked to ensure that it is in the range specified by the limit operand of the case instruction.

11. *Field instructions* replace sequences of shift and bit instructions. They extract and insert up to a 32-bit field into a data word, zero or sign-extend the extracted field, compare fields, and find the first set bit or clear bit in a field. Field instructions may be used to extract and insert digit nibbles in decimal strings. The find the first set bit or clear bit instructions may be used for searching bit maps. Many applications for bit instructions may be found in the operating systems.
12. *Address manipulation instructions* move and push addresses. Push address instructions are used to implement call by reference in a subprogram call. In call by reference, addresses are passed by the caller subprogram to the called subprogram. The push address instruction pushes these addresses onto the stack.
13. *Index instructions* help compilers generate code to address arrays by calculating the index of elements within arrays. At the same time, they check the upper and lower bounds of array dimensions against the index.
14. *Queue instructions* are powerful primitives for the operating system, much like the index instruction is a powerful primitive for the compiler. The VAX 11 contains two instructions to insert and remove entries from doubly linked queues.
15. *Procedure call, return,* and *stack instructions* are universal in the VAX 11; that is, the same instructions are used for calling system procedures (for performing system services) and calling common user-created procedures. To achieve this generality, call instructions and return instructions respectively save and restore the program status word in addition to the program counter. For a system call, the procedure called has at the entry to the procedure a change mode instruction that changes the access mode to a more privileged mode. There are also two types of call instructions: the CALLG instruction and the CALLS instruction. For the CALLG instruction, the argument list does not reside on the stack, and the address of the argument list is an operand of the instruction. The CALLS instruction assumes that the argument list has been built on the stack before it is executed. Other stack instruction on the VAX 11 are the PUSHR and POPR instructions that push and pop registers from the stack. These instructions optimize the switching of environments (program units) where registers need to be saved and returned from stack.

4.5.3 IBM S/360 and S/370 [12]

The IBM S/360 and S/370 machines offer a large variety of instructions, including the basic set of categories of the PDP 11. In addition, they support these types of instructions:

- Packed decimal
- Conversion
- Character manipulation
- Loop
- Special assembly level

1. *General purpose binary integer instructions* include load, store, add, subtract, multiply, divide, and compare. The various types of the general purpose instructions are register-to-memory operations, register-to-register operations, and half-word operations. The load register instructions include load complement register, load positive register, and load negative register. These instructions operate on binary integers. The other IBM S/360 and S/370 instructions may be divided into the following categories.
2. *Bit and logical instructions* include the AND, OR, and XOR instructions and the logical and arithmetic shift (and shift double) instructions.
3. *Branch instructions,* including unconditional branches, are translated by the assembler into the same machine instruction: branch on condition. The assembler supplies the appropriate condition code mask, which determines the type of branch to be made. For example, the unconditional branch instruction is translated to the branch on condition instruction with the mask 1111. Mask 1111 specifies that the branch should occur irrespective of the value of the condition code. Mask 0001 specifies the branch on overflow instruction, where the rightmost mask bit corresponds to the overflow condition code bit. If a given mask bit is zero, a condition code value corresponding to that bit does not cause a branch and is ignored. If a given mask bit is one, a condition code value corresponding to that bit causes a branch.
4. *Subroutine instructions* call subroutines and return from them. To call a subroutine, the caller routine invokes the branch and link instruction to save the return address or link (program counter) in a register before branching to the subroutine entry address. Once a subroutine is entered, the subroutine must save the contents of registers so that it can use the registers without destroying their contents. The subroutine restores the saved register contents before returning to its caller. The IBM 360/370 provides two instructions, store multiple and load multiple, for these purposes. Store multiple stores the registers in the register range specified by two register operands in locations in memory specified by a starting address. Load multiple loads the register in the register range specified by two register operands from the location in memory specified by a starting address.
5. *Operating system instructions* include special input and output instructions and status switching instructions. The input and output instructions initiate the transfer of information between main storage and peripheral devices. They check the status of the peripheral devices and provide control of them. The status switching instructions allow the status of the computer to be switched between the operating system supervisor state and the user state. They also allow the enabling and disabling of interrupts.

6. *Floating-point arithmetic instructions* support the same basic set of operations for floating-point numbers as for binary numbers. They include load, store, add, subtract, multiply, divide, compare, load and test, load positive, load negative, and load complement of single and double precision, normalized and unnormalized floating-point operands. In addition, a halve instruction divides a floating-point number by 2. Furthermore, extended-precision instructions are available. The extended-precision instructions include the load rounded instructions, which round an extended-precision number to a double-precision number, and vice versa.
7. *Decimal arithmetic instructions* can operate on two operands of 16 bytes or 31 digits (plus one sign digit) each. The instructions include add packed, subtract packed, multiply packed, divide packed, and compare packed. The multiplicand of the multiply packed instruction must contain at least one leading zero for every digit (including the sign digit) of the multiplier. The length of a number, however, cannot be determined until execution time. For example, when a pack instruction is generated by the compiler, the length of its operand is not known.

   The IBM S/360 and S/370 machines also provide an execute instruction for specifying the length of an instruction operand at execution time. The execute instruction contains a register operand and a destination address operand. When an execute instruction is encountered, the instruction at the address specified by the destination address operand is executed. The last 8 bits of the register operand are ORed with bits 8 through 15 of the instruction at the destination address. Since bits 8 through 15 are the length field of a pack instruction, the execute instruction allows the pack instruction to have its length field defined at run time. Other uses of the execute instruction are as follows: it permits the modification of immediate operands at run time where bits 8 through 15 form the immediate field of an instruction; it permits the modification of conditions in a branch instruction at run time; and, it permits the modification of the register operands at run time in instructions where the register fields are defined by bits 8 through 15.

   The zero and add packed instruction zeros an area in memory and then adds a decimal number to the zeroed area. The move zones, move numeric, and move with offset instructions shift nibbles within decimal numbers so a number can be multiplied by an odd power of 10. The move zones instruction moves the zone portions of a zoned decimal number or the first 4 bits of each operand byte. The move numeric instruction moves the numeric portions, or the low-order 4 bits of each operand byte, and the move with offset instruction moves an operand into another operand shifted by a nibble. The move zones instruction, for example, could be used in data conversion to insert the sign code from an EBCDIC format into the zone decimal sign nibble. The move with offset instruction is useful for shifting decimal numbers an odd number of decimal places. A more powerful instruction is incorporated in the IBM S/370 series that can shift a decimal number any number of places to thc right or left, inserting the necessary leading or trailing zeros. It also rounds off the last digit of the result in a right shift. This instruction, shift and round packed, allows the rounding factors to be specified as part of the operand.
8. *Conversion instructions* are powerful instructions in the instruction sets of the S/360

and S/370. Input/output devices such as card readers and printers translate Hollerith code into EBCDIC, the internal code of IBM computers, and vice versa. The conversion instructions convert EBCDIC characters into other data formats. The RWD macro instruction causes a subroutine to convert EBCDIC into zoned decimal, packed decimal, and finally into binary. The WWD macro carries out the opposite process. The pack instruction converts a zoned decimal number to a packed decimal number and the unpack instruction converts a packed decimal number to a zoned decimal number. The convert to binary instruction converts a double-word packed decimal number to its binary equivalent. The convert to decimal instruction converts a binary word into its packed-decimal-equivalent double word.

9. *Character manipulation instructions* include move character, which moves a character string from one area of memory to another; move immediate, which moves an immediate byte (character) operand specified by the instruction to a location in memory; insert character, which loads a character; store character, which stores a character byte; compare logical character (and its immediate operand counterpart compare logical immediate), which compare the contents of two character strings.

10. Three *loop instructions* are included in the IBM S/360 and S/370 instruction sets. The branch on count instruction subtracts an implicit count of one from a specified index register operand. If the contents of the register is zero, the program proceeds to the next instruction. Otherwise, it branches to a specified address operand.

    The branch on index low or equal instruction explicitly specifies the count; it is not assumed to be one. Nor does the final value of the loop index have to be zero as it does in the branch on count instruction. The branch on index low or equal instruction explicitly specifies the index register, the count register, and the branch address. The final value register to which the index register is compared is taken to be the count register or the next register past the count register depending on whether the count register is odd or even.

    The third instruction, branch on index high, is the same as the branch on index low or equal instruction except for the condition on which the branch is taken. Whereas the branch on index low or equal instruction is used when the index decreases each time through the loop until it is less than or equal to the final value, the branch on index high instruction is used when the index value increases each time through the loop until it reaches a final value.

11. *Special S/370 instructions* are not found in the IBM S/360 [12]. The insert characters under mask and the store characters under mask instructions allow a 4-bit mask to be specified such that only the appropriate bytes of a word are loaded, stored, or compared. This enhances the use of registers in moving and comparing byte data. Another enhancement to character manipulation is the move character long instruction. Move character long moves very long character strings (16K characters) and allows the padding character to be specified for filling in space in the destination area. Similarly, the compare logical character long compares very long strings.

    The translate instruction specifies the address of a memory table to translate byte by byte a string of bytes in a specified area of memory. The machine assumes the translation table to be 256 bytes long, one byte for each possible 8-bit number.

This instruction may be used in the translation of a character string in one encoding to another encoding (for example, ASCII to EBCDIC). The translate and test instruction allows a byte string to be searched for specified bytes. The translate and test instruction proceeds along the specified string and looks up each byte in a specified translation table. If the corresponding entry in the translation table is not zero, the instruction loads the address of that byte in register 1 and the byte itself into bits 24 through 31 of register 2. It then sets the appropriate condition codes. The translate and test instruction is used to search for illegal or special characters in a character string.

The edit and edit and mark instructions convert packed decimal numbers to their EBCDIC equivalents. The two instructions are identical except that the edit and mark instruction also marks the address of the byte that turned on the significance indicator and saves the address in register 1. This is useful, for example, for printing a character immediately before the first significant digit of a number.

The VAX 11, IBM S/360, and IBM S/370 are examples of CISCs because they include many specialized instructions at a higher semantic level than the basic instructions. These ''complex'' instructions include floating point, packed decimal, conversion, character string, loop and case, field, address manipulation, index, procedure, and edit instructions. They are used for special applications (such as floating-point and conversion instructions for scientific programs; packed decimal and conversion instructions for business programs; and character string field, and edit instructions for text editing programs) and for special high-level-language constructs (including loop and case instructions for loop and case statements, address manipulation instructions for call by reference, index instructions for accessing arrays, and procedure instructions for procedures).

In a RISC architecture, these ''complex'' instructions are not part of the basic instruction set. Packed decimal, floating-point functions, for example, are implemented by subroutines embedded in a library, or are made part of an extended instruction set executed by a specialized, auxiliary processor. Loop and case operations, procedures, and so on, are implemented by a sequence of simple instructions.

4.6 ADDRESSING MODES

In high-level languages, programmers declare data objects and their names. Each declared data object has a lifetime that defines when it exists and a scope that states when it is referenceable. In translating a high-level-language program, the compiler assigns storage for the data objects, associating their names to the memory addresses where they are stored. The storage holding the data objects may be allocated from a stack or a heap depending on the lifetime and scope of the data objects. To support the concept of scope, a display or a static chain may be used for referencing a data object. To reference data objects stored in the stack, various pointers such as (stack pointers, frame pointers, and argument pointers) may be used as base addresses. The addresses of data objects stored in the heap may be stored in the stack. To reference these data objects, the program must first obtain their addresses from the stack. The program must thus generate an address (a stack address) to an address (a heap address). This is called *indirect addressing*.

The addresses of the operands, which are data objects, may be made part of each instruction by the compiler. In many cases, however, it is neither economical nor possible to do so. On a 32-bit machine, each address may have a full 32-bit representation. Storing the full 32-bit addresses as part of each instruction increases the length of each instruction and results in an increase in code size. Often the compiler is not able to generate the address of an operand because the address is known only at run time. Addresses of operands therefore cannot always be made part of an instruction.

An alternative to making an address part of an instruction is the use of *addressing modes*. An addressing mode is a specification for generating an address at run time. Addressing modes are thus also called *operand specifiers* because they specify how to obtain the operand (by generating its address). Addressing modes may be encoded in many fewer bits than a full 32-bit address; for example, VAX 11 addressing modes are encoded in 8 bits. The use of addressing modes is associated with hardware (firmware) support. Hardware (firmware) interprets the addressing mode encoding and carries out the appropriate activities to generate the run-time address of an operand. In a register-based machine architecture, it is efficient to store frequently used base addresses (such as displays, stack pointers, argument pointers, frame pointers, and program counters) in registers. In many addressing modes in this type of machine architecture, the addressing mode specification involves the use of the registers to generate run-time address. Addressing modes are also an effective means of specifying the addresses of data structure elements. Accessing an element of a data structure involves following a path whose length is arbitrary but known at compile time. Each step along the path is an indexing (into arrays or records) or an indirection (through pointers). In the most general case, data structures are arbitrary compositions of scalars, arrays, records, and pointers. In many languages, boundary checks on array subscripts and nil pointers must be performed along the path. Accessing an element of a nonlocal data structure in a block structured language could involve following one path to locate the base address of the data structure and another path to locate the element within the structure.

Unfortunately, most computers do not support addressing modes that specify a general path, but rather support a finite collection of addressing modes that specify special cases of path steps. The compiler's problem is to select the appropriate addressing mode among these finite special cases. For example, some machines have a fixed order for indexing and indirection (for example, index first and then follow the indirection). Other machines implicitly multiply one operand in an indexing operation and limit the size of the literal value in an indexing mode. Compilers must handle the general case and maps the model of implementation into the architectured addressing modes.

Different machines have adopted different approaches to addressing modes [11]. The IBM S/370 uses very few options in addressing modes whereas the DEC VAX 11/780 supports a rich set of addressing modes. The CDC CYBER has an even simpler addressing scheme than the IBM S/370. The IBM S/1 and the DEC PDP 11 machines, on the other hand, have many addressing modes.

The IBM S/370 instruction set has its origin in the IBM S/360 instruction set, which developed in the 1960s when computers were used more for computations than for structuring and organizing data. The CYBER machine, built as a scientific processor, was also optimized for arithmetic calculations. In such an environment, the speed of data fetches from memory is not as important as the speed of the computations once the data is inside the machine registers. Thus, both these machines optimize the register-to-register instructions. The S/370 supports register-to-register and memory-to-register arithmetic but does not support register-to-memory or memory-to-memory instructions. This restriction, plus the small number of addressing modes, allows the S/370 architecture to encode instructions optimally and economically. The CYBER machine also has very efficient register-to-register instructions.

On the other hand, the PDP 11 machine, the VAX 11, and the IBM S/1 were developed for general-purpose applications. They place more emphasis on data structures and are data-oriented rather than computation-oriented systems. Such systems include rich sets of addressing modes at the expense of less tightly encoded instruction sets. Examples of the addressing modes for data-oriented systems are shown in Fig. 4.1 and explained below.

4.6.1 Types of Addressing Modes

Simple addressing modes include the immediate, absolute, and register modes. In the *immediate mode,* the operand itself (not the operand address) is part of the instruction. Figure 4.1 shows a possible encoding of the immediate mode. The immediate operand is placed next to the operand specifier (op. spec.) in the code. When the hardware decodes the operand specifier to be the immediate mode, it treats the bits following the operand specifier as an immediate operand. Immediate operands are useful for implementing arithmetic constants in high-level languages. To ensure reentrant or pure code (that is, code that is not modifiable by its execution), immediate operands should be used only to implement constants since the operands are parts of the code. The S/370, CYBER, PDP 11, and VAX 11 support the immediate addressing mode. Another simple addressing mode is *absolute addressing*. In this mode, the instruction contains the address of the operand as shown in Fig. 4.1. The address of the operand must be known at compile-time. It must be an absolute address (a location fixed in the address space during execution). The CYBER, PDP 11, S/1, and VAX 11 support absolute addressing. Most machines contain a set of general registers for storing operands; the *register mode* is used to access these operands as shown in Fig. 4.1. In the register mode, registers are useful for storing temporary operands generated by the compiler serving as buffers for memory locations. The register mode is supported by the PDP 11, VAX 11, CYBER, S/1, and S/370.

Register deferred or *register indirect,* a more complex addressing mode, specifies the register holding the address of the operand. This addressing mode is used to access operands pointed to by base pointers that are stored in registers. The S/1, PDP 11, VAX 11, and CYBER support this addressing mode. Some pointers are frequently manipulated, especially incremented and decremented. Stack pointers, argument pointers, frame

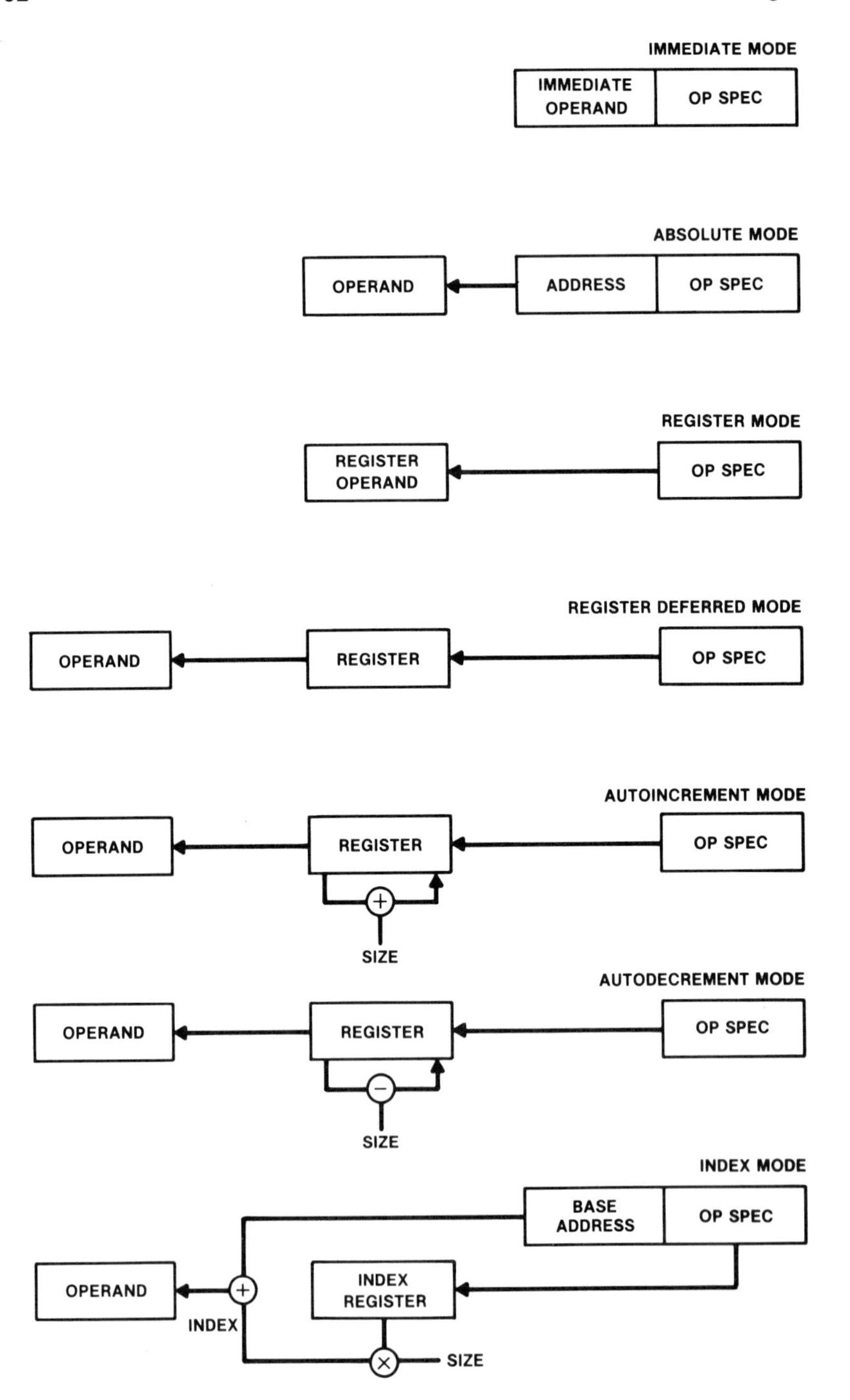

Figure 4.1 Examples of addressing modes.

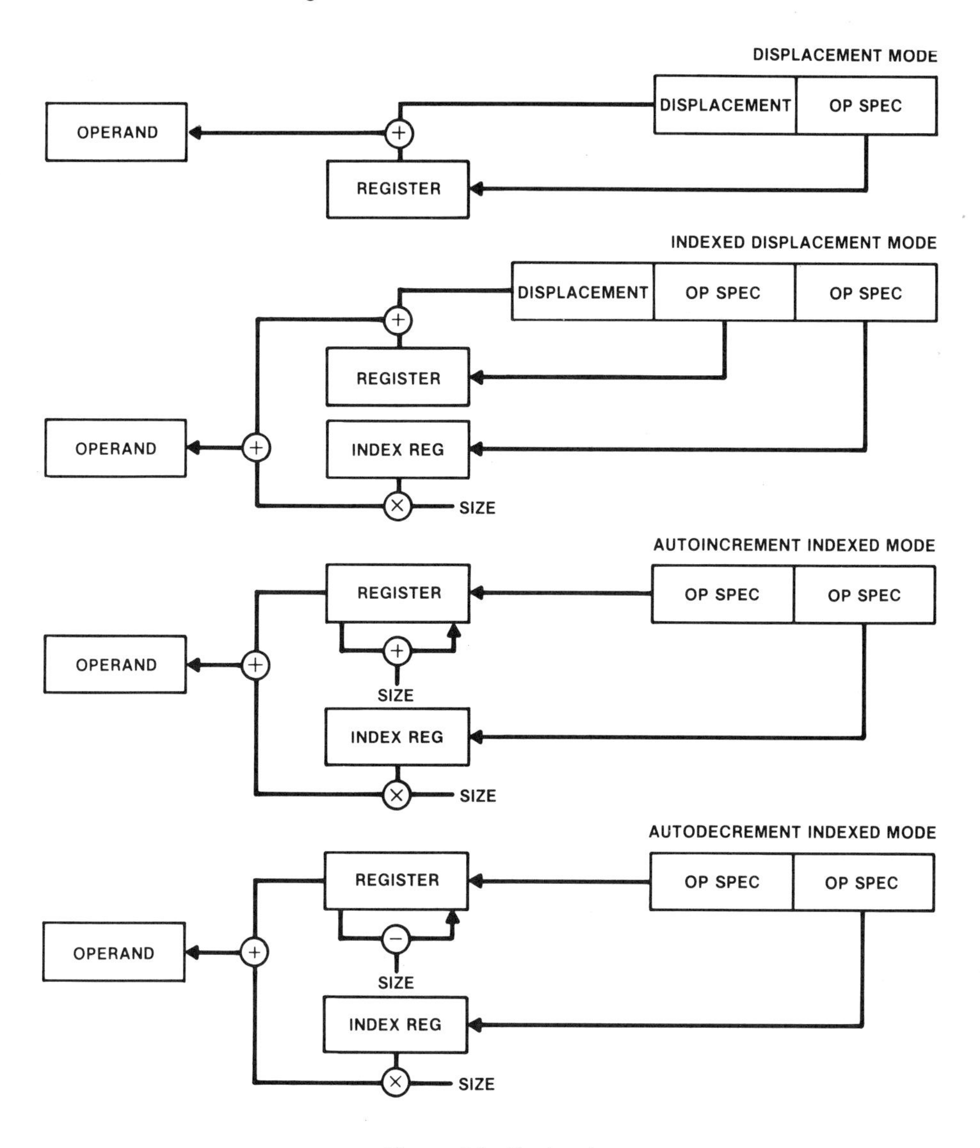

Figure 4.1 Continued.

pointers, and program counters are examples of such pointers. They are usually stored in registers. In pushing and popping information on and off a stack and in accessing array elements, a pointer steps through a series of addresses so that it always points to the next address in the stack or array.

The PDP 11, VAX 11, and S/1 all support the *autoincrement mode*. This addressing mode specifies the register holding the address of an operand. After the operand is accessed, the address in the register is incremented by the size of the operand (pointing to the next operand in an array or the stack). The PDP 11 and VAX 11 also support the *autodecrement mode*. In this addressing mode, the specified register contents are decremented and then used as the address of the operand.

Frequently, an address that is often used but seldom manipulated serves as the base pointer to a data structure. An address that is both often used and manipulated serves as pointer to elements in the data structure. The *index addressing mode* provides the capability to index into a data structure to access a data structure element. In the S/1, PDP 11, and the VAX 11, the address of the operand is obtained by adding the base address, which is part of the instruction operand specifier, to an adjusted index obtained by multiplying the contents of the specified index register with the size in bytes of the operand (Fig. 4.1). This indexing mode is most useful in sequentially accessing the elements of a data structure.

At other times, in accessing an element of a data structure, the compiler generates an offset (displacement) into a table or data structure. For this purpose, some computers (such as the VAX 11) support the *displacement mode*. In this mode, the displacement is a part of the operand specifier. It is added to the contents of a specified (base) register (serving as a pointer to a table or data structure) to form the address of the operand (Fig. 4.1).

In accessing generalized data structures such as PL/I records and C structures, a powerful addressing mode that combines the features of the indexing and displacement modes is used, This mode, the *indexed displacement mode,* forms the operand address by first adding the displacement to the contents of a specified (base) register (pointing to the base of a data structure). The resultant address points to a particular element of the data structure. This address is then added with an index to access a subelement of the data structure. The index is calculated as described in the index addressing mode (Fig. 4.1). The VAX 11, S/360, and S/370 support this powerful addressing mechanism.

Other variations of the indexing mode supported by the VAX 11 are the *autoincrement indexed* and the *autodecrement indexed* modes. In the autoincrement indexed (autodecrement indexed) mode, the hardware automatically increments (decrements) the base register contents after (before) they are added to the index to form the operand address (Fig. 4.1).

The addressing modes discussed thus far are useful for data structures with regular and static elements and subelements. That is, each element of the data structure is of the same size, and the size is known as compile time. In data structures where the sizes of the elements vary, it is easier to represent the data structure as a table of pointers of the same size to elements of variable sizes. For example, an array of pointers can point to variably sized inventory tables. To access an inventory table, an instruction needs to specify the address of the pointer (an address) to the table. Thus, many computers support *deferred* or *indirect addressing* modes in combination with the addressing modes already discussed. In deferred or indirect addressing, the computed or specified address is the address of the address of the operand, rather than the address of the operand itself. Indirect or deferred addressing modes include register deferred autoincrement deferred, autodecrement deferred, displacement deferred, register deferred indexed, displacement deferred indexed, and autoincrement indexed deferred. Register deferred was explained earlier. Register deferred, autoincrement deferred, autodecrement deferred, and displacement deferred addressing modes are the same as the register, autoincrement, autodecrement, and displacement addressing modes except that the result of the address calculation is the address of the operand rather than the address of the operand's address. The *register deferred indexed* mode is the same as the indexing mode except that the base is obtained from a base register specified by the instruction operand specifier. The contents of the base register is added to the adjusted index to form the operand address. In the *displacement deferred indexed* mode, the displacement is added to a specified register to form the address of the base address. To this base address, the index is added to form the operand address. In the *autoincrement indexed deferred* mode, a specified register contains the address of the base address to which the index is added to form the operand address. The specified register pointing to the base address is then incremented by a word size. Many of the indirect addressing modes are supported in the PDP 11 and the VAX 11.

There is no indirect addressing in either the S/370 or the CYBER. Other computers allow indirect addressing to be multilevel. In multilevel indirect addressing, a tag bit is associated with each address to indicate whether it is a direct address or an indirect address. Thus, in indirectly accessing an operand, so long as the address indicates an indirect address, the machine follows the path of indirection (linked addresses) until eventually it reaches the operand.

The PDP 11 and the VAX also support *relative* and *relative deferred* addressing modes. In these modes, the program counter is used as the register. The relative addressing mode is the same as the displacement mode except that the specified register is the program counter. The relative deferred mode is essentially the displacement deferred mode where the specified register is the program counter.

The relative importance of the addressing modes can be seen from their usage frequency as measured by Wiecek [13] on compiler programs executing on the VAX 11 (Table 4.1). Wiecek's results show that 40 percent of the operands are register operands.

TABLE 4.1 COMPILER ADDRESSING MODE FREQUENCY (PERCENT)

Addressing Mode	BASIC	BLISS	COBOL	FORTRAN	PASCAL	PL/I
Register	34.9	38.1	37.9	41.0	45.1	42.2
Literal	9.8	18.5	18.1	18.2	15.5	10.9
Byte displacement	16.3	16.7	10.8	13.6	16.6	11.2
Register deferred	9.0	8.6	15.3	9.1	2.0	2.5
Autoincrement	17.4	3.3	4.8	4.1	2.6	4.4
Index	4.7	3.0	2.1	5.6	7.6	8.8
Long displacement	6.1	6.5	7.3	5.5	3.0	3.5
Word displacement	0.8	2.0	0.9	1.5	6.5	13.9
Byte displacement deferred	0.5	1.5	1.3	0.6	0.4	2.1
Autodecrement	0.5	1.0	1.0	0.5	0.7	0.3
Autoincrement deferred	0.1	0.7	0.2	0.3	0.0	0.0
Long displacement deferred	—	0.1	0.3	0.0	—	0.1
Word displacement deferred	—	—	—	0.0	—	0.1
Totals	100.1%[a]	100.0%	100.0%	100.0%	100.0%	100.0%

[a]Cumulative percentage does not equal 100.0 because of rounding and truncation of data.

(*Source:* Reference 13.)

Other important addressing modes are literal, byte displacement, register deferred, autoincrement, and index. These findings are in general agreement with an independent study by Marathe [14] on the PDP 11.

4.7 INSTRUCTION FORMAT AND ENCODING

Having selected the operations and the addressing modes to incorporate into an instruction set, architects must decide how to format the instructions. The syntax of computer instructions in the most general form is given by

operation code	source operands	destination operand

The operation code (*opcode*) specifies the operation to be performed on the source operands to generate the result, which is written into the destination operand. Instructions that require only a single operand (that is, a single source operand that is also the destination operand) are called unary instructions. Instructions that operate on two operands are called binary or dyadic instructions. These instructions may have two source operands, one of which may also be the destination operand. Or, they may have one source and one destination operand. Instructions that require all three operands, two source and one destination, are called ternary or triadic instructions. Most current processors interpret all three types of instructions using several instruction formats and variable length instructions. The older machines have fixed instruction formats and are classified as either one-, two-, three-, or four-address machines. An address specifies an operand in memory [15,16]. Variable-length instruction formats represent high-level-language operations more closely than do fixed formats. For example, in a fixed-format, one-address machine, the compiler needs to translate a naturally occurring operation with three memory operands into several instructions each able to handle only one memory operand. The introduction of variable-length instructions and variable instruction formats is one step by which, with additional decoding hardware logic, the machine and its instruction set are raised closer to high-level-language syntax and semantics.

The encoding of instructions determines the hardware required to interpret the encoded bits. The instructions must be easy and efficient to decode, and must optimize code density. Three general methods for encoding instructions are available: orthogonal, integrated, and mixed.

1. The *orthogonal* method encodes each field in the instruction (that is, the operation code and the operands) independently. How an operand is encoded does not depend on the operator, and vice versa; operands used with different operators are encoded identically.
2. The *integrated* method does not encode the fields independently. That is, there are no separate fields for the operator code and the various operands.

3. The *mixed* method is a mixture of orthogonally encoded and integrated instructions. Some instructions may even have two fields integrated and an independently coded third field.

The PDP 11 and IBM S/360 and S/370 instructions are encoded in several basic formats and employ the mixed encoding scheme. The interpretation of fields within the operand specifier depends on either the opcode (in the case of IBM S/360 and S/370) or the instruction format (in the case of PDP 11). The VAX 11 employs an orthogonal encoding scheme with a very flexible instruction format. The VAX 11 encodes the opcodes and the operand specifiers independently.

4.7.1 Orthogonal Instruction Encoding

Orthogonally encoded instructions are ideal for pipeline machines because they can decode the opcode and the operand specifiers at different stages of the pipeline. The opcode field consists of subfields that encode the operator type, the number of operands (monadic, dyadic, triadic), and the common information about the operands such as their type (byte, half word, word). Pipeline machines may decode instructions in the following order. First, they decode the subfield of the opcode specifying the number of operands. They then decode the operand specifiers and fetch the operands. Finally they decode the operator subfield of the opcode. The appropriate microcode routine is entered to carry out the specified operation. The instructions in an instruction set may be implemented by microcode, PLA, or hardware logic depending on the number of operators, the number of operand specifiers, and the number and complexity of addressing modes. Microcode is capable of handling more complex instruction sets than PLA or hardwired logic. Besides being suited for pipeline machines, orthogonal encoding has another advantage in needing a relatively small amount of microcode because there is a one-to-one mapping from the opcodes onto the microprogram routines.

4.7.2 Integrated Instruction Encoding

The main advantage of integrated encoding is that microroutines written for integrated combinations of opcodes and operands may be tailored to attain efficiency. With integrated encoding, it is also possible to assign shorter codes to the more common combinations of opcodes and operands, and longer codes to the less common ones. The major disadvantage of fully integrated encoding is its demand on microstore space. The total number of microroutines needed is the full cross-product of the possible opcodes and operand specifiers.

4.7.3 Mixed Instruction Encoding

Mixed encoding combines the advantages of integrated and orthogonal encoding and limits their disadvantages. Some frequently occurring combinations of opcodes and operands may be integrated and assigned short codes; other instructions may be encoded orthogonally.

A methodology for the design of mixed encoding was proposed by Stevenson [17]. The steps of the methodology are: (1) analyze the instruction set for frequencies of opcode and operand combinations; (2) create new, dedicated opcodes from the opcode/operand combinations such that the new opcodes may carry with them one or more operands; (3) quantify the savings of bits for the new opcodes and multiply the savings by the frequencies of occurrence of the opcode and operand combinations; and (4) obtain a sorted list of savings from each combination. Applying the methodology entails creating opcodes out of the best combinations and encoding the other opcodes and operands orthogonally using a radix 256 Huffman Code [18]. The number of integrated combinations must then be optimized by considering the trade-off between program and microprogram sizes, since the former decreases, and the latter increases, with the number of combinations.

Along with the types of encoding for the instruction set, the architect should consider the following.

1. The Boolean functions needed to select the sources, destinations, and opcodes from the input stream should be as simple as possible so that they can be gated into the hardware decoding logic in a simple manner.
2. Immediates should be arranged so that they can be gated directly onto the processor unit's internal bus without requiring shifting logic.
3. Sources and destinations should have the same addressing bit layouts so that the same circuitry can be used to decode both.
4. The opcode set should be as complete as possible since checking for exceptions is expensive.

The encoding of instructions is even more critical when the instructions are decoded by LSI hardware than when they are decoded by microcode.

4.7.4 PDP 11 [9]

The PDP 11 supports instructions whose length may be either one, two, or three words. It has four main instruction formats: operate, single operand, double operand, and branches (Fig. 4.2).

The operate instructions are one word long and have no operands. All 16 bits of the word are part of the opcode. Examples of the operate instructions include wait, reset, input/output trap, return from interrupt, emulator trap, and return from trap.

The single-operand instructions may be one or two words long. The first word contains the opcode (10 bits) and the operand specifier (6 bits), of which the register specification takes 3 bits. The register specification selects one of eight registers; the addressing mode specification (also 3 bits) selects one of eight modes. The eight modes include register, autoincrement, autodecrement, index, register deferred, autoincrement deferred, autodecrement deferred, and index deferred. Only in the two index addressing modes are the single-operand instructions two words long. The second word specifies the base address to be added to the index. Examples of single-operand instructions include clear, complement, increment, decrement, negate, test, jump, and swap bytes.

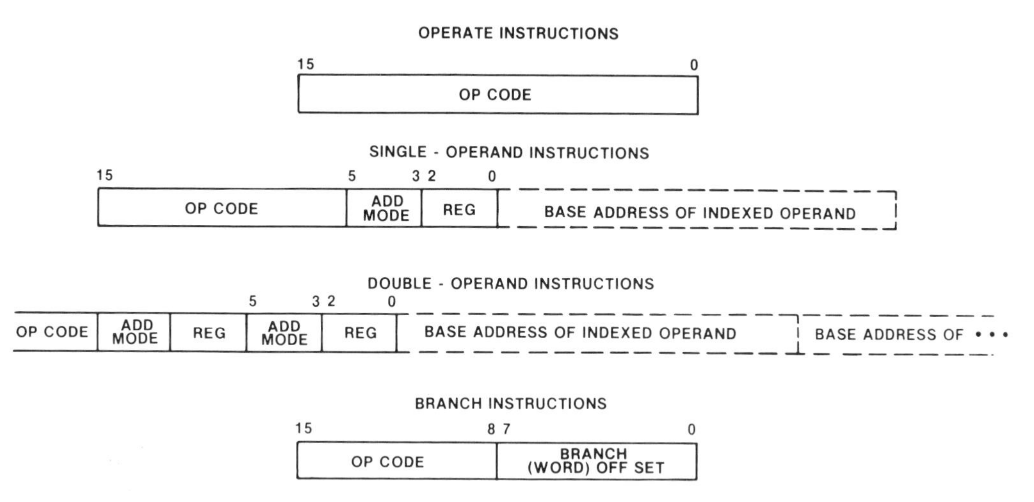

Figure 4.2 Basic PDP 11 instruction formats.

The double-operand instructions range in length from one to three words. The first word contains the opcode (4 bits) and the two operand specifiers (6 bits each). The operand specifiers have the same format as the operand specifier for the one operand instruction. The double-operand instruction may be two or three words long if either one or both of the operands are specified by the indexed addressing modes. Examples of double-operand instructions are move, add, subtract, compare, bit set, bit clear, and bit test.

Branch instructions are one word long. The opcode requires one byte (8 bits); the other byte is the offset relative to the program counter specifying the branch target address. The 8-bit offset allows an instruction to branch 128 words backward from the current location or 127 words forward from the current location. The branch instructions include branch if equal, branch if not equal, branch if plus, branch if higher, and branch if carry.

In addition to these basic instructions, the PDP 11 supports special instructions that use and manipulate the condition bits. These instructions are considered part of the single-operand group. However, they have a special format in which 11 bits are used for the opcode, 4 bits for the condition code, and 1 bit for designating whether the specified condition code bits are to be set or cleared (Fig. 4.3). Combinations of the condition bits may be set or cleared together. Examples of these instructions include add carry, subtract carry, clear carry (C) bit, clear overflow (C) bit, set zero (Z) bit, and set negative (N) bit.

The PDP 11 also has two instructions for subroutine linkage. These instructions are the jump to subroutine and the return from subroutine instructions (Fig. 4.3). Both of these instructions are one word long. The jump to subroutine instruction has a 7-bit opcode. Three bits specify one of eight registers as the linkage register where the program counter of the calling routine is to be saved. Another 6 bits designate the location of the beginning of the subroutine. This destination address specification has the standard 6-bit format in which 3 bits specify a register and 3 bits specify the addressing mode as de-

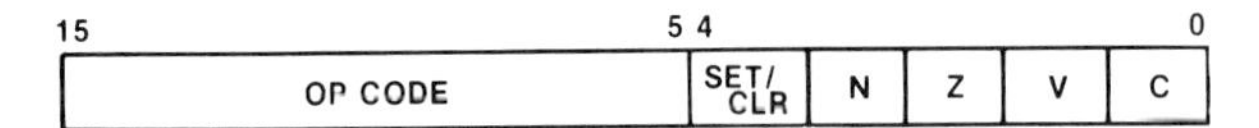

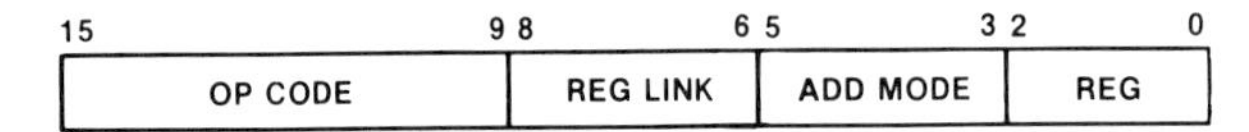

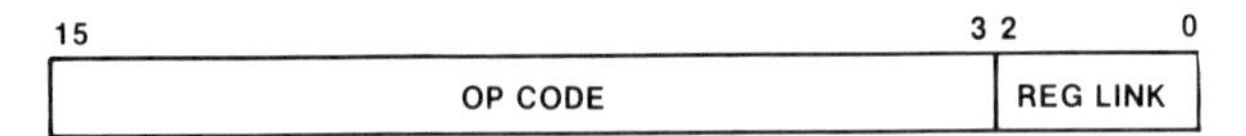

Figure 4.3 Special PDP 11 instruction formats.

scribed above. The return from subroutine instruction has a 13-bit opcode. Three bits designate one of eight registers as the linkage register where the program counter of the program being returned to is stored.

4.7.5 *VAX 11 [10,11]*

The VAX instruction set supports a rich set of instructions with a variable number of operands specified by a rich set of addressing modes (Fig. 4.4). The number of operands ranges from zero in the NOP (no operation) instruction to six in the DIVP (divide packed) instruction. VAX 11 instructions are encoded on byte boundaries. The first byte is the opcode. The opcode encodes the function, the number of operands in the instruction, and the common type of the operands. Operand specifiers from one to nine bytes in length follow the opcode. The first byte is the operand specifier proper; it uses a nibble to denote a register and a nibble to denote the addressing mode. The only exception is the literal operand specifier, which denotes a short immediate operand (6 bits). The operand specifier encoding is shown in Fig. 4.5. The encoding of the literal operand causes the

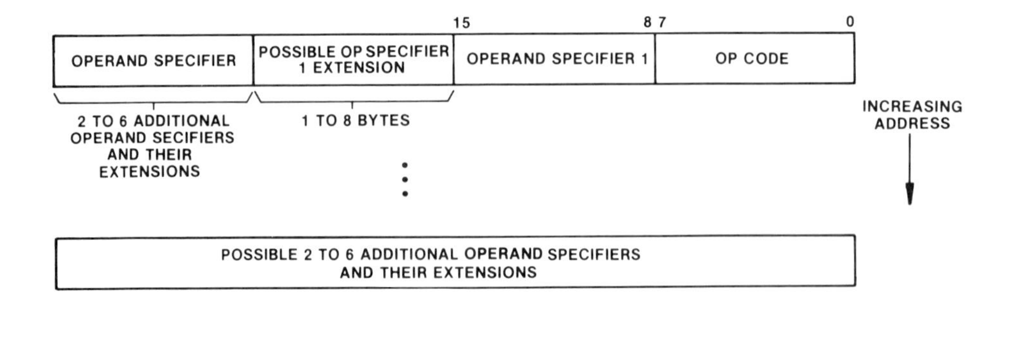

Figure 4.4 Basic Vax 11 instruction formats.

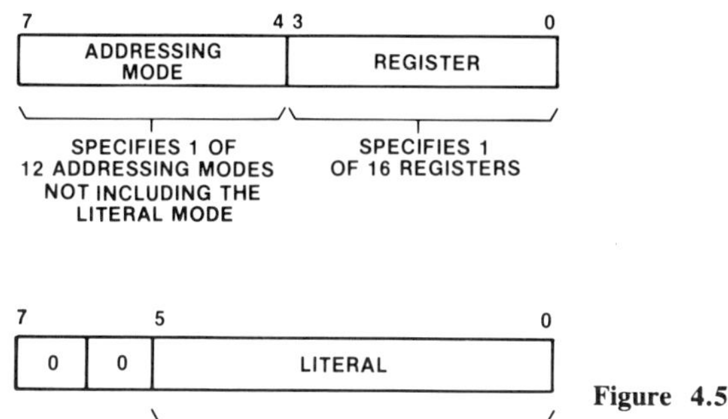

Figure 4.5 General operand specifier and special literal operand specifier formats.

literal mode to occupy four of the 16 possible addressing modes. The operand specifier proper is followed by from zero to eight bytes of specifier extension. Specifier extensions are entities such as displacements, addresses or immediate data. Some examples of operand specifiers with their specifier extensions are shown in Fig. 4.6.

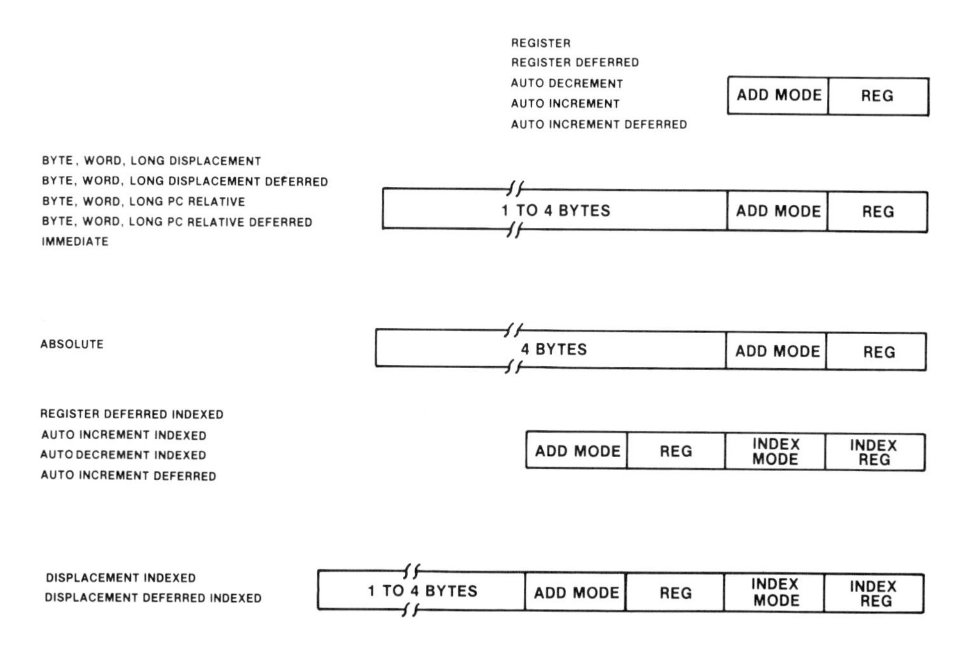

Figure 4.6 Examples of operand specifier and specifier extension formats.

4.7.6 IBM S/360 and S/370 [12]

IBM S/360 and S/370 instructions are encoded in five basic instruction formats. The instructions are of different sizes (two bytes, four bytes, or six bytes) and start on byte boundaries. The five basic instruction formats are:

1. Register to register (RR)
2. Storage, immediate (SI)
3. Register to indexed storage (RX)
4. Register, register, storage (RS)
5. Storage, storage (SS)

All IBM S/360 and S/370 instruction formats have one byte of opcode that is followed by from one to five bytes of operand specifiers (Fig. 4.7). The opcode is divided into several subfields. The length subfield denotes the format and length of the instruction, the type subfield denotes the type of the operands, and the operation subfield denotes the type of operation (Fig. 4.8). The operand specifiers are formed from combinations of the register, immediate, storage, and index fields. The register field is encoded in one nibble denoting one of 16 registers (Fig. 4.9).

The immediate field I is one byte long. The storage field S is encoded in two bytes. The storage field contains fields specifying a base register (B) and a displacement D. The register is encoded in 4 bits; the displacement is a 12-bit address. The storage address is the sum of the contents of the base register and the displacement. The indexed storage field X is the same as the storage field with the addition of an index register field. The effective address is the sum of the contents of the base register, the contents of the index register, and the displacement.

Using these basic fields and subfields, the five instruction formats and their syntaxes are shown in Fig. 4.10. The RR format is used for instructions with two register operands. In the RR format, one byte is used to specify the operands. The byte is divided into two 4-bit specifiers (R1 and R2), each encoding the register number where the operand is found. The SI format is used for instructions with an immediate operand and a store oper-

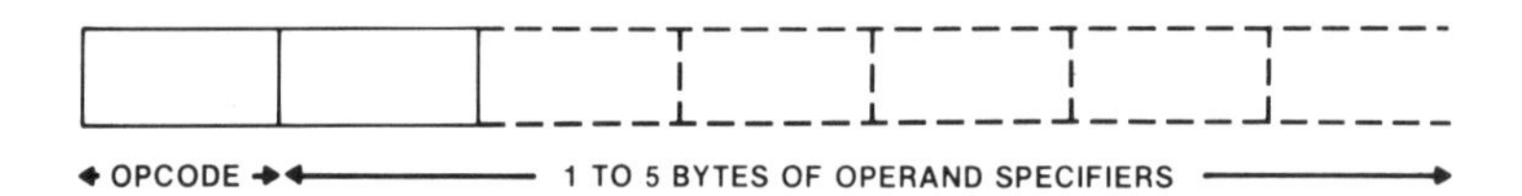

Figure 4.7 IBM 360 and 370 instruction format.

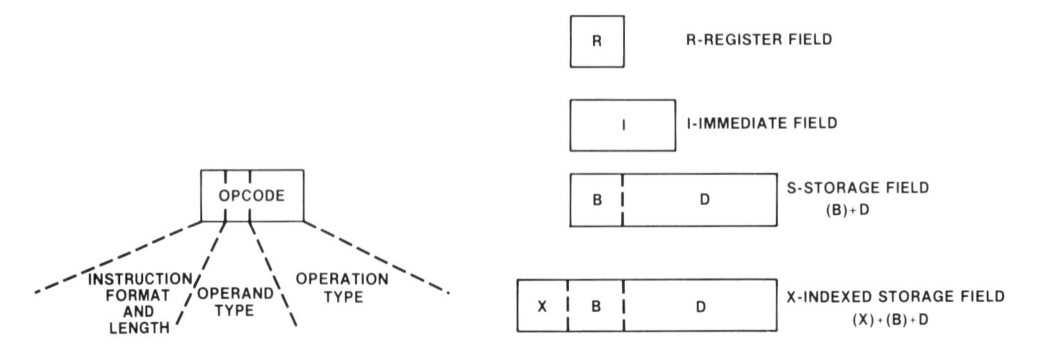

Figure 4.8 OPCODE encoding format.

Figure 4.9 Operand specifier field encoding format.

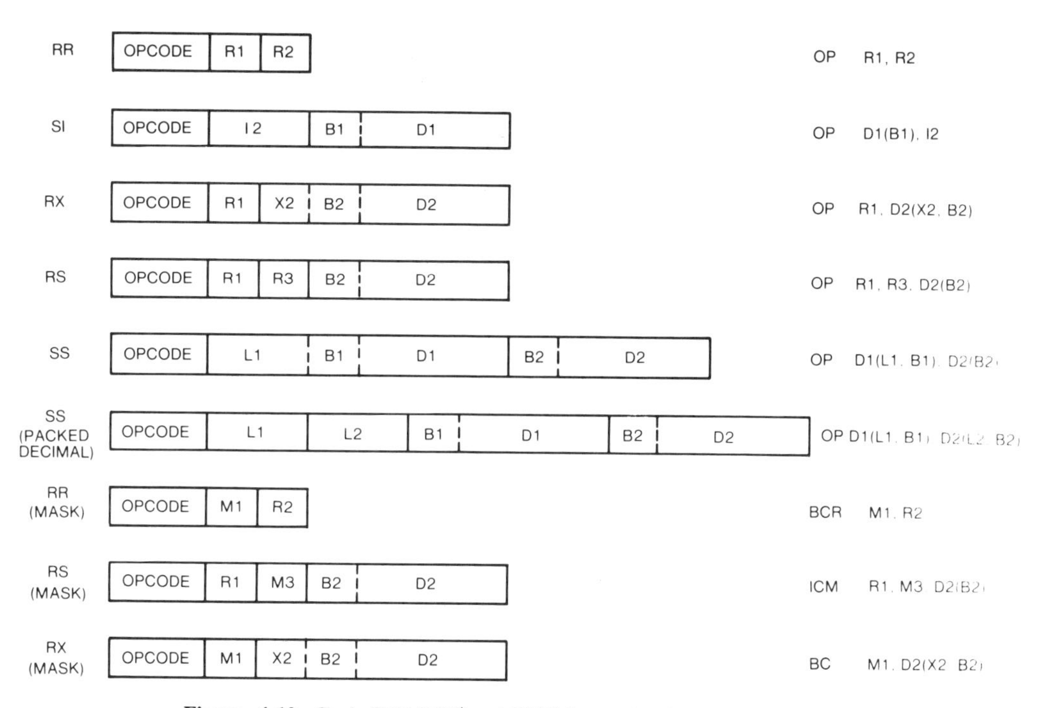

Figure 4.10 Basic IBM S/360 and S/370 instruction format and variations.

and. The SI format uses three bytes to specify the operands: one byte for the immediate operand (I2), and two bytes for the storage operand D1(B1). Instructions with the RX format have one register operand and one indexed store operand. They are, respectively, the 4-bit specifier (R1) and the 12-bit specifier D2(X2,B2). The RS format is used for instructions that require two register operands (R1 and R3) and a store operand D2(B2). An example of a RS format instruction is the branch on index low or equal (Section 4.5.3), where R1 is the index register, R3 is the count register, and D2(B2) is the destination address for the branch. The SS instruction format contains two storage operands [D1(L1,B1) and D2(B2)] with the first operand having a length field that indicates the length of the operand in bytes. Since the length field is one byte long, it can denote, for example, a character string of up to 256 bytes. An example of an SS format instruction is the move character string instruction, where L1 designates the length of the character string, D2(B2) the source location, and D1(B1) the destination location. For instructions involving packed decimal strings, the SS format may specify two length fields (L1 and L2), one for each decimal string operand [D1(L1,B1) and D2(L2,B2)]. An example is the pack instruction to convert a zoned decimal operand D2(L2,B2) to a packed decimal operand D1(L1,B1). L2 and L1 are the lengths of the operands. The register field in the instructions may also be used to denote a mask field (M) in instructions such as conditional branch instructions and insert characters under mask.

4.8 INSTRUCTION SET DESIGN METHODOLOGY

Instruction sets are best designed iteratively by the compiler writer and the computer architect. The compiler writer generates code using the instruction set, and the architect designs the hardware to execute instruction streams composed of instructions from the instruction set. An iterative methodology for instruction set design includes these steps:

Step 1: Construct an initial design of the instruction set based on the intended use of the machine.

Step 2: Construct a compiler for the design.

Step 3: Take measurements to investigate the effectiveness of the opcodes and addressing modes in the design.

Step 4: Combine heavily used instruction sequences into one instruction and replace infrequently used instructions with instruction sequences.

Step 5: Repeat steps 1 through 4 until the instruction set is effective.

To design a machine to support a variety of high-level languages, this methodology may be used with each language. The instruction set designers then tailor the set of iterative designs so that the instruction set is effective for most if not all of the languages.

The measurements obtained in the iterative process indicate the effectiveness of the instruction set design with respect to the set of test programs (benchmarks) selected and the algorithms by which these programs are written. A large number of test sets should be used to minimize the variance of the results obtained from different test programs and algorithms. Some of the significant features of a design that should be exercised by test programs include the following [19]:

1. Integer arithmetic and floating-point operations
2. Character and string processing
3. Bit processing
4. Control expressions
5. Addressing mode flexibility
6. Interrupt handling
7. Input/output
8. Module entry and exit
9. Intermodule communication
10. Type checking and conversion
11. Executive-user interaction

The designers must also select the metrics for evaluating the effectiveness of an instruction set in step 3 of the iterative methodology. The effectiveness ultimately depends on the cost and performance of the resulting architecture. Performance is more easily determined than cost because the cost of a particular design depends on the costs of designing and developing compilers, of designing the architecture, of developing the hardware implementation of the architecture, and of manufacturing the hardware. A complex instruction set that increases the complexity of a compiler or causes less than optimal compiler performance may decrease rather than increase the performance of the compiled code.

4.9 INSTRUCTION MIX

An *instruction mix* is a measure of the frequency of usage of each instruction in a set of test programs. Instruction mixes of existing machines aid in designing the initial instruction set of a new machine before the iterative methodology is applied to it. Instruction mixes are measured from the compiled code (static) or from the execution of the compiled code (dynamic). A static mix has limited usefulness other than relating how much resources (such as registers and memory) are consumed by the static program. Understanding the statistical behavior of programs requires a dynamic mix.

In using instruction mixes for optimizing machine efficiency, the architect should multiply the instruction frequency with the execution time for each instruction. Optimizing only those instructions that are executed frequently is not enough because some rarely executed instructions may consume a large amount of execution time. An example from the VAX 11/780 was given by Clark [2]. In one time-sharing benchmark, the instruction to move a character string accounted for less than 0.47 percent of the instructions executed but required 13 percent of the execution time!

Care must be exercised in interpreting an instruction mix because the instruction mix is affected by the set of test programs, the compiler, and the computer on which it is obtained. For example, a machine with a single accumulator results in a program with a higher frequency of load and store instructions than a machine with a general register set where temporary results may reside without being stored and loaded from memory. As another example, a study by Marathe indicates that the jump instruction is used very often [14]. But a closer look reveals that this occurs because the compiler generates jump instructions rather than branch instructions.

Instruction mix also depends on the application and the language used for it [2,20]. Measurements taken on the VAX 11/780 show that for a FORTRAN benchmark, the top 10 instructions account for 60 percent of all the instructions executed, the top 20 instructions account for 75 percent, and the top 40 instructions account for over 90 percent. But those same top 10 instructions account for only 8 percent of all the instructions executed in a comparable COBOL benchmark; the same top 20 instructions account for 21 percent.

It is thus quite natural for instruction mixes from different studies to vary. The causes of the variation include these:

1. Instruction sets
2. Compilers
3. Application areas
4. Test programs measured
5. Test program segments measured

Because of the variation among the studies, care should be exercised when using instruction mixes for the design and optimization of processors. Making misguided optimizations may be more inefficient than implementing no optimizations. If a designer's own study sample is small, the designer should compare his/her results with the results of others to better understand the possible deviations and variances. It is better to measure the frequency of usage of intermediate language constructs rather than measure an instruction mix. An intermediate language construct mix allows a better understanding of the usage of high-level-language constructs without the dependencies of machines and instruction sets.

If an application area has a significantly different instruction mix from the other application areas, designing a special processor and options for that area may be worthwhile. Even in a single application area, however, all the programs may not exhibit the same instruction mix. If the variance among the individual programs is comparable to the variance caused by application areas, optimizing the processor for these areas will not be possible. Variance resulting from different segments of a single program is usually not important since the sampling for each segment is necessarily small. There should be no need to optimize a processor for a single program or program segment unless that processor is dedicated and running only that single program or program segment.

Marathe compares instruction mixes from different application areas, from different programs, and from different segments in the programs [14]. He quantifies the variance caused by each of these factors. The application areas measured are the following:

1. Scientific FORTRAN (five user benchmarks)
2. Business COBOL (four user benchmarks and one sort program)
3. Operating systems
4. Systems programs (FORTRAN and COBOL compilers, and a BASIC interpreter, macro assembler, and linker)
5. Device-oriented systems (graphics terminals, front-end processor, xerographic printer controller, processor heavily loaded with I/O devices, processor controlling a large collection of other processors)

Marathe measured five representative programs within each area and 24 program segments (512 bytes block) within each program. In all, 10,000,000 instructions were sampled from 25 independent programs. The instruction mix was gathered on the PDP 11.

The results of Marathe's experiments are shown in Tables 4.2 and 4.3. Table 4.2 shows the instruction mix. Only opcodes with more than 0.01 percent usage are included in the table. Table 4.3 shows the instruction mixes by application areas.

One of the results of the study is that there are cases (for example, the MOV instruction) where the variance is affected more by the individual program than by the application area. The study corroborates the results of other studies by concluding that a small number of instructions accounts for a large percentage of the instructions executed and many others are seldom used [21,22].

As can be calculated from Table 4.3, the instruction mix of programs in a scientific application shows that eight PDP 11 instructions account for 79 percent of all the instructions executed and 16 instructions for 92 percent. In the instruction mix of programs in a

TABLE 4.2 INSTRUCTION MIX AND VARIANCE

Name	Overall mean	Overall standard deviation	Variance due to application area	Variance due to programs	Variance due to segments
MOV	31.205	2.170	8	75	8.258
BNE	5.597	1.675	11	12	4.236
BEQ	4.140	.931	3	3	2.776
CMP	4.005	.902	3	2	1.416
JMP	3.940	3.128	48	3	.420
DEC	3.919	1.577	10	11	1.416
ADD	3.684	.092		4	.498
JSR	3.622	.818	2	2	.555
TST	3.492	1.066	3	10	11.441
ASL	3.413	.793	1	8	.445
BR	3.134	1.299	7	3	.393
RTS	3.008	.718	2	1	.342
MOVB	2.024	.591	1	1	1.052
CLR	1.675	.121		.9	.123
BIT	1.675	.531	1	1	.968
BCS	1.587	.500	.8	2	.479
INC	1.409	.290	.1	1	.136
SCB	1.331	1.041	4	4	.758
BLG	1.264	.361	.4	1	.163
BPL	1.233	.885	1	12	14.499
BGT	1.174	.222		1	.828
TSTB	1.169	.510		6	10.540
SUB	1.105	.304	0	2	.888
ROL	1.056	.267		2	.962
BMI	.886	.324	0	2	1.151
BLE	.735	.100		.7	.074
BCC	.619	.284	.4	.2	.274
BITB	.574	.174	.1	.2	.016
BHI	.563	.254	.3	.2	.243
CLRB	.549	.207	.2	.2	.079
CMPB	.504	.193	.1	.2	.100
FADO	.478	.478	1	.1	.030
BGE	.463	.112	0	.2	.028
BIS	.460	.152	0	.2	.236
FMUL	.420	.420	.9	0	.024
SUAB	.414	.205	.2	.2	.143
BLT	.409	.849		.1	.026
ROR	.309	.112	0	0	.244
RTI	.290	.105	0	0	.058
NOP	.281	.130	0	.1	.030
ASR	.235	.072	0	0	.828
BISB	.224	.066	0	0	.010
MFPI	.200	.131	0	.2	.013
MTPI	.175	.130	0	.3	.005
CCNO	.151	.105	0	0	.032
BLOS	.148	.083	0	0	.035
ADC	.115	.050	0	0	.104

TABLE 4.2 *(cont.)*

Name	Overall mean	Overall standard deviation	Variance due to application area	Variance due to programs	Variance due to segments
MEG	.102	.027		0	.001
FDIV	.099	.099	0	0	.001
DECB	.097	.040	0	0	.204
INCB	.096	.030	0	0	.003
FSUB	.082	.082	0	0	.001
TRAP	.073	.036		0	.005
ASLB	.066	.053	0	0	.021
BICB	.048	.011	0	0	.001
WAIT	.039	.021	0	0	.003
ASHC	.035	.026	0	0	.000
EMI	.033	.022	0	0	.000
RORB	.025	.011		0	.001
ASH	.023	.023	0	0	.000
DIV	.020	.008		0	.003
COM	.019	.013	0	0	.003
ASRB	.017	.016	0	0	.000
SBC	.017	.009	0	0	.001
SXT	.012	.007		0	.000
ADCB	.010	.006	0	0	.000
MUL	.010	.007	0	0	.000

Source: Reference 14

business application, eight PDP 11 instructions account for 60 percent of all instructions executed, and 16 instructions account for 76 percent. In the instruction mix of operating system programs, eight PDP 11 instructions account for 69 percent of all instructions executed and 16 for 86 percent. In an instruction mix of system programs, eight PDP 11 instructions account for 62 percent of all instructions executed and 16 for 79 percent. In instruction mix of real-time system programs, eight PDP 11 instructions account for 70 percent of all instructions executed and 16 for 88 percent.

A small number of instructions accounts for a large percentage of the instructions executed. This conclusion is reached in each of the application areas and programming languages. The question remains whether a small group of instructions accounts for most of the instructions executed in running a mix of application programs. Averaging the instruction frequency results in Table 4.2 over the different programs in the different application areas (scientific, business, operating systems, and real time systems), reveals that 8 instructions still account for 60 percent of the instructions executed, 16 for 80 percent, 25 for 90 percent, and 32 for 94 percent.

Instruction mixes are based on instruction sets. By putting instructions performing similar functions into groups, comparisons of instruction mixes based on different instruction sets can be made. This affords an understanding of the frequency of functions being performed independent of the instruction set. The examination of the instruction mixes of various studies shows that instructions concerned with information movement are the

TABLE 4.3 INSTRUCTION MIX BY APPLICATION AREAS

Opcode	Area 1: Scientific	Area 2: Business	Area 3: Operating systems	Area 4: Systems programs	Area 5: Real time systems
MOV	36.859	24.784	30.079	29.161	35.143
BNE	.898	6.916	10.772	6.098	3.301
BEQ	1.428	5.085	2.612	6.601	4.974
CMP	1.666	6.105	2.647	6.085	3.522
JMP	16.430	.484	1.159	1.277	.350
DEC	2.692	4.141	9.897	1.255	1.611
ADO	3.791	3.709	3.546	3.424	3.952
JSR	1.020	5.183	2.984	3.372	5.549
TST	1.799	2.774	1.468	4.053	7.356
ASL	6.373	3.586	1.792	2.591	2.724
BR	8.293	2.048	1.521	1.488	2.319
RTS	.413	4.094	2.992	2.989	4.553
MOVE	.385	3.159	3.364	2.263	.950
CLR	1.264	1.996	1.818	1.626	1.673
BIT	.037	1.696	1.582	3.393	1.667
BCS	1.679	2.723	.650	2.618	.264
INC	1.930	1.940	.378	1.537	1.210
SOB	.007	.251	5.456	.836	.106
BIC	.058	1.053	2.083	1.199	1.926
BPL	.020	.362	.288	.756	4.740
BGT	.655	1.515	1.847	1.040	.812
TSTB	.095	.460	.974	1.275	3.040
SUB	.394	.822	2.191	1.258	.861
ROL	1.948	1.359	.686	.814	.471
BMI	.117	.364	1.535	1.756	.655
BLE	.899	.414	.783	.613	.068
BCC	.222	1.674	.221	.762	.216
BITB	.008	.567	1.004	.506	.707
BHI	.061	1.140	.053	1.202	.360
CLRB	.558	1.257	.185	.654	.892
CMPB	.026	.974	.563	.858	.097
FADO	2.390	.000	.000	.000	.000
BGE	.290	.234	.040	.370	.576
BIS	.192	.328	.132	.828	.818
FMUL	2.09	.000	.000	.000	.000
SWAB	.323	1.205	.233	.314	.195
BLT	.355	.512	.542	.338	.298
ROR	.483	.544	.003	.442	.074
RTI	.047	.247	.091	.519	.546
NOP	.007	.746	.250	.333	.072
ASR	.073	.487	.171	.289	.157
BISB	.161	.465	.069	.193	.229
MTFPI	.000	.355	.000	.645	.000
MTPI	.000	.201	.000	.672	.000
COND	.007	.540	.001	.206	.000
BLOS	.011	.463	.072	.160	.032
ADC	.007	.269	.179	.107	.012
NEG	.177	.034	.123	.048	.125

TABLE 4.3 *(cont.)*

Opcode	Area 1: Scientific	Area 2: Business	Area 3: Operating systems	Area 4: Systems programs	Area 5: Real time systems
FDIV	.494	.000	.000	.000	.000
DECB	.011	.176	.000	.194	.106
INCB	.087	.094	.000	.188	.111
FSUB	.408	.000	.000	.000	.000
TRAP	.000	.052	.093	.015	.203
ASLB	.005	.047	.003	.276	.000
BICB	.005	.050	.059	.073	.054
WAIT	.016	.063	.000	.006	.111
ASHS	.134	.000	.000	.039	.000
EMT	.002	.041	.117	.007	.000
RCRB	.004	.023	.000	.047	.052
ASH	.001	.000	.001	.115	.000
DIV	.033	.001	.000	.038	.030
COM	.000	.066	.000	.028	.000
ASRB	.083	.001	.000	.002	.000
SBC	.002	.041	.004	.039	.000
SXT	.029	.000	.000	.000	.030
ADCB	.004	.032	.000	.015	.000
MUL	.035	.000	.000	.015	.000
ROLB	.000	.045	.000	.000	.000
RTT	.000	.000	.000	.013	.000
BVS	.000	.001	.000	.003	.000
CCMS	.000	.002	.000	.002	.000
IOT	.000	.000	.000	.003	.000
NEGB	.000	.000	.000	.001	.000
XCR	.000	.000	.000	.001	.000
BVC	.000	.000	.000	.000	.000

Source: Reference 14

most prevalent group [14,21–26]. The next most prevalent group consists of the branching instructions, both conditional and unconditional. Another important group is made up of test and comparison instructions. This group is followed by the addition, subtraction, increment, and decrement instructions. Mostly because of differences in compilers and instruction sets, different instruction mixes stress different instructions within each group. However, the functions performed by each group above, irrespective of particular instructions, statistically are the prevalent activities of computers in executing programs.

In a study by S. C. Johnson at AT&T Bell Laboratories, 41 percent of all opcodes generated were moves; 19 percent were branches; 16 percent were call, save, or return operations; 10 percent were comparisons; 10 percent were addition, subtraction, and load addresses; and 4 percent were other opcodes. These results agree with the conclusion in the previous paragraph. In a study by McDaniel on the Mesa instruction set, approximately 50 percent of the instructions executed by the compiler and a VLSI check program were for data movement, 10 to 20 percent were for jumps and conditional jumps, 10 percent were for ALU operations, and roughly 5 percent were for procedure calls and returns [26]. A case study of the VAX 11 instruction set found similar results [13]. Approximately 36 percent of the instructions executed were moves, 25 percent were control (branches), 16 percent were comparisons, 5 percent were arithmetic operations, and 7 percent were procedure calls.

Other empirical observations of instruction set studies show that branch distances are usually very small. The results from Alexander and Wortman's study show that over half the branches were no more than 128 bytes from the target location of the branch instruction [21]. The distribution of branch distances is shown in Table 4.4. The distribution of branch distances on the VAX 11 on compiler programs in another study also shows that branch distance is less than 128 bytes from the branch instruction [13].

TABLE 4.4 DISTRIBUTION OF BRANCH DISTANCES (XPL PROGRAMS)

Distance (Logarithmic)	Frequency Number	Frequency Percentage	Cumulative Percentage
[2**2.2**3]	25,027	2.4	2.9
[2**3.2**4]	146,560	14.2	17.1
[2**4.2**5]	128,798	12.5	29.6
[2**5.2**6]	135,148	13.1	42.7
[2**6.2**7]	120,129	11.7	54.4
[2**7.2**8]	70,331	6.8	61.2
[2**8.2**9]	74,094	7.2	68.4
[2**9.2**10]	40,904	4.0	72.4
[2**10.2**11]	50,452	4.9	77.3
[2**11.2**12]	35,397	3.4	80.7
[2**12.2**13]	22,116	2.1	82.9
[2**13.2**14]	104,612	10.2	93.0
[2**14.2**15]	39,194	3.8	96.8
[2**15.2**16]	32,054	3.1	99.9
[2**16.2**17]	574	0.1	100.0
[2**17.2**18]	118	0.0	100.0
[2**18.2**19]	0	0.0	100.0

Source: Reference 21

Alexander and Wortman also studied the distribution of the values of numeric constants used in a program. Their results are shown in Table 4.5. A major result is that 95 percent of the numeric constants used may be represented by an 8-bit number.

In terms of data references, McDaniel's results on the Mesa system show that local data references outnumber global references by a factor of 4 in a compiler program, and by a factor of 17 in a VLSI check program [26]. In the Mesa architecture, local data refers to data pertaining to a procedure; global data refers to data pertaining to a module. A

TABLE 4.5 DISTRIBUTION OF NUMERIC CONSTANTS (XPL PROGRAMS)

Range (Logarithmic)	Number of bits	Number	Percentage	Cumulative Percentage
Zero	1	7762	15.6	15.6
[2**0.2**1]	1	8459	17.0	32.6
[2**1.2**2]	2	3952	7.9	40.5
[2**2.2**3]	3	2986	6.0	46.5
[2**3.2**4]	4	4747	9.5	56.0
[2**4.2**5]	5	4682	9.4	65.4
[2**5.2**6]	6	5908	11.9	77.3
[2**6.2**7]	7	4715	9.5	86.8
[2**7.2**8]	8	4037	8.1	94.9
[2**8.2**9]	9	1372	2.8	97.7
[2**9.2**10]	10	174	0.3	98.0
[2**10.2**11]	11	39	0.1	98.1
[2**11.2**12]	12	61	0.1	98.2
[2**12.2**13]	13	132	0.3	98.5
[2**13.2**14]	14	92	0.2	98.7
[2**14.2**15]	15	58	0.1	98.8
[2**15.2**16]	16	61	0.1	98.9
[2**16.2**17]	17	1	0.0	98.9
[2**17.2**18]	18	18	0.0	98.9
[2**18.2**19]	19	68	0.1	99.0
[2**19.2**20]	20	71	0.1	99.1
[2**20.2**21]	21	102	0.2	99.3
[2**21.2**22]	22	111	0.2	99.5
[2**22.2**23]	23	40	0.1	99.6
[2**23.2**24]	24	71	0.1	99.7
[2**24.2**25]	25	1	0.0	99.7
[2**25.2**26]	26	0	0.0	99.7
[2**26.2**27]	27	1	0.0	99.7
[2**27.2**28]	28	4	0.0	99.7
[2**28.2**29]	29	2	0.0	99.7
[2**29.2**30]	30	1	0.0	99.7
[2**30.2**31]	31	8	0.0	99.7
[2**31.2**32]	32	68	0.1	99.8[a]

[a]Cumulative percentage does not equal 100,0 because of rounding and truncation of data.

Source: Reference 21

module in Mesa contains a set of related procedures that are compiled as a single unit and share global data. McDaniel also noted that in the two programs he measured, loads from storage occur with two to four times the frequency of writes to storage. Furthermore, the store considers instruction fetches to be store reads. This further biases the comparison of store reads to store writes in favor of store reads.

4.10 EFFICIENT INSTRUCTION SET HEURISTIC

Observations on instruction set characteristics that contribute to efficient architecture include the following [19].

1. A *set of instructions incorporating a small constant into a short instruction*. A study by Tanenbaum found that 81 percent of the constants in the programs studied were 0, 1, or 2 [27]. Thus, even a 2-bit literal field covers most cases. Considerable savings for some instructions are achieved by using a short 4-bit immediate constant mode and a 16-bit immediate constant mode.
2. *Variable-length instructions to represent the most frequently used operations*. Short instructions can usually be used for register to register operations, for local branches for short program-counter relative branch instructions, for short literal instructions, and for instructions with indexed memory accesses. Longer instructions can implement more general branching, memory accesses, and literal operands. General addressing capabilities should be available with the most frequently used operations.
3. *Ability to manipulate operands of various sizes efficiently*. Operands range from the 8-bit byte character to the 64-bit floating-point number. It is desirable for an instruction set to encode these quantities efficiently.
4. *Use of implied registers*. With implied registers, register specification bits can be eliminated from certain instructions. Care must be taken, however, to ensure that instructions with implied registers are not frequently used. Otherwise, register congestion may result, forcing the compiler to generate instructions to save the contents of the registers.
5. *16-bit offsets from registers*. Although most machines can deal with full 32-bit addresses, most processes in general purpose applications have locality of references so that 16-bit offsets can be used effectively.
6. *Ability to access stack elements efficiently*. Addressing optimization that permits easy access to the first 16 integers on a stack frame is desirable because these references represent arguments for function calls, temporary references, and automatic variables. In a recent study, 90 percent of all references from the stack pointer were references to the first 16 words of the stack frame. Of the move instructions, 46 percent were moves of arguments onto the stack to prepare for calls.

These heuristics for efficiency are in many cases in direct conflict with the goals of regularity for ease of compiler design discussed previously. Hence each designer has to evaluate the trade-off between efficiency and design ease for each design situation. The trade-off has to be made based on the goals of the project: whether performance or design interval has the higher priority. Furthermore, the designers must remember that their trade-off decisions affect not only the machine being designed but, because of compatibility and code portability requirements, other machines in the family not yet designed. Finally, it must be remembered that the compiler design principles discussed in Section

4.3 are goals. Exceptions to these goals are possible but have to be justified for the appropriate performance gain when relevant.

4.11 SUMMARY

The design of the instruction set is a key element in the design of a machine architecture to support high-level languages. It affects the complexity and efficiency of the hardware, firmware, and compiler designs. The instruction set has implications in terms of cost, performance, family compatibility, and development cycle.

From a computer architect's viewpoint, the design of an instruction set is related to factors including the following:

1. Machine cycle time
2. Speed of the processing unit
3. Speed of memory
4. Speed of microinstruction execution
5. Size of microstore needed
6. Design difficulty
7. Organization of the machine
8. Technology
9. Compatibility issues

As the instruction set is being designed, the computer architect visualizes how the instructions flow through the machine. The architect reviews the efficiency and cost of the hardware control, data paths, and manipulation units required.

From a compiler writer's viewpoint, the design of an instruction is not only related to efficiency factors but, just as importantly, to compilation ease and correctness. A compiler writer desires a regular, orthogonal, and composible instruction set. The instruction set should provide clear, simple, and consistent choices for the compiler to make when generating code. Special cases and inconsistent definitions should be avoided. A simple compiler is also more likely to be a correct compiler, and is also more easily tunable.

There are currently two philosophies for designing an instruction set, one based on complex instruction sets and one based on reduced instruction sets. Complex instruction sets attempt to narrow the semantic gap between high-level languages and machine instructions. They endow each machine instruction with powerful operators and addressing modes that trigger complex sequences of firmware and hardware activities. They are efficient because their code is tight and they use microcode extensively. Microcode execution is more efficient than software execution. The reduced instruction sets are based on the premise that the execution of simple instructions approaches the speed of the execution of microinstructions. Reduced instruction sets make designing pipelines and controls easier than complex instruction sets. Designers of RISCs examine each instruction to be incorporated into the instruction set in terms of its overall effect on the cycle time of the machine and the additional complexity it introduces into the design. Simplicity often translates to lower costs, shorter development cycles, fewer bugs, and the optimal cost/performance trade-offs.

Instruction set design is an iterative process that requires the cooperation of the compiler writer and the computer architect. The designs of the compiler, the instruction set, and the supporting machine are examined repeatedly and modified to achieve efficient code and efficient implementations of the code. To help select an initial instruction set from which to iterate, the architect reviews instruction mix statistics and observations on instruction mixes (heuristics). The initial choice of an instruction set is then refined by the iterative process.

REFERENCES

[1] D. A. Patterson and D. R. Ditzel, "The Case for the Reduced Instruction Set Computer Architecture," *Comput. Archit. News,* Vol. 8, No. 6, October 1980.

[2] D. W. Clark and W. D. Strecker, "Comments on the Case for the Reduced Instruction Set Computer," *Comput. Archit. News,* Vol. 8, No. 6, October 1980.

[3] W. A. Wulf, "Compilers and Computer Architecture," *Computer,* July 1981, pp. 41–47.

[4] G. J. Myers, *Advances in Computer Architecture,* Wiley, New York, 1978.

[5] D. A. Patterson and R. S. Piepho, "RISC Assessment: A High-Level Language Experiment," *9th Annu. Symp. Comput. Archit.,* Vol. 10, No. 3, April 1982.

[6] G. Radin, "The 801 Minicomputer," *Proc. Symp. Archit. Support Program. Lang. Oper. Syst.,* ACM, March 1982.

[7] D. A. Patterson and C. H. Sequin, "RISC-I: A Reduced Instruction Set VLSI Computer," *8th Annu. Symp. Comput. Archit.,* May 1981.

[8] J. R. Larus, "A Comparison of Microcode, Assembly Code, and High-Level Languages on the VAX-11 and RISC I," *Comput. Archit. News,* Vol. 10, No. 5, September 1982.

[9] R. C. Eckhouse, Jr., and L. R. Morris, *Minicomputer Systems Organization: Programming and Applications (PDP-11),* Prentice-Hall, Englewood Cliffs, N.J., 1979.

[10] C. G. Bell, J. C. Mudge, and J. E. McNamara, *Computer Engineering: A DEC View of Hardware Systems Design,* Digital Press, Bedford, Mass., 1978.

[11] H. M. Levy and R. H. Eckhouse, Jr., *Computer Programming and Architecture, The VAX-11,* Digital Press, Bedford, Mass., 1980.

[12] N. Chapin, *360/370 Programming in Assembly Language,* 2nd ed., McGraw-Hill, New York, 1973.

[13] C. A. Wiecek, "A Case Study of VAX-11 Instruction Set Usage for Compiler Execution," *Proc. Symp. Archit. Support Program. Lang. Oper. Syst.* ACM, March 1982.

[14] M. Marathe, "Performance Evaluation at the Hardware Architecture Level and the Operating System Kernel Design Level," Ph.D. dissertation, Carnegie-Mellon University, 1978.

[15] C. G. Bell and A. Newell, *Computer Structures: Readings and Examples,* McGraw-Hill, New York, 1971.

[16] C. W. Gear, *Computer Organization and Programming,* 3rd ed., McGraw-Hill, New York, 1980.

[17] J. W. Stevenson and A. S. Tanenbaum, ''Efficient Encoding of Machine Instructions,'' *Comput. Archit. News,* Vol. 7, No. 8, June 1979, pp. 10–17.

[18] D. Huffman, ''A Method for the Construction of Minimum Redundancy Codes,'' *Proc IRE,* Vol. 40, 1952, pp. 1098–1011.

[19] W. B. Dietz and L. Szewerenko, ''Architectural Efficiency Measures: An Overview of Three Studies,'' *Computer,* April 1979.

[20] D. W. Clark and H. M. Levy, ''Measurement and Analysis of Instruction Use in the VAX-11/780,'' *9th Annu. Symp. Comput. Archit.*, Vol. 10, No. 3, April 1982.

[21] W. G. Alexander and D. B. Wortman, ''Static and Dynamic Characteristics of XPL Programs,'' *Computer,* Vol. 8, No. 11, November 1975, pp. 41–46.

[22] L. J. Shustek, ''Analysis and Performance of Computer Instruction Sets,'' *Stanford Linear Accelerator Rep. 205,* Stanford University, May 1978.

[23] A. Lunde, ''Evaluation of Instruction Set Processor Architecture by Program Tracing,'' Ph.D. thesis, Department of Computer Sciences, Carnegie-Mellon University, 1974.

[24] L. Svobodova, ''Computer Systems Performance Measurement: Instructions Set Processor Level and Microcode Level,'' *Rep. AD/A000 946/457,* Stanford University, 1974.

[25] R. A. Arbuckle, ''Computer Analysis and Thruput Evaluation,'' *Comput. Autom.*, January 1966, pp. 12–19.

[26] G. McDaniel, ''An Analysis of a Mesa Instruction Set Using Dynamic Instruction Frequencies,'' *Proc. Symp. Archit. Support Program. Lang. Oper. Syst.,* ACM, March 1982.

[27] A. S. Tanenbaum, ''Implications of Structured Programming for Machine Architecture,'' *Commun. ACM,* Vol. 21, No. 3, March 1978, pp. 237–246.

PROBLEMS

4.1 Implement the **and** instruction using a sequence of other instructions. Implement the **add** instruction (addition of two 32-bit operands) using a sequence of other instructions.

4.2 What is the minimal set of instructions needed to support a high-level language?

4.3 What are the various trade-offs and compromises that need to be made between compiler designers and computer architects in designing an instruction set?

4.4 Compare the advantages and disadvantages of CISCs versus RISCs. Which, in your judgment, is a better approach? Present your arguments.

4.5 RISC proponents state that if the instructions in a RISC instruction set can be executed out of a CPU-resident fast store in a single machine cycle just as microinstructions in a CISC machine can be executed out of a CPU-resident fast control store in a single machine cycle, the advantages of CISCs are obtained by RISCs without the need of a complex instruction set. Is this totally true? How are instructions different from microinstructions?

4.6 Instruction sets not only support high-level languages but also operating systems. What is the effect of including special operating system instructions on the RISC philosophy? What about software with frequent usage of floating-point and packed decimal operations? Can these functions be efficiently implemented without special floating-point and packed decimal instructions in the RISC approach? What are possible alternatives?

4.7 Given the following register and memory contents:

(R0) = 100 (100) = 200 (98) = 198
(R1) = 200 (200) = 300 (198) = 298

(R2) = 300	(300) = 400	(298) = 398
(R4) = 400	(400) = 500	(398) = 498
	(500) = 100	(498) = 98

what are the new contents of these registers and memory locations after each instruction below is executed? Assume the same initial register and memory contents at the start of each instruction. For the autoincrement, autodecrement, and indexed modes, assume that the size of one word is two bytes.
The following notation is used for the addressing modes:

Immediate #n (n is immediate operand)

Absolute @#A (A is absolute address)

Register R

Register Deferred (R)

Autoincrement (R)+

Autodecrement -(R)

Index X[R]

Displacement D(R)

Index Displacement D(Rn)[Rx]

Autoincrement Indexed (Rn)+[Rx]

Autodecrement Indexed -(Rn)[Rx]

(a) MOV #1, @#100
(b) MOV R0, (R1)
(c) MOV (R0)+, -(R1)
(d) MOV 100[R1], (R0)
(e) MOV 100(R0), 100(R1)[R0]
(f) MOV (R1)+[R0], (R2)
(g) MOV -(R1)[R0], (R2)

4.8 Compare the advantages and disadvantages of orthogonal instruction encoding, integrated instruction encoding, and mixed instruction encoding. Which in your judgment is the best approach? Why?

4.9 What applications are best suited to run on machines with (a) simple operations and simple addressing modes, (b) simple operations and complex (sophisticated) addressing modes, (c) complex operations and simple addressing modes, and (d) complex operations and complex addressing modes?

4.10 In Section 4.8 (Instruction Set Design Methodology), 11 features of a design are listed. Discuss why you think each feature should be included in the list of features that should be exercised by test programs for benchmarking the effectiveness of the design? Are there other features you think ought to be included? Why?

4.11 Write an assembly program to sort 10 integers in order of their absolute magnitude in an assembly language of your choice. Choose various random sets of 10 integers as input. Count the types of instructions executed by the program. Which is the most prevalent type? Which is next, and so on? Do these agree with studies that the most prevalent group are the move instructions, followed by the branch instructions, followed by the test and comparison instructions?

5

Operating Systems and Architecture

5.1 INTRODUCTION

By abstracting a programmer's view of the computer system from ones and zeros to powerful constructs reflecting algorithms and data objects, high-level languages facilitate programmers' thought processes and enable them to create with greater ease programs that are readable, maintainable, reliable, and portable. A high-level language is a key component in programming methodologies for alleviating the explosive growth of software development costs. Just as important a component is the operating system.

Operating systems are layers of software on top of the hardware; they provide programmers a view of the computer system environment several levels of abstraction above that of the bare machine. An operating system lets programmers concern themselves with programs and information structures rather than with maintaining and manipulating hardware. By creating user-friendly environments, operating systems increase the productivity of the programmers. They are important for applying programming methodologies and they help amortize the cost of software development.

The inadequate design of an architecture for supporting the operating system limits the ways the processor may be used. For example, an inadequate architecture may restrict a processor from being used with a multiprocessing operating system; or, it may restrict the operating system to implementing virtual memory by means of swapping without the "hooks" built in to support a paged operating system [1]. For these reasons, an architecture to support operating systems must be constructed carefully.

Similar to high-level languages, operating systems introduce overhead. A major goal of computer architectures is to reduce overhead by supporting efficiently both high-level languages and operating systems. To do this, the architects must understand not only the concepts of high-level languages and operating systems and their architectural implications, but also how the concepts may be implemented. They must consider alternative approaches for architectural support, and must bear in mind the possibility that elaborate architectural support structures may decrease rather than increase system performance. Chapters 2, 3, and 4 discuss the architectural issues concerning high-level-language support (*language-directed architectures*). Chapters 5, 6, and 7 discuss operating systems and their architectural support (*operating-system-directed architectures*).

5.2 OPERATING SYSTEMS

This chapter introduces the concept of an operating system and examines its functions. Throughout, an attempt is made to explore the implications of designing an architecture to support the various classifications of operating systems. Chapter 6 shows how the concepts of operating systems may be implemented. Chapter 7 discusses portability and efficiency issues, and gives examples of operating-system-directed architectures.

An operating system is a collection of programs that controls the use of system resources. It allocates main and secondary storage to user programs, and accepts I/O commands from various devices. Operating systems manage files and resolve conflicts for resources. Because of its overall view of the processing, the operating system optimizes performance. An interface between the user programs and system resources like an operating system makes systems easier to learn, work with, and change.

In early computer systems, each programmer personally operated the machine by loading card decks and running printers. The execution process consumed the resources of the entire computer and run times were long. As time passed, this approach became unfeasible because the demands on the computer system far exceeded the amount of equipment available. Moreover, the equipment itself was expensive; no user could afford to pay for the entire machine during the period required to process a complete job. The primary objective of early operating systems was to use the expensive physical equipment more efficiently. Architects noted the disparity in the processing speed of the CPU and its I/O devices and suggested that sharing resources would provide the necessary efficiency. Sharing resources efficiently is still the principal task of operating systems. By maintaining a series of queues for the various resources, the operating system coordinates and schedules pending tasks so that all the devices are busy simultaneously. This maximizes the number of tasks completed per unit of time and thereby distributes the cost of running the equipment among many different jobs.

In addition to managing the hardware resources, the operating system implements software resources such as files, processes, and message channels. Software resources provide a useful and reliable programming environment for the user. The term *virtual objects* is often used synonymously with software resources. Although virtual objects appear simple to the user, they may in fact be created by the complicated underlying mechanism of the operating system. Higher productivity in application programming is made possible by the high-level virtual objects created by the operating system.

A file, for example, is a virtual object. It appears to the programmer simply as a set of records that the user may update or read on command from the program. To do these relatively simple tasks, the operating system must format the records and store them in the appropriate type of storage media. In addition, it must establish buffers and procedures to control the transfer of records between main storage and secondary storage. It also must protect the files from unauthorized access or accidental damage. Virtual objects can save the application programmer from a considerable amount of work because the operating system masks all the internal details of the objects and of the task of controlling the devices used to implement them. This results in greater protection from misuse and more reliable operation for all users.

An operating system serves three purposes. It creates from a physical machine a virtual machine that is *personal, extended,* and *reliable* for each user. In creating a personal machine, the operating system multiplexes multiple virtual machines onto a real machine and manages the time sharing of resources. The personal machine is then extended by the operating system to have capabilities far beyond those of the physical machine by providing the user utilities, tools, and library routines. Finally, the operating system makes the personal and extended machine reliable by providing routines for maintenance, error recovery, diagnostics, and audits.

The study of issues in the creation of the extended machine (tools and utilities) is not included in this book because it is independent of the study of machine architecture. Machine reliability is covered in Chapter 8. Chapters 6 and 7 concern the operating system functions of time-multiplexing multiple virtual machines and managing their interactions and sharing of resources.

5.3 OPERATING SYSTEM FUNCTIONS

One of the ways of examining the structure of an operating system views the operating system as a manager of these resources:

1. Memory
2. Processors
3. Devices
4. Information (programs and data)

The operating system allocates these resources efficiently and resolves conflicts in their use. The programs that manage these resources are grouped into four categories: memory management, processor management, device management, and information management. Each manager keeps track of the resources, distributes and schedules them, allocates them, and reclaims them.

The main storage is an important resource handled by the memory manager. The complexity of the main storage depends very much on the sophistication of the memory's hierarchical structure. Advanced operating systems operate on the concept of virtual memory. Virtual memory permits the user to treat the main memory and auxiliary (or secondary) storage, such as disk drives, as a single unit. That is, users view storage as a continuous address space where programs are stored regardless of whether the programs are in main memory or disk. The memory manager (with the help of the information manager and the disk driver) moves information between the disk drives and the main memory according to the needs of the executing program. These transfers are transparent to the user. Although the virtual addresses do not change, the physical location of information within the computer does because of paging and process swapping. Paging and swapping are discussed in Chapter 6. The memory manager keeps track of the continually changing physical addresses of information; it also remembers which parts of the memory are in use. In a multiprogramming environment where multiple programs are active on the machine, the memory manager determines which active program (process) should be allocated memory, when to allocate it, and the amount of memory to be allocated. After the process terminates or no longer needs the memory, the manager reclaims the resource and makes it available to other processes.

Another important system resource is the processor itself; the sharing of this resource is measured by the percentage of available time allotted to a job or program. The job scheduler examines all the jobs submitted to the system and selects the ones allowed into the system. The processor time allotted to a job is the time the job has control of the system resources to execute its program. Figure 5.1 shows a model of the states a job goes through from submission to completion. In a multiprogramming system, the scheduling is divided into two parts: job scheduler and processor scheduler. The job scheduler chooses which jobs will run and creates processes for each job. The processor scheduler decides which of the ready processes receive control of the processor, when they acquire control, and for how long. The life cycle of a process is represented by the transitions between the states shown on the right side of Fig. 5.1. The four states of a process are ready, running, waiting, and complete:

- *Ready:* The process is ready to run. It is waiting for a processor to be assigned.
- *Running:* The process is running and its programs are executing in the processor.

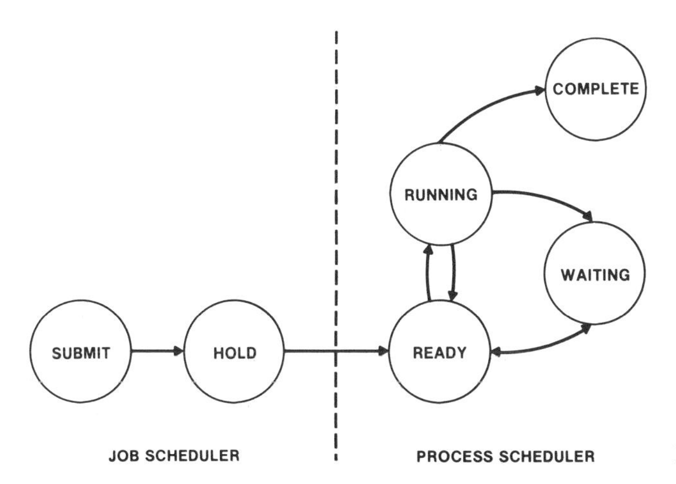

Figure 5.1 State model.

- *Waiting:* The process is blocked or put to sleep. It is waiting for some event (for example, an I/O operation) to be completed.
- *Complete:* The process is terminated. It has completed execution.

Another program module, the traffic controller, resides within the processor manager; its function is keeping track of the status of the process. There is a similar state diagram for every process in the system.

In most computer installations, I/O devices account for over half of the system cost. I/O devices include disks, tapes, printers, card readers, network interfaces, and support devices such as control channels. There are three major types of devices: dedicated, shared, and virtual. A *dedicated* device is assigned to a job for its duration. If a job does not fully and continually utilize the device, this type of allocation is inefficient. Most direct-access storage devices are *shared* by several processes concurrently. Interleaving different jobs on a single device in a multiprogramming environment uses the device fully and hence more effectively in terms of cost than dedicated devices. One drawback of shared devices is they require controls for maintaining status, scheduling policy, and allocating resources; the management of the devices can be rather complicated, particularly if the system requires robust and efficient operation.

Some slow, sequential devices such as printers or card punches lend themselves more readily than disks and drums to the dedicated mode of operation. They may be converted into shared devices through *spooling* techniques. The spooling routine writes, for example, the printer data onto a disk. Later, a routine copies the information onto a printer at maximum speed. Because no interleaving occurs, the spooling may be considered dedicated. But since the disk is shared by several users, it only gives the user the illusion of being dedicated. This combination of shared and dedicated describes the *virtual* device. In the example, one printer changes into many ''virtual'' printers. Creating virtual devices provides a flexible technique for managing and scheduling jobs and devices.

The information manager generates, stores, and retrieves data in a file system. Its basic functions are:

1. Keeping track of the resource (information), including its location, status, size, use, and access rights.
2. Deciding which process has access to the resources, enforcing protection requirements, and providing accessing routines
3. Allocating the resource (for example, opening a file)
4. Deallocating the resource (for example, closing a file)

The management of a file system by the information manager frees users from many of the problems associated with allocating space for their data, physical storage formats, and I/O accessing. In addition, the information manager administers the sharing of information among users and the protection of information from unauthorized accesses.

Figure 5.2 shows the hierarchical structure of the kernel of an operating system [2]. The modules of the information manager are in the outer ring. As has been pointed out, implementing this manager fully can be quite complicated. The file system is divided into

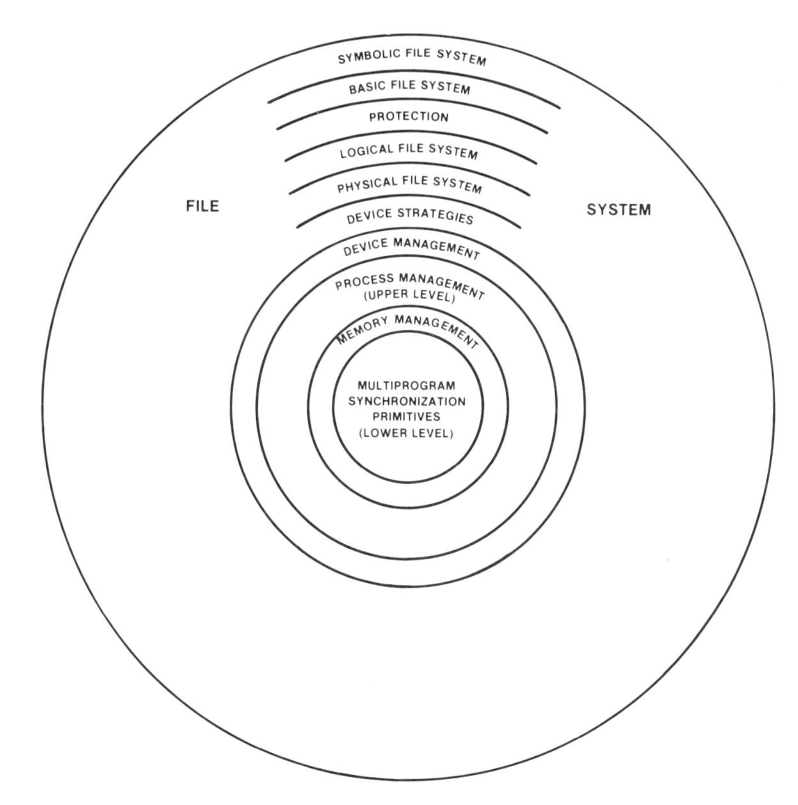

Figure 5.2 Resource management relationship.

layers and each follows structured programming techniques in that each level depends only on the level below it and only calls downward.

5.4 DEVELOPMENT OF OPERATING SYSTEMS

System architects perceived the need for operating systems early in the history of computers. In the 1950s, operating systems reduced system idle time by collecting and submitting batches of jobs, thus eliminating the manual tasks of loading and unloading individual jobs. The operating systems provided the job-to-job linkages. By the end of the decade, computer architects added standard I/O routines for handling the major I/O devices.

In 1961, the concept of virtual memory was introduced by Manchester University on the Atlas computer [3]. It is the seed for the prevalent concepts of virtual resources and virtual machines, and of distinguishing between the virtual and the physical. A virtual memory gives the programmer the illusion that a larger memory than the actual physical memory exists. At the heart of this idea are the principles that virtual addresses are distinct from physical locations. The same information can be paged from disk as needed at different times into different physical locations of main memory. The internal relocation of information in physical memory is transparent to a user program that has the same virtual address to access the information.

Two other major developments came about in the early 1960s. One is the development of a completely on-line transaction processing system, American Airline's SABRE system [4]. The SABRE system strongly influenced on-line transaction operating systems such as the IBM attached support processor [5]. The other major development was the introduction of *segmentation* to support virtual memory. Segmentation is discussed in Chapter 6. Segmentation first was defined on the Burroughs MCP system [6]. This computer supports multiprogramming and allows the I/O activities of one job to overlap with the CPU activities of another job. The Burroughs MCP also introduced the notion of multiprocessing with two identical CPUs in a master/slave mode.

In the mid-1960s, IBM introduced a general-purpose operating system: the OS/360 [7]. This operating system pioneered the concept of a family of computers with a single operating system. The OS/360 provides a complete set of facilities and supporting utilities for a broad range of general-purpose computing needs. Also in the mid-1960s, system architects developed the first time-sharing systems. CTSS and the Berkeley Time-Sharing System introduced the concept of time sharing and became the forerunners of present-day time-sharing systems [8,9]. This innovation began the gradual shift from batch to interactive processing. Another influential system developed in the 1960s, the Multics system, supports general-purpose interactive time sharing [10]. Multics, developed by a cooperative effort involving AT&T Bell Laboratories, General Electric, and MIT, has a sophisticated protection structure implemented in layers called rings. It also fully supports virtual memory with both segmentation and paging.

In the late 1960s and early 1970s, Dijkstra's THE system [11], Brinch Hansen's RC4000 [12], and Hoare's work on monitors [13] laid the foundation for concurrent software systems. Their ideas, and those in Multics, were incorporated in the development of the UNIX™*[14] operating system at AT&T Bell Laboratories. The success of the UNIX operating system results from its simplicity and generality; it provides a small but powerful multiuser operating system. Another operating system developed at AT&T Bell Laboratories in the 1970s is the MERT Operating System [15]. The MERT operating system provides a generalized kernel with extensive interprocess communications; the kernel has stringent requirements for real-time response and supports the simultaneous operation of different operating systems. These ideas were based on the RC4000. MERT is the operating system on which DMERT, the current operating system for the AT&T 3B20D processor, is based [16]. The key milestones in the development of operating systems are shown in Fig. 5.3.

The operating systems discussed thus far are based on functional abstraction. Functional abstraction systems are those in which software is partitioned into modules according to functions. The 1960s and 1970s were dominated by functional abstraction systems. An important development in operating systems is the development of the concept of data

*UNIX is a trademark of AT&T.

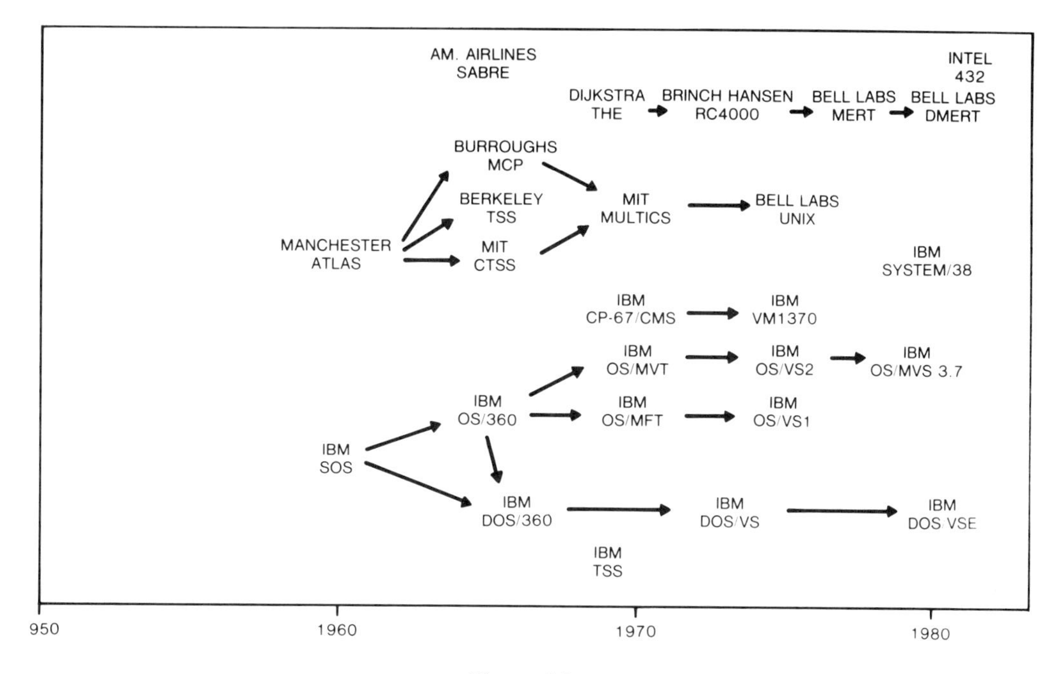

Figure 5.3

abstraction. Data abstraction systems are those in which software is partitioned according to data. Even though the concepts of data abstraction systems originated in the 1960s, few commercial data abstractions systems have been built. The notable ones are Plessey/250 [17], the Intel IAPX/432 [18], and the IBM System/38 [19]. The main drawback of data abstraction systems is that it is difficult to make them efficient. Nevertheless, the concept of data abstraction is important because it enhances the reliability and maintainability of software. Its ideas are adopted in languages such as Ada in several features, including packages and abstract data types.

Operating systems have evolved from merely reducing system idle time to providing multiple virtual machines that are personal, extended, and reliable for multiple users. Current operating systems are taking increasing amounts of system space and time. There is a trend to reduce the size of operating systems by modularizing them so customers purchase only the modules they need; what is considered the operating system will therefore be smaller. Another trend is moving more of the functions of the operating system from software into firmware and hardware, thus alleviating the overhead in system time.

5.5 OPERATING-SYSTEM-DIRECTED ARCHITECTURE

Just as an architecture should support a variety of high-level languages, it should also support multiple operating systems. Because operating systems continually evolve and the many user communities require different operating systems, an operating-system-directed architecture should not be tailored for any one operating system; doing so would compromise the running efficiency of other operating systems. Even when a machine is heavily biased toward a single operating system, the implementation of the operating system evolves with new releases (generics). Furthermore, a machine may be required to be configured in a network or a multiprocessor system; it should therefore also efficiently support distributed operating systems. Therefore, an operating-system-directed architecture should support various operating systems efficiently.

To determine how to construct an operating-system-directed architecture, the common characteristics of the different types of operating systems must be ascertained. How are object-based operating systems, real-time operating systems, transaction operating systems, multiprocessing operating systems, and network operating systems similar? What are their main differences? The architect must understand what it means to raise the level of the hardware/software interface to support the variety of operating systems. Which functions should the architect move from software to firmware or hardware? How is architectural support provided for interprocess communication, synchronization, and context switches? The architect must also consider how the architectural support for the operating system affects compatibility.

To answer these questions, an approach is needed that first classifies the operating systems and identifies their similarities and differences. Next, the architect must examine the implications of the similarities and differences, and attempt to determine the basic activities of operating systems. Compatibility and efficiency issues are then examined to determine their architectural implications on the support of these activities.

5.6 OPERATING SYSTEMS CLASSIFICATION BY APPLICATION

The key operating system functions are scheduling resources and dispatching programs. The type of operating system determines the emphasis placed on the characteristics of these functions and the policies of implementation.

Operating systems may be classified by their applications as general-purpose, real-time, or transaction-oriented. Computer manufacturers supply *general-purpose operating systems* to satisfy the needs of their batch and time-sharing users. A computer center is a prime example of an application of a general purpose operating system. *Real-time operating systems* require each stimulus to result in a response within a prescribed length of time. They are commonly used in process control in various industries and for tracking events in military applications. *Transaction-oriented operating systems* read and update shared data bases. Examples of applications are the airline seat reservations, banking account balance update, and credit card account processing.

An important difference in the characteristics among these systems is the response time to a stimulus. The real-time systems require the quickest responses (milliseconds). Transaction-oriented and time-sharing systems need response times measured in seconds; batch systems are the slowest of all. Each system is thus characterized by its ability to perform functions within time constraints that ensure satisfactory interaction with external events. Table 5.1 compares the characteristics of real-time, transaction-oriented, and general-purpose operating systems.

TABLE 5.1 OPERATING SYSTEMS CLASSIFICATION BY APPLICATION

Real-Time Systems (Process Control, Military)	Transaction-Oriented Systems (Airline, Credit Card)	General-Purpose Systems (Computer Center Time Sharing)
~Millisecond response	~Second response	~Second response
Small process	Data stream input	Friendly user interface
Resident processes	Distributed environment	Tools and utilities
Sophisticated paging	Data base environment	Libraries
Priority levels	Queuing of transactions	Reentrant code
Low-resolution timer	Synchronization of transactions	Group ID
Preemptive scheduler	Well-controlled processes	Job ID
Cycle-time scheduler		Access rights
Contiguous files		Convenient file system
Shared memory communication		Swapping and paging
Controlled environment		

5.6.1 General-Purpose Operating Systems

The two categories of general-purpose operating systems are serial batch and multiprogramming. The *serial batch* system was the first type of operating system developed. Serial batch systems schedule jobs sequentially. Jobs come in from a card reader or a fast, direct-access intermediate device. The operating system collects them into groups called batches. It then processes the jobs singly until all are done. Serial batch systems do not allow multiprogramming; they are used primarily for scheduling input and output.

Multiprogrammed operating systems implement multiple, concurrently operating virtual machines. They enable two or more batch jobs to run concurrently. The system schedules multiple jobs in the CPU that are simultaneously contending for system resources. While one job waits for an I/O event, another job controls the CPU and executes. Multiprogramming maximizes the use of system resources; it is not unusual to see a system with 15 or more jobs running concurrently even though most of them are waiting for I/O events. Multiprogramming is a tremendous improvement over serial batch systems. The key characteristic of a multiprogramming system is the importance it places on the effective sharing of hardware.

A *time-sharing* operating system is a multiprogrammed system that emphasizes user (programmer) efficiency. It is a system with many users interacting with the computer as though each user has exclusive use of it. A time-sharing operating system is characterized by multiple terminal connections to the computer system. The terminal may be a teletypewriter or a video display unit with a keyboard. Often, the users are at large geographical distances from each other and connected through telephone lines to the CPU. Time sharing has the effect of appearing to give users a complete computing system at their disposal at all times, but they pay only for the time they actually use the system.

General-purpose operating systems share many common characteristics. One of their important features is that they support friendly user interfaces and a variety of utilities that make writing, testing, and running programs easy. In addition, they maintain libraries from which multiple users can share programs, files, and routines. In such a system, processes must be able to share reentrant code. General-purpose operating systems should also provide convenient file system facilities for creating, deleting, changing, and sharing files and directories.

Since multiple users share a time-sharing system, the operating system must protect them from each other and allow communication among them. Both the memory management system and the file system should enforce accessing rights and control protection. Concepts such as group and job identifications should be provided to let images be shared among processes in the system, among processes within a group (protected from all other processes), and among processes within a single job (protected from all other jobs).

Finally, general-purpose systems must let users share the limited physical memory. Because users are not always logged on or active, the operating system implements the concept of swapping or demand paging in processes as needed, and provides a virtual address space much larger than the actual physical space.

5.6.2 Real-Time Operating Systems

In many ways, *real-time* operating systems are like time-sharing operating systems. Multiple input sources initiate inputs and the system generates appropriate responses. In a time-sharing system, human users generate the inputs at terminals to run different jobs. In a real-time system, data collection equipment feeds data into the system. The inputs to a real-time system, in many cases, are uniform and repetitive, and less varied than the inputs to a time-sharing system. An electronic telephone switching system is a good example of a real-time system. Telephones represent the input equipment. Their inputs are "on-hook," "off-hook," and dialing information. A common call processing program processes the inputs and provides the appropriate signaling and sets up the connection paths.

One of the major requirements imposed on real-time operating systems is that requests from input equipment must be entered and serviced by the system within a certain prescribed time period (real time) to ensure that the input data is not lost and to ensure real-time (milliseconds) responses. To ensure very fast response, processes in a real-time system are small and reside permanently in memory; otherwise, the system requires a sophisticated paging system. Furthermore, processes are arranged in levels of decreasing priority requirements. The time-critical processes are put at high-priority levels and locked in memory. A preemptive priority scheduler then allows the system designer to specify the order in which processes run. Real-time operating systems also provide high-resolution interval timers for generating events in small time increments [16]. To maximize the efficiency of interprocess communications, the systems allow shared-segment communications. Messages sent between processes have been shown to be inadequate for some real-time problems [21]. Finally, to minimize file access time, real-time systems should store files on contiguous areas of secondary storage.

The schedulers of a real-time operating systems may be either interrupt driven or cycle-time driven. Interrupt-driven schedulers adjust response times by carefully selecting process priorities and context switching* times. The number of interrupts possible should be controlled to minimize unnecessary and time-consuming context switches. In cycle-time-driven schedulers, the longest time interval between two consecutive executions of a process must be less than or equal to a guaranteed response time. This ''worst-case'' time interval is a function of both the maximum number of processes schedulable for execution and the longest execution path of each process, as well as the time expended by system overhead.

In general, real-time operating systems require carefully controlled environments with control over the allocation and assignment of storage to the processes, the execution-time slices and the scheduling priorities of the processes.

5.6.3 Transaction-Oriented Operating Systems

A series of activities generated in a machine by a stream of data that may arrive over data links from a distributed system of machines is called a *transaction*. The data stream is usually machine generated and updates and retrieves data in one or more data bases. Operating systems that handle transactions must be able to acquire data from high-speed devices and links. In contrast, people generate interactive time-sharing commands that are much shorter in length than transactions.

For example, in a telephone company operation support system, a typical transaction consists of 512 bytes of data read from a character device. A pipeline of five processes manipulates the data and writes it to the data base. It is expected that the system does 30 context switches in handling the transaction as processes roadblock for I/O. Each process in the pipeline executes approximately 5000 C-language statements. In comparison, a typical time-sharing system command in the operation support system handles 20 characters of terminal data and spawns three processes. Each process opens a data base file, reads 20 blocks from the disk, and executes 10,000 C statements. The system does about 100 context switches to handle these time-sharing system commands.

A transaction operating system is behaviorally similar to a time-sharing operating system except that emphasis is placed on different computing activities. Both systems require efficient context switches. In general, the processes handling a transaction are well defined and used repeatedly. The interactions among these processes are also well defined. For these reasons, transaction-oriented operating systems tend to be much simpler than time-sharing operating systems. The main emphasis of a transaction system is in its interaction with data bases, queuing transaction requests, synchronizing the requests, and guaranteeing that the data base is correctly updated.

*A context switch is the switching of process contexts. The context of the process that is going from the running state to the waiting state is saved, and the context of the process that is going from the ready state to the running state is brought into the processor. Context switches are discussed in Chapter 6.

5.7 OPERATING SYSTEMS CLASSIFICATION BY CONFIGURATION

Operating systems may also be classified according to the hardware or logical configurations on which they run. Operating systems may be classified as uniprocessor operating systems, multiprocessor operating systems, and network operating systems. Operating systems were first developed on uniprocessor systems as discussed previously to support the management and sharing of the processor resources by multiple users. These are multiprogrammed operating systems. As technology advances and needs for increasing computing performance are realized, architects have begun connecting various processors together into multiprocessors and networks. Hence operating systems must be developed to manage the parallel activities of the multiple processors. Multiprocessor operating systems and network operating systems evolved from the multiprogramming operating systems for uniprocessors. Table 5.2 summarizes the special characteristics of multiprocessor and network systems.

5.7.1 Multiprocessor Operating Systems

Multiprocessor operating systems manage the hardware and software resources of multiprocessing. A multiprocessor configuration is one in which the processors share a single memory. The processors are said to be tightly coupled because each has direct access to the same physical resources (shared memory) and logical resources (shared information). Like the multiprogrammed operating systems, the multiprocessor operating systems switch processes, suspend processes, and respond to interrupts. The major problem of extending a multiprogramming operating system to a multiprocessor operating system is process synchronization. The system must deal with processes executing not only concurrently (interleaved in time) but simultaneously (overlapped in time). The techniques used in uniprocessor systems for synchronizing processes such as masking interrupts and events do not work in multiprocessor systems. In a uniprocessor system, a process may have exclusive access to a shared resource by inhibiting interrupts such that no other processes may be scheduled to run on the machine and access the shared resource. In a

TABLE 5.2 OPERATING SYSTEMS CLASSIFICATIONS BY CONFIGURATION

Multiprocessor Operating System	Network Operating System
Shared and local memories	No shared memory
Semaphores	Distributed synchronization
Multiple-clocks synchronization	Messages
Multiple paths	Mailboxes and pipes
System initialization	Routing
Interprocessor interrupts	Process migration
Load balancing	Flow control

multiprocessor system, however, two processes could conceivably inhibit interrupts in their respective processors and still not be mutually excluded from accessing shared variables at the same time. The problem of race conditions between the occurrences of events and the checking for the occurrences in two different processors also exists. Synchronization based on *semaphores* is therefore required. Semaphores are discussed in Chapter 6. Other differences between multiprogramming and multiprocessor operating systems include the existence of multiple clocks and their need to be synchronized, the existence of multiple data paths to the same destination, system initializations of multiple processors, interprocessor interrupt facilities, scheduling for dynamic load balancing, the existence of both shared and local memories, and the migration of processes and data between them [20-22].

5.7.2 Network Operating Systems

Network operating systems manage the hardware and software resources of a processor connected to a network. Processors in a network do not have shared memories. They communicate by sending and receiving messages. Pipes in the UNIX operating system [15] and mailboxes in VAX/VMS [23] are useful communication mechanisms. Even though pipes and mailboxes are message buffers in virtual memory, they act as files and I/O devices, and they use the same file and I/O system calls as real files and I/O devices. They allow interprocess communications to use the same mechanisms for processes communicating over a network as for processes communicating within the same processor. Network operating systems may pass messages along paths called *links* in the DEMOS operating system [24]. Links allow programmers to define explicitly the logical connections among processes and abstract them from their physical connections. Other considerations for network operating systems include the static and dynamic allocation of processes to processors, the migration of processes among processors, flow control and message routing over alternate paths, and time delays in a geographically distributed synchronization scheme.

5.8 OPERATING SYSTEM COMMONALITIES

There are different types of operating systems, differences in their applications, and different configurations on which they are built. But because they are large and complex software systems, they share many characteristics. All modern operating systems are structured into modules. The modules must be protected from each other, communicate with each other, and be synchronized with each other. Even though a time-sharing operating system and a real-time operating system differ in their scheduling and paging algorithms, and even though a multiprogrammed operating system may implement its synchronizations differently from a multiprocessor system, all the operating systems require intermodule protection, intermodule communication, and intermodule synchronization. The support of these activities forms the nucleus of all operating systems. An operating-system-directed architecture must support this nucleus well. The next two chapters explore what is meant by supporting intermodule protection, intermodule synchronization, and intermodule communication.

5.9 SUMMARY

Like high-level languages, operating systems are an important part of programming methodology. They act as the interface between the programmer and the hardware of the machine. They manage hardware and software resources for the programmers. They keep track of the resources by allocating, deallocating, and scheduling them optimally.

Operating systems have evolved from their original function of relieving the computer operator from loading and unloading jobs to supporting multiple users simultaneously. They allow a single computer to be seen by each user as a personal, reliable, and extended virtual machine. These features are implemented as layers of software between the programmer and the physical machine. In doing so, however, increasing amounts of system time are required to be expended on supporting operating system software.

Concerns with operating system overhead have prompted investigations of machine architectures having features and primitives that support operating systems efficiently. Just as machine architectures should support multiple high-level languages, they should also support multiple types of operating systems. The design of an operating-system-directed architecture, then, requires first categorizing operating systems so that their differences and commonalities can be extracted and understood. Although operating systems are built for different applications and configurations, they have common characteristics. There are three types of operating systems for applications: general-purpose, real-time, and transaction-oriented. By configuration, their categories include uniprocessor, multiprocessor, and network. These different operating systems have different sizes of processes, scheduler algorithms, resource allocation policies, and emphases on response time, but they all manage software modules (operating system modules or user-created modules) and the same hardware resources. In sharing the hardware resources, the software modules must be protected from each other and synchronized with each other, and they must be able to communicate with each other. These functions form the nucleus or fundamental requirements of all operating systems. The architects must ensure that supporting these functions forms the primary design objectives of their operating system-directed architectures.

REFERENCES

[1] J. Hennessy et al., ''Hardware/Software Tradeoffs for Increased Performance,'' *Proc. Symp. Archit. Support Program. Lang. Oper. Syst.*, ACM, March 1982.

[2] S. E. Madnick and J. J. Donovan, *Operating Systems*, McGraw-Hill, New York, 1974.

[3] J. Fotheringham, "Dynamic Storage Allocation in the Atlas Computer, Including an Automatic Use of a Backing Store," *Commun. ACM,* Vol. 4, No. 10, 1961, pp. 435–436.

[4] W. R. Plugge and M. N. Perry, "American Airlines SABRE Electronic Reservations System," *WJCC,* May 1961, pp. 593–602.

[5] *IBM System/360 Attached Support Processor (ASP) System Description,* IBM Publ. H20-0223-0, White Plains, N.Y.

[6] W. Lonegran and P. King, "Design of the B5000 System," *Datamation,* Vol. 7, No. 5, May 1961, pp. 28–32.

[7] *IBM System/360 Operating System Supervisor and Data Management Services,* IBM Publ. GC28-6646-2, White Plains, N.Y.

[8] J. H. Saltzer, "CTSS Technical Notes," *MIT Project MAC Tech. Rep. TR-16.*

[9] W. W. Lichtenberger and M. W. Pirtle, "A Facility for Experimentation in Man—Machine Interaction," *Proc. AFIPS 1965 FJCC,* Vol. 27, pp. 589–598.

[10] E. I. Organick, *The Multics System: An Examination of Its Structure,* MIT Press, Cambridge, Mass., 1972.

[11] E. W. Dijkstra, "The Structure of the 'THE' Multiprogramming System," *Commun. ACM,* Vol. 11, No. 5, 1968, pp. 341–346.

[12] P. Brinch Hansen, *Operating System Principles,* Prentice-Hall, Englewood Cliffs, N.J., 1973.

[13] C. A. R. Hoare, "Monitors: An Operating System Structuring Concept," *Commun. ACM,* Vol. 17, No. 10, October 1974, pp. 549–557.

[14] D. M. Ritchie and K. Thompson, "The UNIX Time-Sharing System," *Bell Syst. Tech. J.,* Vol. 57, No. 6, July–August 1978, pp. 1905–1930.

[15] H. Lycklama and D. L. Bayer, "UNIX Time-Sharing System: The Mert Operating System," *Bell Syst. Tech. J.,* Vol. 57, No. 6, July–August 1978, pp. 2049–2086.

[16] M. E. Grzelakowski, J. H. Campbell, and M. R. Dubman, "DMERT Operating System," *Bell Syst. Tech. J.,* Vol. 62, No. 1, January 1983, pp. 291–302.

[17] D. M. England, "Architectural Features of System 250," *Infotech State of the Art Rep. 14,* 1972, pp. 397–427.

[18] J. Rattner and W. W. Lattin, "Ada Determines Architecture of 32-Bit Microprocessor," *Electronics,* February 24, 1981, pp. 119–126.

[19] *IBM System/38 Technical Developments,* IBM Publ. ISBN 0-933 186-03-7, 1980.

[20] P. G. Sorenson, "Interprocess Communication in Real Time Systems," *Proc. 4th ACM Symp. Oper. Syst. Princip.,* October 1973, pp. 1–7.

[21] L. C. Walker, "Multiprocessor Operating System Design," *Infotech State of the Art Rep. 14,* 1972, pp. 241–262.

[22] J. A. Hawley et al., "MUNIX, a Multiprocessing Version of UNIX," Thesis, Naval Postgraduate School, Monterey, June 1975.

[23] *VAX11 Software Handbook,* Digital Equipment Corp., Maynard, Mass. 1977.

[24] F. Baskett, J. H. Howard, and J. T. Montague, "Task Communication in DEMOS," *Proc. 6th ACM Symp. Oper. Syst. Princip.,* November 1977.

PROBLEMS

5.1 In what ways would elaborate architectural support for operating system constructs decrease rather than increase system performance? Consider also cost/performance trade-offs.

5.2 A virtual object is an abstraction of some physical object in the machine. A file is an abstraction of a collection of disk blocks. Describe the increasing levels of abstraction from disk blocks to a file.

5.3 An operating system is composed of resource managers. All resource managers share the same basic functions of (a) keeping track of the resources; (b) deciding which process has access to the resources, enforcing protection, and providing accessing routines; (c) allocating the resources; and (d) deallocating the resources. What architectural supports are needed for these basic functions?

5.4 Describe the evolution of operating systems from the viewpoint of the evolution of increasing levels of abstractions.

5.5 Is the approach used to design an operating-system-directed architecture the same as that used to design a language-directed architecture? What trade-offs should be considered to support both languages and operating systems well?

5.6 Given the characteristics of real-time, transaction-oriented, and general-purpose operating systems, what would be possible specialized hardware support for each of them? What would be possible common hardware for all of them?

5.7 The basic activity of an operating system is managing resources. How do you relate this view with the view that the basic activities of an operating system are providing intermodule protection, intermodule communication, and intermodule synchronization?

6

Operating Systems: Concepts and Architectural Support

6.1 INTRODUCTION

A computing system constantly activates and deactivates large numbers of processes that are cooperating and competing for resources. The task of the operating system is to manage and control these processes and resources. There are two types of software resources: processes and packages. Processes are sets of activities grouped together; packages are sets of related data structures. Programmers link multiple processes and packages to accomplish jobs. Software resource management ensures that the software resources are protected, synchronized in their use, and capable of communication. Hardware resource management optimizes the use of the physical resources by the software, thus relieving application programmers from such concerns. Despite the differences among operating systems, they all have the same two functions: managing software and hardware resources.

Since operating systems are complex software systems, their functions and utilities may be modularized. For example, one software module executes the compiler program, another executes a terminal command, and a third manages the file system. A part of the operating system must manage not only the user-created modules, but the other operating system modules as well. The part of the operating system that manages the modules is called the *nucleus* or, more commonly, the *kernel* [1]. The kernel controls the interactions among the operating system modules, protects them from each other, and synchronizes them.

Hardware resources include the processor, the memory, and the input/output (I/O) devices. Processor management is performed by the scheduler, memory management by the memory manager, and I/O device management by the device drivers. The scheduler, memory manager, and the device drivers may be part of the kernel or may run as separate processes.

Chapter 5 describes the operating system as the manager of processors, memory, I/O devices, and information. The management of I/O devices is beyond the scope of this book; it is a subject large enough to fill several volumes. Information as a resource is stored as files. Files may be executable or nonexecutable. The algorithms and activities of file management are mostly unrelated to hardware and architectural support and therefore are not covered in this book. However, an executable file may be activated as a process, and process management is a universal activity of operating systems that requires extensive hardware and architectural support. Similarly, the management of the processor and memory requires hardware and architectural support. Process and package management, processor and memory management, and their hardware and architectural support are discussed in this chapter. The discussion covers functional and data abstraction systems and the differences between them, and protection, synchronization, and communication primitives and their architectural support.

6.2 PROCESSES

A program is a list of statements that describes a computation and implements an algorithm. A program in a high-level language (source code) is compiled and assembled into a machine language (object code) and linked with other object programs to form an executable unit. The executable units are stored logically as files and physically in memory or on disks. Activating the executable unit creates a process.

A *process* is thus an activation of an executable program unit. In a multiprogramming system where many processes share a single processor, a process is also a schedulable entity. Once activated, a process may be in various states: actively executing, ready to be scheduled for execution, or waiting for synchronization signals. The operating system defines a *context* for each process to describe its state. The context consists of control and status information about the process; this information is used by the operating system and by the process itself. The context also defines the access environment of the process.

A process context has two components: the swappable context and the nonswappable context (Fig. 6.1). A swappable context is one that may be swapped between memory and disk. Information about a process that is nonswappable (to disk) is kept in a system table that resides in memory at all times; this table (called the process table in the UNIX operating system [2], the software process control block in VMS [3], and the dispatcher control table in the DMERT operating system) allows an operating system to manage all the processes in the system, even those that are swapped out onto disk. For each process, the table in Fig. 6.1 contains the identification of the process (process ID or number) and the size and location of the process (either in memory or on disk). This information allows the operating system memory manager to allocate memory and locate and load the process once it is scheduled to be executed. The process table also contains scheduling and timing information about each process. The operating system

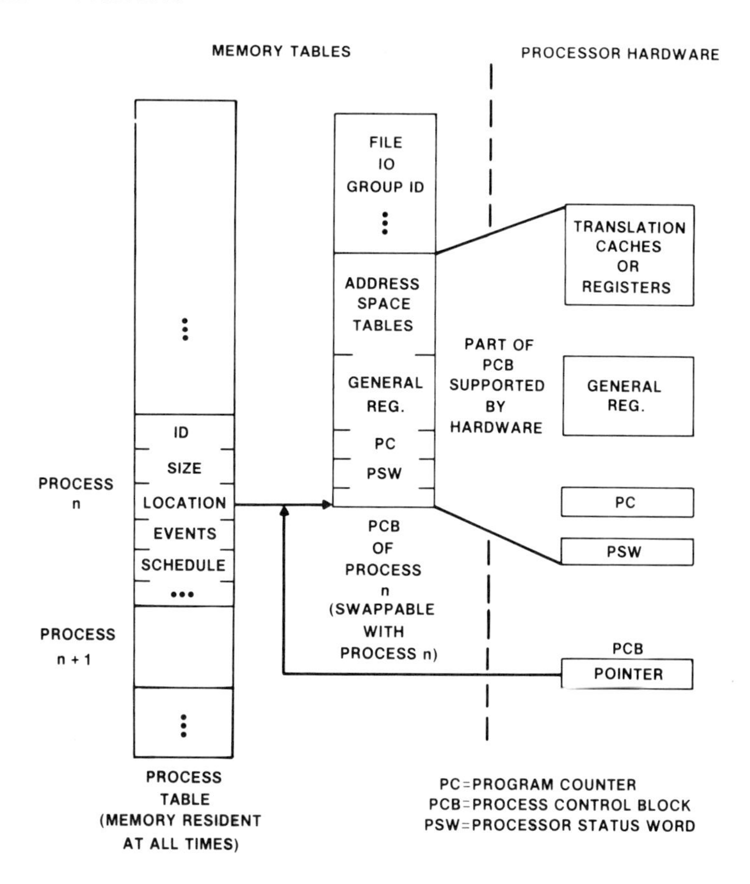

Figure 6.1 Process context.

scheduler determines the state and priority of the process and how long it has been in its current state. Even while a process is in the wait state while swapped out onto disk, it is capable of receiving signals and messages from other processes. Thus the process table must be accessible to the operating system at all times so that processes may post synchronization signals and events to other processes. Some of the events may cause the operating system to change the scheduling status of the receiving process; for example, a "wake up" event causes a process to be switched from the wait state to the ready state.

The other component of a process context is kept in a data structure (called the u_block in the UNIX operating system, the process header in VMS, and the process control block in the DMERT operating system) that is swappable with the process. A pointer kept for each process in the resident process table points to the location of the per-process control block. The per-process control block contains information about the access environment of the process. The access environment is defined by the address translation tables for the process. The address translation tables map the process's virtual address space into physical memory. The per-process control block also may contain information such as the files that have been opened by the process; the user and group identifications of the process; and other memory management data including the working set list, input/output data, accounting and quota information, and the saved hardware context.

The hardware context of a process is that part of the control and status information that is placed in hardware registers for functional and performance reasons while the process is executing on the processor. When a process is preempted (forced from the processor), the operating system saves the hardware context in the swappable per-process control block. The hardware context of the next process is obtained from its swappable per-process control block and loaded into the machine registers.

In many machines, the hardware context consists of four parts: a processor status word (PSW), a set of general registers where the temporary results of the computations are stored, a program counter (PC) that points to the instruction being executed, and a set of registers defining the access environment of the process pointing to the memory-mapping (address translation) tables of the process. The program counter is sometimes made part of the processor status word or the general registers. Some machines also contain buffers (registers or fast static memories) to hold the address translation tables.

The size and complexity of a process hardware context is a cost/performance design trade-off. Status bits are set and reset by special hardwired signals, and thus are automatically part of the hardware contexts. Other information may be stored in software and obtained by following pointers on a table lookup. Information about a process that is used frequently such as mapping information (on every memory access) and program count (on every instruction) is often made part of the hardware context. The computer architect must judge whether the performance improvements of storing this information in hardware outweighs the cost and complexity of additional hardware and the performance degradation that results from saving and restoring information on every context switch.

The hardware context of the PDP 11/45 and PDP 11/70 is shown in Fig. 6.2. The processor status word layout is shown in Fig. 6.3 [4,5]. As can be seen from these figures, the current and previous execution modes (kernel, supervisor, and user) of the process are specified in the processor status word. Depending on the current execution mode, the operating system selects one of the three sets of stack pointer (SP) and memory-mapping registers (kernel, supervisor, or user), as Fig. 6.2 shows. The mapping registers contain the address translation table to map the virtual address space of a process into physical memory space, thus defining the accessible physical space (access environment) of the process executing in the current mode (Fig. 6.4). The register set select bit of the processor status word (Fig. 6.3) selects one of two sets of general registers for the current process (Fig. 6.2). The PSW priority bits define the priority of the current process at which it may be interrupted. The negative, zero, overflow, and carry (N, Z, V, and C) flag bits in the processor status word describe the conditions resulting from computations of the current process. When the PSW trap bit is enabled, a trap occurs after every instruction switching the execution mode of the current process into the kernel mode and invoking a trap-handling routine.

The hardware context for the VAX machines also consists of a set of general registers (including the argument pointer, the frame pointer, and the program counter). It has a set of four stack pointers, one for each access mode (kernel, executive, supervisor and

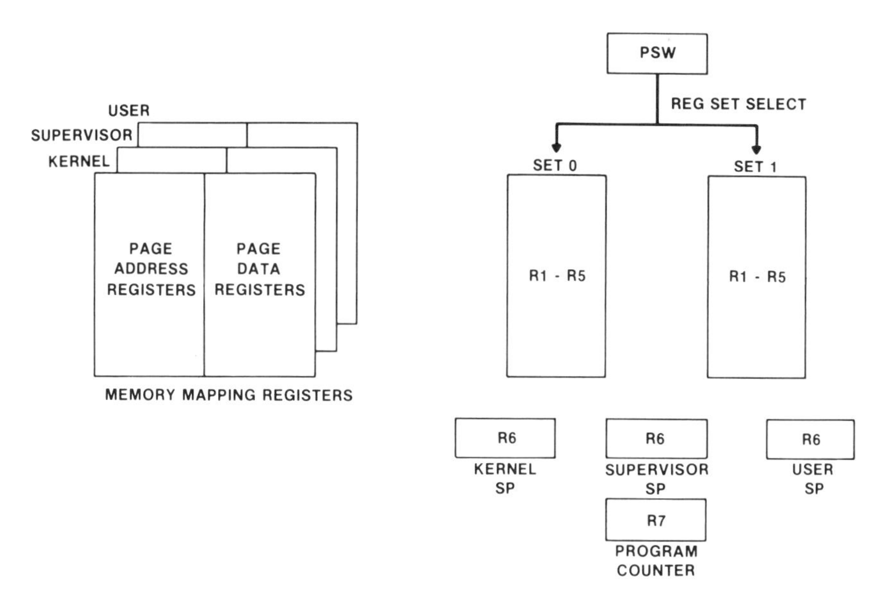

Figure 6.2 Hardware context of PDP 11/45 PDP 11/70.

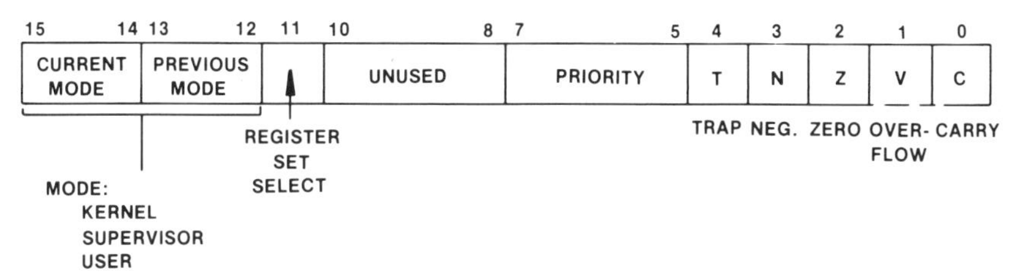

Figure 6.3 PDP-11 processor status word.

user). The processor status longword* and a set of four base and length registers that define the process address space in each of the four execution modes are also part of the hardware context for VAX computers.

The page table base register (0) and page table base register (1) points to the page table that contains the address translation information for the process space regions holding the user program and the user stack. The page table length register (0) and page table length register (1) are the respective lengths of the page tables. The asynchronous system trap levels record pending asynchronous system traps at each level. An asynchronous system trap is an asynchronous call to a routine within the context of a process. An example of an asynchronous call is the notification of completion of the service of an I/O request.

The VAX 11 has a register that points to the hardware process control block of the currently executing process; the hardware process control block in VMS is the part of the

*The VAX 11 defines a longword as a 32-bit word.

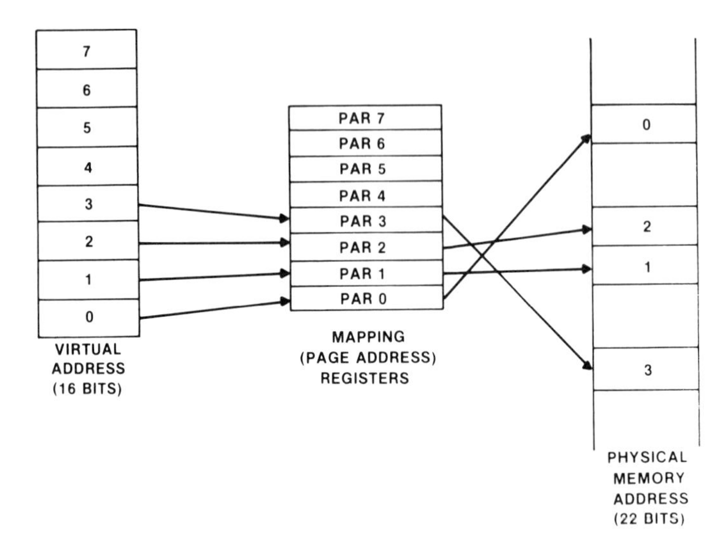

Figure 6.4 Virtual address mapping of physical address in PDP 11.

process header that contains the hardware context. During a context switch, the system loads the hardware context into the current process's hardware process control block and obtains a new hardware context from the next process's hardware process control block. The VAX hardware context is shown in Fig. 6.5 [6]. The layout of the processor status longword is shown in Fig. 6.6. The fields of the processor status longword include a compatibility mode bit (which indicates that the current process is executing the compatible PDP 11 instruction subset), a bit to indicate that a trace is pending, the interrupt priority level of the process, the interrupt stack bit (which indicates that the interrupt stack is being used to service an interrupt or another asynchronous event external to the interrupted process), the previous and current access modes of the current process, a set of four condition code bits (Negative, Zero, Overflow, and Carry), and a set of trap enable bits corresponding to the condition codes. If a trap bit is enabled and the corresponding condition code bit is set, a trap into the kernel occurs.

The hardware context of the 3B20D also consists of the program counter, the general registers (which include the stack, argument, and frame pointers), the processor status word, and the registers defining the address space of the current and the previous processes. The layout of the processor status word is shown in Fig. 6.7. The condition code field contains the four condition code bits: carry, negative, overflow, and zero. The kernel stack and interrupt stack bits indicate, respectively, that execution is currently using the kernel or interrupt stack. As in the VAX, the interrupt stack facilitates interrupt and other asynchronous event handling. When the memory management mapping bit is on, the address space of the current process is virtual and must be translated to access physical memory. The primary and secondary segment base register fields specify the two address spaces that are accessible to the executing process. Normally, all memory addresses are mapped using the primary address space. The source and destination secondary segment

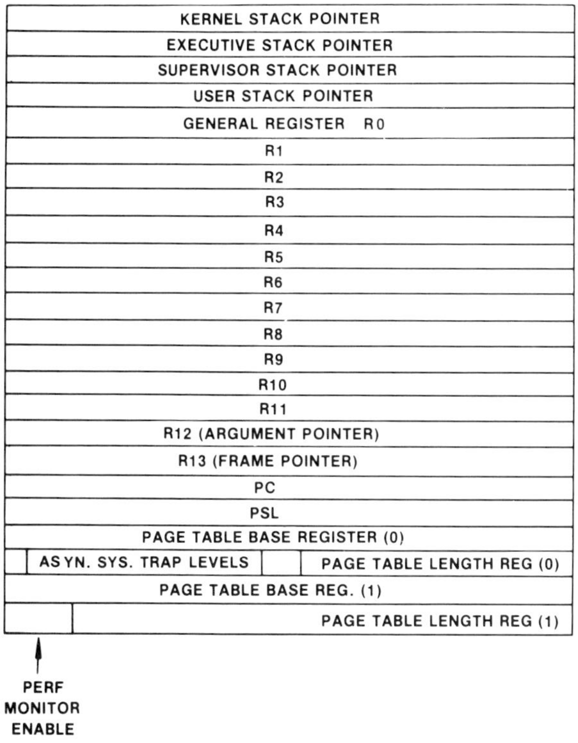

KERNEL STACK POINTER
EXECUTIVE STACK POINTER
SUPERVISOR STACK POINTER
USER STACK POINTER
GENERAL REGISTER R0
R1
R2
R3
R4
R5
R6
R7
R8
R9
R10
R11
R12 (ARGUMENT POINTER)
R13 (FRAME POINTER)
PC
PSL
PAGE TABLE BASE REGISTER (0)
ASYN. SYS. TRAP LEVELS
PAGE TABLE LENGTH REG (0)
PAGE TABLE BASE REG. (1)
PAGE TABLE LENGTH REG (1)
PERF
MONITOR
ENABLE

Figure 6.5 VAX/VMS hardware context (from Ref. 6).

base register bits, when set, cause the read/write memory address to use the secondary address space. This feature allows data to be moved between two address spaces; the operating system uses it to copy data, for example, from the user's address space to its own address space. The emulation control field contains a set of bits that allows the cur-

COMPATIBILITY MODE
TRACE PENDING
INSTRUCTION FIRST PART DONE
EXECUTING ON THE INTERRUPT STACK
CURRENT ACCESS MODE
PREVIOUS ACCESS MODE
INTERRUPT PRIORITY LEVEL
31 30 27 26 25 24 23 22 20 16 15 8 7 6 5 4 3 2 1 0
DECIMAL OVERFLOW TRAP ENABLE
FLOATING UNDERFLOW TRAP ENABLE
INTEGER OVERFLOW TRAP ENABLE
TRACE TRAP ENABLE
NEGATIVE CONDITION CODE
ZERO CONDITION CODE
OVERFLOW CONDITION CODE
CARRY (BORROW) CONDITION CODE

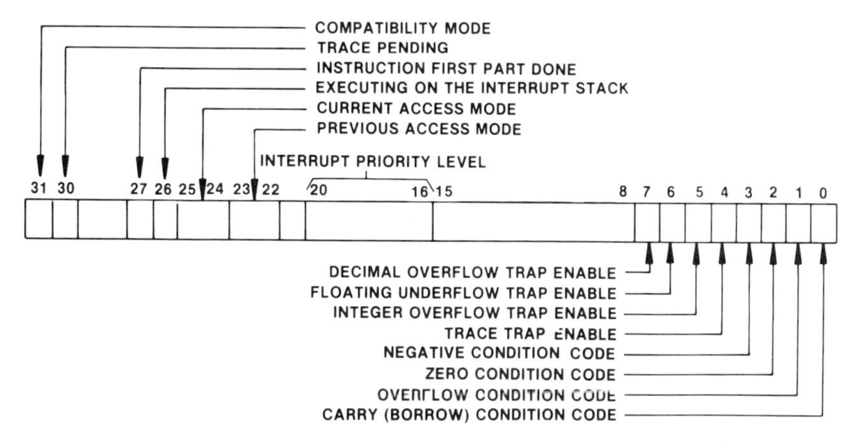

Figure 6.6 VAX process status longword layout.

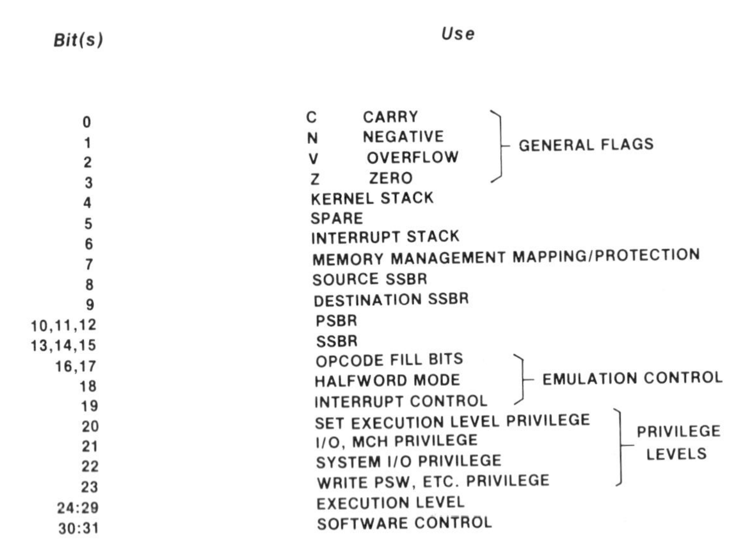

Figure 6.7 3B20 PSW layout.

rent process to execute an emulated instruction set of another machine. The privilege-level fields of the processor status word specifies which privileged instructions the current process may execute. The execution-level field indicates the interrupt priority level of the current process.

6.3 PACKAGES

Information structures are important software resources in most computing systems. Information structures are both data structures representing data objects from the real world (such as bank accounts, airline seats, stock performance records, and computer physical memory spaces) and control structures, which contain control and status information on the resources and activities of the system. Only certain procedures may access and manipulate the information structures. These procedures monitor and guard the information structures and manipulate them for other procedures. A set of procedures *owns* information structures when only the procedures in the set can access and manipulate them. The concept of associating information structures with procedures is crucial to software methodologies for generating more reliable and maintainable software environments. This concept allows software to dynamically check itself for unauthorized procedures attempting to access critical system information structures. It also provides some ‘‘fire wall’’ shielding of information structures from disruptive and error-filled procedures. As a consequence, associating sets of procedures with information structures allow large and complex software systems to be independently developed by many programmers. Their

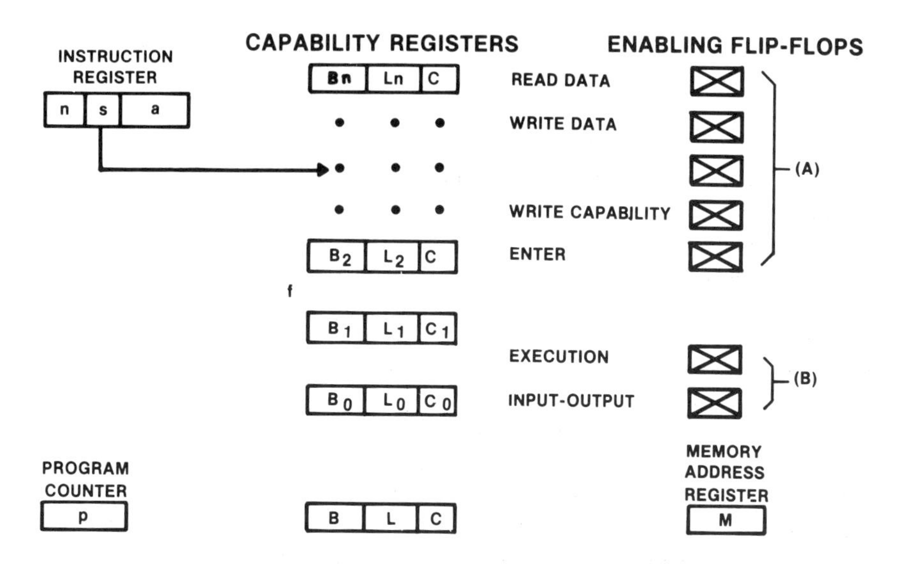

SETTING OF ENABLING FLIP-FLOPS

Cs	READ DATA	WRITE DATA	READ CAPABILITY	WRITE CAPABILITY	OUTPUT ENTER
	*				
RW	*	*			
RC			*		
RWC			*	*	
E					
IO					
EN					*

C	EXE-CUTION	INPUT-OUTPUT
R	*	
RW	*	
RC		
RWC		
E	*	
IO	*	*
EN		

Execution sequence:

Set M = B + p if $p < L$; otherwise trap
Fetch instruction
Set enabling flip-flops (A) from C_s
Set enabling flip-flops (B) from C
Set M = B_s + a if $a < L_s$; otherwise trap
Execute instruction; trap if execution not enabled
Increment p
Repeat

Figure 6.8 Protection architecture using capability registers (from Ref. 7).

procedures may interact with each other only through well-defined and enforced interfaces. The enforced modularity allows greater flexibility in software development environments because the information structures and associated procedures may be changed without creating side effects in the rest of the system.

Both high-level-language designers and operating system designers realize the importance of this concept. The high-level-language designers call a set of information structures and its associated procedures a "class," an "abstract data type," or a "package." Operating system designers call it a "monitor," a "package," or a "domain."

Packages are represented as sets of *capabilities*. A capability defines the address, the range, and the access rights to an object. An *object* is an information structure with a label specifying its *type;* types include procedure, data, and capability objects. The type of an object defines the set of operations that may be performed on it. A procedure object may be executed, a data object may be read or written, and a capability object may be entered, read, or written. The context of a package is the set of capabilities that defines the set of objects in the package, including the data objects and their associated procedure objects, and the capability objects defining the other packages the current context may enter. The context of a package is itself represented as a capability object that is stored in a unique system space address, the capability address. Entering a package causes its context to be loaded into the hardware of the system.

A system that provides architectural support for packages and capabilities is the Cambridge CAP system. Figure 6.8 shows the architecture and execution sequence of the CAP system and the hardware with which it stores the context of the executing package [7]. CAP contains an instruction register, a program counter, and a set of capability registers. The s field of the instruction register selects one of the capability registers. The capability register has a base field (B) pointing to the base address of an object, a limit field (L) denoting the range of the object, and an access code field (C) denoting the operations possible on the object. To generate a memory address for the operand of the executing instruction, the address field (a) is added to the base field. The memory address generated is checked against the limit field of the capability register. If the address is out of range, a trap is generated. To generate a memory address for the next instruction, the system proceeds similarly. It adds the program counter to the base field of the capability pointing to the currently executing instruction object. The instruction memory address is also checked against the limit field of the capability to the instruction object. Hardware in the CAP system checks the access rights of an instruction to an object. A set of flip-flops stores the access rights of the current capability (Cs) to the data object. These access rights include read write (RW), read capability (RC), read write capability (RWC), execute (E), input/output (IO), and enter (EN). An enter capability allows execution control to leave the package owning the capability and "enter" the package designated by the enter capability. Another set of flip-flops stores the access rights of the current capability to the instruction object. The check is made in real time on each instruction execution. The instruction execution sequence is also shown in Fig. 6.8.

6.4 FUNCTIONAL ABSTRACTION AND DATA ABSTRACTION

Software designers divide large and complex software systems into modules; the divisions are based on either functional or data abstractions. In a functional abstraction system, the modules are processes and each process has a functional purpose. In a data abstraction system, the modules are packages; each package contains data and a set of procedures that may operate on it. Thus an execution stream in a functional abstraction system proceeds from process to process following functions it needs to perform, while a stream in a data abstraction system proceeds from package to package following the data it needs to access. Some examples of functional abstraction and data abstraction systems are shown below.

Functional Abstraction	Data Abstraction
Multics operating system	Plessey/250
UNIX operating system	Intel iAPX/432
MERT operating system	IBM System/38
DMERT operating system	CAL
Intel 286	CAP
VAX/VMS	HYDRA
	STAROS

These two types of modularization have different architectural implications in terms of protection, synchronization, and communication. This chapter examines these implications by comparing two functional abstraction systems (PDP 11/UNIX operating system [2] and 3B/DMERT operating system [8]) with two data abstraction systems (Plessey/250 [9] and Intel iAPX/432 [10]).

6.5 PROTECTION STRUCTURES

The two approaches to modularization require the implementation of different protection structures. A protection structure is the structure of the access rights and access environments imposed by the operating system to protect one process's access environment from being overwritten by another process.

The processes in functional abstraction systems are protected from each other because each process has its own access environment. But to perform their functions, processes may have to share resources (software or hardware), which forces their access environments to overlap (Fig. 6.9). Because they share resources, processes or the procedures within a process may have to be grouped into different *privilege layers*. Each privilege layer grants processes a set of privileges and access priorities to shared resources. A functional abstraction system with three privilege layers is shown in Fig. 6.10. The figure shows one, four, and five processes in three layers.

In data abstraction systems, each package also has an access environment. How-

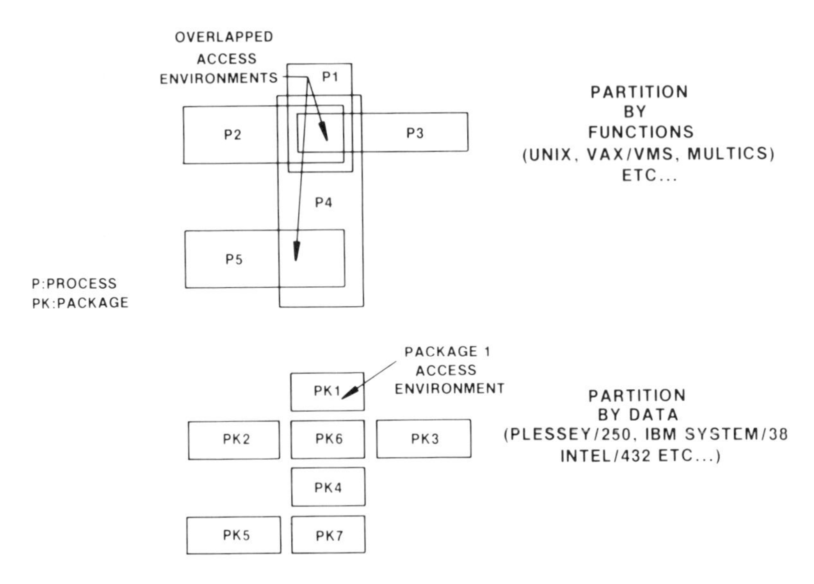

Figure 6.9 Functional abstraction versus data abstraction.

ever, since separate packages encapsulate their own resources, there is no need for the access environments of packages to overlap; hence, there is no need for privilege layers. Figure 6.9 shows how the same system may be partitioned in the functional and data abstraction systems. In the functional abstract system, processes P1, P2, P3, and P4 share a set of resources, and hence their environments overlap. Similarly, P4 and P5 share another set of resources and their environments overlap. In the data abstraction system, PK1 through PK7 all encapsulate their own resources. PK1, PK2, PK3, PK4, and PK5 encapsulate the private resources of P1, P2, P3, P4, and P5, respectively. PK6 encapsulates the shared resources of P1, P2, P3, and P4, while PK7 encapsulates the shared resources of P4 and P5. Whereas a process acquires all the privileges of the privilege layer it is put in, a package acquires only the privileges (capabilities) it needs (Fig. 6.10). The principle of *least privileges* for packages specifies that each package acquires the minimal set of privileges [11]. The advantage of this principle is that it removes privileges from a package that the package does not need but could use to corrupt other modules' access environments. Figure 6.10 shows that in the layered structure, all the processes in a layer have access (shown by a connecting line) to the same set of services of the kernel (innermost layer); in the least privilege structure, a package has access to the services (shown by the connecting lines) of only those packages it needs to do its task.

Since only the procedures within a package can manipulate the resources encapsulated by the package, the package serves as a protective capsule for the resources. Before requesting the resources from the package, other packages must first obtain the privilege (capability) to make their requests. Once the privilege is obtained and the request is made,

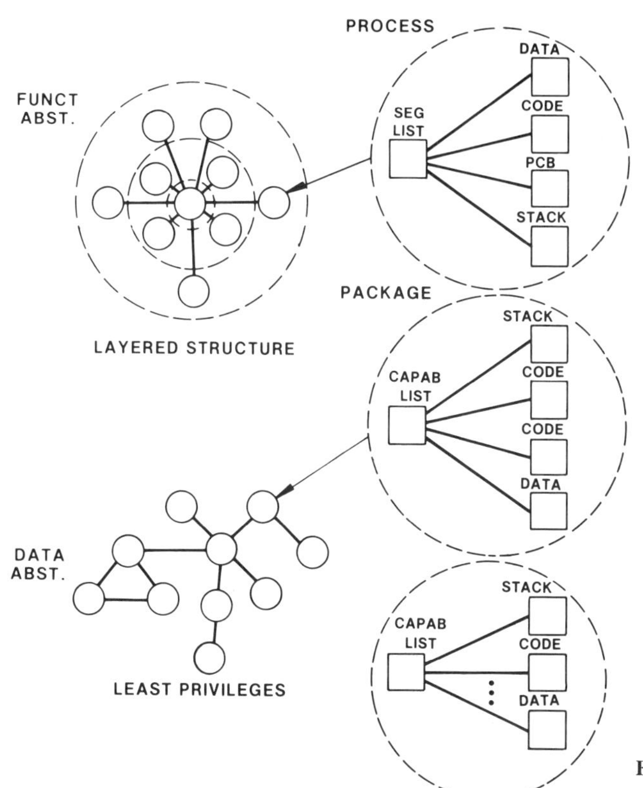

Figure 6.10 Privilege layered and least privileges protection strucrures.

the package manipulates its resources on behalf of the requesting package. Because the resources of each package are hidden from other packages, the data abstraction type of protection is also known as *information hiding* protection [12].

6.5.1 Functional Abstraction Protection

In functional abstraction systems, an access list determines the access environment of each process. An access environment is usually composed of segments, each segment containing logically related information. An access list hence takes the form of a segment list. The segment list contains the descriptors (access rights and addresses) of all the segments that are accessible by the process. These usually include the data, code, process control block, and stack segments (Fig. 6.10). Processes may share the same segment by having the same descriptor in their respective segment lists. The access rights to the shared segment, however, do not have to be the same. There are thus two ways of achieving interprocess protection:

1. Per-process virtual address space
2. Per-segment access rights

Even though the total virtual address space of a process is accessible to the process as a whole, different procedures within the process may have different privileges to the access environment. Procedures are therefore grouped into different privilege layers (called *rings* in Multics [13]). Functional abstraction systems are sometimes referred to as ring-based or layered systems.

The access environment of a process may be divided into subaccess environments. Subaccess environments are the environments accessible by procedures within the process. A subaccess environment may consist of a group of privilege layers (termed an *access bracket of rings* in Multics). Access brackets may be differentiated by types of accesses (read, write, and execute). For example, one access bracket consists of the group of privilege layers containing the subset of segments that may be read by a procedure; another access bracket contains the subset of segments that may be written by a procedure. These access brackets with different types of accesses may overlap. A subaccess environment containing all the procedure (code) segments that can call it may also be defined for each procedure. Multics calls this type of subaccess environment a *call bracket of rings*. When a procedure call crosses ring boundaries within a call bracket of rings, well-defined entry points (called gates in Multics) provide additional protection. That is, a check is performed to ensure that the target address of the call is a specially declared entry point (gate). Thus the facilities provided for intraprocess protection are:

1. Read, write, and execute access brackets
2. Call brackets
3. Gates

The Multics concept of protection structuring has profoundly influenced many of the functional abstraction systems following it, including the PDP 11/UNIX operating system and the 3B/DMERT operating system, which are discussed below.

6.5.1.1 Protection structure of the UNIX operating system [14].

The protection structure of the UNIX operating system has the same philosophy as the protection structure of Multics but is simpler. Like Multics, interprocess protection is achieved by each process owning its own segment list (access environment). For intraprocess protection, the UNIX operating system has two privilege layers or modes of execution: the user mode and the kernel mode. In Fig. 6.11, process N and process M may execute in the user or kernel mode. The dashed lines denote the access environments of the processes. When executing in the user mode, each process has its own segment list (access environment). When executing in the kernel mode, a process switches to the kernel segment list. The kernel segment list is accessible to all processes while they are executing in the kernel mode. A process executing in the user mode has only access to its user segment list contained in its process u_block (process control block). A process executing in the kernel mode has access to the kernel segment list, which resides in the u_block of the UNIX operating system kernel. At any moment, the two access environments are mutually ex-

2 - RINGS SYSTEM (RINGS MODES OF EXECUTION)

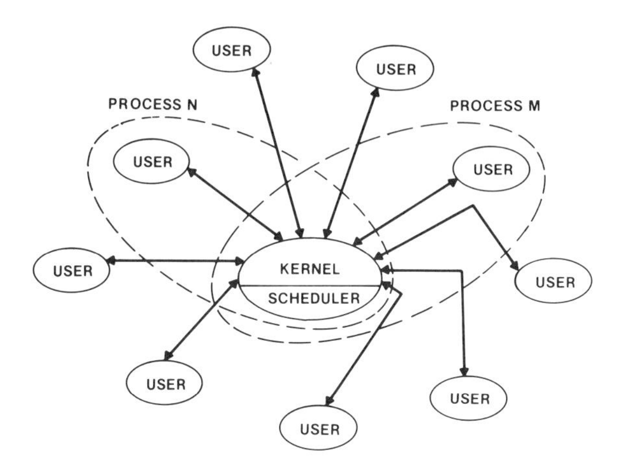

- PROTECTION DOMAIN GRANULARITY: ADDRESS SPACE OF PROCESS MODE
- TO CALL PROCEDURES WITHIN INNER RING (KERNEL), MUST "TRAP" INTO KERNEL
- CAN BE FORCED FROM OUTER RING (USER) TO INNER RING (KERNEL) BY INTERRUPTS OR EXCEPTIONS

Figure 6.11 UNIX structure.

clusive because there is only one segment list base register (KDSA6) that points to either of the segment lists (Fig. 6.12). The access control bits in the access control register (ACR) specify the read access, write access, and read/write access rights to the segment.

The implementation of the two different access environments available to a UNIX operating system process is distinct from the way Multics implements subaccess environments. In Multics, each segment has in its descriptor three associated privilege numbers defining the subaccess environment brackets. The Multics mechanism is more powerful but its complexity increases the probability of errors. The protection structure of the UNIX operating system partitions the segment list into an instruction part and a data part; these partitions further protect the system from executing data or writing into instructions.

6.5.1.2 Protection structure of the DMERT operating system. A segment list defines the access environment of processes running in the DMERT operating system. Exceptions to this general structure are the user-supervisor processes which, like processes in the UNIX operating system, are scheduled as a unit and yet have two mutually exclusive segment lists defining two mutually exclusive access environments. One access environment is used when the process executes in the user mode; the other is used when the process executes in the supervisor mode (Fig. 6.13).

There are four privilege layers in the DMERT operating system: the kernal layer, the kernal process layer, the supervision layer, and the user layer (Fig. 6.14). The user-

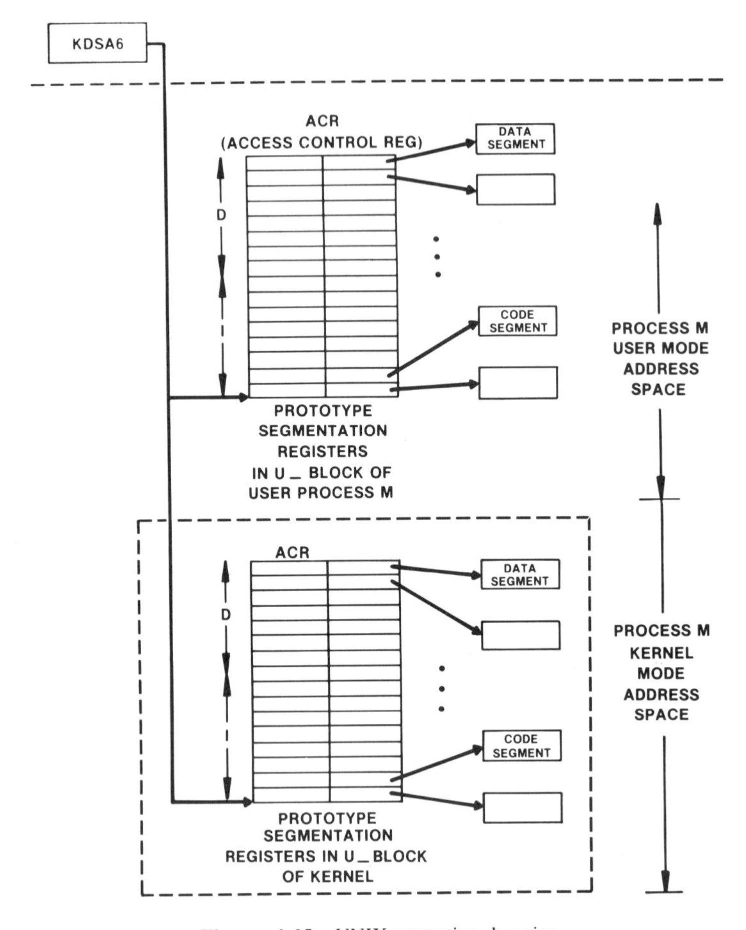

Figure 6.12 UNIX protection domains.

supervisor processes execute in the user or supervisor layer. There are different types of supervisors to which a user may make system calls (UNIX, real-time, etc.). The DMERT structure thus allows multiple (supervisor) environments to be seen by users. The process manager is a special process that executes in the supervisor layer.

The procedures in the kernel process layer are not executed as part of the user-supervisor processes. The procedures are grouped and executed as kernel processes. For example, file management procedures are executed as part of a file manager process, which has its own access environment and is separately schedulable from the user-supervisor processes. I/O drivers and the file manager are kernel process layer processes. The distinction between a process and an execution mode of a process is that a process not only has its own access environment but is a separately schedulable entity. The execution modes of a process are not separately schedulable entities; they define separate access environments only. The DMERT operating system also creates an access environment for

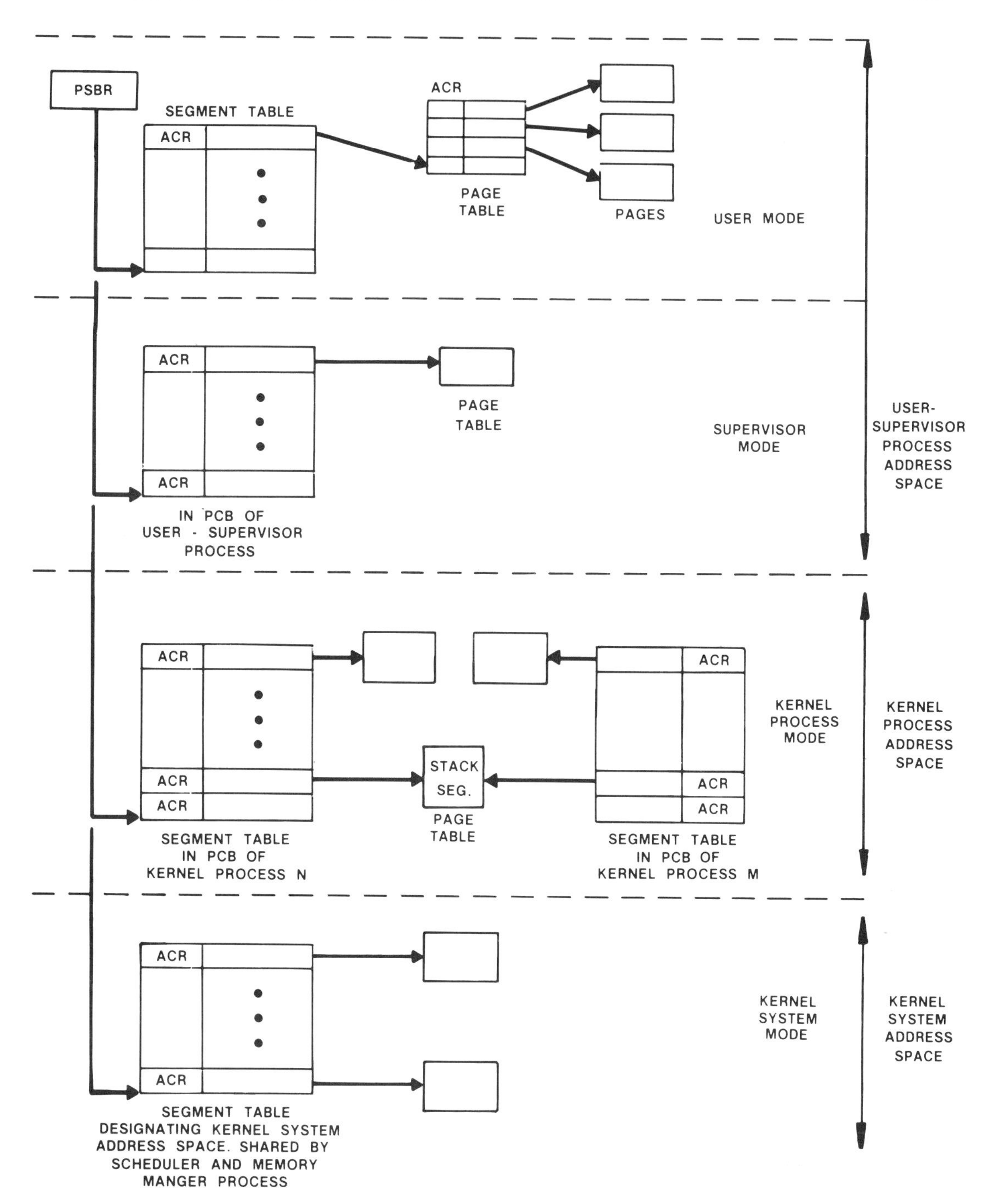

Figure 6.13 DMERT protection domains.

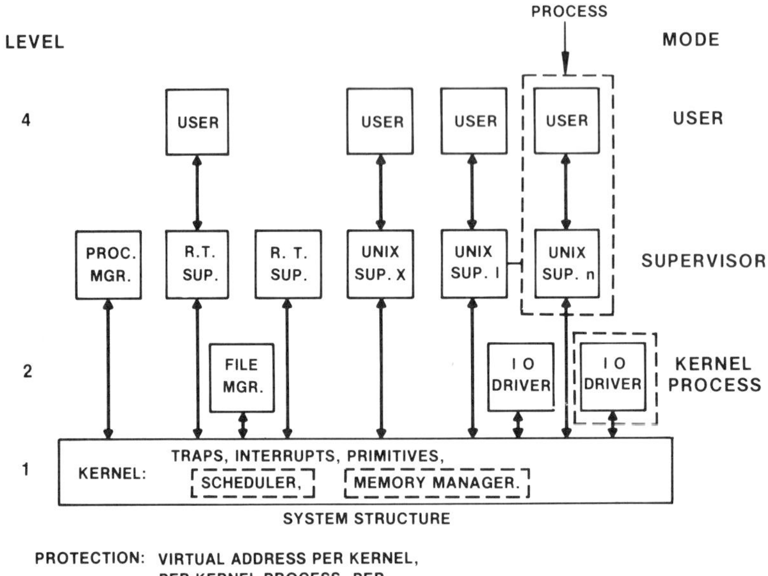

Figure 6.14 DMERT four rings structure.

the kernel that is shared by the scheduler and the memory manager processes. The DMERT operating system treats these processes as special processes that run in the address space of the kernel. The protection structure thus has one access environment per kernel, one access environment per kernel process, and one access environment for each execution mode of a user-supervisor process (Fig. 6.13).

6.5.2 Data Abstraction Protection

A capability list designates the access environment of a package in a data abstraction system. A capability is the protected name of an object. An object is an information structure. Each object has a label specifying its type; the type defines the set of operations that can be used to manipulate the information structure. In other words, a package is a collection of objects and the capability list is a list of the names of the objects in the collection. The capability list is itself an object: a capability object (Fig. 6.15). Data abstraction systems are thus often referred to as object-based or capability-based systems.

A capability within a capability list may be the name of another capability object. This capability object is the capability list of another package and as such, it allows the package with the capability to access the capability list of another package. Access to the other package, however, is usually restricted to the enter capability, which allows execution control to flow to that package. Only selected system packages have the read/write access to a capability object.

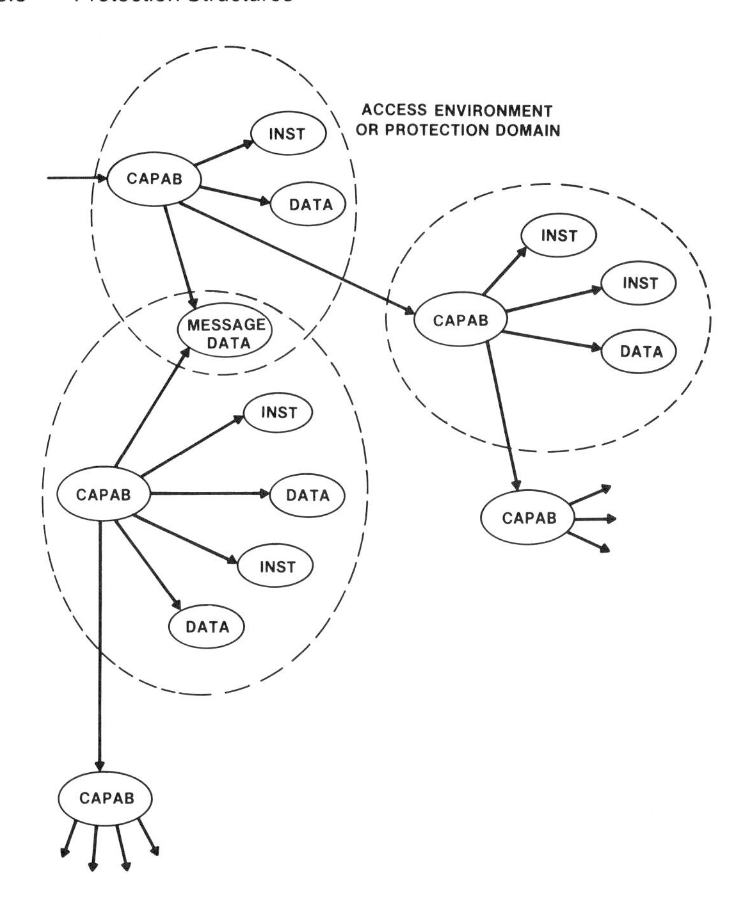

Figure 6.15 Objects-based operating systems structure.

Data abstraction systems protect themselves in two ways:

1. By restricting access to those named in the current capability list
2. By restricting the operations that may be applied to an object to those associated with that type of object

This last feature is made possible because a capability contains not only the access control rights to an object but also the type of object being accessed. Using capabilities to protect data structures obviates the need for modes and rings. For a great many applications, a ring structure is satisfactory, but the price paid is rigidity in structure.

6.5.2.1 Plessey/250 protection structure [9]. The protection structure of a Plessey/250 package is implemented with a set of capability registers (Fig. 6.16). Some of these are designated for a specific functional purpose. Capability register 6 (CR6), for example, acts as the capability list base register for the package; that is, it points to the list of capabilities owned by the package. The capabilities for the currently executing code

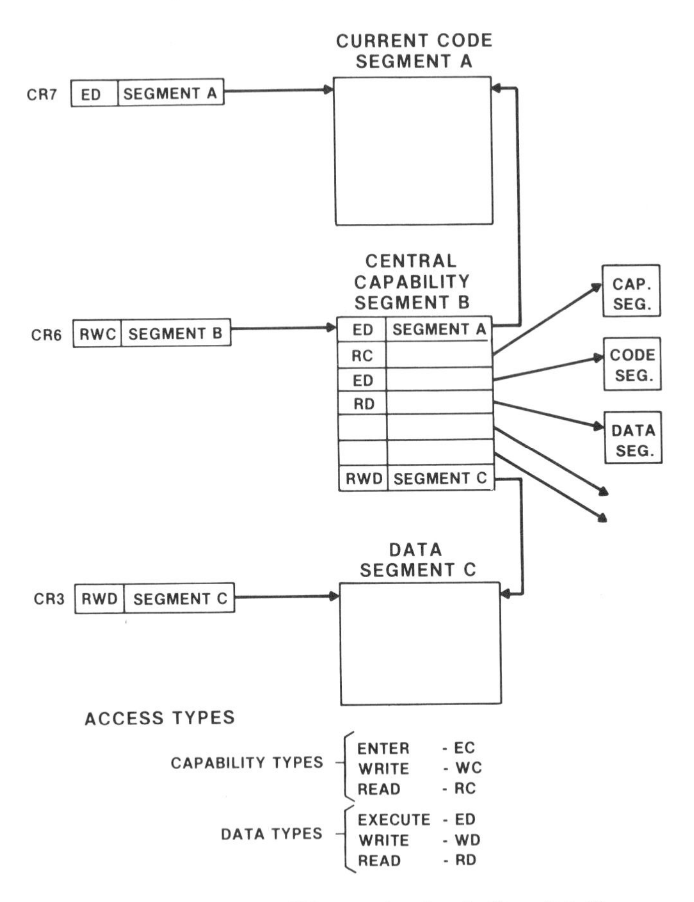

Figure 6.16 Plessy/250 protection domain (from Ref. 9).

object and the current data object are placed in capability registers 7 (CR7) and 3 (CR3), respectively.

Capabilities for different types of objects contain different access types. For data objects, the access types in the capability are the same as those in a segment descriptor: execute, write, and read. For a capability object, the access types in the capability are enter, write, and read. The enter access allows control to "leave" the current package and "enter" the access environment designated by that capability object, that is, the access environment of another package.

6.5.2.2 Intel iAPX/432 protection structure [10,15]. The access environment in the Intel iAPX/432 is different from that of Plessey/250. As shown in Fig. 6.17 [15], the access environment of the current context of the iAPX/432 includes all the objects pointed to by the current context object as well as all the objects pointed to by the current domain object. The *context object* is a hardware-recognized data structure that contains the program counter, the stack pointer, and the list of objects to which the

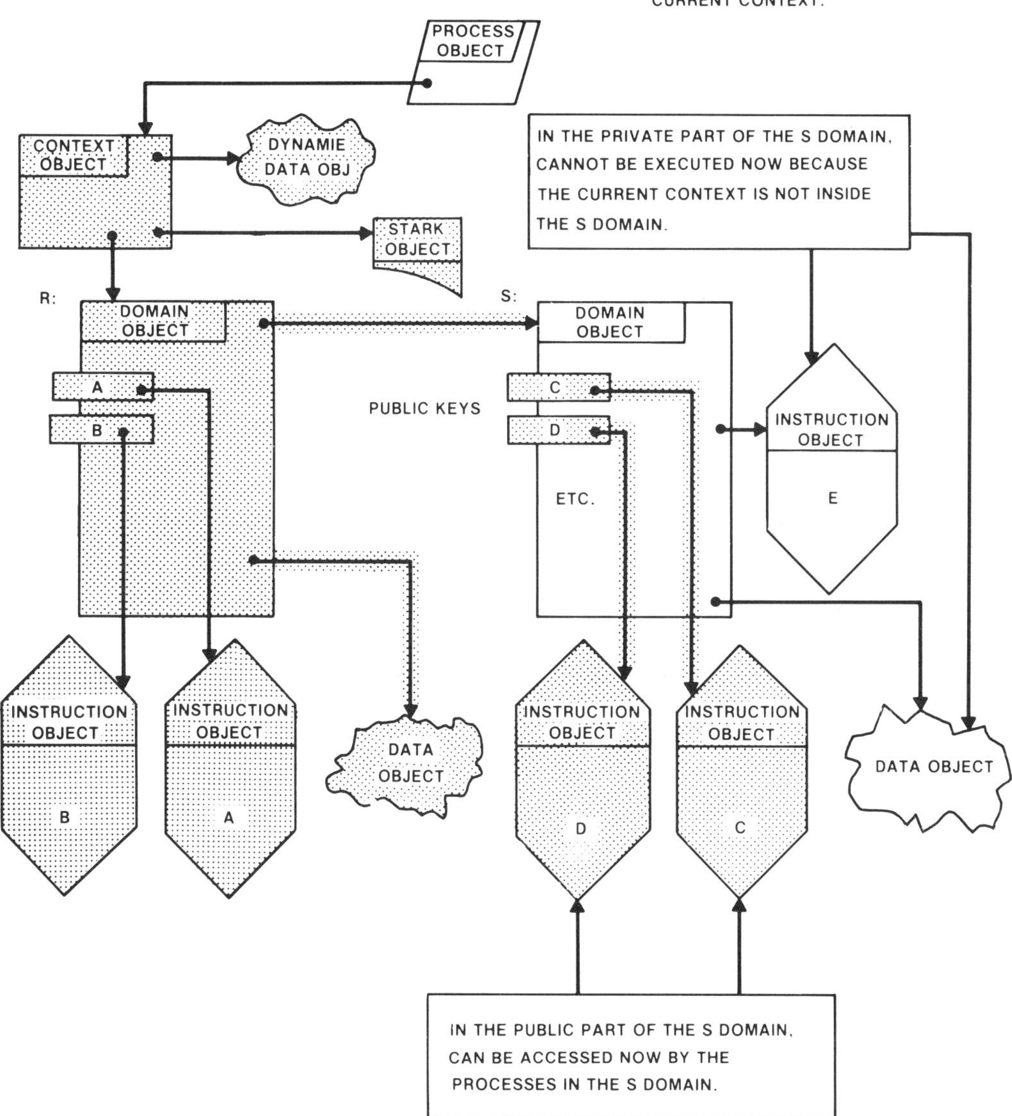

Figure 6.17 iAPX/432 protection domain before call (from Ref. 15).

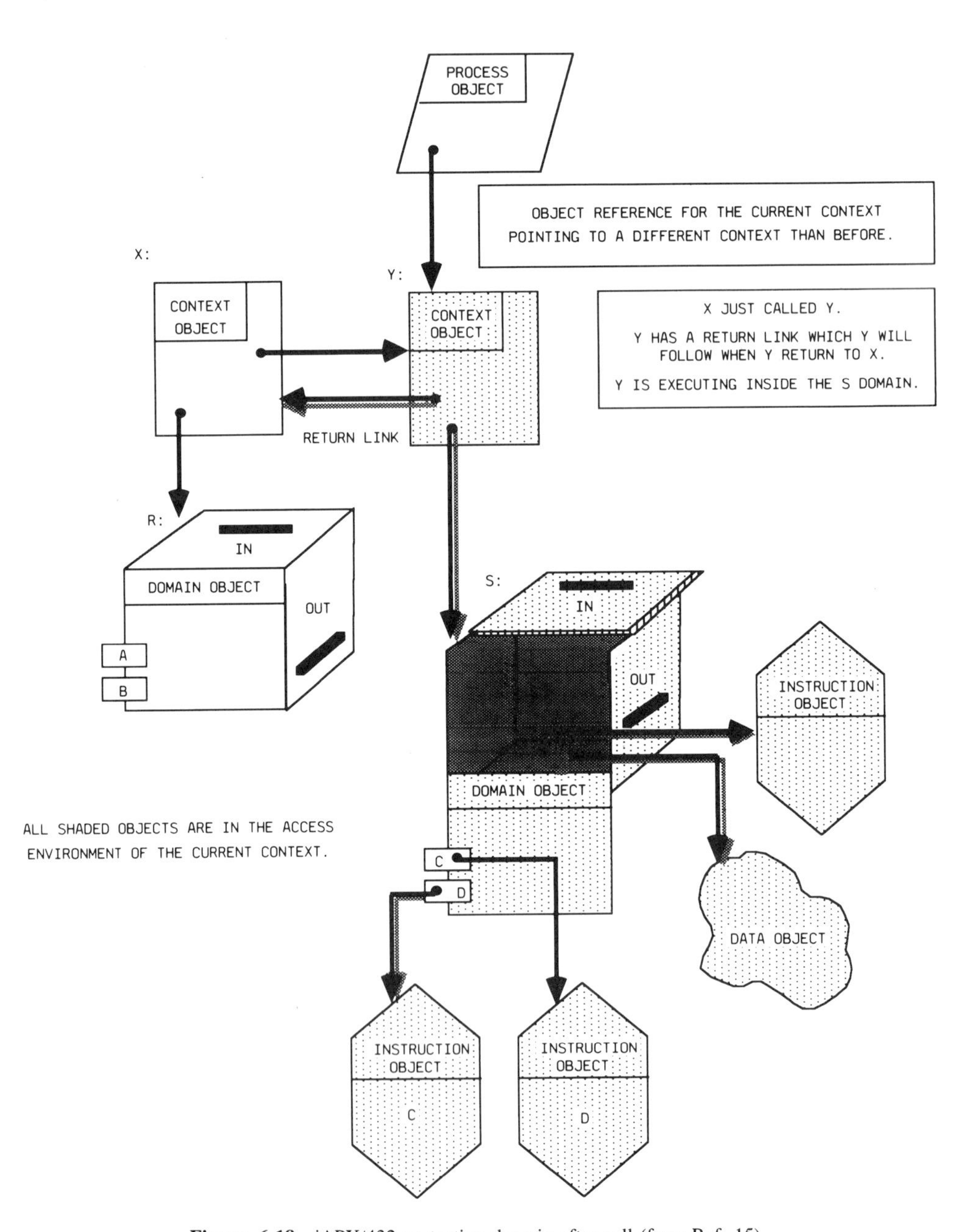

Figure 6.18 iAPX/432 protection domain after call (from Ref. 15).

executing procedure has access. These objects are dynamic in that when the procedure returns they cease to exist. A *domain object* is a hardware-recognized data structure that contains references to all the static objects owned by a package. Static objects include instruction objects describing procedures as well as static data object. Whereas the context object contains references to the dynamic objects accessible by *one* procedure, the executing procedure, the domain object contains references to the static objects accessible by all the procedures within a package, including the executing procedure. A domain object may also contain capabilities to other domain objects. If the current domain object has a capability to another domain object, all the public keys (public procedures) of the domain are in the access environment. A public procedure is a procedure that belongs to a domain but which is callable by procedures of another domain. Public procedures are part of the current context access environment only insofar as they are callable. Once they are called, a new context is brought in with a new access environment (Fig. 6.18) [15]. Within the new access environment, the called procedure instruction and static data objects are accessible (executable, readable, and writable). The private procedures of that domain are also accessible once the domain is entered. In the iAPX/432, the current context access environment is defined by four capability lists (object reference lists). These capabilities are offsets into a system object table that contains pointers to the physical locations of all the objects within the system. The iAPX/432 and the Plessey/250 are different implementations of the same concepts.

6.6 ARCHITECTURAL SUPPORT OF PROTECTION STRUCTURE

The way protection is structured to create access environments for different modules has implications on these architectural issues:

1. Addressing
2. Access environments (context) switch
3. Privileges, rights, and type checking
4. Entering and exiting from another access environment
5. Data movement across access environments

Discussions of each of these issues follow.

6.6.1 Addressing

There are two types of addressing: segment-based and capability based [16]. Their advantages and disadvantages are brought out in the following discussions of the PDP 11/UNIX, the 3B/DMERT, the Plessey/250, and the Intel iAPX/432 operating systems. Segment addresses are context-dependent addresses; that is, segments are bound to each process independently. Since the logical addresses of a segment are independently set for each process, problems result when two processes share the same segment and have different logical addresses for it. Multics solves this problem by using a linkage segment; the trade-off for this solution is that it requires an additional level of indirection (Fig 6.19). Capabilities, unlike segment addresses, are context independent; that is, their names are permanent and the same for all contexts throughout the system. All contexts accessing an object must use the same capability. There may be multiple copies of the same capability to an object. The difference between two addressing schemes is illustrated in Fig. 6.19. The addressing of the PDP 11/UNIX, 3B/DMERT, Plessey/250, and Intel iAPX/432 operating systems is shown in Figs. 6.20 through 6.23 [17].

6.6.1.1 Addressing: Implementation. In the PDP 11/UNIX operating system, the virtual address has three parts: the segment (page), the page (block), and the offset.* The virtual address is mapped into the physical address by the following process. The segment (page) designation part of the virtual address is an offset into the segment (page) table. This offset is used for selecting the appropriate segment (page) descriptor pointing to the base of the segment (page). The page (block) part is then added to the base of the segment (page) to select the appropriate page (block) within the segment (page). The offset part is then concatenated with the physical block address. The hardware support provided by PDP 11 is a set of segment (page) registers (SDR, SAR) where the segment (page) table of the current access environment is loaded. The segment (page) table of the current access environment in main memory is pointed to by the contents of register KDSA6. To access a segment (page) descriptor, only the segment (page) registers—not main memory—need to be accessed.

In the 3B/DMERT system, the virtual address also has three parts: the segment, the page, and the offset. The segment part indexes into the segment table of the current access environment and obtains a segment descriptor. The segment table of the current access environment is pointed to by the segment base register (SBR). The segment descriptor points to the base of the page table for the segment accessed. The page part then indexes into the page table and obtains the physical address of the page. The offset part is then concatenated with the physical page address to obtain the physical address. The presence of the page table allows the pages of a segment to be noncontiguous in physical memory. Hence in the 3B/DMERT system, the pages of a segment are contiguous only in the virtual address space; in the PDP 11/UNIX system, the pages of a segment are contiguous in the physical address space. The hardware support for address development is a set of address translation buffers (ATBs). An address translation buffer is a cache that associates a virtual page address to a physical page address. Thus if a translation is present in an ATB, the address generation described above is bypassed.

In the Plessey/250 system, the three parts of the virtual address are called the capability part, the modifier, and the offset. The hardware support consists of a set of capability registers; each register serves a particular purp ose as discussed above. Capability register 6 (CR6) is loaded with the capability pointing to the current access environment

*A page in PDP 11 teminology is what is called a segment in this book because it is an entity of variable size containing related logical information. A block in PDP 11 terminology is what is called a page because it is a fixed-size quantity related to a disk physical block size. For comparative purposes with the other systems discussed in this book, pages in PDP 11 are referred to as segments, and blocks in PDP 11 are referred to as pages.

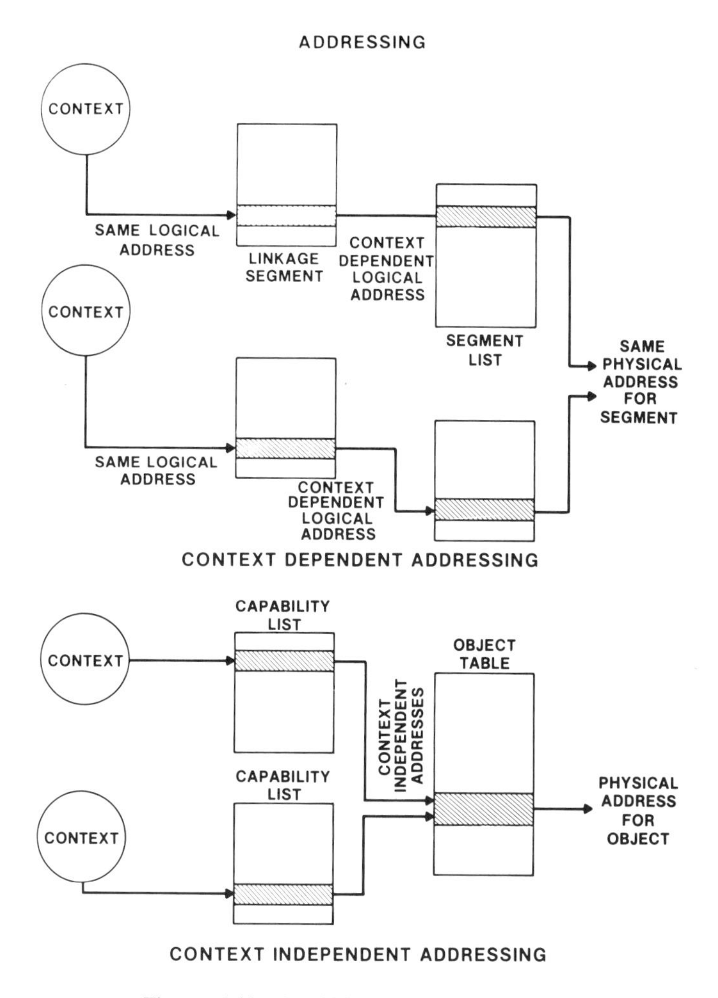

Figure 6.19 Capability based versus segment.

capability list (capability segment); CR7 points to the current code object (code segment); and CR3 points to the current data object (data segment). The capability part of the virtual address selects the capability register that contains the base address of the object being accessed (for example, CR3 pointing to the data segment is selected in Fig. 6.22). The modifier and the offset are then added to the base address to obtain the physical address of the data within the object. The capability registers are hardware support that avoid the table lookup (CR6 pointing to the capability segment pointing to the system capability table) needed on each access.

In the Intcl iAPX/432 system, four capability lists (object reference lists) define each context. The selector part of a virtual address selects one of the four object reference

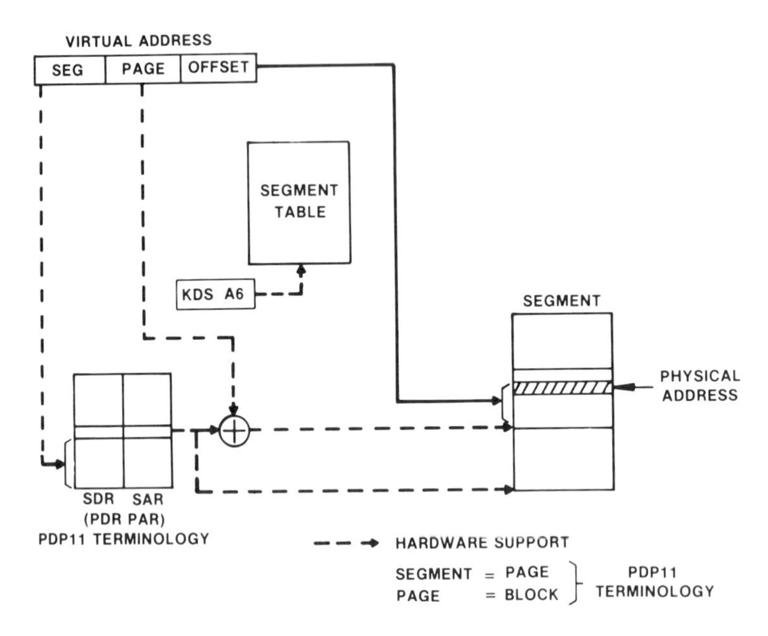

Figure 6.20 PDP 11/70/UNIX address generation.

lists as well as the capability within the selected list. The capability indexes into the system object table and obtains the physical base address of the object. The displacement part of the virtual address is then concatenated with this base address to obtain the physical address. Note that in iAPX/432, the system object table may contain up to 2**24 objects. To minimize storage space requirements, the table is divided into two levels. An object table directory containing 2**12 entries points to 2**12 tables; each table may contain 2**12 objects. To bypass the table lookups for generating each address, there are two sets of hardware base address registers and two sets of associative caches. One set is used for translating between the virtual object address and the physical object address, thus bypassing all the table lookups. The second set is used to bypass the object table directory lookup if the first set of caches indicates a miss during address generation. If both sets of caches indicate a miss, then address generation requires all the table lookups.

6.6.1.2 Addressing: Summary. It can be seen from Figs. 6.19 through 6.23 that even though the protection structure philosophies between functional and data abstraction systems are quite different, the hardware support for address generation is remarkably similar. In all these systems, the hardware support consists of associative caches or registers or both. Thus the hardware support for address generation in the iAPX/432 with appropriate modifications may serve the needs of address generation in the PDP/UNIX, 3B/DMERT, and Plessey/250 operating systems. The difficulty is that since hardware requires that certain signal lines be channeled to the appropriate bits of registers or caches, the sizes of various tables in the different systems are restricted.

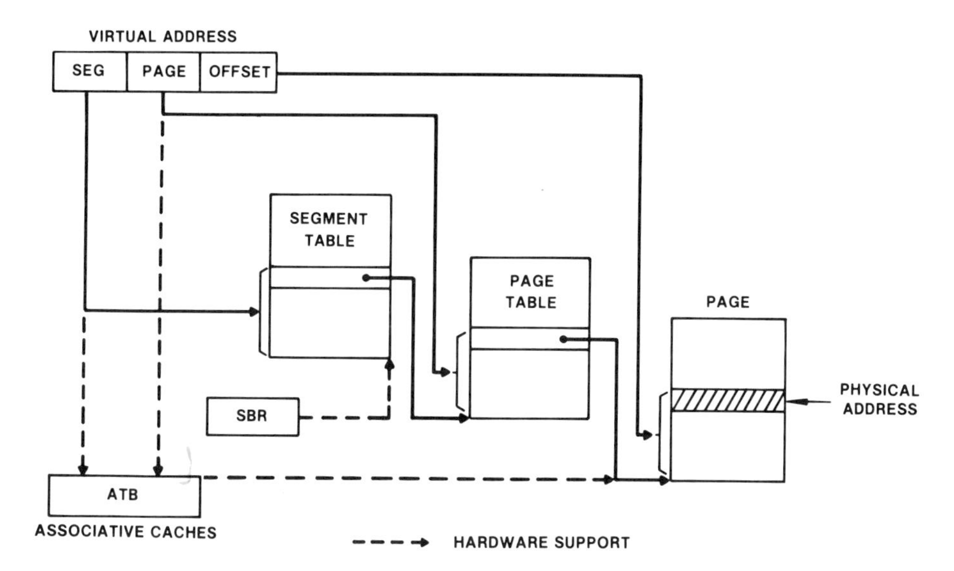

Figure 6.21 3B20/DMERT address generation.

6.6.2 Switching Access Environments (Context Switch)

In all systems, the data in the internal registers of the processor must be saved when switching contexts. Along with saving the registers, switching contexts means switching access environments, which in turn implies switching to the segment or capability list of the new context. If there is no hardware support for address generation, the value of the base register pointing to the new segment list or capability list simply needs to be reloaded. With hardware support, however, either the associative caches and the mapping registers must be flushed and reloaded or a separate set of associative caches and mapping registers must be available and dedicated to the new context. Flushing and reloading is required when multiple contexts share the use of a single set of associated caches and mapping registers.

Ideally, there would be a set of associative caches and registers for each process or package; there would be no need for flushing and reloading, and no overhead would be incurred. But because of the number of processes and packages created in a system, the ideal cannot be attained. Computer architects compromise by including a finite set of associative caches and registers. Each cache is shared by a carefully selected group of processes or packages. One of the characteristics of the processes or packages within a group is that they switch to each other only infrequently. Traditionally, associative caches and mapping registers are associated with privilege layers where, for example, user processes share one associative cache or set of mapping registers and kernel processes share other ones.

Once a process switches to another process using the same associative cache and

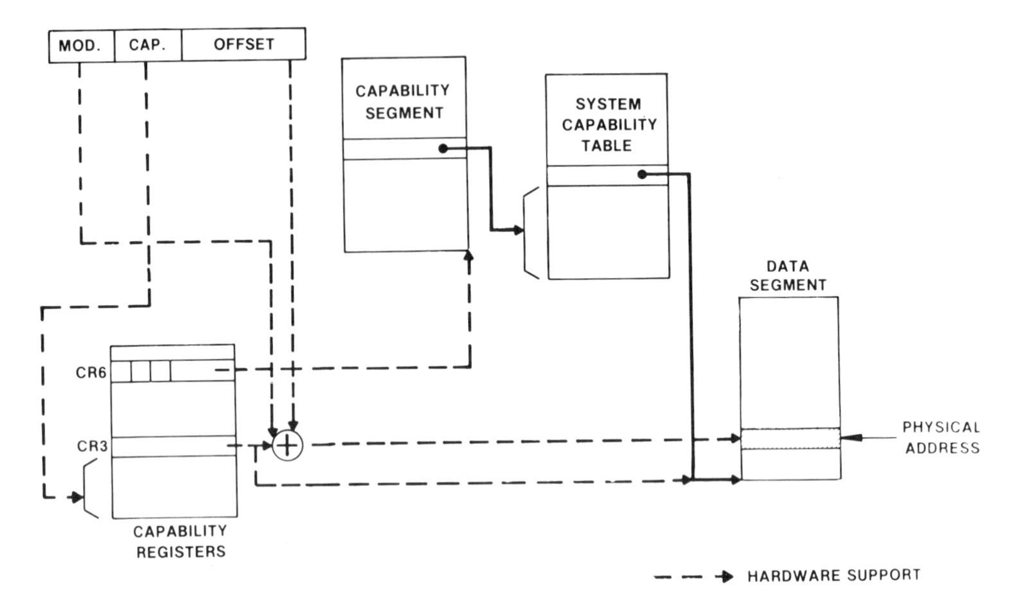

Figure 6.22 Plessey system/250 address generation.

registers, the cache and registers must be flushed and reloaded. There are two methods for doing this. The first method copies the segment list entirely from memory into the registers during the context switch; the PDP 11/UNIX system uses this method. The second method updates the associative caches on demand. The 3B/DMERT, Plessey/250, and iAPX/432 systems use this method. Updating the associative caches on demand means that if information is found to be missing in the cache when it is accessed, the virtual address and the associated physical address are updated into the cache after the address is obtained by referencing memory tables. In the Plessey/250, the CR7 and CR3 capability registers point to the code object and the data object. Each time the code object or the data object changes, the capability list and the system capability table are accessed and a new capability is loaded into CR7 and CR3.

6.6.3 Privileges, Rights, and Type Checking

Although the protection schemes of the different systems are different, the ways they are implemented are similar. The hardware supporting them is also similar. In all four systems, bits designating the access rights to the segment or object are associated with the segment descriptor or the capability. Because each capability has types, a capability to a capability object has different types of access rights than those available in a capability to a data or an instruction object in the Plessey/250. In the iAPX/432, the types are also specifically designated in the capabilities and checked against the types of the objects they reference.

In functional abstraction systems such as Multics, there may be privilege bits in the

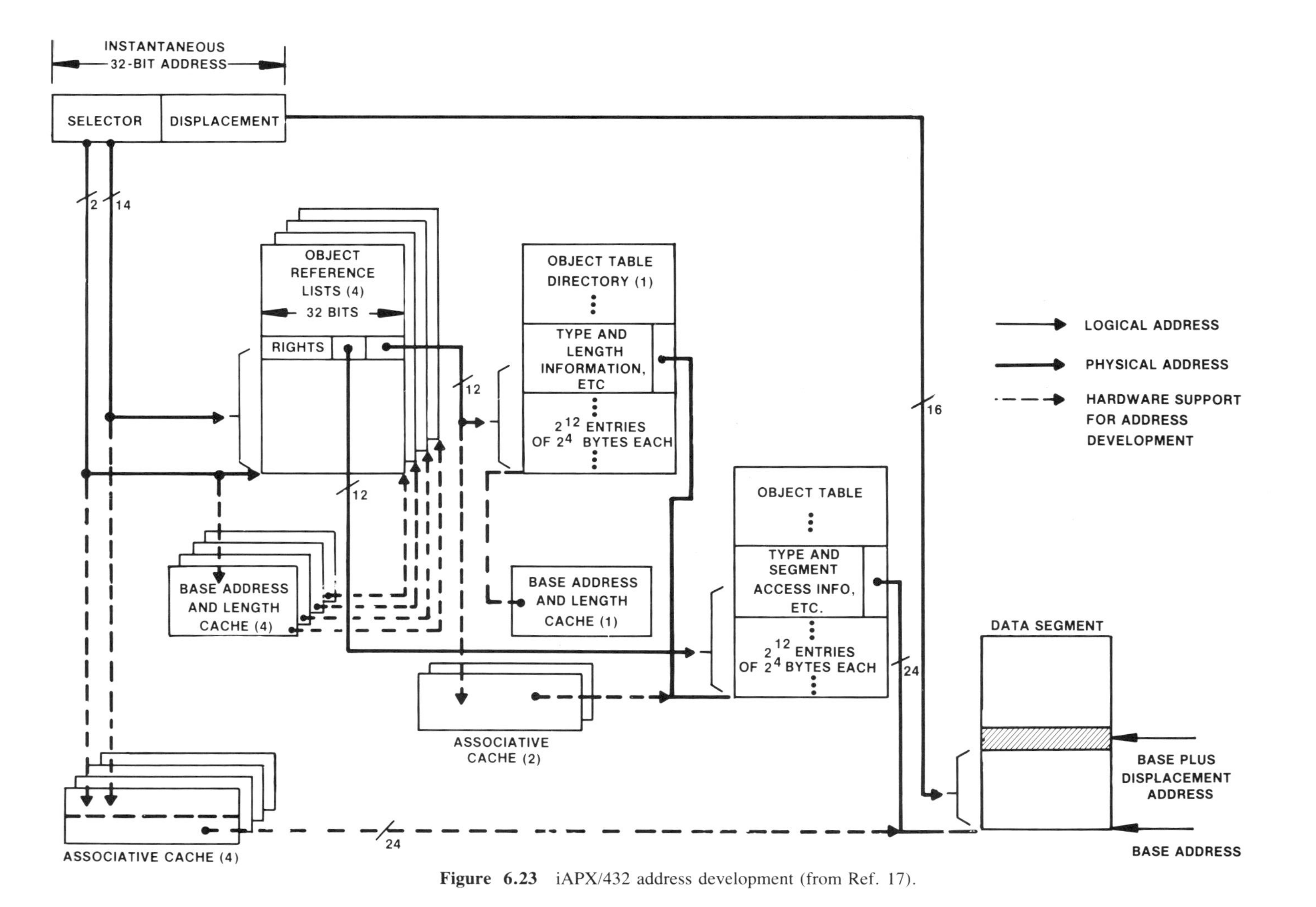

Figure 6.23 iAPX/432 address development (from Ref. 17).

segment descriptor. Or, the instructions themselves may be grouped into privilege instructions and nonprivilege instructions as in the 3B/DMERT system.

6.6.4 Entering and Exiting from Access Environments

In the functional abstraction systems (UNIX and DMERT), a routine in one access environment may request the service of a routine in another access environment (for example, the system access environment) by a system call or an interprocess trap. *Interrupts* also force processes to switch access environments. Both the UNIX and DMERT operating systems handle traps and interrupts similarly. In both cases, a sequence of code (microcode in the DMERT system and assembly code in the UNIX operating system) switches the processor states. It saves the old state on a stack, and brings in the new state designated by the trap or interrupt vector. Then a sequence of assembly code sets up an environment for the called procedure. The appropriate procedure to handle the trap or interrupt may then be entered. Figure 6.24 shows the detailed sequence that occurs on a trap or interrupt in the UNIX system. First, the hardware saves the current processor status word (PSW) and the program counter (PC) in a temporary location and loads a new PSW and PC that is assigned to each device interrupt and to each trap. The sets of PSWs and PCs assigned to interrupts and traps are called interrupt and trap vectors; they are

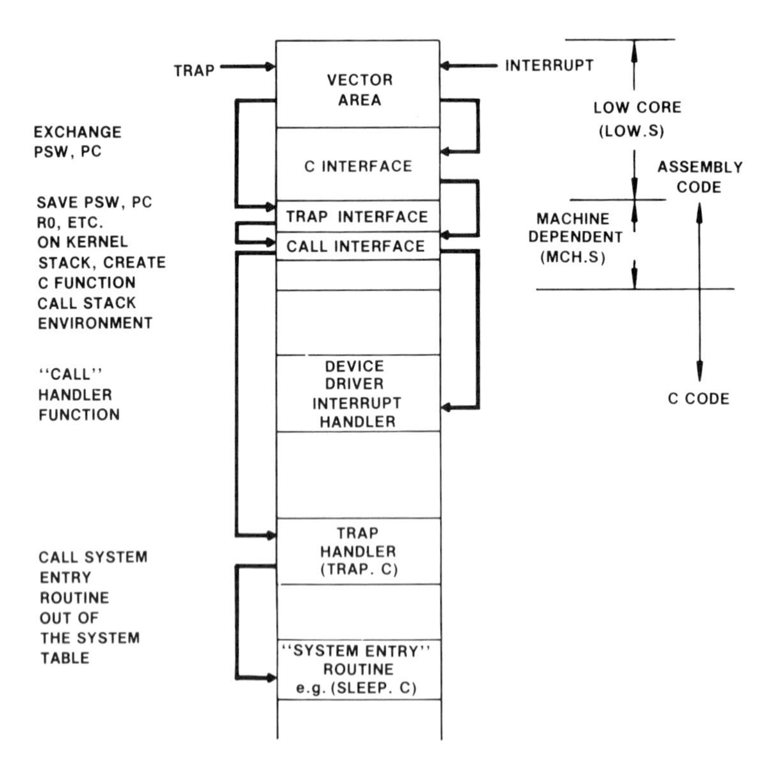

Figure 6.24 UNIX trap and interrupt mechanisms.

stored in storage locations called the vector area. The vector area in UNIX is located at low core (that is, the low-address-range area) in a file named LOW.S. The saved PSW and PC are placed on the kernel stack in the u_block of the currently executing process. The trap/call interface routine (stored in a file named MCH.S) pointed to by the new vector builds an interrupt stack frame on the kernel stack as if it were a function call stack frame. That is, it creates a C function call stack environment. The appropriate trap or interrupt handler routine is then called. This function uses the saved PSW and PC on the stack as arguments. Figure 6.25 shows a similar sequence in the DMERT operating system. Step 3 in the microcode sequence makes the old primary address space the secondary address space. (The use of primary and secondary address spaces are discussed in the next section.) Once the C-function call environment is set up, an interrupt handler routine, an operating system trap (OST) handler routine, or the dispatcher routine is called. The dispatcher routine dispatches one of the kernel processes. Hence in the DMERT operating system a process may trap into a kernel process.

Since there is no concept of privilege layers in data abstraction systems, ''system'' calls are implemented like all interpackage calls. That is, all interpackage calls are the same regardless of whether the package being called encapsulates system resources. Interrupt mechanisms in a data abstraction system are implemented in the following manner. The hardware interrupt signal stops the executing stream and initiates a firmware sequence. The firmware sequence makes a ''pseudo'' call, entering into the procedure of an interrupt handling package. The interrupt-handling package initiates a new execution stream, possibly causing a new sequence of packages to be called and entered.

The Plessey/250 system implements an interpackage call using the enter type capability and the call instruction. As discussed above, a package may own a capability to

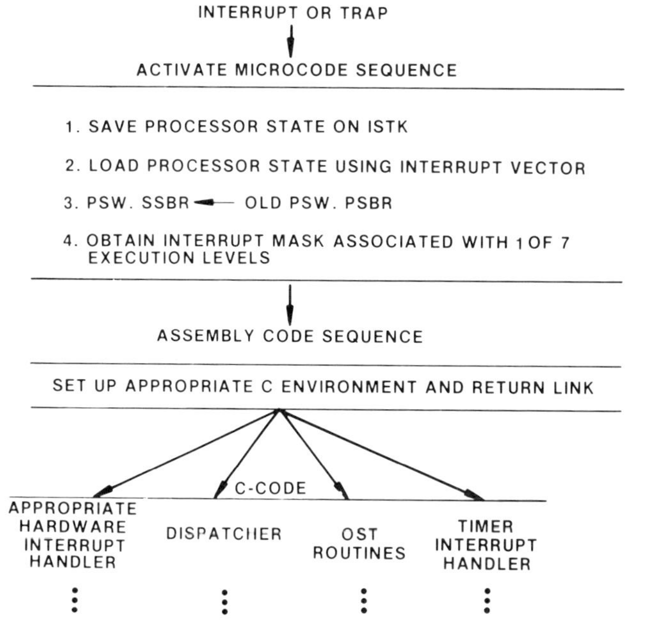

Figure 6.25 3B20/DMERT trap and interrupt mechanism

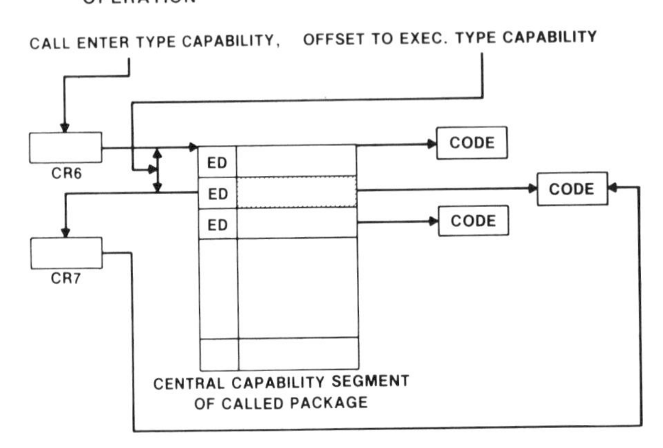

Figure 6.26 Plessey/250 interpackage call.

another capability object with an enter type access. Thus when the call instruction is issued with the enter type capability and an offset as arguments, the enter type capability is loaded into CR6 (Fig. 6.26). Since CR6 contains the pointer to the capability list of the current access environment, switching the value in CR6 essentially switches the capability list, and thus the access environment. After CR6 is loaded with the new capability pointing to the capability list of a different package, the offset argument indexes into the capability list to select the capability for the code segment to be executed. This capability is then loaded into CR7. Before overwriting CR6 and CR7, the program counter (PC), CR6, and CR7 are saved on a stack. The return instruction has no parameters and its action merely restores CR6, CR7, and the program counter.

The Intel iAPX/432 implements a "system call" much like an interpackage (interdomain) call. A domain has public procedures that other domains with the capability to it may call. Thus if a domain contains system resources, and its internal procedures manipulate these resources, a "system call" to manipulate these resources amounts to simply calling on the public procedures of that domain. The processor then switches into the context environment of that domain and the public procedure that has been called interacts with the internal procedures within the domain to act on the resources. An example of a file manager domain protecting a file directory and its public procedures is shown in Fig. 6.27.

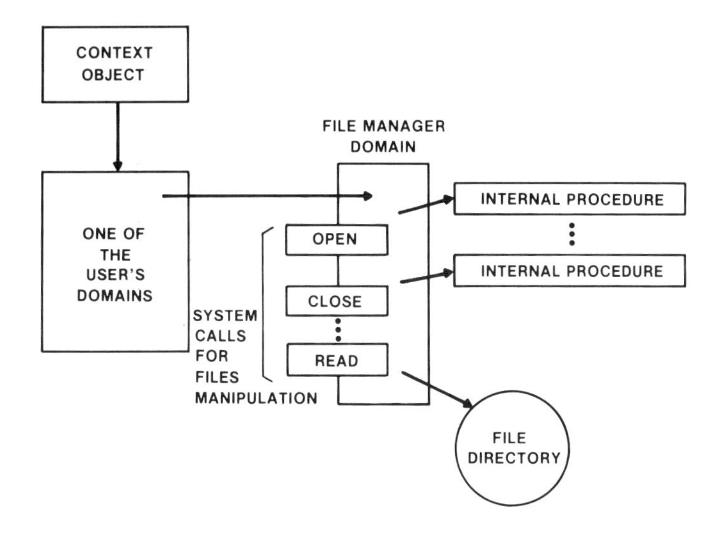

Figure 6.27 iAPX system calls.

6.6.5 Data Movement Across Access Environments

In a functional abstraction system, data from a kernel buffer in one address space may need to be transferred to a user buffer in another address space. Data moves across access environments are possible if both access environments are made available at the same time. Special privileged instructions may then be used to move data or instructions across the environments. In the PDP 11/UNIX system, the two access environments are made available by having two sets of mapping registers, one belonging to the current execution mode, the other belonging to the previous execution mode as specified in the PSW (Fig. 6.28). Each set of mapping registers defines an access environment. Special instructions, move to previous instruction (data) space [MTPI(D)] and move from previous instruction (data) space [MFPI(D)], are used to move instructions and data across access environments.

The 3B/DMERT system supports the concept of a primary (current) address space and a secondary (previous) address space. Even though the access environment of the current process is defined solely by the primary address space, a process may move data between the secondary address space and the primary address space using special instructions while in the privilege mode. This is supported in the 3B20D architecture by having two sets of address translation buffers pointed to by the primary space and secondary space selector bits in the processor status word.

In a data abstraction system, data may move across access environments by passing capabilities. The data to be moved is placed in a data object. The capability for the data

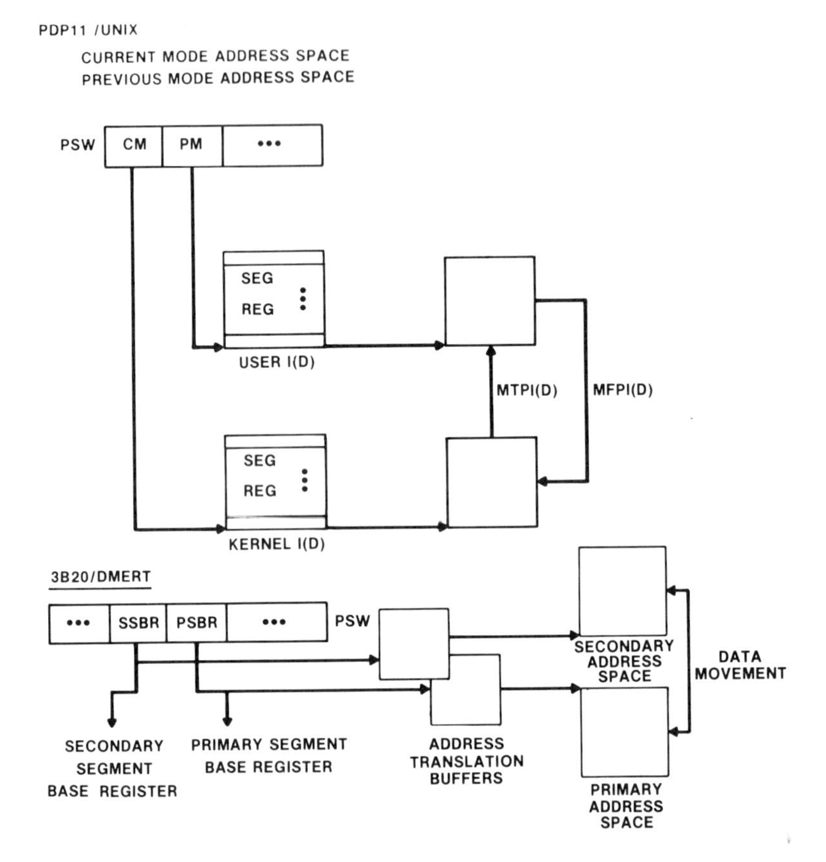

Figure 6.28 Data movement across domains in UNIX and DMERT.

object is then passed from one package to another package. After the capability passes into a new capability list, the data move is complete and the data belongs to a new access environment.

6.6.6 Intermodule Synchronization and Communication

In functional abstraction systems, processes are synchronized with each other by means of events and communicate with each other through messages. In the process environment, a message is a body of information copied from the access environment of one process to the access environment of another. Functional abstraction systems are characterized by their facilities for passing messages and events easily and efficiently among processes, and for queuing messages at the destination processes. They provide processes with several primitive operations, including those to send messages, to wait for any message, and to wait for a particular class of messages.

Packages, in data abstraction systems, are monitors. The use of monitors as synchronization mechanisms is discussed in Section 6.8.5. Packages communicate with each other by passing capabilities through a communication port. A communication port is a special package that buffers, directs, and protects messages sent to it. A message may be implemented as an object with the send and receive operators defined in its type. The mechanism of sending a message may then be implemented by having the package that sends the message pass the capability of the message object to the communication port package. When a package is ready to receive the message, the communication port passes the capability of the message object to the receiving package. This method of interprocess communication is more efficient than that used among processes in functional abstraction systems because only the capability is passed and there is no need to copy the message from one address space to another.

6.7 FUNCTIONAL AND DATA ABSTRACTION TRENDS

Functional abstraction and data abstraction are different types of operating system architectures. The different architectures affect the way modules are partitioned and protected from each other, and the way modules synchronize and communicate with each other. The mechanisms within the two systems, however, correspond closely to each other [18]. This correspondence is shown in Fig. 6.29. The architectural support for the implementation of these mechanisms is also similar.

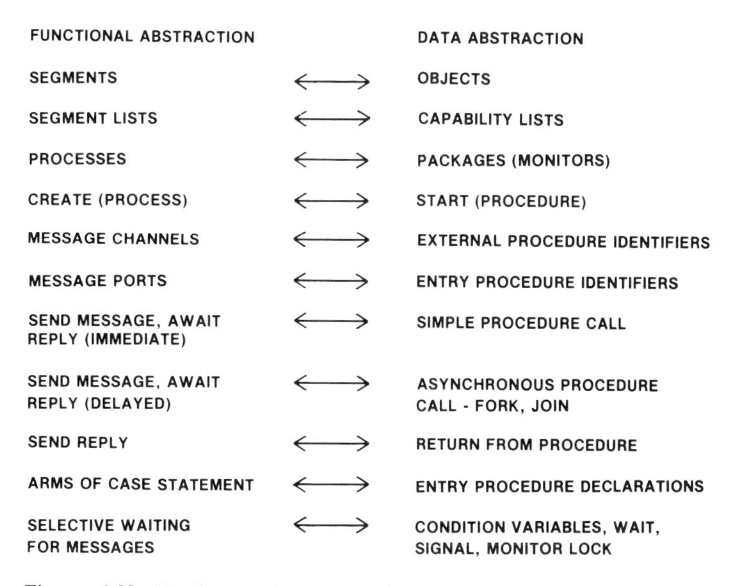

Figure 6.29 Duality mapping between functional abstraction system and data abstraction system.

Functional abstraction systems dominated the 1960s and 1970s and will continue to be dominant in information systems that emphasize the sharing of functional modules. Data abstraction systems such as Ada [19], iAPX/432, and the IBM System/38 [20] are beginning to emerge and dominate systems requiring the sharing of information and data objects. Even in the 1980s, though, functional abstraction will continue to be prominent in the industry.

The proponents of data abstraction systems have shown many reasons why their systems are more desirable than functional abstraction systems. They emphasize that in functional abstraction systems, protection is achieved through a plethora of policies and mechanisms, including privileged instructions, access rights control, per-process virtual address space, and privileged layers. Data abstraction systems implement protection structures using a uniform mechanism. They do not develop the kinds of problems found in a functional abstraction system like Multics. Multics has a nesting structure of privileges on access environments and therefore cannot implement mutually disjoint access environments within the same process [21,22]. Furthermore, an error in a procedure in a high privilege layer may cause critical damage to the system because it can call and access the segments in the less privileged layers. Finally, the layered architecture makes the protection structure rigid.

A simple partitioning example shows that the partitioned modules are smaller in data abstraction systems than in functional abstraction systems (Fig. 6.9). This has both advantages and disadvantages. The advantage is that it provides a finer protection granularity. The disadvantages are that (1) the many objects and their unique names demand a large address space; and (2) switches from one module and its access environment to another module and its access environment become much more frequent. Each switch must be implemented very efficiently so that the overhead does not make the system impractical, as is the case for many of the research systems running without architectural support. Some of the missing architectural support was supplied by hardware for address development (associative caches in the iAPX/432 and the hash generator in the IBM System/38) and firmware and hardware for efficient environment switches (many sets of small associative caches).

6.8 SYNCHRONIZATION PRIMITIVES

With the advent of multiprogramming and concurrent processes, tools were needed to synchronize the processes competing for shared resources. Andler describes the evolution of synchronization concepts and their problems [23]. The concept of *mutual exclusion* of accesses to *shared variables* was developed to implement synchronization primitives. Mutual exclusion means that once a process begins accessing a shared variable, all the other processes must be excluded from accessing the same shared variable. In other words, accessing a shared variable must be an *indivisible* operation. The program code by which a process performs the indivisible operation is called a *critical section* or a *critical region*.

6.8.1 Inhibiting Interrupts

One of the earliest developed and simplest methods by which a process can achieve indivisibility of operation is by inhibiting the interrupts before the operation begins and enabling the interrupts after the operation is finished. The disadvantage with this solution is that a time limit must be imposed on the indivisible operation; that is, the critical region should be short. Otherwise, the processor could remain uninterruptible for a long period of time, and interrupts could be lost. Furthermore, this method works only for uniprocessors. For multiprocessing systems, two processes inhibiting interrupts in their respective processors might still not be mutually excluded from accessing shared variables at the same time.

6.8.2 Locks and the Test and Set Operations

To solve these problems, the concept of *locks* and the *test* and *set* operation were introduced. A lock, often represented by a word in memory, is associated with a shared resource. A process entering a critical region corresponding to a shared resource ''locks'' the resource by performing a test and set operation on the lock. If the lock is already set by another process, the process keeps testing for the lock to be reset (that is, for the resource to become free). When the test and set operation successfully locks the resource, the process may enter the critical region. When it exits from the region, it unlocks (resets) the lock. The main problem with this concept is that there is no queuing mechanism; a process could be wasting processor and memory cycles by repetitively testing for the lock. This is called the *busy wait* problem. Another problem associated with this scheme is the *starvation* problem. Starvation occurs when a low-priority process waits for an indefinite period of time trying to enter the critical region while higher-priority processes running on other processors alternate entering the critical region.

6.8.3 Semaphores and the Signal and Wait Operations

To solve these problems, the concept of *semaphores* and the *signal* and *wait* operations were introduced [24]. A semaphore is a shared integer associated with a shared resource and its associated process queue. It is initialized to be equal to the number of these resources available. A process wanting to acquire one of these resources performs a wait operation, which causes the semaphore to be decremented. If the value of the semaphore is less than zero, the process is placed in the queue associated with the semaphore. Otherwise, it obtains the resource and proceeds. When the process is ready to release the resource, it performs a signal operation, which causes the semaphore to be incremented. If the value of the semaphore is less than or equal to zero, the system sends a signal to wake up a waiting process on the associated queue.

Multivalued semaphores synchronize multiple processes contending for multiple resources. The semaphore concept also solves the busy waiting problem of locks by implementing process queues. The main problem with using semaphores occurs when the code is unstructured, that is, when the critical regions are not easily discernible. When the code is unstructured, it is difficult for the compiler to check for the misuse of semaphores. For example, in the sender and receiver problem outlined below using a shared buffer resource, the signaling and waiting operations on a semaphore are not in the same process and the critical region is difficult to define.

```
sender process                      receiver process
      .                                   .
      .                                   .
      .                                   .
wait (buffer empty)                 wait (buffer full)
      .                                   .
      .                                   .
      .                                   .
signal (buffer full)                signal (buffer empty)
      .                                   .
      .                                   .
      .                                   .
```

6.8.4 Events and the Cause and Await Operations (Conditional Critical Regions)

Brinch Hansen introduced the concept of *conditional critical regions* to extend the concept of critical regions and signal and wait operations [25]. This concept associates a critical region with the occurrence of an *event* (scheduling condition). Processes on a semaphore queue attempt to enter a conditional critical region if a specific event (condition) has occurred. If the event has not occurred, the processes wait for the event in an event queue. When the event occurs, the processes in the event queue are put back into the semaphore queue and allowed to attempt to enter the conditional critical region again.

The await (event) operation, when executed by a process, causes the process to await the occurrence of the event in an event queue. With the wait and signal operations, the only scheduling condition is the availability of a resource. Await and cause operations allow the definition of other scheduling conditions (such as the arrival of a message or the arrival of an interrupt). Each of these scheduling conditions may be represented as a bit in an event flag. Whereas the operations associated with semaphores are the wait and signal operations, the operations associated with events are the *cause* and *await* operations. The cause (event) operation, when executed by a process, enables all the processes waiting for the corresponding event to attempt to enter a conditional critical region. Hence, an event flag is associated with multiple scheduling conditions. Since each event is represented by a bit, it cannot convey quantities. For example, the event associated with a message arrival conveys whether or not a message has arrived. It does not convey the number of message arrivals. A semaphore, on the other hand, is a count variable that keeps track of the number of available resources and the number of outstanding requests (waiting processes). A semaphore conveys quantities. Hence, events and semaphores have different applications.

6.8.5 Monitor (Class, Secretary)

One of the problems with a semaphore is the possibility of its undisciplined use and its being scattered in many processes. Inspired by the *class* concept in SIMULA 67, the concept of *monitors* [26], also known as *secretaries* [27], was introduced. A monitor for a resource collects all the procedures that can operate on that resource into its definition. Only the procedure names (monitor.procname) are known external to the monitor definition. Thus critical regions may be removed from processes and placed into monitors (Fig. 6.30). Mutual exclusion is enforced because only one monitor procedure may be executing at a time. The concept of monitors is exactly the same as that of the abstract data type [28] and package [19]; all three allow the compiler to do extensive type checking. There is a problem with monitors, however. The calling of monitor procedures from outside the monitor is serialized, but within the monitor, the wait and signal operations are still needed to synchronize how the monitor procedures themselves access the shared resource.

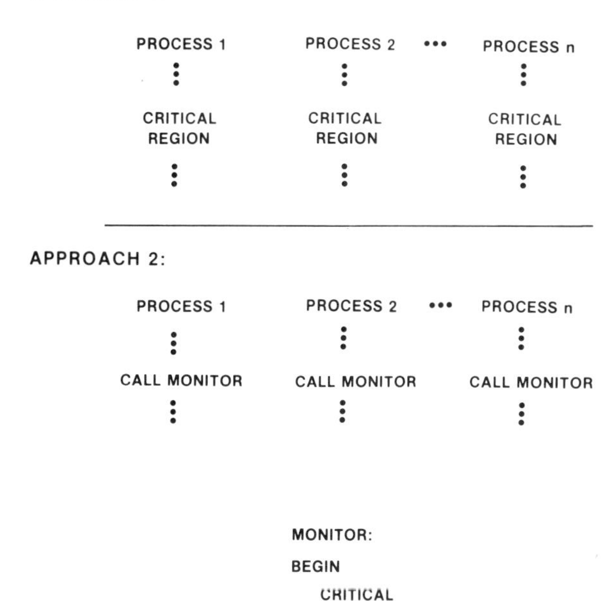

Figure 6.30 Use of monitor.

6.8.6 Path Expression

The concept of *path expressions* resolves the problem of the internal synchronization of the procedures of a monitor [27]. In path expressions, not only are the procedures that may access a shared resource defined in the type, but the permissible order of execution of the procedures is also defined. The synchronization is formulated as an expression [29]:

Path f; (g* + h); i end

In this expression, the execution of operation f may be followed by an arbitrary number of executions of operation g or by a single execution of operation h; an execution of operation i then follows. A path expression, therefore, is nothing more than a monitor with ordered operations. The synchronization is specified in the definition of the shared data object.

6.9 ARCHITECTURAL SUPPORT OF SYNCHRONIZATION CONCEPTS

The architectural development and support of synchronization concepts shows an increasing level of abstraction that makes programming easier because programmers can deal with path expressions and monitors instead of test and set instructions and inhibiting and enabling interrupts. However, the implementation of path expressions and monitors make use of the lower level concepts. Path expressions use counter and state variables, and check them between operations to verify that they satisfy the specified order of operations. Path expressions also associate either a lock or a semaphore with each procedure to ensure that two processes do not access the same procedure simultaneously.

Monitors must associate locks and semaphores with the monitor procedures to achieve mutual exclusion. They may also require signal and wait operations within the monitor procedures themselves. To implement events, the await and cause operations must be mutually exclusive and indivisible. Interrupts may be masked off or accesses to the event flag locked during the posting and checking for the occurrence of an event. Similarly, in the implementation of semaphores, the wait and signal operations must be made indivisible. Thus interrupts may be inhibited or locks used with the sections of code that manipulate and check semaphores. Finally, the test and set instructions must make use of a hardware bus arbiter for serializing accesses and the read-modify-write access as an indivisible operation on a memory cell. Similarly, inhibiting and enabling interrupts require the hardware support of an interrupt mask and interrupt set and clear flip-flops and the operations to manipulate the mask and the flip-flops.

The increasing level of abstraction is simply type extension; that is, more complex extended types are built on simpler, primitive types. At the lowest level, the primitives are on the firmware and hardware level. The indivisible actions needed to obtain mutual exclusion are achieved by appealing to more elementary forms of indivisible actions until the indivisible actions of reading and clearing a memory cell or masking an interrupt are reached (Fig. 6.31).

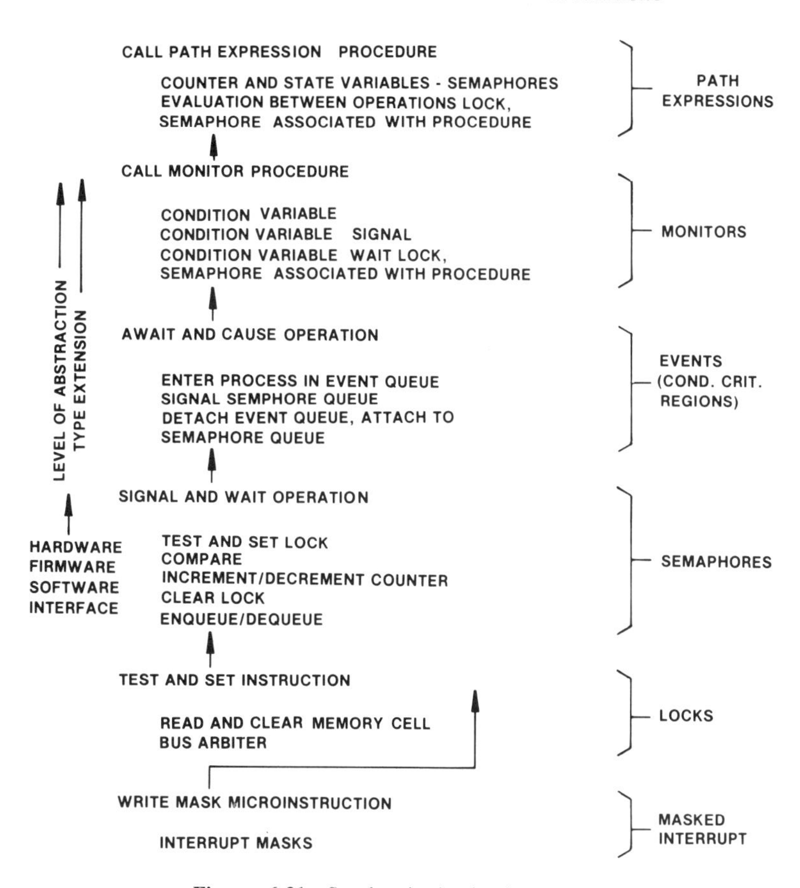

Figure 6.31 Synchronization implementation.

The architects must consider the level at which the hardware/firmware/software interface should be raised. Which concepts should be defined as primitive types with hardware and firmware support? In most conventional machines, the test and set instruction and the interrupt masks are primitive types supported by firmware and hardware. It is possible to raise the hardware/firmware/software interface level so that semaphores may be implemented as a hardware primitive type rather than as an extended type.

6.9.1 Synchronization in the UNIX Operating System

Synchronization in the UNIX operating system makes use of the *event* mechanism. It has two associated system calls: *sleep(event,priority)* and *wakeup(event)*. These calls correspond to the *await* and *cause* operations described previously. A running process issues a sleep system call and waits for the arrival of a specified event. The running process also

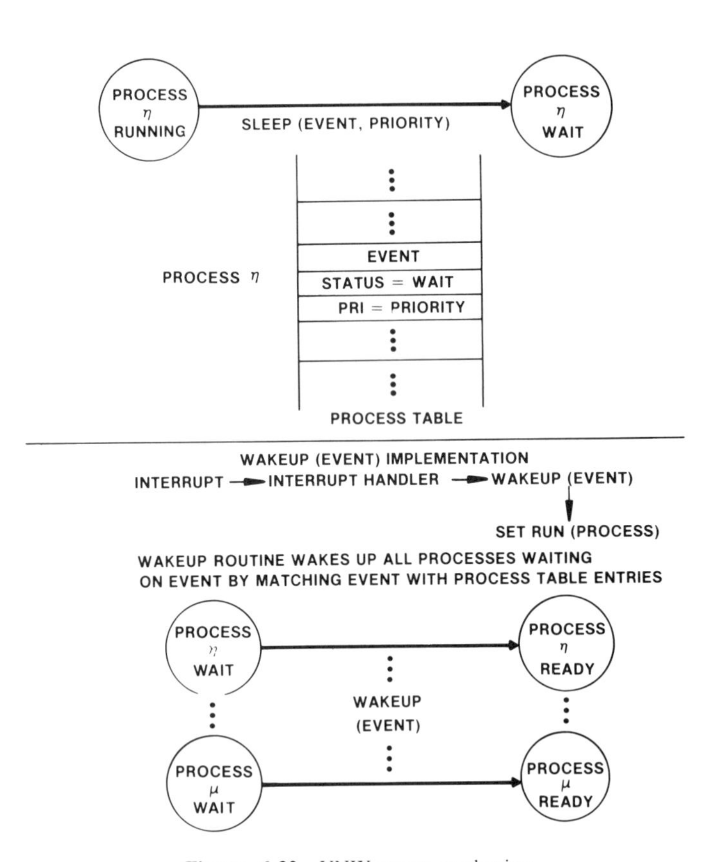

Figure 6.32 UNIX events mechanism.

specifies the priority at which it should be awakened. The sleep system call is implemented by posting the specified event in the process table event entry associated with the calling process. The corresponding process table status flag entry is changed to the wait state and the priority entry is set to the one specified in the system call (Fig. 6.32).

When an interrupt occurs, the interrupt handler is dispatched. The interrupt handler issues the wakeup system call on the event associated with the interrupt. The wakeup system call wakes up all the processes waiting on that event; this is implemented by comparing the event with the posted event entry of all the processes in the process table. When a match occurs, the status flag entries of the associated processes are changed from the wait state to the ready state (Fig. 6.32).

It is important to note that events implemented in the UNIX operating system have no memory associated with them, and thus a process may wait for an event that has already occurred. This condition, called a race condition, may occur when the UNIX system is implemented in a multiprocessor system.

6.9.2 Synchronization in the DMERT Operating System

The DMERT operating system also uses the event mechanism except that it has more features and variations to the basic sleep and wakeup calls. The DMERT kernel process event system calls named *psleep* and *pwakeup* are the same as to the *sleep* and *wakeup* calls of the UNIX operating system. The *sendevent* system call enables a process to send an event to a particular process and the *psignal* call allows a process to send events to all the processes belonging to a control channel. Processes belonging to a control channel have the same channel bit pattern in their dispatcher control entries (DCEs) as are in the dispatcher control table (DCT). This table is similar to the process table in the UNIX operating system. It keeps all the information about a process that is not swappable with the process in the DCE; swappable information is kept in the process control block (PCB) of each process. The difference between the dispatcher control table and the UNIX process table is that the dispatcher control table is implemented as linked lists with one list for each execution level (Fig. 6.33). Each dispatcher control entry in the linked list represents

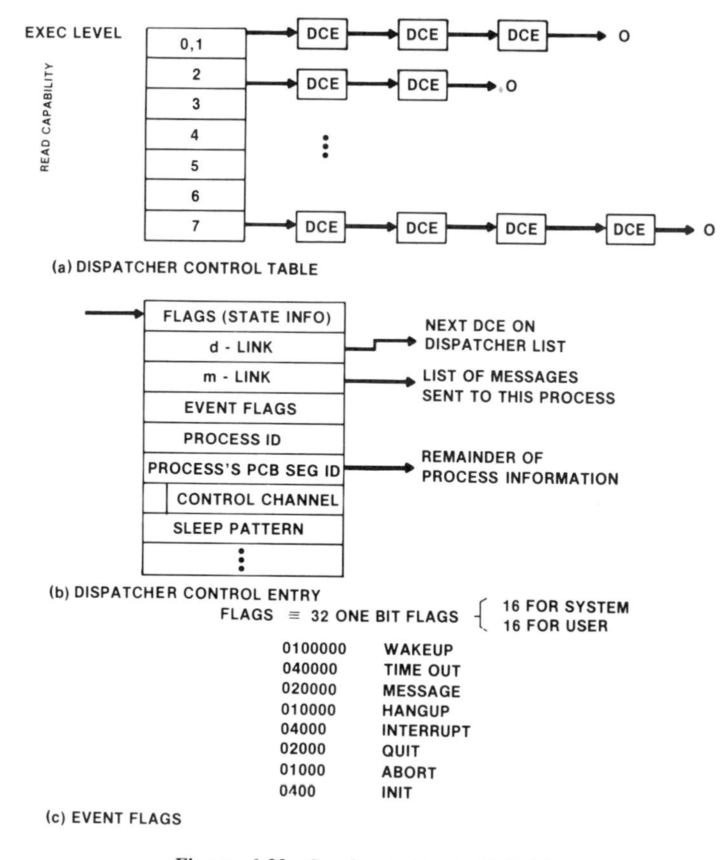

Figure 6.33 Synchronization in DMERT.

a process and contains the process ID, and is a pointer to other information about the process. It also contains the event flags for the process as well as the sleep pattern and control channel pattern. The event flags include wakeup, timeout, message, hangup, interrupt, quit, abort, and initialize. The occurrence of any of these events causes the corresponding event flag bit to be set.

The DMERT operating system also has a set of event system calls available to the supervisor processes. A supervisor process has available a system call that allows and disallows a specific event to affect the process by manipulating an event mask. Another system call allows a supervisor process to wait for either all of a set of specific events or any of the set by manipulating an event wait flag and an event wait mask with the event wait option. Finally, supervisor processes have a choice between roadblocking and waiting. In the DMERT operating system, a roadblocked process may be swapped out onto disk, while a waiting process is guaranteed to be kept in memory. The event system calls are listed in Table 6.1.

TABLE 6.1 DMERT SYSTEM CALLS FOR SYNCHRONIZATION

System Call	Meaning
Kernel OSTs	
Sendevent (process, evflags)	Send events to a process
Psleep (process, pattern)	Put process to sleep on a bit pattern
Psignal (channel, evflags)	Send events to processes on a control channel
Pwakeup (pattern)	Wake up processes sleeping on bit pattern
Supervisor OSTs	
Event (process, eflag)	Send event to a process
Envent (eflag)	Enable event flags that the process can receive
Clrevent (eflag)	Clear event flags; the bit(s) to be cleared normally correspond to the event just received
Crdblk (flag)	Set conditional roadblock for event
Cwait (flag)	Set conditional wait for event (keep process in main memory)
Cyield (flag)	Set conditional yield for event; enter roadblock state if flag is nonnull
Wakeup (pattern)	Wake up all processes sleeping on pattern
Sleep (pattern)	Put process to sleep on bit pattern
Setewait (eflag, opt)	Set event wait mask and event wait option fields in the process's PCB
Cerdblk ( )	Cause process to roadblock for specific events specified by event wait mask
Cewait ( )	Set conditional wait for specific events
Ceyield ( )	Set conditional yield for specific events

The event mechanisms of supervisor processes are similar to those of kernel processes except that:

1. A supervisor can allow and disallow specific events by manipulating an event mask.

2. A supervisor can wait for either all of a specific event or any of a set.
3. Supervisor processes have a choice between roadblock and wait.

The implementation of the kernel process event mechanism in the DMERT system is similar to that of the UNIX system. A sleeping process posts its status and the event it is sleeping on in the dispatcher control table. Unless the process to be awakened is specifically designated, waking up a process requires a search through the linked lists of the dispatcher control table for a matching sleep (event) pattern. Similarly, to wake up a process belonging to a control channel, the system searches through the linked lists and matches the control channel pattern with that specified in the system call. The actions taken by the kernel process event system calls are listed in Table 6.2.

TABLE 6.2 DMERT KERNEL EVENT OSTS

System Call: Description
Sendevent (process, evflags)
• Determine DCE's address of process
• OR the event flags in the DCE (must mask off interrupts)
• Trigger the programmed interrupt at the processor priority of the receiving process
• Enter the process's event handler
Psleep (process, pattern)
• Set sleep pattern in DCE (mask off interrupts)
• Set sleep flag in status
Psignal (channel, evflags)
• Search through dispatcher lists for control channel match
• For each match found, send event to the process as above
Pwakeup (pattern)
• Search through dispatcher lists for sleep pattern match
• For each match, send ''wakeup event'' and clear process's DCE ''sleep'' flag

Supervisor process event mechanisms are built on the kernel process event mechanisms. Additional types of events are obtained by having more words to be manipulated in the process control blocks of the processes. The entries in the process control block for implementing events are shown in Fig. 6.34. Table 6.3 lists the actions taken by some of the supervisor process event system calls.

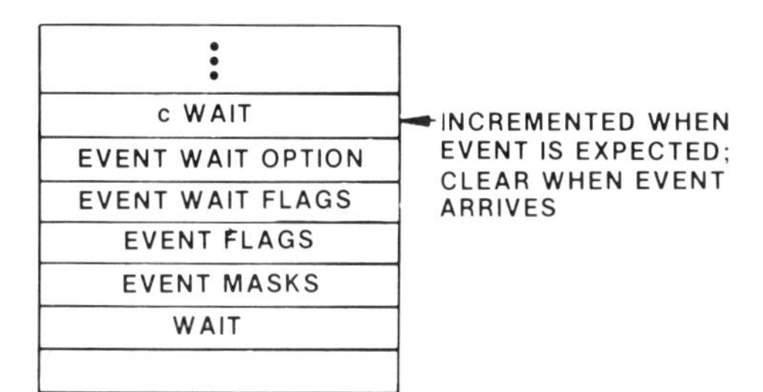

Figure 6.34 DMERT supervisor event OSTs–implementation.

TABLE 6.3 DMERT SUPERVISOR PROCESS EVENT SYSTEM CALLS

System Call: Description
Sleep (pattern)
• Increment cwait in PCB
• Call kernel ''psleep'' routine
Wakeup (pattern)
• Call kernel ''wakeup'' routine
Event (process, eflag)
• Increment cwait in PBC
• Call kernel ''sendevent'' routine
Enevent (eflag)
• Write event mask in PCB
• Clear cwait
Clrevent (eflag)
• Clear specified event flags
• Clear cwait
Setewait (eflag, opt)
• Write event wait mask in PCB
• Write event wait option in PCB
Cwait (flag)
• Set ''roadblock'' and ''job change'' bits in DCT status word
• Restore process priority to 0
• Clear PCB ''timelock'' bit
• Set ''wait'' flag
• Send ''wakeup'' event to scheduler

6.9.3 Synchronization in the VAX/VMS Operating System [3]

The VAX/VMS system also uses the event mechanism for synchronization. It allows processes to (1) set and clear specific event flags, (2) test the current status of event flags, and (3) place a program in a wait state pending the setting of a specified event flag or a group of event flags. Table 6.4 lists the system calls associated with events.

The VAX/VMS operating system supplements the basic event mechanism by defining two types of events: local events and common events. Local events are local to a process; they are represented by two clusters of 32 event flags each and reside in the software process control block of each process. Local events are used for synchronization within a process. Common events are common to groups of cooperating processes that can create and associate common events with two common event flag clusters. A process can read, set, and clear its group's common event flags or its own local event flags. Associated with each common event flag cluster is a control structure containing the information about the creator's user identification, the cluster name, its size in bytes, and a count of the processes in the wait queue. A process may associate itself with the cluster if it knows the cluster name and has proper privileges.

The system determines all the processes waiting for an event from the wait queue. The VAX/VMS system links all the processes waiting for local events in a local event flag

TABLE 6.4 VMS EVENT SYSTEM CALL

System Call	Description
$SETEF	(Set event flag) Sets event flag and causes any process waiting for the flag to be runnable
$CLREF	(Clear event flag) Causes event flag to be cleared
$READEF	(Read event flag) Returns the current state of all 32 event flags in a cluster
$WFLOR	(Wait for logical OR of event flags) Tests the events selected by a mask within a specified cluster and returns immediately if any of them is set; otherwise, process is placed in wait state until any of them is set
$WFLAND	(Wait for logical AND of event flags) Specifies a mask of events; tests and waits for all the events specified
$WAITFR	(Wait for signal event flag) Tests and waits for specified single event; returns immediately if set
$ASCEFC	(Associate command event flag cluster) Associates a process with a common event flag cluster
$DACEFC	(Disassociate common event flag cluster) Disassociates requesting process from common event flag cluster
$DLCEFC	(Delete common event cluster) Releases common event cluster when no processes are associated with it

cluster queue, and all the processes waiting for common events in a common event flag cluster queue. The count of processes in each wait queue facilitates queue scanning and avoids the need for searching through entire process tables.

6.9.4 Implementation of Synchronization and Its Architectural Issues

Even though the three operating systems support many varieties of synchronization services, all are variations of the same event mechanism that requires the system to change the status of processes (1) from the run state to the wait state and (2) from the wait state to the ready state. The systems also need to determine the appropriate processes for which these status changes should occur. The systems appeal to lower-level mechanisms to implement these functions. These mechanisms manipulate and test flags in control data structures, handle system calls and software interrupts, and dispatch new processes. These mechanisms rely on even lower level activities including context switches, linked list manipulations and searches, and stack manipulations. The following architectural features support these activities:

1. Software data structures (process tables, process control blocks, wait queues, and wait queue headers)
2. Stack manipulation instructions
3. Queue manipulation instructions (in VAX)
4. Privilege levels
5. Saving and restoring process environments

6. Creating stack environments (by an assembly sequence in the UNIX system and by microcode in the DMERT operating system)

To support interprocess synchronization in these operating systems more efficiently, the hardware/software interface should be raised to better support the basic mechanisms and activities.

6.10 COMMUNICATION PRIMITIVES

Communication transfers data from one process to another and permits the transfers to occur asynchronously. Event flags may be thought of as the simplest communication mechanism; event flags send one bit of information denoting the occurrence of a particular event (such as an interrupt, the arrival of a message, or a timeout).

6.10.1 Messages

The RC4000 introduced the use of *messages* as interprocess communication mechanisms [1]. A pool of message buffers belongs to and is allocated by the system nucleus for sending and receiving messages. The primary disadvantage of this concept is that memory space must be committed for the pool of message buffers; message buffers are thus not for optimal large amounts of information transferring. Furthermore, each message must be moved twice: once from the sender to the buffer, and once from the buffer to the receiver.

6.10.2 Shared Memory

For an efficient means of passing a large quantity of information from one process to another, an architecture may use shared memory communication. The advantages of shared memory are that there is no need for buffer management and that it is much faster than message communication. The information does not have to be copied. The disadvantages are that it can only be used when actual physical memory is shared. It also requires mutual exclusion synchronization, and tends to be less controlled and thus more susceptible to corruption than message passing when more than two processes are involved.

6.10.3 Pipes

Pipes, introduced in the UNIX operating system, are one form of shared memory communication [2]. A pipe is a one-way interprocess communication channel that behaves like an open file. It is referred to by a file descriptor and used with the same read and write system calls that are used for file system I/O. The disadvantage of a pipe is that it must be set up by a common ancestor of the processes involved.

6.10.4 Shared Files

Files may be shared among users. A user permits access rights to a file and specifies the users that may access the file. A cooperating group of users can share a large quantity of information this way.

6.10.5 Ports

Ports are used for communication among unrelated processes. A port is a globally known name to which a process attaches to receive messages. Neither the message sender nor the receiver needs to know of the other's identity. A port may also be used as a message broadcast facility. Or, it may be used to demultiplex a single stream of data into many streams, and to multiplex many streams of data into a single stream. For example, if a process sends a message to a port to which multiple processes are attached, that message is demultiplexed into multiple messages, one for each attached process.

6.10.6 Links (Paths)

Links were introduced in DEMOS [30]. Access control for links is similar to that for capabilities. Links directly specify the allowable paths over which messages may be sent. That is, a process may not send a message to another process unless it owns a link (path) to that process. The advantage of links (paths) is that they make visible the connections among processes and are especially useful for controlling the interconnectivity of processes in network systems. Links allow the logical connectivity of processes to be abstracted and differentiated from their physical connectivity. A process may own many links and it may group a subset of links into a *channel*. The destination process may select the links over which it receives messages.

6.11 ARCHITECTURAL SUPPORT OF COMMUNICATION CONCEPTS

Different systems use different interprocess communication mechanisms. Three operating systems (UNIX, DMERT, and VAX/VMS) show how interprocess communication concepts may be implemented and supported.

6.11.1 Interprocess Communication in the UNIX Operating System [29]

The basic mechanism of interprocess communication in the UNIX operating system are pipes, signals, and shared files. The UNIX system treats pipes like open files. Pipes use the same facilities as the file system; like files, they may be read, written, and passed from parent to child processes. The reader and writer processes access the pipe file using the same file descriptor pointing to the pipe file. Data passes between them without either process knowing that a pipe, rather than an ordinary file, is involved.

Pipes work like this. The reader and writer processes each have file entries in the system file table. The two entries point to the same *inode* (file descriptor) in the system

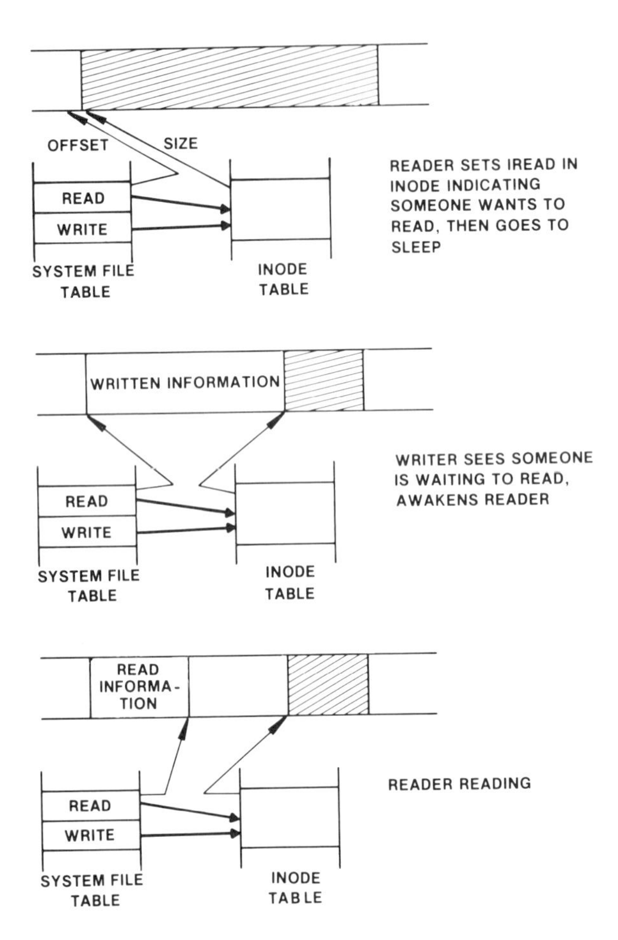

Figure 6.35 UNIX pipe implementation.

inode table describing the pipe file. The reader process sets a status flag in the inode to indicate that it wants to read the corresponding file, and then goes to sleep. The writer process, after it has written into the pipe, checks to see whether a reader process is waiting to read the pipe file. If it finds that a reader has set the read status flag, it awakens the reader process. The reader process then reads until the offset in its file table entry equals the size of the pipe posted in the inode by the writer process (Fig. 6.35).

Another communication mechanism used by the UNIX operating system is *signals*. An entry denoted p_sig resides in each process's process table. When a process (the sending process) wants to signal another process (the receiving process), it writes a value into the latter's p_sig. The value written is a pointer into the receiving process's signal table (u_sig[ ]) in its process control block (u_block). The receiving process specifies the action to be taken when it receives a signal by filling in the address of the procedure that

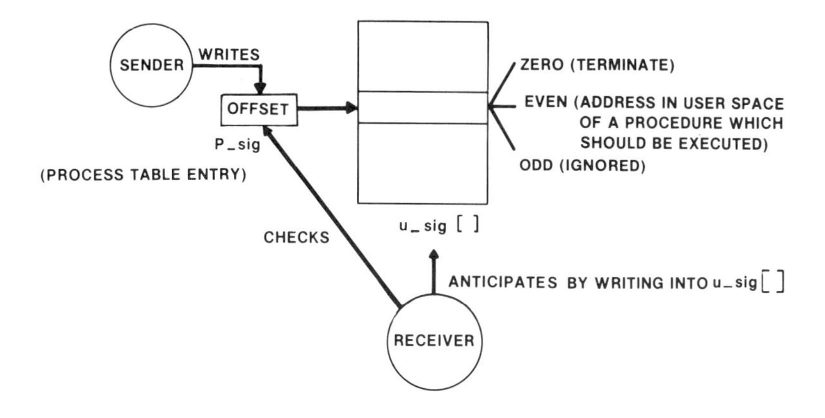

- ASYNCHRONOUS INTERACTION

  KERNEL MODE PROCESS ADJUSTS THE USER MODE STACK TO MAKE IT APPEAR THAT THE PROCEDURE HAD BEEN ENTERED AND IMMEDIATELY INTERRUPTED BEFORE EXECUTING

  SYSTEM THEN RETURNS FROM SYSTEM MODE TO USER MODE

Figure 6.36 UNIX signals implementation.

should be executed in the associated entry in the signal table (Fig. 6.36). This interaction is asynchronous and thus does not serve as a synchronization primitive. That is, the sending process does not wake up the receiving process after a signal is sent. Only when the receiving process is active does it check its p_sig entry to determine whether it has received a signal. If a user procedure is to be executed as a result of the signal, the kernel adjusts the user mode stack to make it appear that the procedure has been entered and immediately interrupted before executing the first instruction. The system then returns from the kernel mode to the user mode and the procedure is executed. The procedures specified by the receiver process are its signal handlers.

6.11.2 Interprocess Communication in the DMERT Operating System

The DMERT operating system processes communicate by means of messages, ports, shared memory, and pipes. These are implemented based on mechanisms developed in the UNIX and MERT systems [31].

6.11.2.1 Message implementation. Each DMERT message consists of a message header and a message body; the message body is filled in by the sending process before it sends the message to the receiving process. After preparing the message, the sending process uses the system call sendmsg, which initiates a request for the kernel to allocate a message buffer from the system buffer pool. The kernel maintains a pool of message buffers and handles the system calls associated with the sending and receiving of messages. The kernel copies the message from the sending process's address space to the allocated message buffer. It then links the message to the receiving process's message queue. The kernel notifies the receiving process by sending it a message arrival event flag. The event causes the receiving process to be dispatched if it runs at a higher priority than the sending process. The message is then copied from the message buffer to the receiving process's address space. The buffer is then unlinked and returned to the system pool. The steps required of a supervisor process sending a message to a kernel process is shown in Fig. 6.37. It shows that sending a message involves various system calls [sendmsg (buf), allocmsg (kbuf), queuem, sendevent (p,f), kevent (f), and deuqueuem (p)], kernel trap-handling routines, dispatching and event mechanisms, buffer allocation mechanisms, and interrupt-handling mechanisms.

6.11.2.2 Port implementation. The DMERT operating system implements ports by using a table in the kernel address space that identifies the processes connected to

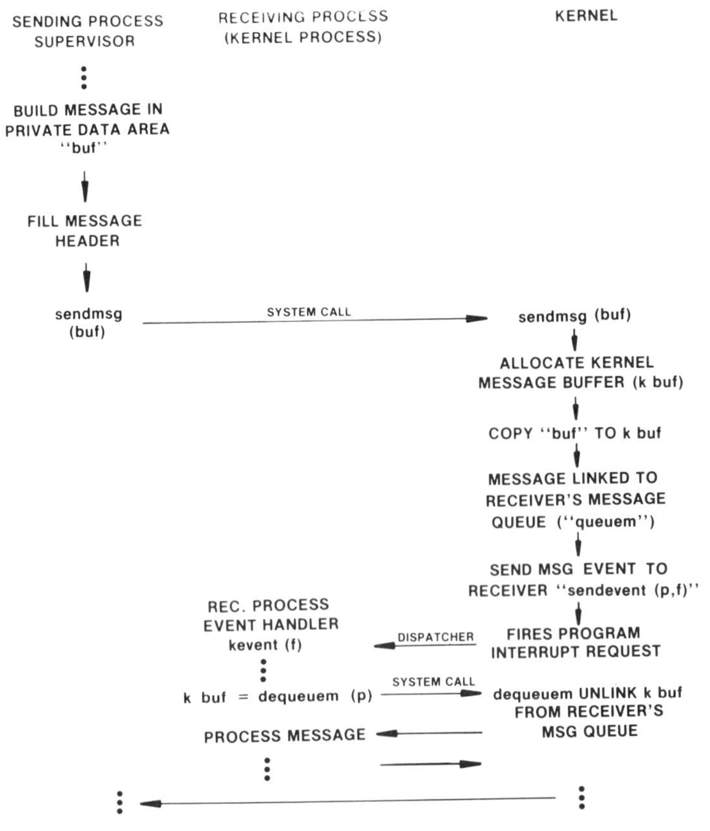

Figure 6.37 DMERT message implementation.

each port. Several system calls manipulate the system port table to connect a process to a port, disconnect a process from a port, and obtain the identity of the processes connected to a port. A port number identifies each port in the system port table. A process is automatically disconnected from a port upon termination. The system call to send a message to a port works in the same way as the system call to send a message; the only difference is that the process identification of the receiving process must be determined by the kernel using the system port table.

6.11.2.3 Shared memory implementation. There are two methods of sharing memory in the DMERT system. The first method, the emulator trap instruction, passes information between a supervisor process and a kernel process. The supervisor process passes to the kernel the process identification of the kernel process with which it wishes to communicate. The kernel then dispatches the kernel process through its emulator trap entry point, passing to the kernel process the identification of the supervisor process and a pointer to an argument list. The kernel process may then access data in the supervisor process address space by setting part of its virtual address space to overlap with that of the supervisor's.

The second method lets supervisor processes communicate with each other. The initiator process passes the identification of the segment to be shared to the receiving process in a message. The receiving process sharing the designated segment then makes a system call that adds the shared segment to its segment list. The shared segment then resides in the address space of both processes.

6.11.3 Interprocess Communication in the VAX/VMS Operating System [3]

Interprocess communication in the VAX/VMS operating system is implemented using messages, mailboxes, and shared memory.

6.11.3.1 Message and mailbox implementation. A mailbox is a buffer in virtual memory used for passing and receiving messages that is treated exactly as if it were a record-oriented I/O device. Mailboxes may be thought of as virtual devices; the system calls for I/O devices apply to mailboxes. A process therefore can read, write, and be notified when something is written into the mailbox. Furthermore, messages may be sent to a mailbox by means of the same system calls used in the VMS system to interface to the I/O drivers. When the mailbox receives a message and a read request is pending, the I/O packet containing the message goes directly to the reading process. If no read is pending when a message arrives, the I/O packet is queued in the mailbox. One major difference between I/O for real devices and I/O for the mailbox is that when a process sends a message to a mailbox, it does not need to wait for a response because the "I/O" completes immediately.

6.11.3.2 Shared memory communication implementation. *Global sections* implement shared memory communication in the VMS system. A global section is a copy of a portion of an image of a data file that may be linked to a process's virtual address space at link time or at run time. Global sections are either permanent or created dynamically by a process. Processes that reference a global section for the first time map the global section into their virtual address spaces. The access privilege to the global section may differ for the processes that map to it. A global section may belong to the group of cooperating processes that created it; it may be shared among the processes in the system, among the processes within a group and protected from all other processes, or among processes within a single job and protected from all other jobs. The permanent global sections are known, linkable images created by the linker. For example, the run-time procedure library is a known linkable image that is implicitly mapped into the virtual address space of the processes that reference the library procedures.

6.11.4 Implementation of Interprocess Communication and Architectural Issues

The interprocess communication mechanisms represent a higher level of abstraction than the synchronization mechanisms, but both are built from the same types of lower-level activities. The DMERT operating system builds the port mechanism on the message mechanism, which uses the event mechanism. To share memory in the DMERT system, a message must first be sent to pass the identification of the segment being shared; this process again relies on the message facilities. Pipes and mailboxes are implemented in such a way that they use the same system facilities as files and devices. Furthermore, they use the event mechanism to wake up processes waiting for messages in the pipe or the mailbox. Finally, signals basically require the manipulation of entries in system tables and the creation of environments for procedures to handle them.

The interprocess communication mechanisms are built on the event mechanism, system calls, and other mechanisms that manipulate system tables. The mechanisms and activities that support interprocess synchronization (Section 6.9.4) also support interprocess communication (Fig. 6.38). In fact, most of the operating system code is concerned with the same activities: switching environments and contexts, searching and manipulating protected control data structures, and handling interrupts. Once the architects identify these universal activities, they explore hardware, firmware, and software mechanisms to support them.

6.12 MANAGEMENT OF HARDWARE RESOURCES

An important function of operating systems is ensuring the efficient use of the hardware resources: processor, memory, and input/output devices. The efficient use of hardware resources has directed the evolution of operating systems into multiprogramming and time-sharing systems (see Chapter 5). In multiprogramming and time-sharing systems,

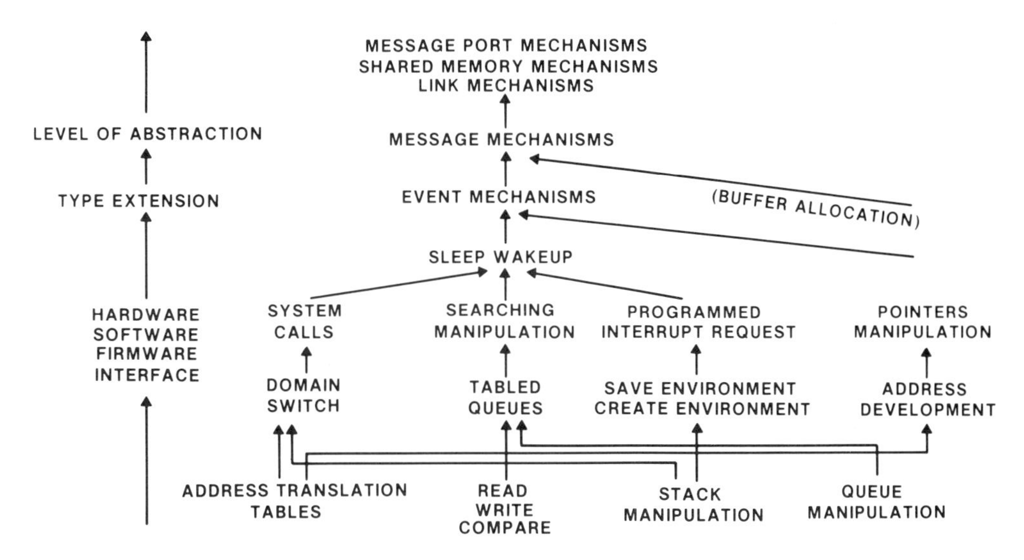

Figure 6.38 Communication primitives implementation.

the operating system manages the use of the hardware resources among competing processes. Its objective is achieving multiple virtual machines that are time-multiplexed on a single physical machine by means of processor, memory, and I/O device management. Processor management functions include keeping track of the processor status, scheduling multiple processes on the processor, and allocating and deallocating processes from the processor. Memory management functions include keeping track of the memory status, allocating memory to active processes, and deallocating memory from terminated processes. The management of I/O devices is directly related to the I/O architecture, controllers, and devices. It is a subject large enough to be its own topic of discussion and is beyond the scope of this book.

6.13 PROCESSOR MANAGEMENT AND ARCHITECTURAL SUPPORT

Processor management assigns processors to processes. Assignments are made at periodic intervals, on demand due to interrupts, or when processes suspend their activities while waiting for synchronization signals. Processor management requires a combination of software and hardware support. The support includes scheduler programs and the data structures required to implement the scheduling policies (for example, queues of waiting processes and queues of runnable processes), a set of software scheduling priority levels, a set of interrupt and hardware priority levels, interrupt mechanisms, timer facilities, process switching mechanisms, and a set of system calls by which processes can request for synchronization for the use of the processor (see also Section 6.8).

6.13.1 *Processor Management in the PDP 11/UNIX System*

In the PDP 11/UNIX system, all the processes in the system have their scheduling statuses in the process table. Various queues linking processes with a certain scheduling status are implemented. Figure 6.39 shows the run queue (RUNQ) linking processes that are ready to run.

A process may execute in two modes: user and kernel. A process executing in the user mode switches to the kernel mode when an interrupt or a trap occurs. The change of access environment during a mode switch was described in Section 6.6.4. Before reverting to the user mode after handling the interrupt or trap, the system checks whether a higher-priority process is ready to run. If a higher-priority process is ready, the scheduler (called the switcher in the UNIX operating system) searches through the runnable processes for the process with the highest priority. A process switch then occurs. The system saves the hardware context of the current process in its u_block. It obtains the hardware context of the new process from its u_block and loads it into the processor.

The PDP 11 timer mechanism generates a timer interrupt at the expiration of each time slice. A time slice in a time-sharing system is the time interval in which the processor is allocated to a process. A process, due to traps and interrupts, may not fully use its time slice. In that case, the timer is reset to begin the next time slice for a different process. In the case that a process fully uses up its time slice, the timer interrupt switches the running process from the user to the kernel mode. The timer interrupt-handling routine calls the switcher to schedule the next process. The CPU time used and other status information are updated in the process table. Periodically, the process manager recalculates the priority of the processes depending on the amount of CPU time each has previously consumed.

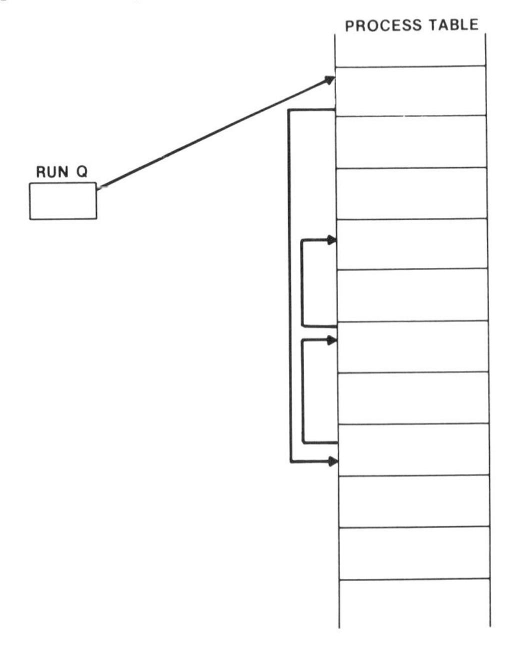

Figure 6.39 PDP-11/UNIX queue of runnable processes.

6.13.2 Processor Management in the 3B20D/DMERT System

Two types of DMERT processes contend for the resources of the 3B20D processor: user-supervisor processes and kernel processes. The kernel processes execute at execution levels 2 through 7; the user-supervisor processes execute at levels 0 and 1. Each execution level has a corresponding interrupt mask. The process manager treats these types of processes differently. For instance, the scheduler does not schedule kernel processes; they are dipatched by either an external interrupt or a software interrupt. On the other hand, the scheduler does schedule the user-supervisor processes by placing each into one of the 256 software scheduling priority levels.

Timer and other interrupts activate the scheduler. When the scheduler receives an interrupt, it saves the state of the user-supervisor process on an interrupt stack, and dispatches the kernel process interrupt handler. As a result of processing the interrupt, the kernel process sends an event to a user-supervisor process; the event is sent at execution level 1. The event mechanism posts a programmed interrupt request at level 1 in the event entry of the user-supervisor process in the dispatcher control table. This interrupt will not fire because the kernel process that sends the event is executing at levels 2 through 7. When the kernel process finishes processing the interrupt and returns control to the interrupted user-supervisor process at level 0, the programmed interrupt request at level 1 fires; control transfers back to the dispatcher. The dispatcher compares the software scheduling priority of the event receiver process with the priority of the interrupted user-supervisor process. If the interrupted user-supervisor process has higher priority, the dispatcher returns control to the user-supervisor process. If the interrupted user-supervisor process has lower priority, the dispatcher sends an event to the scheduler process at level 2. When the dispatcher returns, a level 2 programmed interrupt request fires, and the dispatcher gives control to the scheduler. The scheduler then saves the context of the interrupted user-supervisor process from the interrupt stack in its process control block, and schedules the highest-priority process that is ready to run. It loads the context of the selected process from its process control block into the hardware registers and returns control to the new process. The scheduler also dynamically adjusts the software priorities of the user-supervisor processes to reflect their usage of the machine.

6.13.3 Processor Management in the VAX/VMS System

The software and hardware contexts of a process in VMS are defined in Section 6.2. As shown in Fig. 6.1, part of a process context is nonswappable; this part is the software process control block (PCB). The VMS system implements queues of runnable processes by linking the software process control blocks in doubly linked lists, with one queue for each scheduling priority level [32]. The scheduler uses these queues to select the next process to run on the machine. There are two sets of 32 queues of runnable processes: one set for processes in memory and one set for processes swapped out on disks. Figure 6.40 illustrates the set of 32 queues of runnable processes in memory. There are also 11 queues of nonrunnable processes; these queues are implemented by linking the software PCBs of processes waiting for one of 11 wait conditions. Various events in the system, including interrupts, signal the occurrence of wait conditions; these events cause processes to move

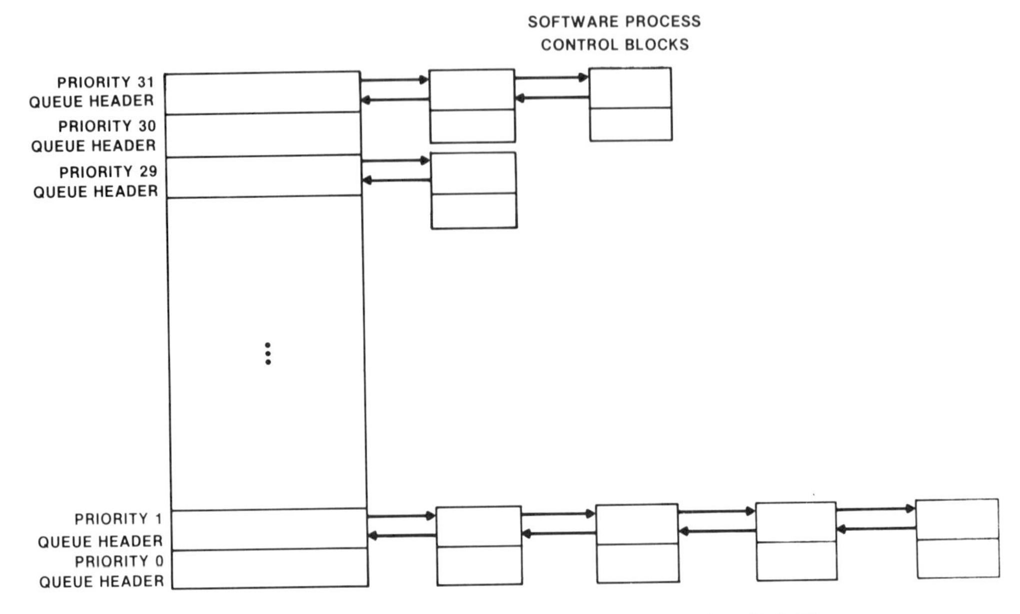

Figure 6.40 VAX/VMX executable process queues (from Ref. 32).

from one of the queues to another. Events may also cause runnable processes to be moved from one priority queue to another as the process manager reevaluates the priorities of the processes.

When the VAX processor becomes available because of an interrupt, the expiration of a time slice, or the suspension of the executing process, it generates an event. The event is detected by a routine in VMS executing at software interrupt priority level 3. When the event detection routine returns to a priority level below 3, an interrupt is generated that causes the execution of the VMS context switching routine. When the context switching routine is entered, its priority is raised to level 7 to ensure that no process state changes occur while the context switch is executed.

The context switch routine first executes a save process context instruction, which stores the hardware context of the current process in its hardware PCB [32]. It then stores the address of the hardware PCB and the priority of the current process in general registers R1 and R2 so that the routine takes advantage of the convenience of VAX addressing modes. A "compute queue status" word indicates whether the queue of runnable processes at each priority level is empty. The context switch routine places the current process software PCB at the end of the queue of runnable processes at its priority level. It does this by updating the corresponding bit in the compute queue status word, calculating the address of the appropriate queue header, and linking the software PCB at the end of that queue. The context switch routine then executes a FIND FIRST SET instruction on the compute queue status field to obtain the highest priority level at which a nonempty queue is found. It computes the address of the header of that queue, and unlinks the first software PCB in the queue. If this PCB is the only entry in the queue, the corresponding bit in the compute queue status word is updated to reflect an empty queue.

The software PCB of each process contains a pointer to its hardware PCB. The context switch routine loads the pointer to the hardware PCB of the selected process into a process control block base register. The process control block base register points to the hardware PCB of the executing process. With this register loaded, the context switch routine executes a load process context instruction; this instruction loads the hardware context of the new process into the machine registers, and pushes the program counter and process status longword of the new process onto the interrupt stack. Finally, the context switch routine executes a return from interrupt instruction, which pops the program counter and process status longword off the stack and causes the new process to "continue" execution.

6.14 MEMORY MANAGEMENT AND ARCHITECTURAL SUPPORT

Multiprogramming enhances CPU and I/O utilization. With multiprogramming, multiple processes may be active simultaneously, which requires storing the address space of the multiple processes in memory. Multiprogramming systems require memory management programs to ensure that processes fill the address spaces in memory efficiently. The simplest way to accomplish this is to assign each process address space a separate contiguous partition of memory (Fig. 6.41). However, since the address spaces of different process vary in size, the free partitions obtained from terminated processes might be either too

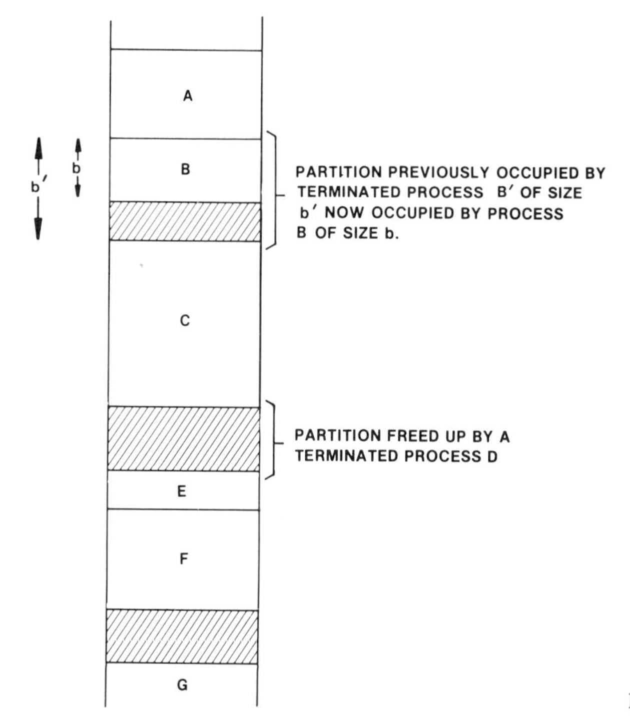

Figure 6.41 Memory fragmentation.

small or too large for the address spaces of newly created processes. A simple algorithm that can be employed is to find the first free partition that is larger than the newly created process address space. A table of free partitions sorted by location may be used for this algorithm. The memory management routine then searches through the table for the first partition that fits. For this reason, the algorithm is called the "first fit" algorithm. Alternatively, a table of free partitions may be sorted by size. When the system requests a free partition for a newly created process, it searches the table for the free partition that best fits the requested space. This is called the "best fit" algorithm.

The problem of *fragmentation* of address space results from allocating storage using either of these algorithms. When an address space is assigned to a free partition, it may not fit exactly. The unused remnant, a fragment, creates a new partition. Eventually, many fragments are created that have little use. Furthermore, they make the table of free partitions larger, which lengthens the execution of the search routine. The solution to the problem of fragmentation is memory compaction. Compacting memory consists of physically relocating the process address spaces (Fig. 6.42).

The capability to relocate an address space is therefore another requirement for memory management. Relocation, however, implies that all absolute addresses within a process be changed to reflect the relocation of the data pointed to by the addresses. To avoid the necessity of adjusting the absolute address of each process to be relocated by

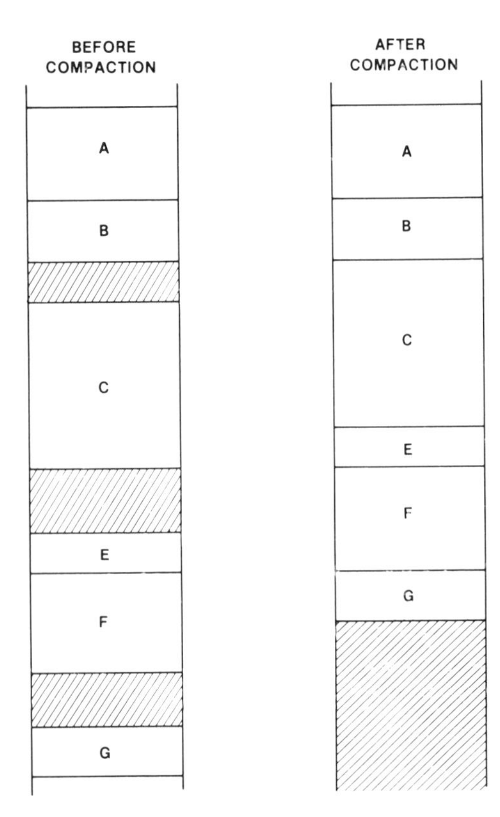

Figure 6.42 Memory compaction.

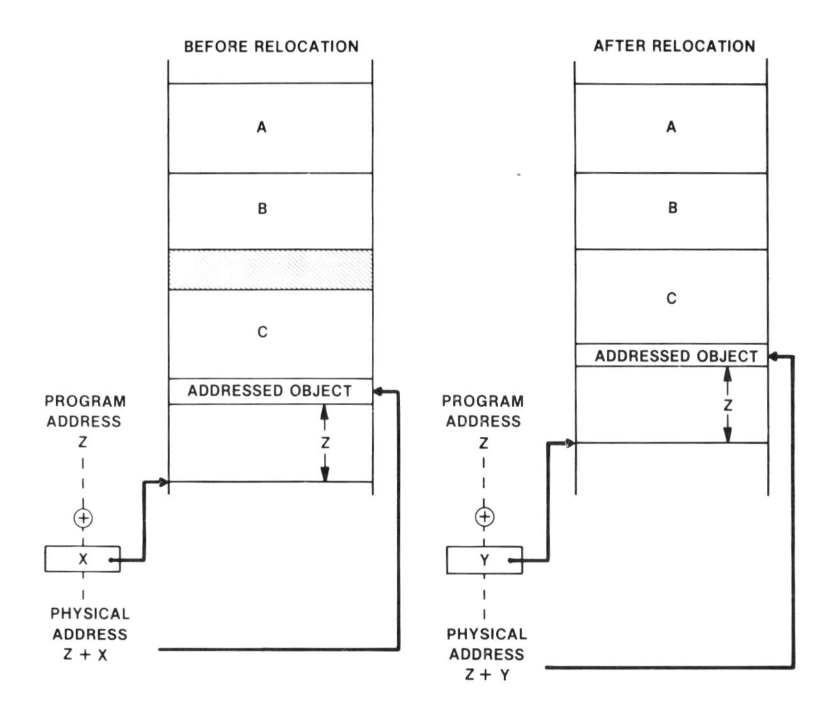

Figure 6.43 Relocation and use of base registers.

reloading the process, machines have base registers. The base registers relocate the address of each memory reference at run time. That is, if a process's address space starting address is relocated from location X to location Y, the base register contents merely have to be changed from X to Y. All memory reference addresses are hence added to the value Y instead of X (Fig. 6.43). The use of base registers, however, affects performance because every memory reference requires an addition operation.

Relocation is not only required for memory compaction but also for process swapping. A multiprogramming environment makes inefficient use of memory if the address spaces of all the active processes must reside in memory. Clearly, suspended processes waiting for events need not reside in memory while they are in the wait state. The address spaces of suspended processes may be swapped out onto disk until the processes are ready to run; then, their address spaces are swapped back. This allows many more processes to be active without being limited by the size of physical memory. When a process is swapped back into memory, however, its previous partition in memory may no longer be available. Its address space must therefore be stored in some other available free partition. This again requires the use of base registers to ensure that all memory reference addresses are relocated correctly.

Another concern of memory management is processes with very large address spaces. If a process has an address space larger than the configured memory, and if its whole address space must be in memory before it is executed, the process cannot be executed. Furthermore, swapping processes with very large address spaces is time consuming; yet, if they are not swapped, they consume large memory spaces while in the wait state. Solving this problem requires partitioning the address space of the large process so that not all the partitions reside in memory.

As discussed in Section 6.2, an address space of a process is its access environment. The access environment may be partitioned into subaccess environments called *segments*. Each segment contains logically related information that has its own set of protection and access rights. Memory management takes advantage of the concept of partitioning address spaces into segments. It views the segments as software resources that may be shared and protected in physical memory. Instead of swapping full processes, only the segments of a process address space are swapped in and out of memory.

Because each segment may be swapped individually, the operating system may not be able to assign all the segments of a process address space to contiguous areas of memory. The operating system may find that there is no space available contiguous to the other segments of the process unless the segments are physically moved, which is a time-consuming activity. To obviate the need for moving segments, segments are generally individually relocatable. This requires each segment to have its own base address. The hardware must provide a set of base registers, one for each segment. A memory reference address to a particular segment is added to the base address of that segment.

Segments, however, do not entirely solve the problem of fragmentation. In fact, because they are logical entities of variable sizes, they may aggravate fragmentation; after all, there are more segments than processes. But research into the way memory references are generated by processes in small time intervals reveals that the memory references of a process tend to be localized in the process's address space. This locality of references implies that only a small subset of the address space needs to reside in memory at any moment in time. This small subset is termed the *working set*. The working set may include small subsets of several segments of a process's address space. So system architects used the property locality of references to alleviate fragmentation. Their solution is the concept of *pages*.

A page is a physical partition of a fixed size. In many minicomputer systems, the size of a page is the same as that of a disk block, that is, 512 bytes. Locality of references implies that only the pages of a working set need to be resident in memory at any one time. Thus, as processes switch from the running state to the waiting state, and vice versa, the overhead of swapping in and out large quantities of unneeded information is avoided by swapping in only the needed pages. This is called demand paging.

The pages of a segment need not be contiguous. It is desirable for each page of a segment to be relocatable. Even though pages tend to be smaller than segments and there are more of them, they are not subject to fragmentation since each page is of a fixed size. The memory manager can view memory as a set of physical pages of a fixed size to be allocated. Pages eliminate the problem of fitting a variably sized entity into another variably sized entity. A variably sized segment partitioned into N fixed-size pages can fit into N physical free pages; only the last page of the segment is fragmented. The fragmentation overhead is thus reduced on the average to only one half-page per segment.

The fact that pages are of a fixed size allows them to start on page boundaries. That is, the base address of each page must be at a page boundary. For example, if the size of a page is 512 bytes, the least significant 9 bits of all base addresses must be zeros. For relocation, the operating system simply concatenates the offset (least significant 9 bits) within a page and the base address of a page to form the memory reference address. This eliminates the overhead of an address addition on each memory reference.

As memory management became more complex, a need developed for dynamic relocatability. The concept of *virtual addresses* met this need. A process views its access environment as a software resource, and accesses objects within this environment with its addresses. These addresses, however, have to be added or concatenated to a base address to obtain the addresses needed to access physical memory. The base address addition or concatenation is essentially a *mapping* of a virtual address (as viewed by a process) to a physical address (as viewed by the hardware logic). Since pages start only on page boundaries, a paged memory system allows a virtual page add ress to be mapped into a physical page address; the least significant bits remain unchanged. The hardware support for memory mapping is hence a set of registers or a set of translation registers storing the mapping of the virtual page address to the physical page address. As discussed in section 6.6, these registers are either loaded during a context switch as in the PDP 11/70, or loaded on demand when a memory reference finds that the translation i nformation is not in the translation registers as in the 3B20D. In the 3B20D, this is termed an address translation buffer (ATB) miss. An address translation buffer miss suspends the executing instruction while the translation information is obtained.

6.14.1 Architectural Support For ATB Miss Processing in 3B20D

The 3B20D is a microprogrammed machine; it executes each instruction by a sequence of microinstructions. ATB misses occur when the machine is in the middle of a microinstruction execution. The ATB miss signal generates a microinterru pt that suspends the microinstruction sequence and saves the suspended microinstruction address on a microstack. The microinstruction address of an ATB miss processing routine is then forced into the microinstruction address register. This microcode routine proceeds to save the address, data, and control information of the memory reference that caused the miss in internal memory of the CPU. Saving this information is necessary because the registers holding it are used by the ATB miss processing routine itself. The contents of the other internal registers used by the ATB miss processing routine are also saved.

The segment number of the virtual address that caused the ATB miss is then added to the register containing the base address of the segment table. This register is selected by 3 bits in the processor status word designating the current access environment (Fig. 6.44). The resultant address is the physical address of the segment table entry containing the base address of the page table for the requested segment. This base address is read into the CPU. It is then added with the page number of the virtual address that caused the miss. The resultant address is the physical address of the page table entry containing the physical address of the requested page. The physical address of the page and its protection bits are loaded into the ATB at the appropriate entry. The saved contents are then restored to their respective registers. The memory reference that caused the miss is restarted and the suspended microinstruction address is popped off the microstack. The microinstruction sequence can then proceed.

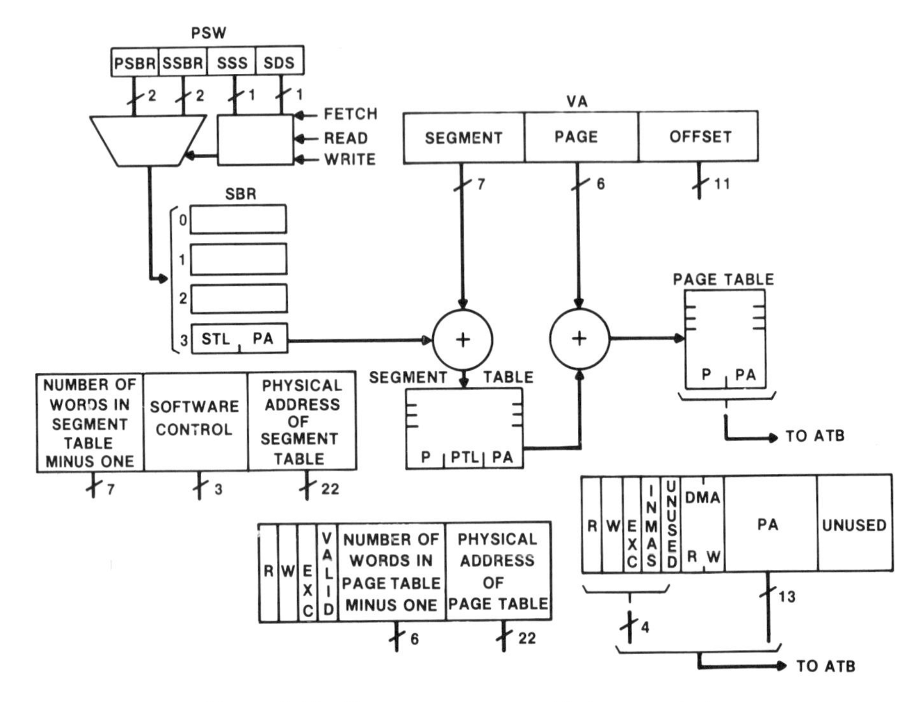

Figure 6.44 3B memory management (miss processing).

The architectural support identified for virtual addressing and memory management include a set of data structures (per process translation tables and a system memory page status table), hardware buffers to store the translation tables (address translation buffers), a bit indicating whether a translation entry is valid, a hardware/firmware fault-handling mechanism to handle ATB translation faults, and software algorithms for allocating and deallocating system memory pages to processes.

6.14.2 Architectural Support for Demand Paging

Demand paging is a memory management mechanism that takes advantage of a process's locality of references by transferring into memory at any point in time only the pages needed for the process execution. When the pages are no longer needed for execution, they are transferred out of memory, freeing up space for other needed pages. It is not possible for the memory manager to know which pages are needed or will no longer be needed by the executing process. Various algorithms are used by memory managers to predict which pages may no longer be needed and are candidates to be replaced. One indicator that uses the principle of locality of references of whether a page may or may not be needed is the length of time since the page has last been referenced. Also, a page that is to be replaced may or may not need to be written out to disk. A page in memory that has not been modified since it was last read from disk need not be written out to disk. The copy in memory and the copy in disk remain identical. By keeping track of the last time that a page has been referenced, memory managers lower the probability of *thrashing:* replacing and writing out pages onto disk and shortly after reading them back in. By keeping track of which pages have been modified, memory managers minimize the amount of disk traffic. Only pages that have been modified need to be written onto disks.

Architectural support for demand paging requires additional tables (per process secondary storage table), additional status bits (modify bit and reference bit to denote that a page has been modified and referenced) a hardware/firmware fault-handling mechanism to handle page faults (a page fault occurs when a page being referenced is currently not in memory), and software algorithms for choosing pages for replacement and for swapping pages out to secondary storage. The relationships among these tables and bits are shown in two examples in Figs. 6.45 and 6.47.

Figure 6.45 shows the IBM S/370 memory management tables [33]. The page map table shown is the per job translation table, the file map table is the per job secondary storage address table, the C (changed) bit is equivalent to the modify bit, and the I (interrupt) bit is equivalent to the inverse of the valid bit. The interrupt bit resides in the page map table (per job translation table). It serves to generate an interrupt during a translation when the table lookup accesses an invalid entry in the translation table. An invalid translation entry could imply a range violation, which occurs if the page tables are of fixed size. The size of the page map table is chosen to ensure that it has enough entries to contain all the page entries of a maximum-size segment. When a segment is not of the maximum size, its page table must have table entries that are not needed. These table entries must be marked invalid so that they will not be used. An attempt to use one of them causes a range violation (Fig. 6.46). An invalid translation entry could also imply a page fault in a paging system (that is, the page belonging to the segment is not in main memory but on disk). The fault- or interrupt-handling routine must determine whether the fault results from a page fault or a range violation. To resolve this ambiguity, some operating systems have a bit specifically indicating whether a page is present in memory. This is called the present bit. Systems using both the valid and the present bits eliminate the ambiguity resulting from using a single bit to indicate two semantically different situations. In the VAX/VMS system, page tables are of variable sizes corresponding to the size of segment. The VMS system keeps a length field for each segment. This method also eliminates ambiguity since a fault in a variable-size page table can only indicate a page fault.

The reference bit indicates that a page has been referenced and, because of the property of locality of reference, should not be replaced. It allows the replacement algorithm to approximate a least recently used algorithm. This algorithm selects for replacement the page that has not been referenced for the longest time. Reference bits are set on page references and cleared periodically. If a reference bit is already clear from a periodic check, the corresponding page has not been referenced since the last time the reference bit was cleared and the page is selected for replacement. Not all operating systems have reference bits, however. The designers of the VAX/VMS system were concerned with the overhead of scanning reference bits in order to clear them periodically [32,34]. Without reference bits, the VAX/VMS system implements a FIFO algorithm, which selects for replacement the page that has been brought into memory for the longest interval. Their architecture maintains a ''cache'' of pages in the form of a free list. The VAX/VMS mem-

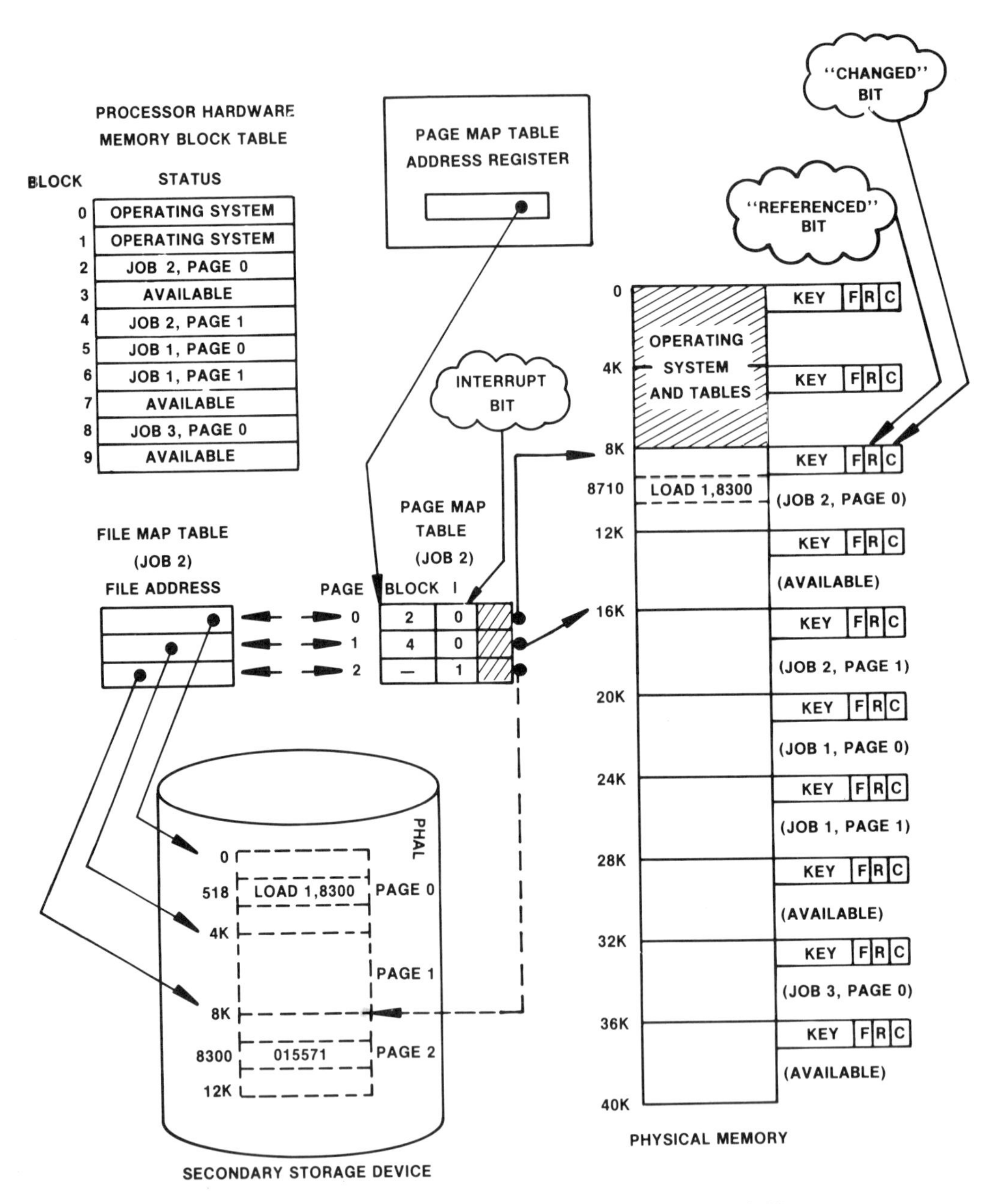

Figure 6.45 Memory management tables (from Ref. 33).

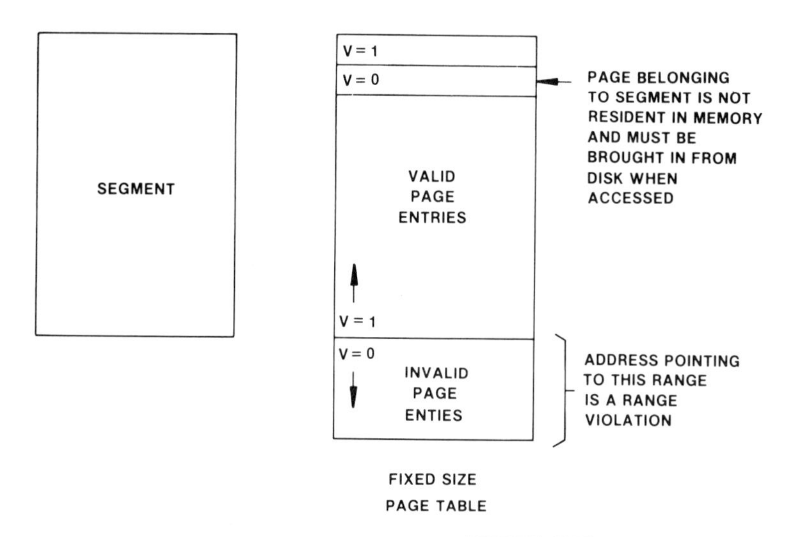

Figure 6.46 Semantics of valid ($\overline{\text{interrupt}}$, $\overline{\text{fault}}$) bit.

ory management tables to support demand paging are shown in Fig. 6.47. When a page is a candidate for replacement, selected by the FIFO algorithm, it is put on the free list (system free page list) or the modified list (system-modified page list), depending on whether the page has been modified during its residency in memory (Fig. 6.47). When a page fault occurs for a page that is on the free list or the modified list, the page may be removed from the list rather than brought in from secondary storage. the time required for a fault from

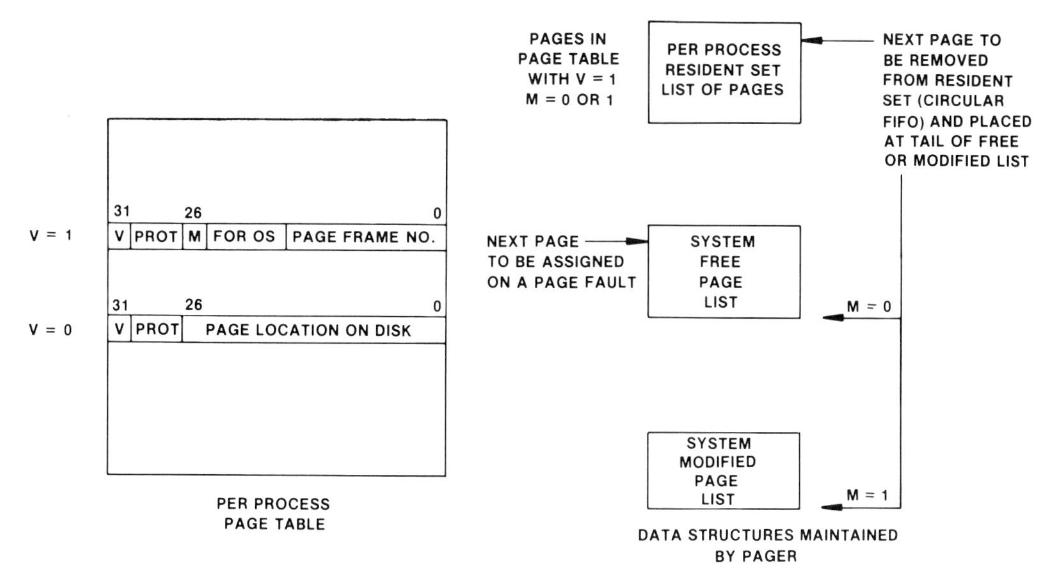

Figure 6.47 VAX/VMS memory management tables for paging.

either list is approximately 200 microseconds on a VAX 11/780 [34]. Only when a page is actually replaced (overwritten) is it removed from the free list, and a page fault requires the page to be brought in from secondary storage. Studies done by the VAX/VMS architects show that the free list can reduce the fault rate of the FI FO algorithm to a level arbitrarily close to that of the least recently used algorithm.

When pages are replaced, only those that have been written need to be swapped out onto secondary storage. Modify (or change) bits allow an operating system to keep track of all pages that have been modified (Fig. 6.47). For systems without a paging device (as a drum), the I/O traffic caused by swapping out modified pages can increase normal file system and swapping response time dramatically. To minimize this penalty, the memory management of the VAX/VMS system attempts to cluster pages together when performing an I/O operation to read or write secondary storage. It keeps a list containing all the pages that have been modified. When preparing to write to secondary storage, the paging software searches the modified list to find contiguous virtual pages. These contiguous pages are then written out onto contiguous disk blocks. If a fault occurs later for a page within the cluster of contiguous blocks, the cluster is read in with one I/O operation.

The presence of reference and modify bits in the address translation buffer implies that care must be taken to keep the bits coherent with their counterparts in the memory tables. For example, when the paging software clears the reference bits in the memory tables, their counterparts in the ATB must also be cleared. Careful synchronization is required in a multiprocessing system if one processor is running the paging software routine clearing the reference bits, while another is actively using its ATB dynamically setting reference bits. The ATBs of the processors must be kept coherent with each other as well as with the memory tables.

6.15 SUMMARY

Operating systems are managers of hardware and software resources. In the operating system, hardware and software resources are represented by data structures manipulated by a set of procedures. A set of procedures and a set of data structures may be encapsulated into a software module. The modularization of program space and data space may emphasize either a functional partitioning or a data partitioning resulting in functional abstraction and data abstraction systems. In either case, the partitioned modules must be protected from each other and be synchronized, and at the same time they must be able to communicate with each other.

Functional abstraction systems are based on modules called processes; data abstraction systems are based on modules called packages. Processes and packages are both represented by data structures, part of which are stored in memory and part of which are stored in hardware. The data structures represent the processes' contexts describing their statuses and the control information required by the operating system.

Processes are protected from each other by having their own access environments in a ring or layered structure. Each layer has a set of privileges of access. Packages also have their own access environments. They have well-defined interfaces to the access environments of other packages. Packages have only a minimal set of capabilities for communicating with other packages. The different protection structure philosophies have architectural implications on the implementation of the access environments in terms of their structures, their addressing, the checking of access rights and privileges, the switching of access environments, the entering and exiting from access environments, and the movement of data among environments. The architectural support for these concepts, however, is similar in the two types of systems although data abstraction systems require more elaborate hardware support for context switching and addressing than functional abstraction systems.

Operating system designers have developed many ideas about synchronizing modules. The synchronization concepts that have evolved to solve the mutual exclusion problem merely represent higher and higher levels of abstraction. In their implementation, they are extensions of simpler mechanisms. Once the architects identify the basic fundamental mechanisms and support them efficiently, all the higher levels' synchronization concepts are more efficiently implemented.

Of the synchronization concepts examined in this chapter, the UNIX, DMERT, and VMS operating systems use the event mechanism (and the mechanism on which it is built; read and clear, and interrupt inhibit). The event mechanism is not sufficient for synchronizing the operating systems of multiprocessor systems. Other synchronization mechanisms, such as monitors or semaphores, must be used.

This chapter also examines the interprocess communication concepts and their implementation in the UNIX, DMERT, and VMS operating systems. It shows that a variety of seemingly different mechanisms are used. On closer examination, however, it is seen that these mechanisms are merely higher levels of abstraction than those used for events, and that they depend on the same fundamental activities (switching environments and contexts, searching and manipulating protected control data structures, and handling interrupts); most of the mechanisms in an operating system depend on these very activities. Thus, architectural support for these activities achieves not only architectural support for interprocess synchronization and communication, but also for most of the mechanisms in operating systems.

Hardware resources such as processors and memory are represented by data structures describing their status and control information. Various operating system procedures control these resources by manipulating the data structures. For example, the scheduler and the pager control the use of the processor and memory with various status information in the tables and linked lists needed to implement algorithms for scheduling their optimal use. Special routines and hardware support are also required to swap context information when different processes are switched to use the resources. Memory management supports the creation and control of multiple access environments of different processes sharing the use of a single physical space. Memory management is also concerned with the efficient use of this physical space (memory). Demand paging is used to bring pages into memory only when needed. The presence of concurrent access environments results in the use of virtual addressing and hardware support to map virtual addresses into physical addresses.

REFERENCES

[1] P. Brinch Hansen, ''The Nucleus of a Multiprogramming System,'' *Commun. ACM,* Vol. 13, No. 4, April 1970.

[2] D. M. Ritchie and K. Thompson, ''The UNIX Time-Sharing System,'' *Bell Syst. Tech. J.,* Vol. 57, No. 6, July—August 1978.

[3] *VAX 11/780 Software Handbook,* Digital Equipment Corp., Maynard, Mass., 1978.

[4] *PDP 11/04/34/45/55/60 Processor Handbook,* Digital Equipment Corp., Maynard, Mass., 1978.

[5] *PDP 11/70 Processor Handbook,* Digital Equipment Corp., Maynard, Mass., 1975.

[6] *VAX 11/780 Architecture Handbook,* Digital Equipment Corp., Maynard, Mass., 1975.

[7] M. V. Wilkes and R. M. Needham, *The Cambridge CAP Computer and Its Operating System,* North-Holland, Amsterdam, 1979.

[8] M. E. Grzelakowski, J. H. Campbell, and M. R. Dubman, ''DMERT Operating System,'' *Bell Syst. Tech. J.,* Vol. 62, No. 1, January 1983, pp. 303–322.

[9] D. M. England, ''Architectural Features of System 250,'' in *Infotech State of the Art Rep. 14,* 1972, pp. 397–427.

[10] P. Tyner, *iAPX 432 General Data Processor Architecture Reference Manual,* Intel Publ. 171860-001, 1981.

[11] J. H. Saltzer and M. D. Schroeder, ''The Protection of Information in Computer Systems,'' *Proc. IEEE,* Vol. 63, No. 9, September 1975, pp. 1278–1308.

[12] T. A. Linden, ''Operating System Structures to Support Security and Reliable Software,'' *Comput. Surv.,* Vol. 8, No. 4, December 1976, pp. 409–445.

[13] E. I Organick, *The Multics System,* MIT Press, Cambridge, Mass., 1972.

[14] K. Thompson, ''UNIX Implementation,'' *Bell Syst. Tech. J.,* Vol. 57, No. 6, July—August 1978, pp. 1931–1946.

[15] D. Kaiser, *iAPX432 Object Primer,* Intel Corp., Santa Clara, Calif., August 1980.

[16] R. S. Fabry, ''Capability Based Addressing,'' *Commun. ACM,* Vol. 17, No. 7, July 1974.

[17] Unpublished information, Intel Corp., Santa Clara, Calif.

[18] H. C. Lauer and R. M. Needham, ''On the Duality of Operating Systems Structures,'' *Proc. 2nd Int. Symp. Oper. Syst.,* IRIA, October 1978; reprinted in *Oper. Syst. Rev.,* Vol. 13, No. 2, April 1979.

[19] *Reference Manual for the Ada Programming Language,* Proposed Standard Document, Department of Defense, Washington, D.C., July 1980.

[20] *IBM System/38 Technical Developments,* IBM Publ. ISBN 0-933 186-03-7, 1980.

[21] E. Cohen and D. Jefferson, ''Protection in the Hydra Operating System,'' *Proc. 5th ACM Symp. Oper. Syst. Princip.,* 1975.

[22] P. J. Denning, ''Fault Tolerant Operating Systems,'' *Comput. Surv.,* Vol. 6, No. 4, December 1976.

[23] S. Andler, ''Synchronization Primitives and the Verification of Concurrent Programs,'' in *Operating Systems: Theory and Practice,* D. Lanciaux, ed., North-Holland, Amsterdam, 1979.

[24] E. W. Dijkstra, ''Cooperating Sequential Processes,''in *Programming Languages,* F. Genuys, ed., Academic Press, New York, 1968.

[25] P. Brinch Hansen, *Operating System Principles,* Prentice-Hall, Englewood Cliffs, N.J., 1973.

[26] C. A. R. Hoare, ''Monitors: An Operating System Structuring Concept,'' *Commun. ACM,* Vol. 17, No. 10, October 1974, pp. 549–557.

[27] E. W. Dijkstra, ''Hierarchical Ordering of Sequential Processes,'' in *Operating System Tecniques,* C. A. R. Hoare and R. H. Perrot, eds., Academic Press, New York, 1972.

[28] V. D. Gligor, ''Architectural Implications of Abstract Data Type Implementation,'' *Tech. Rep. 659,* University of Maryland, May 1978.

[29] R. H. Campbell and A. N. Habermann, ''The Specifications of Process Synchronizatin by Path Expressions,'' in *Lecture Notes in Computer Science,* Vol. 16, Springer-Verlag, New York, 1974.

[30] F. Baskett, J. H. Howard, and J. T. Montague, ''Task Communication in DEMOS,'' *Proc. 6th ACM Symp. Oper. Syst. Princip.,* November 1977.

[31] H. Lycklama and D. L. Bayer, ''UNIX Time-Sharing System: The Mert Operating System,'' *Bell Syst. Tech. J.,* Vol. 57, No. 6, July—August 1978.

[32] H. M. Levy and R. H. Eckhouse, Jr., *Computer Programming and Architecture,* Digital Press, Bedford, Mass., 1980.

[33] S. E. Madnick and J. J. Donovan, *Operating Systems,* McGraw-Hill, New York, 1974.

[34] H. M. Levy and P. H. Lipman, ''Virtual Memory Management in the VAX/VMS Operating System,'' *IEEE Comput.,* March 1982.

PROBLEMS

6.1 Define process context, swappable context, nonswappable context, hardware context, and software context. Describe the relationships among these contexts. Select an operating system other than the ones described in this book and describe its process context, swappable context, nonswappable context, hardware context, and software context.

6.2 The hardware context is an important cost/performance design consideration. Why?

6.3 Compare the advantages and disadvantages of functional abstraction and data abstraction.

6.4 Describe the VAX/VMS protection structure. To which operating system protection structure described in this book is it most similar? Why?

6.5 Why do you think the DMERT operating system designers created the kernel process layer? What are the advantages and disadvantages of having kernel processes?

6.6 Describe the Cambridge/CAP protection structure. To which operating system protection structure described in this book is it most similar? Why?

6.7 What is the difference between a context switch and a process switch?

6.8 Design a program to implement a sender process that writes messages into a queue and a receiver process that reads messages from a queue. Describe the activities of these processes at run time. Describe a design with hardware, firmware, or software support that would optimally implement this program.

6.9 Most of the operating system code is concerned with the same activities: switching environments and contexts, searching and manipulating protected control data structures, and handling interrupts. Do the operating system scheduler, memory manager, and file manager use these samc activities? In what ways?

6.10 Architects must consider the level of abstraction at which the hardware/firmware/software interface should be raised. What trade-offs do architects need to make in designing the level of the interface? Give examples.

6.11 In processor management, what is the difference between software priority levels and hardware priority levels? How are they used?

6.12 Timers play an important role in processor management and other aspects of operating system. Study the features of a commercially available timer integrated-circuit chip. How do these features support processor management?

6.13 What are the trade-offs an architect must make in deciding on the page size? What are the most important considerations?

6.14 Compare the advantages and disadvantages of the PDP 11/70 implementation where the address translation registers are loaded during a context switch and of the 3B20D implementation where the address translation buffers are loaded on demand when a memory reference finds that the translation information is not in the translation buffers.

7

Operating Systems: Architectural Design

7.1 INTRODUCTION

The discussion in Chapter 6 provides an understanding of the fundamental concepts of operating systems and the architectural support for them. Once architects understand these fundamentals, they must consider various trade-offs and constraints in the design of an efficient operating-system-directed architecture. They must consider the compatibility and portability of the operating system in relation to the previous processors of the same family and they must weigh the alternatives of hardware, firmware, and software support. Furthermore, architects must make performance/flexibility trade-offs while recognizing that various operating systems may run on the machine they are designing. Their ultimate goal is creating a flexible design that minimizes the operating system run-time overhead, works efficiently, and remains compatible with machines of the same family. This chapter discusses these considerations, presents heuristics for the design of good operating-system-directed architectures, and reviews the approaches to operating system design taken by the architects of commercial systems.

7.2 COMPATIBILITY AND PORTABILITY

Chapter 4 discusses the concept of a family of machines. This concept was introduced by IBM in the 1960s to protect its large investment in the growing software base on IBM machines. A family of machines is a set of machines that are compatible with each other, and among which software is easily portable. For any new computer belonging to a family, a foremost consideration in its architectural design is protecting the cost of existing software developed for the machines in the family. The architect must ensure that application software and as much system software as possible are portable and compatible. As defined by IBM and other manufacturers, the main feature of a family of machines is a common instruction set. A common instruction set, however, is neither a sufficient nor a necessary condition for family compatibility. In designing a compatible architecture to support high-level languages and operating systems, other issues such as addressing, instruction privileges, time-dependent interaction, and I/O reads and writes need to be considered. These issues are discussed below.

A family of computers has two requirements:

1. Portability
2. Compatible environments

Portability means that software on existing machines can be transported to the new machines of the family. A compatible environment ensures that the same interfaces and functions are available to the software once it is transported to the new machine. The architects must consider portability and compatibility issues at each stage of software generation (Fig. 7.1). This chapter emphasizes the issues related to operating systems and hardware and firmware support.

Software is portable at three different levels:

- Source level
- Assembly level
- Object level

Each level requires different amounts of effort by the programmers to ensure portability. At all levels, the data formats must be the same in a family of machines. That is, the data representations and the effects of arithmetic and conversion operators must be consistent in the machine family. The data format of floating-point numbers with various precisions must be consistent. The addressing, ordering, and alignment of bytes, words, longwords, structures, and members of structures should be the same for all the machines in a family.

Source-level portability does not require the instruction sets of the two machines to be the same. Instead, a source code image is ported from one machine to the other; this image is recompiled, reassembled, relinked, and loaded in the new machine. Source-code-level portability requires each machine to have its own compiler, assembler, and loader.

Assembly-level portability does not require the machines to have their assembly instructions encoded the same, even though the machines are required to have the same assembly instruction set. To accomplish the porting of a program, the assembly-level image from the first machine is run through the second machine's assembler, linker, and loader before being executed.

Object-level portability allows disk packs to be physically moved from one machine to another. The code stored on the disk pack should be executable after it is loaded into memory. Object-level portability requires the encoding of the machine instructions, the address layout, and the data formats to be the same within the family.

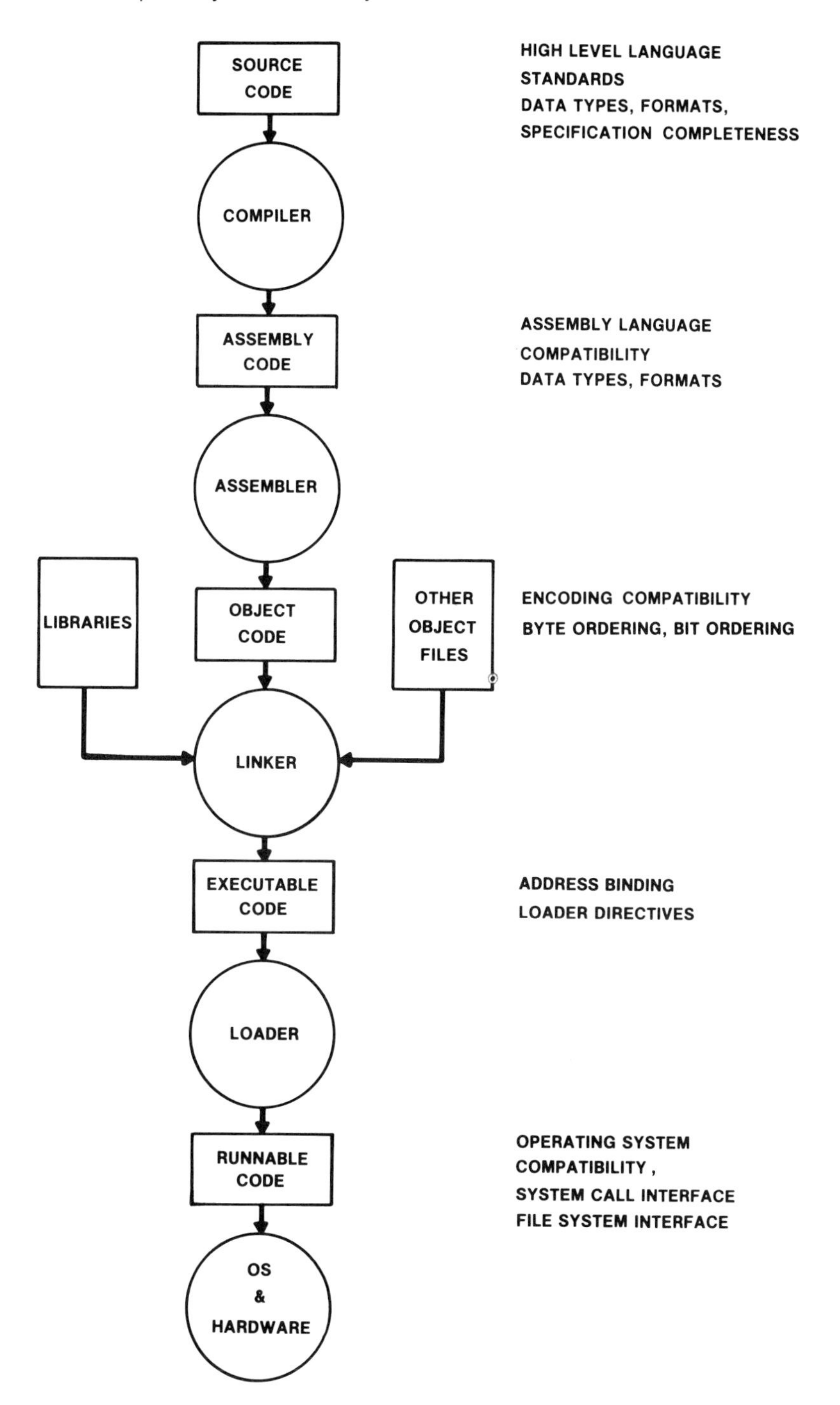

Figure 7.1 Compatibility and portability issues.

Porting a process requires moving a runnable image to a target machine and loading it (the lowest stage shown in Fig. 7.1). Hence the structure of a process image must be preserved. For example, in the DMERT operating system, a process image consists of a process control block segment, a data segment, a stack segment, and a program segment [1]. Once the image is loaded, it must interact with the operating system and hardware of the target machine during run time. For user processes to be portable, the system call interface must remain intact.* The system call interface may remain intact even if the operating system kernel is implemented differently as long as the same system calls are available to the user processes and the system calls provide the same services. Furthermore, even if the kernel is implemented differently to perform the same system call functions, many of the software data structures such as the process management tables and the memory management tables have to contain much of the same information (including status and flags) because they are specifically manipulated by the system calls. When making a system portable, the operating system designer should carefully consider the side effects of each system call.

Portability requires that the I/O drivers, the file manager, and the supervisor remain functionally the same. That is, the I/O or file system calls should invoke the same type of services from the I/O drivers and file managers regardless of how these modules are implemented. Furthermore, the file system's hierarchical structure should remain the same from the user's viewpoint, and the same type of I/O (raw, buffered, character, or block) should remain available to the user.

In addition, portability requires features of the operating system architecture to remain intact. These features include the priorities of the interrupt levels, the program interrupt request levels, and the process execution levels as they are seen by the ported user or system software.

In general, three aspects of an operating system should remain the same for a process that is ported to be compatible with its new operating system and hardware environment.

1. The interface between the operating system modules and the ported process should remain the same. That is, the same system calls should be provided and each system call should provide the same service without side effects.
2. The functional behavior of the modules in response to a stimulus at its interface from the ported process should be the same.
3. The structure of the modules and of the ported process should remain the same. The organization of the address space, the structure of the file system, and the structure of a file image should remain the same.

*The AT&T UNIX System V Interface Definition specifies such an interface. It specifies user process interfaces and the runtime behavior of operating system components seen by the user process. No specification is made of the implementation of the operating system components. User processes can be ported among machines that provide the System V Interface.

Other architectural issues affecting the porting of operating systems include the following:

- Addressing
- Time-dependent process interaction
- I/O reads and writes
- Protection domains

Ensuring that addressing is consistent among machines means defining the virtual address layout and address space organization the same. The machines must have similar segment sharing capabilities and must bind parts of a process to specific virtual addresses consistently. The interaction among time-dependent processes refers to timing relationships between various processes and parts of the systems such as I/O devices. The I/O devices are not guaranteed to be maintained on different members of a processor family. When faster or slower devices are introduced, a timing relationship may be violated. Portable code should not depend on a particular timing relationship to be functional. Finally, the architect should consider the way the family of machines performs I/O reads and writes. The architect must choose between programmed I/O (specific commands to read and write I/O registers) and memory mapped I/O (the same instructions to read and write memory are used to read and write I/O registers; the I/O registers are mapped in the address space). The choice of I/O type affects I/O drivers and their access to I/O registers.

Much of the memory management hardware should be retained in each family member. The hardware should support the same protection structures, access modes, and number of segments per mode. To ensure that the protection and the I/O system structure are the same, the interrupt structure and the programmed interrupt levels should be retained. Hardware and firmware features to enhance the performance of the operating system kernel should not adversely affect portability. With care, the kernel may be reimplemented. The hardware/software interface may be raised within the kernel as long as it provides the same functions without side effects.

In addition to portability, compatibility requires the same system development environment or a superset of the environment available on existing machines of the same family. For example, if a customer has become dependent on certain tools and utilities in the previous environment, the tools and utilities should remain available in subsequent environments. The compatibility requirements include providing the same set or a superset of (1) high-level languages, (2) support functions and high-level-language libraries, (3) utility systems and debuggers, (4) system commands, (5) network services, (6) data base management services, and (7) software generation tools, including compilers, assemblers, linkers, loaders, symbol table dumps, and object and source listers.

7.3 EFFICIENCY

Once the portability and compatibility constraints have been established, the architects strive to support the operating systems as efficiently as possible. Statistics show that a processor spends about 40 percent of its time in the operating system kernel [2,3]. To reduce this large percentage of time and enhance the performance of operating systems, any one or a combination of the following methods may be employed:

- Modifying the architecture of the operating system
- Modifying the algorithms (policies) and tuning the efficiency of the modules
- Providing architectural, hardware, and firmware support
- Eliminating operating system overhead

Because of portability and compatibility issues, modifying the architecture of the operating system is usually not feasible. The other methods are discussed in the next sections.

7.3.1 Modifying Module Algorithms and Tuning

The algorithms of operating system modules may be selectively modified and tuned without an adverse effect on compatibility. Tuning the operating system in many instances means merely rewriting the time-critical sections in assembly code, moving function calls into in-line code, and implementing primitives as macros. Modifying the algorithms of modules and tuning are the methods used by W. Joy to enhance significantly the performance of the Berkeley UNIX operating system [4]. For example, he reported reducing the trap handling time two and one-half times, improving context switching performance by a factor of 7, doubling the performance of interprocess communications, and improving the performance of the paging system by one and one-half to three times. It is thus important that areas for modifying algorithms and tuning be explored thoroughly first and implemented before committing architectural, hardware, and firmware support.

7.3.2 Architectural, Hardware, and Firmware Support

To enhance operating system performance by architectural, hardware, and firmware support, the architect must first identify the activities that are candidates for such support. These activities should have the following properties:

1. They should not compromise compatibility.
2. They should be used by most if not all operating systems.
3. They should be used frequently by the operating systems.
4. They should be real-time intensive and expensive activities.

The activities within the kernel are candidates for architectural support because they do not compromise compatibility. Chapter 6 shows that the activities used by all operating systems are those that support intermodule protection, intermodule communication, and synchronization. The most frequently used activities are switching environments and contexts, queue manipulations and searches, manipulations of linked lists, stack manipulations, address developments, and checks of control bits. This chapter examines real-time intensive and expensive operating system activities that are likely candidates for hardware and firmware support. The DMERT operating system is used as an example because of the extensive measurements done on its performance. From these measurements, an insight into the relative time performance of various operating system functions has been obtained, making the time-consuming operating system functions identifiable.

The system calls of the DMERT operating system that require a large amount of time for execution are *growseg, wakeup, pwakeup, fltclass, termclass, evclass, psignal, getargblk,* and *putargblk*. In addition, the supervisor and user message system calls and the switching of processes (from kernel process to supervisor process and from supervisor process to supervisor process) all require a measurable amount of time for execution. The activities of these system calls are examined in Table 7.1. These expensive functions consume real time by searching through tables, moving bytes, and switching processes. Possible enhancements for these activities include linked list manipulation support, block move and byte count support, and process switching support.

TABLE 7.1 DMERT OPERATING SYSTEM CALLS

System call	Description
growseg	Increase or decrease the size of a segment (requires the service of memory management to search for free swap space or requires a switch to the scheduler process)
wakeup	Wake up all processes sleeping on a pattern (requires searching through the Dispatcher Control Table for matching pattern)
pwakeup	Wake up processes sleeping on bit pattern (same as in wakeup)
fltclass	Fault all processes belonging to a specified class (requires searching through Dispatcher Control Table for all processes belonging to a class)
termclass	Terminate all processes belonging to a given class (same as in fltclass)
evclass	Send an event to a process class (same as in fltclass)
psignal	Sends an event to all pocesses having the same control channel (requires searching through Dispatcher Control Table for processes having the designated control channel)
getargblk	Get argument block from supervisor address space into kernel process address space (requires moving bytes, approximately 4 microseconds per byte, the time required increases almost proportionately with the number of bytes moved)
putargblk	Put argument block from kernel process address space to supervisor address space (same as in getargblk)
All supervisor and user message system calls	(Requires buffer allocation, message copy, queuing message, send event system call, process switches, dequeuing message)
Kernel process to supervisor process switch	(Requires saving the state of the last interrupted supervisor process in that process's process control block, copying the state of the supervisor process to be dispatched to next on to the interrupt stack)
Supervisor process to supervisor process switch	(As in the kernel process to supervisor switch described above, in addition, requires saving of the state of the supervisor process which is being switched from in its process control block)

7.3.2.1 Hardware enhancements. A primary function of an operating system is managing hardware resources in such a way as to achieve the best possible utilization of the resources. Since physical equipment is limited, the operating system sets up virtual resources that compete for the use of the physical resources. However, only one virtual resource assumes full control of the real resource at at time. To enhance the ability of the operating system to carry out its functions, hardware and firmware may be used. Studies have shown that hardware [3] and firmware [2,5,6] can facilitate the administration and control of jobs throughout the system. The following sections discuss these possible enhancements.

Queue Administration. If the system has insufficient resources to satisfy all its users, it needs a queuing mechanism to store the requests temporarily. As soon as a resource is free, the top request on the waiting queue is dispatched to assume control of the newly available resource. There are various queues throughout the system. Figure 7.2(a) shows the general arrangement of the processor manager involving the hold, ready, and wait queues. The user-submitted jobs arrive and are temporarily stored on disk. The job manager takes the selected job and places it in the hold queue according to some preestablished policy. As soon as resources are available and space is available in the ready queue, the top of the hold queue moves into the ready queue. This in effect creates the process and assigns a virtual processor to the job [Fig. 7.2(b)]. The virtual processor is dedicated until the job is completed. After the process moves into the ready queue, the

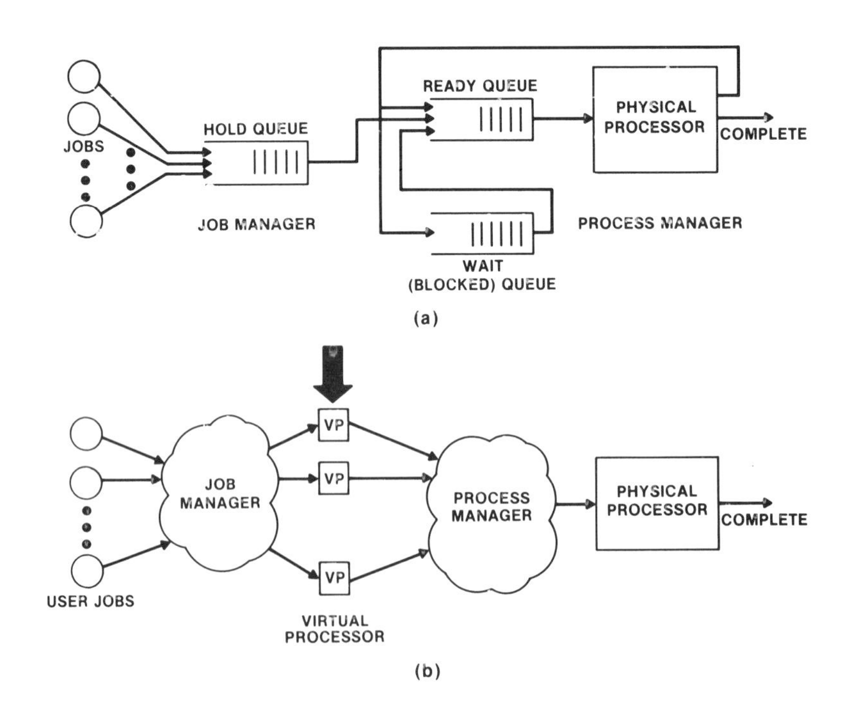

Figure 7.2 Process management structure.

process manager administers and schedules the actual time sharing of the real processor. The process may be in one of three possible states. A running process that has possession of the real processor runs until either the assigned time slice is used up or it cannot proceed any further. In the former case, the process is reinserted into the ready queue and waits for its next time slice. In the latter case, the process is put into the wait queue since it is blocked and must wait until the device becomes idle. As indicated in Fig. 7.2(a), the unblocked process is returned to the ready queue to wait its turn for the use of the processor.

After two years of examining various ways of improving the performance of an operating system, C. C. Foster concludes that the best operating systems supply a good mechanism for holding the queues of processes waiting for resources and provide enough resources that few processes wait on queues [3]. The hardware support for queue implementation is provided by devices called *content addressable memories* (CAMs) [7]. Because they are content addressable, CAMs enable a very efficient search of the memory location containing a desired memory content. The use of CAMs eliminates the conventional searching and sorting routines, a common and expensive part of operating systems. Implementing queues with CAMs allows the operating system to post a request for service in one machine cycle and to return the highest-priority request for servicing in another cycle.

There are three approaches to implementing conventional software queues. The system may keep the ready queue sorted by priority. Or, it may search the ready queue for the highest-priority process each time the operating system wishes to dispatch a process. Third, it may have a separate queue for each priority. When an I/O device becomes idle, the operating system searches the wait (blocked) queue for the highest-priority process waiting for the device and transfers the process to the ready queue, where it competes with all other processes for the CPU.

The use of CAMs simplifies queue implementation. Both the ready and the wait queues may be combined and reside on the same CAM, which eliminates the need to move entries between the queues. When a process is ready for execution, a request is inserted into the CAM. The request contains the job number, process number, priority, and the status bit; the status bit is set to zero or one depending on whether the process is known to be in the ready state (ready to run) or in the wait state (blocked). When the operating system is ready to dispatch a new process to be run, the entire CAM is examined simultaneously (one machine cycle). The request of the ready process having the highest priority level in the CAM is selected, dispatched, and removed from the CAM. If this process involves using an I/O device such as a line printer, the updating of the device status to the busy state includes accessing the CAM and setting all the processes requesting the use of the busy device to the wait state. As long as the device is busy, none of the processes put in the wait state may be dispatched. When the device is released and becomes idle, the inverse operation changes the blocked processes to the ready state and again they may be dispatched.

Using CAMs makes queue manipulations efficient. This substantially reduces the software overhead because queue manipulations are time-critical and one of the more frequently performed operations in an operating system.

Context Switching. The sharing of the processor is achieved by placing several processes together in main storage and providing a mechanism for switching the control of the processor from one process to another. A set of processor registers defines the state of the active process. *Context switching,* the swapping of the contents of these registers for another register image, is done primarily in three situations. It is invoked when an active process calls operating system functions and when an active process is unable to proceed further without requesting a service provided by the control program such as I/O. Context switching also occurs when a process requires cooperation from another process. Multiprogramming environments require frequent context switchings; hence, it is important that the operations of saving one process context and loading another be done rapidly. In modern computers such as the VAX 11/780, the instruction set includes instructions to save and load the hardware context [8]. These two instructions reduce the overhead of the operating system in both system calls and in the dispatching of other processes.

In addition to providing specialized instructions to enhance context switching, some machines provide dedicated hardware to maintain their contexts. Two specific areas in which additional hardware has been provided are the memory management unit and the hardware register set. Chapter 6 discusses the hardware support for memory management. It is possible for a system to supply multiple copies of hardware register sets to facilitate context switching. For example, there are three sets of 16 registers in the UNIVAC 1100 series: A, X, and R. The A registers are used for arithmetic, the X registers for indexing, and the R registers for special functions. To reduce the number of save and restore operations in these registers, the UNIVAC systems provide another three sets of A, X, and R registers for the operating system [9]. The AT&T Bell Laboratories BELLMAC 8 employs an interesting variation of multiple copies of register sets. Its general register set is placed in main memory and is realized as a 16-word area of memory that is considered work space. This area is defined by a work space pointer that is not fixed; that is, the pointer changes dynamically under program control. The activities of context saving and of restoring the general register set involves only the work space pointer instead of the registers themselves. This approach realizes a savings in terms of the number of words transferred in and out of main memory. However, it pays the cost of accessing ''registers'' from memory during program execution between context switches. This approach is aimed at lowering the cost of implementation rather than at increasing the efficiency of execution.

Interrupt Facilities. Context switching is also necessary when interrupts occur. The time interval between the request for the interrupt and the start of the interrupt handling software routines is called the *latency time*. The latency time is basically the time required to change the context of the processor, to determine the source of the interrupt, and to branch into the selected interrupt handling routine. Most systems have a stack facility to help save and restore the hardware context. The operating characteristic of a last-in, first-out stack mechanism provides a direct and straightforward manner for handling priority interrupts: higher-priority interrupts are permitted to interrupt or preempt lower-priority ones. The nesting of interrupts is automatically serviced in the proper order as the interrupts unwind from higher to lower priority. The physical implementation of a stack may take one of three forms [10]:

1. Software in main memory.
2. Dedicated hardware registers.
3. A combination of dedicated hardware registers and software in main memory to handle overflows. Hardware registers are extended into main memory when the hardware stack is exceeded.

By providing a hardware stack facility, the saving and restoring of the processor context may be done quickly. The problem of exceeding the number of hardware registers allocated to form the stack is removed if the hardware stack is allowed to expand into the main memory.

It is possible to achieve a very fast response time for individual priority interrupt requests by associating a separate hardware register set with each interrupt level. Using this technique, there is no need to save the registers on the stack each time a program is interrupted by a higher-priority request. The interrupt hardware simply switches from the register set associated with the interrupted program to the register set associated with the new priority level. The IBM System/7 uses this technique with four priority levels [11]. Each level has a complete set of internal registers. There may be as many as 16 sublevels of priority assigned to each priority level. Current processing is interrupted only by requests on a higher priority level.

In addition to saving its state, the processor must enter the appropriate interrupt-handling routine. For I/O interrupts, the procedure of identifying the interrupting device may be done either by software or hardware polling techniques. The software polling, of course, is a very time-consuming method of having a software routine interrogate each device sequentially from the top of the sequence down to the interrupting device. In hardware polling, the processor and its external devices are physically interconnected so the CPU can interrogate all devices simultaneously to obtain the address of the interrupting unit. The address returned by this hardware handshaking procedure may be used as an index or a vector that is added to the contents of a preassigned processor hardware register. The processor register acts as a base address, and the index points to a full memory word that is treated as an indirect address by the interrupt hardware. Each interrupting device has a unique index into an interrupt vector table. The address found at the table location pointed to by the index is the location of the appropriate device service routine. The use of hardware polling is very effective for determining the highest-priority interrupt that is pending and for generating the program address that handles the selected interrupt.

An architectural approach has been proposed to treat all types of exceptional conditions in the same manner by allowing a single central service routine to be dispatched on any interrupt, trap, or fault [12]. The reason for the interrupt, including the type of interrupt and the pipeline stage in which the interrupt occurred, is made part of the machine state. The reason for the interrupt also contains information supplied by the instructions and external devices that caused the interrupt. This information is termed the *surprise code*; it is read by the single central service routine in handling an interrupt.

Memory Management Hardware. Virtual memory systems typically store the complete virtual-to-physical address translation tables in main memory. The CPU requires a significant amount of time to perform the repetitive tasks of dynamic address translation using the main memory tables. This translation time may be reduced substantially by storing the physical address translations most likely to be used in a high-speed cache called an *address translation buffer* (ATB) which is also commonly referred to as a translation look-aside buffer. The buffer is used when only one process is running at a time. If the buffer contains translation entries for just one process, it must be reset or ''flushed'' to take on new translation data when the processor switches to a new process. A separate set of translation buffers dedicated to the operating system reduces the amount of flushing and reloading when the system switches between a user process and a system process. In the VAX 11/780, the cache containing 128 virtual-to-physical page address translation entries are divided into two equal sections: 64 system space page translation entries, and 64 user process space page translation entries [8].

Memory management chips are available to extend the capabilities and improve the performance of microcomputers. The Motorola memory management chip MC6829 has four sets of preloaded mapping entries with 32 registers per set [12]. Applications that require fast context switching between processes usually dedicate one set of registers to the operating system and the other three to separate processes. Each chip can handle four unique processes, each of which may use up to 64K bytes of memory. The memory is usually defined in terms of 2K-byte pages. Up to eight MC6829s may be connected so the system can accommodate up to 32 simultaneous processes.

Another sophisticated memory management chip is the National Semiconductor NS16082 [13]. The NS16082 is a 16-bit microprocessor; it is referred to as the memory management unit (MMU) when combined with the NS16032 CPU chip to create a virtual memory machine. The MMU includes a translation buffer that contains the addresses of the last 32 virtual pages that were referenced. These two chips support demand paging by means of an aborting function. To understand the importance of this feature, consider the normal operation of the system. The MMU examines all memory accesses. If the requested address does not reside in main memory, the MMU sends an abort signal to the CPU to stop the further execution of the instruction and return the registers changed by the instruction to their original states. The CPU then initiates the search of the needed page from secondary memory and copies it into main memory, where processing proceeds. When the addressed page is in main memory, the virtual address is translated to a physical address. These operations occur at the system level; they are transparent to the users. They ensure that aborted instructions are reexecuted properly with the correct data, even if the data needs to be transferred from secondary storage to main memory.

Real-Time Clock. Maintaining and updating a timing list is another operating system function that can be quite time consuming when it is done entirely by software. Many processes need to be activated periodically or after a certain amount of time elapses. In the meantime, they must sleep quietly in the background using as few resources as possible. Each tick of a real-time clock generates an interrupt. The timers are updated to reflect the passing of another unit of time; the entire timer list is then examined to see if any job needs to be awakened. If the list is not kept in the proper order, it must be searched. Content addressable memories (CAMs) are excellent means of storing the clock wakeup list. The use of a CAM simplifies the ordering or searching problem. A typical timing function available in a system requests to be awakened after N time units have elapsed M number of times. The M events could be once, a predetermined number, or every time. Since the clock interrupts occur very frequently, hardware support for them has relatively large payoffs in system efficiency.

An alternative to content addressable memories for implementing the timing list is the use of a microcomputer such as the Intel 8051. The on-chip program and data memory may be used fully to implement a set of timers and the associated control sequences for administering them. The microcomputer performs the operations of inserting new timers into the list, sorting the list into an ordered set, updating the timing count, signaling to the processor when a timeout occurs, and deleting the timer from the list when it is no longer needed. Allocating special hardware such as a microcomputer to perform these repetitive and time-consuming tasks reduces the load on the main processor and lessens the system overhead of process activation and deactivation.

In the microprocessor area, timing functions are needed in many applications. Special programmable interval timer chips such as the Intel 8253 are available to relieve the CPU of timing internal and external events. These chips are capable of direct interfacing with almost any microprocessor, including the Intel 8080, Motorola 6800, Zilog Z80, PACE, SC/MP, Rockwell 6502, and Intel 8085 [14].

Communication and Scheduling. Hardware support for communication at a low level has also been suggested [15–17]. A proposed approach incorporates a microprocessor into multiprocessor architectures to manage all the internal and external communications among the processes. This microprocessor is called a signaling and scheduling processor (SSP) [18]. It consists of a receiver and a sender hardware controller, and their respective hardware input and wait queues. These hardware queues support all the signaling and scheduling of the system.

7.3.2.2 Firmware enhancements. Microprogramming is another technique used to enhance operating system functions [19]. The benefits derived by casting some of the primitives in firmware include the following:

1. Improved performance
2. Decreased program development cost
3. Security and program correctness

The primitives that are candidates for microprogram implementation are those used fre-

TABLE 7.2 EVALUATION OF HEART PRIMITIVES

Object	Operation	Number of Micro instructions	Execution Time (μsec) Firmware	Software	Firmware: Software
	Load PSW	14	16.2	39.3	1:2.4
	Store PSW	12	12.8	39.3	1:3.1
	VM Scheduler	66	34.2	174.2	1:5.1
	Enter VM Queue	17	15.0	71.4	1:4.8
	Remove VM Queue	25	11.8	44.1	1:3.7
PD	Kcreate	24	8.0	31.1	1:3.9
	Kdelete	13	22.8	85.5	1:3.8
	Kmodify	13	24.0	83.6	1:3.5
	Krefer	16	25.4	89.1	1:3.5
	Find	10	20.0	67.8	1:3.4
	Remove	29	44.0	167.7	1:3.8
VMD	Kcreate	16	5.0	26.5	1:5.3
	Kdelete	25	13.0	66.5	1:5.1
	Kmodify	18	13.6	63.8	1:4.7
	Krefer	14	11.4	55.5	1:4.9
	Find	11	9.0	42.6	1:4.7
CLIST	Kcreate	21			
	(PDP = nil)		32.4	140.8	1:4.3
	(PDP ≠ nil)		34.4	146.9	1:4.3
	Kdelete	13	31.4	138.1	1:4.4
	Kmodify	13	31.4	138.1	1:4.4
	Krefer	18	32.6	131.4	1:4.3
	Find	28	8.8	42.3	1:5.1
	Check Capability	45			
	Kernel Object (T)		25.4	99.0	1:3.9
	(F)		25.6	101.1	1:3.9
	Capability (T)		33.6	149.8	1:4.5
	(F)		33.8	151.9	1:4.5
KLIST	Kcreate	11	7.0	33.4	1:4.8
	Kdelete	14	10.4	58.5	1:5.6
	Kenter PD	36	46.8	175.1	1:3.7
	Kenter SNC	41	52.2	198.3	1:3.8
	Krelease PD	17	13.8	59.4	1:4.3
	Krelease SNC	16	13.0	58.5	1:4.5
	Find	10	6.2	38.3	1:6.2
	Simple Scheduler	44	70.6	198.4	1:5.7
	SP	35	11.4	38.6	1:3.4
	SV	47	8.2	26.2	1:3.2

SEGMENT	Create	21	76.4	330.2	1:4.3
	Delete	23	75.0	320.5	1:4.2
	Kill	11	108.6	488.7	1:4.5
	Export	15	191.6	831.1	1:4.3
	Transfer	46	182.0	797.0	1:4.4
	Find	16	15.6	75.2	1:4.8
SEMAPHORE	Create	20	74.4	323.2	1:4.3
	Delete	22	74.4	319.4	1:4.3
	Kill	9	107.6	484.3	1:4.5
	Export	6	150.0	659.4	1:4.4
	Transfer	39	179.8	794.8	1:4.4
ERP	Create	22	50.4	221.1	1:4.4
	Delete	15	50.8	233.8	1:4.6
	Kill	10	64.8	305.9	1:4.7
	Export	11	66.0	311.0	1:4.7
	Transfer	18	104.0	473.3	1:4.6
	Find	11	14.6	67.0	1:4.6
PROCESS	Create	37	66.6	315.3	1:4.7
	Delete	48	88.6	463.7	1:5.2
	Start	14	70.4	261.2	1:3.7
	Block	26	26.8	91.8	1:3.4
	Wake Up	16	71.6	263.1	1:3.7
VM	Create	27	56.8	259.1	1:4.6
	Delete	20	59.6	278.4	1:4.7
	Start	15	34.0	134.3	1:3.9
	Stop	24	26.4	111.1	1:4.4
PRIMITIVE	Signal	80	48.0	158.4	1:3.3
	Await	132	51.6	196.1	1:3.8
	Advance	23	19.8	93.8	1:4.7
	Consume	101	54.0	189.0	1:3.5
	Observe	34	21.6	88.6	1:4.1
	Advance & Consume	13	19.2	92.2	1:4.8
	Send	76	27.3	120.1	1:4.4
	Receive	68	25.5	145.4	1:5.7
	Force Send	43	23.4	126.5	1:5.4
	Send Answer	43	17.4	106.2	1:6.0
	Force Receive	43	23.1	120.0	1:5.2
	Receive Answer	43	22.5	139.5	1:6.2
	P	18	4.2	26.6	1:6.3
	V	17	3.8	21.3	1:5.6
	Enter Queue	17	10.4	34.4	1:3.3
	Release Queue	10	3.4	13.9	1:4.1

Source: Reference 21.

quently throughout the operating system, are unlikely to change with time, and would suffer from the slower execution rate of software.

A recent study lists fourteen functions that may be implemented as primitives through microprogramming [2]. Some of the functions include queue manipulation, context switching, program synchronization, memory management control, process communication, reconfiguration, protection and checking, and scheduling. As mentioned in earlier sections, some of these functions are also candidates for hardware implementation. In some cases, a combination of hardware and firmware is appropriate. A subsequent paper by the authors of this study shows how to take advantage of the efficiencies gained from microprogramming operating system primitives [5]. They discuss how to select the primitives most appropriate for implementation and how to analyze the trade-offs between software, firmware, and hardware.

When structuring the operating system into hierarchical levels, the architect should recognize the one-to-one correspondence between the logical hierarchy of processes, monitors and resources, and the physical hierarchy of software, firmware, and hardware [20]. This correspondence is shown as follows:

Logical	Physical
Processes	Software
Monitors	Filmware
Resources	Hardware

Logically, monitors reside at a lower level than processes because they govern the accesses of resources by processes. Because processes are implemented in software, firmware is an ideal choice for implementing monitors. The benefits obtained are not only performance improvements, but protection from software routines (since software cannot access firmware) and assurance of mutual exclusion (since control of mutual exclusion is made invisible to processes). Each monitor is responsible for the access control, deadlock prevention, scheduling, timeout, and synchronization for the use of its resource. All these functions are thus automatically subsumed into firmware, which results in increased performance and protection.

An experiment was conducted to confirm the merits of implementing an operating system kernel in firmware. The authors of the experiment implemented an operating system kernel, called HEART, in microcode on a user-microprogrammable minicomputer, the PFU-1500 [21]. They implemented HEART both in firmware and in software, measured the performance of each, and compared the results. They found that the execution speed improvement of the firmware implementation ranged from three to six times that of the software implementation (Table 7.2). They also found that HEART could be implemented with 2276 microinstructions—a relatively small number—and could still provide an efficient and protected mechanism for process multiplexing and scheduling, domain management, segment management and address space mapping, and process cooperation. The set of primitives is shown in Table 7.2.

7.3.3 Eliminating Operating System Overhead

Finally, the operating system performance may be enhanced by eliminating its overhead. The 3B20D system overhead has been classified into five types of overhead [22]:

1. Functional
2. Sanity
3. Preventive maintenance
4. Fault maintenance
5. Service

The total system overhead was measured to be 6 percent of the total CPU usage. It includes such activities as servicing timer interrupts, running the system integrity monitor, running audits and diagnostics, running maintenance programs, serving console interfaces, and providing plant measurements. Except for nondeferrable maintenance, all these activities are unrelated and extraneous to the user process stream. In other words, these activities represent separate streams running on the system behalf or on the behalf of users other than the currently executing user process. They may therefore run concurrently with the executing stream; this concurrency can be achieved by running the overhead processes on a separate processor. In the example of the 3B20D, system performance would be enhanced at least 6 percent. The improvement would be at least 6 percent because running the processes in a separate processor eliminates not only the time the processes consume, but the time needed to switch the processor to and from them. Furthermore, if the overhead processes do not run in the same processor as the user processes, the cache is not polluted with their data, which enhances the overall performance of the cache.

7.4 PERFORMANCE AND FLEXIBILITY TRADE-OFFS

As improvements in technology open up the possibility of implementing more and more system functions in firmware and hardware, the architect is faced with the question of where the hardware/software interface should be. Putting higher-level functions in firmware and hardware makes the implementation of these functions more efficient but less flexible. Three strategies can help alleviate this dilemma:

1. Using firmware rather than hardware
2. Adopting a policy/mechanism separation principle
3. Using modular, exchangeable hardware units and hardware units with option straps

These three strategies are discussed below.

7.4.1 Firmware

The firmware implementation of system functions is an obvious compromise between the inflexibility of hardware and the inefficiency of software. Firmware has been used extensively for implementing low-level system functions since it was introduced in the early

1970s. Earlier in this chapter, the functions that are candidates for firmware implementation are listed. Later, the AT&T WE32000, the Intel iAPX/432, and the IBM System/38 (three current systems making extensive use of firmware implementations of system functions) are discussed. The use of firmware implementations has become increasingly popular [6,23–27].

7.4.2 Policy/Mechanism Separation

Different operating systems have different policies for allocating resources. Often, their policies are more important in dictating their different designs than are the mechanisms for carrying out the policies. For instance, the mechanisms that implement a scheduler (the mechanisms for searching and sorting scheduling lists, for removing and attaching processes to lists, for switching contexts, and for dispatching) may be the same in many operating systems. But the scheduling policies, including the selections of which process to choose and when to choose it, may differ widely. Schedulers in time-sharing systems, for examples are notably different from those of real-time systems. As another example, the many policies governing paging systems (policies determining which pages to page out, the interval between scanning pages, and when to page out pages) can all be implemented using the same mechanisms to maintain the paging tables and lists and to manipulate and update the tables and lists.

It is important for the architect to separate carefully that which is policy from that which is mechanism when designing the system. Policies may be set and tuned by adjusting certain policy parameters; mechanisms may be cast in hardware and firmware without restricting the flexibility of the design to the needs of various operating systems. By considering operating system policies and mechanisms separately, the architect may resolve some questions regarding the trade-offs between performance and flexibility. Various systems adopt the principles of the separation of policy and mechanism [26,27].

7.4.3 Modular and Exchangeable Hardware Unit

The architect should modularize system functions implemented in hardware. VLSI technology makes hardware modularization a desirable design approach. Systems may then be assembled using modular hardware units adapted to particular operating system needs. For example, one of the fundamental differences among operating systems is the memory management hardware unit (see Chapter 6). By carefully designing the hardware and defining the interface, the architect may be able to exchange a different memory management unit to support different operating systems without significantly affecting the hardware of the rest of the machine. The interface to the memory management unit might include, for instance, the virtual address leads, a set of control leads (read, write, initialize, and flush), and the physical address leads. In this way, modular hardware units allow a degree of hardware flexibility.

Another approach to achieving hardware flexibility is the provision of option straps on the input and output pins of a hardware unit. By tying these leads to appropriate voltage levels, the hardware unit could assume slightly different functionality options.

7.5 HEURISTICS FOR OPERATING SYSTEM SUPPORT

Just as architects use instruction mix to obtain insight into the frequency of usage of high-level-language constructs and the compiled instruction sequences, and generate heuristics for instruction set design to support high-level languages efficiently, they can obtain benefits from understanding the activities of operating systems by measuring the time consumed by the most frequent and time-consuming system calls. System call statistics, including the frequency of interrupts, are helpful for generating heuristics for improving operating system performance and developing architectural support.

To support operating systems efficiently without compromising compatibility; an architecture must support context switches and search and manipulate tables well. The architect can enhance the performance of context switching by considering the following during the design of the system. To speed up the loading and saving of contexts, the architecture may include:

- Single assembly instructions to load and save contexts (as in the VAX machine), thus moving the sequence into firmware
- Block move operations on the memory bus
- A wide memory bus and an interleaved memory system

To minimize the need for loading and saving contexts, the architecture may have multiple sets of general registers, address translation buffers, stacks, and an optimized selection of processes to share each set of registers and buffers. The architect should also consider minimizing the necessity for context switches by having a separate operating system processor run asynchronous operating system services so these services do not need to be switched in to the main processor.

To enhance the performance of table manipulations and searches, the architecture may include these features:

1. Hardware support such as that provided by content addressable memories or specially designed hardware (for example, a hardware searcher and sorter, hardware semaphores, and hardware mailboxes [28]).
2. Firmware support so the system needs only one assembly instruction for many table manipulation activities
3. Fast memories (static RAMs) for storing frequently accessed tables
4. Linked lists and searching and sorting algorithms to assist in many of the table searches

In an architectural design, as discussed in Chapter 4, the incorporation of hardware support for high-level-language features should justify its merits; so, too, should the incorporation of hardware support for operating system features justify its merits. The architect must balance performance gain with cost and performance loss (for instance, making a circuit larger or a critical path longer might degrade performance and increase cost). Furthermore, the architect must be careful to include all the hardware support necessary to make the operating system functional. For example, adequate hardware "hooks" (such as interrupt leads, semaphores, and the read-modify-write instruction) must be provided in an architecture to support a multiprocessing operating system.

7.6 ARCHITECTURES WITH OPERATING SYSTEM SUPPORT

This section discusses various architectures (AT&T WE32000, Intel iAPX/432, IBM System/38 and CII-Honeywell-Bull Level 64) with varying degrees of operating system support. These architectures represent conventional architectures as well as object- and capability-based architectures.

7.6.1 AT&T WE32000

The WE32000 (formerly known as the BELLMAC-32) is a high-performance, 32-bit microprocessor developed at AT&T Bell Laboratories [29]. Its architecture supports operating systems and high-level languages; it is reliable and easily maintained because all its components fit onto a single chip. The WE32000 has two mechanisms, the process switch and controlled transfer, to support operating systems. Two instructions handle interrupts and switch processes: the CALL PROCESS and the RETURN TO PROCESS instructions. The process switch and controlled transfer mechanisms use these instructions when handling exceptions.

Before defining the roles of the process switch and controlled transfer mechanisms in exception handling and process switching, a general understanding of the two mechanisms is required. The process switch mechanism does the following:

1. Saves the user and control registers (such as the stack pointer, program counter, and processor status word) in the process control block (PCB)
2. Updates the PCB pointer to the new PCB and loads the control registers from the new PCB
3. Moves blocks of data from the PCB to the translations registers, thereby switching the virtual address domain
4. Loads user registers from the new PCB

The controlled transfer mechanism controls the association of a new processor status word (PSW) with an entry into, or exit from, a procedure or handler. This mechanism has two parts: (1) a controlled call instruction that places the program counter/processor status word (PC/PSW) pair onto the execution stack and transfers into a new routine whose address and PCB are obtained by means of a two-level table lookup using the operands of the instruction (Fig. 7.3); and (2) a controlled return instruction that pops the PC/PSW pair off the stack. The operands of the instruction operate as a double table index. The first-level table exists at a predefined location in memory. The first index operand is an offset into the first-level table selecting an entry containing a pointer to the selected second-level table. The second index operand is an offset into the selected second-level

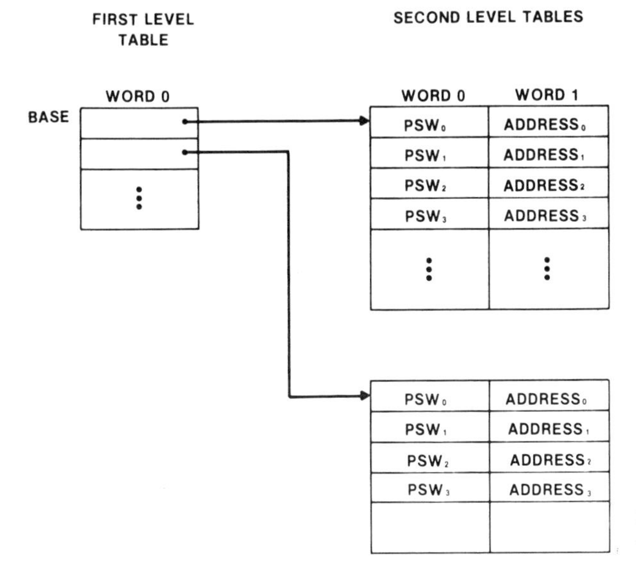

Figure 7.3 WE 32000 controlled transfer tables (from Ref. 29).

table selecting the entry with the PSW and address (PC) of the routine to branch to. The process switch and the control transfer mechanisms support all process switches, interrupt and exception handling, and system calls of an operating system running on the WE32000.

The WE32000 treats interrupts as unexpected calls. A special interrupt device generates an 8-bit interrupt ID and selects from a table one of 256 PCB pointers that correspond to the interrupt handler processes. The selected PCB corresponding to the selected interrupt handler process is passed to the CALL PROCESS instruction. Hence, once the PCB is obtained, process switch and interrupt handling proceeds exactly in the same manner using the CALL PROCESS instruction. The CALL PROCESS instruction switches processes by using the address of the PCB as its argument. The CALL PROCESS and RETURN TO PROCESS instructions use the process switch mechanism described above, saving the context of the current process and loading the context of a new process. In addition, the CALL PROCESS instruction pushes the address of the current PCB onto the interrupt stack and the RETURN TO PROCESS instruction pops the address of the PCB off the interrupt stack. The interrupt stack thus keeps track of the nesting of interrupts and process calls.

The WE32000 handles exceptions by combinations of parts of the process switch mechanism and the controlled transfer mechanism. *Internal exceptions* such as illegal instructions and integer overflow are handled by means of the controlled transfer mechanism to switch to an exception handler routine. The address and PSW of the exception handler routine is obtained from the second-level table as shown in Fig. 7.3 by using the type of exception serving as an index into the table. The first-level index is always zero. A *stack exception* is handled by the process switch mechanism. A pointer to the new PCB is fetched from a predetermined virtual location. The processor switches processes without activating the block move part to change translation tables. The new process with its own stack can then repair or adjust the stack of the process that caused the exception. A *process exception* occurs when the PCB contains an error; it is handled in the WE32000 by a process switch. The process switch scenario is similar to that of handling stack exceptions. A *reset exception* is also handled similarly to the stack exception except that the program counter/processor status word (PC/PSW) pair is not pushed onto the interrupt stack during the process switch since the interrupt stack itself may be faulty. Virtual addressing is disabled and the pointer to the PCB of the handling process is obtained from the fixed physical location.

These two powerful mechanisms also support tasking, exceptions, and packages in high-level languages such as Ada. With appropriate memory mapping, a compiler can represent a task as a WE32000 process. By providing an operating system interface for modifying the controlled transfer tables, a user may insert user-defined exception handlers into the table. These handlers may then be called by the controlled transfer mechanism when a user-defined exception occurs. Finally, the control transfer mechanism may be used to implement entries into common libraries and packages. Each package procedure entry would correspond to an entry in the second level table. Each controlled call then invokes a package procedure.

7.6.2 Intel iAPX/432 [30,31]

The Intel iAPX/432 is a 32-bit microcomputer system designed to support an object-based operating system. One of the goals of the iAPX/432 is changing the hardware/software interface by moving many operating system functions into hardware and firmware. The architecture of the iAPX/432 supports dynamic heap storage management (see Chapter 3). Hardware features dispatch the processes and implement interprocess communications. The software architecture defines small protection domains and run-time environments tailored for specific languages; it also allows data to be abstracted easily. Of the 64K bits of microcode in the microprocessor, 26.4K bits (40 percent) are used to implement operating system functions such as sending messages [30]. Intel calls this the Silicon Operating System (Silicon OS). Table 7.3 shows the allocation of microcode in the iAPX/432 microprocessor.

Another component of the Silicon OS is specialized hardware that recognizes system defined objects. Each object includes a description that defines the properties of the object, including its type, location, and size. Many types of objects are defined by the system: domain objects, context objects, process objects, processor objects, instruction objects, data objects, and others. These objects are discussed in Chapter 6. Their properties are shown in Fig. 7.4 [31]. The iAPX/432 hardware, unlike conventional systems, directly controls the system objects. For each type of system object, the hardware automatically handles certain operations on the object such as type checking and fetching absent memory segments. Other operations are available as specialized instructions. Software handles the rest of the operations.

TABLE 7.3 ALLOCATION OF MICROCODE IN THE IAPX/432

Function	Bits	Percentage
Basic instruction set	3,680	6
Floating-point arithmetic	11,680	18
Run-time environment	6,400	10
Virtual addressing	4,800	7
Fault handling	2,640	4
Silicon operating system	26,400	40
Multiprocessor control	8,640	13
Debug services	1,280	2
Total	64K	100

Source: Reference 30.

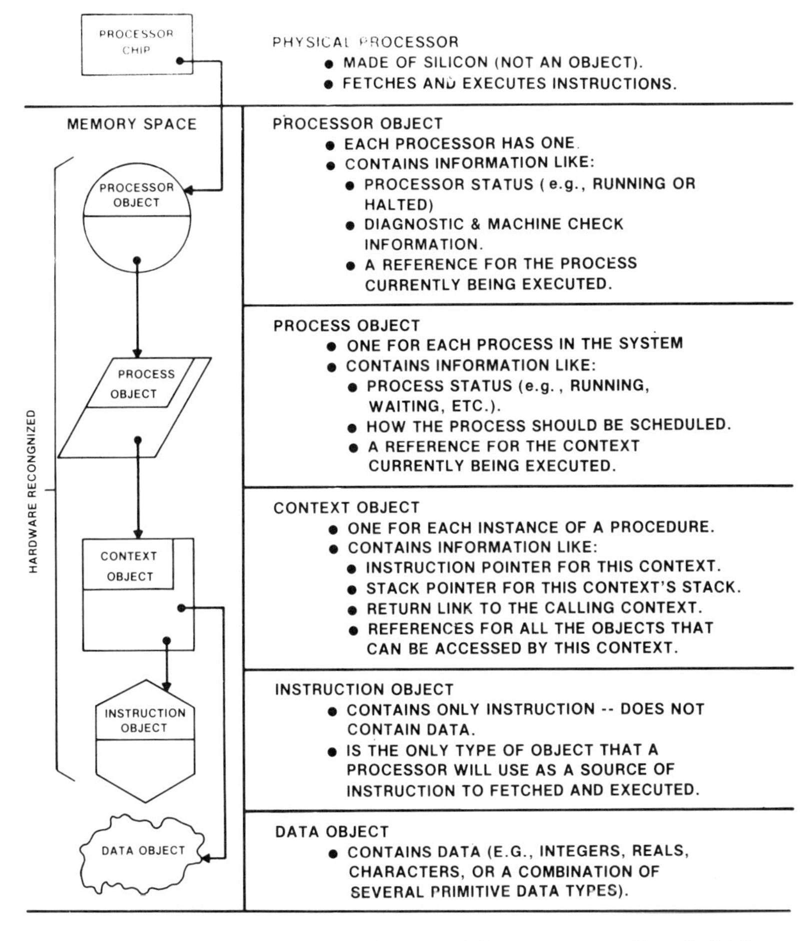

Figure 7.4 Intel iAPX/432—the objects that make up a program (from Ref. 31).

The designers of the iAPX/432 used hardware/software trade-offs to decide which operations on an object the hardware should handle automatically. They considered performance, security, and reliability criteria when making their decisions [30]:

1. *Performance:* An operation that is time-critical and has a large effect on system performance was implemented in hardware.
2. *Security:* An operation that is critical for security to protect the system and isolate the environments of important resources was implemented in hardware.
3. *Reliability:* An operation that must be reliable because it affects the correct operation of the system in delicate programming situations was implemented in hardware.

The iAPX/432 was designed as an operating-system-directed architecture with two main goals: achieving the fast execution of frequently used operating system functions and providing security and reliability with built-in hardware support.

7.6.3 IBM System/38 [32]

The IBM System/38 was designed for the needs of small business data processing systems. One of the important characteristics of these systems is a user interface that is easy to use by nontechnical people; that is, an interface whose complexities are hidden from the users. Many levels of abstraction within the System/38 shield the software and hardware complexities from the user. Two of the levels are implemented in microcode. The first layer of microcode, vertical microcode (VMC), resides in main storage. It is similar in power and format to conventional machine instructions. However, it is not part of the user-visible instruction set. Each VMC instruction has an opcode followed by one to four operands. The second layer of microcode, horizontal microcode (HMC), resides in a control storage inside the processing unit. The HMC is comparable in power and format to conventional system microcode in that it controls the hardware directly. The HMC interprets the VMC. The designers of the System/38 compared cost/performance trade-offs when deciding which functions to implement as VMC and HMC. The VMC/HMC cost ratio is approximately equivalent to the main storage/controlled storage cost ratio; the ratio must be weighted also by the fact that developing a line of HMC code is more expensive than developing a line of VMC code. The execution speed of HMC, on the other hand, is up to 10 times faster than VMC.

These two layers of microcode perform all the system management functions. The VMC layer implements high-level functions such as process management and I/O management. The HMC layer implements the common subfunctions required by the VMC layers as well as frequently executed subfunctions. The two layers of microcode, and the operating system functions they implement, are shown in Fig. 7.5.

Even though storage management is a VMC function, the support for storage management is a combination of VMC, HMC, and hardware. For example, paging programs and data between main storage and disk is a VMC function. The translation of the 48-bit virtual address of a main storage address, however, is accomplished by HMC and hard-

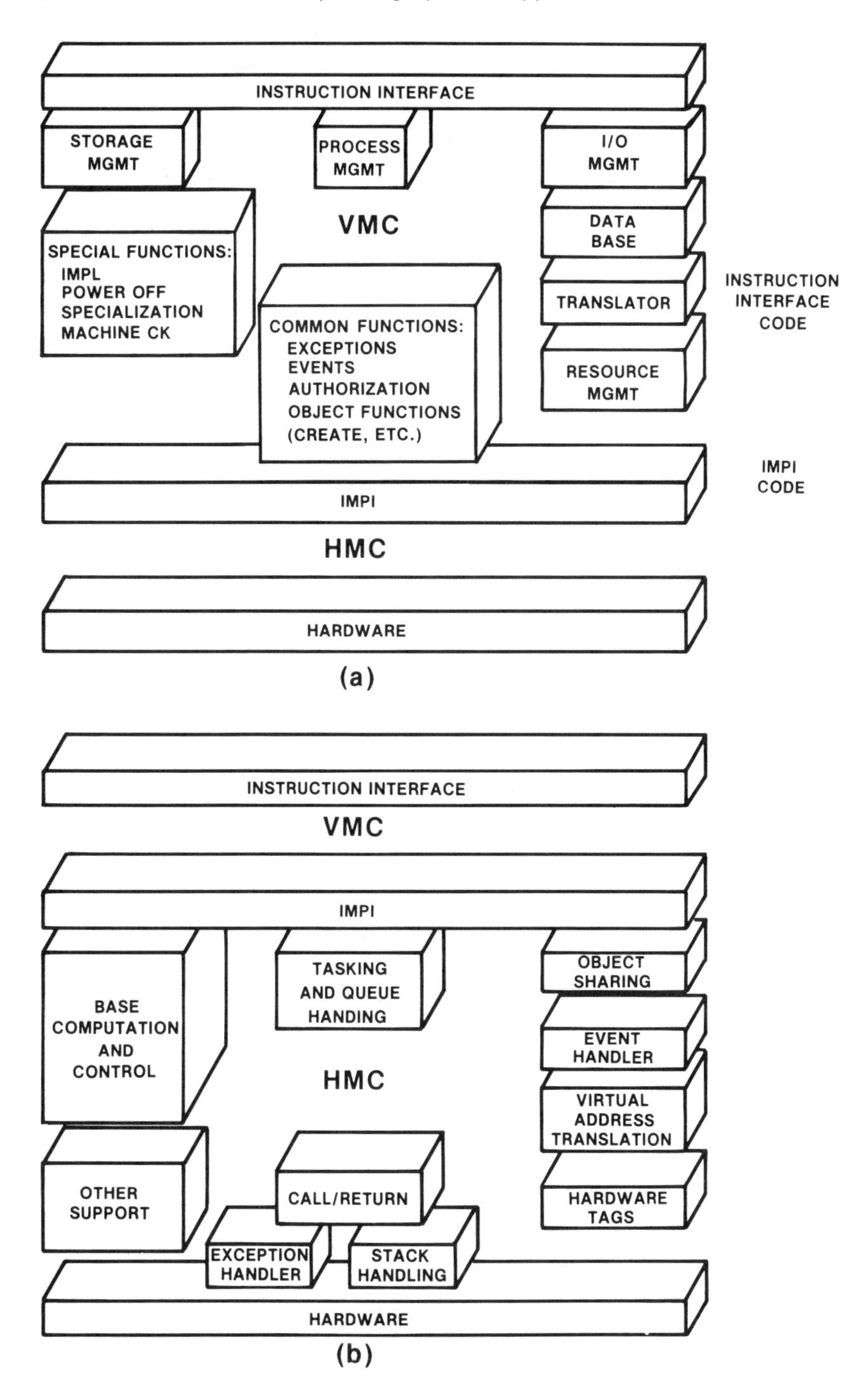

Figure 7.5 IBM System /38—major components in (a) VMC and (b) HMC.

ware. Each HMC and hardware function is defined as an operation code in VMC. Thus whenever a VMC storage management routine uses one of these operation codes, it activates the corresponding HMC and hardware function. The System/38 thus embodies the layered approach (increasing levels of abstraction) in operating system support discussed in Chapter 6. In the layered implementation, low-level functions such as task and queue handling; call/return; exception, event, and stack handling; and virtual address translation are implemented by low-level microcode (HMC). The higher-level functions, such as process management, storage management, exceptions, and events, are implemented by high-level microcode (VMC). Figure 7.5 is an example of an implementation of the layered approach concepts (see also Figs. 6.31 and 6.38).

7.6.4 CII-Honeywell-Bull Level 64 [33]

The CII-Honeywell-Bull Level 64, 64/DPS, and DPS/7 machines introduced an architecture with comprehensive interprocess synchronization and communication facilities. Key to the implementation of this architecture is the concept of *integrated objects*. An integrated object is a data structure built in main memory and initialized by software. Once the data structure is built and initialized, it becomes known to the hardware and firmware of the machine as an operand of specific instructions. Examples of integrated objects are process objects and semaphore objects. The hardware and firmware of the Honeywell architecture implement synchronization and communications facilities by applying a variety of P- and V-instructions to different semaphore objects.

The system implements a semaphore object as a segment with additional capabilities. The semaphore segment is accessible by ordinary instructions at initialization. It is accessible at other times only by semaphore instructions. The semaphore instructions operate on operands within a semaphore segment. The operand of a semaphore instruction is a semaphore descriptor contained in the descriptive area of the semaphore segment. Whenever such an operand is accessed, appropriate checks are done on access rights.

The system defines various semaphore objects. A *lock* semaphore implements mutual exclusion. Each lock semaphore object defines a dispatching priority. Between two matching P- and V-instructions on a locked object, a process has a priority equal to the lock semaphore object dispatching priority. Its original priority is saved by hardware by the P-instruction and restored by the V-instruction. A special semaphore object is defined to implement the event mechanism. Hardware-generated events such as I/O completion or some exception conditions are handled by hardware that simulates a V-instruction. The hardware-simulated V-instruction directly addresses the semaphore object corresponding to the event without the intermediate semaphore descriptor.

The Honeywell architecture defines another type of integrated objects, *semaphores with messages,* to implement interprocess communication. The semaphores with messages serve as hardware mailboxes. The P- and V-instructions on these semaphores send and receive messages. Hardware manages the message containers by means of a semaphore named an FLS semaphore. An FLS semaphore is invisible to programmers and is used to synchronize the use of message container resources. During a V-instruction on a semaphore with message, a hardware simulated P-instruction on the FLS semaphore obtains a container. The FLS semaphore first dequeues a message container and then enqueues it in the designated semaphore with message.

Corresponding to the variety of semaphore objects, there are a variety of P- and V-instructions. There are P- and V-instructions with and without messages. V-instructions with messages queue messages using either the last-in, first-out (LIFO) rule or first-in, first-out (FIFO) rule. Both the P- and V-instructions have a test option. When a process executes a P-instruction, for example, the process may be put in the wait state depending on the availability of the resource. A test P-instruction avoids the wait state and returns a condition code. Thus a P-test instruction may be used to obtain a list of resources by repetitive interrogations.

The Honeywell systems also define a restricted set of semaphore instructions for external addressing, that is, addresses located outside the address space of the process executing the instructions. For example, I/O semaphores are private to each user process. The addresses of these semaphores are made known to the I/O system processes when the I/O is initiated. The I/O system processes can then manipulate these semaphores using external addressing.

Finally, all interrupts, events, and exceptions are handled by hardware-simulating V-instructions. The Honeywell systems also implement an event poller in hardware, which steps in after each execution of an instruction.

7.7 SUMMARY

The design of an operating-system-directed architecture should ensure above all the portability and compatibility of user and system software. Portability means that existing software may be moved to a newly designed machine with minimal effort; compatibility implies portability and a compatible software development environment. To guarantee portability and compatibility, architectural features used by the software should remain invariant and the same software tools should remain available.

Once the portability and compatibility constraints are met, the major goal of an operating-system-directed architecture is to enhance the efficiency of the operating system. Tuning and choosing efficient algorithms for the operating system modules should be attempted. Then, the architect should examine common operating system activities that, given hardware and firmware support, could significantly enhance the performance of operating systems. Some of these activities include queue administration, context switching, interrupt handling, memory management, maintaining the real-time clock, communication, and scheduling. Another approach to operating-system-directed architecture is dedicating a parallel processor to run operating system code, thereby eliminating operating system overhead from the main processor.

In providing hardware support, the architect should consider the issue of flexibility because many types of operating systems may run on a single architecture. Flexibility may be achieved by providing firmware instead of hardware support, by implementing mechanisms in hardware and firmware and policies in software, and by designing modular, exchangeable hardware units and hardware units with option straps.

Examples of operating-system-directed architectures include the AT&T WE32000, the Intel iAPX/432, the IBM System/38, and the CII-Honeywell-Bull Level 64 family. The designers of these architectures placed extensive emphasis during the design phase on providing operating system support. The architectural support they developed include hardware, firmware, and special data structure objects.

REFERENCES

[1] M. E. Grzelakowski, J. H. Campbell, and M. R. Dubman, ''DMERT Operating System,'' *Bell Syst. Tech. J.,* Vol. 62, No. 1, January 1983, pp. 303–322.

[2] G. E. Brown, R. Eckhouse, and R. P. Goldberg, ''Operating System Enhancement through Microprogramming,'' *SIGMICRO Newsl.,* Vol. 7, March 1976, pp. 28–33.

[3] C. C. Foster, ''Hardware Enhancement of Operating Systems,'' *AD-A062462,* University of Massachusetts, U.S. Army Research Office, November 23, 1978.

[4] W. Joy, ''Comments on the Performance of UNIX on the VAX,'' *Electr. Eng. Comput. Sci. Dept. Rept.,* University of California, Berkeley.

[5] G. E. Brown, R. Eckhouse, and J. Estabrook, ''Operating System Enhancement through Firmware,'' *SIGMICRO Newsl.,* Vol. 8, September 1977, pp. 119–133.

[6] R. Chattergy, ''Microprogrammed Implementation of a Scheduler,'' *SIGMICRO Newsl.,* Vol. 7, September 1976, pp. 15–19.

[7] C. Y. Lee and M. C. Paull, ''A Content Addressable Distributed Logic Memory with Applications to Information Retrieval,'' *Proc. IEEE,* Vol. 51, June 1963, pp. 924–932.

[8] *VAX 11/780: Technical Summary,* Digital Equipment Corp., Maynard, Mass., 1977.

[9] B. R. Borgerson, M. D. Godfrey, P. E. Hagery, and T. R. Rykken, ''The Architecture of the Sperry Univac 1100 Series Systems,'' *Proc. 6th Int. Symp. Comput. Archit.,* pp. 137–146.

[10] G. D. Kraft and W. N. Toy, *Mini/Microcomputer Hardware Design,* Prentice-Hall, Englewood Cliffs, N.J., 1979.

[11] *IBM System/7 System Summary,* IBM Corp., Boca Raton, Fla., 1972.

[12] I. LeMair, ''Indexed Mapping Extends Microprocessor Addressing Range,'' *Comput. Des.,* August 1980, pp. 111–118.

[13] Y. Lavi, A. Kaminker, A. Menachem, and S. Bali, ''16-Bit Microprocessor Enters Virtual Memory Domain,'' *Electronics,* April 24, 1980, pp. 123–129.

[14] D. Wicker, ''Programmable Interval Timer,'' *Digital Design,* May 1980, pp. 32–36.

[15] R. Rice, ''The Chief Architect's Reflection on Symbol IIR,'' *Computer,* Vol. 14, No. 7, July 1981, pp. 41–55.

[16] D. R. Ditzel, ''Reflections on the High-Level Language Symbol Computer System,'' *Computer,* Vol. 14, No. 7, July 1981, pp. 55–67.

[17] R. J. Swan, S. H. Fuller, and D. P. Siewiorek, ''CM*—a Modular Multiprocessor,'' *Proc. AFIPS,* AFIPS Press, Arlington, Va., 1977, pp. 637–644.

[18] S. R. Ahuja and A. Asthana, ''A Multi-microprocessor Architecture with Hardware Support for Communication and Scheduling,'' *Proc. Symp. Archit. Support Program. Lang. Oper. Syt.,* March 1982, pp. 205–209.

[19] T. G. Rauscher and P. M. Adams, "Microprogramming: A Tutorial and Survey of Recent Developments," *IEEE Trans. Comput.*, Vol. C-29, January 1980, pp. 2–19.

[20] M. Maekawa et al., "Firmware Structure and Architectural Support for Monitors, Vertical Migration and User Microprogramming," *Proc. Symp. Archit. Support Program. Lang. Oper. Syst.*, ACM, March 1982, pp. 185–194.

[21] N. Kamibayashi et al., "HEART: An Operating System Nucleus Machine Implemented by Firmware," *Proc. Symp. Archit. Support Program. Lang. Oper. Syst.*, ACM, March 1982, pp. 195–204.

[22] W. H. Burkhardt and R. C. Randel, "Design of Operating Systems with Micro-programmed Implementation," *NTIS Rep. PB-224-484*, September 1973.

[23] B. H. Liskov, "The Design of the Venus Operating System," *Commun. ACM*, Vol. 15, No. 3, March 1972.

[24] J. V. Sell, "Microprogramming in an Integrated Hardware/Software System," *Comput. Des.*, Vol. 14, No. 1, January 1975.

[25] W. G. Sitton and L. L. Wear, "A Virtual Memory System for the Hewlett-Packard 2100A," *Prepr. 7th Annu. Workshop Microprogram.*, ACM, September 1974.

[26] A. H. Werkheiser, "Microprogrammed Operating Systems," *Prepr. 3rd Annu. Workshop Microprogram.*, ACM, October 1970.

[27] W. A. Wulf, R. Levin, and S. P. Harbison, *HYDRA/C.mmp: An Experimental Computer System*, McGraw-Hill, New York, 1981.

[28] W. S. Ford and V. C. Hamacher, "Low Level Architecture Features for Supporting Process Communication," *Comput. J.*, Vol. 20, No. 2, pp. 156–162.

[29] A. D. Berenbaum et al., "The Operating System and Language Support Features of the WE32000 Microprocessor," *Proc. Symp. Archit. Support Program. Lang. Oper. Syst.*, ACM, March 1982, pp. 30–38.

[30] J. Rattner, "Hardware/Software Cooperation in the iAPX 432," *Proc. Symp. Archit. Support Program. Lang. Oper. Syst.*, ACM, March 1982, p. 1.

[31] D. Kaiser, *iAPX 432 Object Primer*, Intel Corp., Santa Clara, Calif., August 1980.

[32] F. G. Soltis, "Design of a Small Business Data Processing System," *Computer*, September 1981, pp. 77–93.

[33] P. Guillier and D. Flosberg, "An Architecture with Comprehensive Facilities of Inter-process Synchronization and Communication," *Proc. 7th Annu. Symp. Comput. Archit.*, May 1980, pp. 264–270.

PROBLEMS

7.1 Programmed I/O uses specific commands to read and write I/O registers. Memory-mapped I/O requires that the same instructions to read and write memory are used to read and write I/O registers. Explain how the choice of I/O type affects I/O drivers and their access to I/O registers.

7.2 In implementing conventional software queues, the system may (1) keep the ready queue sorted by priority, (2) perform a search for the highest-priority process each time the operating system wishes to dispatch a process, or (3) maintain a separate queue for each priority. What are the advantages and disadvantages of each approach?

7.3 Operations on queues may be made more efficient by providing hardware support through the use of content addressable memories (CAMs). Searches of memory are made more efficient and ready and wait queues may be combined into one queue that resides on the same CAM. One specific example where CAMs can be used is as a means of storing a clock wakeup list. Discuss in detail another application where the use of CAMs would result in large payoffs in system efficiency.

7.4 Scheduling policies use a set of criteria to determine the priority of a process, which process should execute next, and how long a process should execute. Describe a scheduling policy that would be used in a time-sharing system and one that would be used in a real-time system. How do the two policies differ?

7.5 Policies are used in allocating system resources and mechanisms are used to implement the policies. Policies and mechanisms concerning scheduling and paging are described in Section 7.4.2. Discuss in detail a policy for allocating a specific resource and the mechanisms that could be used to implement that policy.

7.6 Performance, security, and reliability were factors considered in the design of the iAPX/432. Name an operation that is time-critical and has a large effect on system performance. Describe an operation where it is critical for security to protect the system and isolate the environments of important resources. Name an operation in which reliability is critical.

7.7 The iAPX/432 allows domain objects, context objects, process objects, processor objects, instructions objects, and data objects to be defined by the system (Fig. 7.4). For each type of system object, certain operations on the object (such as type checking) are performed. Describe what types of operations and checks can be performed on the various system objects.

7.8 On the iAPX/432, descriptors are associated with system-defined objects. The descriptors define various properties of the object, for example, type, location, and size. Design a protection system where users have different access rights to the same object. For example, one user may only have read access to the object, whereas another user may have both read and write access rights to the same object.

7.9 In the Honeywell architecture, the operand of a semaphore instruction is a semaphore descriptor. Access rights are verified whenever such an operand is accessed. Why can hardware-simulated V-instructions directly address semaphore objects corresponding to hardware-generated events without the intermediate semaphore descriptor?

8

Fault-Tolerant Computing

8.1 INTRODUCTION

Reliability requirements vary considerably from application to application. The computers aboard unmanned missles and spacecraft, for example, must operate continuously without repair. They must have high reliability requirements to ensure successful missions. On the other hand, commercial computers in most scientific and accounting applications may cease to operate temporarily without catastrophic results since nearly all their components are accessible to maintenance personnel and their software is backed up frequently.

One maintenance objective for both scientific and business machines is reducing the maximum length of repair time. This objective requires fault-diagnosis techniques that quickly isolate troubles to within a few replaceable units or circuit packs. For real-time applications such as telephone switching and process control, uninterrupted operation is essential. The systems must function correctly when faults are present and during maintenance. The use of redundant machines provides continuous operation. In electronic telephone switching systems, the central processor is duplicated and both units process the same input data [1]. The outputs come from the active (on-line) machine. If the active machine fails, processing switches promptly to the standby machine. The defective unit is then repaired and put back into operation. The system shuts down completely only if both machines are faulty.

Fault-tolerant computing is defined as the ability to compute in the presence of errors. It is beginning to play an important part in the design of commercial computers for several reasons, including the dramatic advances in LSI technology, the high cost of maintaining sophisticated equipment, a wider field of applications, and user demands for more reliability. Many applications, such as air-flight control, airline reservations, transaction processing, PBXs, and electronic fund transfer systems require more reliable computing. This has led to the development of computers that incorporate more advanced maintenance techniques, including the UNIVAC 1100/60 [2], IBM 4300 processors [3], the VAX 11/780 [4], and the TANDEM 16 [5].

8.2 COST OF RELIABILITY

The most important consideration in the design or purchase of most equipment and systems is cost, specifically the initial cost of the equipment. Emphasizing the initial cost so heavily, however, is often a mistake. Maintenance costs should be considered as seriously. The maintenance and repair costs depend on the reliability of the equipment. As the reliability increases, maintenance costs decrease. But also as the reliability increases, the initial cost of the equipment rises since reliability depends on some form of redundancy or special devices. A trade-off exists between the maintenance costs of a system (that is, how often must it be serviced and by what caliber of service personnel) and its initial cost. Further, maintenance is the expense—because of its dependence on the costs of labor and time—that is most vulnerable to inflation. Labor rates for repair service doubled over the past years (1975 through 1980) from about $30 per hour to $60 per hour [6]. Because of this upward trend, maintenance costs have become increasingly visible to users.

The most significant factor in selecting a system with high reliability requirements is that the cost of the system is not limited to its initial cost but includes its overall operating and maintenance expenses. If the proper maintenance features have been added to the system, the actual total expense (initial cost plus maintenance charges) is held down significantly. This effect is shown in Fig. 8.1 [7]. The initial cost rises as reliability increases, but at the same time, maintenance and repair costs decrease. The total cost of purchasing and maintaining a system first falls with increasing reliability and then rises again, showing that the most cost-effective system is at the minimum point (represented

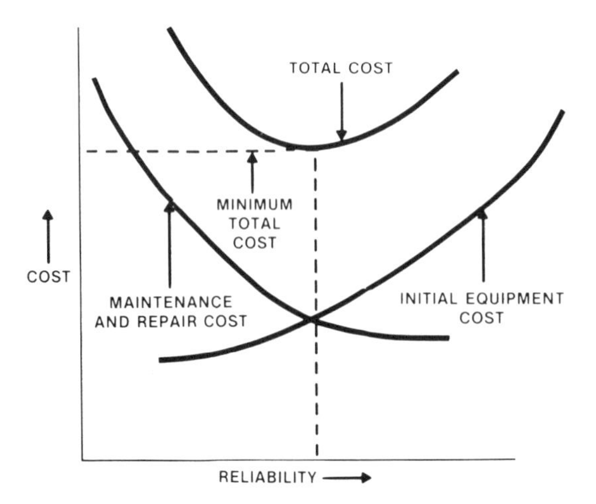

Figure 8.1 System equipment and maintenance cost.

by the dotted lines in the figure). In practice, the optimal balance of cost and reliability is difficult to realize because it involves the many elusive variables of estimating production and maintenance costs.

System designers with considerable experience are usually able to approach the optimal balance of system cost and reliability. Experience is necessary because the relationship between cost and reliability is not always exact; that is, the minimum total cost does not always reflect the reliability of a system. If the results of a failure are likely to be serious, it may be necessary to provide more redundancy to ensure continuous and reliable operation. Conversely, it may be necessary to reduce reliability to the minimum acceptable level for the buyer whose main consideration is initial cost. This, then, is the challenge: to design computer systems, particularly small computer configurations, that satisfy a wide range of applications with different reliability requirements.

8.3 CLASSIFICATION OF ERRORS

There are three major categories of error sources in a system: *design mistakes, component failures,* and *human-operator interaction errors.* [8]. These error sources contribute to system failures. Although design mistakes occur in both hardware and software, software errors are much more predominant; they are also difficult to eliminate from the system. Component failures, on the other hand, are generally the result of aging or environmental influences that cause certain characteristics of the equipment to deviate beyond the specified limits. These failures are referred to as hardware failures. Inappropriate operator actions at control and maintenance panels may destroy the sanity of the system. Operator inputs normally have high priority, and many systems are fatally vulnerable to inappropriate commands and typographical errors.

System failures are functionally classified as *hardware, software,* and *procedural.* The three types of system failures are closely related to the categories of error sources. Component failures occur in just the hardware. Design mistakes, although they occur in the hardware, mostly cause software system failures. Procedural errors are usually caused by mistakes made by the system operator. The percentages of system downtime attributed to each category depend on the system hardware configuration, redundancy structure, software complexity and person-to-machine interface. For example, Fig. 8.2 shows the field experiences of the AT&T's 1ESS™* processor. The percentages in this figure represent the fraction of total downtime attributable to each cause [9]. The software faults account for 50 percent of the downtime compared to 20 percent attributable to hardware and 30 percent caused by procedural errors.

These percentages are reasonable because the 1ESS processor is duplicated. If one of the units fails, the duplicated unit is switched in, thus maintaining continuous operation. Meanwhile, the defective unit is repaired. It is rare when a hardware fault occurs in the duplicated unit during the repair interval but when it happens, the entire system fails. The redundancy structure tolerates a single hardware fault but simultaneous hardware

*Trademark of AT&T Technologies, Inc.

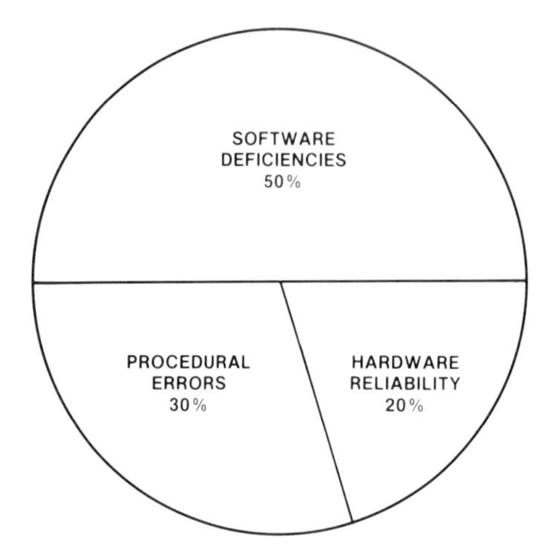

Figure 8.2 Causes of system outages.

faults (one in each processor during the repair interval) cause system outages and contribute to the percentage of system downtime attributed to hardware faults.

Procedural errors account for about 30 percent of the downtime. This figure is comparable to those experienced in commercial computer systems. In commercial computer systems, which are generally nonredundant, a single hardware fault will most likely bring the entire system down. The proportion between hardware and software faults indicated in Fig. 8.2 is considerably different for nonredundant computer systems.

8.3.1 Hardware Faults

Reliability is often thought of as the qualitative judgment of the performance of a device or system. The reliability of hardware components, though, may be measured quantitatively because components fail at statistically predictable rates. The engineering definition of reliability—the probability that a component will perform a required function under controlled conditions for a specified period of time—becomes appropriate for analyzing hardware faults. Statistical analyses generally assume that the hardware being tested is initially free of faults and that it deteriorates with time.

Equipment failures may be plotted against time to form a pattern known as the *bathtub curve* (Fig. 8.3). This pattern has three periods. In the *early life period,* parts that are inherently weak as the result of improper design, manufacture, or usage will fail. The early failure rate, although relatively high, decreases progressively and eventually levels off as the weak components are replaced. Many failing components are detected in the early life period by the burn-in test or by 100 percent inspection. Eliminating all the "weaklings" by subjecting the components to tests under accelerated conditions is a common practice. Systems are also operated for a period of time under varying conditions to ensure the detection of potential failures. This practice is absolutely necessary for equipment aboard airborne missiles and satellites that is nonrepairable during missions. This type of operation is also highly desirable for equipment such as undersea transatlantic

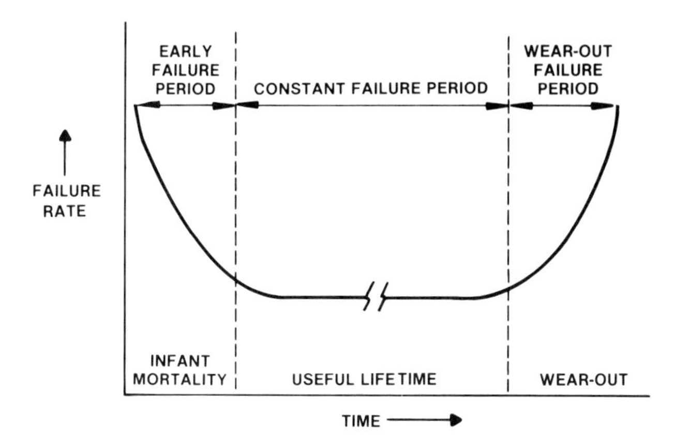

Figure 8.3 Typical bathtub curve of failure rate versus time.

amplifiers whose repair is a major undertaking and very expensive. For small, low-cost computers, a 100 percent burn-in of components may not be economically feasible. However, a certain amount of stressing of components by varying the voltages or increasing the clock rate may identify marginal components in a working system.

After the early failures have been corrected, the components settle down to a long period of relative stability. During this period, called the *useful life period,* the failure rate is low and constant, and the failures are unlikely to have single causes. Failures from a wide variety of causes occur randomly but at a uniform rate. The normal working life of a system occurs during this interval.

In the *wear-out period,* the components deteriorate until each one wears out. The failure rate, as indicated in the bathtub curve, rises again. The wear-out failures may be avoided by replacing components before they reach this period.

8.3.2 Software Faults

In contrast with hardware faults, no software failures result from aging. Software faults are caused by errors in the specifications and the implementation of them. There are many special cases that the software architect may overlook or handle improperly.

The basic elements of software are structures whose behavior does not change with time. Software faults result from design errors by incorrect combinations of instructions. The interactions between instructions are much more complicated than the interconnections of hardware components. A physical machine has a relatively small number of distinct internal states compared with a software system. Software architects usually assume that the hardware designs are correct. The software design, however, has an enormous number of different states to consider; even after extensive validation efforts, the correctness of the design of a large software system cannot be assumed. There are no available techniques for measuring the number of software faults in a program, and every change to a software system creates a new system that has different reliability properties from the original one. The correction of a software error many have side effects in other parts of the system that increase rather than decrease the total number of errors. Obviously, correcting a software error is not as simple as correcting a hardware error by replacing a faulty component with a good one. But once the software faults are corrected, they do not recur as do hardware faults.

Software faults are not predictable except that they exist in every system. Several definitions of software reliability are in use. One definition states that software reliability is the probability that a software system will perform its intended functions for a specified number of input cases under stated input conditions. Since the sequence of code executed depends on the values of the input parameters, the probability of obtaining the correct result also depends on the input data. This definition is probabilistic because of the uncertainty in the selection of input parameters when the system is in operation. Exhaustive testing of all possible input cases is usually not possible. Thus, some software faults manifest themselves only when untested input cases occur in the actual operation of the system.

For a large software system, exhaustive testing is usually not feasible. Some programs always contain residual errors that survive the design, development, and testing stages. The occurrence of software errors in the development of the program may be expected to follow a decreasing pattern (Fig. 8.4). Initially, the system contains a large number of software faults. As the system is used more frequently and is operated at its full capacity, major errors are detected and corrected, thereby reducing the total number of faults in the system. The number continues to decrease asymptomatically with time to a limit of some fixed positive number. One may expect a monotonically decreasing number of software faults toward zero since faults are constantly detected and removed from the program. This is the case for the hardware design faults shown by the dotted line in Fig. 8.4 because the hardware design becomes stable with time. Software, however, is so easily changed that it rarely becomes stable. Each software change introduces new errors, so that the value of the lower limit is a function of the rate at which new capabilities are added to the software. The process of correcting a detected error may unintentionally introduce some subtle errors in other parts of the program. Another reason for constant

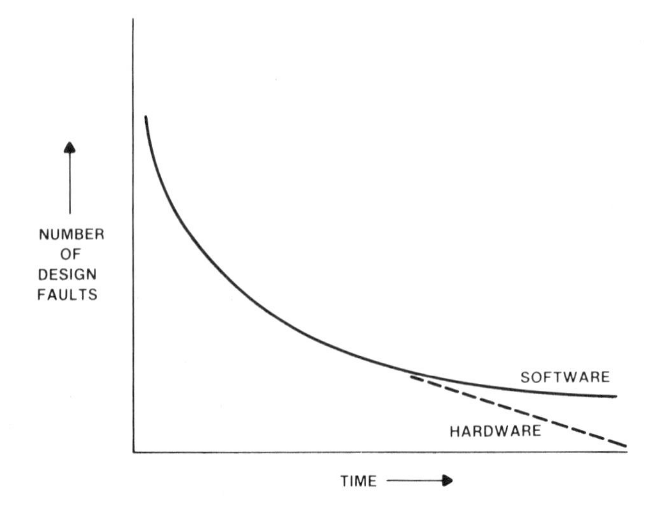

Figure 8.4 Software faults in a large system.

software faults is that a large portion of the program is not tested or exercised. Faults in this portion of the code remain latent for indeterminable amounts of time.

The behavior of the system with several major software releases may follow a pattern similar to that of Fig. 8.5. Each release represents a major revision and update of the program specifications and modifications of the software module to include new features. If more of the residual type of software faults are detected and corrected before a program is released for field or commercial use, the peaks of the curve are reduced and the product becomes more reliable. This is the objective of the evaluation and validation process.

8.3.3 Procedural Faults

Human errors by maintenance personnel and operators also cause system failures. Procedural faults, also referred to as *interaction faults,* are caused by inputs to the system through operator-machine interfaces during operation or maintenance that are not appropriate to the current state of the system. These errors are statistically unpredictable and occur at an unpredictable rate. They may be caused by inadequate and incorrect documentation (for example, user's manuals), or simply by not following instructions in the relevant operating manuals. For example, an operator may mistakenly remove a busing cable between the central processing unit and the main store, completely disrupting the entire system. It is probably impossible to anticipate and provide safeguards against all possible procedural faults.

The problem of procedural faults has continuously remained of great concern to users of information-processing systems. Several approaches help avoid interaction faults. Many companies have extensive operator training and explicit and complete operation and maintenance manuals. Another approach reduces the number of errors by having operators work on more sophisticated and user-friendly systems; sophisticated also in-

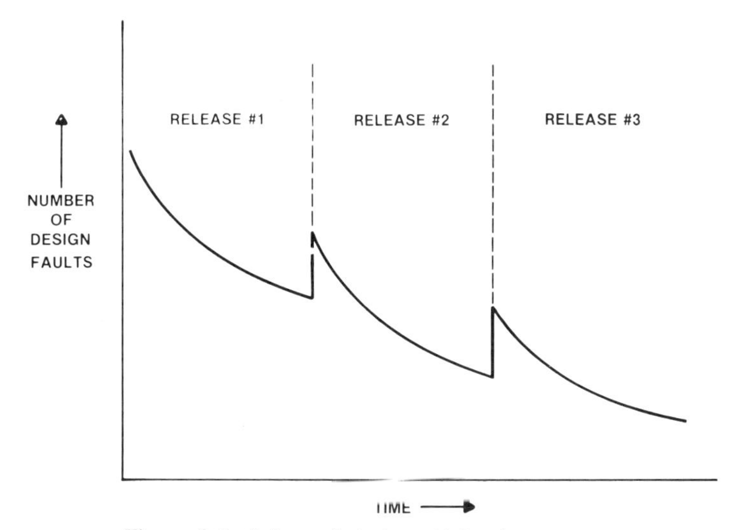

Figure 8.5 Software faults in multiple release program.

cludes the replacement of control panels by more intelligent microprocessor-based consoles. Including well-established protocols into the design of the operator-machine communication interfaces may screen operator inputs for many types of mistakes. But procedural faults still enter systems at high rates.

The occurrence of interaction faults may be expected to follow a decreasing pattern similar to that of software faults (Fig. 8.4). In the early stage, there is a considerable number of interaction errors resulting from inadequate or incorrect documents and inexperienced operators. As these shortcomings are corrected, the procedural errors decrease asymptomatically with time. Also, shortcomings in the software to deal with the operator procedures are corrected to improve the robustness of the system. However, the interaction faults continue to decrease to a fixed number since human operators are not perfect. There is also a continual turnover of operators, which tends to perpetuate procedural errors.

8.4 EFFECT OF SYSTEM UTILIZATION

The failure rates of reliability curves for the hardware, the software, and the procedural operator-to-machine interfaces all are high in the early life period. These faults decrease and settle to a constant level as the system matures. Weak hardware components are replaced, design errors are corrected, and procedural interaction is refined. The wear-out phase is present only in the hardware component curves since each component eventually wears out and is replaced.

Software reliability must take into account the operating environment. A large program contains so many possible flow paths that exhaustive testing is not feasible. Consequently, large programs are not expected to be completely fault-free. Many of their faults are not detected until a specific combination of input variables occurs. The probability of exposing these latent or dormant faults increases with system use. There is a distinct relationship between failure rate and system use for both hardware and software faults. The statistical study done at Stanford Linear Accelerator Center (SLAC) of their computer complex consisting of two IBM 370/168s and one IBM 360/91 in a triplex mode shows an increased system failure rate with higher levels of use [10]. The failure rates are the lowest during nonworking hours. They increase rapidly as the working day begins (8:00 A.M.) and peak before and after the lunch hour. The end of the working day is apparent by the significant decrease in the failure rates. This study shows the direct relationship between the failure rates and the amount of use a particular module or subsystem receives.

Other studies support this relationship between system activity and system failures [11]. These observations indicate that the overall failure rate is composed of two separate quantities. The first is the inherent failure rate as determined through the classical reliability models. The second is the induced failure rate, which depends on system utilization and is cyclic on a daily basis. The classical bathtub curve may be augmented to incorporate this cyclic effect (Fig. 8.6) [10].

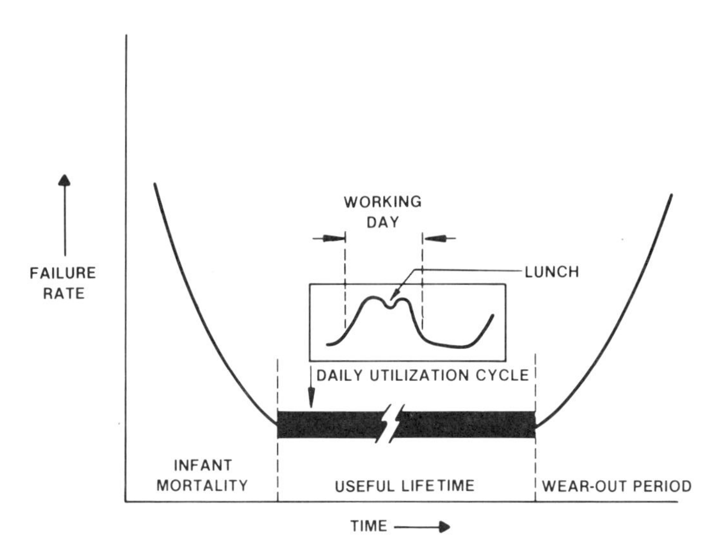

Figure 8.6 Augmented bathtub curve.

8.5 REDUNDANCY TECHNIQUES

If a computer were fault-free, the hardware and software would always behave predictably. The perfect computer has not been built, however, and failures in both hardware and software occur. Hardware failures may affect the control sequence or data words within the machine. This results in errors of two types:

1. The program sequence is unchanged, but the failure affects the final results.
2. The program sequence is changed, and the program no longer executes the specified algorithm.

Software faults are the results of improper translations or implementations of the original algorithms. The flow of instruction execution deviates from the correct control sequence. In many instances, unfortunately, hardware and software faults are indistinguishable. Systems therefore need to be tolerant of faults and able to compute correctly in the presence of faults, regardless of their sources.

A good way of making computers tolerant of faults is by making parts of them redundant. Redundancy allows computers to bypass errors so that the final results are correct. This redundancy, known as protective redundancy, consists of combinations of hardware redundancy, software redundancy, and time redundancy. *Hardware redundancy* consists of additional circuits that detect and correct errors. *Software redundancy* consists of the additional programs that reestablish an error-free working system under trouble conditions. It may include fault detection and diagnostic programs to periodically test all logic circuits of the computer for hardware faults. *Time redundancy* consists of a retrial of an erroneous operation. It includes the repetition of a program or segment of a program immediately after the detection of an error. The retrial is often done by hardware. For example, hardware logic may initiate the automatic reread of a memory location in which a parity failure is detected.

Although protective redundancy is functionally classified into three separate types, one type may encompass one or both of the other types. In the case of software redundancy, the control program requires both memory space (hardware) and execution (time). Each of these types of redundancy and their various combinations have been employed in the design of fault-tolerant computers; the choice of emphasis depends on the user application and the associated reliability requirements.

8.5.1 Hardware Redundancy

There are two types of hardware redundancy: static and dynamic. The static approach uses the massive replication of components, circuits, and subsystems. Error correction occurs automatically. Dynamic redundancy requires additional parts or subsystems to serve as spares. Both static and dynamic redundancy techniques are used in complex computer installations.

8.5.1.1 Static hardware redundancy. In systems where the most frequently encountered type of failure in a component is an open circuit, paralleling two of the components introduces redundancy. Figure 8.7(a) shows a parallel connection of diodes. The failure of a single open-circuit diode does not influence the circuit operation. If most failures are short circuits, a series configuration is necessary to compensate for them [Fig. 8.7(b)]. If the probability of failure is equal for both modes, a combination of the series and the parallel arrangements is the best method for correcting single errors [Fig. 8.7(c)].

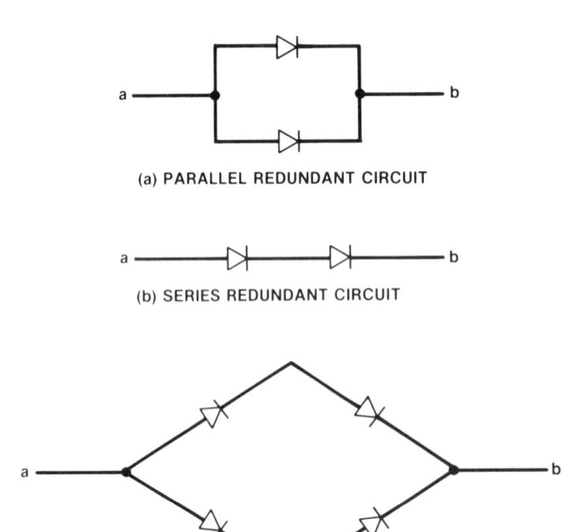

Figure 8.7 Circuits employing static redundancy.

Failure detection is extremely difficult when static redundancy is applied at the component level since the component failure is masked out by the redundant hardware. If the fault is not susceptive to masking and causes an error, however, the fault will go undetected and not be corrected. For a repairable system design, this method of fault correction is undesirable from the viewpoint of fault isolation; that is, a fault may not necessarily be recognized at the system level and isolated to a specific unit.

On the circuit level, one of the fault-correcting techniques to correct this deficiency is the use of quadded logic. Quadded logic is based on the quadruplication of circuitry so the error is corrected within two or three levels of the logic beyond the fault that caused it. Correction is accomplished by logically combining signals from circuits that have not failed with the signal from the faulty circuit (Fig. 8.8). Obviously, this technique makes use of a massive replication of logic gates and is rather complicated. Again, fault detection is inherently difficult because the redundant hardware conceals the faults.

On the subsystem level, von Neumann's original concept of majority logic has been widely studied and enlarged on by many reliability designers, particularly for military

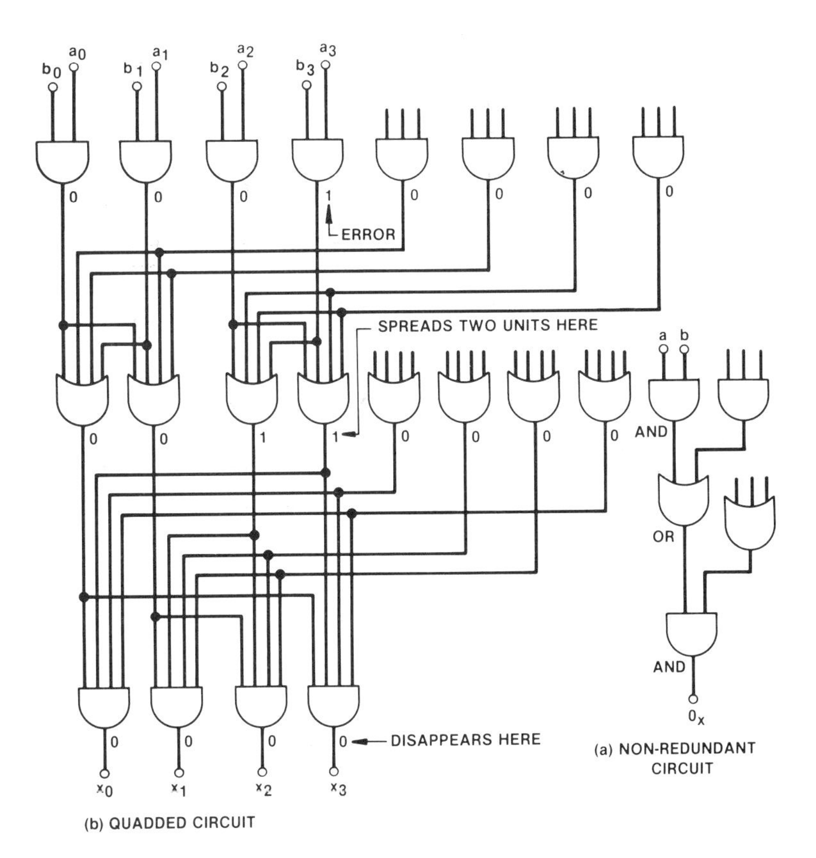

Figure 8.8 Circuit employing quadded logic.

applications. This technique involves the triplication of the functional blocks and the use of voter circuits (Fig. 8.9). Voter circuits restore the proper output when a fault is present in one of the functional blocks. To safeguard against failures in the voter circuit, majority logic is applied to the voter circuits as well.

Error correction codes are another type of static hardware redundancy. Techniques based on error correction codes employ additional hardware and information (data), for example, Hamming correction codes. Figure 8.10 functionally shows the redundant hardware and information for error correction in a memory system.

8.5.1.2 Dynamic hardware redundancy. Dynamic redundancy, also referred to as *selective redundancy,* requires judicious choices to give the most effective protection against failures. In response to an error, the faulty unit is automatically (or manually) replaced with a good unit to correct the trouble. The selected circuit, before its use, may be *active* (powered) or *passive* (unpowered). There are three necessary steps in the dynamic redundancy procedure: error detection, diagnosis, and fault recovery. The foremost step in the procedure is detecting the error quickly. If the fault detection logic points to a fault within a single replaceable unit, the second step (diagnosis) is not needed. But if the fault detection logic embraces a number of replaceable units, diagnosis must be initiated to pinpoint the faulty unit. During diagnosis, the fault is analyzed by either special hardware or software diagnostics; the result of the analysis assigns the fault to a specific device or unit. The third and final step is the recovery action of eliminating the fault by replacing the offending unit with a working unit. In addition, for a real-time control system, if the error occurs in the middle of an operation, some program rollback is necessary to discard the bad data and to recover as much good data as possible.

8.5.2 Software Redundancy

Redundant software protects the system from hardware and software faults by duplicating programs and instructions at both the macro and micro levels. If the hardware of a com-

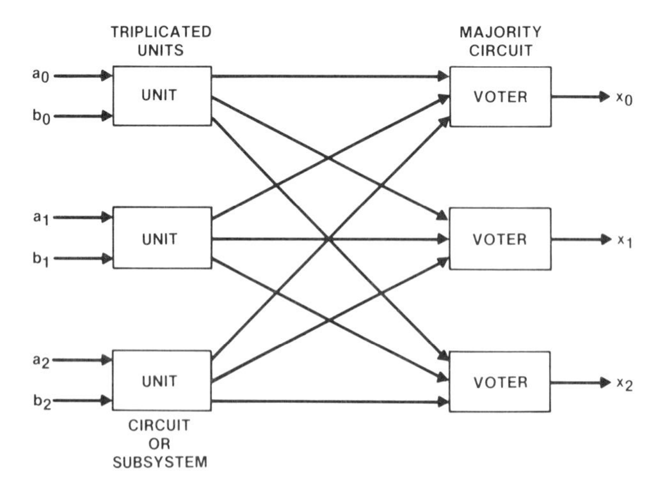

Figure 8.9 Triplicated majority redundancy.

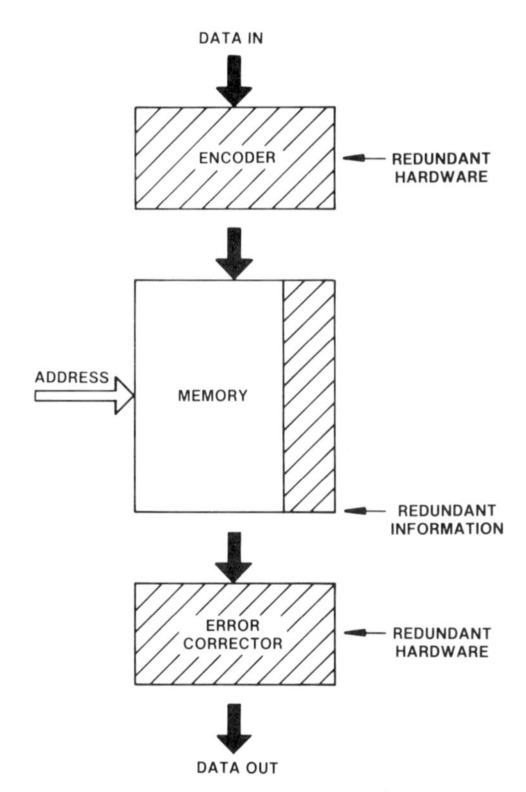

Figure 8.10 Redundancy in error correction scheme.

puter were fault-free, the programs that constitute redundant software may still be necessary [12]. Obviously, the goal of fault-free hardware has not been reached; some degree of software redundancy is therefore necessary to ensure reliability.

Like hardware redundancy, there are two types of software redundancy. Static software redundancy employs extensive replication. Replicated programs are written and executed concurrently on separate hardware facilities. Fault detection is performed by comparison. When more than two programs exist, majority decision by software provides the means of immediate error detection and correction. This is a software equivalent of the triple modular redundant (TMR) system.

Dynamic software redundancy is frequently used in conjunction with dynamic hardware redundancy. When the system detects a failure, error recovery is required to configure the system around the faulty component. Software copies of the state of each system component are made from time to time during normal system operation. To correct the erroneous states of the machine caused by a failure, the system rolls back to the latest software copy of the states.

A rollback operation makes use of the concept of *checkpoints*. A checkpoint is a scheduled point in the execution sequence when the system saves its states. Program rollback forces execution to restart at the last checkpoint and to begin processing the data saved at that checkpoint; it assumes that the data is unmutilated. Error recovery must therefore involve both hardware and software to ensure continuity of operation or, at least, to minimize the disturbance of the system.

N-version programming is an example of static software redundancy [13]. Different versions of a program are written and run concurrently on separate hardware. Their outputs are compared before any action is taken. If one of the versions of the program disagrees with the others, the results of the majority are used, as it is in the triple modular redundant hardware structure. If one version of a program is faulty, it is not necessary to take it out of service, as it is likely that versions of other programs will later agree. The only error recovery that may be necessary is to make the data used by the faulty program consistent with the data used by the other versions. This may be done by copying the data used by one of the other versions. If the fault is in the hardware, the correct result of the majority is used. The N-version, independently written programs provide protection against both hardware and software faults. However, the amount of effort to write N versions of a program, and the amount of processing power required for running the N-versions, is about N times the effort and processing power needed for a simplex program.

Rather than expending N times of effort in program development, a more effective approach is developing a single reliable program using highly structured and formal models to prove the correctness of the software. By developing formal techniques to ensure that the programs operate correctly, the different problems of writing multiple versions of the program, testing them, administering and maintaining the program package, and updating changes are avoided. This approach is taken in the Software Implemented Fault Tolerance (SIFT) system designed by Stanford Research Institute for real-time aircraft control [14–16]. As the name implies, the reliability depends primarily on software mechanisms. The system software is mathematically proven to be correct and is run independently by a number of computer elements. The correct output is chosen by a majority vote implemented by software, in contrast to the hardware voters used in triple modular redundancy structures.

8.5.3 Time Redundancy

Time redundancy or *retrial* is another form of redundancy. Retrial is used to correct errors caused by transient faults. By repeating programs or parts of programs, retrials correct errors caused by transient faults. The system architect must make several decisions about the retrial [17]:

1. Where the retrial must begin to ensure the correction of the error
2. The probability (and necessity) of correcting the error that caused the fault by the rollback action
3. What the cost/benefit ratio is for the rollback in terms of real-time, hardware usage, and software constraints
4. Whether the operating system will permit the rollback
5. The consequences of the rollback in the real world

The machine must be restored to the state of the rollback point; all actions and data changes made after the rollback point as a result of program execution must be restored. Singular events in a real-time system that represent output commands to initiate irreversible actions should not be repeated; for example, an I/O operation in the process control of drilling or cutting a machined part should not be made twice. If such an event is repeated because of a rollback, serious consequences in the real world may result. Provisions to handle singular events must be incorporated into the rollback procedure.

The use of time redundancy in data transfer or I/O communication is much easier to apply and is more effective in correcting transient errors than the use of hardware and software redundancy. For example, if the data received contains an error, the error-check circuitry can initiate a retry. The source or sender retransmits the same data. If no error is detected in the retrial, the system proceeds as if nothing had happened. The event is recorded for later analysis. It is completely transparent to the software.

8.6 HARDWARE FAULT DETECTION TECHNIQUES

Both the static and dynamic redundancy structures described in the previous sections are methods of providing spare parts to enable the system to tolerate failures. When static redundancy is used, the spare units (components, circuits, or subsystems) are permanent parts of the system. They correct errors or *mask* them to prevent them from propagating through the system. The masking function takes place automatically; corrective action is immediate and "wired in." Static types of redundancy have been used primarily in military applications that require high reliability for a short duration.

For commercial applications, the cost of massive redundancy has been too great to justify its use except in special situations. Dynamic redundancy, in which additional subsystems serve as spares within the system, is a far more suitable technique for fault detection in commercial applications. The major components of a repairable fault-tolerant system are fault detection, fault diagnosis (isolation), recovery, and repair. The most important component of all fault-tolerance strategies is fault detection (Fig. 8.11). If all errors were detected and appropriate techniques were applied to recover from them, no fault would lead to a system failure. In practice, this type of coverage cannot be achieved.

The speed of fault detection facilitates the process of fault location and error containment. It is important to perform the next step of fault handling, or isolation, as quickly as possible so that faults do not propagate extensively and are contained within a specified unit. Delayed detection can corrupt important data throughout the entire system. The speed of detection is also important for locating the source of an error: the longer the delay, the harder it is to unwind the system and find the source. Inaccurate diagnosis prevents the working spares from replacing defective units. Furthermore, the speed of detection directly affects system recovery.

In general, error detection is accomplished through the use of hardware, firmware, and software. The type of checking circuitry used depends on the logical structure of the machine as well as the operational and functional use of the data and the control signals.

The hardware error-detection circuitry incorporated in a computer system can take

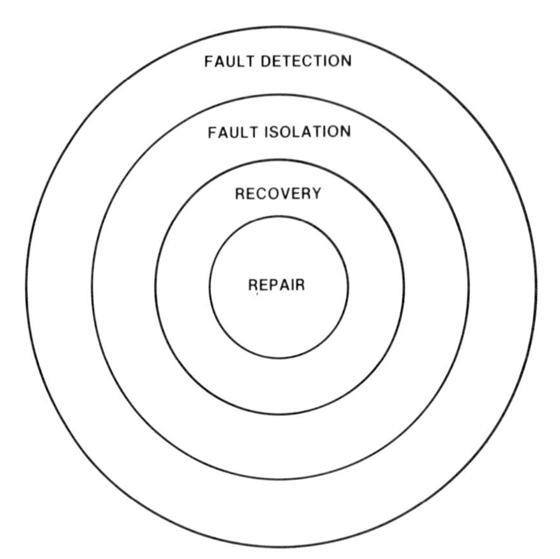

Figure 8.11 Components of fault-tolerance.

many forms. Most of these detection techniques fall into these broad classifications [17]:

- Replication checks
- Coding checks
- Timing checks
- Exception checks

The error detection may be strategically located within a functional unit or at the interface (Fig. 8.12). There are benefits to be gained when detection is done internally at the earliest possible stage, which is during the system activity that generates the results. Internal or early checks minimize the amount of system activity and erroneous transition caused by a fault. There is less time for damage to spread within the system and the actions necessary for fault isolation and error recovery are more likely to be simple. On the other hand, interface or last-moment checks are deployed before any results from a functional unit are transmitted to another functional unit. This prevents any errors from propagating externally to another functional unit and simplifies the more difficult problem of global recovery. The error is contained within the level in which it is detected.

8.6.1 Replication Checks

Replication checking is one of the most complete methods for detecting errors for a computer system. It is also the most expensive redundancy technique because of the hardware required for it. Rapid advances in VLSI and microprocessor technology, however, are beginning to make this type of redundancy cost-effective for many applications requiring high reliability.

Replication checks detect hardware faults. They are based on the assumption that

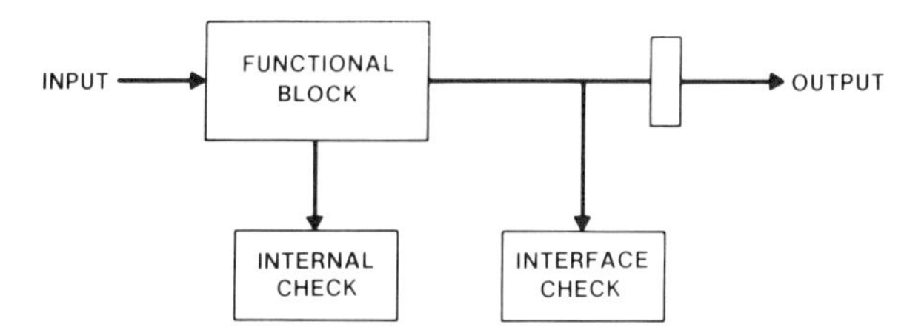

Figure 8.12 Placement of error detection.

the design of the system is correct and that component failures occur independently. A replication check system has an identical copy of a circuit (or subsystem) processing input signals in parallel with an original circuit. The two sets of outputs are then compared by a simple match circuit. No faults in either version of the circuit can remain undetected if the system design is correct and components fail independently.

Replication checks are made at the circuit or subsystem level. The choice of level is influenced to a large degree by the overall fault-tolerant design; the architect must consider reliability, cost, and performance objectives. The arrangement of arithmetic logic units (ALUs) exemplifies replication checking at the circuit level (Fig. 8.13). ALU I is duplicated, and the outputs of the two ALUs are matched after each ALU operation. The outputs from ALU I are used as the actual source of the ALU results to the rest of the processor logic. When the outputs from ALU I are gated onto the output bus, the data is moved into the comparator and matched against the outputs of ALU II. This completely checks the results of the ALU operation. The parity of the result is generated from the outputs of ALU II.

In the AT&T electronic switching systems, replication checks are made at the subsystem level. The approach adopted by the designers of the 1ESS, 1A ESS, 2ESS, and

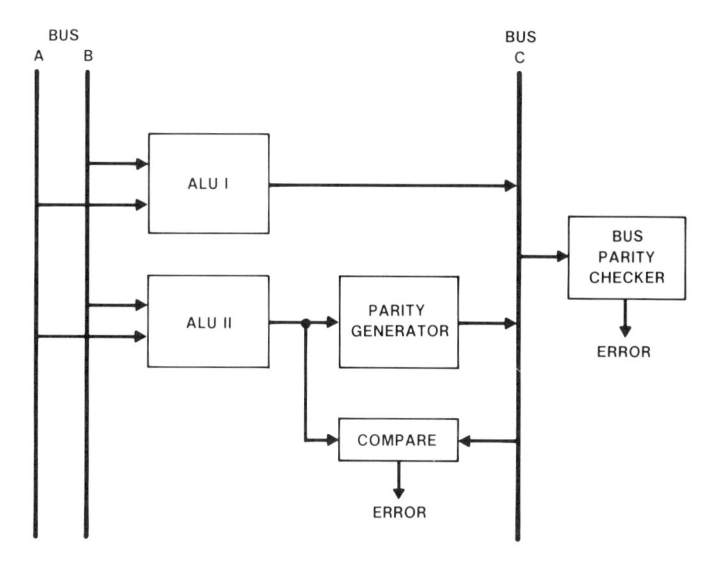

Figure 8.13 Replication at circuit level.

4ESS switching systems is based on the duplication and match philosophy [1]. In this approach, both central processing units handle the same input information and run in synchronism with each other. Critical outputs from each machine are matched against one another at the completion of each internal machine-control operation. Only one CPU, called the on-line machine, actually handles the call processing. The second CPU functions as a standby to the on-line CPU so that matching may be performed. The peripheral equipment is controlled by the on-line CPU. When the outputs from the two CPUs do not match, a fault detection program is called to determine which CPU is faulty. Figure 8.14 shows the 2ESS system configuration, a much simpler structure than that of the later 1A ESS switch. There is only one matcher in the 2ESS switch; it is located in the nonduplicated maintenance center. The matcher always compares the call store input registers in the two CPUs when call store operations are performed synchronously. A fault in almost any part of either CPU quickly results in a mismatch in the call store input register. This occurs because almost all the data manipulation performed in both the program control and the input/output control involves processed data returning to the call store. The call store input is the central point where data is eventually funneled through to the call store. By matching the call-store inputs, an effective check of the system equipment is provided. Compared to the more complex matching of the 1A ESS CPU, error detection in the 2ESS CPU is not as fast since only one crucial node in the processor is matched. Four are matched in the 1A ESS processor [18,19]. Certain faults in the 2ESS processor go undetected until errors are propagated into the call store. This interval is usually no more than tens or hundreds of microseconds. During such a short interval, the fault affects only a single telephone call. The duplication and match approach is cost-effective and practical since the spare unit is required for uninterrupted service.

Replication in a system need not be limited to duplication. Multiple copies of a system module may be used, as in the case of triple modular redundancy systems. When

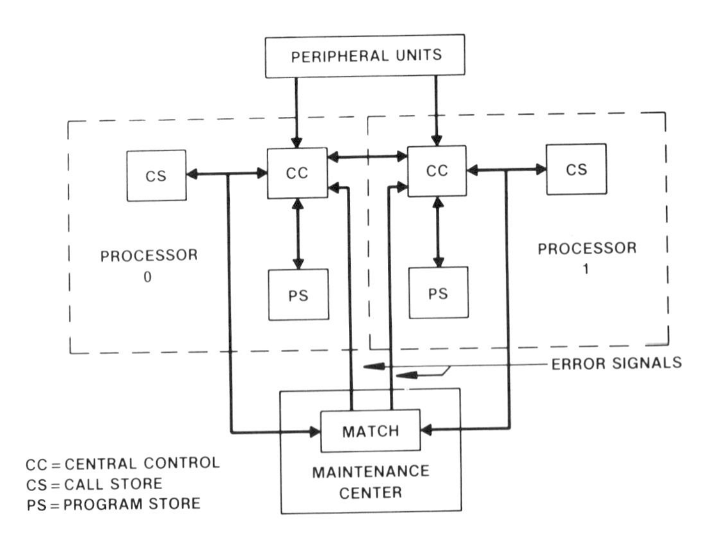

Figure 8.14 No. 2 ESS match access.

three or more copies of a system module are employed, the comparison check is referred to as voting. Voting ensures that erroneous output is suppressed in favor of, or masked by, the majority output. Higher orders of redundancy make error correction possible by identifying which copy of the module is erroneous. The error detection capability is the same whether the unit is duplicated or triplicated. Note, however,that an error check based solely on duplication and matching does not identify which copy of the system unit contains the fault.

An example of replication checks in a triple modular redundant system is the Fault Tolerance Multiple Processor (FTMP) developed for aircraft computers [20]. FTMP is a multiprocessor system consisting of a number of processing modules, global memory modules, and input/output modules connected together by multiple buses. Specialized hardware enables three modules of the same type to be configured to operate together in what is termed a *triad*. Figure 8.15 shows a simplified view of a triad of FTMP modules

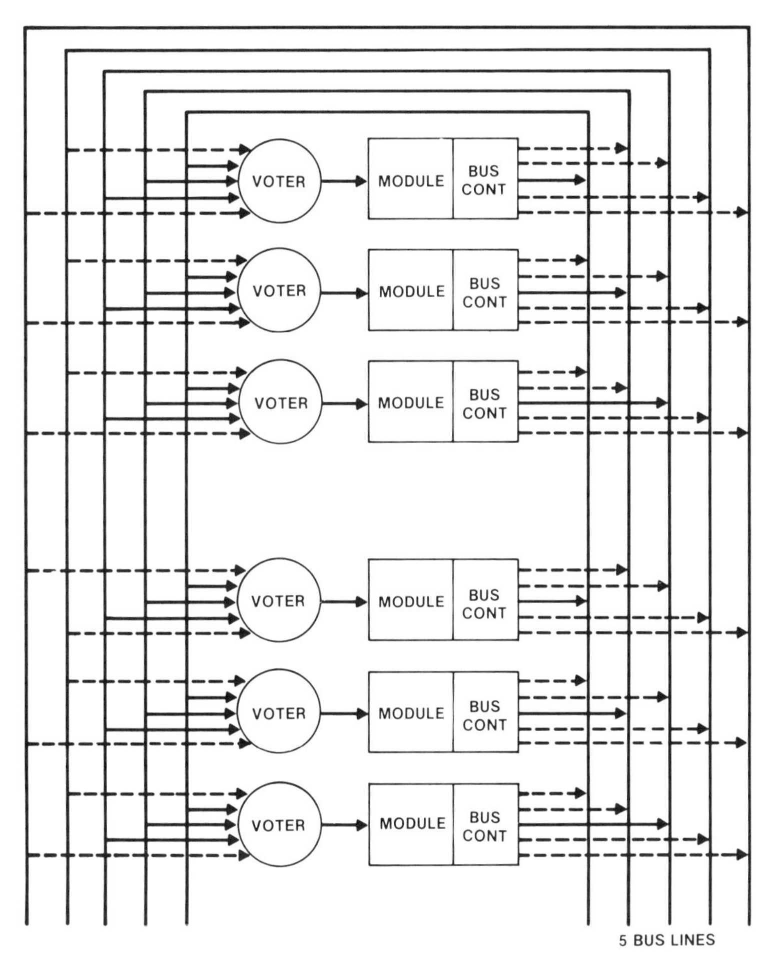

Figure 8.15 Simplified view of triad FTMP modules.

logically connected and operated as TMR units. All activity is conducted by triads of modules and buses. A module triad is formed by associating any three identical modules with one another. This means that any module may serve as a spare in any triad. One triad of bus lines is always active for each of the buses in the system. Each module has access to all the bus lines and contains a decision element to select the correct version of three bus lines. There are five bus lines. Three of the five bus lines (depicted as solid lines in the figure) are enabled. They are connected to a voter in each module, thus constituting a TMR element. The other two bus lines (dotted lines) are not enabled and serve as spares. The three active bus lines carry three independently generated versions of data, each coming from a different member of the triad that is transmitting the data (solid line to the bus) on one specific bus line.

The replication checks based on identical copies of a subsystem do not detect the consequences of design faults. Design faults affect all copies of the unit; hence, they are not detectable by replication. Formal design verification techniques must be employed to ensure that there are no design faults in the structure that could bypass the protection provided by the replication.

8.6.2 Coding Checks

Error detection codes are formed by the addition of check bits to a data word. The error detection capability of this approach is a direct function of the number of check bits included in a word. There are two types of coding checks: separable and nonseparable. *Separable checks,* including parity checking and arithmetic codes, are characterized by the addition of check bits to data words. *Nonseparable checks,* such as m-out-of-n code, are coded in specialized formats.

Parity checking is the most widely used type of coding check because it requires a minimum number of check bits and provides a good error detection capability. Parity checking, a type of separable error detection code, is accomplished by assigning a parity bit to a data word. An odd-parity check requires that both the check bit and the total number of bits in the ones state in the data word be an odd number. An even-parity check requires that the check bit and the total number of bits in the ones state in the data word be an even number. For example, data words 10110100 and 10101000 contain four ones (an even number) and three ones (an odd number), respectively. For an odd-parity check, the check bit must be set to one in the first data word and zero in the second data word, that is, 10110100*1* and 10101000*0*, respectively. In this example, the check bit occupies the least-significant bit position of each data word. For an even-parity check, the check must be set to zero in the first data word and to one in the second data word. Any single-bit errors or odd multiple-bit errors are detectable by a single parity check bit. However, faults caused by an even number of erroneous bits are not detected by the parity checks since an even number of errors appears transparent to the parity check logic. Parity checking is extensively used in data paths and memory systems in electronic switching systems [1].

Another type of separable code that is used for error detection is arithmetic codes

[21]. These codes are based on remainder theorems for residue arithmetic. The major difference between the two code categories is that residue codes are preserved under arithmetic operations. For residue codes, the operands (x,y) and their check symbols (x′, y′) are handled separately; (x,y) generates the result z while (x′, y′) generates check result z′. The checking algorithm computes the residue from the result z and compares it with the check result z′. If the two values match, no error is detected. A disagreement between the two values is considered a fault in either the main arithmetic unit or in the check circuit. Arithmetic codes are rarely used in the LSI and VLSI fault-tolerant system design since the present day trend is toward inexpensive hardware and single-chip CPUs. It is much more economical just to replicate and compare results for error detection [1,22].

The *fixed-weight* or *m-out-of-n code* is an important type of nonseparable coding check. In coding theory, the *weight* of a code word is defined as the number of nonzero components in the code word. Therefore, a fixed-weight code has a fixed number of ones. The unique property of the fixed-weight coding check is its ability to detect all *unidirectional* multiple-bit errors. This type of error occurs when a fault causes all the data bits in the code word either to change from the zero state to the one state or from the one state to the zero state. Unidirectional errors cause the code word to have different weight, which makes the errors detectable by the checking logic. Errors that cause transitions in the states of the data bits in both directions simultaneously are not always detectable using fixed-weight coding checks.

Encoded binary signals used in a computer system represent two types of information: data and control. The data signals, in turn, represent a variety of entities, including numbers, characters, addresses, and labels. These entities may be used directly without modification, or they may be operated by any of the arithmetical or logical functions available on the processor to compute specific values needed by the currently executing program. Separable error detection codes (systematic codes) such as parity allow the original data to be determined without any additional decoding. This characteristic is quite convenient for processing and handling data signals within the computer system. For control functions, the binary encoded signals may similarly employ separable error detection codes. However, these signals are usually decoded at their destinations (that is, the logic gates that generate each of the control signals). Therefore, nonseparable error detection codes with special characteristics are more effective for detecting errors on individual control signals. *M*-out-of-*n* codes have been employed extensively in the 3ESS processor [23] and the STAR computer [24].

A *cyclic code* is a type of separable code that forms a code word from any cyclic shift of the code. Cyclic codes are easy to encode and decode using linear feedback shift registers, and hence they are quite commonly used for checking serial data streams. These codes have been developed to provide efficient error detection for blocks of data. For instance, a cyclic redundancy code check is used in the disk stores of the 1A ESS switching system [25] and the 3B20D disk system [26]. A detailed mathematical treatment of error detection techniques using coding schemes is given by Peterson and Weldon [27].

8.6.3 Timing Checks

Hardware checking procedures, such as replication and coding techniques, are designed to detect physical circuit faults in the arithmetic logic units, the data path(s), the control sections, and a specific subsystem(s). In general, hardware error checks are not capable of detecting software faults. Even when two processors are running in syncronism and are matched for error detection, the same error may appear in the program executing in the on-line machine and in the copy of the program executing in the standby machine. The error can therefore go undetected.

Timing checks are an effective form of software check for detecting errors in duplicated programs if the specification of a component includes timing constraints. The operating system normally oversees and coordinates the activities of the system. For some applications, such as the control of a telephone office, the operating system is cyclic in nature; that is, the operating system program always returns to its basic starting point on completion of the scheduled task. The main program is normally exercised and debugged thoroughly before it is integrated into a system load. Usually, however, every conceivable path in the program has not been checked under all possible conditions. Consequently, some of the less frequently traversed branches of the main program may contain subtle logic faults that may sidetrack the main flow of the execution sequence so it never returns to the main program. This situation, of course, may also result from undetected hardware faults and program bugs.

A hardware timer, also referred to as *watchdog timer,* is used in telephone switching systems to guard against program faults from which the system cannot recover. The concept is relatively simple. A hardware timer runs continuously in the processor; the main program periodically resets it if nothing unusual occurs to deflect the main program from its normal execution sequence. If for some reason (such as a software bug or a hardware fault) the execution sequence never returns to the main program, the timer is not reset. It then issues a high-priority interrupt request and takes the necessary action to reinitialize the system. When a redundant standby processor is provided in the system, the timer interrupt may automatically cause control to switch to the standby machine in an attempt to recover from the system error.

Circuit operations, particularly those involved in the communications between two functional units, also use timing checks. For example, in memory access, the data transfer between the CPU and the main store is usually done asynchronously by handshaking. When a memory-read operation initiates, the CPU waits for a response signal from the memory control unit indicating that the addressed data word is ready to be transferred. If, for certain reasons such as a hardware fault in the control logic, the response signal is not generated, the CPU will wait indefinitely. Since the normal memory read operation only takes a certain amount of time, a hardware timer can be used to detect errors.

In the nonstop Tandem computer, timing checks are integrated into the operating system as one of the major error detection measures [5]. Each processor sends a special message every second to all the other processors in the system. Each processor then checks every two seconds whether messages have been received from the other processors. If a message has not been received, the corresponding processor is assumed to have failed and appropriate action is taken. Timing checks are also made for all input/output operations.

Although timeout signals from a hardware timer indicate a problem in the system, their absence does not necessarily mean that the system is performing satisfactorily. Timing checks on circuit function are not complete system checks. They reveal the presence of faults but not their absence. Consequently, computer architects use timing checks to supplement other checks to cover a higher percentage of faults in a system.

8.6.4 Exception Checks

Programs run in protected environments; they follow sets of prescribed constraints. If the programs are fault-free, they observe the constraints and perform the specified functions accordingly. However, design faults in the software often violate these constraints. The violations may affect the entire system adversely. Some hardware detection circuits are usually designed into the system to recognize design faults and handle them as exceptions. Exception handling, therefore, refers to detecting and responding to abnormal or undesired events.

These constraints may be attributed to either the hardware or the software. Some hardware examples are:

- Improper address alignment
- Unequipped memory locations
- Unused opcode
- Stack overflow

These constraints usually result from the inability of the hardware to provide the services needed by the software. Take, for example, the case of improper address alignment. In many modern computers, integer data types of 8 – , 16 – , 32 – , and 64-bit sizes (byte, half-word, word, double-word) are supported by their instruction set. It is convenient and simpler from the hardware viewpoint to have these data types aligned on the word boundary that matches the layout of the main memory (Fig. 8.16). By aligning the data type on word boundaries, deviations from the format are detected as *exceptions* of improper address alignment. A hardware constraint, of course, places an additional burden on the programmer to observe predefined constraints. As hardware costs continue to decrease, it is appropriate to reduce or eliminate some of the hardware constraints. For example, the VAX 11/780 has integer data types of 8, 16, 32, and 64 bits. The system has been generalized so that these data types occupy one, two, four, and eight contiguous bytes starting on any arbitrary-byte boundary. Considerations like this are becoming increasingly prevalent in modern computer design.

The software structure also places certain constraints on the system to enhance its robustness and provide a protected environment for application programs. Some software exception checks are:

- Illegal execution of privilege instructions
- Out-of-range addresses

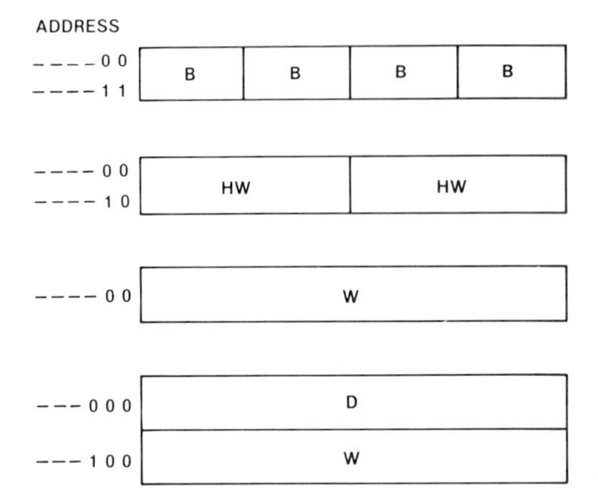

Figure 8.16 Data type layout.

- Memory-access violation
- Illegal operands
- Invalid arithmetic operations such as overflow, underflow, and division by zero.

The detection of an error raises an exception, which is followed by the automatic invocation of the appropriate exception handling facility. In many cases, the exception is attributable to a design fault in the program.

8.7 SOFTWARE DETECTION TECHNIQUES

The need for developing software mechanisms for detecting software errors is increasingly apparent if reliable systems are to be built. Hardware mechanisms, though technologically well advanced, can detect and isolate faults in the hardware but they are not proficient at analyzing software faults. Early software detection schemes rely on hardware protection mechanisms such as exception checks to indicate when program errors occur. This reliance on the hardware mechanisms is inefficient, however, because often by the time a software error causes a hardware exception, the error has propagated to affect an unnecessarily large area. The original error may compound itself so severely that it goes undetected and uncorrected. In large systems, the approach for detecting software errors based on the principle that they eventually cause hardware exceptions is unfeasible [28]. Better software error detection capabilities are needed. But designing them is not easy because software faults are not as distinct as hardware component failures.

Software errors must be detected rapidly during program execution, especially in real-time systems. In many cases, a process stops rather than continues, resulting in a wrong operation since many of the results are damaging and irrevocable. Unlike hardware component failure rates, there are no reliable statistics on the behavior and distribution of various software faults. Design faults are extremely difficult to characterize and enumerate in terms of expected failure modes. Software error detection can only be carried out by recognizing the *abnormal* behavior of the system. A set of standards for *normal* behavior is then required to check deviations from it. By checking the reasonableness of the program behavior at various stages of computation, errors are detected early enough to restrict the propagation of bad data.

There are several general techniques for observing the behavior of a computer system to detect malfunctions [29,30]:

- *Function of a process:* The reasonableness of the outputs for a given set of inputs is checked at the functional block level. Certain performance measures may be used to indicate whether the system is functioning properly. When the applied work load is normal, but measurements that characterize the performance of the system (such as response time, throughput, and time required to perform a standard function) fall outside established threshold values, the system probably has one or more errors.
- *Control sequence of a process:* The sequence of computations made by an executing process is referred to as the control sequence of the process. Each computation changes various system states. By comparing the states changed with valid states, system abnormalities may be detected.
- *Data of a process:* The integrity of the system's data and its structure can be observed while the system executes the program sequence. Mutilation of system data can also be caused by software or hardware trouble.

A *process* is defined here to mean a self-contained portion of a computation which, once initated, is carried out to its completion without the need for additional input.

8.7.1 Functional Checking

The functional aspects of a process may be checked by verifying the reasonableness of the outputs for a given set of inputs. When the relationship between the inputs and outputs is one-to-one, *reversal checks* may be used to check the correctness of the process. A reversal check takes the outputs from the system and computes what the inputs should have been. The calculated inputs are then compared to the actual ones to check for error conditions. In the AT&T 1A ESS switching system, a simple reversal check is applied to a magnetic tape write operation by reading the data written onto the tape and comparing it to the original data. Well-defined mathematical functions often lend themselves to reversal checks. For example, if the output is the solution of a set of mathematical equations, its correctness may be verified by substituting the output into the equation and checking for consistency. In some cases, there may be a simple relationship between the output variables. The output can be verified by checking this relationship. For example, the output of a sorting program may be tested to ensure that the output is indeed sorted (ordered) and contains the correct number of elements.

In many other cases, the correctness of the output can only be verified by an algorithm that is just as complicated as the original algorithm and is therefore subject to design faults of its own. This situation further complicates system reliability. A rigorous check on the correctness of the output is impractical, so only the reasonableness of the output is checked. An unreasonable output usually indicates the presence of errors, but not vice versa.

Timing checks, as mentioned in the previous section, are also used to check given processes. A timing check is a classic way of easily observing the internal performance of a system and detecting bottlenecks and infinite loops. The procedure is to set the interval timer to sound an alarm after an adequate time elapses for the system to perform its function unless something goes wrong. If the timer interrupt occurs before the system has reset it, the interrupt handler must assume that the process has not been carried out properly. Again, it is a check for reasonableness. The lack of a timeout does not imply the absence of errors.

Software functional checking is analogous to a black-box approach in testing a hardware system by examining the relationships between the inputs and the corresponding outputs. Software functional checking, however, is neither efficient nor effective. A better approach in error detection is achieved when a *direct* access of an internal structure monitors its internal behavior, including its control sequence and the dynamic behavior of critical or global variables.

8.7.2 Control Sequence Checking

When each task represents a well-defined set of operations, the correct sequence in which these operations are executed determines the proper output of a process. Any deviation from the specified execution sequence produces a faulty output. A software fault that causes an incorrect execution sequence is called a *control fault*. A control fault may cause the following consequences:

- The execution of an infinite loop
- The execution of a program loop an incorrect number of times
- The traversal of an illegal or wrong branch

These types of error conditions can be detected by various schemes designed for sequence checking. The three types of control sequence that have been implemented are the branch-allowed checks, the relay-runner scheme, and the combined watchdog timer and relay-runner scheme.

A branch-allowed check is a means of detecting the execution of an improper branching operation. This type of check is implemented on several AT&T electronic switching systems [31]. Figure 8.17 illustrates this scheme. A check bit, called the *branch-allowed* (BA) bit, is assigned to each word in the main memory. If the BA bit contains a zero, the contents of that location in main memory may *not* be referenced by any branch instruction; the location, however, may be referenced by the program counter (PC) in its normal sequential addressing mode (that is, the mode in which the PC is incremented by one to point to the location of the next instruction). If the BA bit contains a one, the contents of that location may be referenced by *any* branch instruction located anywhere in main memory. If a branch instruction is being executed in a normal processing sequence, the BA bit of the target location is checked to see whether a branching operation can reference the contents of the target location. If the BA bit is in the zero

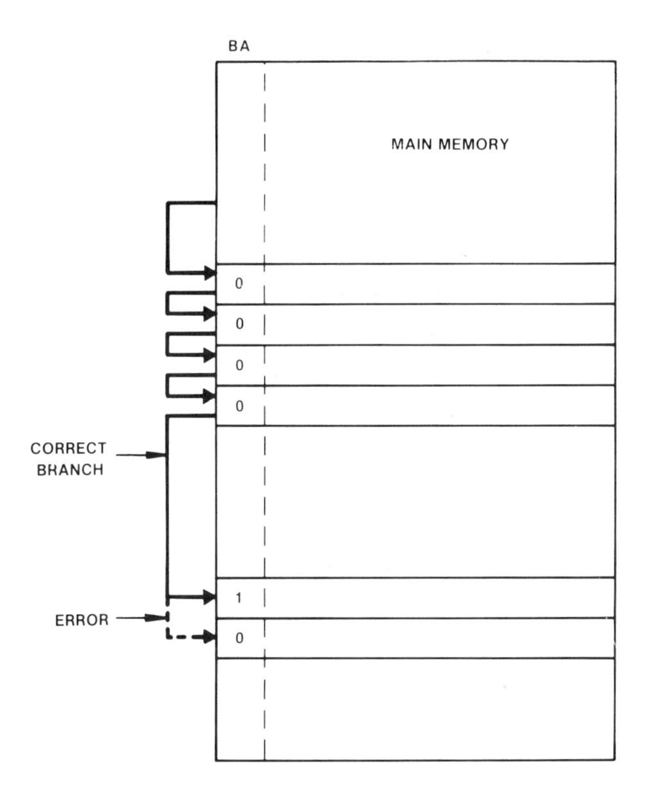

Figure 8.17 Branch-allowed check.

state, an improper branch has been executed, and the BA checking logic indicates that an error has occurred.

The relay-runner scheme also provides protection against illegal jumps that may be caused by software errors or hardware malfunctions [32]. In this scheme, a *baton* which is similar to a password, is carried along with the transfer of control and checked at the appropriate points. When an illegal branch is taken, control does not have the valid baton value. The error is detected at the next checkpoint. Figure 8.18 shows a flow diagram of the relay-runner scheme. The piece of the program is partitioned into functional blocks separated by relay checkpoints. These checkpoints are conditional statements to test whether the program flow carries the valid, up-to-date baton code. The application program enters the first of a series of baton codes in a specified address, for example, CODE1. When program execution reaches the first relay checkpoint, the instruction compares the content at CODE1 with a present code number. If they agree, the content of CODE1 is cleared to zero and a new baton code is stored in location CODE2. If the codes do not agree, an error-trap routine is invoked and normal execution terminates. The process of checking and updating the baton code is performed at various strategic points throughout the program. The scheme is analogous to a relay race, in which one runner does not proceed until receiving the baton from the previous runner.

Branch – Allowed Check

FIGURE 8.17

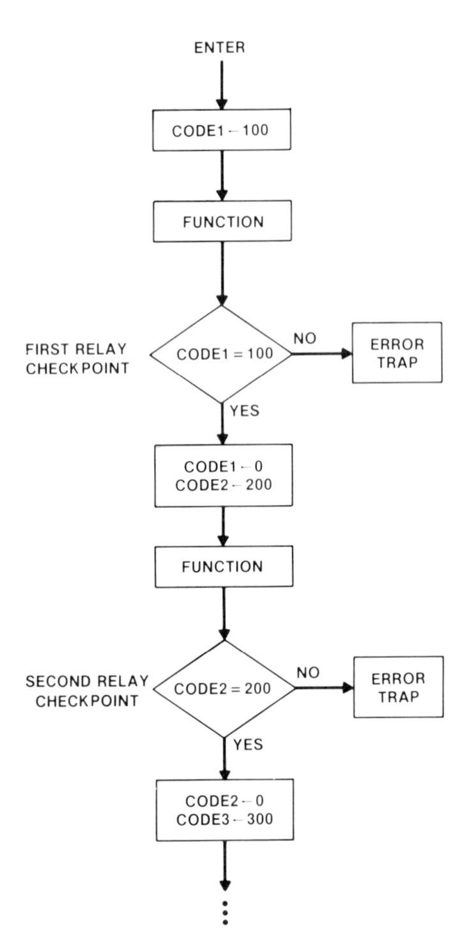

Figure 8.18 Relay-runner scheme.

The *combined watchdog timer and relay-runner scheme* [7] combines the effectiveness of the watchdog timer operation for detecting infinite program loops with the ability of the relay-runner scheme to detect faults in the control structure of program sequencing. Although the operation of a hardware timer is simple to implement in most processors (see Section 8.6.3), additional safeguards to program sequencing and generating timer reset signals is provided by the relay-runner scheme. The hardware timer must be reset only when the system is performing properly; otherwise, the timer should be allowed to request a recovery action. For example, the program may be segmented with relay checks inserted at the appropriate points (Fig. 8.19). In addition, a marker keeps track of the number of checkpoints the program has traversed. The timer is activated at the first program segment. Before a reset timer is generated, the program must pass through

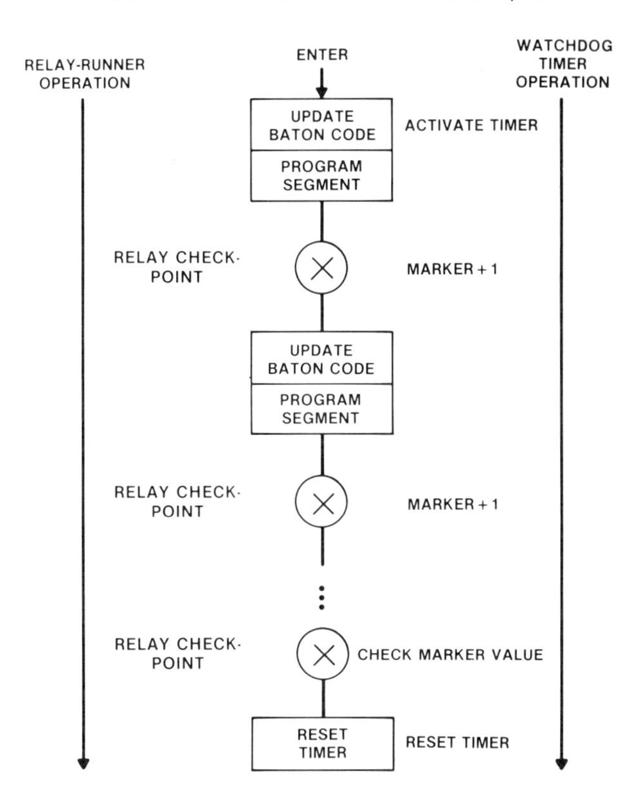

Figure 8.19 Combined relay-runner and watchdog timer scheme.

each checkpoint successfully and have gone through a correct number of checkpoints. The second check is redundant in that the relay-runner scheme ensures that all segments are sequenced correctly. If the program jumps ahead by one or more program segments, the baton code will not match the present code number at the next checkpoint. If the program backtracks one or more segments, the old baton value will be reset to zero; the relay-point check will also detect this condition.

8.7.3 Data Checking

Software errors, as previously indicated, may be caused by residual software design faults as well as by hardware faults. Each can result in the mutilation of memory. Although "data" usualy refers to the information items to be processed by the program, it refers generally to all the information stored in main memory. This means both program instructions and data. Text containing the program instructions may be checked by a functional check or a control sequence check, as described in previous sections. The integrity of the data value of the instructions may be protected easily by coding techniques such as Hamming correction codes and maintaining a check sum of the content of a piece of code. The Hamming correction code is very effective in ensuring the integrity of data values for both instructions and data as they are used and processed.

Besides instructions, data checks may be performed by in-line program checks or by independent software error detection programs called audits. In-line checks include the code in the system to check the validity of data structures each time they are processed by the system routines. If data structures are checked before they are used, errors previously introduced by system components are identified and will not be propagated. If the data structures are checked immediately after they are modified, the routine causing an error is usually identified. For example, if an item is inserted in a linked list, a check can be made on the link in the opposite direction to verify its integrity after the insertion. Properly constructed tests can detect many errors with a small amount of processing. On the other hand, extensive checking often introduces an unacceptable overhead and substantially degrades the perfomance.

Another effective in-line check covers parameters passed to system routines by user programs. It is quite possible that an error in one routine will cause another routine to fail because of an invalid parameter. This conceals the original source of the error. Since checking all the parameters passed between system routines would undoubtedly consume too much overhead, a more structured check with adequate error detection capability may be applied, as is done in the SUE operating system [33]. This approach takes advantage of the levels of structure of the program environment; parameters are checked as they pass from a higher to a lower level. User programs, for example, are at a higher level than system supervisory programs. The checks are not made in the reverse direction. Also, parameters are not checked between routines on the same level. A balance betwen error checking and the overhead of in-line checking is achieved with this straightforward procedure.

An alternative to in-line checking is auditing. *Audits* are integrated in the system software and, therefore, normally consume only a small portion of the total processing capacity of the system. The system invokes audits periodically to run routine checks. Audits may be invoked manually when trouble is suspected. Audit programs check for inconsistencies in the data structures; the inconsistencies usually reflect erroneous system operations. They do not anticipate problems or determine the causes of problems and so they are fast, thorough error detection mechanisms.

Several techniques used by audit programs are similar to those for in-line checking. These techniques include consistency checks, linkage checks, integrity checks, and timeout checks. *Consistency checks* are made on redundant information stored as backup records. For example, if the program and critical data are stored in main memory, a backup recovery copy is placed on a low-cost disk system. When changes are made, records are kept on both the previous and changed versions. The comparison of the updated backup record with the main memory provides a means for detecting an error in the main memory. Correction is done by simply overwriting mutilated data from the secondary storage. Furthermore, if necessary, the previous version of the program may be reloaded to allow a more drastic initialization.

Linkage checks verify that registers associated with facilities are validly linked together by using the redundancy inherent in the linkage structure. For example, when a doubly linked list is audited, redundancy permits the last entry on the list to be identified by the previous entry and by the next entry. Similarly, a loop-around check may be made of the registers linked in a circular list.

Integrity checks are made on state data associated with facilities. These checks are done by verifying the consistency of the data with the actual states of the resources. Error-detecting codes may be employed to code the state of facilities.

Timeout checks locate facilities that may be falsely put into the busy state. If an absolute limit is placed on the holding time of a facility, the facility may be examined at a period equal to the maximum holding time. If the audit finds a facility in the nonidle state longer than the maximum time allowed, it assumes that the facility is lost and can be idled. The audit restores the facility to the operational state.

Audit programs sample, rather than continuously observe, the system's behavior; hence, they require less overhead than in-line checks. They do not, however, provide as timely a detection of errors as in-line checks provide. Many routines may access invalid data before an audit program determines that an error has occurred. Subsequent operations with the erroneous data may cause other system data to become corrupted, making recovery more difficult and drastic. But the relatively low overhead of audit programs allows them to check the system more extensively than in-line checks.

8.8 FAULT RECOVERY

Recovery is the most complex and difficult function of all systems [1]. The shortcomings of either the hardware or software design to detect faults when they occur has a direct effect on the system's ability to recover. When faults go undetected, the system remains impaired until the trouble is recognized. Another kind of recovery problem can occur if the system is unable to isolate a faulty subsystem properly and configure a working system around it. The many possible system states that may arise under trouble conditions make recovery a complicated process.

The more rapidly an error is detected, the easier it is to determine which component is faulty and perform fault recovery. Rapid error detection also helps ensure that errors do not spread. Rapid error detection and good error containment are therefore fundamental to successful fault recovery.

8.8.1 Classification of Recovery Procedures

There are three classes of recovery procedures: full recovery, degraded recovery, and safe shutdown [34]. The recovery procedures may be invoked automatically—with no known interaction between the maintenance operator and the system—or manually. Manually initiated recoveries may make use of extensive program-controlled sequences. The three classes of recovery procedures are described below.

Full Recovery. In a real-time facility, the system providing continuous service must remain operational even in a faulty environment. This means that trouble symptoms must be recognized quickly and faulty units repaired with little or no interference from the user's standpoint. To provide full system capability at all times, appropriate spare subsystems must be available as replacement units for defective ones. A full recovery procedure usually requires all five aspects of fault-tolerant computing: fault detection, fault isolation, system recovery, fault diagnosis, and repair. The sequence of events is depicted in Fig. 8.20. Before the system action, the fault must be *detected*. The objective of *fault isolation* is to identify the subsystem (for example, a memory module, a processor unit, an input/output channel controller, etc.) where the fault occurred. By using automatic program-controlled switching, the system is reconfigured by interchanging the faulty subsystem with its corresponding spare. The *recovery* procedure is then initiated to restore the system to its original computing capability with no loss of hardware or software features. The period of interrupted service during the recovery procedure is minimized and is hardly noticeable to the user. The tasks of *diagnosis* and *repair*—the most time-consuming tasks of the recovery procedure—may be deferred and interleaved with normal system operation (Fig. 8.20).

Degraded Recovery. This is also referred to as *graceful degradation* operation. As in the case of full recovery, all the steps involved with fault-tolerance (detection, isolation, system recovery, diagnosis, and repair) must be included in the procedure. The sequence of events shown in Fig. 8.20 also applies to a degraded recovery, except that no subsystem is switched in. Instead, the defective component is taken out of service and the system is returned to a fault-free state of operation. Selected computing functions in systems using degraded recovery are allowed to operate so that their real-time performance characteristics fall below a normally accepted standard until repairs are made.

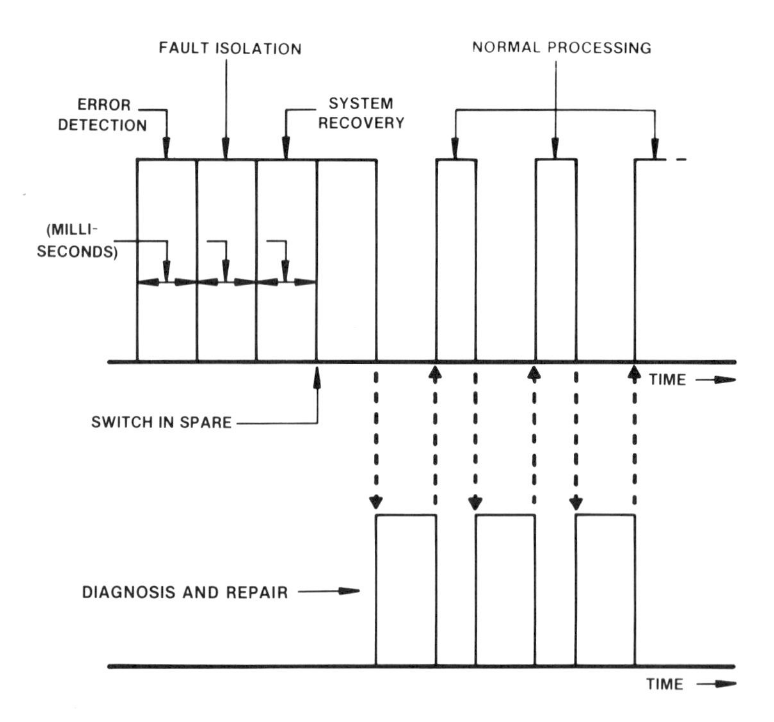

Figure 8.20 Fault recovery sequence (with spare).

Safe Shutdown. This is often called a *fail-safe* operation. It occurs as the limiting case of degraded recovery when the system computing capability has degraded below a minimally acceptable threshold of operation. The goals of safe shutdown are:

1. To avoid damaging any system elements or stored software modules (programs or data) that may still be compromised after degraded operation has been allowed to take place
2. To terminate interaction with any associated systems (users) in an orderly manner
3. To deliver diagnostic and shutdown messages to designated users, systems, and maintenance personnel

The safe shutdown category is similar to a system without any redundancy (Fig. 8.21). Action to isolate the fault must be initiated to determine its identity and location. The normal system operation, which had been momentarily interrupted at the time of fault detection, must now be suspended through diagnosis and repair. The system must then be recovered to a hardware state and program point where normal processing can be resumed.

All three types of fault recovery require certain operations to take place after the fault is detected. A comparison of Figs. 8.20 and 8.21 illustrates some of the maintenance advantages of hardware redundancy. First, the time-consuming task of diagnosis and repair may be deferred and interleaved with normal system processing on a time-shared basis after the system has been restored to the operational state. Second, the availability of a spare permits the fault-free machine to interrogate and diagnose the faulty machine. This type of testing is easily made automatic under program control. Otherwise, it is necessary to have an operator manually force the machine through the diagnostic and recovery steps.

8.8.2 Reconfiguration

In redundant systems, an ensemble of spares or multiple functional units ensure a continuously working system. The simplest structure is a duplex configuration in which every

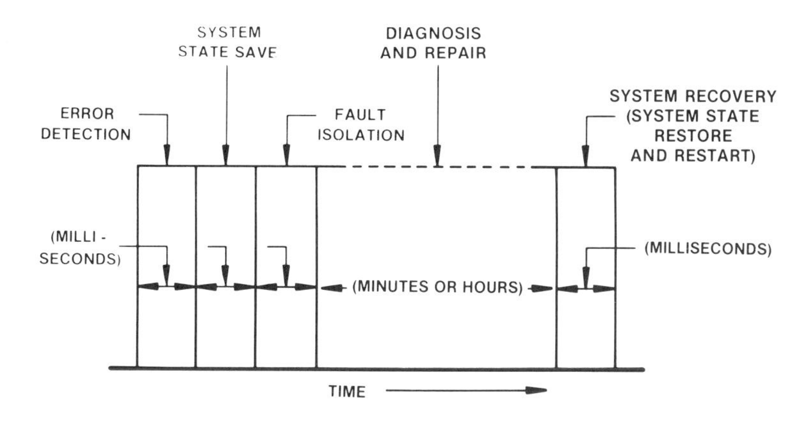

Figure 8.21 Fault recovery sequence (without spare).

functional unit is duplicated. If one of the units fails, the duplicated unit is switched in and continuous operation is maintained. Meanwhile, the defective unit is repaired. Should a fault occur in the duplicated unit during the repair interval, the whole system will, of course, go down. But if the repair interval is relatively short, the probability of simultaneous faults occurring in the two identical units is quite small.

The capability of the system to dynamically reconfigure its modules into a working system provides the continuous operation required for many critical real-time applications. In general, hardware redundancy at the subsystem level is essential to fault tolerance and ease of repair. Several structures have been successfully used to achieve high availability by means of dynamic reconfiguration. Figure 8.22(a) shows the simplest duplex structure. The CPU and its associated bus are duplicated. One machine is in the active mode and controls the system; the spare is strictly a standby unit. In this arrangement, standby machines do not produce or contribute any useful work except in emergencies. Figure 8.22(b) shows a load-sharing arrangement in which both CPUs are actively performing concurrent operations. The faulty processing unit is switched out of service when a hardware error is detected, which reduces the performance capabilities of the system. If the application can tolerate this sort of degradation, the multiple active configuration provides better overall system performance than simple duplex systems.

The combined multiple processors with standby spares is shown in Fig. 8.22(c). The demands for performance and reliability are ideally met by this structure. It is modu-

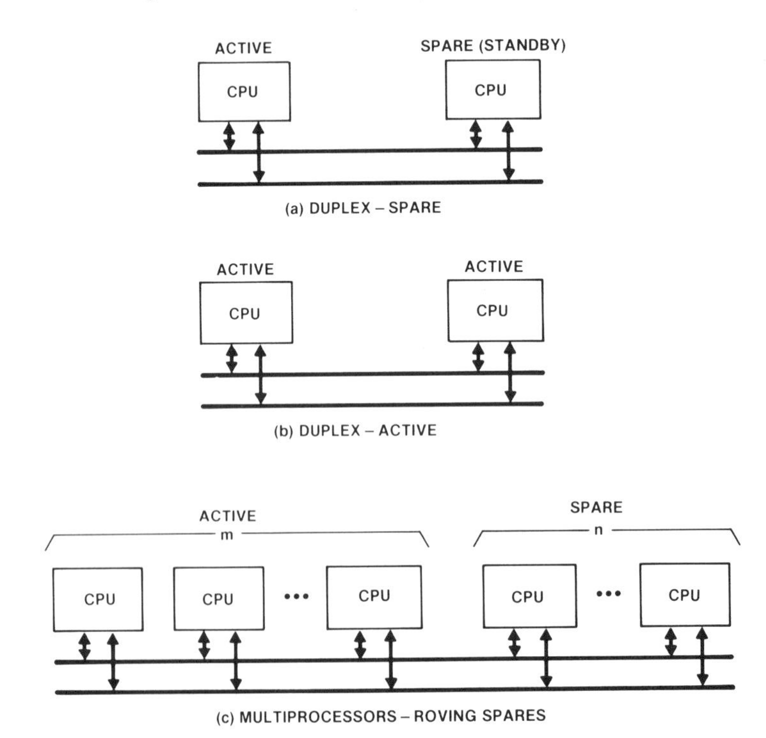

Figure 8.22 Dynamic redundant structures.

lar in that the system can grow gracefully by adding processing modules. High reliability is met by the number of roving spare modules provided in the pool. If one of the active modules fails, a roving spare is substituted and the system recovers to its full capability. Full performance is maintained until all the spares are exhausted.

The active-standby duplex structure as shown in Fig. 8.22(a) is quite simple and straightforward. Because of its simplicity, this redundancy structure has been used throughout each ESS processor [1]. For medium and small ESS processors, Fig. 8.23 shows a system structure containing several functional units that are treated as a single entity. The structure consists of two store communities: *program store* (PS) and *call store* (CS). The program store is in read-only memory and contains the call processing, maintepanance, and administration programs; it also contains long-term translation and system parameters. In this arrangement, the complete processor is treated as a single functional block and is duplicated. This type of single-unit duplex system has two possible configurations. Either processor 0 or processor 1 can be assigned as the on-line working system while the other unit serves as a standby backup (active redundancy). The single-unit duplex configuration has the merit of being very simple in terms of the number of switching blocks in the system. This configuration simplifies not only the recovery program but also the hardware interconnections because the additional accesses required to make each duplicated block capable of switching independently into the on-line system configuration are eliminated.

In the large 1ESS switching system, which contains many components, the mean time to fail (MTTF) becomes too low to meet standard reliability requirements. To increase the value of the MTTF, either the number of components (failure rate) or the repair time must be reduced. The single-unit duplex configuration can be partitioned into a

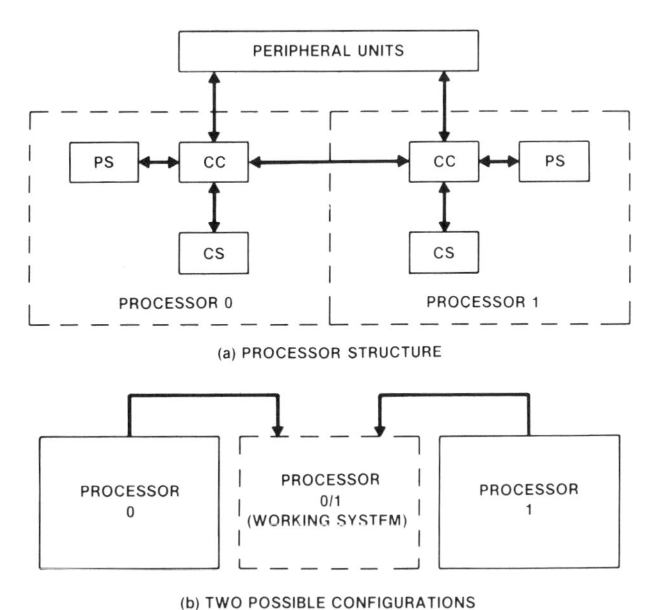

Figure 8.23 Single-unit duplex configuration.

multiunit duplex configuration (Fig. 8.24). In this arrangement, each subunit contains a small number of components and is able to be switched into a working system. The system will fail only if a fault occurs in the redundant subunit while the original is being repaired. Since each subunit contains fewer components, the probability of the two simultaneous faults occurring in a duplicated pair of subunits is reduced. A working system is configured with a fault-free CCx-CSx-CSBx-PSx-PBSx-PUBx arrangement, where x is either subunit 0 or subunit 1. This means there are 2^6 or 64 possible combinations of system configurations. Reconfiguration into a working system under a trouble condition may be an extensive task, depending on the severity of the fault. For example, the processor may lose its ability to make proper decisions. This problem is addressed in the 1A ESS processor by an autonomous hardware *processor configuration circuit* in each CC to assist in assembling a working system [18].

8.8.3 Software Recovery

The objective of error recovery is restoring the system to a consistent state from an erroneous one, thus allowing the system to function properly. There are three error recovery strategies: *backward error recovery, forward error recovery and resets* [17]. The backward error recovery technique, also called *rollback-and-retry,* involves validating and saving the system state (for example, saving the contents of registers within a processor and of main memory in a reliable backup storage) at various stages during program execution. As shown in Fig. 8.25, the points during execution at which system states are saved

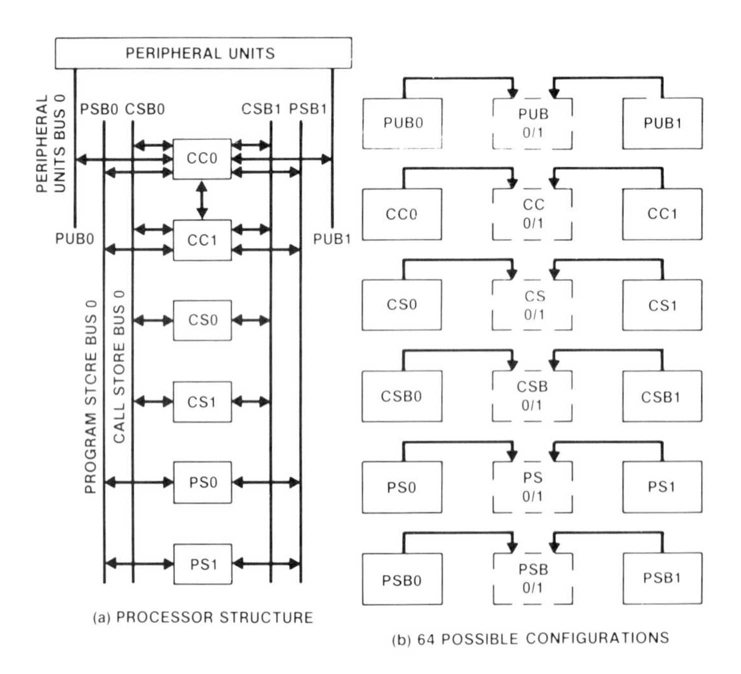

Figure 8.24 Multi-unit duplex configuration.

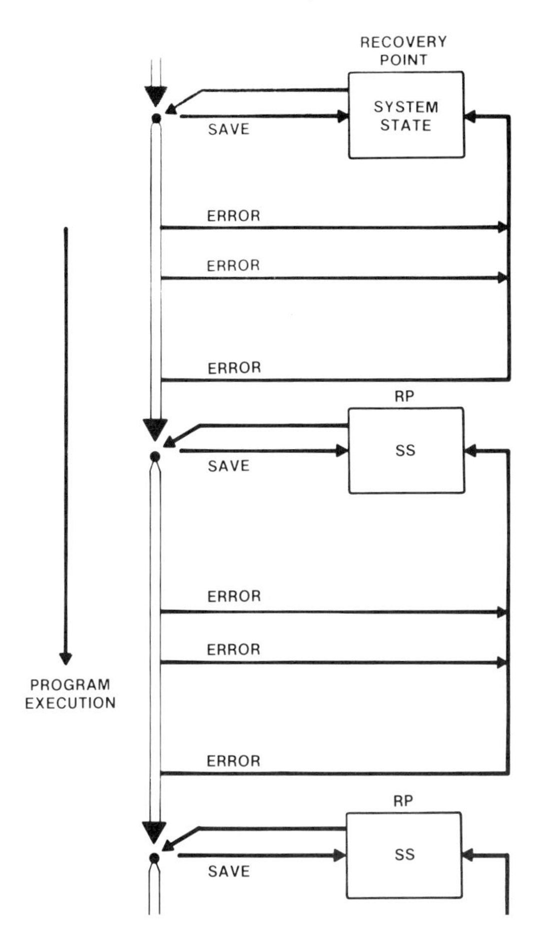

Figure 8.25 Backward error recovery.

are called *recovery points*. If an error is detected, the backward recovery technique reestablishes the system to a previously recorded state and restarts the program execution. It does not identify precisely the source of the error, and after each backward recovery, the work that has been discarded must be repeated.

The rollback and retry recovery technique is not suitable for hardware faults because the same error conditions result. For the backward recovery to work in this situation, the rollback must be done in fault-free hardware. For example, in the Tandem computer system, the program is made up of *process pairs* [35]. One of the processes is considered *primary* and all program execution is done in it. The other process is the *backup* process, which consists of the recovery point and periodic updates of the backup process. The *checkpoint* is data located in different processor hardware. The checkpoints ensure that the backup process has all the information needed to take over control in the event of a failure of the primary process.

In the case of a software fault, a different strategy is needed. Software reconfiguration can overcome the problem of repeating the same errors by replacing a suspected software module with an alternative version. Figure 8.26 shows the *recovery block* scheme, which is a structured method of combining three techniques: the use of error detection routines, backward recovery, and the use of multiple versions of software modules [36]. Multiple versions of software modules produce the same or similar computational results by using an acceptance or validation test as a criterion for determining the acceptability of the execution results of software modules or object blocks. If the acceptance test fails, the process rolls back to the recovery point and makes another try with an alternative object block. An imperfect design of an object block is then bypassed.

Forward error recovery techniques, in contrast, have the system itself make further use of its present erroneous state to obtain another state (Fig. 8.27). Forward error correction is usualy highly application dependent. It relies heavily on knowledge of the nature of the fault and the consequences of it. For example, a real-time control system in which an occasional missed response to a sensor input is tolerable can recover by skipping its response and proceeding immediately to the following input samples. Although forward re-

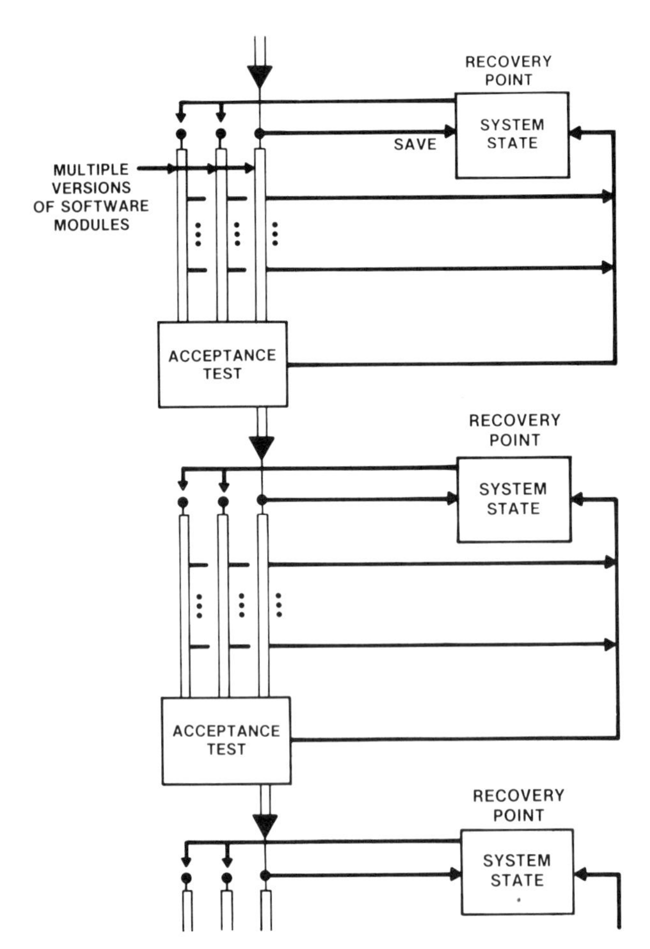

Figure 8.26 Software reconfiguration (recovery block approach).

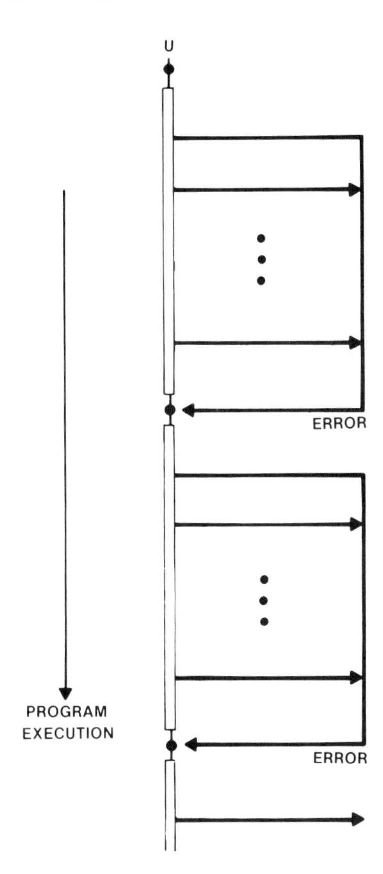

Figure 8.27 Forward error recovery.

covery must be designed specifically for each system, it recovers from faults efficiently when the faults are known and their full consequences anticipated [37].

The most drastic approach to recovery from unanticipated damage caused by system faults is a fixed *reset*. A reset is a comprehensive approach to recovery because it places the system into a predefined (fixed) state. Resets are designed primarily to reduce the effects of failures rather than prevent their occurrence. An example of this is the telephone switching system in which some telephone calls are lost but the system continues to provide service. Figure 8.28 shows a reset arrangement consisting of a set of initialization states to which the system may be reset. The actual reset level used for particular error condition is selected by the system state at the occurrence of the error. If the error is caused by a hardware failure, for example, the selection includes a new hardware configuration to ensure a successful recovery.

In the 2ESS switching system, there are six levels of initialization programs for system recovery [38]. The levels are similar to those shown in Fig. 8.28. At level 1, hardware registers are reset. Levels 2 through 5 incrementally clear call data from the system and reset the corresponding data structures. All transient data in the call stores are cleared at level 6. The level of initialization is done successively in increasing order of severity until no further errors are detected.

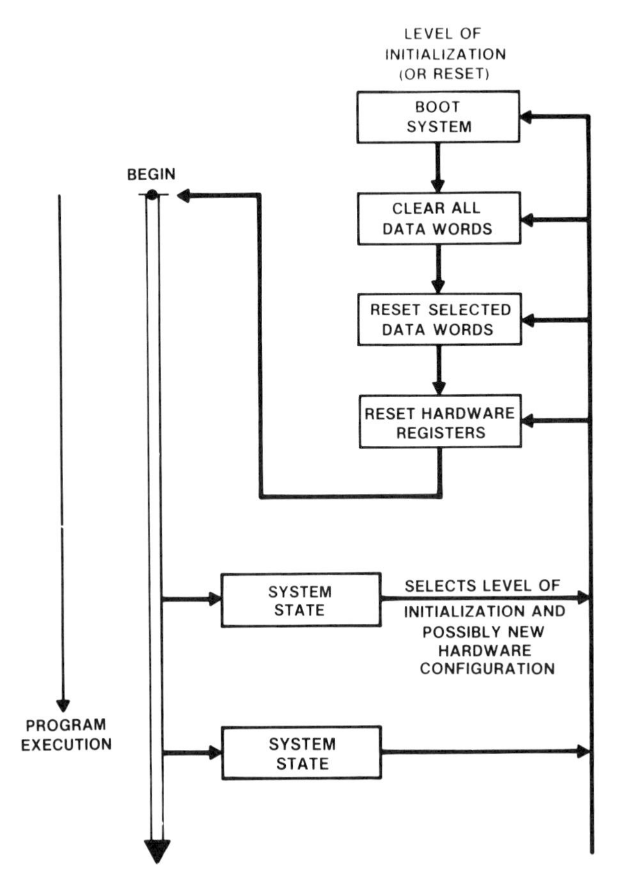

Figure 8.28 Reset recovery.

8.9 FAULT DIAGNOSIS

Whereas fault detection determines whether a circuit is operating correctly, *fault diagnosis* localizes the failure to a replaceable unit. The *replaceable unit* may be a component, a circuit, or a subsystem. The fault diagnosis routine uses fault detection hardware and test sequences to help locate the defective unit. If fault detection identifies a single entity as the source of the fault, diagnosis may not be necessary since the fault can be corrected simply by replacing the entity. If the detection circuit is less specific, however, the fault-diagnosis routine may be required to further isolate the offending unit.

8.9.1 Duplex-Diagnosis Procedure

In a duplex arrangement, as in the case of AT&T's 2ESS switch, the central control (CC) is duplicated; both CCs normally run in synchronism with each other. The CCs are matched at the maintenance center for fault-detection purposes. When mismatch conditions occur, an error is indicated, even though it is not known which CC has taken the fault. The diagnostic routine must be run at this point to attempt to identify the faulty CC. The diagnostic routine is divided into two parts. The first part, which is the more urgent and essential task, is to determine quickly which CC contains the fault. The quick identification of the faulty processor allows the system to recover with a minimum of disturbance. Diagnostics are run in a sequence that examines as much circuitry as quickly as possible. These quick tests can be performed rapidly since their goal is identifying an entire CC and not one of its interior logic circuits. Once the faulty CC has been identified and switched to the off-line state (that is, the unit is no longer involved in real-time control operations; its healthy duplicate has taken on the processing responsibilities), the real-time requirements of the diagnostic are relaxed considerably. For example, if the on-line CC contains the fault, the system reconfigures itself by switching the standby CC to the on-line state and placing the former on-line CC in the off-line state. While the real-time response requirement of the diagnostic has been reduced, however, the second part of the diagnostic (fault resolution) has increased in importance.

Fault resolution attempts to isolate a fault to one or two replaceable units such as circuit boards by using off-line tests. Typically, off-line diagnostics are stored in low-cost bulk memory units such as tapes or disks; they are brought into main memory only when needed.

When the CCs are self-checking in a duplex system, the two processors do not have to be run in the synchronous match mode for effective fault detection. The hardware check circuitry both detects a fault and identifies the defective unit down to the circuit-board level. On-line diagnostics, in this case, are not necessary to determine which one of the two CCs contains the fault. The self-checking hardware provides the diagnostic information without further testing.

The modern packaging technique of using LSI and VLSI circuits to implement both memories and processors has encouraged the use of large circuit boards. Fault resolution does not need to be as precise when the standard repair procedure is to replace the circuit board containing the fault. First, a processor is typically implemented on one or two large circuit boards. If a fault occurs and is isolated to one of the two processor boards, repair by replacement is a quick, simple, and cost-effective approach to servicing the faulty unit. The cost of replacing an entire circuit board is justified when the advantages of faster repair times and savings realized by not having to develop additional fault diagnosis hardware and software are considered.

When the detailed fault resolution requirement is relaxed because of the use of large boards in the processor's implementation, a basic problem still exists. That is, after the faulty unit has been replaced, the integrity of the replacement unit must be verified to ensure that it does not also have a fault. The complete system, including the replacement unit, must be exercised exhaustively to ensure that the difficulty has been corrected. This may often amount to a complete diagnostic test sequence being applied to the repaired system. Even though the processor hardware incorporates additional logic to act as an aid in detecting faults and isolating the faults to a specific unit in the processor, a complete evaluation of the hardware by the processor diagnostic program is still required.

8.9.2 Diagnostic-Test Inputs

A logic circuit is tested by using a diagnostic either to verify its logical integrity (that is, how it performs its prescribed logical function under all possible sequences of inputs) or to detect any faults that may be present in the circuit. A diagnostic test that detects a specific fault corresponds to a combination of input signals that cause an incorrect output from the logic circuit if a fault is present. Any nonredundant logic circuit with n inputs may be completely tested by applying all 2^n possible input combinations to the circuit. As n becomes large, this procedure becomes inefficient. By examining the physical behavior of the circuit, a smaller set of tests may often be identified that will be sufficient to detect all the faults that are likely to occur.

For example, the input combinations required to completely check a three-input AND gate is shown in Fig. 8.29. The classical faults associated with a logic gate are the stuck-at-1 and stuck-at-0 faults for each of the inputs and the output. In general, there are $2(n + 1)$ possible faults for an n-input gate, and $n + 1$ input combinations are required to detect these faults. As indicated in Fig. 8.29, the input of all ones detects any input or will detect any input or output stuck-at-zero faults. The other input combinations check each input's ability to cause the output to change to the opposite state. For an OR gate, the set of input combinations are the complement of those for checking the AND gate.

A logic circuit such as an arithmetic unit is made up of logic gates interconnected in a specified manner. The complete circuit may be verified by an input sequence that permits the inputs and the output of each gate to assume all its possible states. Many of the internal gates are not directly influenced by variations in the input signals and the output. The control of the inputs and the observation of the output must therefore be done indirectly. This indirect evaluation involves examination of logic signals in the logic chain from the input leads through the entire logic chain to the output lead. To check gate X in the circuit shown in Fig. 8.30, for example, the three input combinations must be generated by setting the other inputs in the circuit appropriately. The output of gate X is allowed to propagate to the output OR gate for observation. To do this, the other input to the output OR gate must be held in the 0 state. The input combinations check the behavior of gate X completely; they also check faults along the logic gating chain from the input signals to the output of the final OR gate.

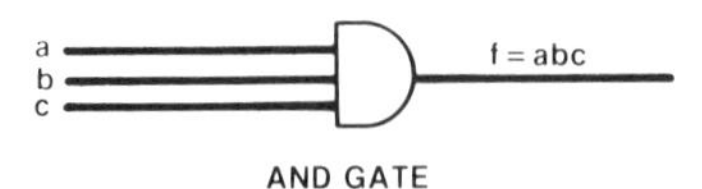

AND GATE

INPUT			OUTPUT	FAULTS								OUTPUT
a	b	c	f	a S-a		b S-a		c S-a		f S-a		f
				0	1	0	1	0	1	0	1	
1	1	1	1	✓		✓		✓		✓		0
0	1	1	0		✓						✓	1
1	0	1	0				✓				✓	1
1	1	0	0						✓		✓	1

Figure 8.29 Input combinations required for checking AND gate.

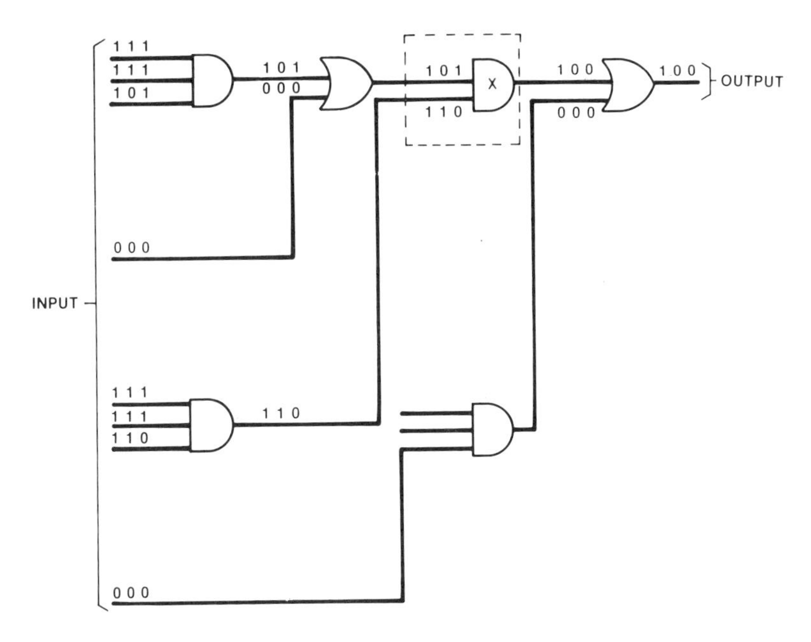

Figure 8.30 Test inputs required to check gate X.

Test generation for digital logic circuits has been studied extensively since the mid-1960s. The objective of these studies has been to develop a systematic procedure that allows a designer to derive a set of tests that exposes all possible faults in a logic circuit. The basic philosophy observed by such test sequence designers is to apply an input sequence (test vectors) to a specific logic circuit that causes the output(s) to differ from those of a normal, fault-free condition. The identification of the appropriate test sequences for a complex LSI logic circuit can be a highly laborious procedure, even with the use of sophisticated computer programs. There are essentially four techniques that are used extensively: the path sensitizing technique, the D-algorithm technique, the Boolean difference technique, and Poage's technique. These procedures are described in considerable detail in several excellent references [39,40].

One of the most important aspects of diagnostic design in the early planning stage is the specification of features to be incorporated in the hardware (such as test points, observation points, and private control points) that the diagnostic uses to evaluate the hardware. These features must be specified and agreed on during the hardware design phase by both the logic designer and the diagnostic programmer.

8.9.3 Microdiagnostics

Microdiagnostics is defined as the set of diagnostic procedures implemented as microprograms on a microprogram-controlled computer. Microinstructions provide access to the individual microoperations or control primitives of the processor. These control primitives represent the *elementary* control signals of the machine. A test sequence (diagnostic) written in microcode may be directed to check the individual hardware-control steps. A microinstruction sequence would be capable of checking the result at each microstep. Consequently, a more detailed evaluation of the hardware may be performed with microdiagnostic routines.

The use of a diagnostic written in microcode may be enhanced further by providing test points in the hardware and along each logic path. A logic signal may then be monitored by the microinstruction sequence as the logic signal propagates through the logic network. Such observation points provide an efficient means of testing a logic circuit when it has to be diagnosed. To isolate the circuit fault to a particular circuit module, the diagnostic program must be capable of obtaining the test result and determining whether an error has occurred. Diagnostic observation points strategically located in a logic circuit help monitor the behavior of the circuit. Without these observation points, it would be difficult for the diagnostic routines to check certain portions of the logic. In a self-checking design, the hardware-detection circuits are clearly the most appropriate points for observing the behavior of the circuit.

The identity of each error-indicating signal must be maintained throughout the system. Keeping the signals unique provides useful diagnostic information, and the error signals serve as observation points for the diagnostic programs. The error signals are usually collected from throughout the system as the diagnostics are run and stored in one or more dedicated hardware registers. The diagnostic accesses the error-indicating registers to determine which of the hardware detection circuits produced an error signal during the execution of a test sequence.

The microdiagnostic programs are very effective for testing the internal logic of the processor. However, as other functional units (such as memory modules and I/O devices) are included in the system diagnostics, macroinstructions may be required to diagnose them. Macroinstructions, also called machine instructions, are used instead of microinstructions because the individual microinstructions normally relate to internal processor operations.

The costs of repairs are directly related to the adequacy of the diagnostics to pinpoint the faulty unit. Special attention has been focused in this area to simplify the repair procedures with additional maintenance hardware support. The costs of repairs are directly related to the adequacy of the diagnostics to pinpoint the faulty unit. Special attention has been focused in this area to simplify the repair procedures with additional maintenance hardware support. General Automation, Inc., developed an integrated hardware, software, and firmware diagnostic tool called "Isolite" in 1979 to eliminate field service calls for routine circuit board failures [41]. Circuit boards are equipped with a small ROM chip and LED indicators. The ROM chip contains testing logic that is activated each time the board is powered up. The LED indicators display whether the test sequences are successful. If the tests are not successful, the LED indicators let the system operators quickly identify and replace the faulty boards. This type of support is becoming increasingly popular because it makes maintaining systems easy for relatively unskilled operators.

A commonly used procedure in performing fault diagnosis is based on the bootstrap approach. The diagnosis starts from the point where the integrity of the "hardcore" has been ensured. The hardcore is defined as that part of the hardware that must be functioning correctly for diagnostic functions to be initiated. The bootstrap approach involves using the hardcore portion of the processor to start a diagnostic evaluation of another portion of the machine and to expand the validation process to the subsystem level as each successively larger level is found to be fault-free. The bootstrap approach starts evaluating a small section of the processor and expands the diagnostic process to include more and more hardware with each succeeding step until the entire machine has been tested. An effective method of validating the processor hardcore is to have the necessary diagnostic test sequences automatically run on the hardcore under the control of another intelligent controller, the maintenance processor. Many current computer systems include a dedicated, intelligent maintenance processor as an integral part of the system for diagnostic purposes [3,42–44].

With the high cost of labor, the concept of remote and centralized maintenance appears attractive for many installations. In this approach, the expertise necessary to perform system maintenance is concentrated at a central location. Instead of dispatchng technicians to the site of a faulty machine, faults are diagnosed remotely. Standard telephone lines are used as the data links to the centralized maintenance facility. Computer systems such as the VAX 11/780, IBM 4300, IBM System/38, and HP 3000 Series 33 all provide remote diagnostic capabilities [42,43,45].

8.10 MAINTENANCE FUNCTION IN HIGH RELIABILITY REAL-TIME SYSTEMS [46]

Software and hardware maintenance features must effectively function together to ensure reliability in a real-time system. Software features include fault recovery programs, audits, and diagnostics; hardware features include redundant processors, self-checking circuits, maintenance access and controls, and diagnostic microcode. These components contribute to effective maintenance design. The relationship between hardware and software is continually changing because some maintenance software is implemented by hardware, appropriately assisted by firmware. The combination of software and hardware reliability features must be carefully examined before designing a system.

8.10.1 Maintenance Hierarchical Structure

Maintenance architecture is typically organized in a hierarchical structure. Figure 8.31 shows the hardware and software maintenance features that form the hierarchical system. It is partitioned into the following levels:

1. The *hardware level* is the lowest level; it consists of functions that are implemented directly in hardware, including parity check circuits, maintenance access circuits for diagnostics, and redundant self-checking hardware.

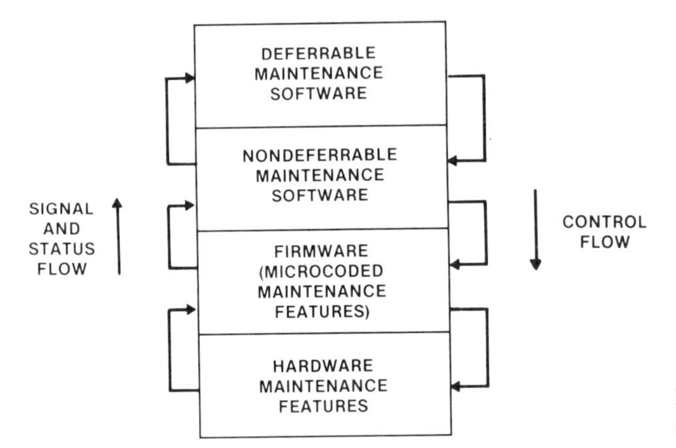

Figure 8.31 Functional hierarchical structure.

2. The *firmware level* consists of maintenance functions that are implemented in firmware, assuming that the system is microprogrammed. An example of a microcoded function is an initialization sequence for a disk controller.
3. The *software nondeferrable level* consists of software functions that must be handled immediately when a signal is received from the hardware. A common example is an error interrupt handler. Another example is a system reconfiguration program that switches redundant units into service when a fault is detected in an active unit.
4. The *software deferrable level* consists of maintenance activities that are deferrable and noncritical in real time. These activities include diagnostics, audits, unit restoral, and human/machine interface programs.

The upward flow of signals and status information from the hardware maintenance circuits is shown in Fig. 8.31. A large part of this flow at the lowest level consists of error interrupts that are generated by hardware check circuits. These interrupts are initially processed by microcoded interrupt handlers. They in turn pass control to nondeferrable software handlers and a software message is sent to the deferrable maintenance structure.

On the other hand, the control information flows down from the higher levels to the lower levels. Deferrable maintenance sends software control messages to nondeferrable maintenance. Nondeferrable maintenance issues commands that initiate microprogram sequences; and at the lowest level, microcode manipulates the hardware directly.

The flow of information up and down the maintenance hierarchy is best illustrated with a specific example. In the AT&T No. 3ACC processor, a technique for correcting memory faults known as "double store read" is used [1,23]. In this technique, the processor automatically redirects the read operation to the off-line memory when bad parity is detected on a memory read. The No. 3ACC processor is operated as a duplex pair in which the write operations are directed to both memories. Therefore, the off-line memory normally contains the same data as the on-line memory. The handling of the double store read operation that relates to Fig. 8.31 is as follows:

1. The parity detect circuit detects a single bit error during a memory read. The error indicating signal causes a microinterrupt. A signal is sent from the hardware to the firmware level.

2. The microcoded interrupt handler records the location of the error in a scratch register and directs the memory read operation to the off-line memory. The bad word, at this point, is left in memory. This microinterrupt may occur between microinstructions within a complex instruction containing many store references. The microinterrupt handler causes a software interrupt that is handled within the nondeferrable maintenance structure.
3. The nondeferrable error interrupt handler reads the scratch register and determines the location of the error. The memory module that contains the faulty word is removed from service and replaced with a backup module. This function takes longer than the memory reread described in step 2 (milliseconds versus microseconds). Nondeferrable maintenance notifies the deferrable maintenance of the error by means of a software message.

   Based on the message sent by nondeferrable maintenance, the system initiates a memory diagnostic of the faulty module. This diagnostic requires many seconds to execute. Appropriate reconfiguration actions are then taken and the results are reported to the operator by a teletypewriter message.

Figure 8.31 shows a natural signal flow from the lowest to the highest level to accomplish all the related maintenance functions.

There has been a greater use of structured design principles in defining the total maintenance subsystem from the highest levels to the lowest levels of hardware. This results in an overall structure that is not only inherently better partitioned at the boundary between the hardware and the software, but also globally within the entire maintenance system. Although structured design was not entirely neglected in the past, it is the best approach and will ensure that future systems are easier to maintain and more reliable.

8.10.2 Basic Maintenance System Structure

There are two basic system architectures that appear in various forms in many systems. Figure 8.32 shows a hierarchical system. The highest level of this system is a processor. The next level down is a channel such as a direct memory access (DMA) unit. Further

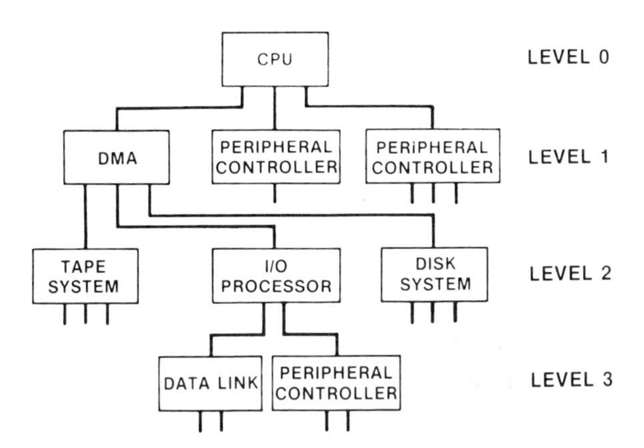

Figure 8.32 Hierarchical system.

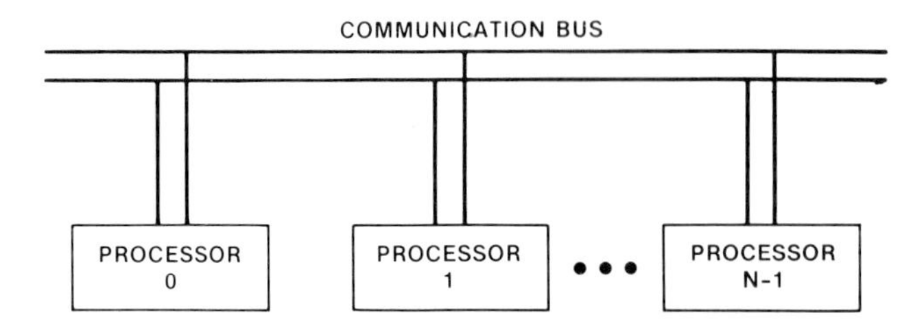

Figure 8.33 Parallel processing system.

down in the hierarchy are peripheral controllers, disk units, and so on. The lowest level in the structure are data terminals. This hierarchical arrangement is under the control of a centralized CPU. The advent of inexpensive microprocessors, however, has led to a hierarchical system with more levels and considerably more intelligence at each node. This presents interesting maintenance control problems that are quite different from earlier problems. For example, it is no longer practical for the CPU at the top node to directly diagnose a bottom node. Instead, a message must flow down the hierarchy with a diagnostic request, and then a response must flow up with the result of the diagnostic.

Parallel or multiprocessing systems are at the opposite end of the spectrum from hierarchical systems. Figure 8.33 shows a simple view of a parallel processing system arrangement. Parallel processing system architecture is expected to become more widespread because a very effective large processor may be obtained simply by paralleling small processors that share a common (redundant) communication bus. This is particularly true if there is no prior assignment of tasks to the small processors.

Both hierarchical and parallel processing systems require the joint efforts of hardware and software designers to achieve an effective maintenance system design. The movement of software functions into hardware or firmware is continuing. Microdiagnostics, self-checking circuits, error correction hardware, and well-structured hardware and software interfaces will allow maintenance programs to be greatly simplified and will allow software designers to take a more functional view of the hardware system.

8.11 TECHNOLOGY IMPACT

A great deal of work in the area of fault-tolerant computing has been done in recent years, much of it in support of the U.S. space program [34] and special applications such as electronic telephone switching systems [47]. Reliability is of primary importance in these applications. A large collection of design techniques has been developed for implementing these systems, including the following [48]:

1. Duplex self-checking configurations [1,49]
2. Triple modular redundancy (TMR) with voting [50]
3. Error-correcting codes for concurrent processes [21,27]
4. Software-implemented fault tolerance [14]
5. Fault-tolerant memory systems [51,52]

The system architect should use the fault-tolerant techniques appropriate to the requirements of the system in terms of reliability, available technology, users, and cost/benefit trade-offs.

Older systems such as the general-purpose commercial computers have very few built-in maintenance features other than memory parity. Fault detection in such machines is often done by the users, who note only that the output had stopped or was obviously incorrect. The prime objective of the manufacturers of these machines is minimizing the purchase price. Since hardware was expensive in early years, maintenance features that did not contribute directly to the performance of the system were excluded.

As improved integrated-circuit technology becomes available and users demand greater reliability, maintenance features are being integrated into even general-purpose computer designs. Most fault-tolerant design techniques developed for space application and other real-time high-reliability applications are directly applicable to the designs of reliable and highly maintainable computer systems. Figure 8.34 shows the maintenance design trend of special- and general-purpose computers. The top curve represents the fault-tolerant computer systems dedicated to special applications. The cost of these systems continues to decrease as technology improves. The second curve represents general-purpose commercial computers. It starts with the same slope as the top curve (assuming constant functionality). With greater demands from users, more maintenance features are incorporated into the system, increasing the functionality (more hardware) and the slope changes. With continued cost reduction of integrated circuits, new applications with high reliability become economically feasible. The third curve represents further increases in functionality (more hardware). For example, the nonstop Tandem computer is the first commercial fault-tolerant computer system [5]. It fills the need of those applications requiring nonstop computing operation. The market is ready for more computer

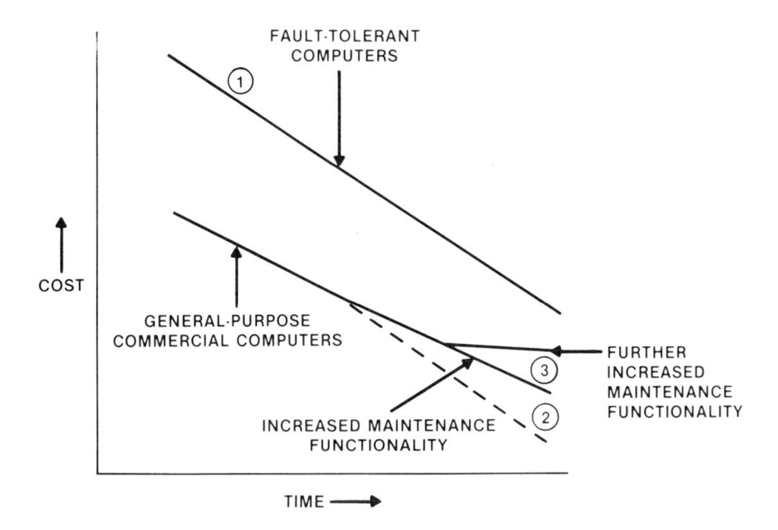

Figure 8.34 Maintenance functionality trend.

companies in this area represented by the third curve. The trend of the future will be more of the nonstop type of computer systems.

8.12 SUMMARY

Fault-tolerant computing is defined as the ability to compute correctly in the presence of a failure, regardless of its source. Errors are classified as hardware faults, software faults, and procedural faults. To achieve fault tolerance, redundancy in hardware or software or both is required so that errors are bypassed and the final results are correct. A design including fault tolerance must be considered from the very beginning of the architecture to yield an integrated, cost-effective system that meets the specified reliability requirements.

The major components of a fault-tolerant system are fault detection, fault recovery, fault diagnosis, and repair. The most important component is fault detection because the success of all fault-tolerant systems depends on the effectiveness of error detection. Fault detection may be accomplished by either hardware or software techniques. A majority of detection schemes for hardware faults fall into the following categories: replication, coding, timing, and exception checks. These checks may be strategically located internally within a functional unit or at its interface. The concurrent error detection by hardware with system operation gives immediate error detection capability. This limits the error propagation to other functional units, thereby simplifying the more difficult problem of system recovery. Detection techniques for software faults have not been developed as extensively as those for hardware faults. Design faults are extremely difficult to characterize and enumerate. Detecting software faults can only be carried out by recognizing the *abnormal* behavior of the system. By checking the reasonableness of the program behavior at various stages of a computation, errors are detected sufficiently early to restrict the propagation of erroneous data. There are several general techniques for observing the behavior of a computer system to detect software faults including checking the reasonableness of the function and the control sequence, and checking the data structure of a process.

The second component of a fault-tolerant system is fault recovery. It is the system's most complex and difficult operation. The recovery procedure may be classified into full recovery, degraded recovery, and safe shutdown. Full recovery requires appropriate spare subsystems to be available as replacement units for defective ones. The system must be capable of restoring itself to its original computing capability with no loss of hardware or software features. Degraded recovery returns the system to a fault-free state of operation, but the computing capability of the system is reduced or degraded. Safe shutdown is often referred to as ''fail-safe'' operation. The system is rendered incapable of performing its functions and must be shut down until the appropriate corrective actions restore it to an operational state. When spare modules are provided, the system is capable of dynamically reconfiguring its modules into a working system. Reconfiguration is part of a recovery procedure of isolating and removing a defective module from an ensemble of modules that make up a working system. In addition, error recovery includes the restoration of the system to a consistent state from an erroneous one, thus allowing the system to continue functioning correctly. This may be accomplished by means of backward recovery techniques that reestablish the system to a previously recorded state and restart it from that point. A more drastic approach to recovery is reinitializing a system from a reset state.

The third component of a fault-tolerant system is fault diagnosis, wich localizes the failure to a replacement unit. The replaceable unit must be a component, a circuit, or a subsystem. The fault diagnosis routine uses fault detection hardware and test sequences to help locate the defective unit. The most commonly used diagnosis procedure is the bootstrap approach, which begins by checking the hardcore portion of the machine. Once the hardcore has been checked and found to be fault-free, the bootstrapping tests another portion of the system. It progressively extends out to include more and more hardware until the fault is pinpointed. Diagnostic test programs are very effective when written as a microcode module in which individual control primitives may be manipulated. When the fault has been diagnosed and located to within a few circuit packs, maintenance personnel must replace the packs one at a time until the defective one is found. The completeness and accuracy of the diagnostic directly affect the active repair time.

Fault-tolerant computing features have been implemented in large machines and have gradually migrated into single-chip microprocessors and multichip devices. Duplication and triplication of microprocessors have become economically feasible for realizing high reliability and performance in distributed processor arrangements. This is evidenced with the recent commercial product offerings of Stratus/32 [53] and August Computer Systems [54].

REFERENCES

[1] W. N. Toy, ''Fault-Tolerant Design of Local ESS Processors,'' *Proc. IEEE,* 66, No. 10, October 1978, pp. 1126–1145.

[2] L. A. Boone, H. L. Liebergot, and R. M. Sedmak, ''Availability, Reliability, and Maintainability Aspects of the Sperry UNIVAC 1100/60,'' *Proc. FTSC-10,* October 1980, pp. 3–8.

[3] H. Cordero, Jr., ''4341's Intrastructure Is New from the Substrate Up,'' *Electronics,* November 8, 1979, pp. 110–115.

[4] D. P. Siewiorek and R. S. Swarz, *The Theory and Practice of Reliable System Design,* Digital Press, Bedford, Mass., 1982.

[5] J. A. Katzman, ''A Fault-Tolerant Computing System,'' *Proc. Hawaii Int. Conf. Syst. Sci.,* 1978, pp. 85–102.

[6] G. Danler and R. McGowan, ''The Case for Self-Testing Computers,'' *Mini-Micro Syst.,* July 1980, pp. 97–101.

[7] G. D. Kraft and W. N. Toy, *Microprogrammed Control and Reliable Design of Small Computers,* Prentice-Hall, Englewood Cliffs, N.J. 1981.

[8] A. Avizienis, ''The Methodology of Fault-Tolerant Computing,'' *First USA–Japan Comput. Conf. Proc.,* 1972, pp. 405 413.

[9] R. E. Staehler and R. J. Watters, ''1A Processor—An Ultra-dependable Common Control,'' *Int. Switch. Symp. Rec.,* Kyoto, Japan, 1976.

[10] S. E. Butner and R. K. Iyer, ''A Statistical Study of Reliability and System Load at SLAC,'' *Proc. FTCS,* October 1980, pp. 207–212.

[11] X. Castillo and D. P. Siewiorek, ''Workload, Performance, and Reliability of Digital Computing Systems,'' *Proc. FTCS-11,* June 1980, pp. 84–89.

[12] A. Avizienis, ''Fault-Tolerance and Fault-Intolerance: Complementary Approaches to Reliable Computing,'' *Proc. Int. Conf. Reliable Software,* Los Angeles, April 1975, pp. 458–464.

[13] L. Chen and A. Avizienis, ''N-Version Programming: A Fault-Tolerance Approach to Reliability of Software Operation,'' *Proc. FTCS-8,* June 1978.

[14] J. H. Wensley, ''SIFT—Software Implemented Fault Tolerance,'' *Fall Joint Comput. Conf. Proc.,* 1972, pp. 243–253.

[15] C. B. Weinstock, ''SHIFT: System Design and Implementation,'' *Proc. FTCS-10,* October 1980, pp. 75–77.

[16] J. H. Wensley, L. Lamport, J. Goldberg, M. W. Green, K. N. Levitt, P. M. Melliar-Smith, R. E. Schostak, and C. B. Weinstock, ''SHIFT: The Design and Analysis of a Fault-Tolerant Computer for Aircraft Control,'' *Proc. IEEE,* October 1978, pp. 1240–1254.

[17] T. Anderson and P. A. Lee, *Fault-Tolerance Principles and Practice,* Prentice-Hall, Englewood Ciffs, N.J., 1981.

[18] A. H. Budlong, B. G. Delugish, S. M. Neville, J. S. Nowak, J. L. Quinn, and F. W. Wendland, ''1A Processor-Control System,'' *Bell Syst. Tech. J.,* Vol. 56, February 1977, pp. 135–180.

[19] H. J. Beuscher, G. E. Fessler, D. W. Huffman, D. J. Kennedy, and E. Nussbaum, ''Administration and Maintenance Plan,'' *Bell Syst. Tech. J.,* October 1969, pp. 2765–2864.

[20] A. L. Hopkins, Jr., T. B. Smith III, and J. H. Lala, ''FTMP—A Highly Reliable Fault-Tolerant Multiprocessor for Aircraft,'' *Proc. IEEE,* Vol. 66, No. 10, October 1978, pp. 1221–1239.

[21] A. Avizienis, ''Arithmetic Error Codes: Cost and Effectiveness Studies for Applications in Digital Systems Designs, *IEEE Trans. Comput.,* Vol. C-20, No. 11, November 1971, pp. 1322–1331.

[22] L. E. Gallaher and W. N. Toy, ''Fault-Tolerant Design of 3B20 Processor,'' *NCC-81 Proc.,* Chicago, May 1981.

[23] R. W. Cook, W. H. Sisson, T. F. Storey, and W. N. Toy, ''Design of a Self-Checking Microprogram Control,'' *IEEE Trans. Comput.,* Vol. C-22, March 1973, pp. 255–262.

[24] A. Avizienis, G. C. Gilley, F. P. Mathur, D. A. Rennels, J. A. Rohr, and D. K. Rubin, ''The STAR (Self-Testing and Repairing) Computer: An Investigation on the Theory and Practices of Fault-Tolerant Computer Design,'' *IEEE Trans. Comput.,* Vol. C-20, No. 11, November 1971, pp. 1312–1321.

[25] C. F. Ault, J. H. Brewster, T. S. Greenwood, R. E. Hagland, W. A. Reed, and M. W. Rolund, ''Memory Systems,'' *Bell Syst. Tech. J.,* Vol. 56, No. 2, February 1977, pp. 181–206.

[26] R. E. Hagland and L. D. Peterson, ''3B20D File Memory Systems, *Bell Syst. Tech. J.,* Vol. 62, No. 1, February 1983, pp. 235–254.

[27] W. W. Peterson and E. J. Weldon, Jr., *Error-Correcting Codes,* MIT Press, Cambridge, Mass., 1972.

[28] H. Kopetz, *Software Reliability,* Springer-Verlag, New York, 1979.

[29] D. E. Morgan and D. J. Taylor, "A Survey of Methods of Achieving Reliable Software," *Computer,* Vol. 10, No. 2, February 1977, pp. 44–51.

[30] S. S. Yau and R. C. Cheung, "Design of Self-Checking Software," *Proc. Int. Conf. Reliable Software,* Los Angeles, April 1975, pp. 450–457.

[31] T. E. Browne, T. M. Quinn, W. N. Toy, and J. E. Yates, "No. 2 ESS Control Unit System," *Bell Syst. Tech. J.,* Vol. 48, October 1969, pp. 2619–2668.

[32] C. V. Ramamoorthy, R. C. Cheung, and K. H. Kim, "Reliability and Integrity of Large Computer Programs," Electronics Research Laboratory, College of Engineering, University of California, Berkeley, *Memo ERL-M430,* March 12, 1974.

[33] K. L. Sevcik, J. W. Atwood, N. W. Brushcow, R. C. Holt, J. J. Horning, and D. Tsichritzis, "Project SUE as a Learning Experience," *AFIPS, Proc. FJCC,* Vol. 41, Part 1, Fall 1972, pp. 331–339.

[34] A. Avizienis, "Fault-Tolerance: The Survival Attribute of Digital Systems," *Proc. IEEE,* October 1978, pp. 1109–1125.

[35] J. F. Bartlett, "A Non-stop Operating System," *Proc. Hawaii Int. Conf. Syst. Sci.,* 1978, pp. 103–117.

[36] J. J. Horning, H. C. Lauer, P. M. Melliar-Smith, and B. Randell, "A Program Structure for Error Detection and Recovery," *Lecture Notes in Computer Science,* Vol. 16, Springer-Verlag, New York, 1974, pp. 171–187.

[37] T. Anderson and B. Randell, *Computing Systems Reliability,* Cambridge University Press, Cambridge, 1979.

[38] P. J. Kennedy and T. M. Quinn, "Recovery Strategies in the No. 2 ESS," *Dig. Pap., 1972 Int. Symp. Fault-Tolerant Comput.,* Newton, Mass., June 1972, pp. 165–169.

[39] M. A. Breuer and A. D. Friedman, *Diagnosis and Reliable Design of Digital Systems,* Computing Science Press, Woodland Hill, Calif., 1976.

[40] H. Y. Chang, E. G. Manning, and G. Metze, *Fault Diagnosis of Digital Systems,* Wiley-Interscience, New York, 1970.

[41] G. Danler and R. McGowan, "The Case for Self-Testing Computers," *Mini-Micro Syst.,* July 1980, pp. 97–101.

[42] *VAX 11/780: Technical Summary,* Digital Equipment Corp., Maynard, Mass., 1977.

[43] A. Durniak, "Computers," *Electronics,* October 25, 1979, pp. 164–177.

[44] R. Coyle and J. Doyle, "A Self-Diagnosing Minicomputer," *Mini-Micro Syst.,* July 1980, pp. 90–94.

[45] D. L. Nelson, "A Remote Computer Troubleshooting Facility," *Hewlett-Packard J.,* September 1978, pp. 13–15.

[46] D. C. Plisch and F. M. Goetz, "Hardware versus Software Design Tradeoffs for Maintenance Functions in High-Reliability Real-Time System," *COMPSAC 1978,* Chicago, pp. 607–613.

[47] B. E. Briley and W. N. Toy, "Telecommunication Processors," *Proc. IEEE,* Vol. 65, No. 98, September 1977.

[48] D. A. Rennels, "Distributed Fault-Tolerant Computer Systems," *Computer,* March 1980, pp. 55–65.

[49] D. A. Anderson, "Design of Self-Checking Digital Networks Using Code Techniques," *CSL Report R527,* University of Illinois, Ph.D. thesis, October 1971.

[50] R. E. Lyons and W. Vanderkulk, ''The Use of Triple-Modular Redundancy to Improve Computer Reliability,'' *IBM J. Res. Dev.*, Vol. 6, No. 2, April 1962, pp. 200–209.

[51] W. C. Carter and C. E. McCarthy, ''Implementation of an Experimental Fault-Tolerant Memory System,'' *IEEE Trans. Comput.*, Vol. C-25, No. 6, June 1976, pp. 557–568.

[52] D. B. Sarrazin and M. Malek, ''Fault-Tolerant Semiconductor Memories,'' *Computer*, August 1984, pp. 49–56.

[53] R. Freiburghoue, ''Making Processing Fail-safe,'' *Mini-Micro Syst.*, May 1982, pp. 255–264.

[54] J. H. Wensley, ''Fault Tolerant Systems Can Prevent Timing Problems,'' *Comput. Des.*, November 1982, pp. 211–220.

PROBLEMS

8.1 The reliability function, $R(t)$, for devices with a constant failure, λ, is given by the negative exponential distribution function as follows:

$$R(t) = e^{-\lambda t}$$

A physical system normally consists of many different types of components: integrated circuits, connectors, switches, and so on. Typically, each type of component has a different instantaneous failure rate. One means of characterizing a physical system is to treat each component as being in *series* with other components in the system. Consequently, when a single component fails, the entire system fails. Assume a system with n components and failure rates of λ_1, λ_2, λ_3, and λ_n, respectively. What is the overall system reliability function?

8.2 In a triple modular redundant (TMR) system as shown in Fig. 8.9, what are some of the design problems that must be solved to have a working system?

8.3 If one branch of a TMR system becomes faulty, would you continue to run the system in the TMR configuration or run only one of the two good units? Explain why your choice is the appropriate strategy for continuing system operation.

8.4 As shown in Fig. 8.2, software deficiencies account for 50 percent of system outages. What are the factors contributing to these deficiencies? State the steps you can take to reduce this number.

8.5 The telephone switching system must function continuously, without interruption, until the equipment is replaced at the end of its life or for some other reason. Since service must be provided 24 hours a day, there can be no scheduled system down time for repair or maintenance. In contrast, the life span of an airborne missile is equivalent to the duration of its mission, which can be quite short when compared with the long life of telephone switching equipment. If you were to design a computer system for each of the two applications above, what redundancy techniques would you choose for each application? Explain.

8.6 Uniquely representing the 10 decimal digits 0 through 9 requires a minimum of 4 binary bits; six binary bit patterns are treated as unused combinations. An additional parity check bit could be added to provide error detection over each binary-coded digit. However, the usage of the check bit would bring the total number of bits required in a binary coded digit to 5 bits. Devise another coding scheme using only 5 bits to represent the decimal digits 0 through 9 that has a greater error detection capability.

8.7 The 3-line-to-8-line decoder is shown in Fig. P8.7. For any single logic fault of the type stuck-at-0 or stuck-at-1, what are the output error results?

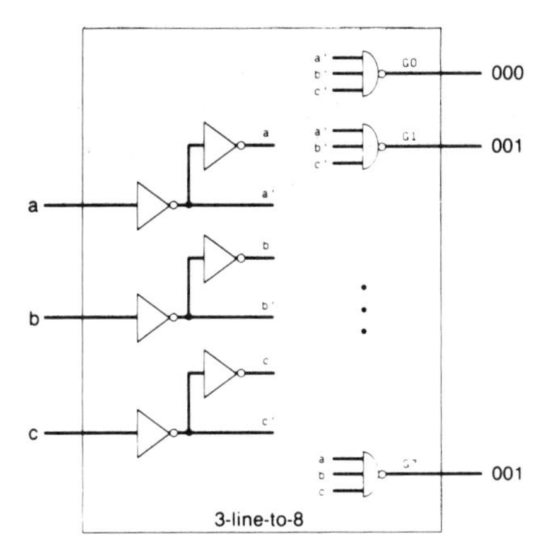

Figure P8.7 Binary decoder.

8.8 For Problem 8.7, devise an error detection circuit for detecting single stuck-at-0 or stuck-at-1 faults of the 3-line-to-8-line decoder circuit.

8.9 N-version programming requires N versions of a program to be written independently and run concurrently on separate hardware. The results of the majority are used. This redundant technique provides both hardware and software fault protection. List advantages and disadvantages of N-version programming and identify specfic applications for which this type of redundant technique is most appropriate.

8.10 Retry is used to correct errors caused by transient faults. Transient faults are usually attributed to a noisy environment. In a computer system, however, the circuit boards and backplane interconnections are well controlled, and noise problems due to crosstalk can be reduced to a negligible amount. What other factors in a computer system generate transient-like types of faults? Provide solutions to these problems.

8.11 In a duplicated system, as in the case of electronic telephone systems, both processors operate in step and perform identical operations. Selected outputs are continually matched for error detection. Work out a recovery strategy that will ensure a working system when a mismatch between the two processors has occurred.

8.12 A commonly used procedure in performing fault diagnosis is based on the bootstrap approach. A portion of the computer, referred to as the *hardcore,* must be established as functioning correctly before the diagnostic test procedure can be initiated. The bootstrap approach uses the hardcore portion of the processor to start evaluating another portion of the machine and expand the diagnostic process to include more and more hardware with each succeeding step until the entire machine has been tested. Identify the components of the hardcore and explain why they must be operational before the initiation of the bootstrap diagnostic procedure.

8.13 In duplicated systems, two techniques have been used for error detection. One is the synchronous and matched mode of operation. Both processors operate in step and perform identical operations, and selected outputs are matched continually. An error occurring in either processor is detected immediately. A second technique is the deployment of extensive self-checking hardware as an integral part of the processor. Faults occurring during normal operation are discovered quickly by detecting hardware. Compare the advantages and disadvantages of these two techniques.

8.14 A self-checking circuit requires that two outputs be generated that provide an output signal of the form 1-active-out-of-2. The two outputs are combined to give a single error using the 1-active-out-of-2 encoding if both signals are active or if neither signal is active as shown in Fig. P8.14. The combining XOR gate is not self-checking in that some fault conditions in the XOR gate will prevent the checking circuitry from giving any error indication; faults normally detected will be ignored. Modify the circuit shown in Fig. P8.14 to allow the XOR gate to be tested to ensure that it is fully operational.

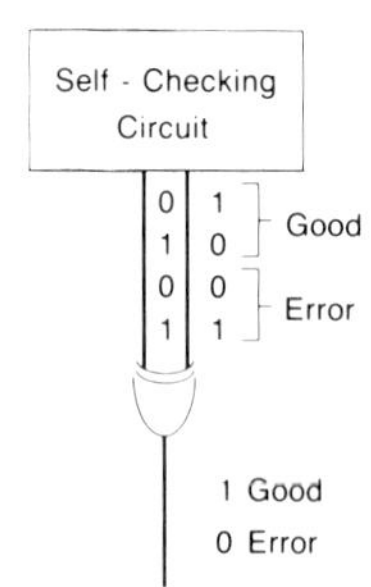

Figure P8.14 Error output circuitry.

9

AT&T 3B20D Processor

9.1 INTRODUCTION

The 3B20D processor is the first member of a family of processors designed for a broad range of AT&T applications. Its development is a natural outgrowth of the continuing need for high-availability, real-time control of electronic switching systems for the telecommunications industry [1–3]. The 3B20D architecture takes advantage of the increased efficiency and storage capabilities of the latest integrated-circuit technology to significantly reduce its maintenance and software development costs.

Figure 9.1 shows the trend of processors for electronic switching systems (ESSs) for the past three decades. The first-generation processors, the No. 1 and the No. 2, were designed specifically for controlling large (several thousand to 65,000 lines) and medium (1000 to 10,000 lines) telephone offices. The predominant cost of these systems, as in most early systems, was the cost of the hardware. The advent of silicon integrated circuits in the mid-1960s was the technological advance needed for dramatic performance improvements and cost reductions in hardware. Integrated circuits led to the development of the second generation of processors: the No. 1A and the No. 3A. These processors, unlike the first-generation machines, were designed for multiple applications; the third-generation machines have even greater capabilities.

The 3B20D processor, the first member of the third generation, is a general-purpose system. Its versatile processing base fulfills the varied needs of telecommunications systems. Along with its Duplex Multienvironment Real-Time (DMERT) operating system, the 3B20D is now (January 1984) targeted for 12 different network applications. Over 200 3B20D sites are currently providing real-time data base processing for enhanced 800 service, network control point (NCP) systems, high-capacity processors for the Traffic Serv-

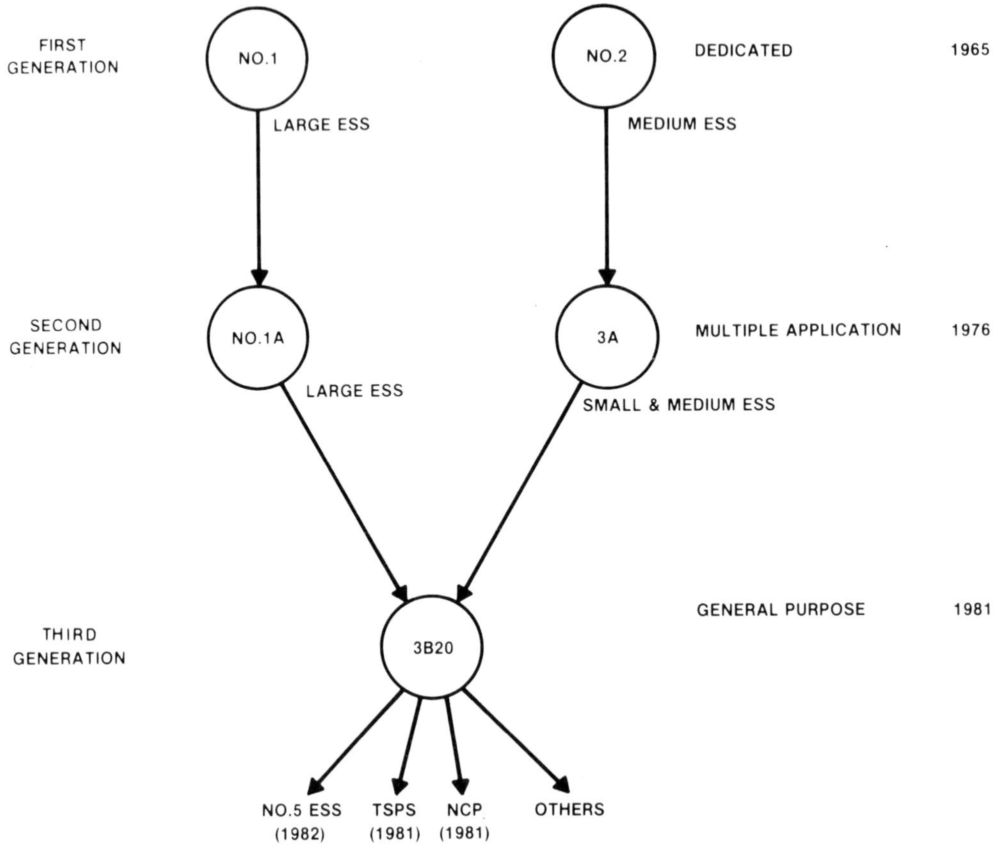

Figure 9.1 ESS processors.

ice Position System (TSPS), central controls for the 5ESS offices, and support processors for the 1AESS and 4ESS offices.

The development of the 3B20D processor started in early 1977; it is currently in production at AT&T Technologies, Inc. A set of papers describing the 3B20D processor and the DMERT operating system appear in the January 1983 issue of the *Bell System Technical Journal*. This chapter is extracted from those papers.

9.2 OVERVIEW OF 3B20D PROCESSOR ARCHITECTURE [4]

The successful deployment and field operation of many electronic switching systems and processors (notably the No. 3A) have contributed to the design of the 3B20D. Previous systems have demonstrated the simplicity and robustness of duplex configurations in meeting stringent reliability requirements [5,6]. Hence, a duplex configuration forms the basic structure for both the hardware and software architecture of the 3B20D. The 3B20D processor also has a concurrent, self-checking design. Extensive checking hardware is an integral part of the processor. Faults occurring during normal operation are quickly discovered by detection hardware. Self-checking eliminates the need for fault-recognition programs to identify the defective unit when a mismatch occurs; therefore the standby processor is not required to run synchronously. This simplifies system maintenance because reconfiguration into a working system is immediate. Another advantage of the self-checking design is that it permits more straightforward expansion from simplex to duplex or multiple-processor arrangements.

As opposed to the hardware-dominated costs of the first- and second-generation processors, the costs of the 3B20D, as is typical of current systems, are dominated by software design, updating, and maintenance expenditures. To reduce these costs as much as possible, the 3B20D supports a high-level language, a customized operating system, and software test facilities. By combining the software and hardware development efforts, an integrated and cost-effective system has evolved.

9.2.1 High-Level-Language Support

The most common approach to increasing software productivity and reducing software maintenance costs is the extensive use of a high-level language. The 3B20D processor instruction set was designed knowing that the C language would dominate the programming environment. C is a general-purpose language. The C language has a rich set of operators; it requires many function calls and subroutines. The language is well suited for the structured programs required for large systems. Its straightforward control makes programs compact and easy to manipulate [7].

Before the instruction set of the 3B20D was designed, considerable studies were made to determine the characteristics of a large, diverse sample of C programs. Based on these studies, the instruction set was designed to be space and time efficient for compiled C programs. Features of the instruction set handle:

1. Symmetrical resources
2. Addressing modes
3. Address manipulation
4. Flexible data structures
5. Stack instructions
6. Procedural instructions

From the compiler's viewpoint, the most important attribute of a processor instruction set is *regularity*. Regularity is the key feature needed to abstract the various processor resources for treatment by the compiler. the 3B20D instruction set includes a wide range of addressing modes (including direct, indirect, and index) covering various data structures. The uniform treatment of the addressing modes applied to all data types (bytes, half words, and full words) without exception makes it possible to compile compact and efficient code. The instruction set of the 3B20D handles subroutine entries and exits, and stack manipulations.

9.2.2 Operating System Support

Higher productivity in application programming is made possible by the facilities of the operating system. The DMERT operating system is a general manager of processor, memory, input/output, and software processes. Its functional description is presented in Section 9.5.

The 3B20D supports memory management that lets programs use virtual addresses without regard to where they actually reside in memory. A high-speed address translation cache memory called the address translation buffer (ATB) reduces the overhead associated with address translation.

The operating system also supports context switching when interrupts occur. A memory stack saves and restores the hardware context. In the 3B20D processor, a local high-speed 8K-byte RAM is provided for context switching. The addressing of the stack is part of the kernel virtual address space; it has been assigned a fixed segment number and pages 0 through 3. Whenever the kernel virtual address falls into this range, the store operation is directed to the high-speed RAM; otherwise, the virtual address is translated by the ATB and directed to the main memory. The combination of fixed mapping by a special circuit and dynamic address translation by the ATB allows the high-speed stack to be extended into the main memory when the use of the high-speed RAM is exceeded.

9.2.3 Software Test Support

The software test facility is an option at both the microprogram level and the macroprogram level. The microlevel test set (MLTS) attaches to the microcontrol section of the central control. By means of direct access to a support computer system, the MLTS assembles and loads the writable microstore. The MLTS is a development tool used for the initial debugging and troubleshooting of the processor core hardware and subsequently of the microprogram sequences. The MLTS steps through microprograms, freezes and examines them, and traces through the execution of microprogram sequences before they are included in the operational system.

The utility circuit (UC) provides a similar set of facilities at the macroprogram level for software debugging and troubleshooting. The UC and its associated software form the extensive Test Utility System (TUS). A number of matchers are incorporated into the UC for tracing and monitoring a variety of system conditions so programmers can observe and follow the execution of a program sequence. Much of the program debugging can take place in real time concurrent with program execution. The UC thus directly extracts and records information such as transfer traces from the internal data buses, thereby ''capturing'' the history of the machine while it is running at normal speed.

9.2.4 Duplex Configuration

Figure 9.2 shows the general block diagram of the 3B20D processor. The central control (CC), the memory, and the I/O disk system are duplicated and grouped as a switchable

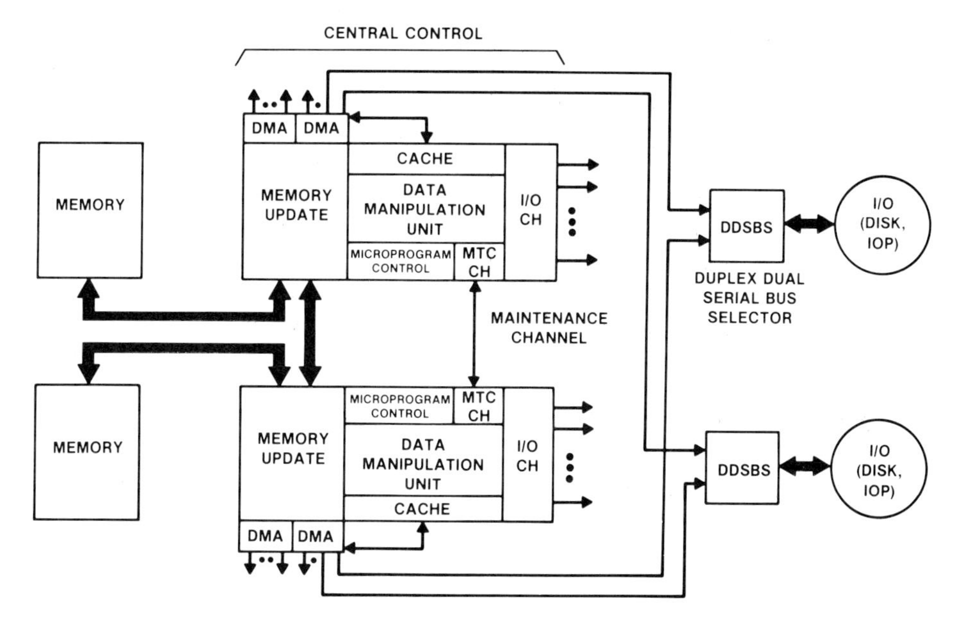

Figure 9.2 3B20D processor general block diagram.

entity, although each CC may access each disk system. The quantity of equipment within the switchable block is small enough to meet stringent reliability requirements, thus avoiding the need for complex recovery programs. Each CC has direct access to both disk systems; this capability, however, mainly provides a valid data source for memory reloading under trouble conditions. The processors are not run in the synchronous and match mode of operation as is done in early systems [1–3]. However, both stores (on-line and standby) are kept current by memory update hardware that acts concurrently with instruction execution. When memory data is written by the CC, the on-line memory update circuit writes into both memories simultaneously. Under trouble conditions, the memory of the standby processor contains up-to-date information; complete transfer of memory from one processor to another is not necessary.

The direct memory access (DMA) circuits interface directly with the memory update circuit to have access to both memories. A DMA write also updates the standby memory. Communicaton between the DMA and the peripheral devices is accomplished by using a high-speed dual serial channel (DSCH). The duplex dual serial bus selector (DDSBS) allows both processors to access a single I/O device. For maintenance purposes, the duplex 3B20D central controls are interconnected by the maintenance channel (MCH). This high-speed serial path provides diagnostic access at the microcode level. It transmits streams of microinstructions from the on-line processor to exercise the processor. Other microinstructions from an external unit help diagnose problems.

9.3 THE 3B20D PROCESSOR [8]

The 3B20D processor performs all the functions normally associated with a CPU and others, including duplex operation, efficient emulation of other machines, and communication with a flexible and intelligent periphery. The microprograms in the processor minimize the amount of hardware decoding and simplify the writing of microcode. There is substantial flexibility in the choice of instruction formats that may be interpreted.

The CPU is a 32-bit machine with a 24-bit address scheme. Most of the data paths in the central control (CC) are 32 bits wide and have an additional 4 parity check bits. The CC architecture is based on registers; multiple buses allow concurrent data transfers. Separate I/O and store buses allow concurrent memory access and I/O operations.

9.3.1 Central Control Structure

A block diagram of the central control is shown in Fig. 9.3. The major subsystems and their associated functions are:

1. Microprogram control
2. Data manipulation unit
3. Special registers
4. Store interface circuit
5. Store address translation
6. Cache store unit
7. Main store update
8. Main store
9. Input/output interface
10. Maintenance channel

These functions and subsystems control the central control and all interactions with it.

The *microprogram control* subsystem provides nearly all the complex control and sequencing operations required for implementing the instruction set. The microcode supports up to three different emulations in addition to its native instruction set. Other complicated sequencing functions are stored in the microinstruction store (MIS), or microstore. The microcontrol (MC) unit sequences the microstore and interprets each of its words to generate the control signals specified by the microinstruction. Execution time depends on the complexity of the microinstruction. Each microinstruction is allocated execution times of 150, 200, 250, and 300 nanoseconds. The wide 64-bit word allows a sufficient number of independent fields within the microinstruction to perform a number of simultaneous operations. Some frequently used instructions are implemented with a single microinstruction.

The *data manipulation unit* (DMU) contains the rotate mask unit (RMU) and the

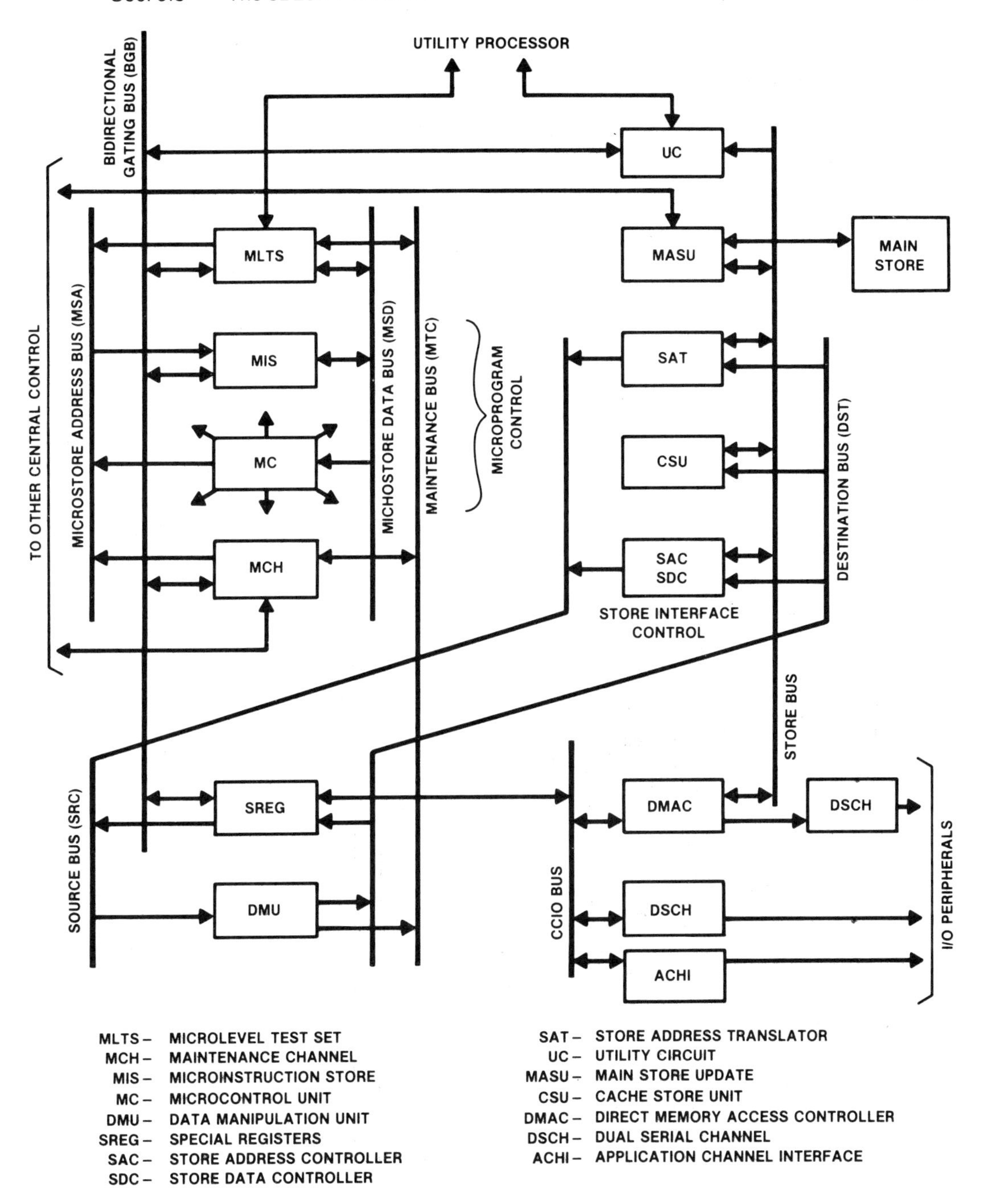

Figure 9.3 3B20D central control.

arithmetic logic unit (ALU), as shown in Fig. 9.4. These units perform the arithmetic and logic operations of the system. The RMU rotates or shifts any number of bits from positions from 0 through 31 through a two-stage barrel shift network. In addition, the RMU performs AND or OR operations on bits, nibbles, bytes, half words, full words, and miscellaneous predefined patterns. The RMU outputs go directly into the ALU. The ability of the RMU to manipulate and process any bit fields within a word greatly enhances the power of the microcode.

The other component of the DMU is the ALU, which is implemented using AMD Co.'s 2901 ALU slices. The 2901s are bipolar 4-bit ALUs (Fig. 9.5) [9]. Eight 2901 chips provide two key elements: the two-port, 16-word RAM and the high-speed ALU. Data in any of the 16 words addressed by the 4-bit A-address input may be used as an operand to the ALU. Similarly, data in any of the 16 words defined by the 4-bit B-address input may be simultaneously read and used as a second operand to the ALU. Because the internal 16-word RAM is dedicated as general registers, the result may be directed to the RAM word specified by the B-address. This optimizes the performance speed of the arithmetic and logical operations involving general registers and the output of the RMU.

The logic blocks of Fig. 9.4 depict the self-checking capability of the RMU and ALU. The first-stage byte rotate unit of the RMU is checked for byte parity, which it preserves; the mask unit, including the second-stage bit rotate, is checked by duplication. The ALU is also checked by duplication. The data is taken from one ALU and parity is generated from the other. The data from one ALU is also matched with the duplicate. The

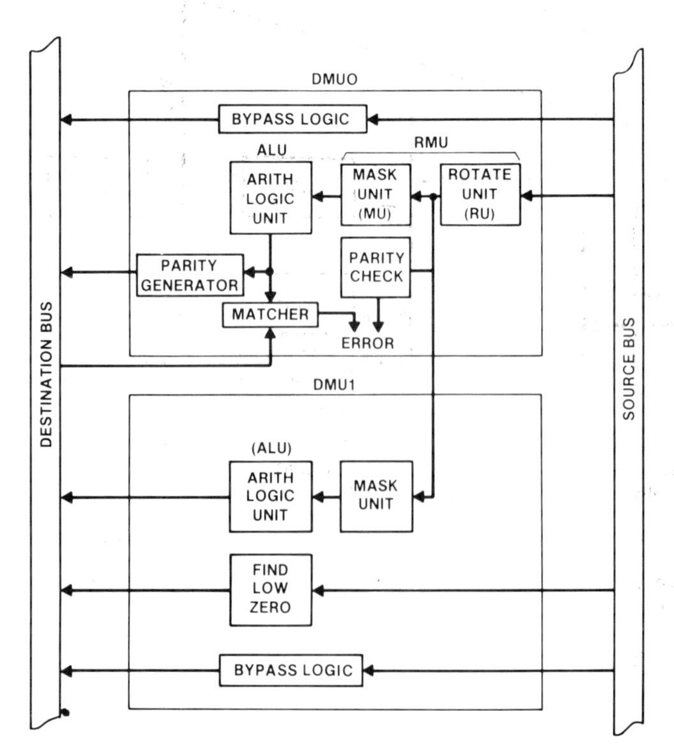

Figure 9.4 Data manipulation unit (DMU).

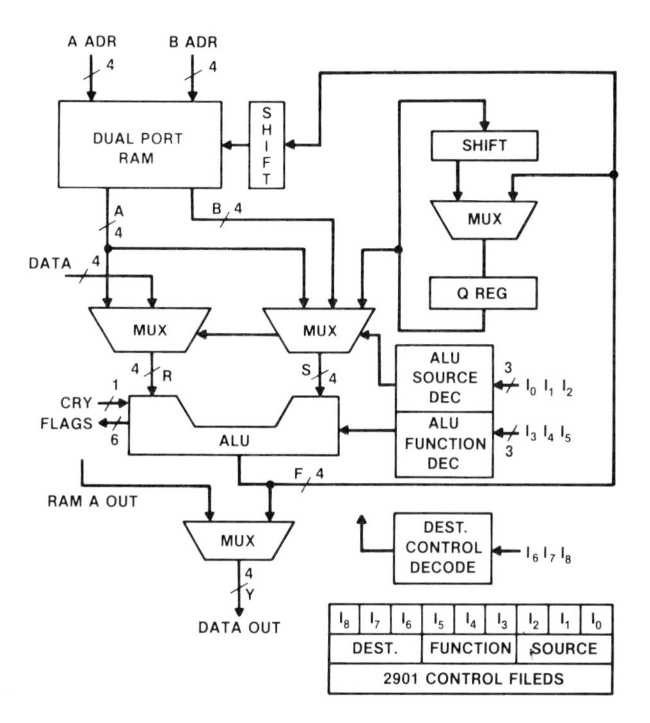

Figure 9.5 2901 internal architecture.

underlying self-checking strategy, illustrated here and used throughout the CPU, is using parity checking where parity is preserved and duplication of logic where parity is not preserved.

The *special registers* (SREG) associated with the operation of the CC are external to the DMU, unlike the 16 general registers inside the DMU that are available to the programmer. Most of the special registers are not explicitly specified by the 3B20D instruction set. They are characterized by their special dedicated functions and receive their inputs from sources other than the internal data bus. They control and direct the operation of the processor. Some of the special registers are:

1. Error register
2. Program status word
3. Hardware status register
4. System status register
5. Interrupt register
6. Timers

In addition to these registers, a 32-word RAM that is available only at the microcode level is provided within the SREG block. It is used for scratch-pad space and it is preassigned registers such as those supporting memory management to facilitate and enhance the power of microprogram sequences.

The *store interface circuit* controls the transfer of data and instructions from system memory to the CC. Two controls, the store address control (SAC) and the store data control (SDC), handle memory addressing, update the program counter, and fetch instructions. Associated with the store address control are the program address (PA), the store address register (SAR), and the store control register (SCR). Associated with the store data control are the store data register (SDR), the store instruction register (SIR), and the instruction buffer (IB). These circuits ensure a continuous flow of instructions to the microcontrol unit.

Memory mapping is required in the implementation of a virtual address multiprogramming system. The *store address translation* (SAT) facility is the mechanism that provides memory mapping between a program-specific virtual address and its corresponding physical address. Address translation hardware is included in the SAT by the address translation buffer (ATB) to facilitate memory management. A detailed description of the ATB is in Section 9.3.3.

The *cache store unit* (CSU) is an optional circuit that improves overall system performance by reducing the effective memory access time. The cache is a four-way set-associated memory containing 8K bytes. A detailed description of the CSU is in Section 9.3.4.

The *main store update unit* (MASU) provides a multiport interface to the memories as both DMA and CC circuit attempt to use the memory. The update circuit arbitrates asynchronous requests from the on-line CC and the on-line DMA. The cross-coupling between the memory update units permits the on-line CPU to access either memory, or both memories, for concurrent write operations.

The *main store* uses AT&T 64K dynamic memory devices and high-speed TTL-compatible gate-array integrated circuits. The main store consists of a single circuit board main store controller and a 1M-byte main store array circuit board. Up to 16 main store array boards (16M bytes) may be equipped within the central control frame. Throughout the central control, byte parity is maintained over each byte of the data word. By adding 4 additional error correction code bits (in addition to the byte parity bits), the main store in a modified form of Hamming code performs a single-bit error correction and double-bit error detection.

Input/output interface is done in several ways in the CC. The communication path between the CC and the I/O channels is through the CCIO bus, which is a local, high-speed, direct-coupled, parallel bus. Direct memory access between the main store and peripheral units is provided by a direct memory access controller (DMAC) that communicates with intelligent peripheral units via dual serial channels (DSCHs). I/O channels including user-specific interfaces may be connected directly to the CC by means of the CCIO bus. Two standard interfaces are the DSCH, a high-speed multiport serial interface, and the application channel interface (ACHI). The ACHI is a high-throughput, parallel bus, peripheral communication path.

The *maintenance channel* (MCH) circuit provides diagnostic access to the CC at the microinstruction level. It also controls basic fault recovery and system sanity functions in the off-line processor.

The processor structure diagramed in Fig. 9.3 allows three kinds of transfers to proceed simultaneously. The first is a microcontrol path through the microinstruction store

(MIS). The second is a computation path through the data manipulation unit (DMU). The third is a memory path through the cache. The CPU is pipelined at both the microstore and store levels; microinstruction execution is overlapped with microstore read, and instruction execution is overlapped with fetch. In addition, there are separate transfer paths for maintenance and input/output.

9.3.2 Memory Management Architecture

The memory management architecture of the 3B20D is one of the most crucial functional areas of the system. It is the product of numerous design iterations that resulted in a balanced compromise among software simplicity, real-time performance, and hardware economy.

The 3B20D processor supports a modern multiprogramming operating system. Such a system implements multiple, concurrently-operating virtual machines. The multiple virtual machines enable the concurrent running of two or more processes, with each having a full range of virtual address space. To accommodate these needs, the 3B20D provides 16M bytes (24 bits) of virtual address space per process. Virtual memory allows a process to resume execution after being swapped out of the main memory and relocated. Virtual memory is a more flexible and efficient technique of time sharing the physical memory among processes than the overlaying technique that is commonly used because it does not require the continual replacement of the memory during processor switches. More importantly, this form of memory management is an effective technique of realizing memory protections among independent processes to minimize the probability of system outage due to memory mutilation.

The 24-bit virtual address as shown in Fig. 9.6 is divided into three fields. The segment index identifies a specific segment, the page index specifies a page within a segment, and the byte offset specifies the byte within a page. The virtual to physical address translation is done by the segment and page tables, both of which reside in main memory. The layout of the translation sequence is shown in Fig. 9.7. Each process has its own segment

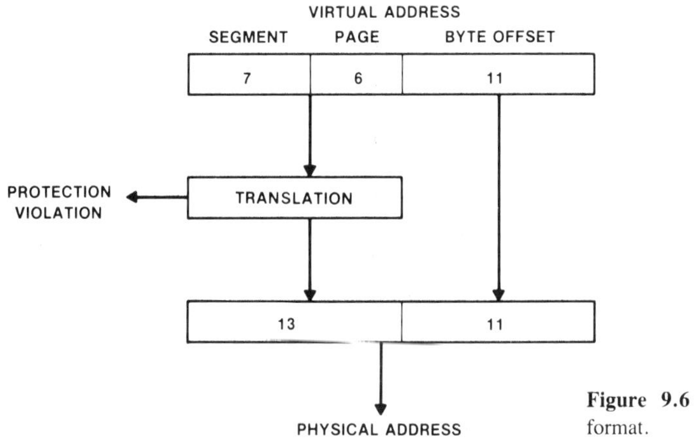

Figure 9.6 Virtual to physical address format.

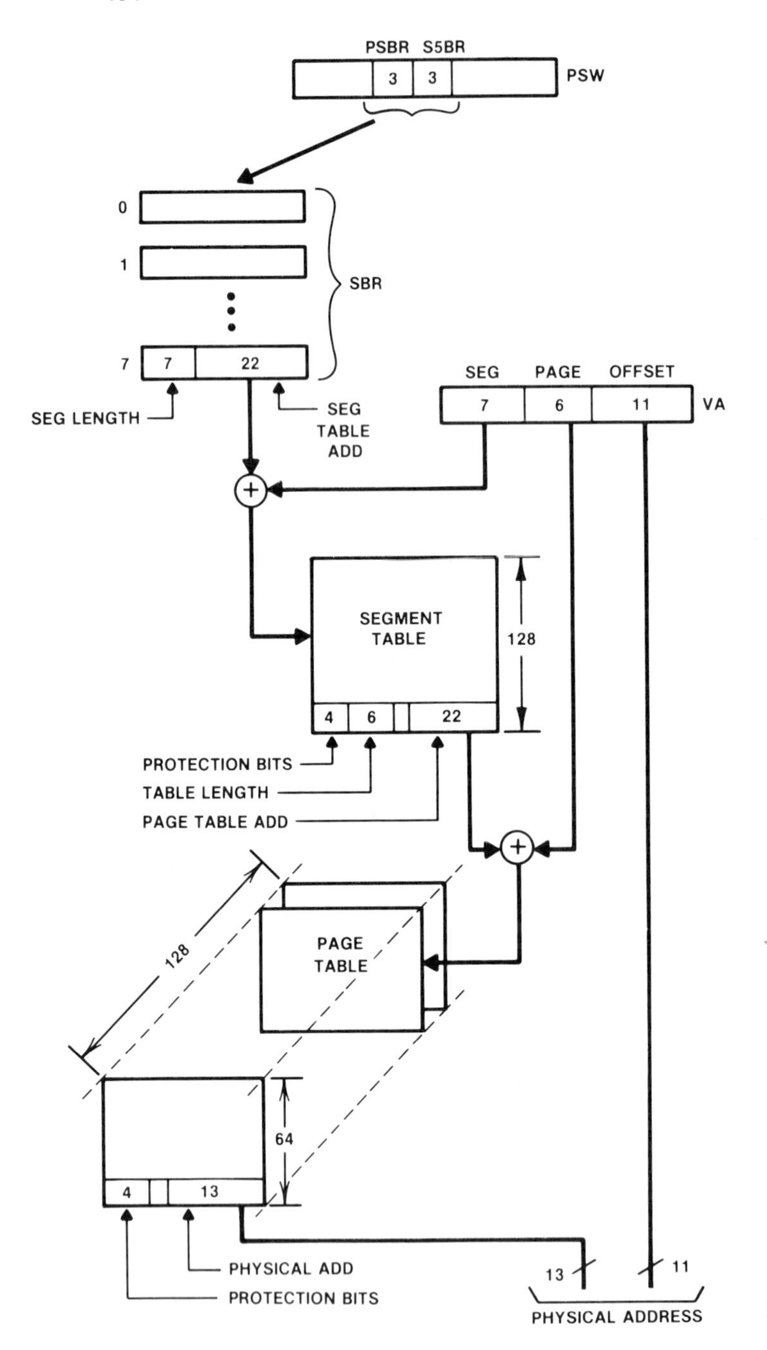

Figure 9.7 Address translation.

table and each segment has its own page table. The page table of a segment is shared by all the processes that share the segment. The address space of the currently executing process address is defined by the hardware segment base registers (SBR), a 32-bit register in main memory that contains the physical address pointing to the beginning of the process's segment table and its length (which is equal to the number of segments allocated to the process). The segment field of the virtual address and the segment table address in the SBR are used to index the segment table and access an entry. The fetched segment table entry and the contents of the page field of the virtual address index the page table. The physical address is generated by concatenating the relocation address field of the fetched page table entry and the byte offset field of the virtual address. During each step of the translation process, the length fields and the protection bits are checked for possible table length errors and protection violations. An error-handling routine is initiated when an error occurs.

The 2K-byte pages are the smallest relocatable entities in the system. This definition minimizes external memory fragmentation and simplifies memory allocation. A contiguous segment in virtual address space does not have to be contiguous in physical memory. Therefore, memory may be allocated one page at a time. The need for shifting segments in main memory to create enough contiguous free space is eliminated.

Each virtual address space (VA) as indicated in Fig. 9.7 has 7 address bits for segments (allowing 128 segments) and 6 address bits for up to 64 pages per segment. The two-stage translation allows the operating system to allocate a fixed 64-word block for each page table independently and allows the page tables for different segments of the same process not to be adjacent in physical memory. Consequently, the algorithm for allocating page tables is simple. If there were no segment table, each process would have a large single contiguous page table whose size was able to vary from one word to 8K words depending on the largest virtual address space allocated to the process. In a two-stage translation, the software algorithm to handle the allocation and deallocation is simple.

9.3.3 Address Translation Buffer [10]

To minimize the overhead of the virtual to physical address translation, high-speed address translation buffers (ATBs) store the physical addresses and access permissions of the most recently accessed pages (Fig. 9.8). When the processor initiates a store access, part of the virtual address is used to read the ATB and determine whether the corresponding physical address is available in its memory. If the physical address is present (called a *hit*), it is catenated with the page offset to form the complete physical address for accessing the main store. If the physical address is not present (called a *miss*), a microroutine is initiated to do the segment and page table lookups and load the obtained physical address, the protection field, and the tag field into the ATB. The access is then restarted and subsequent access to the same page results in a hit. The translation time for a hit in the ATB is 200 nanoseconds; for a miss, it is 6 microseconds. The ATB hit ratio has a significant effect on the real-time performance.

The two-way, set-associative 64-word ATB is capable of storing the address trans-

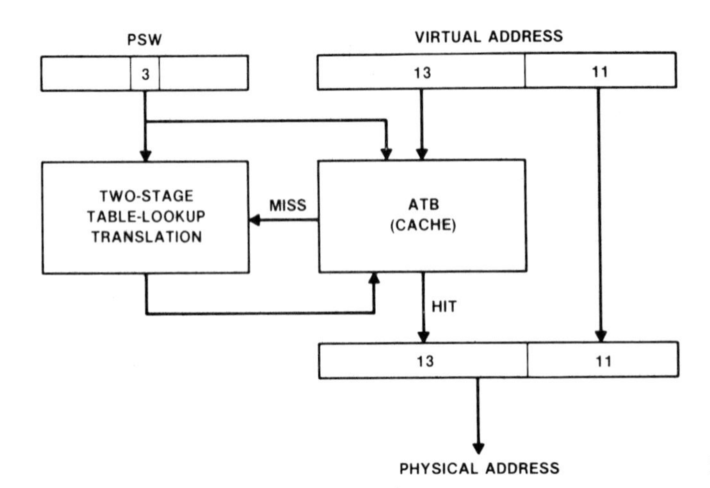

Figure 9.8 ATB general block diagram.

lation information of the 128 most recently accessed pages. Eight blocks of ATBs accommodate eight separate and independent address spaces for a total of 1024 entries. Figure 9.9 is a more detailed block diagram of the ATB and associated translation process of the table-lookup sequence. Two 3-bit fields contained in the program status word (PSW) provide control for the memory management. At times, the operating system must execute code in one address space and fetch or store data in a different address space. The primary and secondary segment base register fields (PSBR and SSBR) in the PSW allow two separate address spaces to be defined. Generally, the PSBR is used to select one of the eight blocks of the ATB for address translation. Under PSW control, however, the SSBR may be used to read or write data in a different address space. Special instructions manipulate the PSW; this hardware feature allows data to be moved very efficiently between two address spaces.

When an access is initiated by the processor, the ATB is accessed using 3 bits of the PSW (PSBR or SSBR, selecting one of eight address spaces), the low 3 bits of the segment field, and the low 3 bits of the page field of the virtual address. The address tag field tag bits of both sets of ATBs are matched against the corresponding bits of the virtual address. When a successful match with one of the two comparators occurs, the corresponding ATB outputs (the high 13 bits) are concatenated with the low 11 bits of the virtual address to form the physical address. If a miss is detected, the ATB miss microroutine is initiated by the processor. The corresponding 3-bit field (PSBR or SSBR) of the PSW that selects one of eight ATBs is also used to select one of eight segment base registers for the two-stage table-lookup address translation, which is shown on the left side of Fig. 9.9. The new entry from the page table and its associated tag field are loaded into the specified ATB. The memory access is restarted on return from the microroutine.

Since an ATB miss takes 6 microseconds (compared with the normal ATB cache access time of 200 nanoseconds), the ATB hit ratio affects the memory cycle time significantly. The two-way (four-word) ATB is capable of storing the address translation informaton of the 128 most recently accessed pages. For normal-sized processes with reasonable locality in addressing, the ATB hit ratio should be over 95 percent. When an ATB

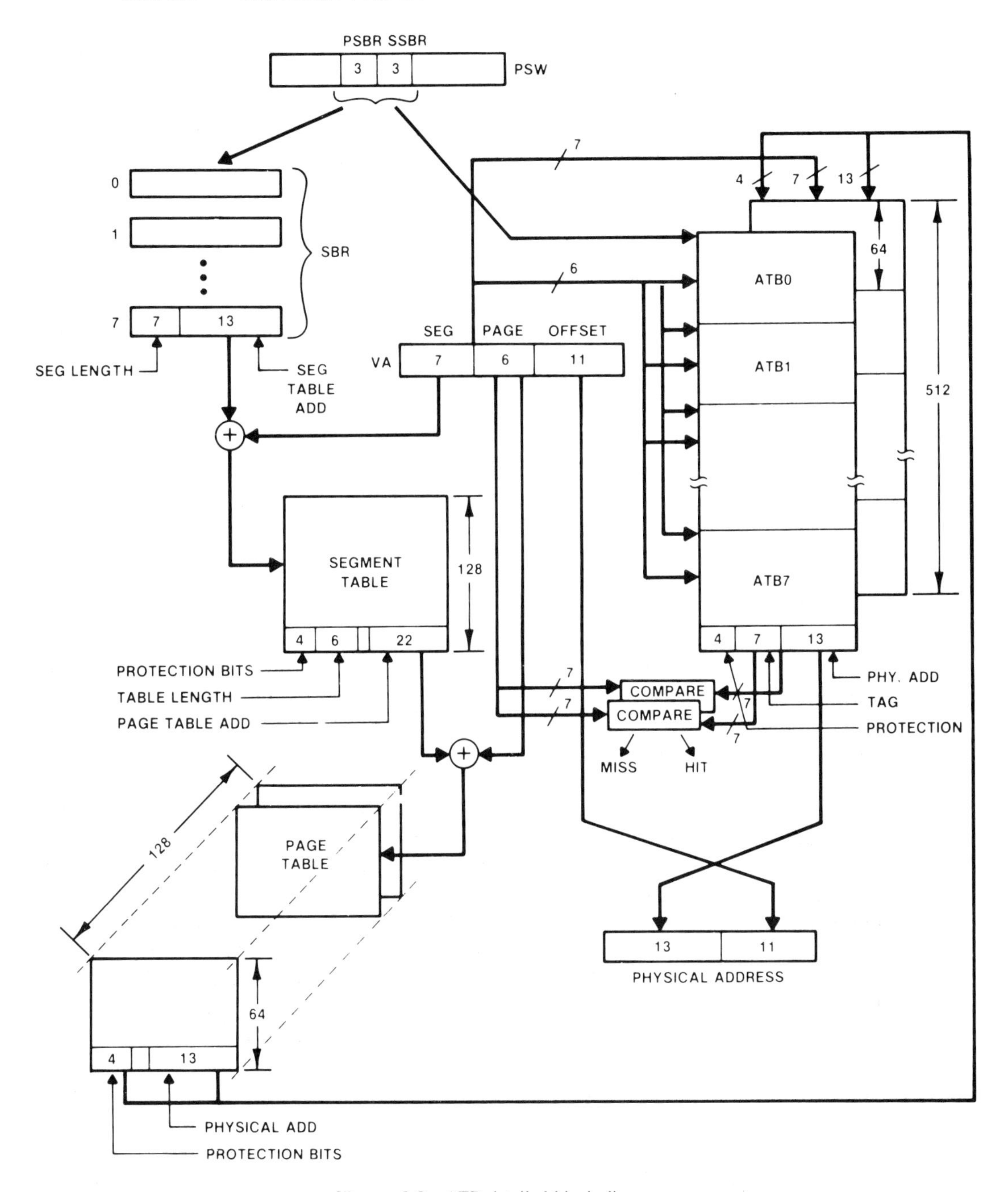

Figure 9.9 ATB detailed block diagram.

is assigned to a different process during context switching, however, the ATB is flushed and there is a temporary low-hit period while the ATB is accumulating addresses for the new process. The existence of eight ATBs reduces the probability of total flushing because the operating system preserves the contents of the current ATB by switching to a different one if control needs to be transferred to a different process temporarily. This architecture works especially well in a multienvironment operating system such as DMERT.

9.3.4 Cache Store Unit [10]

The cache store unit (CSU) is an optional circuit that improves the effective access and cycle time of store operations. Caches take advantage of the general programming characteristic of *locality of reference*. Most references to memory are highly localized or clustered into small groups at any given time. Regions tend to change relatively slowly during the course of program execution. Thus, a relatively small, high-speed cache store unit containing the most often used words from the main store reduces the average access time of the reference.

The CSU is organized as a four-way, set-associative memory. The design of the CSU is easy to maintain because it uses high-speed static memory parts. The mapping between the cache and the main memory is shown in Fig. 9.10. Each cache word may be assigned to a main memory word having the same page offset address. Any main memory word may be stored in any of the four cache words. For example, word 0 from the first cache modules may correspond to word 0 of any page in main memory. The mapping function compresses the main memory address range into the much smaller CSU. The compression is achieved by adding a *tag* field that contains the top 13 bits of the physical address to each word of cache data.

The size of each of the four sets of caches is 2K bytes (512 words) for a total of 8K bytes for the CSU. Access of the ATB and the cache unit simultaneously is possible because the 13-bit page offset used to address the cache is the same for both the virtual address and the physical address; hence, there is no need to wait until the virtual to physical address translation is completed before accessing the cache. As shown in Fig. 9.11, the access of the ATB and the cache is performed in parallel. A cache access uses 9 of the low 11 bits of the virtual address (invariant in the translation) to select a unique word from one of the four cache modules. The specific byte is identified by the lowest two address bits. The upper portion of the virtual address (high 13 address bits) are concurrently translated by the ATB. Each of the four cache tag modules is matched to the two translated high 13 bits of physical addresses. The ATB indicates to the cache which of the two translated addresses is valid. If cache tag module matches this translated high 13-bit physical address, the CSU generates a "hit" signal and gates the associated word to the CC. If a miss occurs, the physical address generated is used to access the main memory. The partition of the address field enables the hardware parallelism of accessing both the ATBs and the CSU simultaneously. It therefore has a direct effect on system performance.

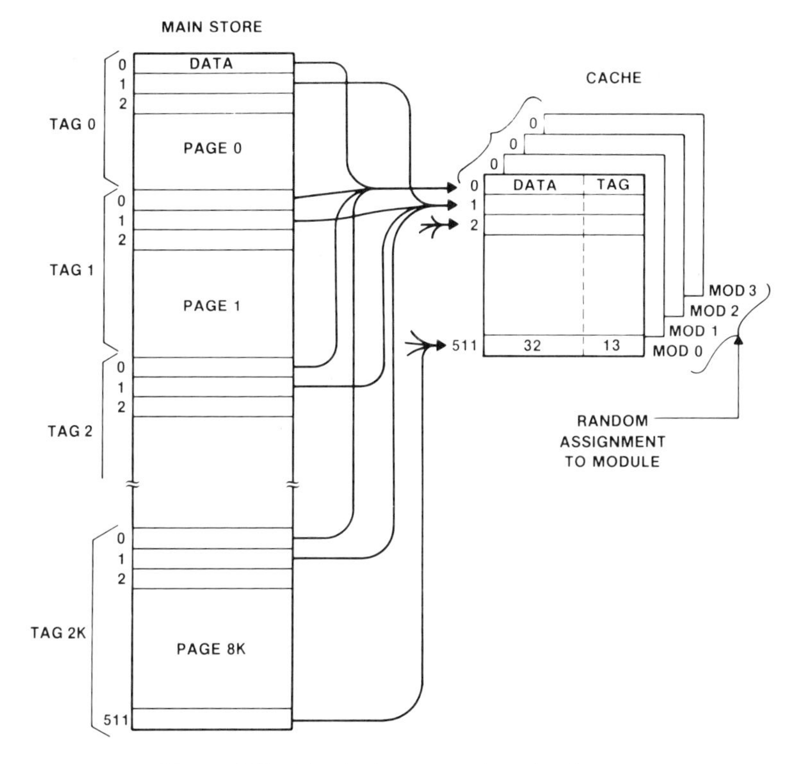

Figure 9.10 Mapping between cache and main store.

9.3.5 Interrupt Stack [10]

As hardware and software interrupts occur, some processes are suspended in favor of higher-priority processes. The machine state of a process to be suspended is saved on the *interrupt stack* and is restored when control is returned to the interrupted process. A separate segment of storage is allocated for the interrupt stack. As a series of interrupts occur, machine states are added to and removed from the stack. Frequent interrupts affect system performance because they require the overhead operations of storing and restoring the internal states of the machine.

The interrupt stack is an 8K-byte storage mechanism for saving the machine states of suspended processes. The stack is located physically on the bottom half of four memory planes that have lengths of 1K words and widths of four bytes. The four 512-word pages are catenated to form the 8K-byte interrupt stack. The top halves of the four memory planes are the four modules of the cache store unit (CSU). The 3B20D designers used this approach (sharing memory devices between the CSU and the interrupt stack) because of the efficiency and availability of 1K- by 4-bit memory devices.

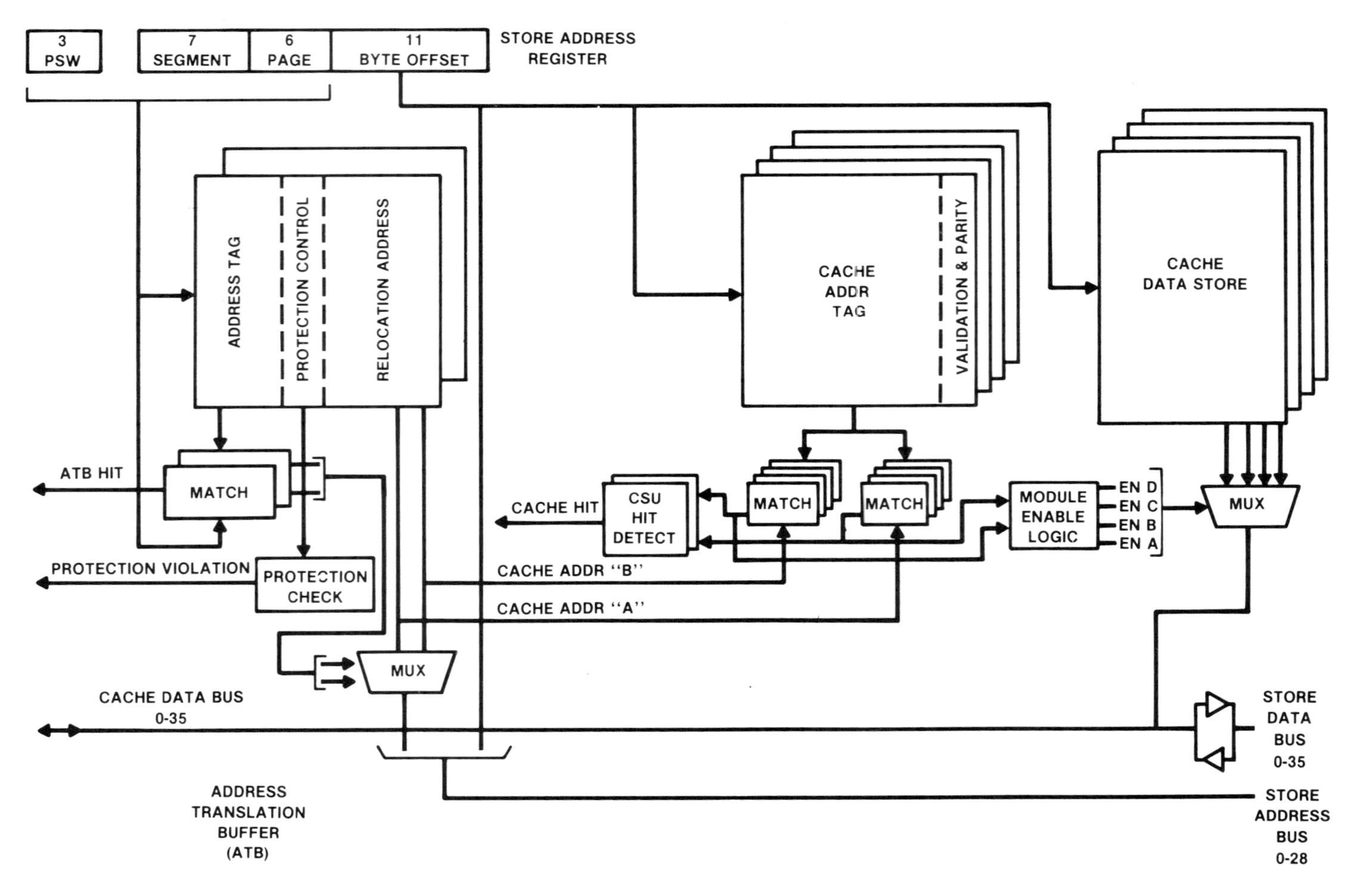

Figure 9.11 3B20D store address translator and cache block diagram.

Figure 9.12 shows the functional implementation of the stack. Since the interrupt routines are handled completely in the kernel program, the addressing of the stack is part of the kernel virtual address (VA) spectrum (segment 32 and pages 0 through 3). Whenever the kernel virtual address falls in this range, the store operation is directed to the high-speed RAM. An AND gate detects this address range and tests several conditions. When the system is operating in the kernel mode and contains a high-speed cache that is not bypassed, the virtual address is mapped directly (fixed mapping) and pointed to the high-speed RAM. Otherwise, the virtual address is translated by the ATB and pointed to the main memory. The combination of fixed mapping by special logic gates and dynamic address translation by the ATB allows the high-speed stack to be extended into the main memory when the high-speed RAM is exceeded. When the processor does not include the optional CSU, address translation is done completely by the ATB and the interrupt stack is located in the main memory.

9.3.6 Instruction Set Overview

The 3B20D is a complex instruction set computer (CISC). Its instruction set supports a large set of opcodes, addressing modes, and data types. The power of the 3B20D derives from the richness of its instruction set. The architecture supports high-level languages, particularly C. Before developing the instruction set, 3B20D architects measured a large sample of C programs to determine their characteristics. After examining the measurements, the architects chose seven programs as their benchmarks. They used the benchmarks to evaluate various combinations of instruction sets. The size of the instruction sets and the execution of the benchmark programs were judged and, through an itera-

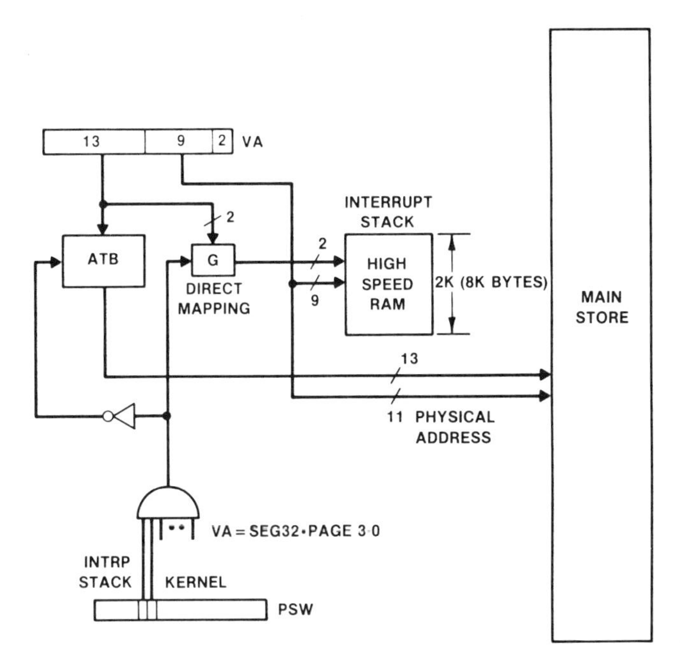

Figure 9.12 High speed interrupt stack.

tive process, the architects designed an instruction set that uses memory space and executes instructions efficiently.

The general instruction format is shown in Fig. 9.13. It consists of the opcode, source operands, and the destination operand. The opcode defines the operation to be performed on the source operands; the result is stored in the destination operand. The operands may be one of three data types: byte, half-word (16 bits), and full-word (32 bits). The data type is implied by the opcode definition; the instruction set has a separate opcode for byte, half-word, and full-word operations. There are three address mode categories: memory, immediate, and register. Memory mode operands give the memory location of data for the instruction. Various memory address modes, such as index, indirect, and absolute, are used in generating the effective address for accessing the memory. The data read from the derived address is used to execute the instruction. Immediate mode operands provide direct data as part of the instruction. Register mode operands specify the register in which the desired data is located.

Immediate mode operands apply only to the source field, whereas the operands of the memory or register may specify sources of data as well as the destination for completed calculations. The source field may contain zero, one, or two operand(s) while the destination field may just contain zero or one (Fig. 9.13).

The 3B20D processor supports a variety of instructions for efficient program execution. Most instructions are one of the following functional types:

- Arithmetic
- Logical
- Jump/branch
- Load/store
- Function call/return
- Stack manipulation
- I/O
- Bit insertion/extraction
- Maintenance
- Special
- Floating point

The instructions implemented by microprogram sequences allow the flexibility to modify or add new instructions easily and quickly. This is evidenced by the inclusion of floating-point instructions at a later stage of development.

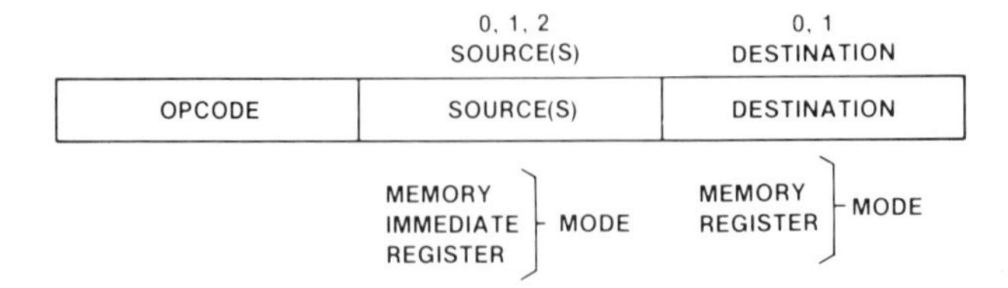

Figure 9.13 Instruction format.

Function call instructions support C language functions. They automatically save registers, set up the argument list for the called function, and set up registers to point to the environment of the new function environment. The environment is implemented with a stack in memory pointed to by a stack pointer register. The stack grows in a positive direction. The following registers are explicitly manipulated by the function instructions.

1. *Stack pointer (SP):* The stack pointer points to the top of the stack and is properly set so a new function may be called.
2. *Frame pointer (FP):* The frame pointer points to just above the top of the save area. This is a region created on the stack by the function call instructions for saving registers. Just past the save area frame is a region on the stack where a function may store local variables.
3. *Argument pointer (AP):* The argument pointer points to the beginning of a list of arguments to the function.
4. *Program counter (PC):* The program counter is set to the address of the first executable instruction of the instruction.

A sample stack frame is shown in Fig. 9.14.

A bit field 1 to 32 bits in length within one word is another data type. The format is shown in Fig. 9.15 with the *offset* specifying the beginning and the *number* specifying the length of the bit field. Instructions are provided both to extract and to insert a bit field from and to storage. Most of the necessary bit manipulation functions for high-level languages are implemented easily with the bit, byte, half-word, and full-word data fields.

Floating point is supported and is consistent with the proposed P754 IEEE standard [11]. Data representations, semantics, and the precision of floating-point operations adhere to the P754 standard.

9.3.7 Microcode Features

The large microstore address space (16 bits) in the 3B20D processor provides a relatively inexpensive means of specifying complex instructions and special system functions.

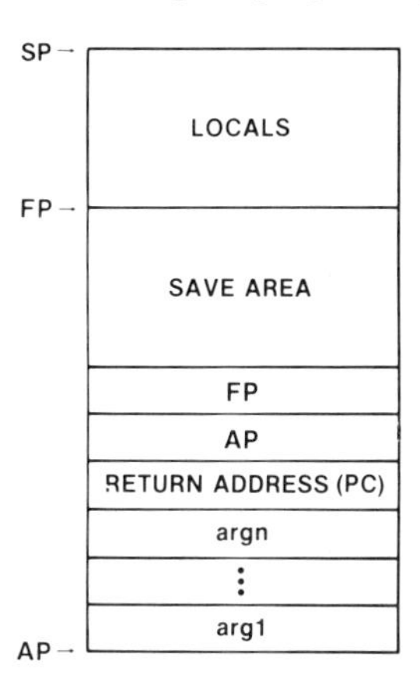

Figure 9.14 Sample stack frame.

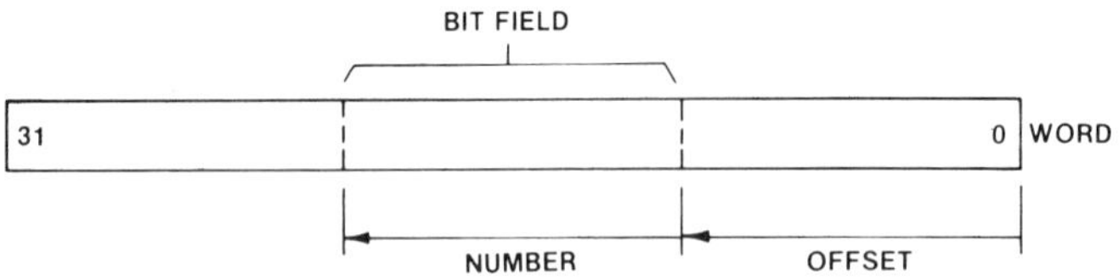

Figure 9.15 Bit field format.

These may be added or modified with little difficulty compared to hardwired functions.

Microcode may reside in either read-only memory (ROM) or the writable control store (WCS). The following sequences have been implemented in the 3B20D microcode:

1. The *microboot* sequence of code initializes the processor and loads the writable control store and the first-level bootstrap program from disk. If it is unable to load from the primary disk, it automatically tries to load from the backup disk.
2. The *tapeboot* sequence of microcode initializes the processor and copies data from a standard nine-track magnetic tape to the disk. The microboot routine may then be used to initiate program execution.
3. The *basic instruction set* is microcode that implements the native instruction set and special instructions that are specific to the 3B20D processor.
4. The *external interrupt routine* is invoked only on completion of an instruction with an interrupt pending. The microcode saves the state of the system, then transfers control to an interrupt event handler routine.
5. The *error interrupt routine* is entered when a hardware or software error occurs. The microcode saves the state of the machine and then transfers control to a routine that attempts to recover processing without switching to the other machine. This interrupt may be encountered between any microinstructions.
6. The *memory management trap* is entered if the virtual address of the memory fetch cannot be translated directly to a physical address by the address translation hardware. The microcode reads the segment and page tables of the active process, loads the hardware translation unit with the translation information, and reactivates the memory access.
7. *Maintenance channel instructions* allow the processor to communicate with its duplex mate via the maintenance channel.
8. *Diagnostic sequences* are contained in a section of the writable control store; they load and execute special microcode diagnostics.
9. Several *miscellaneous routines* are used for functions such as loading the writable control store and loading the hardware matcher registers in the utility circuit.
10. Up to three *emulation routines* may be loaded to allow the 3B20D to emulate other machines.

During the development of the 3B20D, several new software and hardware tools evolved to generate and debug microcode with relative ease. Of principal importance are the MICA [12] bit-sliced assembler and the microlevel test set (MLTS). These tools allow laboratory utility computers to assemble microcode and control the 3B20D. The MLTS loads writable microstore, accesses main store, accesses registers and controls sequencing at the microcode level, sets breakpoints, and provides trace capability.

During the development of the 3B20D processor, substantial benefits were realized because the system was microprogrammed. Major improvements in the instruction set architecture were accommodated by microcode changes. Features have been added to enhance error recovery, permit transferring bootstrap programs from magnetic tape to disk, and improve system performance.

9.4 I/O FACILITIES [13,14]

The I/O facilities meet a wide range of applications with different needs and capabilities. The I/O communication structure is modular and flexible; it operates by means of dedicated point-to-point channels. The loose coupling of the processor to the peripherals allows considerable freedom to expand the system with minimal physical constraints.

The I/O architecture is shown in Fig. 9.16. Although the channel address ranges from 0 to 19, the processor may only be equipped with seven programmed I/O channels

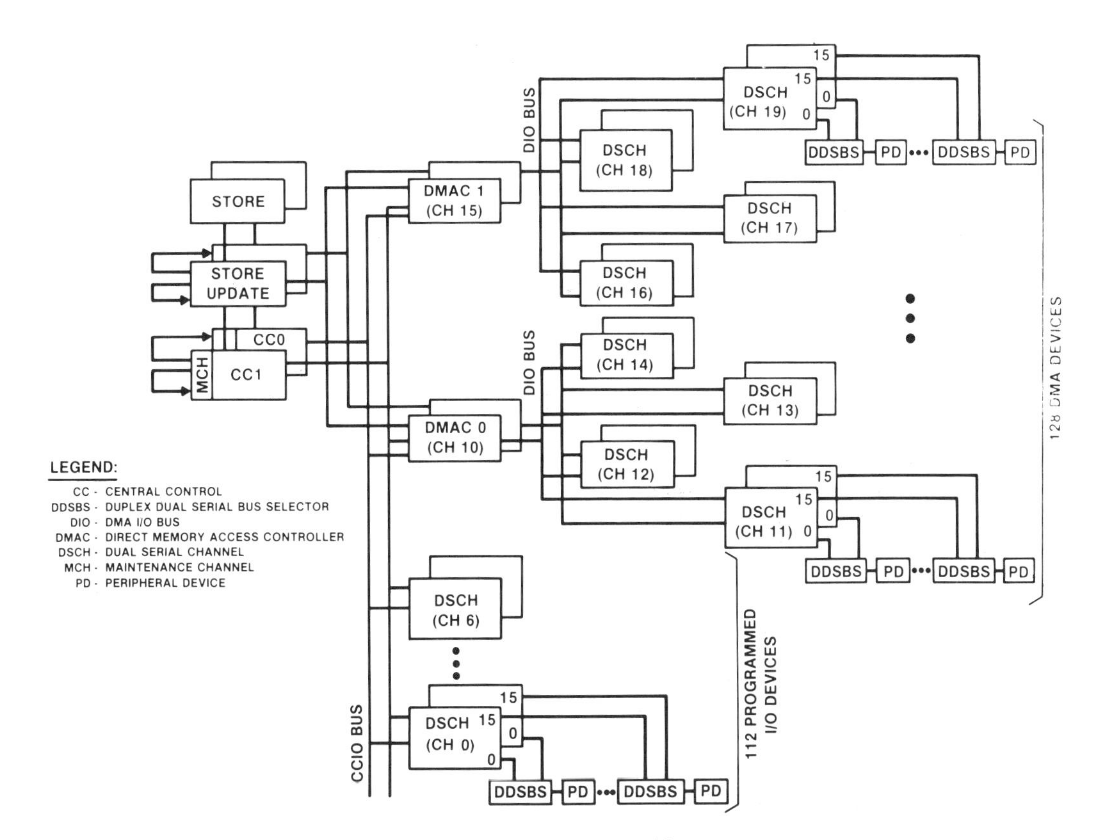

Figure 9.16 3B20D I/O architecture.

and eight direct memory access (DMA) channels. The other five channels are not currently allocated because of space restrictions. Each channel may control up to 16 devices; the maximum configuration, therefore, has 128 DMA devices and 112 programmed I/O devices. Programmed I/O channels are directly controlled by microcode via the CCIO bus. The DMA facility provides autonomous control of data transfer between the main store and peripheral devices, thus alleviating the constant need for the CC to process I/O requests. A common controller (DMAC) controls up to four dual serial channels (DSCHs); each DMAC corresponds to a DMA channel.

9.4.1 Dual Serial Channel

All standard peripheral devices use the dual serial channel (DSCH) for communication. It is a semiautonomous unit providing up to 16 private serial point-to-point data transmission paths, giving a unique link for each device (Fig. 9.17). Each link consists of two bidirectional data leads, a transmitting clock, a receiving clock, and a request lead. Each of the two data leads operate at 10 mHz for cable distances of up to 100 feet. For devices up to 250 feet away, a 5-mHz clock rate is used.

The normal data transfer operation is a 32-bit word message. The dual serial channel allows the concurrent transmission of 16 data bits each to form 32-bit words. In addition to the 16-bit data, the transmission includes 3 start code bits plus 2 parity bits (one for each byte). When the DSCH transfers words, its transfer time (including the overhead of additional bits for propagation delay) and synchronization timing is about 4.5 microseconds per 32-bit word. The DSCH may also transfer blocks; in this mode, it is able to transfer sixteen 32-bit words at a rate of 3.0 microseconds per word as a single sequence. Although the addressing and loading of data are performed under program control, the actual transmission is done autonomously under control of the DSCH hardware.

Data is transmitted using RS-422-compatible signaling. The other end of the cable connects to a duplex dual serial bus selector (DDSBS) that converts the signals from the DSCH into a parallel format. Each DDSBS may serve two DSCHs; this configuration allows each peripheral device to connect to both CPUs of the duplex processor.

The programmed I/O operation is controlled directly by the processor; except on DMA operations, devices do not initiate action on their own. Service request functions are included in the DSCH to allow a device to signal the processor via the interrupt mechanism. The signaling is transmitted over the request line of the DSCH link. The DSCHs are used for processor-to-processor communication in multiple processor configurations. Also, DSCHs attach directly to peripheral devices, so communication may be initiated by either end.

9.4.2 Direct Memory Access

The DMA circuit consists of a controller and from one to four DSCHs (Fig. 9.16). A DMA may accommodate up to 64 devices, all of which may be active concurrently. The DMA controller (DMAC) supports virtual addressing, word or block (16-word) transfers, device-initiated transfers, and multiple jobs for a given device. The latter function allo-

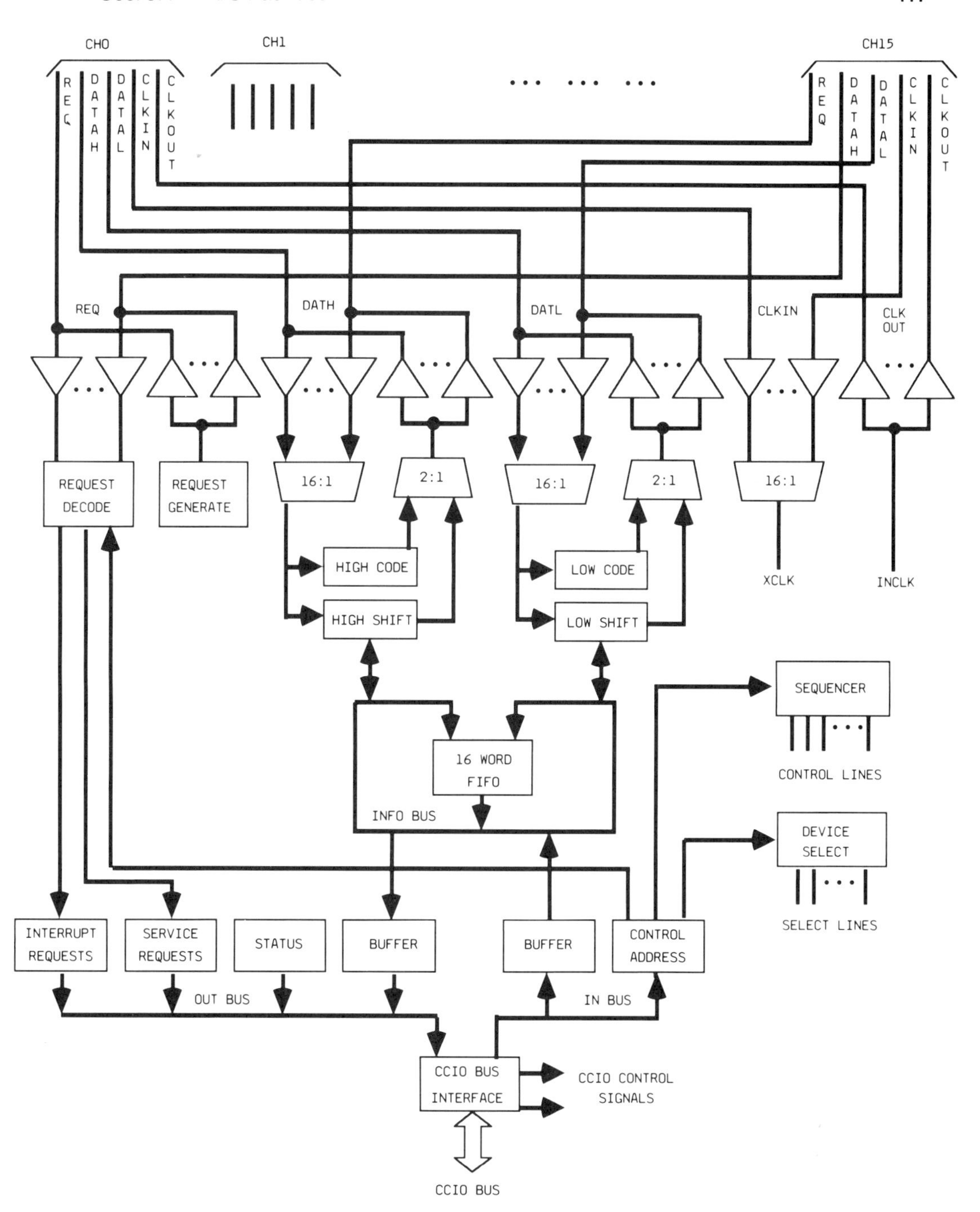

Figure 9.17 Dual serial channel (DSCW) block diagram.

cates a unique segment in memory to each job for a device, which prevents one job from mutilating the memory of another job.

A DMA transfer is a two-step operation. The first step involves passing data between the channel and peripheral device; the second step concerns passing data among the channel, DMAC, and main store. While the first operation is in progress, the DMAC may be loading or unloading another channel from main store. The DMAC has a hardware priority circuit that gives channel 0 priority over channel 1, which has a higher priority than channel 2, and so on. The devices on a given channel are assigned priorities in the same manner; that is, device 0 has the highest priority and device 15 the lowest. The channel does not permit interleaving devices on less than a block or word boundary. Once a transfer of a block or word starts, it must be completed before another device on that channel may be serviced.

A DMA transfer is initiated by a device passing to the DMAC a starting virtual address and, optionally, a transfer count. The DMAC translates the address into a physical address as described below. The transfer count is used as a check to verify that the device and DMAC are in agreement about the number of transfers to take place.

The address translation process used by the DMAC is the same as that used by the central control; both use the translation page tables that are stored in main memory (see Section 9.3.3). Each page has protection bits defining the DMA read/write access capability. The maximum-size transfers that may be accomplished with a single address setup is one segment or 64 2K-byte pages. As part of the initialization process for the DMAC, the processor passes a unique page table pointer to the DMA for each of its active devices. The DMAC uses the page table pointer and the virtual address to obtain the desired physical page pointer. As the DMA transfer crosses a page boundary, the DMAC automatically accesses the page table to obtain the next physical page pointer.

After setting up the DMAC, the device initiates the transfer by sending a transfer request. The DMAC asks for the data from the device or sends the data to the device in the word (32 bits) or block (16 words) mode. The device then sends another transfer request and the handshaking continues until the entire job is completed.

9.4.3 Peripheral Devices

The 3B20D processor accommodates a broad range of general-purpose peripheral devices that are reliable and easy to maintain. The critical hardware components are duplicated and the software preserves all the valid data sources. Duplex dual serial bus selectors (DDSBSs) permit the controlled replacement of a working standby device for a faulty on-line device when the duplication of a peripheral device is needed. The following peripheral devices are available for the 3B20D system.

1. The *moving-head disk system* provides a reliable and flexible mass storage medium for programs and data. A backup copy of system programs and critical parameters may be reloaded quickly in the event of a duplex main store failure. The disk system comprises the disk file controller (DFC) and the moving head disk drive (MHD). The DFC interprets and executes commands from the processor to transfer

informaton to and from the MHD. Each DFC occupies 1 of 128 channel slots and supports up to 16 MHD drives, which are available in 80M- and 300M-byte sizes.

2. The *I/O processor (IOP)* controls a wide range of data link facilities and is the most flexible member of the family of devices. An IOP supports up to 16 peripheral controllers (PCs), which are microprocessor-based controllers programmed to handle specific terminals or devices. For example, one type of PC is the line controller (LC); each LC supports up to four independent lines (data links or terminals).
3. The *magnetic tape system* includes a tape drive and a controller. The tape drive accepts the industry-standard (IBM-compatible) nine-track tapes at a density of 1600 bits per inch. The tape controller is a type of PC and occupies one of the 16 slots of the IOP.
4. The *scanner/signal distributor (SC/SD)* monitors and controls power, equipment states, environment conditions, and so on. The SC/SD circuit board has 48 scan points and 32 signal-distributor points. It occupies one of the PC slots of the IOP. When an IOP is fully equipped with 16 SC/SD circuit packs, it provides a total of 768 scan points and 512 signal-distributor points.

9.4.4 Craft Interface [15]

The maintenance interface is commonly referred to as the *craft interface* in the telecommunications industry. The craft interface of the 3B20D is markedly different from previous systems developed at Bell Laboratories because it relies almost exclusively on video displays and keyboard controls. The earlier systems have key-lamp panels and teletypewriters in their master control centers (MCCs).

The craft interface includes hardware, firmware, and software that enables maintenance personnel to obtain the status of, and exert control over, the system. Status information is presented visually as graphical displays and text messages on various terminals and printers; audible alarm circuits may also be connected to the 3B20D. System control is exerted primarily through a keyboard attached to the video display terminal. System control is also possible from remote locations called switching control centers. The data links to the remote sites use the international standard message protocol (X.25) because of its low vulnerability to noise and other data communication failures. The adoption of the X.25 message protocol standardizes remote access to the 3B20D processor for packet switching networks.

Figure 9.18 is a functional block diagram of the craft interface. Each of the duplex processors is connected to both IOPs which, as mentioned previously, support up to 16 peripheral controllers (PCs). The IOP software driver (see Section 9.5) contains "handlers" that deal with the specialized functions of the PCs. Maintenance personnel use the read-only printer (ROP) and the maintenance CRT (MCRT). The ROP logs all important status messages. The MCRT is a keyboard display terminal. The system contains only one ROP and one MCRT because the port switch keeps the ROP and the MCRT connected to the active on-line processor.

All capabilities of the craft interface are accessible from a remote switching control

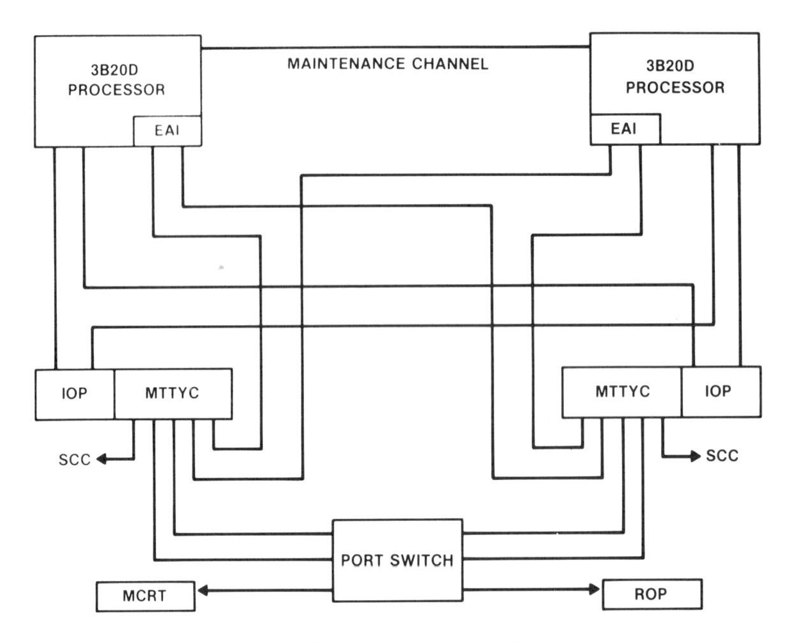

Figure 9.18 Craft interface hardware overview.

center by means of a dedicated data link. The data link is duplicated; it includes a primary link and a backup link. Both links use the CCITT X.25 communication protocol. The MCRT, ROP, and X.25 links are attached to a peripheral controller known as the maintenance teletype controller (MTTYC). The craft interface handler controls the transfer of data to and from the peripheral devices associated with the MTTYC. The MTTYC is connected directly to the emergency action interface (EAI) in the central processor. The EAI menu on the MCRT gives basic status information and manual control of the processor regardless of DMERT software sanity; this access is controlled totally by the firmware in the MTTYC. This reliable, high-capacity data link for remote maintenance makes the 3B20D well suited for unattended operation.

9.5 DMERT OPERATING SYSTEM [16,17]

The operating system used in the 3B20D is the Duplex Multi-environment Real-Time (DMERT) operating system, which is now called the UNIX RTR operating system. It has a process-oriented structure that emphasizes high data availability. It is designed for both real-time and time-shared operations. The basic architecture of the DMERT operating system is based on an earlier system named MERT [18] and the UNIX operating system [19]. Both the UNIX and the MERT operating systems were developed to execute on commercial equipment. Currently, the UNIX operating system is widely used and the MERT operating system has been replaced by its duplex successor, the DMERT operating system. Experience gained from the operating system of the earlier No. 3A processor, a real-time monitor known as the Extended Operating System (EOS), also benefited the designers of the DMERT system [20]. The DMERT operating system has a sophisticated architecture that draws on the proven design concepts of the EOS, MERT, and UNIX operating systems (Fig. 9.19).

9.5.1 Process Structure

The DMERT operating system consists of modular and independent processes, each having localized data known only to itself. The concept of a *process* is therefore fundamental to understanding the DMERT architecture, which is composed of a kernel and many cooperating, concurrent processes.

A process is a collection of related, logical segments (programs and data) that may be brought into memory to form an executable entity. It is the basic memory entity in the DMERT system. A segment has from 1 to 64 pages; each page is 512 32-bit words in length. Segments grow dynamically in increments of pages. Each process has at least three segments: a code or text segment, a stack segment, and a process control block segment. The stack segment stores temporary data. The process control block is a special type of data segment that contains information identifying the process to the operating system. The information in the process control block includes the process number, the type of process, its priority, and address space qualifiers that define the virtual address space needs for the process. Each process has its own virtual address space of up to 128 segments. The virtual addresses are mapped to physical addresses by hardware under the control of the DMERT operating system.

In the DMERT operating system, segments are the basic swappable entities; that is,

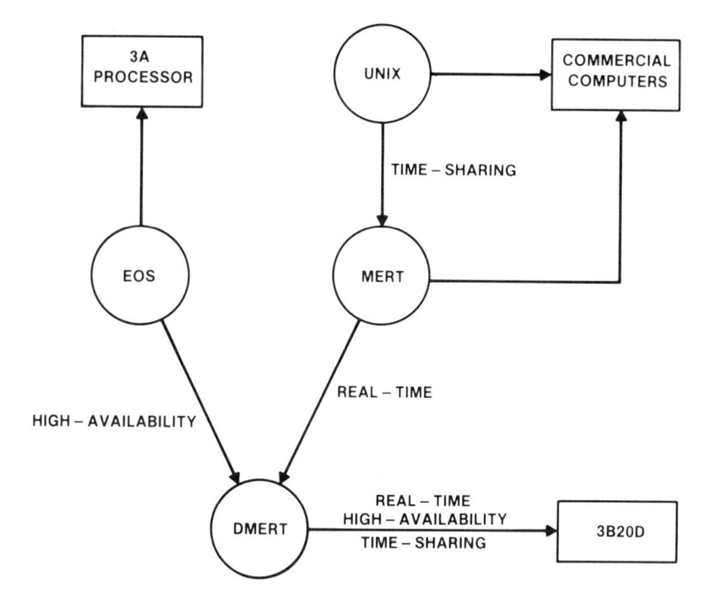

Figure 9.19 Bases of DMERT architecture.

individual segments of a process are swapped in and out of main memory as needed. Although a segment may be swapped out to secondary memory if main memory is needed for a higher-priority process, the system keeps track of it and executes it when possible.

A process may be created dynamically to perform a set of functions. When its task is finished, the process terminates itself. Other processes continuously perform work. These processes are called *live processes* even though they may be inactive until an interrupt occurs. The two types of processes constitute a feature of the DMERT operating system that allows main memory to hold only the processes necessary to support the application.

9.5.2 Multilayer Virtual Machines

As a general-purpose operating system, the DMERT system is structured as a series of cooperating processes that form different levels of virtual machines. Protective mechanisms are built into the structure that prevent the virtual machines from interfering with each other. To ensure that all the processes accomplish their tasks simultaneously, the DMERT operating system has a rich set of interprocess communicaton and synchronization mechanisms, including messages, events, process ports, interprocess traps, and shared memory. These communication primitives supply system services to requesting processes.

There are four levels of virtual machines: the kernel, kernel process, supervisor, and user levels (Fig. 9.20). Successive levels have increasing restrictions on the access rights of the system resources. The four process levels free programmers from the task of programming detailed manipulations of the physical machine. The higher levels take advantage of the services provided by the lower levels.

In general, more services are available to the application programmer at high levels.

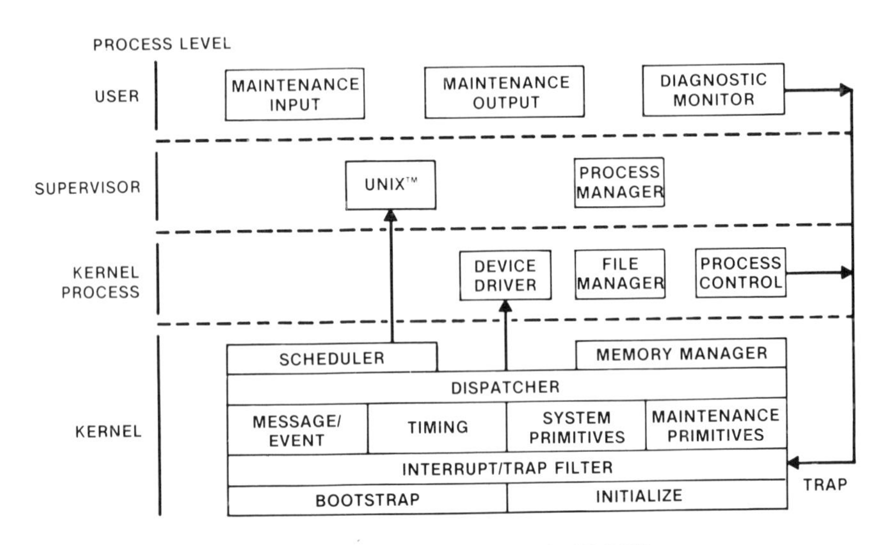

Figure 9.20 Hardware supporting the DMERT struture.

Lower levels use real time more efficiently for program execution. The leveling structure of the virtual machines permits the DMERT system to manage real-time applications and, at the same time, provide a time-sharing system for background tasks. This approach avoids contention for system resources with the high-priority task and simplifies the implementation effort for lower-priority tasks.

1. The *kernel* level is the most primitive virtual machine. Programs at this level directly control the system hardware and do not have access to other system functions. The kernel handles hardware interrupts, timer interrupts, and operating system traps in which services are provided to requesting processes. The kernel is used during initializations. It supplies system and maintenance primitives, schedules processes, and assists with memory management, timing routines, message, and events. The kernel services are primitive yet efficient in their execution. Users may not introduce code at this level.
2. The *kernel processes* form a virtual machine that is hardware-related and structured to provide critical processing efficiently in a real-time environment. Kernel processes are completely driven by interrupts. They have their own virtual address spaces but share the kernel's stack and the kernel's message buffer segment. Swapping is not necessary with kernel processes because their segments are locked in memory to ensure rapid response to interrupts. The various peripheral device drivers and the file manager, which implements a hierarchical file system, are examples of kernel processes. When processes are built, kernel processes are set up to access the operating system's stack and message buffers. This design allows quick access to the arguments of operating system traps and fast message communication between processes. Since kernel processes use the kernel's stack, they must run until they complete their tasks. They then return control to the kernel. Users may add kernel process code.
3. *Supervisor processes* form the third level of virtual machine. The programs of this level are generally independent of the hardware. These processes may use all the services provided by the kernel and kernel processes. Supervisor processes provide time-sharing services that are considered *background* tasks. They share the real time of the processor with each other according to priorities administered by the scheduler, which is a special process in the kernel. In general, supervisor segments are not locked in memory but may be swapped in and out. They therefore take much longer to dispatch than either special or kernel processes.
4. Supervisor processes may run alone or they may be used to implement *user processes,* which make up the fourth virtual machine level. The DMERT process manager is a supervisor process that does not support a user level. However, the UNIX operating system supervisor provides a user environment identical to that seen by UNIX programs. This is done through code at the supervisor level that calls on the services of lower virtual machine layers. The DMERT operating system can simultaneously support multiple supervisors, each supporting its own user processes. It treats a supervisor-user process combination as a single process with a dual address space. Code at the supervisor level executes more efficiently than user-level code

because a supervisor has direct access to the lower-level primitives; the user interface to these primitives is coordinated by the user's supervisor. All application programs that do not have stringent time constraints are written at the user level.

9.5.3 Interprocess Communication

The DMERT operating system has a rich set of interprocess communication and synchronization mechanisms including messages, events, interprocess traps, and shared memory. These interprocess communication primitives are fundamental to the DMERT structure. Most of the system services are requested by an exchange of events and messages between a requesting process and either a system process or the kernel.

Processes are usually separate and distinct entities but two processes working together on a task must be able to exchange informaton. The DMERT operating system allows *messages* to be sent from one process to any other process, regardless of which levels the processes are on. The messages may be up to several hundred bytes long (seven blocks of 64 bytes). The sender must only know the target process number and a predetermined message format to send a message. An optional acknowledgment capability allows the sender to synchronize actions with the receiver.

Communications between processes may also occur using *events*. An event is a single bit that is set by the operating system or by a process; an event is usually interrogated by a receiving process. Presently, 32 bits are available to record events; but the DMERT operating system reserves 16 bits for its use. Events (for example, the reception of a message) are frequently used to communicate interval status between processes.

The operating system also contains mechanisms known as *interprocess traps* to allow lower-level processes to support high-level processes. A user-level process may ''trap'' to a supporting supervisor and a supervisor may ''trap'' to a kernel process. A trap transfers control from one process to another and passes input parameters to the target process. The lower-level process returns status information and control to the trapping process after it has completed its work.

Processes have a view of their own virtual address space and, in general, may not access the address space of any other process. Although this design protects against faulty processes, it makes sharing large amounts of data difficult. Cooperating processes that must exchange information at rates higher than those supported by messages or events may share segments. A shared segment is a part of the virtual address space of several processes simultaneously. The application must control access to the shared data.

9.5.4 Multiple-Environment Support

Application programmers may add code at the kernel process, supervisor process, and user levels. The multilevel structure makes the DMERT operating system flexible and efficient in its use of real time. The structure of the virtual machines permits the management of both real-time applications and time-shared background tasks. For example, Fig.

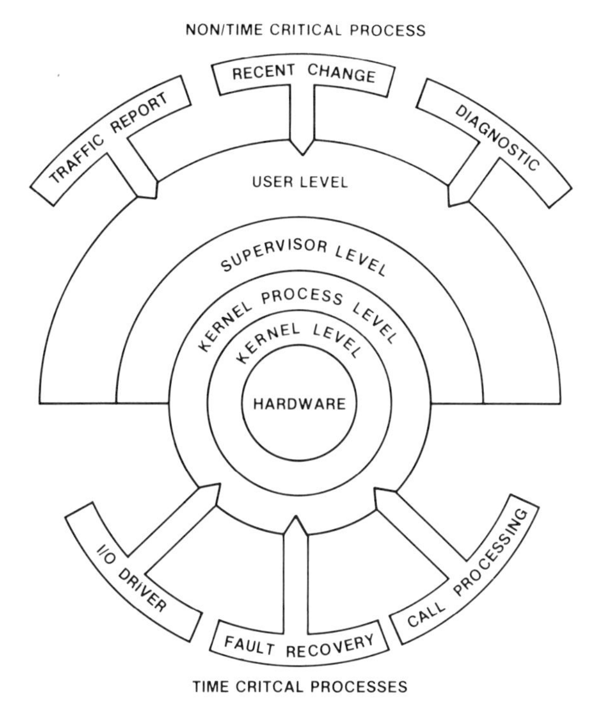

Figure 9.21 Example of DMERT multi-environment structure.

9.21 shows how telephone switching software is allocated to the different levels. The operating system maintains a process hierarchy based on 16 execution levels. Time-critical functions such as the I/O drivers, fault recovery, and call processing are implemented at the kernel process level. A kernel process may belong to levels 3 through 15 (levels 0 through 2 are reserved for the time-sharing environment). By means of this hierarchical execution-level structure, applications are able to customize their control and distribution of real time.

The portion of real time that is not used by the kernel or kernel processes is time-shared among supervisor and user processes. Deferrable jobs such as traffic reports, recent changes, and diagnostics are implemented at the highest user level. Processes supporting the time-sharing environment are run at execution level 2. These processes are run just beneath the real-time hierarchy; they gain control of the processor only after all the real-time work is completed. By supporting both real-time and time-sharing environments, the DMERT operating system makes efficient use of its physical resources.

9.5.5 DMERT Overhead

The efficiency of the DMERT system depends on the overhead it requires to perform its tasks. There are five types of system overhead:

1. *Functional overhead* handles the timing-based facilities for interrupt servicing, scheduling, craft terminal polling, and data link polling.
2. *Sanity overhead* monitors and resets the hardware sanity timers, monitors the operating system and application sanity timers, and checks for process lockout conditions.
3. *Preventive maintenance* is a type of overhead that exercises the system (routine preventive maintenance) and runs routine software audits.
4. *Fault maintenance* detects faults and recovers from them by removing faulty units from service and testing and restoring the replacement units. This overhead is incurred only when faults occur.
5. *Other nonelectable services* not covered by the previously described overhead types include craft interface services and plant measurements services.

The DMERT operating system overhead is characterized in terms of CPU time and is expressed as a percentage of the overall system use of CPU time. The first two types of overhead (functional and sanity) are continuous; they cannot be controlled or throttled by the application. Functional and sanity overhead use less than 5 percent of the CPU time allocated to the DMERT operating system. Preventive maintenance is intermittent. It may be controlled in two ways: by throttling routine software audits so their peak resource usage is limited to a desired value, and by exercising routine diagnostics during times of light call processing loads.

The fault maintenance overhead is measured as a single-fault, worst-case scenario that includes fault detection, isolation, recovery, testing, and restoring the repaired unit. The total resource usage is averaged over the specified 2-hour repair interval. The services overhead includes normal administrative activities necessary to maintain and administer the processor complex. The total system overhead for functional, sanity, preventive, fault maintenance, and services is less than 15 percent (Fig. 9.22).

9.6 FAULT RECOVERY [21]

When any of the unique fault detection circuits detects an error condition, an error interrupt (or error report in the case of certain peripherals) is registered in the processor. The most severe error interrupts result in automatic hardware sequences that switch the processing activity between the processors (hard switch). Less severe errors result in microinterrupts that activate the microcode and software to recover the system. This layered approach constituting the recovery architecture is depicted in Fig. 9.23. Microcode provides low-level access to the hardware and the recovery software provides the high-level control mechanisms and decision making.

Figure 9.24 illustrates the principal architecture and features of the recovery software. The bootstrap and initialization routines contain a fundamental set of microcode and software algorithms that control initializations and recoveries. These actions are stimulated by a maintenance restart function (MRF), which represents the highest-priority microinterrupt in the system. An MRF sequence may be stimulated from either hardware or software recovery sources.

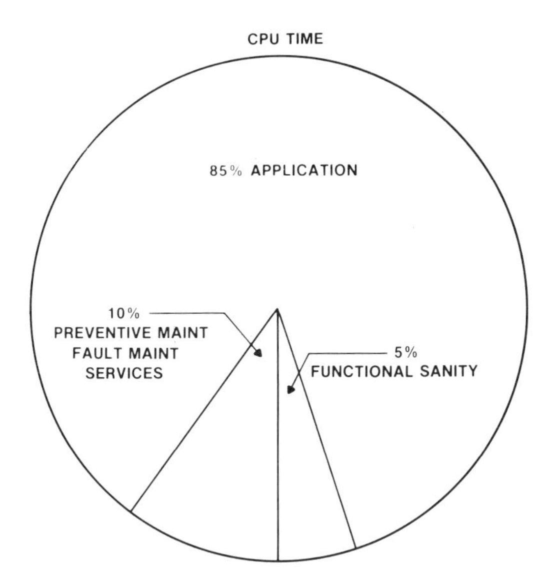

Figure 9.22 DMERT overhead.

The fault recovery and system integrity packages control fault detection and recovery for hardware and software, respectively. The error interrupt handler (EIH) is the principal hardware fault recovery controller. It receives all hardware interrupts and controls the recovery sequences that follow. The configuration management program (CONFIG) determines whether an error is exceeding the predetermined frequency thresholds. If a threshold is exceeded, CONFIG requests a change in the configuration of the processor to

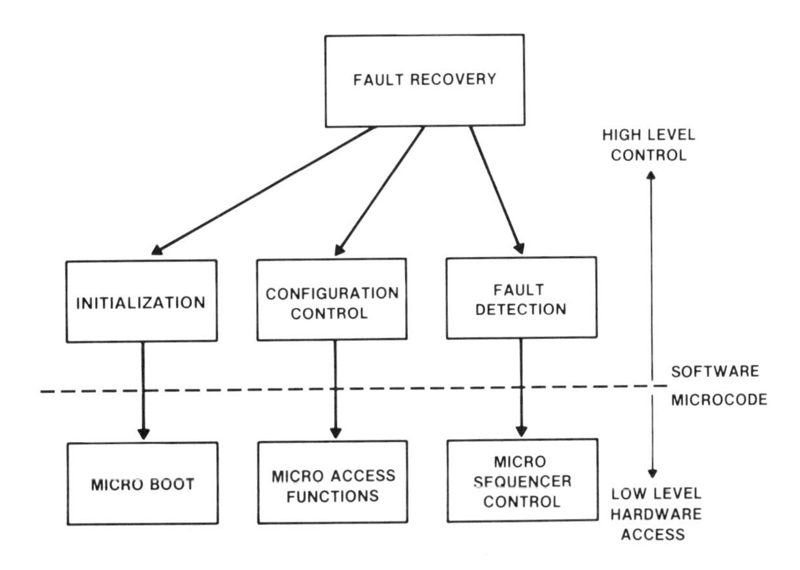

Figure 9.23 Recovery software structure.

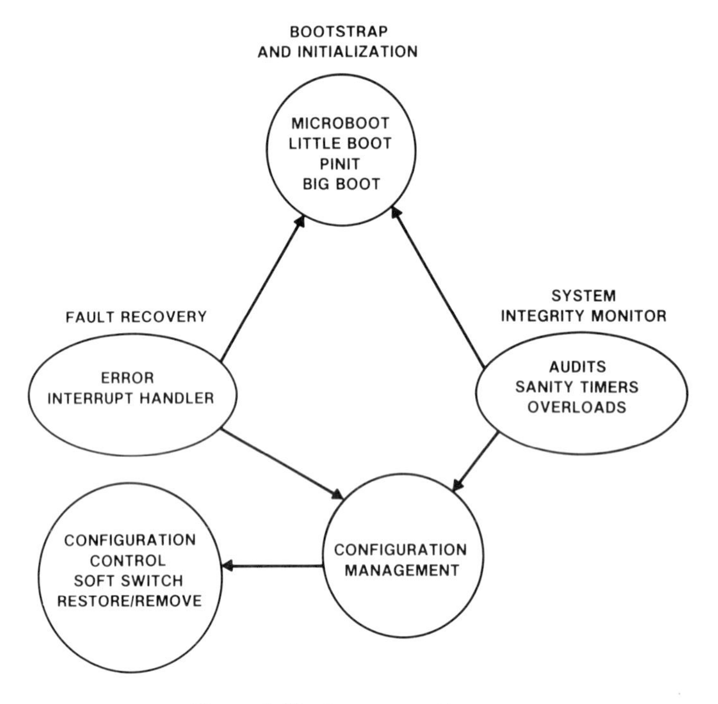

Figure 9.24 Recovery architecture.

a healthy state. Thus, CONFIG serves as an error-rate analysis package for both hardware and software errors.

9.6.1 Hardware Fault Recovery

The 3B20D has built in self-checking circuitry that detects hardware faults as soon as they occur. This circuitry simplifies recovery since early detection limits the damage done by the fault. Faults in this category indicate that the processor is no longer capable of proper operation and results in an immediate termination of the currently running processor and a switch to the standby processor. Since the standby processor does not match the active processor instruction by instruction, an initialization sequence is required to start execution properly.

Some types of faults and errors are not severe enough to justify an immediate termination and switch of the processors. Examples of errors of this kind are hardware faults detected in the standby processor memory and software errors such as write-protection violations. Other errors in this category are the hardware faults that are handled by the self-correcting circuitry. Although most units have self-checking circuits, some units (such as main memories) have fault rates that justify the addition of self-correcting capabilities. Disks also are self-correcting through the use of cyclic redundancy codes. All errors in this class are reported to the recovery system as error interrupts.

All error interrupts are reported to the configuration management program

(CONFIG). Errors are logged against the failing unit and error rates are compared to allowed error thresholds. If the affected threshold is exceeded, further action is required based on several factors, including the importance of the faulty unit and whether a mate exists for it. If the faulty unit is essential to the system and a mate unit is available, the faulty unit is removed from service and scheduled for diagnostic testing. If there is no available mate unit, the faulty unit is initialized and returned to service until the mate is restored. When the mate is restored, it is switched on-line and the faulty unit is scheduled for diagnostic testing. In the case of essential units, it is better to have a faulty unit than no unit. Unessential units are removed from service and scheduled for diagnostic testing whenever their error thresholds are exceeded.

Each processor has a sanity timer that causes an initialization if it expires. The active processor maintains both its own timer and the timer of the standby unit. If the active processor cannot recover from a fault, the sanity timer triggers the initialization of the standby processor.

9.6.2 Special Microcode for Recovery

A large fraction of the microcode in the central control (CC) handles system recoveries. Most of this recovery microcode is in read-only memory because most of the recovery functions are required regardless of the past history of the CC or its boot devices. Functions that are required even if the CC is not ready to execute its instruction set include:

1. Microinterrupt processing
2. Maintenance channel assists
3. Microcode to initialize hardware systems

Microinterrupt processing handles errors in the address translation buffer to microinstruction store sequence (see Section 9.3.1). Maintenance channel assists allow one processor to access the other processor. Microcode initializes the hardware systems; additional recovery microcode that resides in writable microstore (WMS) extends the processor's instructions set to provide convenient diagnostic and recovery software access instructions. When diagnostic performance requirements do not justify a special instruction, a microstore scratch area is made available. Arbitrary microsequences loaded into the scratch area are then executed as special tests or functions. Before the software can run, however, the WMS must be loaded from disk. The WMS is loaded as part of the processing of the MRF microinterrupt.

9.6.3 Software Fault Recovery

Software fault recovery is architecturally similar to hardware fault recovery. Each major unit of software has associated with it error detection mechanisms (defensive checks and audits), error thresholds, and error recovery mechanisms (failure returns, audits, and data correction and initialization techniques). Both the system integrity monitor (SIM) and the error interrupt handler (EIH) oversee the proper execution of the process. An error threshold in SIM ensures that a process does not put itself into an infinite execution loop or excessively consume a system resource (for example, message buffers). The EIH, through the use of hardware and microcode detectors, ensures that processes do not try to access memory outside defined limits or execute restricted instructions. Each process has initialization and recovery controls (analogous to hardware) to effect recoveries. Figure 9.25 illustrates this software recovery architecture.

If recovery actions result in the removal of hardware units, diagnostics are dispatched automatically to analyze the specific problem. Audits are the software counterparts for hardware diagnostics; the major difference is that routine audits run more frequently than diagnostics, and they correct certain errors.

9.6.4 Software Audits

The DMERT audit package verifies the validity of critical data structures. Most audits exist throughout the system within the processes that control the data to be audited. In some cases, several audits are invoked consecutively to form a sequenced mode audit. Most requests for running audits comes from an audit control structure, the audit manager.

Audits in the DMERT operating system verify data, not functions. The basic types

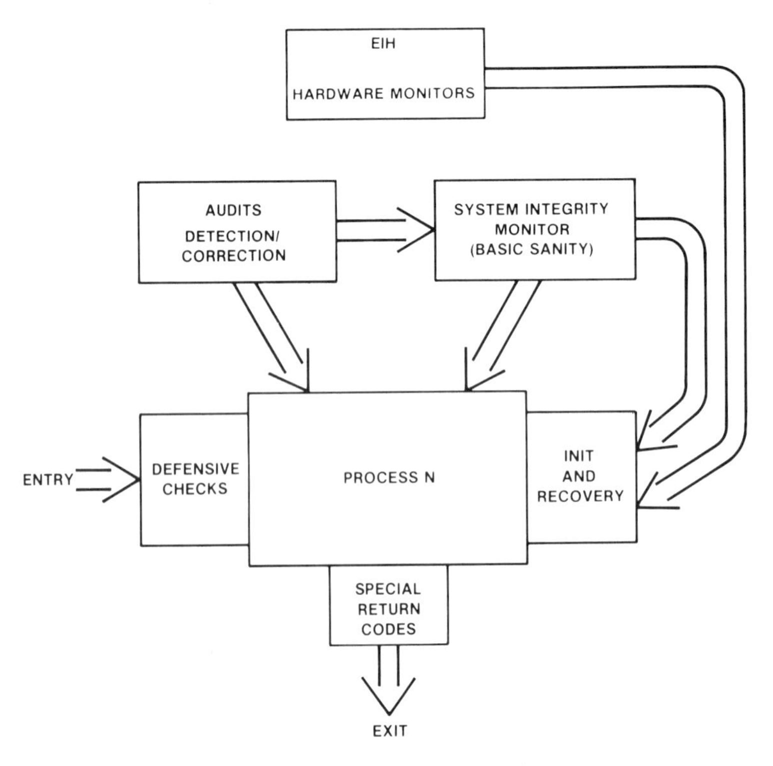

Figure 9.25 Software fault recovery architecture.

of auditable data are system resources and stable data. Though most of the auditable data in the operating system resides in the kernel, additional data resides in critical processes such as the file manager and device drivers. Smaller amounts of auditable data reside in supervisor processes such as the UNIX operating system and the process manager.

Some audits, scheduled on a regular basis, are known as routine audits; others, scheduled on request, are known as demand audits. Audits within the DMERT operating system include the following:

- The *message buffers audit* finds and frees lost message buffers, that is, messages that have been on the queue of a process for extended periods of time.
- The *scheduler audit* checks for linkage errors in the ready and not-ready lists of the scheduler.
- The *memory manager audit* recovers lost swap space and corrects any overlap of swap space.
- The *file manager audit* checks all internal file manager structures, including task blocks, buffers, and the mount table. It corrects the information and can back out aborted tasks to free their resources.
- The *file system audit* is demanded by the file manager whenever a file system is mounted in the read/write mode. It checks and corrects the file system's super block free list and its free-block bit map. The audit verifies the integrity of the mounted file systems concurrent with their use.

9.6.5 System Initialization

When a maintenance restart interrupt occurs, a long sequence of microsteps begins to establish system sanity. Both processors may be in their maintenance restart function (MRF) sequence at the same time and each one may try to become the active processor. The MRF code decides which processor should become active and whether to do an off-line initialization or an on-line initialization. If a processor determines that it has just powered up, it clears main store and does an off-line initialization unless it is forced on-line by an operator command.

A number of tests are made on data in the system status register (SSR) to select one of four possible actions:

1. Processor initialization
2. Stop and switch
3. Microboot
4. Tapeboot

The simplest actions are initializing a processor and stopping and switching to the other processor. Switching to another processor is accomplished by sending a switch command over the maintenance channel to the other processor. If an initialization does not recover the system to an operational state, another and more severe initialization is triggered automatically. The initialization interval determines whether escalating is necessary. Any initialization that occurs within the initialization interval (that is, within a specified time interval after an initialization) escalates to the next higher level. The length of the initialization interval is a system generation parameter that is established by the application.

The *microboot program* uses information on the DMERT disk to initialize the writable microstore and read in the first software boot program called little boot. To do this, it must first select the disk drive to use as the boot device. If the craft interface has forced either the primary or the secondary boot device active, it uses that device. Otherwise, the microboot program selects a disk drive based on the state of the initialization status control bits in the system status register. Alternate boots use alternate devices. Microcode is read from the disk and then copied to the writable microstore. Finally, the little boot program is read from the boot partition and given control.

The *tapeboot program* is a complex sequence of microcode that is only used when requested manually from the craft interface. Its function is to create a new system disk from tape. Tapeboot initializes the tape device and disk device selected by the craft interface and initializes the writable microstore from tape. The load disk tape program is read from tape into main store; memory management tables are created to allow it to run the hardware complex without the operating system present. The load disk tape program then reads the tape to make a DMERT disk image.

9.6.6 Emergency Mode

The emergency mode on the 3B20D refers to the facilities and procedures that prevent the system from experiencing a total outage. For example, emergency facilities are applied when the system is unable to recover automatically. The most frequent emergencies encountered include duplex failures of the control unit, duplex failures of the system disks, duplex failures of the essential I/O devices, and failures of fault recovery to find a working configuration of the hardware. Other problems requiring the emergency mode include software faults that do not allow the system to operate properly, errors that destroy the integrity of the disks, and software overwrites that introduce catastrophic errors into the software.

Emergency mode capabilities are built into the system to address problems that may cause the failure of the 3B20D as a system. The emergency action interface (EAI) on the 3B20D provides manual initialization capabilities that can recover the system from several of the conditions mentioned above. The EAI allows the maintenance personnel to demand a specific processor and disk configuration if a certain configuration is causing problems. The EAI also allows the craft to reconfigure the system to handle maintenance hardware failures. For example, the craft may inhibit error sources and sanity timers through EAI commands, thus allowing recovery from certain maintenance failures even though both processors are affected. The EAI also provides capabilities for craft initializations to deal with the loss of subsystem capabilities.

The 3B20D provides other emergency mode capabilities through the port switch select, the disk power inverter select, and the unit power switches. These devices are used by maintenance personnel to manually reconfigure the system to handle certain problems.

Under unstable bootstrap conditions, the 3B20D outputs diagnostic information called *processor recovery messages*. These messages provide a general set of diagnostics in the event of a complete system outage.

The final backup repair procedure consists of the dead start diagnostics. Primarily used as installation tools, the dead start diagnostics allow a nonworking processor to be repaired from a remote host processor.

9.7 FAULT DIAGNOSTICS [22]

As with earlier processor designs, 3B20D processor diagnostics detect faults efficiently and effectively, provide consistent test results, protect the contents of memory, do not interfere with normal system operation, allow automatic trouble location, and are easy to maintain and update. In addition, the 3B20D diagnostics are:

1. *Portable* because the diagnostic software must execute in several environments
2. *Flexible* because the diagnostics test multiple system configurations containing various types of circuits
3. *Modular* because standard control interfaces are required to accommodate various test access facilities, input/output facilities, and DMERT application processes that diagnose application-dependent hardware interfacing with the 3B20D processor.

To meet these design objectives, the diagnostic control structure is an integral part of the DMERT operating system and supports the evolutionary stages of development.

9.7.1 Diagnostic Environments

As shown in Fig. 9.26, the 3B20D processor may be diagnosed from several execution environments. During the early phase of its development, a local host computer was used to support hardware, software, and diagnostic design. This arrangement continues to be used in factory testing. Later in the development phase, more efficient use was made of the host computer by providing access to a remote 3B20D processor over a dial-up telephone line. In the final development stage (the standard duplex system configuration), the active control unit is capable of diagnosing its own peripheral controllers and the standby control unit. Each of these access arrangements is discussed below.

Figure 9.26(a) shows three local host access arrangements. In the first arrangement, diagnostic programs executing in a host computer send test inputs and receive test results through a standard communications port to a microlevel test set (MLTS). The MLTS connects directly to the 3B20D control unit backplane, and provides complete access to and control of the processor's microprogram control circuitry. The second access arrangement uses a circuit designed to simulate the central control input/output (CCIO) internal bus. The CCIO bus simulator (BS) is accessible using a standard communication input port. A dual serial channel (DSCH) connected to the CCIO/BS can then communicate directly with a maintenance channel (MCH), the circuit designed for control unit access. Like the

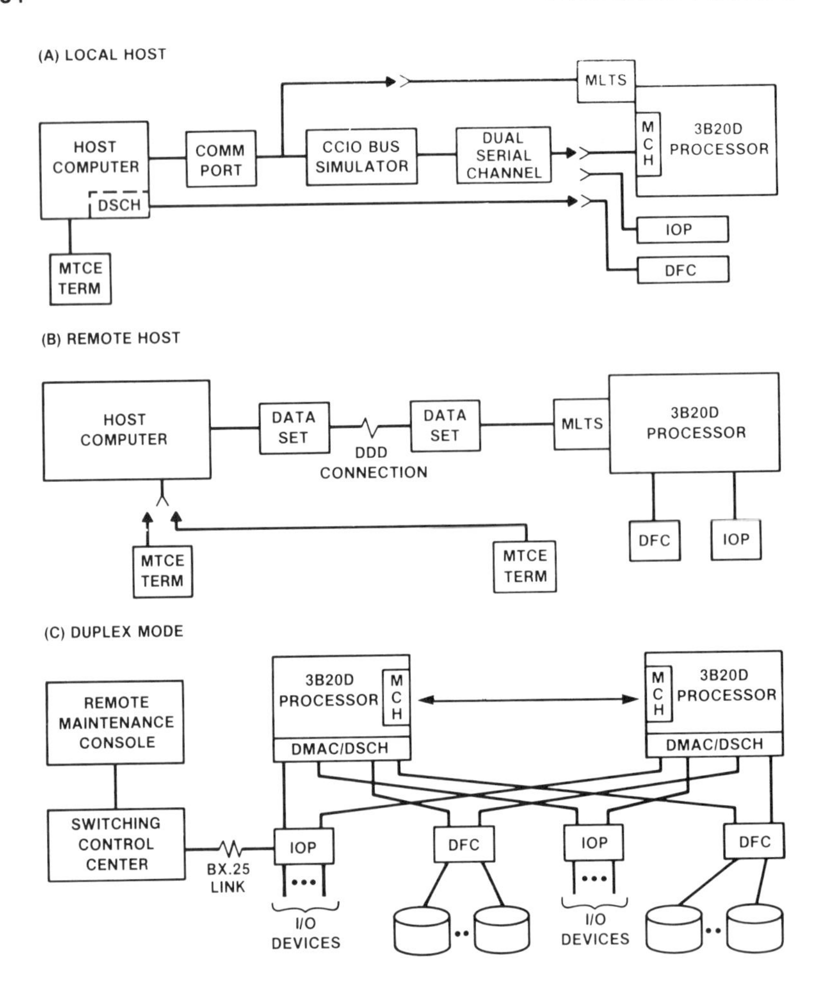

Figure 9.26 3B20D processor diagnostic environments.

MLTS, the MCH can access the central control at a low level. Only the MCH, however, is used in the duplex configuration; it communicates with either another MCH or a DSCH. As shown, the CCIO/BS-DSCH access path is also used to diagnose the input/output processor (IOP) and the disk file controller (DFC). The third access arrangement is used when the local host is a 3B20D processor. The path in this case is from the DSCH of the host processor to the MCH, IOP, or DFC of the target machine.

The DSCH communicates over distances of approximately 100 feet. Remote host [Fig. 9.26(b)] access arrangements are used for diagnosing over longer distances. Using data sets and a telephone line, tests stored and executed on a remote computer are applied through the MLTS to the control unit. Peripheral controllers (IOP and DFC) may also be diagnosed by downloading tests into the control unit and executing them. Although remote host diagnostics are useful when a local host is unavailable, execution performance is limited by the transmission facilities used.

The primary diagnostic execution environment is the duplex mode of the 3B20D [Fig. 9.26(c)]. The active (on-line) processor acts as a local host for diagnosing the standby (off-line) processor. A link between maintenance channels provides the access path for testing the control unit. In the duplex mode, the DFC and IOPC are diagnosed from the on-line control unit using the operational interface path, which is a DSCH attached to the direct memory access controller (DMAC). Tests of the links from the off-line processor to the peripherals may also be run under the control of the active processor. As shown in Fig. 9.26(c), the duplex system configuration also supports remote monitoring and control of diagnostics over a dedicated link to a switching control center.

9.7.2 Diagnostic Control Structure

The diagnostic control structure is depicted in Fig. 9.27. The modules that provide access to the equipment configuration data base (ECD) are at the kernel process level. All the information relevant to the diagnostic tests that should be applied to each hardware unit is contained in the ECD. This information includes the name of each hardware unit; its subsystem, subunits, and their logical interconnections; equipage options; and auxiliary information such as channel address and baud rate. Whenever a circuit design is originated or updated, diagnostic tests are designed and appropriate ECD changes are made.

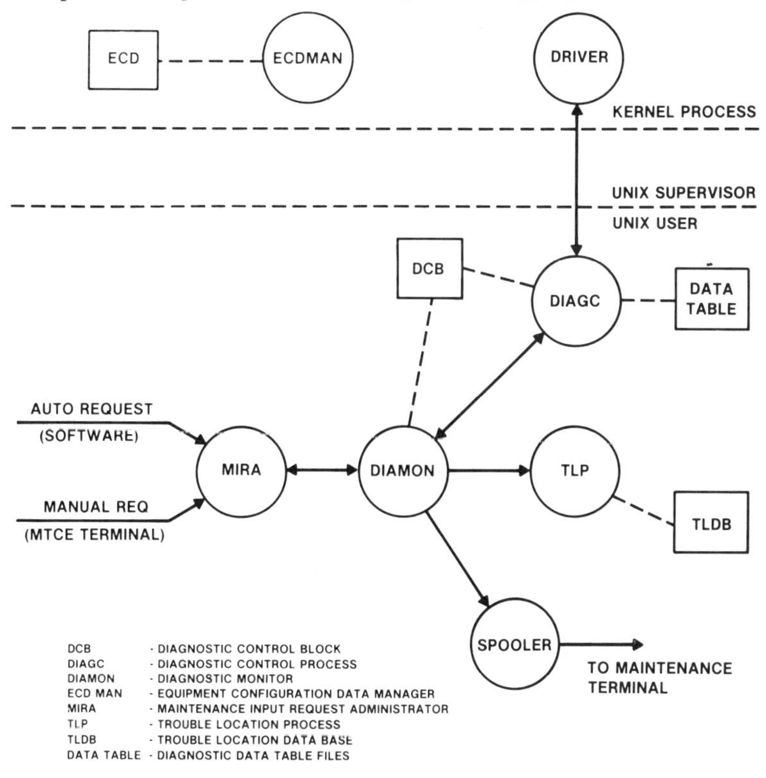

Figure 9.27 Diagnostic control structure.

The UNIX operating system supervisor resides at the supervisor level, and provides a protected environment and operating system service for the higher-level processes. The modules operating under the UNIX operating system that pertain exclusively to diagnostics are the maintenance input request administrator (MIRA), the diagnostic monitor (DIAMON), the diagnostic control process (DIAGC), and the trouble locating process (TLP). Output messages from the diagnostic structure are sent to the system spooler for printing.

The maintenance input request administrator (MIRA) schedules and dispatches all the maintenance requests. MIRA has two queues, a waiting queue and an active queue, to administer maintenance requests. Requests are serviced according to their priorities and the availability of resources. Manual requests have higher priorities than requests initiated automatically. For each service request, MIRA creates a DIAMON process and sends it a message. When the request is completed, DIAMON sends a message back to MIRA. Interfaces are provided in MIRA to administer routine exercise requests and inputs from the error interrupt handler. Execution of each diagnostic is directed from start to finish by DIAMON.

DIAGC is a generic name that refers to a class of diagnostic control processes. The DIAGC is a unit or application-dependent module that controls the execution of tests. DIAGC contains all the application-dependent task routines, translates the interpretive diagnostics, and provides the interface with DIAMON. A unit's diagnostic phase table (DPT) contains the name of a particular DIAGC process to be used in the diagnosis. DIAMON imposes no limit on the number of processes that may interface with it.

If the diagnostic request specifies the TLP option, the trouble-locating process is invoked after the diagnostic testing is completed. The TLP compares characteristics of the failures found by the diagnostics with a resident data base of fault signatures. In each data table, the tests are partitioned into groups. A test failure in a group sets a flag bit, called a key, which is permanently assigned to the group. The TLP searches the results of the diagnostics and, based on the phase and key information, creates an ordered list of the closest signatures and ultimately of the suspected faulty equipment. This approach makes the data base and sorting processes less sensitive than earlier methods of testing changes to circuits and marginal failures. During the development of the 3B20D, the trouble-locating data base (TLDB) was generated by physically inserting faults into units in a test laboratory. The TLDB of operational systems may be modified directly by inserting information into the test data table.

9.7.3 Diagnostic Features

The combination of hardware access circuits and modular control programs just discussed provide the 3B20D processor with considerable maintenance flexibility. Tests are selected according to the type of circuit under diagnosis. Requests may diagnose an entire unit, a particular subunit, or all the subunits in a specified community. Individual test phases or ranges of phases may be executed and the results printed with optional amounts of detail. Some diagnostic test phases, because of their long execution time requirements or their dependence on the availability of other system hardware resources, are restricted to manual initializations. Interactive features such as stepping, pausing, and looping facilitate difficult repairs. Units are restored to service automatically if they pass all tests. Several host computer versions of the software are supported along with application-dependent interfaces.

Diagnostics are initiated manually or automatically. Manual requests may be entered from a local maintenance terminal or through a workstation at a switching control center that is connected to the processor with a synchronous data link. Automatic requests originate from other software modules, including the error interrupt handler, the routine exercise scheduler, and the application software modules.

9.7.4 Evaluation

The stringent availability requirements of AT&T applications using the 3B20D processors have a significant effect on all the aspects of the system design. The diagnostic and maintenance designers were actively involved in meeting these requirements from the initial architectural planning and requirements generation. Many hardware features monitor system integrity, detect errors, reconfigure the system, and facilitate repairs. Although some of the features isolate faults during pack repairs, most are used at the system level to effect repairs through pack replacement. Diagnostics, the primary repair capability for the system, make extensive use of these hardware features for control and observation of the circuitry.

During the development of the processor, diagnostic tests were generated manually and with the aid of hardware logic simulators. To ensure that the diagnostics met the objective of detecting 90 percent of the simulated faults, an extensive evaluation process was carried out. Thousands of faults were inserted at the dual-in-line package (DIP) terminals (pins). These faults provided timely and effective feedback on the design of the diagnostic tests and the development of the trouble locating data base.

9.8 OPERATIONAL RESULTS OF 3B20D PROCESSOR

The 3B20D processors have been in commercial operation since September, 1981. Over 200 systems are providing real-time, high-availability telecommunication services. The performance of the 3B20D improved tremendously during the first two years of operation. Figure 9.28 shows the results of field data accumulated over many machine operating hours [23]. When the first system began commercial service, outages occurred because of software and hardware faults that could only be corrected with field experience. The sharp inverted spikes shown in the figure were caused by combinations of design faults that showed up under unusual sets of system conditions. The one for May 1982, for example, resulted from a hardware problem (noisy power supply) that forced a recovery that was too drastic for the fault. The curve in the figure shows that the availability factor improved as the processor design matured and the operating personnel gained experience.

Figure 9.29 shows downtime data for three AT&T processors, including the

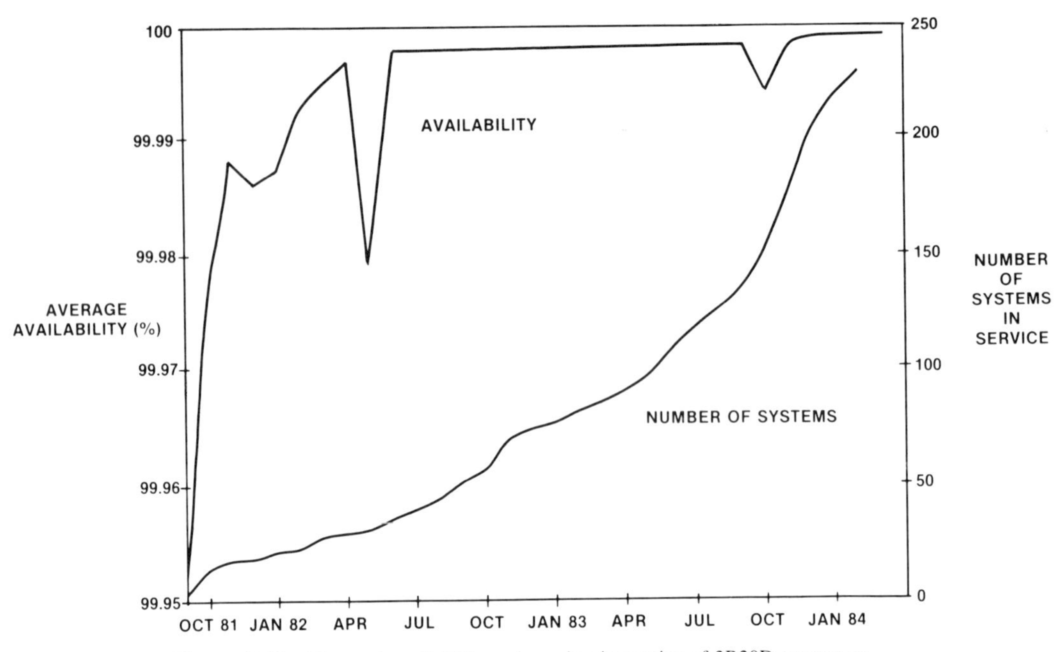

Figure 9.28 Observed availability and number in service of 3B20D processors.

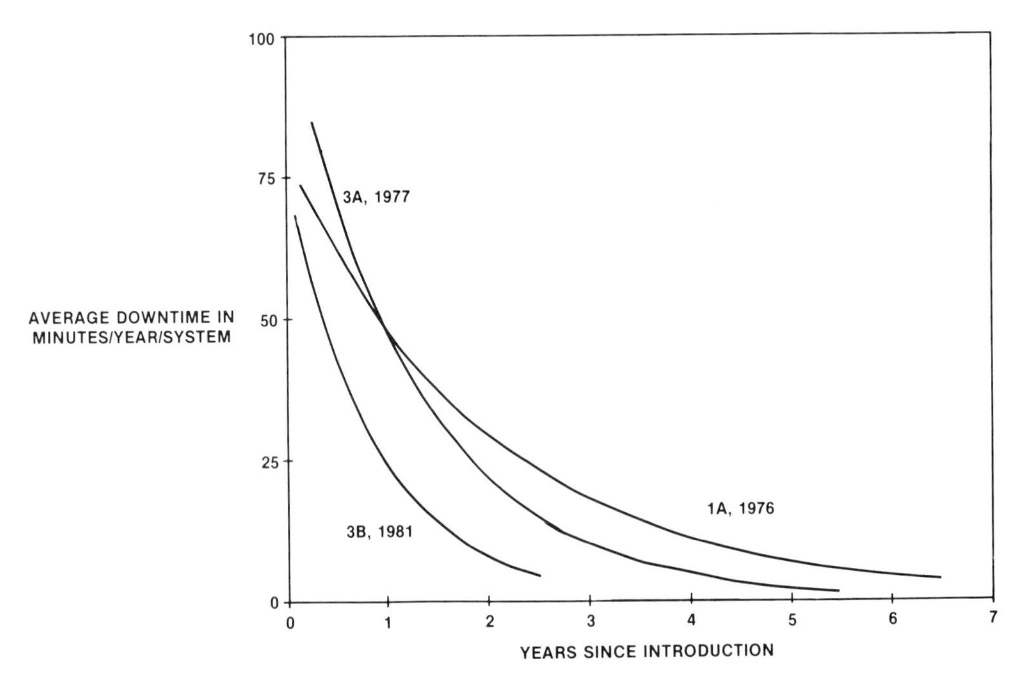

Figure 9.29 Downtime versus time since introduction for three high availability processors.

3B20D. The experience gained in the design and field operation of earlier electronic switching systems (notably the 1A and the 3A processors) have contributed to the design of the 3B20D. The reliability (downtime) curves show that each processor approached its downtime objective more quickly than its predecessor. The data has been smoothed and fit to an exponential decay function for the comparison.

9.9 SUMMARY

The 3B20D processor is a general-purpose, high-availability machine that supports many types of applications. A comprehensive set of software tools and facilities improves programming productivity and reduces the cost of software development and maintenance. The hardware architecture efficiently supports high-level languages, particularly the C language.

The processor is a 32-bit machine with a 24-bit addressing scheme. Hardware features support a modern, general-purpose operating system, that is, an operating system with good virtual-to-physical address translation. Other features include microprogram implementation, emulation capabilities, high-speed data caches, high-speed interrupt stacks, self-checking circuits, extensive diagnostic access, a craft interface for emergency manual control, and duplex operation.

The standard I/O communication between the central control and the peripherals is over a dedicated point-to-point dual series channel that transmits at an effective rate of 20 megabits per second. The dual series channels operate in a word transfer mode or a block transfer mode. The loose coupling of the channels between the processor and the peripherals permits considerable freedom in expanding a system. A wide range of peripherals further extends the capabilities of the processor. The peripherals include a moving-head disk system, a magnetic tape system, a high-speed printer, a scanner and signal distributor, and data terminals.

The 3B20D processor uses the DMERT operating system. This operating system was designed concurrently with the hardware to meet the needs of switching and telecommunication systems. The procedures of the DMERT system enable users to efficiently share the 3B20D processor and its physical resources, including processor time, storage space, and peripheral devices. The DMERT operating system is a multiple environment system that permits time-critical, real-time code to coexist with time-shared background tasks.

An important provision in the 3B20D processor is a complete set of maintenance facilities, from error detection through fault recovery and diagnostics. Approximately 30 percent of the internal central control logic is devoted to self-checking. This allows concurrent error detection and immediate recovery. The combined hardware and software of the DMERT operating system and the 3B20D processor includes an integrated package of maintenance facilities to meet the high-reliability requirements of electronic switching systems.

REFERENCES

[1] "No. 1 ESS Description," *Bell Syst. Tech. J.*, Vol. 43, No. 5, September 1968.

[2] "No. 2 ESS Description," *Bell Syst. Tech. J.*, Vol. 48, No. 8, October 1969.

[3] "No. 1A Processor Description," *Bell Syst. Tech. J.*, Vol. 56, No. 2, February 1977.

[4] W. N. Toy and L. E. Gallaher, "Overview and Architecture of 3B20D Processor," *Bell Syst. Tech. J.*, Vol. 62, No. 1, Pt. 2, January 1983, pp. 181–190.

[5] W. N. Toy, "Fault Tolerant Design of ESS Processors," *Proc. IEEE,* Vol. 66, October 1978, pp. 1126–1145.

[6] T. F. Storey, "Design of a Microprogram Control for a Processor in an Electronic-Switching System," *Bell Syst. Tech. J.*, Vol. 55, February 1976, pp. 183–232.

[7] B. W. Kernighan and D. M. Ritchie, *The C Programming Language,* Prentice-Hall, Englewood Cliffs, N.J., 1978.

[8] M. W. Rolund, J. T. Beckett, and D. A. Harms, "3B20D Central Processing Unit," *Bell Syst. Tech. J.*, Vol. 62, No. 1, Pt. 2, January 1983, pp. 191–206.

[9] AMD, *The AM 2900 Family Data Book,* Sunnyvale, Calif., 1979.

[10] I. K. Hetherington and P. Kusulas, "3B20D Memory Systems," *Bell Syst. Tech. J.*, Vol. 62, No. 1, Pt. 2, January 1983, pp. 207–220.

[11] D. Stevenson, "A Proposed Standard for Binary Floating Point Arithmetic," *Computer,* Vol. 14, No. 3, March 1981, pp. 51–62.

[12] J. T. Beckett and S. W. Ng, "A General Purpose Microcode Assembler," *IEEE COMPAC Proc.*, 1978, pp. 84–89.

[13] A. H. Budlong and F. W. Wendland, "3B20D Input/Output Systems," *Bell Syst. Tech. J.*, Vol. 62, No. 1, Pt. 2, January 1983, pp. 225–274.

[14] R. E. Hagland and L. D. Peterson, "3B20D File Memory System," *Bell Syst. Tech. J.*, Vol. 62, No. 1, Pt. 2, January 1983, pp. 235–254.

[15] M. E. Barton and D. A. Schmitt, "Craft Interface," *Bell Syst. Tech. J.*, Vol. 62, No. 1, Pt. 2, January 1983, pp. 383–398.

[16] J. R. Kane, R. E. Anderson, and P. S. McCabe, "Overview, Architecture, and Performance of DMERT," *Bell Syst. Tech. J.*, Vol. 62, No. 1, Pt. 2, January 1983, pp. 291–302.

[17] M. E. Grzelakowski, J. H. Campbell, and M. R. Dubman, "DMERT Operating System," *Bell Syst. Tech. J.*, Vol. 62, No. 1, Pt. 2, January 1983, pp. 303–322.

[18] H. Lycklama and D. L. Bayer, "The MERT Operating System," *Bell Syst. Tech. J.*, Vol. 57, No. 6, Pt. 2, July 1978, pp. 2049–2086.

[19] D. Ritchie and K. Thompson, "The UNIX Time-Sharing System," *Bell Syst. Tech. J.*, Vol. 57, No. 6, Pt. 2, July 1978, pp. 1905–1930.

[20] C. H. Elmendorf, "Meeting High Standards with Extended Operating System," *Bell Labs Rec.*, March 1980, pp. 97–103.

[21] R. C. Hansen, R. W. Peterson, and N. O. Whittington, "Fault Detection and Recovery," *Bell Syst. Tech. J.*, Vol. 62, No. 1, Pt. 2, January 1983, pp. 349–366.

[22] J. L. Quinn and F. M. Goetz, "Diagnostic Tests and Control Software," *Bell Syst. Tech. J.*, Vol. 62, No. 1, Pt. 2, January 1983, pp. 367–382.

[23] J. J. Wallace and W. W. Barnes, "Designing for Ultrahigh Availability: The UNIX RTR Operating System," *Computer,* August 1984, pp. 31–39.

PROBLEMS

9.1 Figure 9.2 shows the general block diagram of the AT&T 3B20D processor. Each functional unit is duplicated to serve as a backup under trouble conditions. The backup is strictly a standby unit. In this arrangement, the standby does not produce or contribute any useful work except in emergencies. Describe a load-sharing arrangement with the same configuration as shown in Fig. 9.2 in which both central controls are actively performing concurrent operations. What is the expected increase in performance?

9.2 Floating-point operations can be implemented by subroutines, microinstruction sequences, or additional hardware support. When higher performance is needed, the provision of a hardware floating-point unit is usually offered on an optional basis. In the 3B20D processor functional diagram shown in Fig. 9.3, where should the floating-point hardware fit in the architecture to achieve the best possible performance?

9.3 The data manipulation unit (DMU) shown in Fig. 9.4 contains the rotate mask unit (RMU) and the arithmetic logic unit (ALU). These units perform the arithmetic and logic operations. The RMU rotates any number of bits from positions 0 through 31 through a two-stage barrel shift network. In addition, the RMU performs AND or OR operations on bits, nibbles, bytes, half words, full words, and predefined patterns stored in ROM. Implement the RMU unit using standard logic gates.

9.4 For maintenance purposes, the duplex 3B20D central controls are interconnected by the maintenance channel (MTC CH), as shown in Fig. 9.2. This high-speed serial path, compatible with the standard I/O serial channel (I/O CH), provides diagnostic access at the microcode level. It transmits streams of microinstructions from the on-line processor to exercise the off-line processor. Assume a system consisting of up to 16 simplex 3B20 processors. Show a system configuration in which the duplex 3B20D controls all the simplex 3B20s through their maintenance channels. Also show the I/O interconnections that allow communication among all the processors.

9.5 The virtual to physical address translation is done by the segment and page tables, both of which reside in main memory. The layout of the translation sequence is shown in Fig. 9.7. Show a functional block diagram of the implementation of a virtual to physical address translation if the translation is done only by page tables and the page addresses have 13 bits instead of 6. Compare the advantages and disadvantages of these two arrangements.

9.6 The cache store size of each of the four sets shown in Fig. 9.10 is 2K bytes (512 words). Accessing the address translation buffer (ATB) and the cache unit simultaneously is possible because the 13-bit page offset used to address the cache is the same for both the virtual address and the physical address; hence, there is no need to wait until the virtual to physical address translation is completed before accessing the cache. As shown in Fig. 9.11, the access of the ATB and the cache is performed in parallel. Suppose that the cache store size of *each* of the four sets needs to be increased from 2K bytes (512 words) to 8K bytes (2048 words) and that the virtual address format and size of the ATB needs to remain the same. Develop a scheme that would allow the concurrent access of the ATB and the cache store.

9.7 The DMERT operating system is a multilevel structure of virtual machines. There are four levels of virtual machines: kernel, kernel process, supervisor, and user. Successive levels permit the management of both real-time applications and time-shared background tasks. List the advantages and disadvantages of this architecture.

Index

A

B

C

D

E

F

G

T

U

V

W

X